THE ESSEX REGIMENT
1929–1950

THE ESSEX REGIMENT
1929–1950

BY
Colonel T. A. MARTIN
M.B.E.

The Naval & Military Press Ltd

Published by

The Naval & Military Press Ltd
Unit 10 Ridgewood Industrial Park,
Uckfield, East Sussex,
TN22 5QE England

Tel: +44 (0) 1825 749494
Fax: +44 (0) 1825 765701

www.naval-military-press.com
www.military-genealogy.com
www.militarymaproom.com

In reprinting in facsimile from the original, any imperfections are inevitably reproduced and the quality may fall short of modern type and cartographic standards.

AUTHOR'S PREFACE

For this story of the Regiment between 1929 and 1950 the author has to express his indebtedness to all those who, often at great personal inconvenience, found time to give the details without which the book could not have been completed.

It is not possible to mention all the names of those who have helped nor yet would they wish it, but three must be singled out. Colonel S. C. W. W. Rea, who laid the foundations on which the book was built; Major R. H. A. Painter, who is responsible for the many excellent and accurate maps and sketches, and Major S. H. Andrew.

Major Andrew was of invaluable assistance at every turn and no appeal for help went unanswered. He was a tower of strength in this as in every matter of Regimental interest and well-being, and I, with all the Regiment, owe him a very great debt of gratitude for his work at Warley since 1939.

I also thank Captain F. C. Pryor for his aid over the complicated matter of printing and publishing.

I acknowledge Lieutenant-General Sir Geoffrey Howard's kindness in writing the Foreword. The kindness of Brigadier J. S. Nichols, General Sir Evelyn Barker, Lieutenant-General Sir Francis Tuker, Lieutenant-General Sir Dudley Russell, and Lieutenant-General Sir Willoughby Norrie in writing a short preface to the chapters dealing with the 1st Battalion, 2nd Battalion, 1/4th Battalion, 1/5th Battalion, and 2/5th Battalion, respectively, is also gratefully acknowledged.

Finally, my thanks are due to the Colonel of the Regiment, Brigadier C. M. Paton, C.V.O., C.B.E., for his constant interest and invaluable advice.

I make no excuse for including chapters on our old Territorial battalions and the Essex Home Guard in this story of the Regiment. A change to an anti-aircraft role cannot alter the fact that these old Volunteer units were part of the Essex Regiment from 1883 to 1939, and even now share the Regimental badge with that of the Royal Artillery. The Home Guard, wearing the badge of and affiliated to the Essex Regiment, was very much a part of the defence forces of the County of Essex, and must have its share in this history. We are indebted to Major P. Finch for his contribution.

I have also included chapters on the Allied Regiments of the Dominion of Canada and the Commonwealth of Australia, and the Essex Regiment Chapel, without which no history of the Regiment would be complete.

T. A. MARTIN.

LITTLE CHESTERFORD,
 1st *November*, 1951.

In memory of All Ranks of
THE ESSEX REGIMENT
who, between 1929 and 1950, were
killed in action or died in the service
of their King and Country

CONTENTS

Author's Preface — v

Foreword by Lieutenant-General SIR GEOFFREY W. HOWARD, K.C.B., C.M.G., D.S.O., D.L. — xvii

Introduction — xix

1. The Inter-war Years, 1929–39 — 1
   - Section I 1st Battalion The Essex Regiment, 1929–39
   - II 2nd Battalion The Essex Regiment, 1929–1939
   - III The 161st Infantry Brigade T.A. 4th, 5th, 6th, and 7th Battalions The Essex Regiment, 1929–39

2. The 1st Battalion The Essex Regiment, 1939–48 — 25
   Foreword, by Brigadier J. S. Nichols, D.S.O., M.C.
   - Section I Egypt, 1939–40
   - II The Sudan, 1940
   - III Operation against Gallabat, 1940
   - IV Palestine, January–May 1941
   - V Operations in Iraq, 1941
   - VI Operations in Syria, 1941
   - VII Tobruk and Ed Duda, 1941
   - VIII India, 1942–43
   - IX The Arakan, May–June 1943
   - X Long-range Penetration. Assam and Burma, 1944
   - XI India and England, 1944–48

3. The 2nd Battalion The Essex Regiment, 1939–48 — 129
   Foreword, by General Sir Evelyn Barker, K.B.E., C.B., D.S.O., M.C.
   - Section I England, France, and Belgium, August 1939–April 1940
   - II France and Belgium, May–June 1940
   - III Home Defence and preparation for the Counter-offensive, June 1940–June 1944
   - IV Operations in North-west Europe, June 1944–May 1945
   - V Germany, Italy, and England, 1945–48

CONTENTS

4 The 1/4th Battalion The Essex Regiment, 1939–46   247
  Foreword, by Lieutenant-General Sir Francis Tuker, K.C.I.E., C.B., D.S.O., O.B.E.
  Section I Home Defence, 1939–40
    II West Africa, 1940–41
    III Egypt, Cyprus, and Palestine, 1941–42
    IV The Western Desert, June–October 1942
    V El Alamein and the Advance to Tunis, 1942–43
    VI The Italian Campaign, 1943–44
    VII Greece, 1944–46
  Appendix A Honours and Awards, 1/4th Battalion The Essex Regiment
    B Battle Casualties, 1/4th Battalion The Essex Regiment
    C Battle of Djebel Garci

5 The 2/4th Battalion The Essex Regiment, 1939–45   348

6 The 5th (1/5th) Battalion The Essex Regiment, 1939–50   356
  Foreword, by Lieutenant-General Sir Dudley Russell, K.B.E., C.B., D.S.O., M.C.
  Section I Home Defence, 1939–41
    II The Middle East, 1941–43
    III The Italian Campaign, 1943–44
    IV The Middle East, 1944–45
    V North-west Europe, April–May 1945
    VI May 1945–June 1946
    VII The Post-war Story
  Appendix A Battle Casualties, 5th Battalion The Essex Regiment
    B Location by Date, 5th Battalion The Essex Regiment

7 The 2/5th Battalion The Essex Regiment, 1939–42   439
  Foreword, by Lieutenant-General Sir Willoughby Norrie, K.C.M.G., C.B., D.S.O., M.C.
  Section I Home Defence, 1939–40
    II West Africa, 1941
    III The Middle East, 1941–42
    IV The Battle of Deir-el-Shein, 1st July, 1942

8 Old Battalions in a New Role, 1939–50   474
  Section I 59th (The Essex Regiment) H.A.A. Regiment R.A. (Late 7th Battalion The Essex Regiment)

CONTENTS

    II 64th Searchlight Regiment (Late 1/6th Battalion The Essex Regiment), 1938–45
   III 65th Searchlight Regiment (Late 2/6th Battalion The Essex Regiment), 1938–45

9 The New Battalions, 1940–45   485
    Section I The 8th Battalion The Essex Regiment (the 153rd Regiment R.A.C.) and "C" (Essex) Squadron 107th Regiment R.A.C.)
    II The 9th Battalion The Essex Regiment (11th (Essex) Medium Regiment R.A.)
   III The 10th Battalion The Essex Regiment (9th Parachute Regiment)
   IV The 19th Battalion The Essex Regiment

10 Home Defence Battalions The Essex Regiment, 1939–43   505
    Section I The National Defence Companies
    II The 7th and 30th (Home Defence) Battalions The Essex Regiment
   III The 70th (Young Soldier) Battalion The Essex Regiment

11 The Regimental Centre, Warley, 1939–50   517

12 The Essex Regiment Chapel   527

13 The Allied Regiments from the Dominion of Canada and the Commonwealth of Australia   538
    Section I The 1st Battalion The Essex Scottish Regiment of Canada
    II The 11/44th Infantry Battalion (City of Perth Regiment) of Australia

14 The Essex Home Guard   546
    By Major P. R. Finch, T.D., R.A. (T.A.)

15 The Essex Regiment, 1945–50   561
    Section I The Regiment, 1945–50
    II The Six Freedoms
   III The Amalgamation of the 1st and 2nd Battalions
   IV The 1st Battalion The Essex Regiment (44th and 56th Foot), 1948–50
    V The 4th Battalion The Essex Regiment (T.A.), 1948–50

APPENDICES

I	Roll of Honour, 1939–45	574
II	Honours and Awards, 1939–45	602
III	Award of the Victoria Cross to Lieutenant-Colonel A. C. Newman	615
IV	Commanding Officers, 1929–50	617
V	Regimental Dates, Service, and Battle Honours since formation	622
VI	"Ed Duda: our Action outside Tobruk," by Lieutenant P. P. S. Brownless, 1st Battalion The Essex Regiment	630

LIST OF ILLUSTRATIONS

1st Battalion The Essex Regiment entering the barracks of the French 106th Regiment of Infantry. Rheims. 20th February, 1935 — 16

2nd Battalion leaving H.M. Tower of London for Chelmsford and the presentation of silver bugles by the County of Essex. 2nd October, 1937 — 17

2nd Battalion march off after the presentation. Chelmsford. 2nd October, 1937 — 17

The Colonel and Commanding Officers, Mytchett, August 1929 — 32

1st Battalion after the occupation of Fort Gallabat (Sudan). November 1940 — 33

Facsimile of the Surrender of Palmyra received by the 1st Battalion. 3rd July, 1941 — 33

1st Battalion. The capture of Palmyra (Tadmor) 2nd/3rd July, 1941 — 80

1st Battalion headquarters, Ed Duda. December 1941 — 81

1st Battalion. On Ed Duda after the battle. December 1941. — 81

1st Battalion. Lieutenant M. D. Lough and his platoon, 44 Column, on conclusion of operations in Assam and Burma. July 1944 — 96

1st Battalion. The officers, 44 and 56 Columns, on conclusion of operations in Assam and Burma, July 1944 — 96

Officers, 2nd Battalion. Meurchin. April 1940 — 97

2nd Battalion. Personnel pass a knocked-out German Panther Tank near Tilly-sur-Seulles. 19th June, 1944 — 240

2nd Battalion. Tilly-sur-Seulles immediately after its capture by the Battalion. 19th June, 1944 — 240

2nd Battalion in Zetten after its capture. 22nd January, 1945 — 241

2nd Battalion cross the Neder Rijn in the Second Battle of Arnhem. 14th April, 1945 — 241

LIST OF ILLUSTRATIONS

1/4th Battalion in co-operation with Churchill tanks move into the attack. Medjez-el-Bab. 6th May, 1943	256
H.R.H. The Duke of Gloucester inspects the 1/5th Battalion. Mosul. May 1942	256
1/4th Battalion in the Western Desert, 1942	257
His Majesty King George VI inspects the 1/4th Battalion. Tripoli–Castel Benito Road. 19th June, 1943.	336
1/4th Battalion. The area of Monte Cassino and the Abbe D'Monte Cassino. March 1943	337
1/4th Battalion. A group of survivors of "B" and "D" Companies after the assault of Monastery Hill, 18th/19th March, 1943	337
Drums of the 5th Battalion. Latakia, Syria. May 1943	352
5th Battalion near Lanciano (South Italy) 9th December, 1943	352
5th Battalion. Road draining and repair near Lanciano. 9th December, 1943	353
5th Battalion. A section relief on the River Arielli, near Villa Grande. 15th January, 1944	353
2/5th Battalion. A belated Christmas Dinner. Mosul. January 1942	464
The Essex Regiment Chapel, Warley	465
Lieutenant-Colonel A. C. Newman, V.C.	616
Lieutenant-Colonel R. B. James, D.S.O. (and two Bars)	617
Regimental Sergeant-Major C. J. Rose, D.C.M. (and Bar)	617
L/Corporal E. B. Hazle, D.C.M. (and Bar)	617
The Drums of the 2nd Battalion beat Retreat in the Piazza San Marco, Venice. 20th March, 1947	between pages 568–9
The return of the Salamanca Eagle to the Regiment. 28th September, 1947	,,
The Colours of the 4th Battalion being received from the Colour Party of the Regimental Depot. Gordon Fields, Ilford. 17th May, 1947	,,
The King's and Regimental Colours of the 1st, 2nd, 4th, 5th, 6th, and 7th Battalions of the Regiment, The Salamanca Eagle, and the Silver Drums of the 2nd Battalion. 25th May, 1946	,,

LIST OF MAPS

The Anglo-Egyptian Sudan and Italian East Africa	31
The Battle of Gallabat. Diagram of British Dispositions at 6 p.m., 6th November, 1940	36
1st Essex, Movements in Palestine, Iraq, and Syria, May–August 1941	52
1st Essex, Operations around Falluja and Baghdad, May 1941	57
1st Essex, Tobruk and Ed Duda, October–December 1941	82
1st Essex, Movements in the Arakan, May 1943	93
1st Essex, Assam and Burma	96
1st Essex, 44 and 56 Columns in Burma and Assam, April–June 1944	103
1st Essex, Operations against Phekekrima, April 1944	108
2nd Essex, France and Belgium, May 1940	*facing page* 156
2nd Essex, Normandy, the Initial Break-in, 6th–9th June, 1944	166
2nd Essex, Juaye Mondaye and Verrières (Essex) Wood, 10th/11th June, 1944	171
2nd Essex, Tilly-sur-Seulles, 16th–20th June, 1944	178
2nd Essex, Les Orailles–Bois de St. Germain, 28th June–10th July, 1944	182
2nd Essex, Parfouru L'Eclin–Launay Ridge, 11th July–1st August, 1944	187
2nd Essex, Crossing of the Orne–Forge à Cambro–Bas Breuil–Esson, 8th–17th August, 1944	196
2nd Essex, The Advance to and Crossing of the River Seine, 24th August–2nd September, 1944	200
2nd Essex, Pont Audemer, 26th/27th August, 1944	202
2nd Essex, The Capture of Le Havre, 3rd–12th September, 1944	207

LIST OF MAPS

2nd Essex, Ryckevorsel, 25th/26th September, 1944	213
2nd Essex, Operations in South-west Holland, October–November 1944	*facing page* 224
2nd Essex, Nijmegen and the Island, 30th November, 1944–12th April, 1945	231
1/4th Essex, Operations on the El Alamein position, July–October 1942	270
1/4th Essex, El Alamein (Operation "Supercharge"), 2nd 4th November, 1942	282
1/4th Essex, Mareth and El Hamma, March 1943	287
1/4th Essex, The Wadi Akarit, March 1943	290
1/4th Essex, Movements in Tunisia, 1943	293
1/4th Essex, Djebel Garci, March 1943	296
1/4th Essex, The Battle for Cassino, March 1944	310
1/4th Essex, Italy, 1944	323
1/4th Essex, Greece, 1944–45	334
5th Essex, Italy, 1943–44	374
5th Essex, The Crossing of the River Trigno, November 1943	377
5th Essex, The Crossing of the River Sangro, November 1943	394
5th Essex, The Battle for Villa Grande and Subsequent Operations, River Arielli, December 1943–March 1944	408
5th Essex, North-east Germany, April–May 1945	*facing page* 432
2/5th Essex, Deir-el-Shein, 1st July, 1942	462

FOREWORD

BY LIEUTENANT-GENERAL SIR GEOFFREY W. HOWARD
K.C.B., C.M.G., D.S.O., D.L.

WHEN in 1836 the War Office first authorised the publication, at their expense, of the historical records of Regiments, they did so to encourage Regimental *esprit de corps* which the fighting throughout the Napoleonic Wars had shown to be of supreme importance. It was unfortunate that War Office funds ran out before the exploits of our Regiment, up to that date, could be recorded. Nevertheless, we have been fortunate in that capable and public-spirited men have always been found willing and ready to come forward to undertake the task of writing up our history, on which the whole "tradition" of our Regiment depends.

The Regiment owes a debt of the deepest gratitude to these friends of past years, perhaps to none more so than to Mr. J. W. Burrows for his masterly work. The chronicling of a Regiment's doings is a labour of love, involving an immense amount of hard work, research, and the sorting and sifting of a mass of detail, much of it irrelevant. The thanks, therefore, of the whole Regiment are due to Colonel T. A. Martin, M.B.E., for so willingly coming forward to bring up to date our history and carry on the good work so ably performed by our former historians. The success with which he has carried out his task needs no commendation, it is there for all who read these annals to see for themselves.

As the narrative unfolds, readers will not only note how splendidly in World War II the Regular and Service Battalions upheld the highest traditions of our Regiment, but they cannot help but be profoundly stirred by the exploits of our Territorial Battalions. The prominent part played by these Battalions in World War II has added immense lustre to the annals of our Regiment; not only is the whole Regiment appreciative of what they have done, but their performances must be particularly gratifying to the leaders of the County, as well as to its ordinary men and women who have always given their County Regiment so much encouragement.

G. W. Howard.

INTRODUCTION

THIS book has as its main purpose the forging of yet one more link in the long history of the Essex Regiment. The period to be covered is extensive and varied, embracing as it does the years of calm before the Second World War burst upon an unprepared Western world. It must paint a fair and accurate picture of the fortunes of war as they affected the battalions of the Essex Regiment during those six years of struggle, and finally it must include a survey of the post-war years. Here, then, we have the three pegs on which to hang our story. A story in which we can relive those vital years, not a dull narrative of events, merely a War Diary, but a record of achievement secured against odds of varying degree. This book must not be one that spends its life on the bookshelf of a reference library, but a volume whose pages recall incident and anecdote, to be read with pride and pleasure.

The presentation of bald facts does not normally produce any feeling of enthusiasm or the desire to investigate their portent; facts must be presented to show their physical, moral, and mental effect on the individual. One may read that a certain battalion captured a certain place on a certain day, and that may be all, but to the reader this statement would convey nothing of the effort of blood and toil that must have been expended, nor the feelings of those who knew that they were facing probable destruction. It is clear, then, that our goal has a somewhat different approach to that of many regimental histories of the past, which tabulated events with consistent and mathematical accuracy and at the same time produced a feeling of lassitude and a lack of enthusiasm to finish reading the final chapter. The facts will in no way be presented less accurately; but they will, so far as is possible, be shown in their proper setting, enabling us to assess the effects of the elements and the fog of war on the outcome of an action and to look at it in its true perspective. In this way the continued story of our Battalions will emerge.

When we study the final pages of those admirable histories written by Mr. John Burrows, we find that in November 1929 the 1st Battalion moved from Colchester to Pembroke Dock, and that in February 1937 the 2nd Battalion returned to England from Khartoum and was stationed at Warley Barracks. Here we have something on which to build.

With regard to the Territorial battalions, we know that the Essex Infantry Brigade was reconstituted in February 1920 and consisted of the 4th, 5th, 6th, and 7th Battalions. The last note that we have of them tells us that the Brigade was in camp at Worthing in 1930 carrying out annual training. The 8th Battalion, which had been operating as a cyclist battalion, was disbanded after the First World War.

In order to bring the Regular and Territorial battalions up to date, we will have to tie up the loose ends and give a quick survey of what they were doing in the inter-war years up to the time when Great Britain declared war on Germany. This will cover a period of years from 1929 to 1939. It is proposed to do this in the first chapter.

Each Battalion is then dealt with separately and in sequence, and its story during the war years and immediately after told as one complete narrative. This is followed by some account of the activities at the Depot, of the Regimental Chapel, and of the Allied Regiments of Canada and Australia. We are proud to remember that the Victoria Cross was awarded to Major F. A. Tilson, The Essex Scottish Regiment of Canada, during the campaign in North-west Europe.

Finally, we have some account of the post-war period.

The Essex Regiment fought in many parts of the world: Europe, the Middle East, Assam, and Burma. We remember its great and gallant victories, such as Verrières Wood and the Bois de St. Germain in France, Ed Duda, El Alamein and El Blida in Africa, Cassino, the Sangro, and Villa Grande in Italy. The withdrawal from Dunkirk is also not forgotten. These and many others were the high-lights, but there were numerous successes which did not receive the blaze of publicity.

> *"At the going down of the sun and in the morning*
> *We will remember them."*
>
> T. A. M.

Chapter One

THE INTER-WAR YEARS, 1929-39

IT is necessary, at the opening of this chapter, to link up with the latest of our published histories so that no gaps are left in the Regimental Records.

As already mentioned in the Introduction, the Burrows histories cover the period up to the moves of the 1st Battalion to Pembroke Dock in November 1929, and of the 2nd Battalion to Warley in 1937 on their return after a foreign tour lasting nearly eighteen years.

The 161st Infantry Brigade T.A., re-formed after the First World War and consisting of the 4th, 5th, 6th, and 7th Battalions The Essex Regiment, had passed through a period of difficulty and frustration. War seemed far distant, if not impossible, and both volunteers and equipment were lacking. No praise is high enough for those Territorials of all ranks who served through those years of disinterest and so preserved the continuity, spirit, and corporate feeling of each detachment, company, and battalion.

For Regular battalions, too, the years from 1920 to the early thirties were not easy. Keeping the foreign service battalion up to strength meant the home battalion was under-staffed and under establishment. Training for war was difficult, but meticulously carried out. Individual training gave place to platoon, platoon to company and eventually to battalion and higher training. This was the yearly round both at home and abroad.

It might be thought that the battalions would have had phases of dullness and boredom, but one can see that this was not the case. Keenness and enthusiasm were never in doubt, and the spirit of the Essex Regiment remained high. Games and sporting events of every kind were sedulously fostered at every level from platoon to battalion. To an outsider it might appear that an undue proportion of time, energy, and funds were being spent on sport, but this was not so. Apart from the general physical fitness and moral well-being achieved, games played by all ranks build up a mutual trust and are invaluable. They are a factor in the production of a state of high morale in a unit, a quality without which a unit is poor in peace and weak in battle.

In tracing the movements and activities of units through the years before 1939, for the sake of clarity each Regular battalion will be dealt with separately.

Up to 1939, battalions of the Territorial Army will be grouped together in the entity of the 161st Infantry Brigade T.A., as all Territorial battalions during this period were doing much the same things.

And so during those peaceful years little thought of war passed through minds free of care and worry. Excitements were few and far between, and a move from one station to another was an important event. But throughout these years the Essex Regiment, recovering from the stress and change of the First World War, was building itself up again to withstand the shock and turmoil of the Second.

As these pages unfold, it will be seen that as the peaceful years passed to the uneasy days which preceded the outbreak of the Second World War, a firm foundation was being laid from which came that spirit and high morale that made sure our future victories.

Section I

1st BATTALION THE ESSEX REGIMENT, 1929-39

COLCHESTER · PEMBROKE DOCK · CATTERICK CAMP · THE SAAR
PALESTINE · EGYPT · CYPRUS

In November 1929 the 1st Battalion The Essex Regiment moved from Colchester to Pembroke Dock. Twenty years later it was to be back again in Colchester. Much could be written of its exploits in the interim, but the aim is only to produce a picture which will give the reader an insight into its activities in peace and war, its victories, its set-backs, and its final achievements.

Before leaving Goojerat Barracks, Colchester, the Battalion had a farewell message from the Lord-Lieutenant of Essex, Brigadier-General Sir Richard Colvin, K.C.B. This message was read out on parade by Lieutenant-Colonel F. H. D. C. Whitmore, C.M.G., D.S.O., D.L., who had always identified himself with the County Regiment in all its activities. Since himself becoming Lord-Lieutenant, his interest and active help have never wavered.

During its stay in Colchester the Battalion took the greatest interest in everything to do with the county, and there were not many functions with which it was not connected in one way or another. There were few who left Colchester without real regret. Pembroke Dock sounded not too encouraging, and to an East Anglian it was a move to a far country. It was the Battalion's first introduction to the people of Wales.

However, the 1st Battalion, under the command of Lieutenant-Colonel A. E. M. Sinclair-Thomson, D.S.O., had to say *au revoir* to Colchester and entrain for Pembroke Dock. From being members of a large military community, they now found themselves the only Regular battalion in the whole of the Western Command, but the Battalion quickly settled down in its new station.

The Battalion stayed exactly four whole years in Pembroke Dock. This was an overlong time in a one-battalion station, but never was there any sign of deterioration or looking back. It was a period of hard work and play, of healthy rivalry between companies, and of a team spirit within the Battalion which showed that the unit was fundamentally sound. The interest in games within the Battalion was most marked, and the active participation of the officers gave the necessary leadership. It was also a period of weapon-training success in the Army Rifle Association competitions. The Company Shield and the Hopton Cup were both won in 1932.

In September 1931, Lieutenant-Colonel G. H. Wilmer, D.S.O., M.C., took over command of the Battalion from Lieutenant-Colonel A. E. M. Sinclair-Thomson. The new Commanding Officer began to turn his attention more and more to tactical training both in and out of doors. There were lectures and discussions in the winter evenings, and these, which were followed by all with the greatest interest, produced a real feeling of confidence when the Battalion took the field during the annual manœuvres.

The years passed by and the time approached for another change of station. It was in March 1933 when the Battalion learnt it was to move to Catterick Camp during the following winter. At that time Catterick was little more than a hutted camp on a large scale. Today great improvements have been made. In Catterick the Battalion would become part of the 5th Division, whose Headquarters were in the camp and whose commander was soon to be Major-General G. W. Howard, C.M.G., D.S.O., in 1935 to be appointed Colonel of the Essex Regiment.

The stay at Pembroke Dock had proved a pleasant one, but all realised that it was time to leave a one-battalion station and enter once more upon the round of competition—both military and sporting—existing in a large garrison.

At 7.30 a.m., on a cold morning, the Battalion saw Catterick for the first time. Its first impressions were quite unprintable. Huts seemed to be a very poor exchange for Llanion Barracks at Pembroke Dock. It was indeed a great change, but it did not take long for the Essex men to settle down. There was tremendous competition both in work and games, and this was a splendid thing for the general good of the Battalion. Great efforts were made to brighten up the lines; every hut had a garden of its own and there was continued striving to produce the best layout.

The winter of 1933/34 was spent mainly in individual training and in the normal activities of a unit in winter quarters, with a month's leave at Christmas, a form of amenity that no longer exists today.

By the spring, however, the Battalion was ready with all the other units of the station to commence training in earnest. In May 1934 it moved to Strensall Camp for a month and completed the annual weapon-training course, together with A.R.A. and Command competitions. When it returned it began the normal routine leading to battalion, brigade, and divisional training.

In the early autumn the Battalion had a taste of combined operations in which the Army, Navy, and Air Force took part. The 13th and 14th Brigades, reduced in strength for this exercise, were the invading force and the 15th Brigade was defending the shores of England. The men very much enjoyed the Navy's hospitality. Such exercises, apart from their military value, are a great help in fostering the *esprit de corps* of all fighting services. At that time nobody could have anticipated history, and North Africa, Salerno, Anzio, and the Normandy beaches were still a long way off.

Shortly after the return to Catterick on the conclusion of this exercise, the Battalion received orders to move to the Saar, where it was to be part of an international force sent to supervise the Plebiscite. As this was an event of historical importance, it would be well to deal fully with their experiences.

It will be remembered that the Plebiscite of the 1st January, 1935, was taken to allow the people of the Saar a free vote as to whether they wished to be under French or German rule. That the preparations for the voting and the ballot itself passed off successfully and peacefully was largely due to the hard work of the Battalion and the tact of the troops. It is truly said that the British soldier is one of our best ambassadors.

By the 20th December, 1934, the Battalion, comprising 20 officers and 470 men, under Lieutenant-Colonel Wilmer, was ready to move. An advance party, under Captain T. E. Hearn, had left on the 17th. This was followed by one company, which entrained at Richmond on 20th December. The rest of the Battalion proceeded by rail from Richmond to Dover on the following day. Here the 1st Essex joined the 13th Infantry Brigade Headquarters and the 1st East Lancashires and sailed for France. The adventure had begun. On the 22nd December, the Battalion detrained and found itself alone in Neunkirchen, where the reception was anything but friendly. Neunkirchen was the centre of the area for which the Battalion was responsible and was reputed to be a potential danger-spot.

The 1st Essex was then split up into detachments and proceeded to its several stations. Battalion Headquarters was established at Grube Heinitz, four miles from Neunkirchen. With it was the Headquarters Wing (Captain T. E. Hearn), "A" Company (Brevet-Major F. A. S. Clarke, D.S.O.), and "C" Company (Captain C. A. Gregory). In Hamburg was "B" Company (Major A. W. W. Row), and in St. Wendel "D(S)" Company (Major G. A. M. Paxton, M.C.). The layout of the Battalion was that the two outlying detachments, "B" and "D(S)" Companies, were at the two extremities of an inverted equilateral triangle, each situated about one mile from the German frontier, with the other point of the triangle comprised by "A" and "C" Companies and Headquarters Wing. The area included hilly and wooded country, and was in many places, especially at Grube Heinitz, thickly studded with coal-mines and chemical works.

The Battalion quickly settled in, and preparations for the Plebiscite were started almost at once. At all times 25 per cent. of the Battalion was ready to move at thirty minutes' notice. The period between the 25th and 31st December was utilised for embussing practice and in visits by the Commanding Officer and other officers to the burgomasters of the local towns. Their reception was now much more friendly. On Christmas Day, "A" and "C" Companies were inspected by Mr. G. G. Knox, the Governor of the Saar Commission, and received his high praise for their steadiness and turn-out. He asked Lieutenant-Colonel Wilmer to convey his best wishes for a Merry Christmas and a Happy New Year to all ranks. While inspections and reconnaissances were going on, the band and drums had been visiting various towns in the Battalion area. A crowd of over four thousand assembled one afternoon in Neunkirchen to hear them play.

For the purpose of voting, the whole of the Saar territory was apportioned into districts corresponding with the areas of responsibility of the various military units. Each village had one or more voting stations, and each station in turn had one or more polling booths attached to it. The duty of collecting the ballot boxes from these stations and providing an adequate escort devolved upon the units stationed in each district. The 1st Essex had been allotted the largest and most difficult area. Everything was now ready for the big day, the 1st January, 1935, which unfortunately was a day of thick snow and ice. Each booth was provided with small armed parties, but otherwise there was no display of force, the troops being kept in hand, out of sight, but ready for any emergency. As was to be expected after such detailed arrangements, the Plebiscite went off without a hitch. After the voting the local inhabitants desired to be as friendly as possible. There were many opportunities for sport. One major event, for example, was the football match which the Battalion played against the Borussia Club of Neunkirchen. A large crowd of both soldiers and the civilian population turned out to see the local club win by seven goals to four. There were also many incidents of generosity and hospitality.

On the 14th February, 1935, a regretful farewell was said to Lieutenant-Colonel Wilmer, who went home preparatory to taking over command of the 161st Infantry Brigade (T.A.) and was succeeded by Lieutenant-Colonel A. E. Maitland, D.S.O., M.C.

The Battalion left the Saar on the 19th February, 1935. On arrival at Rheims, honours were exchanged with the French 106th Infantry Regiment. All ranks were entertained magnificently and many visits were paid to places of interest, including the famous Cathedral and the War Memorial, where Colonel Maitland laid a wreath on behalf of the Battalion.

The 1st Battalion ultimately arrived back in London and was greeted at Victoria Station by Major-General A. J. Hunter, C.B., C.M.G., D.S.O., M.C., Director of Personal Services, who conveyed the thanks of the Secretary of State for War and of the Army Council for the impeccable way in which the 1st Essex had performed its duties in the Saar. On arrival at Wellington Barracks, the Lord-Lieutenant of Essex, Brigadier-General Sir Richard Colvin, addressed it and said, "The whole country rejoices at the success you have attained in the Saar. We know it was a difficult position and you have done much. We hope that perhaps you have provided a bridge over the gulf between France and Germany which other people have failed in their efforts to provide." The Battalion then marched from Wellington Barracks to King's Cross Station with "Bands playing and Drums beating," an occasion both for the Battalion and the London crowds.

At York, General Sir Alexander Wardrop, G.O.C.-in-C. Northern Command, met the Battalion at the station and congratulated all ranks on their good work. Finally, at a late hour on Friday, the 22nd February, the Battalion arrived once more at Catterick, where it was met by Major-General Howard.

From this time the year 1935 had little of battalion interest to place on record. There was the usual cycle of training and the normal round of sport, but to those with foresight signs of potential war clouds began to appear in the autumn of that year. On the 12th September, three battalions of the 5th Division received sudden orders to proceed to Malta. Italy had embarked on war with Abyssinia. Had League of Nations action been taken against the aggressor nation, Malta would have been of the greatest strategic importance, and a strengthening of her garrison was an urgent necessity. The safety of the Middle East, particularly the Suez Canal, was also vital to British interests.

Then the Headquarters of the 13th Infantry Brigade received orders to proceed to Egypt, and it was soon known that the whole of the 5th Divisional Headquarters, together with tanks and artillery, would also leave for Egypt about Christmas Day. In actual fact the remainder of the troops of Catterick Garrison, less the 1st Essex, some Gunners, Tank Corps and Signals, joined Divisional Headquarters in Egypt in the New Year of 1936. But the Essex Regiment was to be represented in Egypt, not by the 1st Battalion with the 5th Division from England, but by the 2nd Battalion which had been hurriedly dispatched with other reinforcements from India and which was by now established at Sidi Barrani.

In the summer of 1936 Lieutenant-Colonel Maitland was placed on the retired list for reasons of ill health, and command of the Battalion was taken over by Lieutenant-Colonel R. V. Read, D.S.O., M.C.

The big event of 1936 which marked the first part of the year for those remaining at Catterick was the Northern Command Tattoo held at Ravensworth, near Gateshead. For this the 1st Battalion produced a "Regimental Historical Display" which was a most popular item. Major R. E. G. Carolin was the officer in charge of the display and great credit was due to him for the final result.

In the summer of 1936 the 1st Battalion received orders to move to Palestine. Landing on the 31st October, 1936, there was a short stay in

Mishmah Ha Emek Camp, but by Christmas the Battalion was installed in Peninsular Barracks, Haifa, with a detachment at Carmel Camp.

The 1st Essex now formed part of the 16th Infantry Brigade (Brigadier J. F. Evetts, C.B.E., M.C.), and its role was that of internal security, preventing Arabs from murdering Jews, protecting transport, and keeping the main roads open for traffic. This entailed having troops at immediate notice to move so that incidents could be dealt with quickly and before bandits had time to disperse. It was found that a hard-hitting mobile column was the best antidote.

Months went by with the Battalion engaged in these arduous duties, and it was with pleasure that it heard that it was to take over from the 2nd Queen's Own Cameron Highlanders in the Citadel Barracks, Cairo, during the trooping season of 1937/38. The 1st Essex had already done sixteen months in Palestine. No one could know the Battalion would very soon be back.

The last months of the first period of service in Palestine passed quickly. They were fully occupied, as the situation in the country had not in fact improved. This was due to many reasons: unsuitable organisation and insufficient numbers of the British; intimidation of the Palestine Police, and wholesale assassinations of informers. The 16th Infantry Brigade (1st Essex, 2nd Hampshire Regiment, and 2nd Royal Ulster Rifles) was much too small to compete with what was in fact a divisional area. The Battalion took part in seven brigade operations alone, and there were numerous other operations of like importance but on a smaller scale. The killing and maiming of Jews by Arab road ambushes and bomb throwing were almost daily occurrences. Mobile columns of the Battalion were continually on the move rounding up suspects and dealing with incidents. There were many illustrations of courage and leadership. For example, No. 16 Platoon (Lieutenant D. A. C. Wilkinson) encountered a large armed band near Fasula in November. Two bandits were killed and many wounded. Just before Christmas there were detachments of five battalions occupying some twenty villages at night and observation posts in the hills by day. Even so there were not more than 800 troops, police, and Transjordan Frontier Force holding the area at any time; a number quite inadequate for the purpose. Although Christmas was spoilt as a festival, the Battalion had the satisfaction of knowing it was instrumental in ridding the Acre area of bandits and that it had put a brake on the Arab rebellion in Damascus.

By the middle of January 1938 the Battalion was on the way to

Cairo. Before leaving, Brigadier J. F. Evetts addressed it and thanked all ranks for the excellent work which they had done during their tour in Palestine, under very difficult conditions. Major-General A. P. Wavell, the G.O.C. in Palestine, also had a few words of praise to say before it left. "I am sorry to lose such a fine and excellent Battalion which was handed over to me by my predecessor (Lieutenant-General Sir J. G. Dill) as a thoroughly efficient and well-disciplined unit; and, in everything you have done, you have fully proved it during the time you have been under my command."

By midnight on the 14th January, 1938, the Battalion had settled into the Citadel Barracks, Cairo. It was not long before it was out on collective training, and all ranks quickly accustomed themselves to the new conditions of mechanisation and desert warfare. After manœuvres, Major-General E. A. Osborne said, "I am confident that you are among the very best of the County Regiments in the British Army. Your work during the collective training season has been first class and you have been remarkably quick in adapting yourselves to new conditions."

Barely six months had elapsed from the day of arrival in Cairo when sudden orders were received to prepare for a move to Palestine for emergency duties, and on the 11th July, 1938, the Battalion was once more *en route*. Lieutenant-Colonel G. A. M. Paxton, M.C., was now in command, for he had taken over from Lieutenant-Colonel Read, who in May 1938 had left the Battalion on being appointed British Military Attaché to the United States.

On arrival in Palestine for the second time, the Battalion, less two companies, was stationed at Nazareth: "D" Company was sent to Tiberias and "B" Company to Kadoori School at the foot of Mount Tabor.

The Battalion was then reorganised on the basis of a Headquarters and three mobile columns, comprising one hundred men in each column. These columns had many duties: searching villages for arms or bandits, engaging bands operating against Jewish colonies or attacking convoys on roads. They met with considerable success. In an action near Kafr Kanna, on the 23rd August, 14 Arabs were killed and a quantity of arms and ammunition captured.

On the 27th September, 1938, the Battalion was ordered to return to Egypt forthwith owing to the uncertainty of the political situation, and on the 29th embarked in H.T. *Neuralia*, for Alexandria, arriving at Mersa Matruh on 1st October, where it bivouacked. Work there consisted of digging trenches and putting the allotted sector in a proper state of defence.

Before leaving Palestine, the G.O.C., Lieutenant-General R. H. Haining, and Brigadier J. F. Evetts, sent farewell and congratulatory messages.

A few months earlier Private J. E. Mott had been awarded the M.B.E. A bomb had been thrown into a café in Haifa crowded with troops and civilians. Private Mott had shown the utmost coolness and presence of mind in picking it up and throwing it through the window into the street, where it exploded violently but without loss of life. This award was subsequently changed to that of the George Cross.

Ultimately the Battalion arrived back in Cairo on the 16th October, where there was a good deal of refitting to be done. But the 1st Essex was soon on the move again, for orders were received to proceed to Moascar, Cyprus, and Port Said. Headquarters were to be at Moascar, but 4 officers and 175 other ranks had to be found for Cyprus and 1 officer and 75 other ranks for Port Said.

Before Christmas, Lieutenant-General Sir Geoffrey Howard, K.C.B., C.M.G., D.S.O., Colonel of the Regiment, visited the Port Said detachment and the Battalion at Moascar, on his way out East.

Nineteen thirty-eight had been a disturbed and restless year. The Battalion had served in Haifa, Cairo, Nazareth, Tiberias, Mount Tabor, Mersa Matruh, Moascar, Port Said, and Cyprus, and 1939 brought no prospects of a more settled way of life.

Training competed with crises of growing intensity. Perhaps the Cyprus detachment had the most peaceful time, worthily upholding the name of the Regiment by good discipline, fine ceremonial, and sound training. There were two ceremonial guard-mounting parades on the Main Square of Nicosia before His Excellency the Governor during the first half of 1939.

In March 1939 the Battalion was pleased to hear of the award of the Military Medal to Private Attwood and Private Lygett for outstanding gallantry in Palestine.

And so the spring and summer of 1939 passed away crisis by crisis. Only a miracle could prevent the threatening war, but there was no miracle. September 1939 found the 1st Battalion The Essex Regiment efficient and alert.

Section *II*

2ND BATTALION THE ESSEX REGIMENT

MALTA · TURKEY · INDIA · EGYPT · SUDAN · WARLEY

In the spring of 1937 the 2nd Battalion The Essex Regiment (The "Pompadours") arrived in England from a foreign tour of seventeen and a half years. Their history up to that date has been written by Mr. J. W. Burrows. However, as this excellent history is at present out of print, it may be desirable to deal briefly with the service overseas of the 2nd Battalion before considering its further service at home.

Re-formed at Colchester after the First World War, the 2nd Battalion arrived at Malta on the 13th September, 1919, under the command of Major A. G. L. Pepys, M.C.

Lieutenant-Colonel A. P. Churchill took over command in March 1920. This month saw the first public post-war ceremonial parade of the Battalion—"Trooping the Colour" on the Palace Square, Valetta, on the second anniversary of Arras Day, the 28th March, 1920, before Field-Marshal Lord Plumer, the Governor and C.-in-C. Malta. This parade and the preparation before may be said to have welded the young Battalion into a well-disciplined and proud unit. It was a foundation-stone on which the success of the "Pompadours" in the years between the wars was built.

The stay in Malta was short. By mid-1920 the Army of the Black Sea had been reduced below safety limits and reinforcements were necessary to enable the army of occupation in Turkey effectively to function. On the 25th June, 1920, the 2nd Essex sailed for Constantinople. Although on active service, the Battalion was not engaged in active operations, and six months later returned to Malta for a further tour of pleasant peace-time garrison duty.

A year later, on the 15th November, 1921, the 2nd Battalion again went to Turkey, as a unit of the Allied Army of Occupation under General Sir Charles Harington, K.C.B., D.S.O. There they were to undergo the excitements and arduous experiences caused by the threat to Constantinople and the Dardanelles by the victorious Turkish Nationalist armies, which, flushed with their victories over the Greek armies in Asia Minor, were threatening an attack on the British forces in their defensive positions on the Ismid peninsula and at Chanak. It was only the able negotiations of Sir Charles Harington with Mustapha

Kemal Pasha and the resolute and disciplined front presented by the British forces that prevented war. With the signing of an armistice agreement at Mudania, the crisis passed, and with the lessened tension normal trooping was reintroduced. In March 1923 the 2nd Battalion left the Army of the Black Sea and moved to India.

From 1923 to 1926 the 2nd Essex was to be stationed at Ambala, in the Punjab, coming under Lahore District. Hot-weather detachments to the Simla Hill stations of Kasauli, Solon, and Jutogh, and special detachment duty to Amritsar broke the monotony of three years in the plains of India. The Battalion was exceptionally smart and well disciplined in those years even for the Essex Regiment and earned high praise from General Sir William Birdwood, the Army Commander. It is said that the annual training report on the "Pompadours" for the year 1923/24 was displayed for years in an office at Army Headquarters as an example of the standards that could be reached.

On the 20th February, 1924, the period of command by Lieutenant-Colonel A. P. Churchill came to an end, and it was Lieutenant-Colonel C. R. Roberts-West who was in command when the Battalion moved to Cawnpore, in the United Provinces, on 26th March, 1926.

Throughout the years at Cawnpore a permanent detachment of one company had to be found at Benares, together with hot-weather detachments at Kailana, Landour, and Chaubuttia. There were thus only two companies at Headquarters for many months at a time, a disadvantage in training, sport, and sociability. But the 2nd Battalion did not look back, and it was a highly efficient and happy unit that Lieutenant-Colonel H. R. Bowen, D.S.O., took to Landi Kotal in the Khyber Pass on the 28th October, 1928. He had taken over command in March of that year.

Here the Battalion came under Brigadier C. A. Milward, C.B., C.I.E., C.B.E., D.S.O., who was later to have it under his command through the operations on the Kajauri Plain in 1930.

The year in the Khyber soon passed, and on 1st December, 1929, a move was made to Nowshera, in the North-West Frontier Province, as the next peace-time station. It was not to be very peaceful. The Battalion was involved in the Kajauri Plain operations 1930 and in serious internal security duties in Peshawar City. A full account of these operations is given in the history of the 2nd Battalion The Essex Regiment by Mr. J. W. Burrows (2nd Edition, 1937).

The Indian General Service medal was awarded to all ranks serving in these operations. Lieutenant-Colonel H. R. Bowen was awarded a bar to his D.S.O., Regimental Sergeant-Major A. J. Mobbs received the M.B.E., Sergeant F. Field the Military Medal, and the following officers, warrant officers, and other ranks were mentioned in dispatches for distinguished services during the operations:

> Lieutenant-Colonel H. R. Bowen, D.S.O.
> Captain G. V. L. Prowse.
> Captain C. J. I. F. Hopegood.
> R.S.M. A. J. Mobbs, M.B.E.
> Sergeant F. Field, M.M.
> Sergeant R. Wash.

After the excitements and exertions of the North-West Frontier the Battalion, on the 16th December, 1931, moved to Nasirabad in the Central Provinces, where in January 1932 it bade farewell to Lieutenant-Colonel Bowen, and welcomed Lieutenant-Colonel H. Gordon who had come from the Worcestershire Regiment to take command.

Before Colonel Bowen relinquished command he had had the satisfaction of receiving a letter saying, "In the official order of the best British battalions in the Northern Command (including the *Jhansi* Brigade temporarily in the Northern Command for the Kajauri Plain operations) was:

> "2nd Battalion The Essex Regiment. First."

Nasirabad was one of those small internal security stations where a battalion might so easily go downhill. This was not the case, and indeed regimental sports history was made there. The "Pompadours" won the Indian Football Association Shield at Calcutta and the Vizianagram Tournament in Delhi.

The stay at Nasirabad passed peacefully by until in 1935 the 2nd Battalion learnt the Indian tour was nearly over and that it was to move in the cold weather of 1935/36 to the Sudan.

In the event its departure was expedited, since by the 16th October, 1935, it was on the high seas. The Battalion did not know where it was going. The baggage was marked "Khartoum," but everybody sensed they were not going there. The trooper was under sealed orders, for it was a time of crisis, the time of the Italian attack on Abyssinia. There was the chance of war, and the Middle East, that area so vital to Britain's interests, was threatened.

The destination of the 2nd Essex was not to be Khartoum, but the Western Desert of Egypt. Disembarked at Suez, the Battalion moved first by train to Sidi Bishr Camp, ten miles from Alexandria, and then on to Mersa Matruh. A short stay, and then even farther west into the desert to Sidi Barrani. Here it was set to work on the construction of a battalion-defended locality, which, although not to be needed in 1935 and 1936, was to be of value in 1940 when war with Italy did in fact break out.

This was a period of real importance, and the Battalion deserved, and got, many tributes for its excellent work in the Western Desert. Great credit was due to Lieutenant-Colonel C. C. Spooner, D.S.O., who had taken over from Lieutenant-Colonel H. Gordon at Sidi Bishr before the Battalion moved.

As the threat of immediate war lessened, the 2nd Essex was released from the desert and moved south to Khartoum, arriving there on the 28th March, 1936, eighteen years since the Battle of Arras, 1918. It was a year of gathering storm. In Abyssinia, Palestine, and Spain there was war or civil war, and Europe was restless under Italian bombast and German rearmament. But Khartoum was peaceful and the last year of the foreign tour passed quickly.

As a fitting conclusion to the Battalion's foreign tour, the King's Colour was trooped at Khartoum on the 27th January, 1937, the salute being taken by His Excellency Lieutenant-Colonel Sir Stewart Symes, K.C.M.G., K.B.E., D.S.O., the Governor-General of the Sudan.

On the evening of the 6th February, 1937, the 2nd Battalion The Essex Regiment sailed from Port Sudan. Suez was reached on the 9th February, where good-bye was said to the large "turn-over" draft which was to join the 1st Battalion in Palestine.

The 2nd Essex marched into Warley on the 20th February, 1937, where it had a splendid welcome. The band of the 4th Battalion played it away from the station and also as it marched past Colonel F. H. D. C. Whitmore, the Lord-Lieutenant of Essex, who afterwards gave an address of welcome.

It was not long before everybody was off on leave, and on their return great preparations were put in hand for the Coronation. The Battalion found three parties for this duty:

"A"—Processional Troops: Lieutenant-Colonel C. C. Spooner, D.S.O., and 7 other ranks.
"B"—Street-lining Troops in Pall Mall: Captain and Brevet-Major H. L. H. Boustead, Lieutenant T. L. G. Charles with the King's Colour, and 43 other ranks.

"C"—Street-lining Troops (Reserves): Major W. G. Cowley, 5 officers and 150 other ranks.

After the Coronation the Battalion returned to Warley, but a week later it was moved to the Tower of London in relief of the 2nd Battalion Scots Guards. This was an event of historical importance and counted as a distinction. The advance party took over on the 18th May, 1937.

Life in the Tower proved somewhat monotonous, as military activities were wholly confined to guard duties. The Main Guard took part in the Ceremony of the Keys each night.

It was not an uncommon thing to see the children of the Royal Family being shown around. Her Majesty Queen Mary brought her grandchildren, the Princess Elizabeth and the Princess Margaret, and the Duke and Duchess of Kent also paid a visit while the Battalion was there. The Lord Mayor of London was quite a frequent visitor, and it may not be generally known that as the Tower is within the city walls, the Lord Mayor has a right to go there whenever he likes. On certain evenings the band and drums in full-dress uniform would beat Tattoo, this display being followed by the Ceremony of the Keys and the sounding of the Last Post on Massed Bugles. As the band and drums were floodlit, the whole parade was most impressive, and will always remain in the memories of those who saw it.

In October 1937 the Battalion took part in an impressive ceremony at Chelmsford. Thirty silver bugles, raised by voluntary subscription from the people of Essex, were presented as an expression of pride in the services abroad of the 2nd Essex during its foreign tour. Each bugle bears the inscription "Presented by the County of Essex to the Officers and Men of the 2nd Battalion The Essex Regiment in commemoration of their distinguished Service abroad from 1919 to 1937," followed by a facsimile signature of the Lord-Lieutenant of Essex.

It was the morning of Saturday, 2nd October, 1937, when the Battalion left Liverpool Street Station in a special train headed by the L.N.E.R. engine "The Essex Regiment," being joined at Brentwood by H.Q. Company, which was not doing duty at the Tower.

On arrival at Chelmsford the "Pompadours" detrained and marched through the crowded and beflagged streets to the County Cricket Ground, where, drawn up in line, they received with a General Salute the Lord-Lieutenant of Essex, Colonel F. H. D. C. Whitmore, C.B., C.M.G., D.S.O., who was accompanied by General Sir Harry Knox,

K.C.B., D.S.O. (Adjutant-General to the Forces), Sir Herbert Creedy, G.C.B., K.C.V.O. (Permanent Under-Secretary of State for War), Lieutenant-General Sir Geoffrey Howard, K.C.B., C.M.G., D.S.O. (Colonel of the Essex Regiment), Major-General R. M. Luckock, C.B., C.M.G., D.S.O. (Commander 54th Division and East Anglian Area), and Commander Coventry, R.N. (A.D.C. to the Lord-Lieutenant).

The presentation was followed by the Ceremony of "Trooping the Colour," and then, headed by the band and drums playing "The Essex Bugles," the Battalion marched to the Drill Hall, where it was entertained to tea by the County.

In a concluding speech the Lord-Lieutenant was good enough to congratulate the 2nd Battalion on its display and said the whole occasion had been an unqualified success. The Adjutant-General also spoke. He said he would like to make mention of the great work of the county of Essex. He had started his soldiering at Colchester, he looked upon Essex as his military home, and he knew there existed in the county a magnificent County Spirit. "There are no counties in England which can do things so well as Essex, and I know of no regiment fortunate enough to have such a magnificent presentation as this today."

Nineteen thirty-eight saw increased facilities for training. Battalion training at Colchester followed platoon and company training, and after battalion training there was a period of brigade training with the 11th Infantry Brigade in Suffolk. A most valuable year in which the Battalion acquitted itself well. The experience gained was to prove invaluable in the coming years.

Nineteen thirty-eight was a period of increasing international tension, including the alarms and unreadiness of the Munich crisis. Had the 2nd Essex moved overseas at forty-eight hours' notice as was at one time its orders, the Battalion would have undoubtedly given a good account of itself despite the extreme difficulties under which it would have served and fought.

The year 1939 opened quietly, and on the surface the normal life of the Service was continued. The 2nd Battalion was selected to take part in the Aldershot Tattoo, and rehearsals competed with training parades and schemes, filling the soldiers' day to overflowing. But in the orderly room and company offices the preparation of all measures for mobilisation went on apace. Throughout the summer reservists and supplementary reservists were attached for refresher training, for new equipments such as Brens and mortars, the 15-cwt. truck and Bren carrier

1st Battalion The Essex Regiment entering the Barracks of the French 106th Regiment of Infantry. Rheims. 20th February, 1935. Lieutenant-Colonel A. E. Maitland, D.S.O., M.C., Captain T. A. Martin, Captain L. A. G. Bowen, M.C. (O.C. "A" Company), R.S.M. C. T. Sparrow.

2ND BATTALION THE ESSEX REGIMENT LEAVING H.M. TOWER OF LONDON FOR CHELMSFORD AND THE PRESENTATION OF SILVER BUGLES BY THE COUNTY OF ESSEX. 2ND OCTOBER, 1937.

2ND BATTALION THE ESSEX REGIMENT MARCH OFF AFTER THE PRESENTATION, THE SILVER BUGLES BEING PLAYED FOR THE FIRST OCCASION. CHELMSFORD, 2ND OCTOBER, 1937.

were now beginning to reach units. The training reservists received was to stand them in good stead only a few months hence.

Field engineering was an important part of the training, as during the summer the 2nd Essex had been warned to be prepared on mobilisation to carry out the role of a pioneer battalion in addition to the normal role of infantry.

The calling-up of the Militia under a recent Act of Parliament came into effect on the 15th July, 1939, when the young men of Essex began to flow into the depot at Warley. The first batch to complete its initial training was posted to the 2nd Battalion very shortly before the outbreak of war.

And so, as the declaration of war upon Germany became a matter of days or even hours, we see a proud and confident battalion being joined by reservists and supplementary reservists all knowing their place and role, and strengthened by drafts of young, fit, and partially trained militia already inculcated with the spirit and traditions of the Essex Regiment during the period at the depot. This was a very different picture from that seen only a year earlier, when the Munich crisis found the nation uncertain and unprepared. The task had not been easy. The 2nd Battalion, down to bedrock after passing the majority of its personnel to the 1st Battalion in February 1937, had been re-formed from a nucleus of about one hundred old hands by the summer of 1939. When the time came, Lieutenant-Colonel Spooner handed over a battalion second to none. "This was largely due to my two Adjutants, Captain C. S. Mills and Captain T. L. G. Charles, and to Major H. L. H. Boustead, the Battalion training officer, and the 'Pompadours' of the 1940 campaign owe these three a great debt of gratitude." Lieutenant-Colonel A. H. Blest took over command from Lieutenant-Colonel Spooner on 1st August, 1939.

Section III

THE 161ST INFANTRY BRIGADE T.A.: 4TH, 5TH, 6TH, AND 7TH BATTALIONS THE ESSEX REGIMENT, 1929-39

The 161st Infantry Brigade with the rest of the Territorial Army was reconstituted on the 16th February, 1920, and on this day the 4th, 5th, 6th, and 7th Battalions of the Essex Regiment again came into being.

The organisation and general layout of battalions remained the same from 1918 until 1929, when changes were made with a view

B.R.—2

to the organisation of each battalion into three rifle companies and one machine-gun company.

It is not proposed to deal with each battalion separately, as this would lead to much repetition, the battalions following the same routine year after year. Better to select the outstanding items of each Territorial year and so picture the Essex Territorial Brigade through the "years of disinterest" to the days when with rising danger to the British Commonwealth the volunteer spirit quickened once more into life.

The Territorial year was divided into two parts: the pre-camp period of drill-hall parades, range work, and exercises without troops, followed by the annual camp. A very high proportion of those on the strength managed to attend camp. The nation owes a debt of gratitude to those employers of labour who gave special leave to Territorials to enable them to attend, and to the many who placed country before self and family, and spent their yearly holiday from normal work attending camp with their unit.

Numbers in camp were not high in the "dog days," but, weak or strong, the Territorial battalions always entered into the spirit of camp. To work hard and play hard might have been their motto. The inter-unit spirit was strong. Whether athletic championship or Drums competition, the interest and friendly rivalry were very great.

The 1929 camp at Mytchett deserves a special mention. It so happened that Mytchett Place was the residence of the then Colonel of the Regiment, Major-General J. C. Harding-Newman, C.B., C.M.G. Also all the Commanding Officers of the Regular and Territorial Battalions were able to meet in the Officers' Mess of the 7th Battalion. Lieutenant-Colonel H. R. Bowen, D.S.O., Commanding the 2nd Battalion, was home on leave from India, and thus able to join the other Commanding Officers. Such a gathering, probably, has few precedents in the British Army. General Harding-Newman was photographed with the assembled Commanding Officers, who were Lieutenant-Colonel A. E. M. Sinclair-Thomson, D.S.O. (1st Battalion), Lieutenant-Colonel H. R. Bowen, D.S.O. (2nd Battalion), Lieutenant-Colonel J. L. French (4th Battalion), Lieutenant-Colonel C. Portway, M.C. (5th Battalion), Lieutenant-Colonel E. A. Loftus, O.B.E., T.D. (6th Battalion), and Brevet-Colonel G. Shenstone, T.D. (7th Battalion).

Every year, every Battalion celebrated Gaza Day. As the anniversary of the 26th March, 1917, comes round, there are many in Essex whose thoughts go back to the days when the Essex Infantry

Brigade, consisting of the 4th, 5th, 6th, and 7th Battalions of the Essex Regiment, was fighting the First Battle of Gaza. Remembrance generally took the form of a commemoration service at the Regimental Chapel, Warley, or at a parish church in the town where the headquarters of the Battalion was situated. In 1929, the 4th and 7th Battalions had their service at the Regimental Chapel, while the 6th Battalion had its at West Ham Parish Church. With the yearly observances, those who fell at Gaza are never forgotten.

Voluntary training in those days was a success, and it makes pleasant reading to find what zeal the Essex Territorials put into their work, whether at drill hall or at camp. Competition for vacancies at tactical exercises without troops, for attachment to regular units, and for ceremonial parades on the occasion of some important happening was extremely keen.

It is perhaps not realised how great a part the Territorial Army has taken in the ceremonial of the county. Hardly a State occasion passes without the appropriate Territorial battalion playing its part, whether by lending its band and drums or providing a Guard of Honour. It would be interesting to have the full details of all battalions, but certainly the record of the 4th Battalion in finding Royal Guards of Honour would be hard to beat, not only within the Essex Territorial Brigade, but within the whole army. In the fourteen years between 1925 and 1939 the 4th Battalion was called upon to find no fewer than seven Royal Guards of Honour:

1. *25th March*, 1925: H.R.H. Prince Henry (later Duke of Gloucester) —Opening of the new Southend Road.
   Guard Commander—Major J. L. French.
2. *21st October*, 1926: The Duke of York (later King George VI), to present Ilford's Charter.
   Guard Commander—Major J. L. French.
3. *9th May*, 1929: The Duke of York (later King George VI), to receive Freedom of the Borough of Ilford.
   Guard Commander—Captain G. M. Gibson.
4. *18th July*, 1931: H.M. King George V opened King George V Hospital, Ilford.
   Guard Commander—Major G. M. Gibson.
5. *5th October*, 1931: H.R.H. Prince George (afterwards Duke of Kent) to present Barking's Charter.
   Guard Commander—Captain J. S. Cox, M.C.

6. *14th October*, 1937: H.R.H. the Duke of Gloucester to present Wanstead and Woodford's Charter.
Guard Commander—Captain A. Noble.
7. *6th June*, 1939: H.R.H. Princess Alice (Countess of Athlone), deputising for H.M. Queen Mary, visited King George V Hospital, Ilford.
Guard Commander—Captain E. J. Sheldrake.

In each of these Guards of Honour the band and drums were on parade with the King's Colour of the Battalion. There is no doubt that these Guards of Honour and the preparation for them set a tradition throughout the Battalion for drill, military bearing, and turn-out. It was so, too, in the other battalions of the Essex Territorial Brigade.

And so the years moved on from 1929. In 1932 the country was suffering from a financial crisis of some magnitude, and as an economy measure there were no Territorial camps. This, however, did not deter the Territorial Army. As an example of keenness it is hard to beat the effort of the 5th Battalion, who decided to finance and hold its own camp at Brackenbury Banks, Felixstowe. Nineteen officers and 200 other ranks attended voluntarily without pay and allowances. This fine example stirred public imagination, and the Army Council expressed their thanks to the Battalion.

In 1933 annual camps were reintroduced, and records show the strength of the 54th East Anglian Division was 6,720, a very large percentage of which attended camp. All four Essex battalions were about 500 strong at this date, and again a very high proportion of those "on the books" attended the 161st Infantry Brigade Camp at Dibgate, Shorncliffe.

Changes in command took place in 1933-34, Colonel F. R. Waller, T.D., handing over the 7th Battalion to Lieutenant-Colonel C. D. Martin, T.D., and Lieutenant-Colonel P. L. Grimwood, M.C., taking over the 6th Battalion from Colonel C. A. Bailey, O.B.E., T.D. The Army List for 1934 shows that the Commanding Officers and Adjutants within the Essex Brigade were:

4th Battalion: Lieutenant-Colonel J. L. French.
    Captain N. R. Salew.
5th Battalion: Lieutenant-Colonel C. Portway, M.C.
    Captain R. E. G. Carolin.

6th Battalion: Lieutenant-Colonel P. L. Grimwood, M.C.
Captain L. W. W. Marriott.
7th Battalion: Lieutenant-Colonel C. D. Martin, T.D.
Captain A. H. Blest.

The big event of 1935 was the celebration of His Majesty King George V's Silver Jubilee in May. Each Battalion celebrated in its own particular way. The 4th Battalion paraded for a thanksgiving service at Valentine's Park, Ilford, after which there were Jubilee celebrations. A detachment of the 5th Battalion took part in a parade of the various units of the Colchester Garrison, and the 6th Battalion attended a service at Upton Cross.

Territorial camp 1935 was again at Dibgate, and it was to be the last Territorial camp in which four Essex Territorial Battalions were to be present. The first of an inevitable series of changes which were to eat away Essex infantry was about to take place. It was the last time that the 7th Battalion The Essex Regiment (T.A.) could take part in annual training as infantry and form part of the 161st (Essex) Infantry Brigade.

Responding to a request by the Army Council that it accept conversion to an anti-aircraft unit, the 7th Battalion undertook this important duty. An account of the Battalion's last departure from camp is worth quoting. "At an early hour, when the tents were shrouded in mist and the usual bustle of camp had not come to life, the 7th Battalion marched out. Almost mechanically the orders were obeyed. ... '7th Essex. Advance in fours from right of companies.' The band began to play and then stopped. Silent, they marched until suddenly there came another sound—cheers! Round upon round of cheers growing louder every minute. It was the Brigade's farewell gesture. It was a scene which gave evidence of the fact that no matter what happened, the 7th Battalion would always be a part of the Essex Regiment." They were, and still are, men of Essex, although they had become 59th A.A. Brigade (7th Battalion The Essex Regiment).

The year 1936 was a normal one. The following year was noteworthy owing to the Coronation of King George VI and Queen Elizabeth. All three Essex Territorial Battalions took some part in it, either finding detachments to line the route or for other duties. A number of officers and N.C.O.s of each battalion were awarded Coronation Medals.

By the spring of 1938 recruiting was definitely improving. Both the

4th Battalion and the 5th Battalion had strengths well in excess of 500, strengths greater than they had had for many years. The nation was awakening to the trials that lay ahead.

In this year the 6th Battalion made history. It was "adopted" by the Worshipful Company of Carpenters. It is very seldom that one hears of an army unit being "adopted" by a Livery Company. The object was that the Company should give both moral and financial aid to the Battalion of its choice. On the 5th January, 1938, the Master of the Worshipful Company of Carpenters invited Lieutenant-Colonel R. W. Wren to meet the Court at a luncheon at the Carpenters Hall, where he was allowed to explain to the Court the needs of the Battalion and suggest ways that the Company could be of assistance.

Later that year the 161st (Essex) Infantry Brigade was sad to see the 6th Battalion follow the 7th Battalion into an anti-aircraft role. After the annual camp of 1938 the 6th Essex was to join Anti-Aircraft Command and undergo conversion into two Searchlight Units—1/6th Battalion The Essex Regiment (64th Searchlight Regiment) and 2/6th Battalion The Essex Regiment (65th Searchlight Regiment). The conversion was marked by considerable ceremony and ceremonial, which included a march past before the Mayor of West Ham at the Town Hall, Stratford. The new units were still to remain part of the Essex Regiment. In his final words to the 6th Battalion, Lieutenant-Colonel R. W. Wren said, "We have to make up our minds to do our job as well as, if not better than, we have been doing our infantry training up to now."

In 1938 the 5th Battalion was sorry to lose Lieutenant-Colonel W. L. Ridley, who gave up command after the annual camp. Lieutenant-Colonel H. C. N. Trollope, D.S.O., M.C., took over command.

And so through the Munich crisis of September 1938 to 1939, a year that opened in an uneasy calm and was to end with an embodied and mobilised Territorial Army.

Events were now to move fast. Early in the year battalion organisation which had remained almost unchanged since 1929 was altered. The Territorial Army was reorganised and brought into line with the Regular Army, a change that was long overdue. This had hardly been digested when an even greater decision was reached—the Cabinet resolved to double the Territorial Army.

The road ahead was now clearly signposted "Danger." Despite the Munich agreement and Hitler's protestations for peace, Germany marched, on 15th March, 1939, into Bohemia. Czechoslovakia, weakened by the loss of her fortified positions under the Munich agreement of 1938, was unable to resist, and Hitler, arriving in Prague, proclaimed a German protectorate over the country.

The British Government took prompt action to strengthen the armed forces. On the 29th March, 1939, Mr. Neville Chamberlain, the Prime Minister, announced in Parliament the immediate doubling of the Territorial Army, a planned increase by voluntary enlistment of some 210,000 men.

Recruiting was already brisk. The 4th Battalion was now over 600 strong and up to peace establishment. The 5th Battalion was not far behind. The 1/6th Battalion, the 2/6th Battalion, and the 7th Battalion, under the impetus of a drive to strengthen the anti-aircraft defences of London, were enlisting a steady stream of recruits. The spirit of voluntary service was indeed alive.

That the Territorial units of the Essex Regiment were efficient and capable of meeting the new crisis that lay ahead was mainly attributable to that small cadre of all ranks who gave both time and devotion to their battalions in the years leading up to the Second World War, in particular the commanding officers—Lieutenant-Colonels J. L. French and G. M. Gibson (4th Battalion), Lieutenant-Colonels C. Portway and W. L. Ridley (5th Battalion), Lieutenant-Colonels C. A. Bailey, P. L. Grimwood and R. W. Wren (6th Battalion) and Lieutenant-Colonels F. R. Waller and C. D. Martin of the 7th Battalion. The success of their work is set out for all to see in the records that follow.

By the end of April 1939, barely four weeks after the decision to double the Territorial Army, it was decided by Parliament to introduce conscription into the country. It might have been thought that the inevitability of being called up under the new scheme would have affected the voluntary enlistment of men into the Territorial Army, but it was not so. There was a continued rush of recruits. Very soon the 4th Battalion was in a position to anticipate being able to go to camp as two full-strength battalions with waiting lists. The position in the 5th Battalion area was almost as good.

The second line of the 4th Battalion was raised side by side with the first line battalion, except that "B" Company of the 2/4th was raised in the Romford area. Lieutenant-Colonel G. M. Gibson, was in command of the 1/4th Battalion, and command of the 2/4th Battalion was given to Major Lord Edward Hay, the Second-in-Command of the 4th Battalion. Lord Edward Hay was later to lose his life in the destruction by enemy action of the Guards' Chapel in Wellington Barracks, London.

The 5th Battalion did not raise its second line side by side with the first line. The Battalion area was divided geographically into two parts. In one was the 1/5th (West) Battalion The Essex Regiment; in the other the 2/5th (East) Battalion. Lieutenant-Colonel H. C. N. Trollope, D.S.O., M.C., commanded the 1/5th (West) and Lieutenant-Colonel C. Portway, M.C., T.D., took command of the 2/5th (East) Battalion.

There was much to do. Doubling the Territorial Army did not of itself produce an army. Numerically stronger, the force was for a time weaker in the terms of fighting formations, because experienced officers and non-commissioned officers and trained soldiers, never plentiful, had now to go doubly far. But difficulties are there to be overcome, and this was never more true than with the Territorials in 1939. Camp lay ahead—that year to be held at Wannock—and over all lay the shadow of war.

The 64th Searchlight Regiment (1/6th Essex) and the 65th Searchlight Regiment (2/6th Essex) were busily recruiting and training at drill hall, camp, and searchlight site. The 59th A.A. Brigade (7th Essex) trained that year at Cleave anti-aircraft camp in North Devon, and then at the end of the training period was partially embodied and dispersed to war stations. They were released in July on relief by another brigade and returned to their homes. But not for long.

In August the international situation rapidly deteriorated. On the 21st/22nd of the month the Soviet news agency published the fact that Germany was about to sign a non-aggression pact with the Soviet Union. This was a danger signal that the British Government could not ignore.

"Key parties" of Territorial anti-aircraft and coast defence batteries were called out; the guarding of vulnerable points (V.P.s) was ordered. Two days later, on the 23rd August, certain regular reservists to complete units overseas to war establishment were called up, and the full manning of radar and anti-aircraft positions was ordered. Reception at unit headquarters of the various code-word telegrams authorising the various stages of the "Preparatory to War" period was at shorter and shorter intervals as the hours of peace grew less and the morning of the 3rd September, 1939, grew remorselessly nearer. As the days of August 1939 ran out and September came in, it was clear that war was inevitable.

Chapter Two

THE 1st BATTALION THE ESSEX REGIMENT, 1939-48

FOREWORD

by Brigadier J. S. Nichols, D.S.O., M.C., *Officer Commanding 1st Battalion The Essex Regiment, 1940-41*

In November 1940 I had the honour and good fortune to be selected by General Wavell to take over command of the 1st Battalion The Essex Regiment, then on service on the Sudan–Abyssinian border, and to remain in command of the Battalion throughout the rest of its service in the Middle East, a period of fourteen months.

During this period the Battalion's record must have been unique, for I doubt if any other unit had such a varied and momentous career in such a short space of time. During that period we took part in four separate campaigns, served in eleven or more different formations, and travelled more than 15,000 miles, entering eight different countries.

I am convinced that no unit in the army had finer personnel than the 1st Essex. The initiative, resourcefulness, efficiency, and endurance displayed in the Iraq and Syrian campaigns were remarkable, but the crowning feat was the Battalion's performance in the Tobruk corridor. It was with a very sad heart but with very proud memories that I left the 1st Essex Regiment in January 1942. The period of my command had been for me the most important and the happiest period of my life.

J. S. Nichols

31st July, 1951.

Section I

EGYPT, 1939-40

THE 1st Battalion The Essex Regiment, commanded by Lieutenant-Colonel G. A. M. Paxton, M.C., was, with the exception of a strong company (4 officers and 175 other ranks) in Cyprus and one company at Port Said, quartered in Nelson Lines, Moascar, Egypt, when in the early hours of the 24th August, 1939, messages denoting the introduction of the "Precautionary Period" were received and the mobilisation of the Battalion on to a war footing began.

The Battalion was at this time under the orders of the Canal Brigade, commanded by Brigadier W. T. Brooks, M.C., A.D.C.

Officers serving with the Battalion on the outbreak of war were Lieutenant-Colonel G. A. M. Paxton, M.C.; Majors C. J. I. F. Hopegood, S. O'C. Mallins, W. P. Williams, K. F. May; Captains A. H. Kelly and H. J. K. Genders; Lieutenants F. H. B. Webster (Adjutant), R. B. James, J. I. Houston, J. F. Higson, W. N. C. Waite, P. H. A. L. Franklin; and 2/Lieutenants K. P. L. Wilson, J. S. Greene, C. H. Robinson, I. J. D. Stevenson Hamilton, C. J. S. McMillen, M. D. O'Reilly, and T. D'A. Muirhead. Captain B. O'Hagen was Quartermaster. Others "on the strength" but away from the Battalion included Major T. O'C. Doherty, Captain N. R. Salew, Lieutenants A. J. M. Littledale and P. A. Sinclair-Thomson. Those with the Cyprus detachment were Major K. F. May, Captain H. K. J. Genders, Lieutenants P. H. A. L. Franklin and J. I. Houston.

Mobilisation orders had been anticipated ever since Italy's invasion of Albania in April 1939 had made her eventual participation in any future war almost inevitable, and all plans for administrative details, such as the storage of the Battalion's heavy baggage, the safe custody of regimental plate, and the transfer of funds to the custody of the United Services Trustee, had been made. Mobilisation was thus an easier process than otherwise would have been the case.

On the same day that the order "prepare to mobilise" was received, the 1st Essex, less "C" Company, the Cyprus Detachment and "D" Company, left Moascar for Port Said. Here Battalion Headquarters was established in the Cold Storage, no doubt a good place whence to wage a cold war in a hot climate.

The Battalion was employed in occupying strategic points between

Moascar and Port Said. The primary task of the Canal Brigade was at that stage to keep a watch on Italian and other neutral shipping to prevent sabotage, particularly the scuttling of a ship in the Suez Canal, that vital lifeline of the Empire.

Italy was still busily reinforcing her garrisons in Abyssinia, Eritrea, and Italian Somaliland, and the passage through the Canal of Italian troop and store ships was an almost everyday occurrence. Italians, throwing insults from their ships to the British shore garrisons, little thought that they would be dead or prisoners of war within the next eighteen months.

There was little to report during September 1939. On the 17th a convoy brought to the 1st Essex 3 officers and 103 reservists as reinforcements, and the arrival of these reservist reinforcements in Egypt fourteen days after the outbreak of war is an enlightening commentary on the efficiency of our mobilisation arrangements. It will be remembered that to recall to the colours some six thousand reservists as reinforcements for overseas garrisons was one of the earliest acts of H.M. Government during the precautionary period.

At the end of September 1939 the Cyprus detachment, having been relieved by the 1st Sherwood Foresters from Haifa, rejoined the Battalion. Cyprus, a Crown Colony of great strategic importance in the eastern Mediterranean, had been held on the outbreak of war by a company of the 1st Essex armed with its rifles, nine Bren guns, and three Boyes anti-tank rifles. Not exactly a strength compatible with the strategic importance of the island.

The 1st Essex was to remain in the Port Said–Moascar area until January 1940. The role allotted to the Battalion was neither exacting nor spectacular, but nevertheless essential.

Battalion headquarters moved from Port Said to Moascar during November, and there were various inter-company changes from time to time, but generally speaking the layout and role of the 1st Essex did not alter until the 3rd January, 1940, when a warning order for a move was received.

The second draft to reach the Battalion since the outbreak of war had been welcomed on 27th November, 1939. It was from the 4th Battalion, which earlier in the year had been called upon to find a volunteer draft for overseas. This was the first of the many interchanges between Regular and Territorial battalions that were to be a feature of the war years, and which were to do so much to fuse the battalions of the Regiment into one spiritual entity. This does not mean there was not strong battalion rivalry. There was, and it is right that this spirit should always exist. But over all lay, as lies today, the feeling that loyalty to the Regiment as a whole is of greater importance than loyalty to one battalion. And so, throughout the war, officers and men, deeply attached to the battalion with which they served, accepted attachments and postings within the Regiment without question. As it was for the good of the Regiment that they were posted, so all of their loyalty and endeavour went with them to their new unit. Thus will the regimental spirit for ever live on.

Section II

THE SUDAN, 1940

On the 22nd January, 1940, the 1st Essex moved to Suez, where it was embarked in the Polish ship *Batory* for Port Sudan. Families had been embarked for England earlier in the month.

On leaving Moascar, Lieutenant-Colonel Paxton received the following message from Brigadier Brooks, Commander of the 23rd (Canal) Infantry Brigade:

> "On leaving the Brigade, I wish you and all ranks of your Battalion all good luck. I hope you will have many happy soldiering days in front of you, and I ask you to accept my thanks for the cooperation you have given me whilst under my command."

Disembarked at Port Sudan on the 24th January, 1940, the 1st Essex arrived at Khartoum twenty-four hours later, having dropped a detachment at Atbara on the way. This Atbara detachment consisted of "A" and "B" Companies, a machine-gun platoon, an anti-tank platoon, and a mechanical transport section, together with some signallers. Major K. F. May was in command, with Lieutenant P. A. Sinclair-Thomson as detachment adjutant and quartermaster. The Battalion soon settled into Khartoum Barracks (North), well known to many from their stay in Khartoum Barracks (South) with the 2nd Battalion in 1936/37.

Atbara, where there was to be this two-company detachment, is 200 miles north of Khartoum.

Three British battalions garrisoned the Sudan in those early days of 1940: 1st Essex in Khartoum (North), 2nd West Yorkshire Regiment in Khartoum (South), and 1st Worcestershire Regiment at Port Sudan. The G.O.C. the Sudan was Major-General W. Platt, C.B., D.S.O., who carried out a "marching-in" inspection on 13th February, 1940. General Platt was afterwards to gain fame by his victories over the Italians in East Africa and from his conquest of Abyssinia.

While at Khartoum the Battalion carried out training with renewed vigour. Desert mobile patrols and the organisation of defensive positions for the protection of Khartoum were the order of the day, but nevertheless the war seemed far away and much less pressing than it did in Europe.

It is difficult to be at war and yet at peace. Too much and too premature emphasis on war and training for war will lead to staleness through being overtrained; too little emphasis on war and too much reliance on a peace programme of work will result in a perhaps imperceptible falling away of morale. To find the mean is part of the art of command.

As the spring of 1940 passed into early summer, it was evident that German action in Western Europe would not be long delayed, and that the success or failure of the expected offensive would determine Italy's future course of action. Training became more intensive despite the onset of the Sudan hot-weather season. Exercises with the Sudan Defence Force were held frequently, and generally took the form of mobile columns fighting delaying actions against greatly superior enemy forces advancing against Khartoum from the east (Eritrea). An air of urgency was apparent, but despite the calls upon them the 1st Battalion—as with the other battalions of the Regiment—spared time to remember the great deeds of the past.

The 25th of April, 1940, the twenty-fifth anniversary of the landing of the 1st Battalion as part of the immortal 29th Division at Gallipoli in 1915, was indeed a day to commemorate. It was an incentive and inspiration for the days of battle that lay ahead.

It was now apparent that the period of inaction was ending, and steps were taken to send the garrisons of the Middle East to their war stations. This order reached the 1st Essex at 11 a.m. on the 1st May, 1940, and by 7 p.m. the Battalion had entrained for Atbara. It detrained early next morning, and that afternoon, when it had been joined by the mechanical transport road party, the Battalion was concentrated at its war station.

The initial task was to link up air defence and air-raid precautions with the civilian authorities. This was very important, as Atbara, a junction of railway lines from the north and east, is a focal point of communication within the Sudan. It will be appreciated how difficult it was, in a country of deserts and before the introduction of radar, to get information about approaching aircraft which could draw near to the few strategic points from any direction without giving prior warning.

Arrangements were made with the Sudan Railways that stationmasters should report when they saw or heard aircraft, and similar arrangements were made with outlying police posts. One of the first duties of the intelligence section was to go to Adarama, seventy-six miles south-east along the track to Kassala, and deliver a wireless set to the local police post. This network of wireless outposts and railway telephones was expected to give due warning, not only of air, but ground approach.

Concurrently, work on the defences was undertaken, and defences were manned by one platoon in each sector. These works involved, among other things, the laying of sixteen miles of buried cable by the signal platoon, and it still rankles with the signal officer, Lieutenant I. J. D. Stevenson-Hamilton, that his idea of digging the trench for the cable by towing a borrowed Arab plough behind a 15-cwt. truck did not work. After a very few miles the vehicle's clutch burnt out and the platoon had to dig the remaining miles.

On the 19th May, 1940, it was learnt that mobilisation had been ordered throughout Italian East Africa, and all ranks must have had mixed feelings when they remembered that only a few weeks before they had watched a procession of Italian troop and store ships passing through the Suez Canal on the way to Italian East Africa. Many must have known that the original British garrison of three line battalions and approximately 5,000 men of the Sudan Defence Force had as yet only received small reinforcements from Egypt and India, and many, too, must have known of the 300,000 Italians in East Africa and of 200,000 in Libya.

By the 25th May, 1940, Italian mobilisation in East Africa was complete. In Europe the retreat to Dunkirk was in progress. A declaration of war by Italy could not long be delayed, and on the 10th June, 1940, she declared war. Full precautions were taken in Atbara. A semi-blackout was ordered and all anti-aircraft defences manned. Italian subjects were rounded up and sent to Khartoum for internment.

It was now that the following message was received from Lieuten-

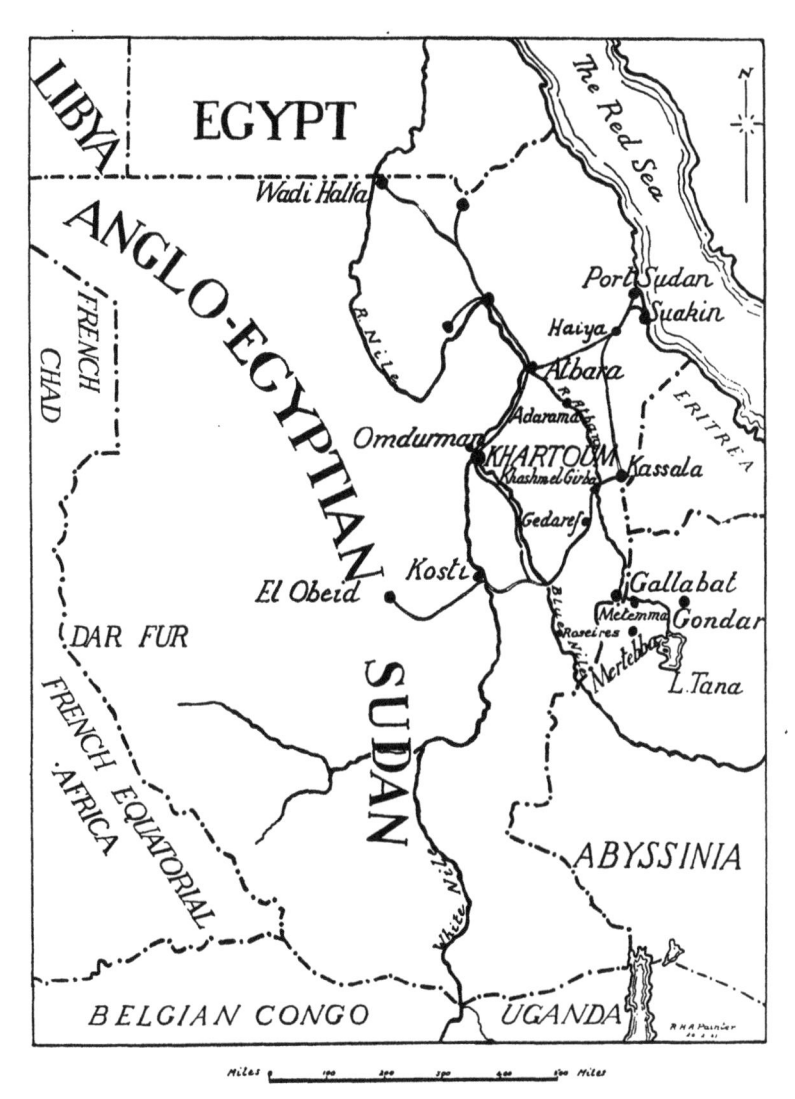

THE ANGLO-EGYPTIAN SUDAN AND ITALIAN EAST AFRICA.

ant-General Sir Geoffrey Howard, K.C.B., C.M.G., D.S.O., Colonel of the Essex Regiment:

"To Lieutenant-Colonel G. A. M. Paxton, M.C. Whatever is in store for you and your Battalion, I can only wish you Godspeed and good luck, confident in your ability to maintain unsullied the proud annals of the Regiment."

By the 18th June, 1940, it was clear that the Italians were effecting a concentration of troops in North Eritrea, and a counter regrouping of the Sudan Defence Force was ordered accordingly.

On the 6th July, 1940, "C" Company, under Captain J. F. Higson, was sent to reinforce the garrison of Khartoum. On the following day Atbara had its first air raid, some twenty bombs being dropped with the bridge over the River Atbara as the target. No damage was done. The net result was that the officers who were enjoying an after-breakfast cigarette outside the mess, about a mile from the bridge, had to make a hasty dive for cover as the aircraft unexpectedly appeared and bombs fell. The only casualty was sustained by Major W. P. Williams, a bomb splinter passing through his Wolsey helmet as he was cycling to his company office.

In August an important reconnaissance was carried out to find a suitable route for convoys from Egypt to the Sudan by way of Aswan and Wadi Halfa as an alternative to the Nile River route. This reconnaissance was carried out under Captain P. H. A. L. Franklin, and was highly successful.

Brigadier J. C. O. Marriott, C.V.O., now commanding the newly formed 21st Infantry Brigade, was at Atbara on the 16th August, and carried out a thorough inspection, both of the Battalion and of the defences for which it was responsible.

The 1st Essex now began to see a little action. Platoon patrols in M.T. were sent out towards Kassala in order that they might draw the enemy fire, which was very inaccurate, and thus experience a little battle inoculation at no cost to our own ammunition supplies.

In the first real action, Captain H. J. K. Genders, who had left Atbara on the 20th August with one full war-scale platoon to join a Sudan Defence force detachment on the Eritrean border, came into contact during the night of the 26th/27th August with Italian forces near Adaradeb. In the ensuing action Captain Genders, Lance-Corporal Jay, and Private Davis were killed, the first casualties in the Battalion since the outbreak of war.

THE COLONEL AND COMMANDING OFFICERS, THE ESSEX REGIMENT. MYTCHETT. AUGUST 1929.

Standing (L. to R.) Lieut.-Colonel (Bt.-Colonel) G. Shenstone, T.D. (7th Battalion), Lieut.-Colonel J. L. French (4th Battalion), Lieut.-Colonel C. Portway, M.C. (5th Battalion), Lieut.-Colonel E. A. Loftus, O.B.E, T.D. (6th Battalion).
Sitting (L. to R.) Lieut.-Colonel A. E. M. Sinclair-Thomson, D.S.O. (1st Battalion), Major-General J. C. Harding-Newman, C.B., C.M.G. (Colonel of the Regiment), Lieut.-Colonel H. R. Bowen, D.S.O. (2nd Battalion).

(Imperial War Museum)
1ST BATTALION THE ESSEX REGIMENT AFTER THE OCCUPATION OF FORT GALLABAT (SUDAN). NOVEMBER 1940.

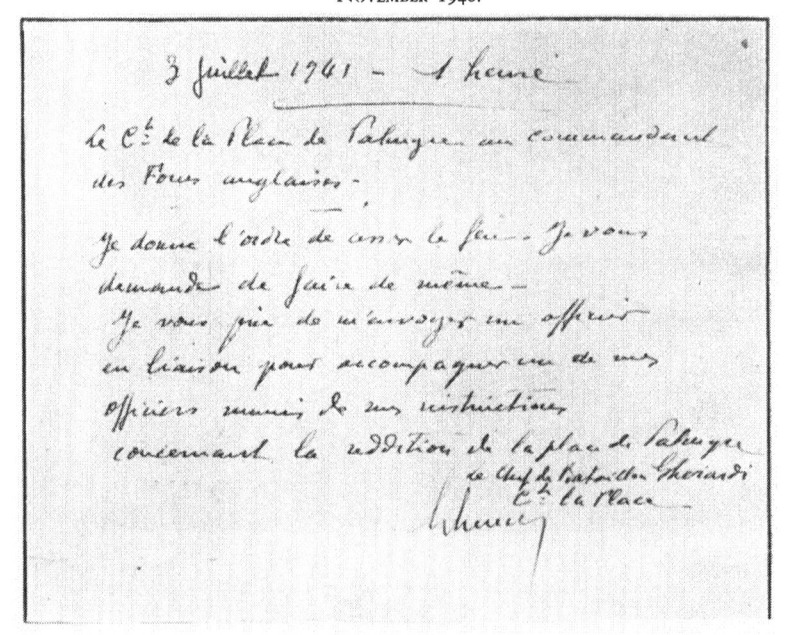

FACSIMILE OF THE SURRENDER OF PALMYRA RECEIVED BY THE 1ST BATTALION THE ESSEX REGIMENT. 3RD JULY, 1941.

Sergeant A. J. Burgar distinguished himself by successfully withdrawing the platoon after he had first taken all means of identification off the body of his commander whilst under heavy fire. For his conduct he was granted an immediate award of the Military Medal.

The 3rd September, 1940, the first anniversary of the outbreak of war with Germany, found the Battalion still uncommitted to action on any scale, but despite the inactivity, heat, and lack of mail from home, it remained in good heart, greatly cheered and excited by the sight of large-scale reinforcements now passing through Atbara.

These were elements of the 5th Indian Division under Major-General L. M. Heath, C.B., C.I.E., D.S.O., M.C., which were passing south and eastwards to the borders of Italian East Africa. Headquarters of the 5th Indian Division had been established at Gedaref, the obvious centre of communication by road and rail, both for the recapture of the frontier posts of Gallabat and Kassala which had earlier been occupied by the Italians, and for a subsequent advance towards Asmara or Gondar.

On the 22nd/23rd October the 1st Essex, warned for possible operations in the Roseires area, was relieved by the 6/13th Frontier Force Rifles of all duties at Atbara. A few days later the warning order to move was cancelled, but only temporarily, for a few hours later fresh orders sent the Battalion forward to Gedaref. By the 30th October it was concentrated and encamped some six miles outside Gedaref. Major W. P. Williams was in command, for he had taken over from Lieutenant-Colonel Paxton, who had remained at Atbara.

The 1st Essex was by now transferred to the 5th Indian Division, and in the 10th Indian Infantry Brigade, with the 4/10th Baluch Regiment and the 3/18th Royal Garhwal Rifles. The Brigade Commander was Brigadier W. J. Slim, M.C.

Whilst in bivouac at Gedaref, the Battalion was visited by the Secretary of State for War, Mr. Anthony Eden. He expressed his great satisfaction at the smartness of the men and thanked the Battalion for all its good services since it had been in the Middle East.

Section III
OPERATIONS AGAINST GALLABAT, 1940

Immediately after arrival in Gedaref rehearsals of possible operations against the Gallabat area were held, for an actual attack was to take place at dawn on the 6th November, 1940. During the final days before this attack, officer reconnaissance parties went forward to the area of the knoll known as Signal Hill, from where good observation of the area of attack was obtainable.

The two frontier posts of Gallabat and Metemma, the former in the Sudan and the latter in Eritrea, faced each other across a khor (ravine) in a valley about two miles wide. Both forts were on forward slopes. Gallabat had been captured and occupied by the Italians since July 1940.

The countryside was largely covered by elephant grass as much as eight feet high, and in places visibility was as little as one yard. This elephant grass was at the time of the attack bone-dry and easy to kindle by the dropping of incendiary bombs. There was little soil on the small features, and rock was near the surface, so that any defensive position could only be attained by the building up of small stone sangars. These became very visible once the surrounding elephant grass had been burnt away by incendiary bombing.

Shortly after arrival at Gedaref the 1st Essex moved up another eighty-odd miles to a harbour area in the Ghor Otrub, west of Signal Hill. Brigadier Slim then issued orders for the attack on Gallabat. The plan was for the 3/18th Royal Garhwal Rifles to attack and capture the fort at Gallabat and for the 4/10th Baluch Regiment to secure the left flank and patrol forward to Um Zareba. Abyssinian irregulars (the Bunda Buka) under British officers were to operate on the right flank of the 10th Indian Infantry Brigade. On the capture of Gallabat the 1st Essex was to pass through and capture Metemma. The attack on Gallabat was timed for dawn, the 6th November, and was to be prefaced by air and artillery bombardment.

About 10 p.m., on the 5th November, the Battalion left its harbour area in the Ghor Otrub and began to move in single file down the narrow rocky track leading to Gallabat. The night was pitch dark, and shortly after the start of the approach march it began to rain. As dawn broke the Battalion was resting astride the Gallabat track about 1,200 yards west of the fort. Here it lay as the guns of the 28th Field Regiment and the British aeroplanes—ancient single-engined Wellesley bombers escorted by Gladiators of the South African Air Force—bombarded and bombed Gallabat and Metemma. The Essex watched the Gladiator fighters pass over with particular interest. The South African pilots, on their way through to collect their planes in Egypt, had been guests of the Essex Regiment at Atbara, and a very close liaison had been established. And so it was with personal interest that the Essex watched the fortune of the air battle that immediately followed. But the Italian C.R.42 fighters were too much for the obsolescent Gladiators and Wellesleys, the great majority of which were soon shot down. Air superiority was thus lost.

The attack by the 3/18th Royal Garhwal Rifles then went in with great dash, but unfortunately the supporting tank squadron ("B" Squadron 6th Royal Tank Regiment) ran into a minefield and suffered heavy losses. Other tanks damaged their tracks in charging the low walls of the fort. There were thus no tanks immediately available with which to attack Metemma. The 1st Essex then moved forward according to plan and occupied a second battalion position on Gallabat Hill. The 4/10th Baluch Regiment moved forward on the left. It should be explained here that the total area on Gallabat Hill was extremely small for two battalions, so that when both the Essex and the Garhwalis were deployed, a company area was a space about fifty yards square. A perfect air target.

Now very heavy air attacks came in, as all Italian aircraft in range were switched to aid the Italians in Metemma. They met with no opposition, for there were now no British fighters left and there were no ground anti-aircraft defences, save infantry small arms.

The area occupied by the 1st Essex was bare rock. There were no power tools and no hand digging could produce adequate cover from the air. The maximum cover possible was a six-inch head-cover scrape of rubble. The inevitable result was heavy casualties from air attacks during the 6th/7th November.

Unfortunately the Regimental aid post (R.A.P.) had become detached in the move forward from Signal Hill and had got lost, so the many casualties had to be sent back by returning Bren carriers and trucks and any available transport down the battalion main axis— not an inspiring sight for those in the rear areas.

The position on Gallabat was held throughout the 6th and 7th November, but during the afternoon of the 7th orders were received from 10th Indian Infantry Brigade Headquarters to evacuate Gallabat Fort. Lieutenant I. J. D. Stevenson-Hamilton, as Signal Officer, stayed till one of the last, when, engineer demolition having been carried out, he withdrew with his wireless set. On his way back to Battalion Headquarters he met Brigadier Slim standing to one side of the track and said how sorry the Battalion was not to have had the chance of attacking Metemma. The Brigadier agreed, but said that in view of the heavy belts of wire surrounding the fort and because most of the British

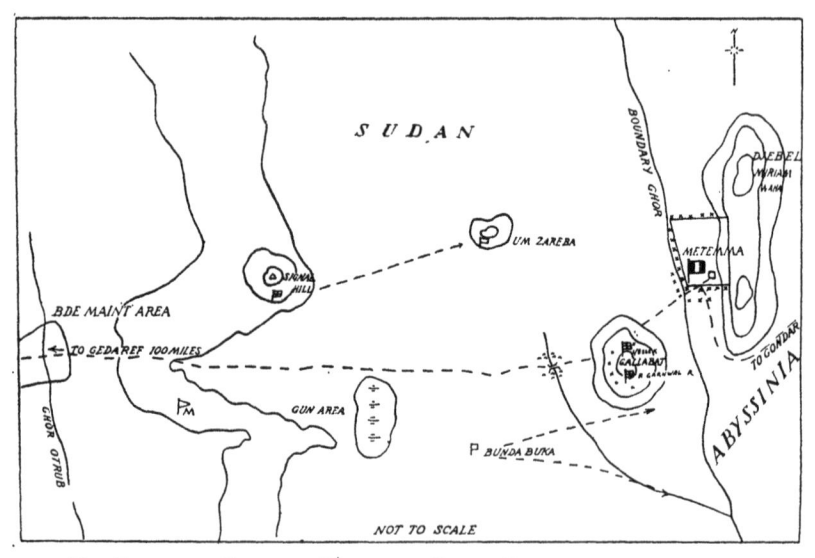

THE BATTLE OF GALLABAT. DIAGRAM OF BRITISH DISPOSITIONS AT 6 P.M., 6TH NOVEMBER, 1940.

tanks were out of action any attack on Metemma was quite out of the question.

This view is taken by "Strategicus" in his book *A Short History of the Second World War* published in 1950, when he says: "Only the failure of his tanks prevented him from taking Metemma."

During the operation the 1st Essex had 12 killed, 3 died of wounds, 47 wounded, and 6 missing, a total of 68 casualties. Considerable casualties had also been sustained by the 3/18th Royal Garhwal Rifles, but nevertheless morale on Gallabat Hill had remained high.

Lieutenant Stevenson-Hamilton says: "The spirit of the troops in the Fort was excellent, and I was asked on many occasions when we were going forward to attack Metemma. It is my opinion, and I know it is the opinion of many other officers, that Gallabat proved by far the nastiest experience which the Battalion ever went through—even remembering the bitter fighting around Tobruk, the actions in Syria and Iraq, and later the actions against the Japanese in Burma."

Unfortunately, this satisfactory state did not obtain in the rear areas of the Brigade, and the sight of considerable numbers of wounded being ferried back in every kind of transport disheartened some men, and a move of rear elements of all battalions towards Gedaref might easily have occurred.

To quote from the dispatches by General Sir Archibald P. Wavell, K.C.B., C.M.G., M.C., C.-in-C. in the Middle East, and published as a supplement to the *London Gazette* of Tuesday, the 11th June, 1946:

"39. The operation, although it resulted in our retaking Gallabat and inflicting very heavy losses on the enemy, was not as successful as had been hoped owing to certain factors which could not be foreseen.

"The first of these was the breakdown, mainly from mechanical causes, of all the tanks except one light tank during the capture of Gallabat. The chief causes of the breakdown were damage to the tracks by the rough ground or by enemy mines. The second factor was a temporary loss of command of the air due to six of our fighter aircraft being shot down in a combat with the enemy.

"40. Gallabat was captured early on 6th November by the 3rd Garhwal Rifles and the squadron of the Royal Tank Regiment with few casualties, one enemy colonial battalion being practically destroyed. The further advance on Metemma had, however, to be postponed owing to the breakdown of the tanks. The enemy positions at Metemma were heavily wired and defended by a large number of machine guns, and without tank support it was considered inadvisable to attempt their capture. The further advance was therefore postponed till the afternoon, when it was hoped that some of the tanks would be repaired.

"41. During the morning, however, the enemy gained control of the air and developed an extremely heavy bombing attack on our forward troops, the Garhwal Rifles who had captured Gallabat and the 1st Essex Regiment who were in process of relieving them. There was little cover and the ground was too rocky to dig shelter trenches. Both battalions suffered heavy casualties and their morale was temporarily affected. Also the workshop lorry of the tank squadron was destroyed by a bomb and three fitters were wounded, which greatly hampered the task of repairing the tanks.

"42. The Brigade Commander therefore decided that he must cancel the attack on Metemma, and that in view of the enemy's continued command of the air and the target offered by Gallabat, it would be necessary to withdraw the somewhat shaken troops from that area.

"A withdrawal was therefore made to the high ground west of Gallabat on the evening of 7th November."

On withdrawal of the 1st Essex and 3rd Garhwal Rifles from Gallabat Hill, the Battalion made its way back to its old bivouac area in the Ghor Otrub.

These operations cannot be called satisfactory from the Battalion's point of view. Heavy casualties had been incurred from enemy air attacks, and yet the Battalion was denied the satisfaction of the advance on and capture of Metemma.

Back in the bivouac area Major Williams had to report sick, and on the morning of the 9th November, 1940, Major K. F. May took over command. He remained in command until the 6th December, when Lieutenant-Colonel J. S. Nichols, M.C., assumed command.

On the night of the 6th/7th November, whilst holding Gallabat Fort, the troops were without mosquito nets in a highly malarial area, and as a direct result more than 250, all ranks, went down with malaria in the latter part of November.

The 1st Essex remained in the bivouac area until the end of November, companies taking over patrol work in the Gallabat area from the 4/10th Baluch Regiment.

One patrol deserves special mention. On the 19th November "C" Company was operating in the Gallabat area as a fighting patrol. The leading platoon under 2/Lieutenant A. M. Williams surprised and attacked an enemy standing patrol on the outskirts of Gallabat Fort. After a sustained action, in which all platoons were engaged, "C" Company broke off the engagement and withdrew, having taken prisoners and inflicted heavy casualties on the enemy. The success of this action can be attributed to the fearless example set by 2/Lieutenant Williams and Company Sergeant-Major C. W. Small. Unfortunately 2/Lieutenant Williams was wounded and 3 of his platoon killed.

On the following day a special message was received from Major-

General L. M. Heath, the commander of the 5th Indian Division, congratulating "C" Company.

It is interesting to note that one of the prisoners taken subsequently directed artillery fire on to detailed targets in Metemma apparently with the greatest good-will.

On the 28th November all units received through Headquarters 10th Indian Infantry Brigade a congratulatory message from the War Cabinet relayed by General Sir Archibald Wavell, the C.-in-C. Middle East Forces, on the conduct of operations and the capture of Gallabat.

During the period after the main attack, forward companies saw some of Haile Selassie's official drummers brought up and heard messages being "drummed off" by the African drummers far into the interior of Abyssinia. These "drummings" were messages of encouragement to partisans or invitation to Italian Colonial troops to desert, and were picked up by other drummers across the border and so relayed across Ethiopia. These messages, which infuriated the Italians into heavy retaliatory fire, resulted in a steady trickle of deserters through the Essex lines.

On the 11th December the 10th Indian Infantry Brigade was relieved and started to move from the Gallabat front to the Butana Bridge area. The 3/12th Royal Frontier Force Regiment took over the left forward positions (some 2,000 yards west of Gallabat Fort) from the 1st Essex who, on the 13th December, moved out of the battle area. They moved by various stages to Gedaref and then to Khasm-el-Girba and on to Butana Bridge. There for some ten days a defensive position was occupied covering the bridge from any Italian intrusion from the direction of Kassala. At this time the 5th Indian Division was holding some 200 miles of front. Here it was possible to carry out some mobile training, as positions were only held by lookout posts during the day.

At Butana Bridge the 1st Essex was relieved in the 10th Indian Infantry Brigade by the 2nd Highland Light Infantry, which had moved down from Egypt to join the 5th Indian Division before the advance into Eritrea.

On leaving Butana Bridge the Battalion travelled in two troop trains to a bivouac area near Haiya Junction, a somewhat grand-sounding name, but in reality a water-tank, a signal box, and some sidings and railway sheds right out in the desert. Here quite a happy Christmas was spent waiting for the battalion M.T. to reach Port Sudan.

At Port Sudan the Battalion was embarked on the transport *Dunera* on the 30th December, and moved to Port Said and thence to Palestine, the Battalion's third visit to that country in a little over two years. The five-day voyage was very pleasant, the ship's staff doing their utmost to make the Battalion happy and comfortable.

Section IV

PALESTINE, JANUARY–MAY 1941

On arriving in Palestine, the area selected by Lieutenant-Colonel Nichols for training, the Battalion was first moved to Haifa, and took over from the 1st Buffs on the 6th January, 1941.

Before dealing with the period in Palestine, it is necessary to give some account of the state of the Battalion on its arrival from the Sudan. First, owing to battle casualties, malaria, and other sickness the 1st Essex was below war establishment by about 15 officers and 350 other ranks. Battalion Headquarters was almost non-existent, partly owing to casualties and partly due to the fact that it had been necessary to retain a number of key personnel at Headquarter Troops Atbara when the Battalion moved to join the 5th Indian Division, and there had been no time nor opportunity to train replacements. Then, owing to its employment since the outbreak of war, there had been no chance to develop a proper war routine, nor to carry out any realistic training for modern war, nor even to train as a complete unit. Also the moral effect of heavy air attack in the open without any adequate means of countering it had been considerable. Equipment, too, was worn and out of date and transport badly in need of replacement. On the other hand, the personnel of the Battalion was, says Lieutenant-Colonel Nichols, "absolutely first class, about 85 per cent. to 90 per cent. being regular soldiers, many of whom had just completed their normal colour service in 1939 and had been recalled or retained."

Shortly after arrival in Peninsular Barracks, Haifa, the Battalion was inspected by Lieutenant-General Sir Phillip Neame, V.C., K.B.E., C.B., D.S.O., the G.O.C.-in-C. Palestine. Then came a period of guard duty, a time of struggle between Lieutenant-Colonel Nichols who wished to train his battalion and Sub-Area Headquarters who required men for duty of every type. So many cooks were demanded that Colonel Nichols lost his patience, and sent a signal saying, "Please note that this unit is a battalion of infantry and not a corps of cooks."

It did nearly lose him command of the Battalion, but it did check the perpetual call for cooks and other administrative personnel.

Recreation, leave, and welfare were all given equal importance to training, and it was a confident, fit battalion that left Haifa at the end of February for a period near the Dead Sea, where a training area just south of Jericho was taken over from the Royal Scots Greys. Here the 1st Essex came directly under Headquarter Troops Palestine for training and under Jerusalem sub-area for administration.

This month of training in the Dead Sea area was to be the culmination of the stay in Palestine and Lieutenant-Colonel Nichols was warned that from April onwards the Battalion was likely to be moved back to a war area.

The move to the training area entailed a road move of about 120 miles, the last eighty-five miles being marched. This march did more to harden up the Battalion than almost anything else, and in addition very useful training was carried out during the move. Particular attention was paid to measures against hostile air attack, with the result that all ranks felt they need not worry unduly about enemy air action, even if they had nothing with which to reply. The result was to be proved in Syria.

The other infantry unit then in Palestine, 1st Bedfordshire and Hertfordshire Regiment, was also training in the Dead Sea area, and the training period terminated by inter-battalion exercises set and conducted by Major-General G. Clark, C.B., M.C., and the Staff of Headquarters 1st Cavalry Division. The final exercise is of interest. It was an operation in which the Battalion was instructed to attack and capture positions held by the 1st Bedfs Herts which were partially protected by ground considered impassable even for infantry at night. The exercise, starting one afternoon, was intended to last for thirty-six hours. By dawn of the first morning the scheme was over, two companies of the Essex having crossed the "impassable" ground by night and destroyed the defending garrison. A patrol under 2/Lieutenant B. F. H. Grimley captured the commanding officer of the opposing battalion. This was an interesting forecast of what was to happen at Palmyra.

Major-General Clark was to be a very good friend to the Battalion and the help he gave in Palestine was considerable. This was followed by the interest and consideration shown in the forthcoming campaigns in Iraq and Syria.

On return to Haifa, a further inspection of the Battalion was held, this time by Major-General Clark, who reported that he was very pleased with its state. He informed Lieutenant-Colonel Nichols that the 1st Essex in turn-out, general cleanliness, and administration in barracks was as near perfection as he considered possible in war-time.

The 1st Essex was now under the command of the 1st Cavalry Division, but under Haifa sub-area for administration.

Section V

OPERATIONS IN IRAQ, 1941

On the 3rd April, 1941, a group of Iraqi officers, known as "The Golden Square" and under the leadership of Rashid Ali, who was working with the Germans, seized power, and Rashid Ali Ghailani became Prime Minister of Iraq.

Iraqi treaty obligations with Britain allowed the transit of British troops through Iraq in war, and on the 18th April an Indian infantry brigade group landed at Basra, covered by the 2nd King's Own Royal Regiment (Lancaster), which had landed from the air at Shaiba the day before. Later in the month Rashid Ali was warned that another brigade from India would land at Basra on or about the 30th April.

Rashid Ali then threw off any pretence of pro-British feeling, forbade the second landing and, in anticipation of German assistance by aircraft and even airborne troops, launched the Iraqi army on the 2nd May against Habbaniya, the Royal Air Force training base in the Iraqi desert.

This news reached Haifa the same day. There was also a report that part of the Iraqi Army was advancing on Rutbah Wells, 300 miles east of Haifa and about half-way between Haifa and Baghdad. There was also believed to be an Iraqi threat to Ramadi, 200 miles east of Rutbah and about 100 miles from Baghdad.

On the 2nd May, Lieutenant-Colonel Nichols, whilst on a visit to the Haifa Staff College, received, at 10.30 a.m., a sudden order to proceed immediately to Sub-Area Headquarters. "Here," he says, "I was given the following instructions: I was to assemble my battalion at H.4 where I would form a firm base from which I could operate against the Iraqi rebels, drive them from Rutbah and so on. On arriving at H.4, all troops there, including the R.A.F. armoured cars (one section) would come under my command, and I would be directly under the

G.O.C. Palestine and Transjordan. One company would move by train from Haifa at 12.15 p.m. All transport, including certain additional R.A.S.C. vehicles, would move by road at 5 p.m. and the remainder of the Battalion would entrain at 8 p.m. to Lydda. From Lydda the move to H.4 would be by air.

At 4.15 p.m. that day Lieutenant-Colonel Nichols received written confirmatory instructions from the G.O.C. Palestine: "Your task is to assemble your Battalion at H.4 with a view to occupying Rutbah and preventing Iraquian troops from assisting a German landing should one take place there. You should go from H.4 to Rutbah by air if possible, but your landing at Rutbah must be protected by our troops, probably Arab Legion in M.T."

Lieutenant-Colonel Nichols was also given a situation report on Iraq which confirmed that two Iraqi columns had been sent towards Rutbah Wells and gave the first official news of the outbreak of fighting at Habbaniya. H.4 was one of the pumping stations between Haifa and Iraq. These stations are maintenance and "booster" points on the oil-pipe lines from the Iraq oilfields to the ports of Haifa and Tripoli and are numbered in sequence. H.4 was, for example, the fourth camp from Kirkuk on the Haifa pipe-line.

On receipt of the message the Battalion prepared to move as ordered. There was, however, a period in which the task became obscure, for instead of being permitted to carry out the first orders to concentrate the whole of his battalion at H.4, Lieutenant-Colonel Nichols was told to remain at short notice to move, only one company ("C" Company, Captain J. F. Higson) actually moving to Mafraq on the 2nd May. This order cancelling the move of the Battalion and ordering the return of the transport was received at 8 p.m. the 2nd May.

Captain Higson says: "The orders of this move were rather startling. I was summoned to the Orderly Room 'at the double,' and instructed 'to move "C" Company to Lydda. Your train is in Haifa railway station. From Lydda you will move to an unknown destination in Iraq—that is all.' In a few hours 'C' Company was airborne."

Of this Colonel Nichols says: "The value of battalion standing orders for war was well illustrated. I had just finished issuing a revised edition of these and was in consequence able to tell Captain Higson to move his company immediately on Scale B. I think that the company was on the move in less than one hour.

On arrival at H.4, "C" Company came under the command of Air Vice-Marshal J. H. D'Albiac, who was then in charge of operations from H.4 eastwards, and Lieutenant-Colonel Nichols was informed that the R.A.F. had a call upon additional companies of his battalion if required.

During the period between the dispatch of "C" Company on the 2nd May and the receipt of fresh orders on the 8th May, the extent and importance of the Iraqi rebellion were becoming fully appreciated.

The original British garrison in Iraq was besieged in Habbaniya and the second force—the Indian infantry brigade landed on the 18th April —was still at Basra. The third force, the Indian brigade due on the 30th April, was still embarked. The Habbaniya garrison consisted of the R.A.F. personnel of the training base, some 1,500 Assyrian Levies and the 2nd King's Own, which on the outbreak of the rebellion had been flown up from Shaiba over the heads of the revolting Iraq army into Habbaniya. The task of this small garrison was not made easier by the presence of some 9,000 civilian refugees from Baghdad and elsewhere.

Active assistance to the rebels by Germany was expected, first by the provision of aircraft and crews and then by the landing of airborne troops.

Unless the rebellion could be quickly quelled, a grave situation imperilling the Middle East might well arise. This, then, was the situation on the 8th May, when Lieutenant-Colonel Nichols was given fresh instructions and warned that the 1st Essex was to be ready to move in forty-eight hours. But within the next two days orders again were changed.

To meet the new situation in Iraq, Lieutenant-General Sir Henry Maitland Wilson took over command of Palestine and Transjordan. Major-General G. Clark was sent by air to report to General Wavell, where he was told to make plans for the relief of Habbaniya and Baghdad.

As a result of this the following took place:

A special force was formed for operations in Iraq from 1st Cavalry Division and other troops in Palestine, all under the command of Major-General George Clark, and was given the code name of "Habforce." This was divided into two separate columns:

Striking Force "Kingcol." Commander: Brigadier J. Kingstone, D.S.O., Commander 4th Cavalry Brigade.

Troops: (1) 4th Cavalry Brigade with Headquarters and Signal Section. (Composite Household Cavalry Regiment, the Warwickshire Yeomanry, and the Wiltshire Yeomanry.)

(2) 237th Battery (25-pounder) of 60th Field Regiment R.A.

(3) "A" and "D" Companies 1st Essex, with two Bren carriers, all under Major K. F. May and carried in R.A.S.C. lifting transport.

(4) One anti-tank troop R.A. (2-pounder).

(5) Eight R.A.F. Armoured Cars.

(6) Two supply companies R.A.S.C.

Main body. Commander: Lieutenant-Colonel J. S. Nichols, M.C.

Troops: (1) Headquarters 1st Cavalry Division (part).

(2) 1st Essex (less two companies) in lifting transport (requisitioned Palestine buses driven by battalion personnel).

(3) 60th Field Regiment (less one battery).

(4) One battery (less a troop) anti-tank artillery.

(5) Ancillary Services necessary to maintain the force across 600 miles of desert.

(6) Detachment of the Arab Legion (some 400 strong) under Glubb Pasha.

The assembly area for both parts of the Force was to be at Mafraq, the main body first collecting at Irbid.

It is proposed first to deal with "A" and "D" Companies as part of "Kingcol" and thereafter deal with the follow-up to Habbaniya of the remainder of the Battalion as part of Habforce main body.

Major May's detachment ("A" and "D" Companies and two Bren carriers) left Haifa on the morning of the 11th May, 1941, with orders to rendezvous with the rest of "Kingcol" at Mafraq in Transjordan the same evening.

The day was fine. The road skirted the lower slopes of the Mount Carmel range and then plunged down into the plain of Esdraelon. This wide, open, clay-covered plain has played an important part in the history of Palestine from the days of the Israelites and the Philistines to General Allenby's mighty victory against the Turkish army in 1918.

The road ran along the south of the plain, hugging the northern slopes of Carmel until it crossed the eastern part of the plain to reach Beisan. From there it began to wind down to the Jordan which was bridged at Jisr-el-Majame, an unimposing little bridge compared to the Allenby bridge at Jericho. The road surface was good, and on the way down the "Sea Level" sign was seen by the side of the road.

From river level the road started to climb straightway into Transjordan. The surface still remained good, but the countryside was now rugged, wild, and inhospitable. The climb from the Jordan Valley was long, and it was 9 p.m. before the tail of the long column reached

Mafraq. By now the brown rocks of the Transjordan side of the valley had given way to flat desert, and the last few miles of the long journey were along a road "like a large piece of black ribbon pinned on a sand-table."

Staging at Mafraq, the detachment, with the remainder of "Kingcol," reached H.4 on the afternoon of the 12th May.

These stations consisted of an area of some ten acres of desert fenced by high perimeter wire in which were situated large pumping units for boosting the oil flow. The living quarters of the staff were well-appointed, and provided all requirements and refinements against the climatic conditions. The stations were completely deserted. The staff had evacuated when the Iraqi trouble had started, and the local Bedouins had looted and damaged the buildings considerably.

After refilling all vehicles with oil, petrol, and water, "Kingcol" moved farther east on the 13th May to Rutbah Wells. The tarmac road ceased about forty-five miles east of H.4. The rest of the journey was by desert tracks of the worst description, but nevertheless there was no mechanical trouble in any of the vehicles of the 1st Essex.

The township of Rutbah consists of the normal squalid collection of Arab hutments with its quota of bedraggled children and dogs. The Rest House was reasonably smart, but had been ransacked by Bedouins, and nothing of any value remained.

Staging in Rutbah for less than twenty-four hours for maintenance, "Kingcol" pushed on another 200 miles towards Ramadi, across the desert. The going was hard and good, and vehicles were able to disperse, each driver picking his own course across the hard surface. An average speed of seventeen miles per hour was maintained.

First acquaintance with the enemy was made during the 15th May, when a Blenheim bomber with Iraqi markings flew down the column machine-gunning. It also dropped one bomb which fell between two platoon trucks of "D" Company, but no damage was done and there were no casualties.

On the 16th May Major May's detachment, with the anti-tank troop Royal Artillery under command, had the task of escorting "Kingcol's" supply companies and "B" Echelon vehicles. They were to be taken along a track yet to be located, from a point approximately fourteen miles west of Ramadi across country to Mafri and thence to Habbaniya. It was no easy task. No track of any nature could be discovered, and recourse had to be made to a cross-country desert march by compass bearing.

Captain J. S. Greene says: "The only sign of habitation was an occasional signpost to Ramadi, which was known to be held by the Iraqis. That night we reached the western end of the road to Baghdad, a metalled road once again, and halted some kilos short of Ramadi. We were informed that some R.A.F. armoured cars would meet us and guide us round the south of Lake Habbaniya the next day. They never showed up. We tried to get round, but the column became badly bogged down in soft sand, and we had to return to our starting-point. Here we were bombed by the Luftwaffe, but no damage was sustained.

"Arab Legion guides reached us the next day (17th May) and the column set out to cross the difficult route south of the lake. It was most difficult. The normal firm desert gave way to numerous small serrated wadis which appeared to run across our main axis, and, except for their main course, were of very soft sand. Unless a vehicle took them at high speed the wheels sank to the axles. Most of that day was spent on this most uncomfortable ride. By late afternoon the column reached the firmer ground of the plateau surrounding the lake, and arrived at Habbaniya by the late evening."

Before the main body of "Habforce" moved on from H.4, Major-General Clark sent for Lieutenant-Colonel Nichols and asked if he had an officer who could take charge of the large "B" Echelon transport columns to which would be added a special supply column, and who could be relied on to get the column through to Habbaniya within forty-eight hours of "Kingcol." He pointed out that both enemy ground and air action was probable and that in places the going would be very bad.

"I told him," says Colonel Nichols, "that I was confident that my transport officer, Lieutenant Lovelace, would do the job." After some questioning General Clark agreed to this, and issued the necessary orders. He pointed out that the success or failure of the whole operation depended on Lovelace's ability to get the transport and supplies through in time.

"When I gave Lieutenant Lovelace his orders," continues Colonel Nichols, "I told him that if he succeeded I would recommend him for the M.B.E. When I told General Clark about this, he said he would do his utmost to see that the recommendation went through, which I am glad to say it did."

On the morning of the 18th May, 1941, "Kingcol" entered Habbaniya, the two 1st Essex Companies leading the column. The first object, the relief of and linking up with the garrison of Habbaniya, had been accomplished. The second object, a salutary lesson to the rebels, had yet to be accomplished.

The Essex camping area was by the lake-side over a ridge separating the bivouac area from the main landing-ground and the air station beyond. The Lake of Habbaniya is a very large stretch of water lodged in a huge basin as if scooped out of the sand by some enormous hand. The edges are steep and in some places sheer. It was from these heights above Habbaniya that the Iraqis had shelled the air station and the cantonment at the beginning of the rebellion.

On the 18th May the 1st Essex (less "A" and "D" Companies) as part of "Habforce" main body also entered Habbaniya. They had moved by M.T. to H.4 on the 14th May, and they remained there until the morning of the 17th. By then four "Bombay" troop-carrying aircraft had arrived, and the move by air of the 1st Essex was started that day. On the 18th those who had not been lifted the day before were sent forward in M.T. to H.3. This was to enable the R.A.F. to make certain of two round trips a day, and thus enable the concentration of the Battalion to be effected as quickly as possible. It was done, and by the evening of the 18th May Battalion Headquarters was established in the officers' club at Habbaniya. The air-lift had necessitated a drastic reduction in kit. Before leaving Palestine Colonel Nichols had been told that his battalion was to reduce its kit well below the normal field scale, but when the air-lift took place, kit had to be still further reduced. The Commanding Officer ordered the shedding of greatcoats and one blanket per man. These were not recovered till well on in the Syrian campaign.

Although geographically close together, "Kingcol" and "Habforce" main body were to remain separate entities for the fighting that lay ahead.

In order to understand what happened in Habbaniya, some explanation of the situation there is now necessary. It was what Colonel Nichols calls "a most remarkable situation." The whole station was under command of Air Vice-Marshal D'Albiac. There were some 600 to 700 R.A.F. personnel with about twenty aircraft, mostly training machines, a battalion of Iraq Levies under R.A.F. command, and a section of R.A.F. armoured cars.

Army personnel consisted of the 2nd King's Own Royal Regiment, a battalion of Gurkha Rifles, a battery of mountain artillery, and a light anti-aircraft battery. These had been grouped and called the

Habbaniya Brigade, and were under command of Colonel O. L. Roberts, the G.S.O.I. of the 10th Indian Division, who with four or five junior staff officers had been flown up from Basra.

An Iraqi brigade group was holding the little town of Ramadi on the Haifa route some ten miles west of Habbaniya and barring all movement westwards. Another Iraqi brigade group was holding the town and bridge of Falluja, some ten miles away on the road to Baghdad.

On the north Habbaniya was bounded by the Euphrates and on the south by Lake Habbaniya and an area of soft almost impassable sand. The Iraqis had broken the river banks in various places, which had caused floods to both the east and west of Habbaniya so that the area in which the Essex found themselves was practically an island about ten miles long and three to four miles deep.

Officers were quartered in the main R.A.F. officers' mess and troops in R.A.F. barracks, while "Kingcol" was bivouacked on the shores of the lake.

The various clubs in the cantonment were all functioning in spite of frequent enemy low-flying air attacks. All were well stocked with drink, but there was a shortage of food and all ranks were feeding on hard rations almost at minimum scale. Being cut off from the surrounding country, they could buy nothing.

The 1st Essex, less "A" and "D" Companies with "Kingcol," was in R.A.F. barracks in the centre of the area. It maintained a platoon (later a company) holding the causeway leading to Ramadi and a platoon holding the causeway to Falluja Bridge.

Forty-eight hours after the arrival of "Habforce" main body, Major-General Clark with Force Headquarters flew in and took command.

In the meantime Falluja Bridge and town had been captured.

"This," says Colonel Nichols, "I consider was one of the most brilliant operations in the history of the 1939–45 War. The plan was made entirely by Colonel Ouvry Roberts in his capacity as Commander Habbaniya Brigade."

The problem of capturing the bridge at Falluja appeared to be almost insoluble without landing craft, specialised equipment, and considerable artillery support. The approach to the bridge was limited to a single causeway. Colonel Roberts's plan was as follows: On the night of the 17th/18th May the Gurkha battalion in Habbaniya was ferried across the Euphrates east of Habbaniya by improvised means and under cover of darkness. By daylight they had got into positions surrounding most of the perimeter of Falluja. By making use of the aircraft bringing up the 1st Essex from H.4 and H.3, during the short stay in Habbaniya between flights, he landed the 2nd King's Own, less two companies, behind Falluja astride the road to Baghdad in the early hours of the morning. Falluja was then bombarded from the air from 7 a.m. to 3 p.m. Artillery from "Kingcol" which had arrived on the lakeside that morning joined in the later stages of the bombardment.

At 3 p.m. one company of the Iraq Levies was ordered to advance along the causeway to Falluja Bridge under cover of "Kingcol" artillery, and as this company arrived near the bridge a party of Iraqis with a white flag met the company commander, surrendering the whole of the Iraqi force in Falluja. By this brilliant operation Falluja and the bridge were captured without a single casualty.

But on the morning of the 22nd May an Iraqi force—an infantry brigade group moved up in M.T. from bivouac areas many miles north of Baghdad—counter-attacked without warning from the air or intelligence. It is interesting to note that this particular operation had been the subject of an exercise held two years previously, set and conducted by the British Military Mission. It was subsequently discovered that the Iraqi commander carrying out the operation had used the directing staff solution drawn up by the Military Mission.

The small tanks broke into the town and fierce fighting followed, principally with the Assyrian Levies, sworn enemies of the Iraqis. The situation was obscure and Brigadier Kingstone was ordered by Major-General Clark to proceed to Falluja and take over. This he did, ordering the 1st Essex "Kingcol" Detachment and part of the Household Cavalry Regiment ("C" Squadron) to support the 2nd King's Own and the Assyrian Levies. The way up to Falluja lay along the main Baghdad road which runs into low ground near the Euphrates outside Habbaniya. The Iraqis, taking full advantage of this fact, had opened the bunds and flooded an area west of Habbaniya. This necessitated the Essex companies wading and ferrying themselves and their equipment as best they could. By dint of improvised rafts the non-swimmers were got across the worst parts, together with all arms and ammunition.

Major May says: "The operation involved complete stripping, and swimming and wading about 600 yards. With improvised rafts of old oil drums and planks made up by Indian Sappers, first "A" Company crossed. We piled arms and ammunition and all clothing on top and got over in parties of ten to fifteen; it took about two hours to get the company over."

By early afternoon the enemy attack on Falluja had spent itself. The 2nd King's Own had suffered heavily, losing almost half their officers, but the situation was in hand. The enemy had been held except for some infantry who had established themselves on the outer edge of the town.

These "A" Company, 1st Essex, commanded by Major R. B. James, was ordered to attack. Major James ordered a platoon under Lieutenant T. D'A. Muirhead to clear the right side of the main road up to the eastern limit of the town. A further platoon was ordered to contain enemy opposition to the south of the main road which was proving troublesome. The remaining platoon was employed in guarding a number of Iraqi prisoners, on anti-sniping duties, and on keeping the main road to the river clear for the evacuation of wounded and for replenishment of ammunition and supplies.

Throughout this time, Major James showed complete disregard for his own safety in reconnoitring well forward of his Company Headquarters, and directing the course of the company battle as it developed. His Company Headquarters was established immediately in rear of the platoons in action, and the men at Company Headquarters formed his only immediate tactical reserve.

Lieutenant Muirhead's platoon made good progress towards the east end of the town with only few casualties, but was held up by stubborn resistance from some enemy established in trenches dug on the outside fringe of the town. The main source of trouble lay on the north side of the main road, where two L.M.G. sections had established themselves on the roof-tops, and made any further movement in that area impossible without heavy casualties.

Major James decided to destroy these two light machine guns by the use of his Company Headquarters, his only reserve. He led his party across the main road which was under fire, and into a side alley leading towards the position from which the L.M.G.s were firing. Progress was slow, as the party had to clear each house before any forward movement could be made.

The L.M.G.s could still be heard firing at Lieutenant Muirhead's platoon, and the task became more and more urgent. It was when the party was fifty yards short of its objective and moving close to the wall up the alley with Major James in the lead that a L.M.G. opened up from a window on the other side of the alley. The fire caught

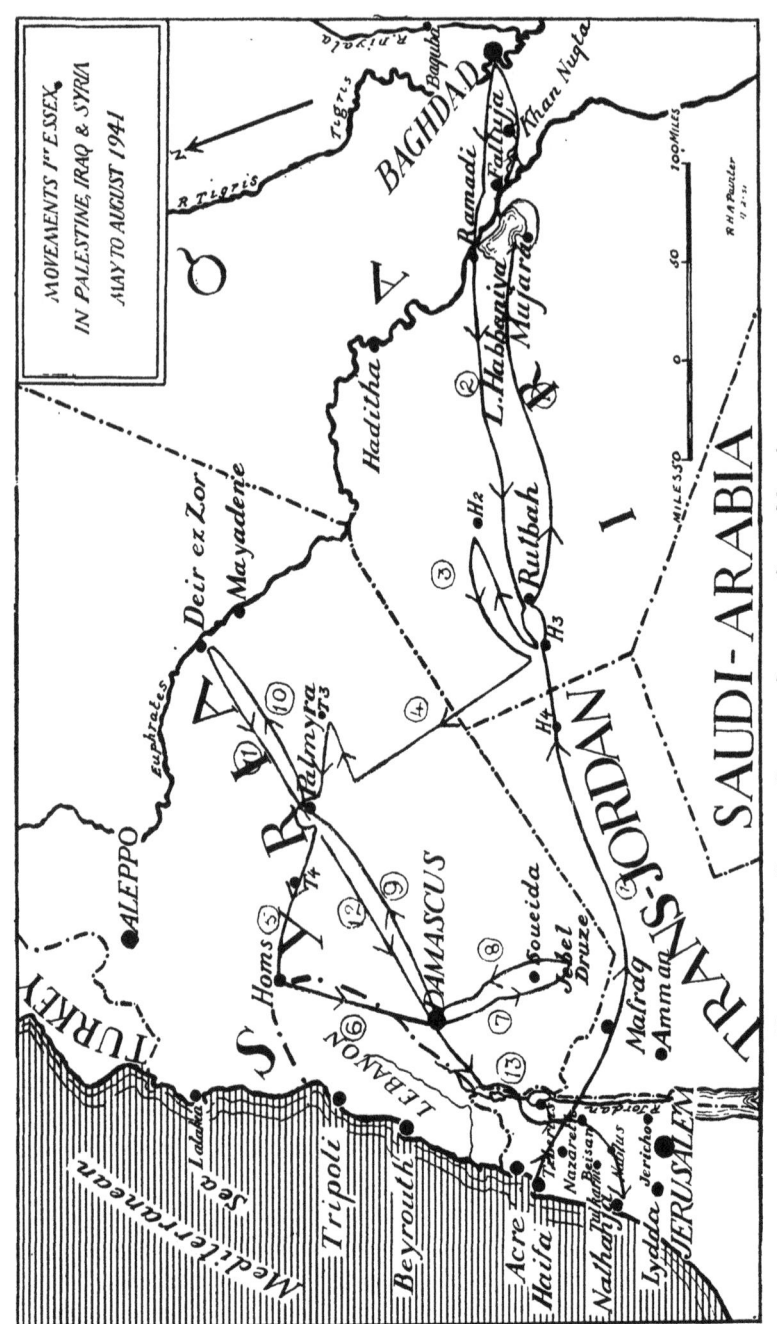

MOVEMENTS, 1ST ESSEX, IN PALESTINE, IRAQ, AND SYRIA, MAY–AUGUST 1941.

Private Sibbald, badly wounding him in the back, and whilst he was bundled into a nearby doorway, fire was directed into the window which had the effect of silencing the L.M.G. temporarily.

The whole of the party took refuge in a house opposite. This proved to be occupied by Iraqis, all of whom had to be liquidated. Major James organised its defence, and took the remainder of the party to the top of the house. From here it was possible to engage the two L.M.G.s with rifles. The gun crews, being fired on from an unexpected quarter, retired from the fray, leaving their dead and wounded behind. Fire was then directed at the windows of the houses occupied by the Iraqis. It was not long before a white flag was put out of one of the windows and the whole Iraqi garrison of those houses surrendered.

For his gallantry and leadership in this operation, Major R. B. James was to be awarded the D.S.O. while Lieutenant T. D'A.Muirhead was to win the M.C., and Private A. W. G. Eldridge, batman to Major James, the M.M. Major James was twice more to win the Distinguished Service Order before being killed in command of the 5th Battalion the East Yorkshire Regiment in Normandy. A large amount of enemy war material, including six light tanks, was taken, as were 2 officers and 100 other-rank prisoners. Altogether it was a most satisfactory operation.

"A" and "D" Companies next proceeded to the outer defences of Falluja. Enemy artillery shelled Falluja Bridge without effect intermittently throughout the 23rd May, and low-flying Messerschmitts attacked the town three times, but there were no enemy infantry counter-attacks.

On the 24th "D" Company sent a fighting patrol out to a hamlet, three-quarters of a mile from the company position, where a large body of enemy was reported to be gathering. After inflicting 5 casualties on the enemy, the patrol had to withdraw because of the enemy's greatly superior numbers. The patrol was not followed up during its withdrawal, and during the night of the 24th/25th May the enemy evacuated his position.

On the 23rd or 24th May (the exact date is uncertain) Major-General Clark sent for Lieutenant-Colonel Nichols and told him that he had decided to withdraw the Essex detachment from "Kingcol" and return them to battalion command. He explained the situation to him, which at the time was confused.

Briefly: Major May had taken command of the 2nd King's Own

when their commanding officer and second-in-command were wounded, and was still in Falluja; "A" and "D" Companies and the detachment of carriers, 1st Essex, were commanded by Major James. Brigadier Kingstone, without his headquarters and accompanied by only one staff officer, was commanding the troops in Falluja. No proper reorganisation had taken place there after the Iraqi force had been beaten off.

General Clark ordered Colonel Nichols to proceed to Falluja with the 1st Essex, where the detachment from "Kingcol" would revert to his command, and to take over command of all troops in Falluja, organise the place, clean it up, and carry out such offensive action as was possible.

"This I did," says Colonel Nichols. "It was a difficult task, as Falluja was in an appalling mess and troops were very much mixed up. The heat was considerable, the place was infested with mosquitoes, and troops were without mosquito nets. There were no N.A.A.F.I. supplies, and we were all still living on battle rations."

With the restoration of the situation at Falluja the way for the advance on Baghdad was now open and Major-General Clark was anxious to push on.

"Kingcol" was re-formed, Major R. B. James being placed in command of the two companies of the 1st Essex as Major K. F. May was still commanding the 2nd King's Own.

On the 28th May "Kingcol" left Falluja for Baghdad in two columns. The south column consisted of the 25-pounder battery (less a troop), a squadron of the Household Cavalry, the two Essex companies, the Anti-tank Troop R.A., some of the R.A.F. armoured cars, and a detachment of the Field Ambulance. It was to cross the gap in Hammonds Bund and after leaving Falluja to advance direct to Baghdad. The north column, which comprised the Household Cavalry (less a squadron), the Arab Legion, and the R.A.F. armoured cars, was to cross the Euphrates and then operate on the north flank. Here General Clark initiated a very clever move. He employed Glubb Pasha's Arab Legion to ride round the countryside ahead of and to the flanks of the advancing columns, taking with them several thousands of pounds for distribution to the local sheiks and headmen, announcing that the force advancing from Habbaniya was only the minute advance guard of a mighty British force advancing against Iraq from Egypt. With every pound that was handed out the reputed size of the force grew, so that by the time that "Kingcol" was approaching Baghdad the enemy commander thought that a large proportion of the British Middle East Forces was advancing against him.

The route of the south column lay across a further long stretch of desert where there was no metalled road, but the going proved good and firm. The cultivation and the irrigation canals started again at Khan Nuqta, some twenty kilometres from Baghdad, and progress began to get slow, as these irrigation canals proved to be "blown."

On the morning of the 29th May the column reached a twenty-yard-wide canal across which the road was breached and the bridge blown. The enemy was strongly entrenched on the far side. "A" and "D" Companies went into action. "D" advanced to the banks of the canal, but owing to heavy fire an immediate crossing was not possible. The 25-pounders then came into action, but were at first unable to deal with the many unlocated M.G. posts that were the chief factors in holding up the advance. But after some hours the artillery fire began to take effect, and at 10 a.m.—the first move towards the enemy had taken place at 4.45 a.m.—2/Lieutenant B. F. H. Grimley led two sections across the damaged bridge. As the artillery fire lifted they were able to press on, the enemy withdrawing in the face of the Essex advance. Lieutenant T. D'A. Muirhead had also got his platoon across, and he and 2/Lieutenant Grimley occupied a bridge-head position.

Engineers came up to repair the bridge, but by early 30th May so little repair had been possible that it was decided to continue the advance with the 1st Essex companies on foot. By 10 a.m. the bridge was sufficiently repaired to allow transport to cross. The transport soon caught up "A" and "D" Companies, who by this time had advanced some six miles to another canal-bridge area very similar to that which had held up the advance the day before. The bridge was, however, undefended and unblown. The leads to the charges were quickly cut by Major R. B. James, and a bridge-head was established under command of Captain J. S. Greene. As soon as the Royal Engineers had declared the bridge safe, transport began to cross and the advance on Baghdad was resumed.

Iraqi fighters attacked the bridge-head during the day. Captain J. S. Greene and "A" Company Headquarters were chased in a somewhat undignified manner round and round the house they occupied by an aeroplane closely resembling a British "Gladiator" fighter. But so soon as it was realised that this was no playful British pilot, fire was opened up and the Iraqi pilot remembered an appointment elsewhere.

In compensation, an abandoned Government Experimental Farm

housed countless hungry chickens who were soon hungry no more. Nor yet were "A" and "D" Companies.

On the 31st May, 1941, as "Kingcol" closed on Baghdad, the Iraqi Government requested an armistice.

Meanwhile in the Falluja area where 1st Essex (less "A" and "D" Companies with "Kingcol") still were, there had also been operations against a very elusive enemy. There were constant patrols and skirmishes, but with floods, snipers, and an extremely mobile enemy, it was more "hide and seek" than normal fighting. However, there were exceptions, and one quite considerable action took place on the 28th May.

The rebels had cut several bunds and had flooded the Baghdad road for many miles. Orders were received to send out a fighting patrol to close the regulator on the Abu Ghuraib Canal and thus control the flood water over the Baghdad road. The rebels, estimated at a company but in fact in much greater strength, held a large oasis and were well dug in, with both flanks protected, quite near to Falluja.

Major K. F. May was sent out with two platoons and a M.G. Section from the Assyrian Levies, and got within half a mile, but could not progress farther owing to the strength and accuracy of the enemy fire. Artillery and air support were then asked for and obtained. In the evening of the 28th a second attempt was made under Major A. H. Kelly, who ordered a limited advance under cover of artillery concentrations, hoping the enemy might give way and retire with the evening light. However, the enemy, by now reinforced by additional M.G.s and some light artillery, did not retire. Major A. H. Kelly was seriously wounded and a withdrawal of our forces had to be ordered.

On the morning of the 29th May Major-General Clark arrived and decided that the enemy would be bombed for an hour, after which another two-company attack could go in with Major May in command.

In the event, the bombing was so inaccurate and the low-flying M.G. attacks so ineffective that the enemy positions were not only undisturbed but he was able to bring up reinforcements. To add insult to injury the 1st Essex companies, not the rebel positions, were showered with pamphlets in Iraqi calling upon them to surrender.

The attack was not put in, and there was a pause in which a better bombing plan was to be formulated, but before the answer to the rebel position had been found, the problem was solved by an Iraqi request for an armistice.

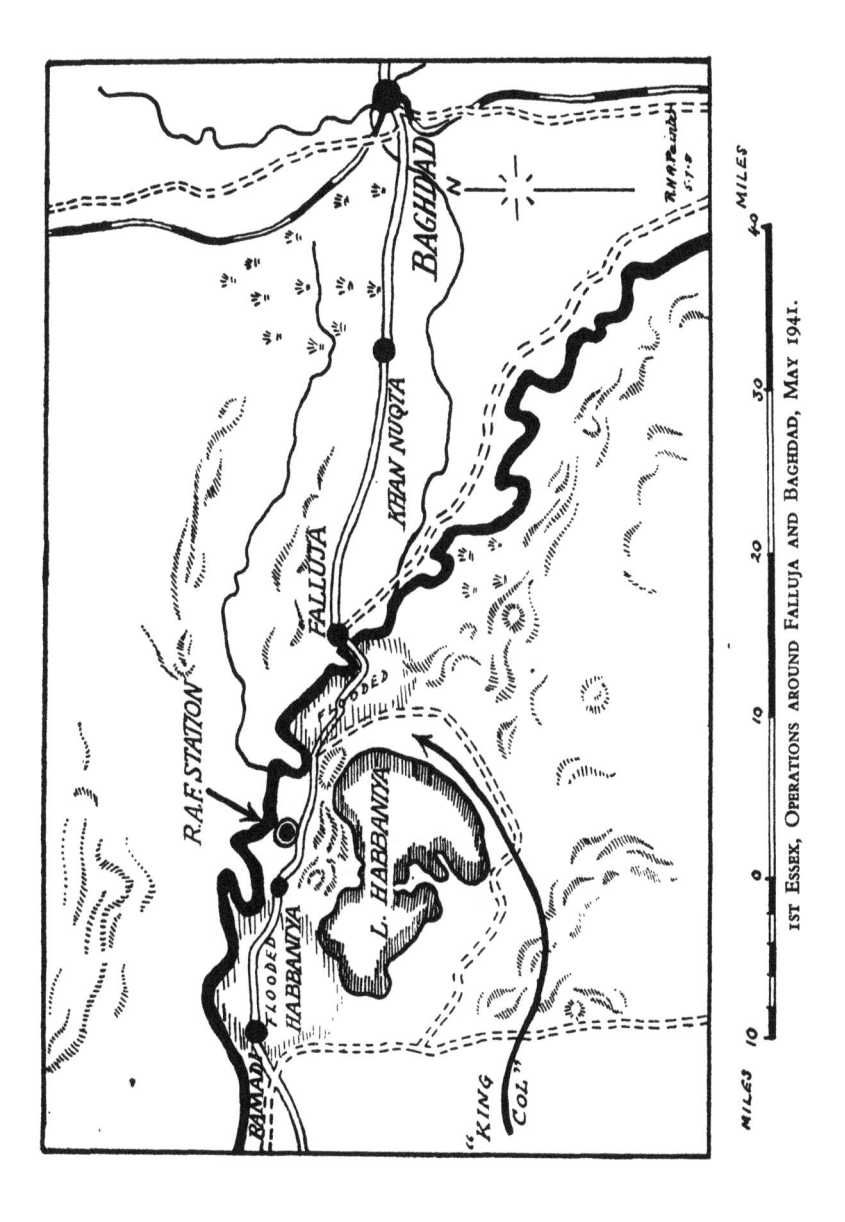

1st Essex, Operations around Falluja and Baghdad, May 1941.

At 4.30 a.m. on the 5th June, 1941, "Kingcol" left bivouac, and at 7 a.m., moving in order of army seniority, began to enter Baghdad. Major May returned from Falluja in time to reassume command of "A" and "D" Companies before their entry into the city.

On the 7th June "Kingcol" paraded in hollow square, and after inspection by His Excellency the British Ambassador, all ranks were thanked by him for their good work in raising the siege and restoring the situation in Baghdad. On the 9th June a Guard of Honour of 50 rank and file under Captain C. H. Robinson and Lieutenant T. D'A. Muirhead paraded in the British Embassy grounds for the occasion of rehoisting the Union Jack over the Embassy. On the 12th June "Kingcol" left Baghdad for Habbaniya, where command of "A" and "D" Companies reverted to the Battalion Commander.

Summing up the Iraq campaign, Brigadier Nichols says:

"The Iraq campaign, though little has been heard of it, was of great importance to the war as a whole; had Iraq been lost, and occupied by the Germans, the effect can well be imagined. The Iraq Army were employing five complete divisions in this campaign, with a small but efficient air force, backed by Germans. Our total forces consisted of 'Habforce,' two battalions from the 10th Indian Division, and the troops and personnel comprising the R.A.F. Station of Habbaniya.

"The part played by the 1st Essex was undoubtedly of vital importance. It was a part which called for continual improvisation, considerable endurance, and ability to put up with great discomfort. The lack of mosquito nets, shortage of food, and complete absence of N.A.A.F.I. supplies, also the shortage of medical equipment, made life hard.

"Although eventually from fifty to sixty all ranks went down with malaria, not a man reported sick with this until the fighting was finished. This throws an interesting light on the spirit which existed in the Battalion.

"I would also like to draw attention to the consideration and kindness shown to the Battalion by Major-General Clark. I had known him since Staff College days, where he was on the directing staff whilst I was a student.

"He particularly asked for the Battalion to be included in 'Habforce'; he always asked for my opinion and comments before setting us out on any difficult task, and was insistent that no operation should be undertaken which would entail heavy casualties."

Section VI

OPERATIONS IN SYRIA, 1941

Concentrated in bivouac on the shores of Lake Habbaniya, the Battalion rested and refitted. It was a pleasant change, and it was now possible to send foraging parties into the surrounding country, where the inhabitants were only too pleased to sell fruit and vegetables of which there was an abundance.

But by now the general situation in the Middle East had changed. A new theatre of operations had been opened up since the 1st Essex left Haifa for Iraq. During the fighting in Iraq, not only had German and Italian aircraft participated, but they had used French airfields at Damascus and Palmyra for refuelling and rearming. This was not all: the French authorities in Syria had openly supplied arms to the rebels. This could not be tolerated, and with the agreement of General de Gaulle, the leader of the Free French, Britain had decided to occupy Syria and the Lebanon.

On the 11th/12th June Major-General Clark sent for Lieutenant-Colonel Nichols and said that "Habforce" had received orders to take part in the Syrian campaign and would move to a concentration area in and around H.3. The move started on the 17th June.

Had an intelligent observer counted the 1st Essex transport on the westward journey toward Haifa, he would have noted there was now an additional Bren carrier named "Southend-on-Sea" beside its more experienced mates, "Chelmsford" and "Colchester." Perhaps it can now be disclosed that an Iraqi carrier had been captured, brand new, at Falluja. Too good to miss, it was quickly hidden away and subsequently brought into Baghdad on a lorry, covered with a thick tarpaulin and bulked out with boxes to disguise its shape. Major May there enlisted the aid of the Chief Engineer, Iraq Railways, who supplied desert-coloured paint to hide its present dark olive-green. In its new guise and rechristened "Southend-on-Sea" the "liberated" carrier took part in the capture of Palmyra.

By the evening of the 17th June the column had moved westwards some 170 miles along the desert road between Baghdad and Haifa, and the Battalion bivouacked for the night of the 17th/18th June at a point about forty-five miles east of Rutbah Wells. The day's trek had gone very smoothly, for the Battalion transport vehicles were travelling with light loads, a part of the troops having been lifted on the troop-carrying lorries of No. 3 Reserve M.T. Company, R.A.S.C.

On the 18th June the move took them to staging post H.2. Here an unexpected quantity of water was found in various tanks, which helped men and vehicles considerably, and all ranks were very glad of the unlooked-for opportunity to wash.

The attack into Syria was to be four-pronged, two from Palestine and two from Iraq. The 7th Australian Division had entered Syria on the 8th June and had advanced up the coast road. The Free French, farther inland, were directed on Damascus. "Habforce" was now to cross the Syrian Desert with its object Palmyra and the large airport. Palmyra stands guarding the only good crossing through a range of hills immediately to the west of it, running north and south. It has also the only large water supply for many miles. In consequence it has been a town of strategic importance for thousands of years and many roads and tracks from all directions converge there. The fourth prong of the attack was to be the advance of the 10th Indian Division under Major-General W. J. Slim up the River Euphrates.

It is of interest to note the remarkable rise of the Commander and principal staff officers of this formation. Major-General Slim was subsequently to command the Army in Burma and be C.I.G.S. The G.S.O.I., Colonel O. L. Roberts, became a divisional commander in Burma and subsequently a Lieutenant-General; the A.A. and Q.M.G., Lieutenant-Colonel A. Snelling, became the Major-General Administration Fourteenth Army, Burma; while Major Cariappa, the D.A.A. and Q.M.G., became the first C.-in-C. of the army of India. Indeed, a remarkable record.

On the 19th June, 1941, the westward move of the 1st Essex was halted, and Lieutenant-Colonel Nichols was called forward to a conference at "Habforce" Advance Headquarters at H.3. Here he was told that on the following day his Battalion was to move to the neighbourhood of H.3, bivouac for one night and move forward towards Palmyra the next day. The Battalion was to remain, as at present, completely motorised. The distance from H.3 to Palmyra is approximately 150 miles.

For the advance, "Habforce" was divided into three parts. The 4th Cavalry Brigade, with one battery of the 60th Field Regiment and one troop of a field squadron and detachments of other arms, moved with a detachment of the Arab Legion from H.3 at 4 a.m. on the 21st June. The main body (1st Essex; 60th Field Regiment less a battery; a field squadron less two troops; one Australian anti-tank battery; one light anti-aircraft battery less two sections; Divisional Headquarters) moved at 7.30 a.m. It was followed by "B" Echelon transport and supply column.

Leaving the "start-line" outside H.3 at 8 a.m. on the 21st June, the head of the 1st Essex column crossed the frontier into Syria at 12.25 p.m. that day. The going was good, and 120 miles across desert were covered before the column was ordered to halt, about 4 p.m.

Meanwhile, the 4th Cavalry Brigade had reached the vicinity of staging post T.(Tripoli)3, which was found to be held stoutly. Whilst in this area the 4th Cavalry Brigade was attacked from the air several times and suffered casualties. About 5 p.m. the main body was once more ordered to move forward, and the advance towards Palmyra continued for about one hour. The 1st Essex was then ordered to bivouac for the night at Jouffra, some twenty miles from T.3. Jouffra is merely a small oasis with a few wells. Shortly after halting, a number of casualties from the 4th Cavalry Brigade were brought in which Colonel Nichols says, "was rather a shattering sight after our very peaceful day's move."

On the 22nd June the 1st Essex, with the main body, moved on towards T.3, but slowly and with many halts. About midday they were ordered to halt within sight of T.3, and also within sight of Palmyra. Here the Battalion received the first air attack.

Palmyra lies approximately south of a range of steep hills. Cutting through the range the main road to Damascus and Homs winds its way through the imposing ruins of ancient Tadmor built by the Romans. There is, to this day, a fine Roman bathing pool fed by a mountain stream which all the troops sampled after the capture of the town. To the north-east of Palmyra lies the fort of Poste Weygande guarding the approaches to the north and east. Next facing east is the aerodrome, also well defended, whilst lying back and facing south-east was the Poste Restion or Arab fort. Furthermore, north-west of Palmyra and perched up in the hills was the imposing Château Turcq. The château dominated any attempt to pinch out Palmyra by an advance from the north-east, and covered the approach up an obvious wadi, of which, luckily, the French had not realised the importance.

A company of the Foreign Legion held Poste Weygande with a platoon at the fort at T.3, and a further party in the château.

General Clark's plan for the 23rd June was for the 4th Cavalry Brigade (less one squadron investing T.3) to move on Palmyra and attack it. He decided to move his reserve (1st Essex with anti-tank and anti-aircraft artillery detachments) three hours in rear. The plan involved a night march to within striking distance of Palmyra, as by now the enemy air force had made all movement by day impossible.

At 7.45 p.m. the start-line for the night march was passed, and after moving for nearly five hours at six miles in the hour Colonel Nichols was met by a staff officer and given orders to halt the Battalion indefinitely. The 1st Essex was then approximately ten miles north-east of Palmyra.

Lieutenant-Colonel Nichols was given the choice of "tucking into" the wadis in the hills as all units of the 4th Cavalry Brigade had done or remaining dispersed in the open. He decided to do the latter in the plain about eight miles from Palmyra. Here the 1st Essex remained for nearly a week, and during that time sustained some pretty concentrated bombing. Nearly 300 bombs of the 100-kilo variety were dropped on the Battalion in the first three days. Not a casualty was sustained, for both men and vehicles were well dispersed and well dug in in soft ground, and protected by four Bofors and many Brens. Lieutenant-Colonel Nichols said in his report on the Syrian Campaign: "In spite of repeated daily air attacks there were no casualties to personnel in the actual bivouac area and only one vehicle was put out of action. Other units which were partially hidden in hills and wadis, but in much harder ground, suffered a number of casualties to men and vehicles, although less frequently attacked. . . . If I had to choose again, I would choose the flat open ground, and my troops agree."

The only casualties during this period were when a small convoy of "B" Echelon had just left the bivouac area. Lieutenant (Quartermaster) W. L. Ambrose and Private E. Fountain were killed and 2 other ranks were wounded.

During this period General Clark had made two attempts to take Palmyra with the 4th Cavalry Brigade, both of which failed. There was, however, no general attack for the moment, because the British had no air support while the enemy had ample bombers and fighters. On the 25th June a message was received "Expect own aircraft," but it was not until the afternoon of the 26th that three British "Tomahawk" fighters were seen over the area, quickly shooting down the opposition.

General Clark in the meantime had sent for Colonel Nichols and told him that Palmyra must be taken, that he considered it to be an infantry task, and that Colonel Nichols was to submit his plan, using any supporting arms he might want.

Lieutenant-Colonel Nichols continues:

"My first plan was to move by night, assemble in the gardens and groves on the south-east side of Palmyra and attack at first light with the whole Battalion. He turned this down as likely to cause too many casualties and told me to think again.

"I came to the conclusion, after several reconnaissances, that the key to the whole position was the Château Turcq, and I decided that the first step must be its capture by night. If this was successful I planned to move the Battalion round the north side of Palmyra and occupy positions to the west of the town, astride the road to Homs. This would also put us in possession of a good water supply, four miles west of Palmyra on the Homs road.

"I decided that the best way of capturing the Château Turcq was a silent night attack by two platoons; but that a reconnaissance the previous night was essential. For this 2/Lieutenant B. F. H. Grimley was selected.

"I thought that after getting astride the Homs road it would not be difficult to work our way into the ruins of Palmyra, from which Poste Weygande could be attacked with support of the field regiment, and with adequate observation.

"I explained this plan to General Clark, which he approved, and after some discussion decided that the operation would be carried out in the following phases, all of which were to be carried out by night:

"Phase I. Capture of Château Turcq, and move-up of one company to supporting distance.

"Phase II. Capture of the enemy posts on the hills south of the Homs road, and move-up of the whole Battalion to position west of Palmyra.

"Phase III. Final attack on the ruins and forts from the west."

2/Lieutenant Grimley was accordingly detailed to take out a reconnaissance patrol, and by a very daring and successful action travelled over eight miles by night to the château area. He then led his patrol up the extremely steep hill leading to the château and entered the château itself. There they saw 3 of the enemy asleep, but these they did not disturb for fear of compromising the raid planned for the next night, and successfully withdrew.

The following night 2/Lieutenant Grimley returned at the head of the fighting patrol. The château was entered and captured and the garrison of the Foreign Legion was taken prisoner, including 6 captured while still asleep. One light and one heavy machine gun were also captured. 2/Lieutenant Grimley's patrol had no casualties. For this and other gallant actions during the fighting in Iraq and Syria 2/Lieutenant B. F. H. Grimley was granted an immediate award of the Distinguished Service Order.

The next night Phase II was carried out according to plan without casualties.

The third phase laid down that one infantry company would move into the ancient ruined city of Tadmor and secure a position in the native village if possible, later endeavouring to enter the forts, supported by carriers, artillery, mortars, and bombing. So on the night of the 1st/2nd July, "C" Company pushed forward into the ruined city area and captured the ancient theatre, a key point, without a casualty. Major James and 2/Lieutenant P. J. B. Savill with carriers, mortars, and two infantry platoons moved up in support, and the following day the sweep of the intervening ground between the ruined city area and the town of Palmyra started.

Of this action Lieutenant-Colonel Nichols says: "This proved a tougher proposition than was expected. There were plenty of snipers who were difficult to locate, and this slowed up the advance. The carriers tried to locate them by several sweeps, but found the ground pretty bad going. In addition they were peppered by armour-piercing bullets, and eventually one carrier got hopelessly ditched and came to rest partially on its side within short range of the enemy, and here a very gallant little episode occurred. After several sweeps, some of which were within 100 yards of the enemy, the ditched carrier was located. Carriers then came up and shielded it while the crew were hauled out. This action necessitated two trips and all the crew were taken off, but the carrier had to be abandoned. This little action was pretty warm while it lasted, as some of the crew were wounded whilst being hauled out." His leadership in this episode won the M.C. for the carrier platoon commander, Lieutenant C. H. Lawrence.

Lieutenant-Colonel Nichols then decided, in view of the strength of the opposition encountered, that he would not press any further advance in daylight. Major James had been wounded, 1 other rank had been killed, and 5 wounded.

That morning of the 2nd July, 1941, as the 1st Essex advance was halted, a message was received from 1st Cavalry Division which said, "Very satisfied with the operations carried out by your unit. Commander does not wish you to occupy 'Temple' tonight, as further progress without fresh troops would not be possible, and the possibility of an attempt to relieve Palmyra from Homs is ever present."

But the end was near. At 5.30 a.m. the 3rd July, 1941, two French envoys bringing with them three prisoners from the Royal Wiltshire Yeomanry came out of Palmyra into the lines of "B" Company 1st Essex. They stated that the French Commander wished to make terms of surrender and a white flag was flying from the Fort. This message was passed back to Major-General Clark, who met the envoys and arranged surrender.

At 12 noon the 3rd July, 1941, the 1st Essex moved into Palmyra and occupied the town. Major May was detailed to take the surrender at the Poste Weygande, the headquarters of the 6th Foreign Legion who had been the backbone of this stout defence. The Legion was commanded by a 100 per cent. pro-German, and officers and N.C.O.s were tough and efficient. They had fought stubbornly until ordered by General Dentz, the French C.-in-C. Syria, to stop. They were given the choice of being prisoners of war or joining the de Gaulle forces. Few joined.

Major-General Clark was quick to send a personal message of congratulation to Lieutenant-Colonel Nichols on the success of his plan and on the offensive spirit of the 1st Essex who so successfully put the plan into effect.

On the 9th July all ranks were pleased to hear of the following immediate awards for gallantry in action during operations in Iraq:

> Major R. B. James—Distinguished Service Order.
> Lieutenant T. D'A. Muirhead—the Military Cross.
> 6010866 Private A. Eldridge—the Military Medal.

The Battalion remained responsible for the defence of Palmyra, and, with the move of Headquarters "Habforce" to Qaryateine, the troops in Palmyra came under Essex command. These included a squadron of the Wiltshire Yeomanry, a section from an Australian anti-tank regiment, a troop of the 169th L.A.A. Regiment, a troop of 239th Battery R.A., and detachments of R.E., R.A.S.C., R.A.M.C., R.E.M.E., and Provost Corps.

On the 14th July changes in command took place. "Habforce" came under the 1st Australian Corps and Palmyra garrison became part of the 6th Division.

The next day, the 15th July, 1941, an armistice with Syria was signed and the campaign was officially over. That same day the 1st Essex was told that it would be relieved in Palmyra by the 1st King's Own and would come under the 85th L. of C. Sub-Area. It was to be prepared to move at short notice to Homs and then on to Damascus.

On the same day that the armistice with Syria was signed, the Prime Minister, Mr. Winston S. Churchill, made a speech in the House of Commons in which he said:

"I hope it will soon be possible to give fuller accounts to the public than they have yet received of the Syrian fighting, marked as it was by so many picturesque episodes such as the arrival of His Majesty's Life Guards and Royal Horse Guards, and the Essex Yeomanry (*N.B.*—A mistaken reference to the Essex Regiment) in armoured cars across many hundreds of miles of desert to surround and capture the oasis of Palmyra. If anyone had predicted two months ago, when Iraq was in revolt and our people were hanging on by their eyelids at Habbaniya and our Ambassador was imprisoned in his Embassy at Baghdad, and when all Syria and Iraq began to be overrun with German Tourists, and were in the hands of forces controlled indirectly but none the less powerfully by German authority—if anyone had predicted that we should already, by the middle of July, have cleaned up the whole of the Levant and have re-established our authority there for the time being, such a prophet would have been considered most impudent."

There can be little doubt that the 1st Essex had contributed very largely indeed to the success of British arms in Iraq and Syria.

On the 18th July they left Palmyra for Homs and Damascus. The route was along the Tripoli pipe-line, where the going was found extremely rough. Damage was done to vehicles, one 3-ton lorry being destroyed by fire. After Homs the going improved, and five hours later the Battalion reached Douma, outside Damascus, where it bivouacked.

Here it came under command of 85 L. of C. Area, but not for long. On the 20th fresh orders came in to place it under the 5th Cavalry Brigade which, under the terms of the Armistice agreement, was about to take over the Jebel Druze from the Vichy French Forces.

On the 23rd July the move-up was carried out, and Lieutenant-Colonel Nichols met Brigadier Dunn, Commander of the 5th Cavalry Brigade, to be told that the Brigadier had specially asked to have the 1st Essex for the relief of the Jebel Druze from the French, as he wished to make an impressive show of strength and smartness.

The following day the Battalion debussed some three and a half miles outside the town of Soueida, and marched to the outskirts of the town. Then, led by the Yorkshire Dragoons and 5th Cavalry Brigade Mounted Party, the 1st Essex made a ceremonial entry into the town, marching with fixed bayonets whilst eighteen R.A.F. bombers demonstrated over the town. After a short halt whilst the French troops marched out of Soueida by a different route, the Battalion marched past Brigadier Dunn. The strength on the march-past was 19 officers and 442 other ranks. The Brigadier the next day expressed his pleasure at the way the Essex had staged the march-in.

A show of force had to be made two days after the march-in, because it was believed that the French forces had not handed in all their arms in accordance with the convention. All precautions for a possible clash were taken, but luckily proved unnecessary, as the French yielded a large quantity of arms and ammunition without further persuasion.

A more peaceful operation took place the following day, when the 1st Essex paid a liaison visit to the ancient Druze village of Salkhad, some twenty miles from Soueida. There was much ceremonial and many speeches. The Moudir, or Head Man of the District, said that he welcomed the British troops on behalf of the Vinn, that it was a very happy day to have them in their country once more, and that they would offer everything to help the Allies win the war. Lieutenant-Colonel Nichols replied and said how proud we were still to have the Druze as our allies after over a hundred years of friendship between the two peoples. There was much fraternisation after this ceremonial opening to the visit, and there is little doubt that the visit of the 1st Essex did a great deal to aid the Allied cause and to cement the traditional friendship of the Druze to the British nation.

But as so often happens, sudden move orders were received during the journey back to Soueida. The 1st Essex was to replace the 2nd Royal Fusiliers in the 5th Indian Infantry Brigade on the 1st August, and be prepared to move with that formation to Deir-ez-Zor in relief of the 10th Indian Division.

On the 1st August the G.O.C. Palestine and Transjordan, General Sir H. Maitland Wilson, G.B.E., D.S.O., M.C., arrived and inspected the Battalion drawn up in a hollow square. As the Battalion presented arms, General Wilson was heard to say, "Well done, Crasher."

Addressing the parade the General congratulated them on their part in the relief of Baghdad, the capture of Palmyra, and the arduous journeying across desert country. He said the Battalion's forthcoming move to Deir-ez-Zor would only be temporary, and that upon its return it would take its place in the fighting forces of the Middle East, where the recent experiences would, he hoped, stand it in good stead. This of course meant a move into the Western Desert.

Next day, the 2nd August, the 1st Essex moved northwards via Palmyra to Deir-ez-Zor. It was another arduous desert journey, and another 310 miles for the Battalion's hard-worked mechanical transport. It is interesting to note that since leaving Haifa on the 11th May, the Battalion M.T. had done 3,500 miles over country which was mostly untracked desert or track of a very primitive nature, and yet not one vehicle had been lost or abandoned through mechanical trouble. This was a fine achievement, which reflected great credit on the transport personnel.

On entering Deir-ez-Zor on the 9th August, 1941, the 1st Essex took over, from the 4/13th Frontier Force Rifles, the duties, including patrolling and internal security within the 5th Indian Brigade boundary south of the River Euphrates.

On the 16th August the Battalion found a guard of honour of 100 rank and file commanded by Captain J. S. Greene at the airport for the arrival of General de Gaulle, who was accompanied by Brigadier W. Lloyd and Chef de Battalion Reyniers. After his inspection General de Gaulle expressed high admiration for the turn-out, drill, and smart bearing of the guard of honour. The Brigade Commander also expressed his pleasure.

On the 30th August, 1941, yet another airport guard of honour had to be provided, again commanded by Captain J. S. Greene, this time for the arrival of General Sir Claude Auchinleck, G.C.I.E., C.B., C.S.I., D.S.O., O.B.E., the C.-in-C. Middle East Forces, who was accompanied by General Sir Henry Maitland Wilson. At the conclusion of the inspection, the C.-in-C. complimented the Commanding Officer on the smart turn-out, drill, and steadiness of the guard of honour.

The two months in Deir-ez-Zor soon went by, the stay being enlivened by the news of further immediate awards to the Battalion for gallantry in action, this time during operations in Syria:

Lieutenant-Colonel J. S. Nichols, M.C.—Distinguished Service Order.
2/Lieutenant B. F. H. Grimley—Distinguished Service Order.
2/Lieutenant C. H. Lawrence—Military Cross.
Platoon Sergeant-Major W. E. Cornell—Distinguished Conduct Medal.

In mid-September orders were received that the 5th Indian Infantry Brigade would shortly move to Egypt and that the 1st Essex would remain temporarily and take over the whole brigade area, coming directly under Headquarters British Forces in Palestine, Transjordan, and Syria.

The 5th Indian Infantry Brigade was relieved in the Syrian desert by the 3rd Indian Motor Brigade, but during the interval between the departure of one and the arrival of the other the 1st Essex had to control and patrol the whole area, which was about 300 miles deep and 350 miles wide.

Now another signal came in. The 1st Essex had been selected to relieve a Czech battalion in the 23rd Infantry Brigade of the 6th Division and was to be ready to move from Deir-ez-Zor to Aleppo on or after the 3rd October.

Lieutenant-Colonel Nichols went and paid a visit to the Commander of the 23rd Infantry Brigade in Aleppo (Brigadier C. H. V. Cox, D.S.O., M.C.). There he learnt that the 6th Division was to be renamed the 70th Division, and that it was being moved by sea for a special operation in an unspecified area, which, however, was almost certain to be Tobruk.

The last weeks in Syria were enlivened by a rising of local tribesmen against the collection of taxes by the Free French authorities. Deir-ez-Zor had to be put in a state of defence, mobile columns had to be organised and sent out, and altogether the 1st Essex had their hands full. But they felt this was not their war, and when a company had to be sent to Meyadin to intervene, it was preceded by an armoured car flying an enormous Union Jack. Luckily the tribesmen, fully armed and some thousands strong, were content to await a negotiated settlement.

From Deir-ez-Zor two companies went out to Hassetche in Assyrian territory on a tributary of the Euphrates where they patrolled forward to the Turkish border. A very good liaison was made with the intensely pro-British and Christian Assyrians. From Deir-ez-Zor it was possible to go on leave to Aleppo, where, at the nearby frontier railway station, it was possible to go on board the restaurant cars of the Orient express, or its wartime equivalent, and drink a bottle of iced beer loaded on the car at the train's starting-point—Berlin.

On the 12th October, 1941, the 1st Essex crossed from Syria into Palestine after a stay of nearly four months. The re-entry into Palestine almost coincided with the anniversary of the Battalion's first arrival in that country five years previously.

At the staging camp near Hadera all heavy baggage had to be packed and handed in, for the Battalion was only allowed to take forward a very small scale of baggage.

Their experiences in Iraq and Syria had been valuable. They had done extremely good work and had brought new credit to the Regiment. It was a battleworthy and confident Battalion that passed westwards across the Suez Canal on the 14th October, 1941.

Section VII

OPERATIONS IN THE WESTERN DESERT: TOBRUK AND ED DUDA, 1941

The 1st Essex entrained immediately the ferry crossing of the Suez Canal had been made, with destination Amriya. Here the 15th/16th October was spent in refitting the Battalion with new battledress and leather jerkins. All ranks were confined to camp and there was a great air of secrecy. "When we got our final orders to move," says Colonel Nichols, "all ranks, including myself, were only allowed to carry what we could manage on our back and in one hand. One hand had to be kept free. (We afterwards discovered the reason for this, when we started to disembark in Tobruk harbour.) I decided therefore that kit-bags should be tied in pairs, so that one man could carry two men's kit-bags, leaving the other free to carry much-needed equipment and stores."

On the 17th October, 1941, 7 officers and 258 other ranks embarked at Alexandria in the destroyer *Havoc* and sailed for Tobruk. The following day the remainder of the Battalion came into the fortress also by destroyer and the whole Battalion was established with the 2/24th Australian Infantry Battalion.

On the next day orders were received to relieve the 2/17th Australian Infantry Battalion in the line, and by midnight of the 21st/22nd October the relief was complete, the 1st Essex coming under command of the 20th Australian Infantry Brigade.

We are indebted to Major J. S. Greene for a full and interesting account of the move into Tobruk and of life in the fortress, but before giving this story it is probably opportune to interpose a short account of the general situation in the Western Desert in the autumn of 1941, and to give, too, the names of those commanding companies in the Battalion as it entered Tobruk.

Depleted by calls to Greece, Crete, and the Sudan, General Wavell's Desert Army which had captured Benghazi in the spring of 1941 had been pushed back by General Rommel's Afrika Korps and the Italians, and had regrouped on the border of Egypt. By a daring decision, General Wavell had left a force in Tobruk as he fell back. This force, which was maintained by sea, had held Tobruk all through the summer of 1941.

In June 1941 General Wavell had launched a limited offensive with a view to relieving Tobruk. It failed. General Wavell had been succeeded by General Sir C. J. Auchinleck. During the rest of the summer the Western Desert Force, under Lieutenant-General N. Beresford-Peirse, remained active with a view to distracting the enemy's attention from Tobruk. At midnight on the 26th September command of all troops in the Western Desert, less the Tobruk Garrison, passed to the newly formed Eighth Army, with Lieutenant-General Sir Alan Cunningham as its commander.

As the 1st Essex moved into Tobruk in October 1941, General Auchinleck was about to launch his first offensive (operation "Crusader"), the objective to be a link-up of the Eighth Army and the garrison of Tobruk, and the defeat of the enemy forces. These at this time consisted of seven Italian and three German divisions. The enemy was no longer superior in numbers, but possessed a great advantage in the quality and armament of the German tanks.

As the Battalion moved out of Amriya, "A" Company was commanded by Major J. S. Greene, "B" Company by Captain I. J. D. Stevenson-Hamilton, "C" by Captain C. Nelson, and "D" Company by Major C. H. Robinson. Major J. F. Higson had Headquarter Company and was also acting as Battalion second-in-command, and Captain P. H. A. L. Franklin was the adjutant.

Now Major Greene goes on:

"We left Amriya by M.T. in the early morning. The freshness of the morning made us thankful for our newly acquired battledress. The men were great value, irrepressibly cheerful, and glad to be on the move again. The waiting around had been unpleasant.

"Our route took us through the more disreputable part of Alexandria and thence to the docks, where we debussed on the quayside alongside which were the destroyers which were to take us to Tobruk.

"The Royal Navy then took us over, and we were embarked without any fuss or bother on to our destroyers. Ours was the *Kandahar*—most appropriate—two companies to each destroyer. 'B' Company came with us and the men settled themselves on the deck sitting on their kit, gaining what shelter they could from the superstructure of the destroyer. The usual check showed we were all aboard. Life-jackets were issued and adjusted.

"It was about 7 a.m. when we slipped out of the harbour. Our send-off was a noisy affair with most of the craft in the harbour blowing their sirens. Our convoy consisted of three destroyers, and a mine-layer carrying stores and ammunition bringing up the rear. Guns were manned, and it was interesting to see the Navy at work—most impressive. We were allowed on the bridge from time to time. This helped to pass the hours, and provided us with a splendid insight into the workings and handling of a destroyer. Many of us were distressed to read later in the year that this gallant little ship was sunk off Bardia, and one wondered how the crew had fared.

"The day was fine but cold, the sun shone, and life somehow seemed very peaceful. Our route took us close to the coast, and we were able to recognise Mersa Matruh, where many of us had been in October 1938 during the Munich crisis. Some of our fighters came out from Mersa Matruh to have a look at us. It was very reassuring.

"The men fed from the galley. We were lucky enough to be able to use the wardroom for our meals, which were delicious and well served, our last civilised meal for some months.

"At dusk we passed Sollum, which was the high-tide mark of Rommel's advance in 1941. It was dark when we passed Bardia, and as we approached Tobruk flashes of gun-fire and Very lights could be seen plainly against the darkness of the night. We altered course and reduced speed outside Tobruk, and gradually approached the harbour. The entrance was marked by two red lights which slipped past us in the darkness. It was incredible how our ship threaded its way through the wrecks in the harbour to the quayside to rub its side against another wreck next to the quay. The loud-hailer instructed us to disembark forthwith. We stumbled with our kit across the wreck and on to the quay. It was 11 p.m., and we were in Tobruk. The Company formed up in silence. We were guided by an Aussie guide through the town, to where some M.T. was parked. 'Bardia Bill' was silent that night, and the bombers left us alone, though they had been over earlier that night. The town had certainly had a pasting. Buildings created a fantastic silhouette against the night sky, a real surrealist's paradise.

"The march through this ruined town seemed endless, uphill the whole way. My valise seemed to get heavier and heavier as we went along, and it was a relief to get to the M.T. The Company was loaded on to the trucks, and the convoy moved out of the town along a twisty road liberally punctuated by bomb and shell craters. We debussed at Sidi Mahmoud, close to the junction of the El Adem–Bardia–Tobruk road, where existed a large P.W. cage. The person who originally sited that camp must have had a warped sense of humour, as the road junction was constantly shelled through the siege, particularly after the breakout.

"At Sidi Mahmoud, our advance party met us, and guided us to our company dispersal area, where we doubled up with an Australian battalion for the night. The Aussies' welcome was splendid, and they produced hot tea from somewhere. Despite the fact that it tasted very odd, it was wet and warm, and very welcome. It was our first introduction to the water in Tobruk, where, as the popular saying said, 'Mr. Eno would have been put out of business.'

"It was 2 a.m., before we 'got down to it,' in a shallow dugout, which gave one sufficient room to sit up only. The light consisted of a round cigarette tin full of paraffin with a piece of rope as a wick. The night, or what remained of it, was spent battling without much success against the hordes of fleas left by the Italians in that dugout.

"The next morning gave us our first view of the area which was to be our home for some weeks. The area of ground known as Sidi Mahmoud was most inhospitable. It was boulder-strewn, covered in small stunted bushes, and sloping downwards towards the sea, which could be seen about a mile away. The area was strewn with shell splinters, grenades, wire, broken rifles, blown-up tanks and other impedimenta of war. On the way over to breakfast, one of the company kicked a small Italian grenade, which exploded, wounding about four men. These were our first casualties.

"It was about midday when we had our first Stukas raid. About twelve machines came over and plastered a gun area, which, we afterwards learnt, was the Essex Yeomanry position. These Stukas circuses were to become almost part of our daily life, but to see one for the first time was a little unsettling.

"We received orders at midday to relieve an Australian battalion on the perimeter that night. We were to commence moving up as soon as darkness had fallen. The Battalion was to be deployed with three companies forward, 'D' right, 'B' centre, 'C' left, with 'A' Company in reserve and counter-attack company.

"The move-up commenced at about 6.30 p.m., and we left our dispersal area at about 8.15 p.m. in transport down the El Adem road. There was no interference by the enemy with our move forward, and it was not long before we reached a point on the road past which no M.T. could move. We marched from there until we met our guide on the road, who led us to our company area. The Australians were 'standing-to' when we arrived. The take-over didn't take long. I was bequeathed a jar of rum by the Company Commander from whom I was taking over, a very useful addition to our meagre supplies. After a handing over of maps, traces, patrol reports, etc., he disappeared into the darkness. I rang Battalion Headquarters that our take-over was complete, and then went round the platoon areas.

"The morning found us well settled in with the men in good form. As reserve company, our position was on the reverse slope of the main ridge on which the forward defended localities were situated, which enabled us to move around freely during the hours of daylight. Occasional shells pitched into our company area without causing any great inconvenience.

"Then followed a period of days which lengthened into weeks that were spent either on the perimeter or in the reserve area. One quickly adjusted one's self to a completely new and novel sort of existence—when one just lived from day to day.

"The perimeter consisted of a thin line of positions which were based on the old Italian positions sited for the defence of the town. These positions were built of concrete, and provided a reasonable amount of shelter from the elements as well as the enemy. The normal company frontage was far in excess of that laid down in all textbooks. This made it necessary to hold the frontage with all three platoons forward, depth only being provided by the reserve section of each platoon being echeloned to the rear. Additional section positions were dug between the original Italian positions in order to cover the front by fire. Each section position had additional L.M.G.s allotted to it. These took the form of a variety of captured automatic guns, including Spandaus and Bredas, and gave the platoon greatly increased fire power. The section positions were self-contained units with reserves of ammunition, water, and food. Rations were so arranged to enable section cooking to be organised. This gave rise to cooking competitions between the sections, who would vie with each other to produce the most palatable concoction from the basic ingredients of bully beef and biscuits, bread and jam. Mrs. Beeton had nothing on some of those dishes! It was a great morale booster, and provided much fun.

"Routine became rigid in many respects, and life on the perimeter must have proximated to the state of affairs during some parts of the 1914-18 War. We 'stood-to' at an hour before dawn each and every morning, and watched the sun rise up again to start our day for us. Then the excitement of breakfast, which invariably consisted of porridge, bacon, bread and jam, and some Tobruk tea. The monotony of our diet was rarely broken, but the men were grand, and rarely grumbled, and we all 'mucked in' on what was going and enjoyed it. We were very thankful for our supply of fresh bread from the bakery in the town. It was a great luxury.

"Breakfast was followed by shaving, and everyone shaved in about a third of a mug of water. Then followed the cleaning up of one's dugout, weapon inspection, checking of ammunition, water, reserve rations, and the hundred and one odd jobs to be done in a defensive position. I endeavoured to get round the platoon positions each day with my batman, a progress of events which took most of the morning. Jerry was not worried about one or two bodies moving about the position, but he would mortar and shoot up any groups of men seen in the position. We in our turn kept reasonably quiet, and did not open up any more than necessary. Occasionally the gunner forward observation officer would want to re-register or change a defensive fire task, and we felt a little guilty about starting the war off again. German guns and mortars, after their morning or evening 'hate,' were reasonably well behaved. Lunch was a light meal, and we aimed at resting as many men as possible during the afternoon, providing a single sentry in each section position only. The afternoon was invariably spent completing the numerous returns, reports, etc., which were required by 'the powers that be,' and getting ready for the night's activities. Our evening meal we organised to finish before dark, and before 'stand-to.' It was usually bully in some form or other, with perhaps prunes—very healthy—or tinned fruit if you were lucky. Because of the lack of vitamins in our diet, the doctors made us swallow a vast variety of pills which were reputed to do all sorts of interesting things to one.

"That night brought a whole host of activities in the form of double sentries, listening posts out, 'wire and ditch' patrols, deep reconnaissance patrols, and fighting patrols. Most of one's company was engaged in this programme through the night. After a number of weeks this became most exhausting. The C.Q.M.S. was always a very welcome visitor. There was always a chance that he might bring us some mail, or some cigarettes or something different to eat. He was always like a breath of fresh air, providing us with news from the battalion and the outside world, which seemed very remote. He disappeared just as unobtrusively as he had arrived, leaving us a new stock of bully, bread, jam, and water—perhaps tomorrow he might bring some letters.

"We relied entirely on the 'Tobruk Truth' for our news. This was printed in duplicated form down in the town, a survival of the Aussies, and gave us news of the outside world. It was very welcome. Mail was an event of the first magnitude, but it only came in twice while we were in the fortress. In my first lot I received a demand from the Paymaster for the sum of 3/3, which appeared to be outstanding on an account I had handled whilst Camp Adjutant and Quartermaster at Atbara. The letter eventually was blown up with me on Ed Duda. A big batch of mail came through just before the attack on Ed Duda.

"Cigarettes were difficult to obtain for the men, and supplies had to be carefully husbanded.

"The usual Stukas raids came at regular intervals, and usually when the Northumberland Fusiliers (a machine-gun battalion) had been firing from our company area during the previous night—how unpopular they became. Before dawn they had packed up bag and baggage, and disappeared to some safer area leaving us to take the proverbial 'can back.' The 'Bush artillery' was another method of becoming very unpopular with the opposition. It consisted of captured Italian artillery pieces of dubious vintage sited close behind the main ridge and manned by the Anti-Aircraft Platoon. After a short course on these weapons they were entrusted with their management. From their behaviour it seemed to take them to a higher social plane. They surrounded themselves in an air of mystery comparable to the normal gunner 'hoodoo'! However, they appeared to produce the goods, and to hit where it hurt Jerry most. He invariably 'came back' with an assortment of shells and mortars until we persuaded our 'gunners' to pack it in.

"Our one amusement was to sit on our ridge at night and watch Tobruk being bombed. It was almost a nightly performance, and the barrage our gunners put up was splendid, and very pretty to see. It was rather a macabre sort of amusement.

"Sand storms were one of the most unpleasant features of our period in Tobruk, but luckily they were few. We normally stood-to whilst they blew, and after the storm had passed the difficulty of cleaning one's self up in a small bowl of water can be imagined. Flies were abundant, but thanks to the sanitary personnel and field-hygiene section, our sickness rate was surprisingly low.

"The complete lack of any air support during the siege was a little depressing to begin with, though one accepted the fact without question. We had one plane in the fortress, a Hurricane, which was a very treasured possession. It would appear in the early morning, scurry round the perimeter for a quick look round, and come down again on the airstrip to be tucked away in a cave until it went off again on its morning task the next day. It was splendid to see some of our own aircraft again once the November offensive started with our fighter sweeps working along the Trigh El Abaid. The trail of burning vehicles left behind was evidence of their success.

"In front of our forward defended localities ran a continuous anti-tank trench of a depth which varied considerably. The barbed-wire fence was of some considerable depth and liberally booby-trapped throughout its length. Our minefields covered the whole front in great depth, consisting of a variety of mines, some being Egyptian-produced mines which exploded on the slightest provocation. Each section post had a 'spoke' minefield running out from the position like clock rays, which proved most effective. A number of uncharted minefields also did exist, which made movement off recognised tracks a risky business.

"Few comforts were forthcoming during our time in the fortress. One saw tins of Barclay's lager flattened by M.T. lying round the desert, which suggested that Tobruk had seen better days.

"I was detached from the Battalion and under command of the 4th Border Regiment when we had orders to concentrate for the breakout. It meant handing over very quickly, and a long march back in the gathering darkness to Sidi Mahmoud, where the Battalion was concentrated.

"Orders were issued for our attack on Ed Duda. These were cancelled later in the night, and we settled down to a night's sleep. The future looked difficult, but most of us slept well. The next morning was spent waiting and wondering. Weapons were checked, ammunition sorted out, and orders were eventually issued at midday. We moved off as darkness was gathering, and took our place in the enormous convoys of vehicles passing out through the original gap made by the Black Watch. That night we spent outside the perimeter dispersed in company blobs. Morning found us spread over a large area in the original Italian positions. It was interesting to see the conditions under which the opposition had been living. The Black Watch had had bad casualties during the breakout. Evidence of this was shown by the many impromptu graves round the desert. It was interesting to find letters in the enemy positions from Italy and Germany dated the middle of November 1941; it was then 26th November, 1941."

For the actual account of the part played by the 1st Essex in these operations there are fortunately two contemporary narratives. The first of these accounts is by Lieutenant-Colonel J. S. Nichols, D.S.O., M.C. It is the Commanding Officer's battle story. The second, by Lieutenant P. P. S. Brownless, is a platoon commander's battle picture, and so is complementary to the first. It is given as Appendix 6 in this history.

Lieutenant-Colonel Nichols writes:

"About the middle of October 1941, the Battalion moved to Tobruk to form part of the 70th Division, and took over a portion of the southern perimeter defences from the 2/17th Australian Infantry Battalion, remaining in a static role until 24th November.

"On 20th November, a series of operations were undertaken on the south-eastern portion of the perimeter in order to form a corridor which was intended to join up with the advancing troops of the Eighth Army. These operations were to be in five phases, and were to be undertaken by the 32nd Army Tank Brigade, the 14th Infantry Brigade, and a portion of the 16th Infantry Brigade, together with supporting arms. The fifth and final phase of these operations was to be the capture of a commanding portion of the El Adem escarpment, known as Ed Duda. On this feature it was intended that the Tobruk Garrison would effect a junction with troops of either the 13th or 30th Corps.

"It did not appear likely that the Battalion would take part in any of the operations at Tobruk, as at that time it was in Brigade Reserve, in the southern sector; but on 24th November orders were suddenly received that as all the battalions of the 14th Infantry Brigade had already been expended, the fifth and final phase would be undertaken by the 1st Essex, which would come under command 32nd Army Tank Brigade for this operation. During that afternoon the Battalion moved to a concentration area at Sidi Mahmoud, and was there

joined by the following troops, which came under command of the Battalion:
One Section Lifting Transport, R.A.S.C.
One Troop 439th Anti-Tank Regiment, Royal Artillery.
Two Sections 2nd Field Company, Royal Engineers.
One Section 215th Field Ambulance, R.A.M.C.

"The whole of this party was to move in M.T. under cover of darkness to the forming-up positions, between two of the most advanced positions which were distant about 2,000 yards from the original perimeter posts and about 10,000 yards distant from the concentration area at Sidi Mahmoud.

"Late that night, orders were received postponing the operation for twenty-four hours.

"On 25th November, the Battalion and attached troops moved at 6 p.m. to an assembly area near the original perimeter defences.

"On arrival there, instructions were received that once more the operation would probably not take place as planned, owing to an alternative operation which was being undertaken that night by the Tank Brigade, in which the Battalion would not take part.

"The Battalion then moved to a dispersal area about one mile south-east of the original perimeter defences, ready to undertake any operation which might be ordered.

"On 26th November, at 11 a.m., orders were received that the Battalion and attached troops would move forward immediately to the forming-up position, ready for the attack on Ed Duda. The Battalion moved at 11.45 a.m. and formed up at 12.30 p.m., ready to follow the 32nd Army Tank Brigade when ordered.

"At 12.45 the tank advance started and the enemy commenced to shell the Battalion at its forming-up position, but this caused no damage or casualties.

"The objective was about 7,000 yards distant from the forming-up line. The attack was, at the time, an isolated operation, as no troops were advancing on the right or on the left.

"At 1.15 p.m. our tanks could be seen on the objective, and at 1.45 p.m. the Battalion was ordered to advance. The advance was carried out at a speed of about 10 m.p.h. in the following formation: Carrier Platoon leading; 'D' Company; Troop 439th Anti-Tank Regt., R.A.; 'B' Company echeloned to the right; 'C' Company echeloned to the left; Battalion Headquarters in the centre, about 100 yards in rear of the Anti-Tank Troop; 'A' Company (reserve) in rear of Battalion

Headquarters, followed by remainder of 'A' Echelon Transport Vehicles, R.E., and Section Field Ambulance.

"The advance was carried out across the plain without interruption until the leading troops were about 200 yards from the near edge of the escarpment, where they were heavily bombed. This bombardment destroyed half the Carrier Platoon, about one platoon of 'D' Company, killing the Company Commander (Major C. H. Robinson) and the Carrier Officer (Lieutenant C. H. Lawrence, M.C.), and inflicting about 35 other casualties. This did not check the advance, and all companies, on reaching the escarpment, debussed according to plan and went forward rapidly to seize their respective objectives.

"At this time the whole Tank Brigade had withdrawn to the left flank, and was formed up ready to support the Battalion if required.

"As the remainder of the Battalion reached the escarpment, it came under heavy artillery fire at fairly short range, both from field and heavy artillery. Many of the guns could actually be seen, and some of them were undoubtedly firing over open sights.

"By 3 p.m. all companies had reached their objectives without much opposition, about 50 prisoners being taken. The position taken up by the Battalion was in the form of a box. 'B' Company on the west, commanded by Captain I. J. D. Stevenson-Hamilton, held position astride the by-pass road, reaching up to the northern edge of the escarpment, supported by the Anti-Tank Troop less one section. 'D' Company (Lieutenant P. F. M. Parry) seized positions facing south some 300 yards south of the road. 'C' Company (Captain C. Nelson) held positions astride the road facing east.

"During this time Battalion Headquarters and troops in the Headquarters area continued to come under heavy artillery fire, from which very little cover could be found, and in consequence casualties were heavy.

"At about 3 p.m. 'D' Company was counter-attacked from the south by enemy infantry and tanks. A party with Lieutenant Parry (who was then commanding the company), which was some 200 yards in advance of the rest of the company, was wiped out, all being killed, but the attack was driven off before it reached the remainder of the company.

"About 3.30 p.m. 'B' Company (Captain Stevenson-Hamilton) on the west was attacked by enemy infantry brought up in lorries (estimated at about two companies). This attack was held up about 200 yards from the forward defended locations—heavy casualties being

Palmyra

(Crown Copyright)
1st Battalion The Essex Regiment. The Capture of Palmyra (Tadmor) 2nd July, 1941.

1st Battalion The Essex Regiment. (centre) Lieutenant-Colonel J. S. Nichols, D.S.O., M.C., and (right) Captain P. H. A. L. Franklin at Battalion Headquarters, Ed Duda. December 1941.

(Imperial War Museum)
1st Battalion The Essex Regiment. On Ed Duda after the Battle. December 1941.

inflicted on the enemy, and several vehicles being destroyed. A sharp and spirited counter-attack was then put in by a platoon commanded by 2/Lieutenant B. G. Gingell, and about 80 prisoners were taken.

"Meanwhile, an attack by lorried infantry from the east developed on the front of 'C' Company, but this was also driven off, several enemy vehicles being destroyed and about 30 prisoners being taken.

"In the Battalion Headquarters area temporary positions had been obtained which were not very satisfactory. Communication to forward companies was maintained by pack wireless sets until L/T (Line) communication was established at about 4 p.m.

"By 3.30 p.m., in spite of casualties and some confusion among M.T. drivers, Major J. F. Higson, who was acting Battalion Second-in-Command, had succeeded in getting back all unwanted transport, reorganising it, and dispersing it about 1,000 to 1,500 yards north of Battalion Headquarters.

"At 4.30 p.m., finding considerable gaps between 'B' and 'D' Companies ('D' Company had by this time been reduced to a strength of about 40), I moved up 'A' Company, less one platoon, to fill the gap. The remaining platoon was kept in Battalion reserve, and took up defensive positions facing north-west and protected the rear of Battalion Headquarters.

"One Company of Royal Northumberland Fusiliers which had advanced under immediate orders of the 32nd Army Tank Brigade was incorporated into the defence and support of the Battalion.

"At about 5.30 p.m., as the daylight was fading, enemy shelling ceased, and it became possible to establish Battalion Headquarters in what then proved to be a more sheltered position.

"During the night, the enemy remained in close contact on the west and south. Several lorries with troops on board which entered the Battalion position were captured, and personnel taken prisoner. Shortly after midnight, the 19th New Zealand Infantry Battalion, accompanied by one squadron of tanks, and one troop anti-tank guns, reached Ed Duda from the east, having marched over ten miles by night, passing through positions believed to be held by the enemy but without any interruption. Their Commander, Lieutenant-Colonel Hartigan, visited Battalion Headquarters, but did not move his battalion up, as he had received instructions from the 32nd Army Tank Brigade to remain in reserve in the valley to the north-east.

"On the morning of the 27th November the enemy was found to be in close contact with the front of 'B' Company, and the whole Battalion area was kept under constant artillery and M.G. fire, so that no work or improvement of positions was possible. During the morning, a patrol of 'D' Company, commanded by 2/Lieutenant K. W. M. Mann, was established nearly 2,000 yards to the south across the Trigh

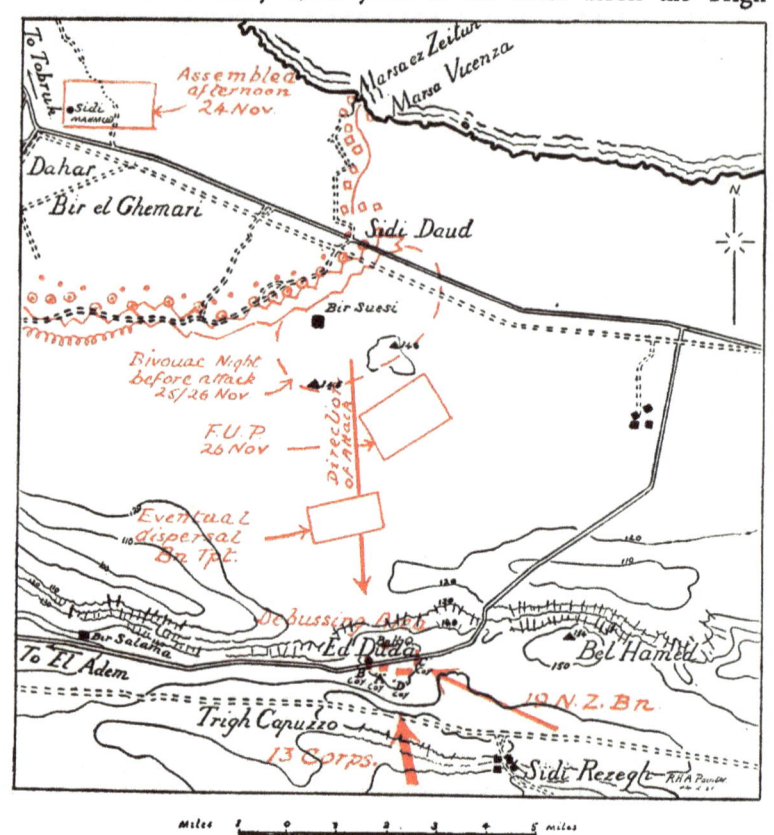

1ST ESSEX, TOBRUK AND ED DUDA, OCTOBER–DECEMBER 1941.

Capuzzo, and remained there most of the day, although parties of enemy infantry made two attempts to drive it back.

"During the night of the 27th/28th November active patrolling was carried out, and defences considerably strengthened.

"On the morning of the 28th it was found that the enemy had withdrawn to a distance of about 4,000 yards on the front of 'B' Company, and shelling was not so heavy. Patrols obtained contact with the enemy both to the west and to the south.

"Meanwhile the 19th New Zealand Battalion, less two companies, two mortar detachments, and the Carrier Platoon, had been withdrawn to join the 4th New Zealand Brigade, which had moved up on to Bel Hamed some 3/4000 yards east of Ed Duda. Remaining two companies established themselves in positions some 1,200 yards north-east of 'C' Company.

"Nothing further of importance occurred until about midday on 29th November, when a patrol of 'B' Company, who were well to the west, observed large clouds of dust coming from Sidi Mamun. A little later a large number of M.T. vehicles could be seen moving from Sidi Mamun. At first little notice was taken of this, as it was thought that it was a party of enemy withdrawing towards El Adem, but at 12.45 p.m., about 40 enemy tanks could be distinguished, followed by about 40 or 50 lorries, and at 1.30 p.m. these got into position in the west astride the El Adem road and started to advance on the Battalion positions. About 2 p.m. 15 tanks had got to within 300 yards of 'B' Company's forward defended localities, and from 2 p.m. for nearly 2½ hours these bombarded 'B' Company's forward defended localities with gun-fire, causing a number of casualties and destroying the forward defended localities (all of which consisted of sangars, owing to the rocky nature of the ground, which had made digging impossible).

"During this time, one or more troops of 'I' (Infantry) tanks were moved forward to engage the enemy. But their fire had no effect, several of our own tanks being knocked out.

"About 4.30 p.m. between 25 and 30 tanks, followed by infantry who had debussed in the valley to the south-west and moved up behind these tanks, advanced and overran most of the positions of 'B' Company and 'A' Company. By this time all our anti-tank guns had been knocked out, and most of the posts containing anti-tank rifles had been destroyed. The remnants of 11 and 12 Platoons of 'B' Company were taken prisoners, also 8 and 9 Platoons of 'A' Company, and most of 'A' Company's Headquarters. These platoons had withstood a heavy and close-range bombardment for 2½ hours, and could effect nothing against the heavy tanks (Mark IV) which moved over and through them, closely followed by parties of infantry with sub-machine guns.

"The enemy continued to advance slowly, and by 5.30 p.m. 25 tanks had penetrated the centre of the Battalion's position, whilst infantry established themselves in the forward posts of 'A' and 'B' Companies. The remnants of 'B' Company, under command of Captain Stevenson-Hamilton, were still hanging on at the extreme right of the position. 'D' Company, having driven off enemy infantry who had advanced south on 'D' Company's front at about 5 p.m., and actually reached the wire, was holding firm on the south-east portion of the position, some of the posts being within 100 yards of the enemy tanks, and 'C' Company, on the eastern portion of the defences, remained intact, also Battalion Headquarters. During the enemy advance the whole Battalion area was kept under constant gun and M.G. fire from tanks, also from enemy artillery. At 5.45 p.m. about one squadron of Infantry tanks came up from the east to counter-attack, and a sharp battle ensued. Our tanks had several casualties and were forced to withdraw. At 6 p.m., after the daylight had faded, more enemy infantry moved up and started to dig in around the tanks, which had halted astride the road.

"At 6 p.m. a small party had been assembled for the local defence of Battalion Headquarters, consisting of pioneers, signallers, and runners, and two machine guns manned by personnel of the Royal Northumberland Fusiliers Company Headquarters. The situation as known at Battalion Headquarters was as follows:

"On the extreme right of the position, remnants of 'B' Company (Company Commander and 8 other ranks), plus one platoon of 'A' Company and one M.G. section, were still hanging on. Within 100 yards of this party were three enemy tanks, whilst about a company of enemy infantry was consolidating in the positions previously held by 10 and 11 Platoons. 'A' Company, less one platoon, had been destroyed or taken prisoner, and their positions were being consolidated by enemy infantry. Communication had been lost with 'D' Company, and it was not known what had happened to that company. 'C' Company was holding firm and was intact. All anti-tank guns had been knocked out. At least one M.G. platoon had been destroyed or taken prisoner—1½ platoons were known to be intact. The R.A.P. located between Battalion Headquarters and 'B' Company was still functioning and evacuating casualties.

"Twenty-five enemy tanks, 18 of them heavy, were in the middle of the Battalion position, within 400 yards of Battalion Headquarters. About one company of enemy were digging in half-way between the tanks and Battalion Headquarters.

"Two companies of 2/13th Australian Infantry Battalion were in reserve near Headquarters 4th Royal Tank Regiment, and at 6 p.m. I asked for these to be sent up for counter-attack purposes. They arrived at 10 p.m., and were formed up into position, right and left of

Battalion Headquarters, ready for counter-attack should opportunity occur.

"Communication to Headquarters 14th Infantry Brigade and to Division was intact by line, and the situation was explained. Line communication was also maintained with 'B' and 'C' Companies.

"At about 9 p.m. a message was received from 14th Infantry Brigade that strong help was forthcoming, but that it would take time. It appeared, therefore, that it would be best for the remnants of the Battalion, together with the Australian companies, to keep very quiet, as there was a full moon, and should our positions be known to the enemy, they would have immediately overrun them and destroyed the garrison. I therefore issued orders to this effect.

"At 1.30 a.m. a large number of our own tanks arrived from the north-east, and when they approached the enemy tanks started up and hastily withdrew. A counter-attack was immediately put in by the two Australian companies against the enemy infantry in front of Battalion Headquarters, and directed to the old positions of 'A' Company. This was completely successful, the enemy infantry all surrendering or running away. Meanwhile, Captain Stevenson-Hamilton, with one platoon of 'A' Company and the remnants of 'B' Company, succeeded in re-establishing his original position. By 2 a.m. the whole position was completely reoccupied and the enemy driven off.

"Colonel Burrows, commanding the 2/13th Australian Infantry Battalion, had come up with the two Australian companies, and after the counter-attack had succeeded, he decided to leave the companies under the command of the Battalion, and so for over forty-eight hours the Battalion was a composite unit, which included two companies of Australian infantry. These were 'B' and 'C' companies of the 2/13th Australian Infantry. On the morning of the 30th November, while these two companies formed part of the Battalion, a second attack with about 50 tanks followed by lorried infantry was launched again from the west on Ed Duda, but this time, owing to increased and very effective artillery support, the advance was held up 800 yards from the Battalion and beaten off. Meanwhile, all troops on Ed Duda had been placed under the command of the 1st Essex, and three regiments of artillery and one regiment of 'I' tanks placed in direct support of the Battalion."

(The new second-in-command, Major G. H. Walker, arrived up at the Ed Duda position during the night of the 30th November/1st December. Lieutenant-Colonel Nichols put him in charge of the patrolling programme, the visiting of the battalion perimeter, and to look after the New Zealand companies. "He was," says Colonel Nichols, "very quickly in the picture, and within a few hours was taking an active part in the battle." Major Walker was destined to stay with the Battalion as second-in-command and later as commanding officer, apart from a period away as Commandant 70th Divisional Battlecraft School and General Staff Officer, Grade I, until March 1945.)

"Some active patrolling was carried out during the next two days to the south and west, and there were indications that an attack was being prepared on the south.

"On 3rd December, at 6 p.m., two companies of the 19th New Zealand Battalion relieved the two Australian companies, and came under command of the 1st Essex, and for eight days the Battalion was a composite unit incorporating 'A' and 'B' Companies of the 19th New Zealand Battalion.

"During this period, a party from Headquarters Company, 19th New Zealand Battalion, consisting of signals, mortars, and carriers, commanded by Major McLaughlin, was also operated under command, although it did not form an integral part of the Battalion.

"On the morning of the 4th December another attack developed on the Battalion front. A battalion of infantry, supported by heavy artillery concentrations and mortar fire, advanced from the west on top of—and to the north of—the escarpment. The leading enemy got to within 200 yards of the western forward defended localities, but were beaten off with heavy loss by the combined fire of infantry, M.G.s, and artillery. They were subsequently 'cleaned up' by a troop of 'I' tanks and the New Zealand carriers.

"Later in the morning a further attack by infantry, supported by armoured fighting vehicles, developed on the front of 'C' Company to the south, but this also was beaten off by the co-ordinated fire of all arms; very effective support was given by one troop of tanks which had been located in 'C' Company's area and which were in close touch with the Company Commander. I was, at this stage, more or less immobile by a bad desert sore, and Major Walker's constant supervision and presence in the forward areas were most helpful.

"The Battalion, with two New Zealand companies, continued to hold the position until 8th December, on which night, the 1st D.L.I. and 4th Border Regiment passed through the Battalion and captured positions farther to the west, thus disengaging the Battalion from immediate contact with the enemy.

"Between the 4th and 8th December, long-distance patrols had been carried out by all companies, several parties of prisoners being taken, and enemy columns retreating from east to west were considerably harassed.

"On the 9th, 10th, and 11th December the Battalion remained on Ed Duda, but carried out salvage operations, and continued to contact parties of enemy who were taken prisoner.

"On the morning of the 11th December, the two New Zealand companies were recalled, and on the 12th December the Battalion was drawn into rest inside the original Tobruk defences.

"During the period of operations on Ed Duda from the 26th November to 9th December the following casualties occurred:

Officers Killed

Major C. H. Robinson; Lieutenant P. F. M. Parry; Lieutenant C. H. Lawrence, M.C.; Lieutenant R. C. Browne.

Died of Wounds

Captain P. J. B. Savill.

Officers Missing

Lieutenant T. D'A. Muirhead, M.C.; 2/Lieutenant J. W. Milton.

Other Ranks

Killed in action	31
Died of wounds	4
Wounded	70
Missing (many of these wounded and a few killed)	90 (5 now reported 'Missing at Sea')."

Such, then, was the battle in which the 1st Essex made history. They had fought the best the Germans could put against them and had prevailed. In spite of the weight of the German armour and his superiority in numbers, they had stuck it out through thick and thin.

For the Ed Duda operations the Battalion received the following awards:

Bar to D.S.O.—Lieutenant-Colonel J. S. Nichols, D.S.O., M.C.
    D.S.O.—Captain I. J. D. Stevenson-Hamilton.
    M.C.—Captain J. F. Higson.
        2/Lieutenant K. W. M. Mann.
        2/Lieutenant B. G. Gingell.
        Captain N. Pedersen, R.A.M.C.

D.C.M.—Sergeant F. Applebee.
L/Sergeant C. Hayes.
M.M.—Sergeant G. Marchint.
Sergeant G. Smith.
Corporal T. Mead.
L/Corporal S. Furnival.
L/Corporal E. White.
L/Corporal C. A. Churan.
Private G. Grantshaw.
Private A. F. Cordery.
Private M. Calvert.

The award of the M.C. to Captain Nils Pedersen was particularly gratifying to the Battalion. It was due to the fact that he sited his regimental aid post in the centre of the much-shelled battalion position that so many badly wounded individuals were able to survive. His work in the R.A.P. was beyond praise, and in his work he was most ably assisted by the Padre. Despite the fact that the R.A.P. area was shelled continuously during the daylight hours, Pedersen carried on his work unperturbed by all that was going on around him.

Lieutenant-Colonel Nichols, writing to the Colonel of the Regiment on the 3rd January, 1942, says:

". . . I received a message from both the G.O.C. 70th Division (Major-General Scobie) and G.O.C. 13th Corps (Lieutenant-General Godwin-Austin) congratulating the Battalion on its work."

The importance of Ed Duda can be judged from a message sent by the Commander of the Eighth Army on the 30th November or 1st December to the effect that "if our troops can continue to hold Ed Duda the battle will be won."

Major J. F. Higson here interposes: "On 29th November I (acting Battalion Second-in-Command) received a message from Headquarters 70th Division to the effect that it was considered that Ed Duda would shortly become untenable and that we were to make plans for withdrawal back within the Tobruk defences.

"I informed 'Crasher' accordingly, and without a moment's hesitation he replied, 'Take a message——

'Ed Duda growing stronger every hour, feel confident we can resist attack from any quarter. Strongly deplore any suggestion of withdrawal.'

"This reply was received by Major-General Scobie at a time when he was about to order our withdrawal. On receipt, however, he immediately changed his plans and decided to retain Ed Duda to the great advantage of the main forces advancing from Egypt. He replied: 'Greatly admire your spirit.' This action of Lieutenant-Colonel Nichols was probably the turning-point in the campaign, for whether the main forces would have ever linked up with Tobruk had the Germans been in force on Ed Duda is very problematical."

The Battalion was now withdrawn to rest and refit with their morale extremely high. They had fought Italians, Iraqis, and French, and now they had proved they were better than the best the Germans could put against them. They only waited for reinforcements to complete the task so well begun.

But it was not to be. As 1942 came in, they were back in Qassassin, Egypt, and they were not to return to the Western Desert.

As in earlier months troops had to be sent from Egypt and North Africa to the Sudan, Greece, Crete, Iraq, and Syria, so now with the entry of Japan into the war were reinforcements urgently needed in India and the Far East. The 1st Essex was among those to go with the 70th Division. It was still part of the 23rd Infantry Brigade (Brigadier C. H. V. Cox, D.S.O., M.C.).

Before leaving the Middle East, the Battalion had to say good-bye to Lieutenant-Colonel Nichols who had commanded for the past year. He had been selected for command of a brigade in the Eighth Army, and his well-merited promotion was a source of pride to the Essex.

Section VIII

INDIA, 1942–43

With the relief of Tobruk the whole of the 70th Division had been withdrawn to Egypt, and many were the rumours in the early weeks of 1942 as to the next role. Cyprus, the Western Desert, the Far East, and Syria all figured in the betting, but as the situation in Malaya and Burma got progressively worse, so the odds on the Far East shortened.

Early in February the 70th Division was, however, standing by to go to Syria, and a reconnaissance party from the Battalion had actually moved, when later in the month these orders were suddenly cancelled and the Division told to embark at a week's notice for the Far East.

Lieutenant-Colonel E. W. Towsey, O.B.E., the West Yorkshire Regiment, was now in command, and on the 25th February, 1942, he took the Battalion on board H.M.T. *Mauretania*, which sailed three days later from Port Tewfik bound for Rangoon.

During the voyage news was received that Rangoon had fallen to the Japanese, and so the ship was diverted to Bombay. The 1st Essex disembarked there on the 8th March and moved up to Poona.

Three weeks later, on the 31st March, orders were received saying the 70th Division would concentrate in North-east India. On the 7th April the 1st Essex left Poona, detrained four days later at Barkakawa and moved into Khunti Camp. This was near Ranchi, about 200 miles west of Calcutta, and in this area the Battalion, with the majority of the 70th Division, was to spend the greater part of the next twelve months.

The 70th Division was at the time the only trained, battle-experienced formation in India, and was held in reserve to provide a mobile striking force against any Japanese landing on the coast of Bengal between Calcutta and Cuttack.

This invasion did not materialise, but the monsoon did. The Battalion spent a very wet three months under canvas, after having spent every pre-monsoon moment on intensive training.

There were few highlights, and, indeed, these long months were somewhat wearisome, but there was at least the consolation that they did not suffer alone, for the whole of the 70th Division was similarly placed.

In early September 1942, the so-called "Congress Revolution" broke out in Bengal. The 70th Division, in reserve to the Fourteenth Army, was available to deal with the situation. The whole of the 23rd Infantry Brigade was deployed, Brigade Headquarters with the 4th Border Regiment and 1st South Staffords in and around Patna, and the 1st Essex around Dhanbad, a town near the centre of the coalfields west of Calcutta.

Lieutenant-Colonel E. W. Towsey says, "I think it is about the only time in history that soldiers were given a completely free hand in dealing with civil disturbances, with the result that the revolution fizzled out in a matter of three weeks or so." There is little doubt that resolute action without delay for parleying or legal quibbles resulted in the minimum of bloodshed, for all knew the troops were in earnest and would not be diverted from their task.

One particularly successful, though bloodless, operation was when the Battalion was called upon to arrest disloyal elements of the civil police force in Tatanagar, the site of the second largest steel works in the world. It was a case of an approach march by night, infiltration, as unobtrusively as possible, into the town, and the isolation of each police-station. Despite the lack of preliminary reconnaissance, the operation went like clockwork. The disaffected police were awakened and spirited out of the town almost before anybody realised anything unusual was afoot.

The Battalion returned to Khunti in October and spent the next five months in jungle training. There was an area of thick jungle about 100 miles from Ranchi. Brigades of the 70th Division marched to this training area at Daltongunj in succession, put in six weeks in the jungle and then marched back. The 1st Essex did the 110 miles from Daltongunj to Khunti Camp in four and a half consecutive days.

Section IX

THE ARAKAN, MAY-JUNE 1943

On the 11th April, 1943, the 23rd Infantry Brigade, now under Brigadier P. C. Marindin, left the Ranchi area and moved to Jhingergacha in Eastern Bengal, where a brigade box was formed for the defence of the frontier of India.

In December 1942 the 14th Indian Division had advanced into the Arakan with the object of retaking the Mayu Peninsula and the port of Akyab. The advance was checked by the Japanese, who had dug in and fortified very effectively the tip of the Dombaik Peninsula. A Japanese counter-offensive starting in the Kaladan Valley and then crossing over the Mayu Range met with considerable success. It threatened the lines of communication of the forces operating towards Akyab, and also threatened an invasion of Bengal.

It was this threat that brought the 70th Division forward into Arakan as part of the 15th Indian Corps reserve.

The 1st Essex, the leading battalion of the 23rd Brigade, embarked at Kiddapore Docks, Calcutta, on the 1st May, and arrived at Chittagong three days later.

There was, however, a limiting proviso as to the use of the Brigade, for, as the Essex heard at Chittagong, G.H.Q. had laid down that, in view of the role then being planned for all the 70th Division, the 23rd Infantry Brigade would not be committed to action unless a situation of really grave emergency arose.

The Battalion spent the night of the 4th/5th May at Chittagong, and then set out by rail and road for Bawli Bazaar, which was to become its base. It was at the height of the hot season, but the heat was not so oppressive as had been expected. Indeed, apart from its then sinister associations, the Arakan is a pleasant country with its paddy-fields, green clumps of bamboo and mango trees, and its bamboo villages.

The two days at Bawli Bazaar were busy ones. It was here that the Battalion was first introduced to mules and put on a mule basis. Personal equipment and company stores had to be organised on a very light and independent scale. Each man had to carry essentials on his back, including two days' rations. About a dozen mules were allotted to each company for carrying ammunition, picks and shovels, and rations. "Utter confusion followed," says Major Stevenson-Hamilton, "since very few officers or men had had any previous experience of loading or handling mules."

However, with every minute spent in learning to tie mule loads and load mules by day and night, the job was done. This was just as well, for in confirmation of the visual evidence of a constant flow of wounded and stragglers through Bawli Bazaar, an order was issued saying that a grave situation had arisen and the corps reserve would be deployed.

The 1st Essex was instructed to proceed immediately to defend the pass Bawli Bazaar–Goppe Bazaar. Now that the lateral road between Maungdaw and Buthidaung was in Japanese hands, this pass was the only one with a proper mule track connecting the two sides of the Mayu Range.

The Battalion set off in single file up the dusty track, each company with its complement of mules. The foothills were reached and the climb up the 1,500-foot pass began. "The morning was very hot, and the Battalion, unused to hill climbing, found this a stiff march with its frequent pauses to make room for mules coming the other way. A new form of friendly address came into being as little groups of Indian soldiers greeted Essex with 'Hullo, Johnny, Thik Hai,' to which the equally good-humoured answer was, 'Thik Hai, Savage.' "

At the top of the pass Battalion Headquarters under Major Higson and a ration dump were established around a small village. "B" and "D" Companies took up positions at the top of the pass, while "C" Company went right forward to occupy and hold Goppe Bazaar

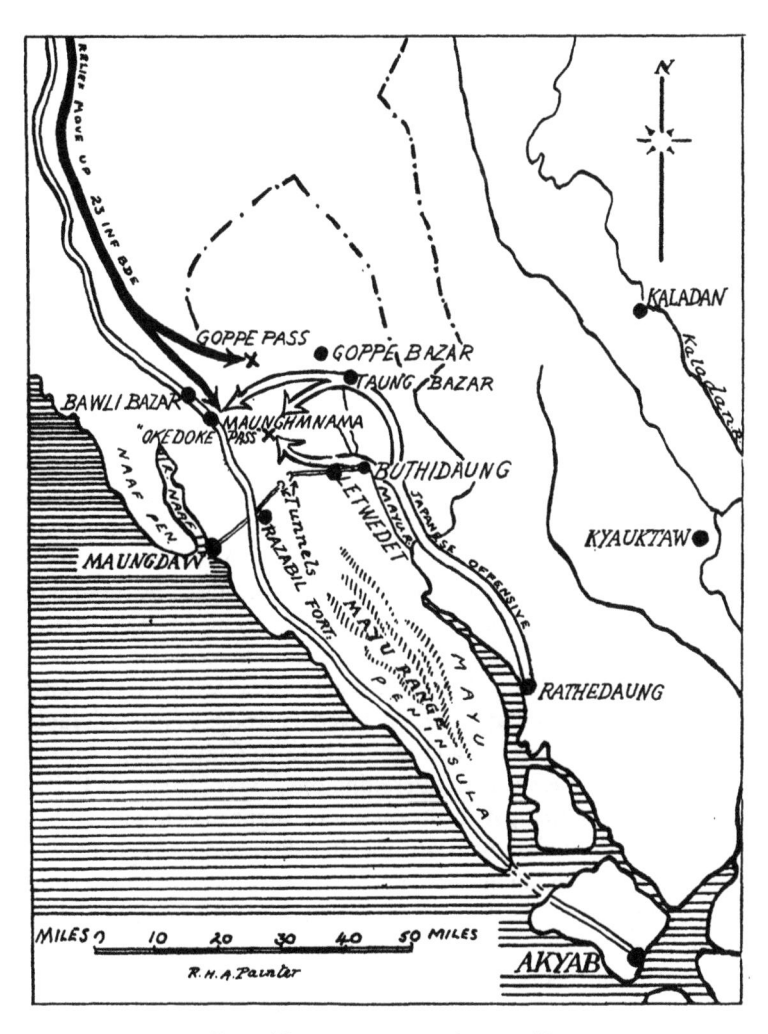

1ST ESSEX, MOVEMENTS IN THE ARAKAN, MAY 1943.

against all comers. "A" Company remained half-way down the pass some two and a half miles to the west of "C" Company.

Platoon positions were cut into the jungle hillsides, and the jungle thinned out to provide fields of fire. Section positions were, as always in the jungle, grouped close together. "One platoon headquarters heard some queer noises the first night, and discovered a panther's lair fourteen feet below them. However, neither seemed to worry the other, and when it got dark in the evening the snorts of the beast were always to be heard."

One night a message was received saying that a Japanese force was making its way round the Taung Bazaar position (held by a battalion of Dogras) and was making its way up to Goppe Bazaar.

"In Goppe Bazaar," says Major Stevenson-Hamilton, "all was confusion. Streams of sick and wounded men were passing back through our company position and the ground was littered with discarded weapons. In the village we buried over six hundred rifles, four 3-inch mortars, and a quantity of mortar ammunition to prevent them falling into Japanese hands."

The expected attack did not materialise. The front, at the beginning of May perilously near disintegration, held, and with the Japanese attack losing its impetus, stability was achieved in advance of Goppe Bazaar. So the firm base provided by the 23rd Brigade was not tested in battle.

The Battalion's main activity was patrolling. Standing patrols were put out at night well down to the Taung River. After a sweaty march they would lie up during the hours of darkness, bitten by mosquitoes and entertained, once the men were used to them, by many strange noises of barking deer and other animals and insects.

The 23rd Infantry Brigade remained in the area Bawli Bazaar–Goppe Bazaar until the 24th May, when, relieved by troops of the 26th Indian Division, it was pulled out and moved back to Chittagong.

"The journey back was an interesting one," says Lieutenant P. P. S. Brownless. "The first part of it was a long night march with all baggage carried on mules. At dawn the Battalion and its baggage were embarked (at Zinbindjung) on a river steamer and two lighters and sailed slowly up the Naaf River. They were disembarked in the evening (at Taunbro Ghat on evening 26th May), and after two days in some small hills beside the main road, travelled by lorry to railhead. While the Battalion was bivouacking in paddy-fields near the railhead the monsoon broke. Within an hour everything was under water, and by the evening the paddy-fields in which it had been hoped to spend a not uncomfortable night were six inches deep in water and inhabited by thousands of croaking frogs."

The Battalion reached Chittagong on the 29th May, the Battalion remaining there until the 13th June, when it was finally embarked to sail for Kiddapore. It was to be the 21st June before the 1st Essex reached its final destination—Bangalore, or rather Bidadi Camp, twenty-three miles south of the town.

The uneventful part played by the Battalion in the Arakan was not unimportant. The arrival of leading elements of an experienced British division at a time of appalling disorganisation and battle-weariness contributed much, in a critical few days, to the security and morale of the theatre of battle.

Section X

LONG-RANGE PENETRATION. ASSAM AND BURMA, 1944

Following a brief period of rehabilitation and refit, the 23rd Infantry Brigade again got down to training. At first it was thought that they were to carry out intensive jungle training, suitable areas being reconnoitred and selected.

Then, on the 6th August, it was announced that the brigade was going to turn over to combined operations. "Mock-ups" were built, and a staff planning course held at Headquarters 2nd Division at Ahmednagar. This plan was, however, short-lived. On the 6th September it was announced that the 70th Division was being turned over to L.R.P. (Long-range penetration) duties. The news was broken to the Battalion by the Divisional Commander, Major-General G.W. Symes, M.C.

"Special Force" to which they now belonged was commanded by Major-General O. C. Wingate, D.S.O., and the inclusion of 70th Division within this force ushered in a period of reorganisation and very intensive training.

First, all over forty years of age were to be posted away. This meant that Lieutenant-Colonel Towsey had to leave the Battalion. His place was taken by Lieutenant-Colonel G. H. Walker.

Next, units were to be formed into columns, each infantry battalion forming two columns, a depot party, and an air-base party.

Lieutenant-Colonel Walker says:

"Eventually organisation within the Battalion established itself. A depot party from each unit in the brigade was formed, commanded by the Battalion Adjutant (Captain W. E. Tanner), to maintain unit records, heavy baggage, and to keep touch with 2nd Echelon. Air

Base required a unit staff of the quartermaster and staff, post-corporal, and so on. Apart from these two administrative groups, the Battalion comprised two columns. After much change and discussion, the happy solution of numbering them 44 and 56 was arrived at. The columns

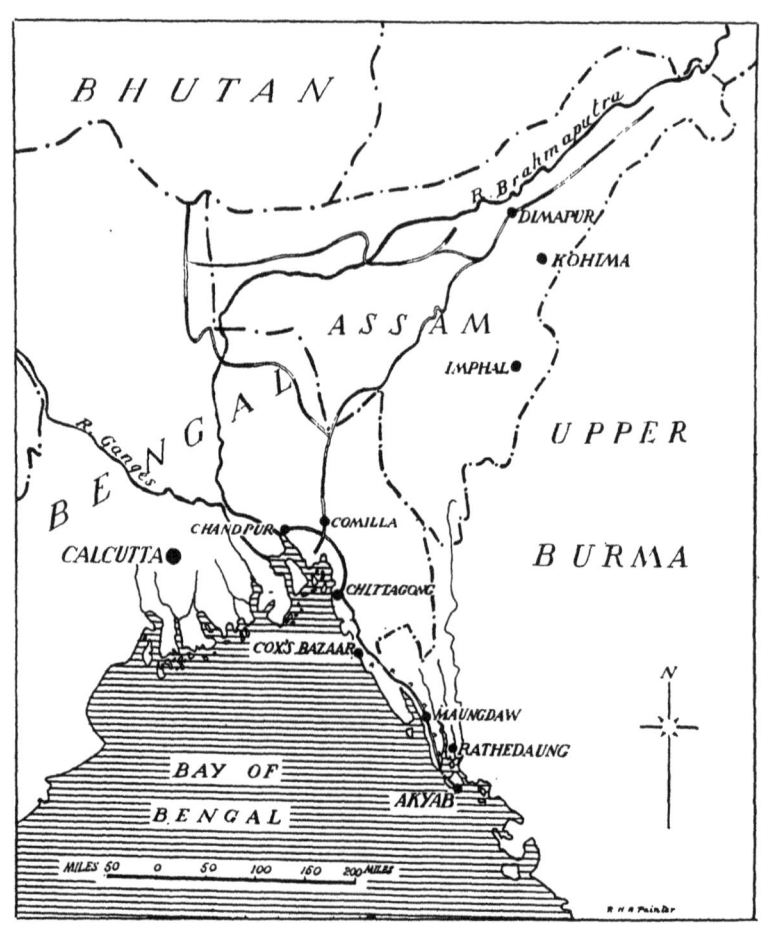

1ST ESSEX, ASSAM AND BURMA.

were identical and modelled in the larger sense on those operated by General Wingate in the preceding campaign. No. 44 was commanded by the Commanding Officer and 56 by the Second-in-Command" (at this time Major A. Lovelace, M.B.E.).

"In our early training, command direct by Brigade to columns was

(Crown Copyright)
1ST BATTALION THE ESSEX REGIMENT. LIEUTENANT M. D. LOUGH AND HIS PLATOON, 44 COLUMN, ON CONCLUSION OF OPERATIONS IN ASSAM AND BURMA. JULY 1944.

(Crown Copyright)
1ST BATTALION THE ESSEX REGIMENT. THE OFFICERS, 44 AND 56 COLUMNS, ON CONCLUSION OF OPERATIONS IN ASSAM AND BURMA. JULY 1944.

Included in the group are: Lieutenant-Colonel G. H. Walker, Majors A. Lovelace, M.B.E., M.C., C. Nelson, J. D. J. Sammons, Captains G. J. M. McCrossan, White, P. H. C. Clark, G. J. Athill, K. M. Grant, Robinson (R.A.M.C.), Berry (R.E.), Donaldson, P. C. Haskins, Lieutenants P. P. S. Brownless, M. D. Lough, S. M. Pitchford, C. H. P. Mantell, Rice, H. W. Wilson, Hawkes (R.E.), D. F. Early, W. R. Swallow, Captain The Rev. Beveridge (R.A.Ch.D.), Mr. D. Price, R.S.M. G. Wildey.

2ND BATTALION THE ESSEX REGIMENT. MEURCHIN. APRIL 1940. *(Imperial War Museum)*

The Rev. Harvey, Lieutenant A. J. M. Parry, Captain J. W. Duerdon (R.A.M.C.), 2/Lieutenant G. C. Mcares, 2/Lieutenant D. E. Long-Price, Major C. L. Wilson, M.C., Lieutenant D. G. Calvert, 2/Lieutenant D. B. Jemings, Lieutenant G. L. M. Petre, Captain J. F. Cramphorn, Captain H. F. H. Jones, Lieutenant-Colonel A. H. Blest, Captain R. H. A. Painter, 2/Lieutenant P. R. Barrass, Lieutenant A. W. Palmer, Captain G. H. N. Sheffield, 2/Lieutenant A. J. Baines, 2/Lieutenant G. H. Watson, Captain P. C. Hinde, Lieutenant (Q.M.) E. H. Crane. Interpreter.

[97]

practised, but it soon appeared that it was best to work the two columns as a Battalion group under the C.O., and this policy was followed throughout operations. The fact that each column was independent and a separate entity made for extreme flexibility within the Battalion and contributed much to its success."

Major-General Wingate personally visited the 23rd Infantry Brigade on the 26th September during the reorganisation period and decided the future composition of the Brigade. It was to consist of Brigade Headquarters and Defence Company (32 Column), the 60th Field Regiment R.A. (66 and 88 Columns), 2nd Duke of Wellingtons (33 and 76 Columns), 1st Essex (44 and 56 Columns), and the 4th Border Regiment (34 and 55 Columns).

Battalion columns were to be approximately 18 officers and 400 other ranks. These numbers, with the addition of the depot and airbase parties, made the Battalion stronger than at any time since the beginning of the war.

Columns were completely self-contained and were on a mule and air supply basis.

By the end of October the 1st Essex, with other units of the 23rd Brigade, left the Bangalore area for the Central Provinces of India, and settled in to camp at Chhartapur. Here training was supervised by Major-General Wingate and Major-General Symes, and by Brigadier L. E. C. M. Perowne, who had taken command of the 23rd Infantry Brigade.

The air supply was a great factor in the training, and Lieutenant-Colonel Walker says:

"The most novel aspect of L.R.P. as conceived by General Wingate was the supply of columns by air and the use of aircraft as a substitute for artillery. The Battalion had trained extensively with aircraft for supply dropping and in close support, and all ranks were confident that the methods to be used were sound and feasible. They were also told that the U.S.A.A.F. Task Force would provide light aircraft for couriers and evacuation of casualties, but there was no opportunity to train with these aircraft.

"It is due to the untiring efforts and skill of pilots of the R.A.F., U.S.A.A.F., and Dominion Air Forces that the Battalion was so magnificently served in all three branches. The monsoon began after a month of operations, when both columns were operating at an average height of 5,000 feet, and consequently in the clouds for most of the day. Yet the aircraft still came over, and it is to be recorded that 56

Column was never once without rations for a single meal. Unfortunately, towards the latter part of operations, 44 Column did miss a number of supply drops due entirely to dense low cloud. Even when the men were exhausted, sick, and hungry, they still admired the great courage of the air crews."

Although to some degree anticipating future events, it may be convenient here to give a short account of the organisation for and method of supply dropping.

Each column had an officer and 3 N.C.O.s of the R.A.F. and a powerful R.A.F. wireless set. At least seventy-two hours before a supply drop was required, a demand in code was made on Rear Brigade, who passed it to Air Base. The following day an acceptance, modification, or refusal of the demand was made. Additional demands might be submitted up to the day preceding the drop. When the aircraft (three were usually required for a column drop) had left the airfield, the column was notified by W/T and their time of arrival calculated.

Early in the operations aircraft were guided to the dropping area by an "L"-shaped line of fires, but this arrangement was eventually abandoned because of cloud, and W/T control was used. "Free drop" of mule fodder usually came first, followed by statichutes of rations, ammunition, mail, and rum. The aircraft sometimes arrived in close succession, and would circle, dropping one after the other. If bad visibility prevented the drop, an arrangement was made between ground and air to try later in the day.

Drops were normally at five-day intervals, and included four days' "K" or jungle rations, and one day's compo and bread. Important or fragile stores, such as wireless sets or blood-transfusion sets, were dropped with coloured statichutes. For the majority of the operations it was unnecessary to arrange collection parties, all such work being done by Nagas, who were overjoyed at receiving the containers and silken statichutes. When the columns passed through the Somra Tracts, an area stripped bare by the retreating Japs, it became necessary to arrange supply drops of rice for the local population.

Captain F. W. Waddell, Quartermaster of the 1st Essex and senior quartermaster in the 23rd Brigade, was specially selected by Lieutenant-Colonel Walker to be the quartermaster responsible for the organisation of supply at the Brigade Air Base. It is not too much to say that all columns in the Brigade owe him a great debt for his work of organisation, work that gained him the award of the M.B.E. when the 23rd Brigade was withdrawn from Burma and Assam.

January 1944 saw the Battalion in another camp—Shargarh—but still in the Central Provinces, and still engaged in most arduous training. Much was very different from that to which they had been accustomed. All ranks knew no slackness could be tolerated which on operations would risk the safety of comrades. Even mules had to be taught discipline at the cost of their leader's liberty. "If a mule leader or groom allows his animal to run away, he will be automatically placed upon a charge." How the mules would have laughed if they could have read that battalion order.

At the end of March 1944 both columns moved to Saugor, and on the 31st entrained for a move to the forward areas of Eastern India and Burma. One of the very last Battalion orders before entraining said:

"Attention is drawn to the fact that women members of the U.S.A. Forces are not allowed to marry without first obtaining the approval of the Commanding General U.S. Forces, China, Burma, and India. Before contracting a marriage with a woman member of the U.S.A. Forces, any officer or other rank will therefore make sure that permission has been obtained."

No doubt Lieutenant-Colonel Walker was right in being prepared for all eventualities, even behind the enemy lines in Assam or Burma.

The original intention of this eastward move was that concentration would be effected in the Haicakandi area, but whilst the 23rd Brigade was being concentrated and moved forward as a preliminary to a move by air into Burma, the strategical and tactical situation in Burma was altering in favour of the Japanese.

On the 16th March, 1944, General Mutaguchi's Fifteenth Army had crossed the Chindwin with the intention of reaching Imphal and Kohima before Allied reinforcements could arrive, and then, by breaking into the Brahmaputra Valley, accomplishing an invasion of India. This advance, by early April, was threatening Assam and the Manipur Road running parallel to and behind the Burma frontier. The L. of C. of General Stilwell's American-Chinese force was also menaced.

It was this situation that caused the switch and early deployment of the 23rd Brigade. At Agartala Station on the 6th April the 1st Essex was met with the news they were being diverted on changed orders, and would proceed to Mariani, as the threat to General Stilwell's L. of C. was steadily increasing. Lieutenant-Colonel Walker was told by the staff officer who met the train that in all probability the railway line would by now be cut by the Japanese. However, such was not the case. This was the first encounter with the pessimism they were to meet during the next week.

Arriving at Mariani on the 8th April, after having been in transit for eight days, the Battalion was spread out on the polo ground, men, transport, and equipment just as it had come out of the train. The first evening "we were all surprised to find a few local Englishmen wearing dinner jackets solemnly playing their customary game of Bridge and drinking their chota pegs...."

Twenty-four hours later the 1st Essex was inspected by the Supreme Commander South-East Asia Command, Lord Louis Mountbatten, who greatly impressed all ranks with his personality, confidence, and cheerful candour, saying that great things were now asked and expected of the Battalion.

A few weeks later, when the Battalion was many miles deep into the jungle, the following letter was dropped from the air.

"SOUTH-EAST ASIA COMMAND HEADQUARTERS.
"21st April, 1944.

"DEAR WALKER,

"I am writing to thank you for the arrangements you made to enable me to see the 44th and 56th Columns of the Essex Regiment at Jorhat on the 8th April. It is most encouraging finding your men in such good heart, and I feel sure that they will add to the great traditions of the Long Range Penetration forces.

"I am sorry I have been unable to write before, but on completion of my tour I only had two days in Delhi before transferring my Headquarters to Ceylon, and this has been the first opportunity of attending to private correspondence.

"I wish you all the best of luck in your great adventure.
"Yours sincerely,
"(Sgd.) LOUIS MOUNTBATTEN.

"LIEUTENANT-COLONEL G. H. WALKER."

On the 10th April the Battalion received orders to entrain for a small station called Bokajan, some ten miles back towards and north of Dimapur. The Battalion was ordered to prevent the enemy from penetrating to and cutting the road and railway in this area. There was a new unmade-up track from Bokajan up to the foothills. It was thought that the Japanese, known to be moving a force in this direction, might select this route.

Just as the train was due to move off, Lieutenant-Colonel Walker was whisked out of the train and sent off by jeep to receive instructions from the General Officer Commanding the L. of C. at Dimapur. On his arrival at the Headquarters the Commanding Officer found the whole Headquarters packing up, the staff being somewhat despondent and pessimistic. However, the G.O.C. gave Lieutenant-Colonel Walker a concise picture of the general situation as it was then known to him.

The Battalion was now to operate in the Naga hills, starting off up the Bokajan track. Never before had anything more than small parties with porters crossed this particular territory. There were some tracks that even a jeep could use, but these all ran in the wrong direction and were not in the Battalion area. The General also gave Colonel Walker a free hand to take what assistance he might require. The Commanding officer thereupon collected two more jeeps, a 3-ton truck, some Naga interpreters, and an Indian Jemadar.[1] He also arranged to have sent to the Battalion a party of 75 Gurkhas and 120 Indian porters. These were the L. of C. Headquarters camp staff. And so the 1st Essex now comprised British, Indians, Gurkhas, and Nagas.

The Commanding Officer got back to the Battalion that evening. The next day he took 44 Column up to Mohumi, a 2,000-foot climb. 44 Column was to give early warning of and to stop any Japanese move northwards from the Kohima area. 56 Column, with Major A. Lovelace in command, was ordered to remain in the dense jungle at the base of these foothills astride the track, patrolling actively to prevent any Japanese penetration to the main L. of C. road and railway. The two columns, apart from being surprised by wild elephants, took up positions without interference from the enemy on the 11th and 12th April.

44 Column, after their 2,000-foot climb to Mohumi, commenced patrolling and the establishment of O.P.s linked by wireless. They found the country in this area covered with dense bamboo and scrub jungle; once off the game tracks or small Naga trails, it was impossible to move even a few men more than a mile a day, cutting all the way. The mountains were 2,000–5,000 feet high and very steep. 56 Column found itself in the dense jungle of the foothills. Trees often reached 100 feet in height, and everywhere was dense undergrowth

[1] Viceroy-commissioned native officer.

and a mass of creeper. It was a highly malarious area. This country has since been described as the wildest and most trackless in the Himalayas, which means in the entire world.

In addition to the physical handicaps of climate and terrain, there was the additional handicap of weight. Away from normal lines of communication, each man had to be independent for a period of five days, and in addition to normal clothing, a weight of 63½ lb. had to be carried. Each man was loaded with a blanket, groundsheet, gas cape, pullover, two pairs of socks, vest and pants, a pair of canvas shoes, a toggle rope, jack knife, half mess-tin, spoon, soap and towel, toothbrush, anti-louse powder, anti-mosquito cream, camouflage cream, gas wallet, water-sterilising outfit, and five days' rations. Then there were the personal arms of each individual, a machete or entrenching tool, two grenades No. 36, one Bren magazine, 50 rounds S.A.A., and an escape map and compass. All were burdened with "Mae Wests" to start with, but these were abandoned early in the campaign.

On leaving the Assam Plain at Bokajan, the Battalion entered the country of the Nagas and Kukis. These two peoples, independent as hill men the world over, comprise many tribes speaking different languages, and are practically unspoilt from contact with the white man. The Kukis are alleged headhunters, and there is little doubt that the ancient pastime received a new lease of life when their country was invaded by the Japanese. The Nagas are friendly to the white man.

As if to discourage visitors, all villages in this country are perched on hill-tops. Indeed, a village is rarely, if ever, seen under 2,000 feet. The houses are solidly constructed of wood, with excellent thatch and built on stilts in the Kuki country. The villagers' paddy is far below in the valley, and daily excursions to and fro had made the Nagas hill climbers of incredible performance.

44 Column, established at Mohumi, spread its observation posts over an area with a radius of fifteen miles. One O.P. near Keruma established a W.T. post overlooking Keruma on the M.T. road from Kohima to Phekekrima. It first observed the enemy on the 14th April moving north, presumably to the line of the Assam–Bengal Railway.

On the 15th April, 44 Column made the first contact with the Japanese for the 23rd Brigade. This was at Phekekrima, the head of the M.T. road north from Kohima. The road was incomplete from Phekekrima northwards for a few miles, and then was broken by a series of bad landslides.

THE 1ST BATTALION THE ESSEX REGIMENT 103

Lieutenant L. J. Bristow-Jones and two detachments of the Reconnaissance Platoon with a wireless set had the task of obtaining identification of the Japanese troops moving north towards the Assam-Bengal

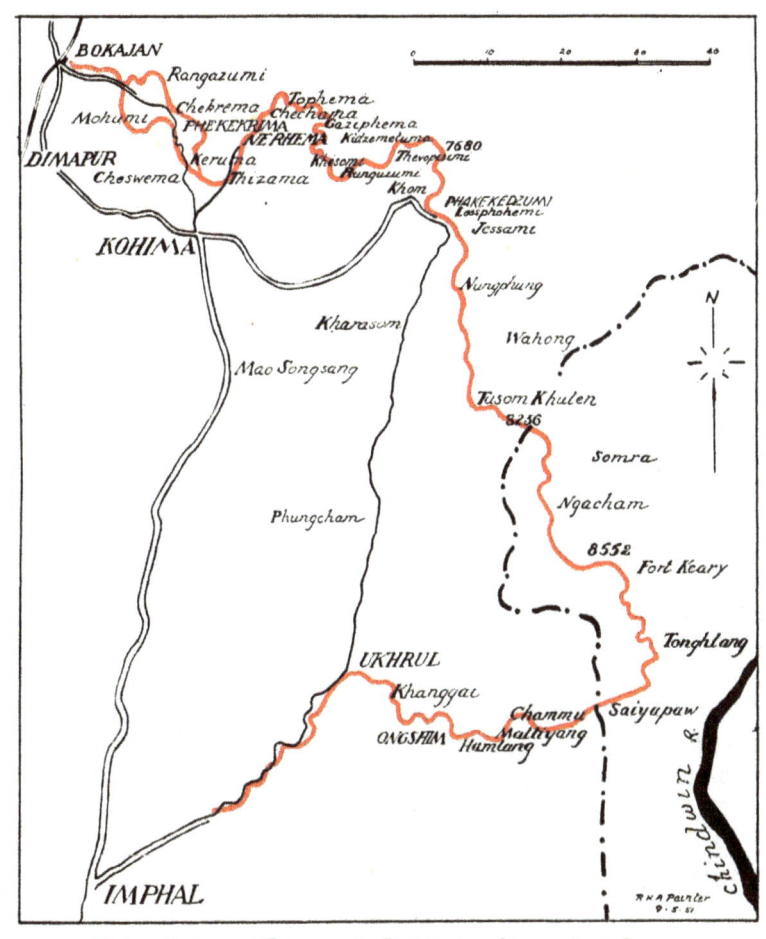

1ST ESSEX, 44 AND 56 COLUMNS IN BURMA AND ASSAM, APRIL-JUNE 1944.

Railway. This was in accordance with 2nd Division operation instruction No. 7, dated 13th April, 1944, which said:

"5. 44 Coln, 23 Bde, will operate from their present posn at H.Q. at Mohumi 3895, to obtain all possible information about enemy localities in the area Cheswema 4875-Merema 4872; it is of paramount importance that an identification be established as early as possible, as there are indications that troops operating from this area are NOT from 3 Regt of 31 Div, but another formation.

"6. 44 Coln will push forward a patrol to obtain information as follows:

(*a*) whether village at Keruma 4682 is occupied;

(*b*) whether rd block has been established at Cheswema and exact location.

"The patrol will annihilate small parties of foraging enemy met with, and if it is found possible to occupy Cheswema unopposed will do so."

Lieutenant Bristow-Jones's patrol consisted of Sergeant G. Puxty and Privates Mower, Martin, and Bergin. Near Phekekrima they contacted a patrol under Sergeants Churan and Hervey, and about 8 a.m., the 15th April, Bristow-Jones moved his patrol into the village of Phekekrima, taking with him a wireless set from the Reconnaissance Platoon operated by Private C. Mariner.

Shortly afterwards 5 Japanese approached the village and were fired on. They then withdrew. Towards midday another Japanese came towards the village, and "when he was within 100 yards he apparently noticed something suspicious, for he suddenly turned and ran. Our men fired, and the Jap dived over the edge of a steep bank and returned a few rounds."

Then, says Sergeant Puxty, "Lieutenant Bristow-Jones crawled over the bank and found the Jap lying against a tree, wounded. As soon as he saw the officer the Jap tried to shoot but Bristow-Jones fired first." On the dead body was the required identification, which was quickly got back to 44 Column.

At this stage some fifty Japanese who had crept up unobserved suddenly attacked the patrol. Although outnumbered nearly four to one, "the patrols formed up in a defensive position about twenty yards square," says Sergeant Puxty. "The Japs used small mortars, L.M.G.s and a M.M.G., and raked the position with fire. The Bren gunner, Private Mower, lay in an exposed position where three tracks converged into one, and kept up a deadly fire, supported by Privates Bergin and Martin with rifles. On the flanks Lieutenant Bristow-Jones and Sergeant Puxty with a Sten gun were also busily engaged, the former doing deadly work with hand grenades.

"During the action Private Mariner broadcast a running commentary to Column Headquarters. He interrupted the broadcast once when he saw a good target, picked up his rifle and killed his Jap. Private Mariner only ended his running commentary on the battle when he was charged by the Japanese and had to smash the set with a pick-axe.

"Private Martin was wounded twice during his support of the Bren gunner. After this he broke up a bayonet charge of 8 Japs to the rear of our L.M.G., aided by Sergeant Puxty. As Martin was moving to a new position, he was killed by rifle fire."

The Japanese fought hard to encircle Bristow-Jones's party, but the latter fought their way out. They had lost 1 man killed to a minimum of 12 Japanese killed and wounded.

This clash has been told at length, partly because we have a first-hand account of the action, and partly for the fact that the first encounter with the Japanese had very definitely shown that the 1st Essex were the better men.

In fact, Lieutenant-Colonel Walker writing a little later to the Colonel of the Regiment is quite unkind to the Japanese: "He is a poor shot except at very close range. Grenades are poor. He is easy meat if ever you can catch him in the open."

However, further operations around Phekekrima were not going to be so easy, for the enemy was not to be caught again in the open, but to be attacked in his defensive positions. Of this Lieutenant-Colonel Walker says in another letter to General Howard:

"The Jap sites his positions most cunningly. Field of fire Max. 20 x—holds his fire till you are sometimes a yard away. Goes deep into the earth very quickly with top cover 4 ft. thick and one entrance and exit, and the fire slit. Can live for weeks on rice, jungle spuds, and water."

To resume the account of operations. Up to now 44 Column had been under the command of one L. of C. and 56 under another. Now the Battalion was to come under command of the 2nd Division. On the 16th April, 44 Column began moving forward from Mohumi to Chekrema with a view to the assault of Phekekrima, and on the morning of the 18th 44 Column battle group of three rifle and one support platoons (one M.M.G., and one 3-inch mortar) moved to the attack.

Phekekrima stands 4,000 feet above sea-level. The track from Chekrema was on the top of a ridge with extremely steep gradients on either side. Landslides had taken place at frequent intervals.

By the afternoon it was clear that the enemy had been strongly reinforced and a combination of enemy fire and difficult terrain made further progress impossible.

The inaccessibility of the enemy positions had rendered the task of the attackers most arduous, and one platoon had an officer and 4 men injured by a fall down a cliff. However, in addition to these injuries, only 2 had been slightly wounded for an unknown number of Japanese killed by 3-inch mortar and small-arms fire. The Column dug in on the next ridge in the village of Chekrema.

56 Column was now released and came under direct command of the Commanding Officer. It was impossible to get even unloaded mules across the valley, so 44 Rear and 56 Column, assisted by Indian porters, manhandled all loads up a 4,000-foot hill to Rangazumi and from there advanced to join the battle group of 44 Column.

The plan now was to attack the south-east flank of Phekekrima via the Nro River. The track to the Nro River, 2,000 feet down, was very steep, and as no real path existed along the nullah, the assault group was continually wading in water waist deep and climbing over large boulders. There was no alternative, for the steep gradients on either side of the track made encircling movements impossible.

On the 21st April both columns had their first supply drop, which was 90 per cent. successful. This same day the attack on Phekekrima took place.

Lieutenant-Colonel Walker says:

"A probing attack by one platoon of 56 Column at 5 a.m. drew enemy fire, making him disclose his positions, but after this reconnaissance had withdrawn, he advanced his positions, a favourite manœuvre of his as we learned later.

"The Commanding Officer, who was with Major Lovelace throughout the day, established a Command Post with W.T. sets direct to both columns, the 3-inch mortars, the M.M.G.s and 'soft'[1] left behind. This post was an excellent O.P., with a good view of Phekekrima across a short intervening lower ridge, all thickly covered with trees and undergrowth. As it turned out, the 56 Column battle took place only about 100 to 150 yards below this O.P., but, although all the noise of battle and shouts could be heard, nothing could be seen because of the thick jungle.

"56 Column was in position about 100 yards from the first of the Japanese positions astride a causeway or 'knife-edge' approach—the

---

[1] "C" group comprising wireless team, farriers, spare mule leaders and mules, medical party, R.A.F personnel, etc.

only possible one from the north. Mortars and M.M.G.s took up positions and ranging commenced.

"Zero was scheduled for 11 a.m. Only five supporting aircraft arrived instead of the squadron hoped for, and strafed the target area, which was very accurately indicated by 3-inch mortar smoke. Harassing fire was kept up by the mortars and the village was set on fire. The Japs replied with M.M.G.s and L.M.G.s.

"44 Column Rifle Company under Captain R. J. Haynes, after successfully accomplishing the most exhausting climb, eventually came up against a cliff, and found the only approach up a steep track which would only permit single file. This was covered by heavy and light machine guns from which we sustained 1 killed and 1 wounded. One platoon had got astride the main M.T. road one mile to the south. All efforts to get round to a more favourable approach failed.

"Meanwhile, the Rifle Company of 56 Column were attacking frontally (from the north). One platoon commanded by Captain B. B. French succeeded in getting on to the causeway and assaulted the Jap positions with flame-throwers. Both operators were killed, also the Platoon Commander and others. The enemy had left 2 L.M.G.s. and several snipers who let the leading platoon pass and then came into action between them and the following platoon. The leading platoon had to be withdrawn before supporting mortar fire could be put down.

"44 Rifle Company reported that the only other route to the objective meant an eight-hour climb down to the valley and up again. They were now out of food and water and had a two-day climb to get back. They were therefore ordered to recover their wounded men and to withdraw. This was done.

"All 3-inch mortar bombs were now expended: 56 Column had suffered 1 officer and 14 other ranks killed and 9 wounded. I therefore ordered 56 Column to withdraw, leaving two platoons under Major Lovelace to advance again under cover of darkness to recover any wounded. This was carried out, but only our dead were found. 56 less one stop platoon returned to Chekrema and 44 came in next day."

The officer killed was Captain B. B. French.

All through their occupation of Chekrema the 1st Essex found the villagers very friendly and helpful and glad to act as stretcher-bearers to take the wounded to road-head.

During the 22nd, 23rd, and 24th April there was active patrolling, and many efforts were made to get in those reported wounded and missing during the attack on the 21st. Unfortunately these efforts were without avail, the enemy being extremely alert and quick to outflank any patrol pushed forward by the 1st Essex.

On the evening of the 23rd, Lieutenant-Colonel Walker ordered a new attack for the 24th/25th April with strong direct air support, but early on the 24th April a message came in from Rear Brigade, "No D.A.S. for at least four days."

The aircraft provided by the U.S.A.A.F. under Colonel Cochran for the close support of Special Force included Mitchell bombers and Mustangs for ground strafing. The Battalion, being now divorced from Special Force, had no call on these aircraft. However, demands could be made on Corps through Brigade for Hurri-bombers, and Hurricanes fitted with cannon. Once the demand had been sanctioned by Brigade, and passed to Corps, the column itself was in direct W/T with A.A.A.C. and could modify the time of sortie according to local weather conditions. Twelve planes, bombing and strafing, was a normal demand. Indication to aircraft was by 3-inch mortar smoke, and since the column had no V.H.F. set, there was no W/T communication.

In this instance the call for direct air support could not be met, but in general the direct air support provided for the Battalion was most accurate and had good effects, but the 250-lb. bomb, unless a direct hit, did no damage to bunkers. However, the harassing effect of repeated reconnaissance sorties after bombing was great, and it is felt that this air support contributed much to the Battalion's success.

Despite the negative message from Rear Brigade, six Hurri-bombers bombed and fired on Phekekrima on the evening of the 24th and again on the morning of the 25th April.

On the 24th Lieutenant-Colonel Walker issued orders for a fourth attempt on Phekekrima. This time 56 Column under Major Lovelace was to move east and round to the south of the village and then attack up the spur which ran along the M.T. road. 44 Column was to hold frontally. Strong direct air support was asked for and promised.

On the morning of the 25th, 56 Column left complete with mules, but with equipment reduced to a minimum. They were to by-pass Phekekrima by way of the Nro nullah, and were to establish themselves on the road south of the village.

It was essential for 56 Column to take a supply drop after it was established on the south side of the objective. So it was arranged that both columns would take a supply drop on the day before the attack

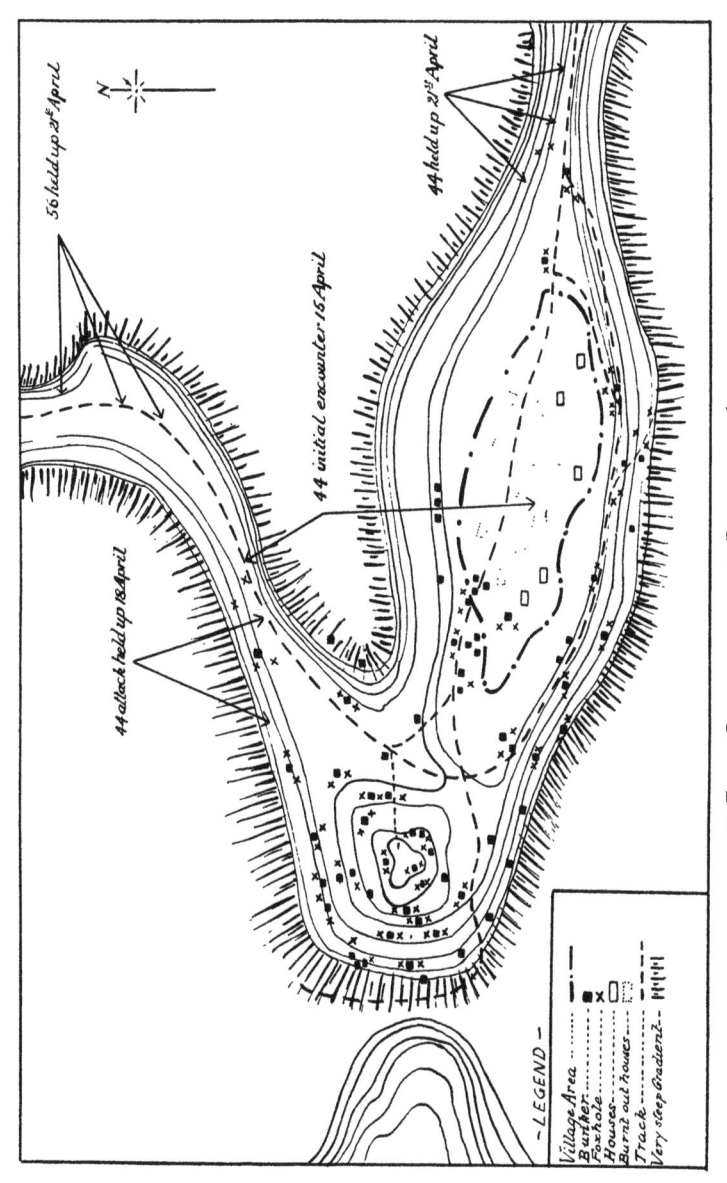

1ST ESSEX, OPERATIONS AGAINST PHEKEKRIMA, APRIL 1944.

to give the impression of a larger force both to the north and now to the south of the enemy position.

They found the going from Chekrema downhill to the nullah very difficult for the mules which had to be unloaded and their loads manhandled for the steepest part. It was no better in the nullah itself, where for the most part the Column had to wade waist deep in water. Out of the nullah the gradients were too steep for loaded mules, and once more all loads had to be manhandled, but by the evening of the 26th they were clear of the most difficult country and bivouacked 400 yards from the road south of Phekekrima. It had been a most unpleasant and difficult thirty-six hours.

Next morning 56 Column marched along the road to Gurkha Farm, a house on a small feature west of the road. It provided not only an O.P. for Phekekrima and an excellent bivouac area, but some cover for a R.A.P., for by reason of the appalling country and conditions in which they had been operating since being committed to action on the 11th April, 56 Column had now nearly 100 malaria cases.

On the morning of the 28th, 56 Column observed parties of 20–30 Japanese leaving Phekekrima and they found themselves checked by enemy positions situated between themselves and 44 Column now near the village, for 44 Column had advanced to Phekekrima.

During the 26th and 27th information from patrols and observation had led Lieutenant-Colonel Walker to believe an evacuation was in progress. Finally, a reconnaissance patrol of 3 Nagas, led by Lieutenant Bristow-Jones, was sent forward with orders to go on into Phekekrima until fired on.

On their return they stated that the Japanese were not in the village area, but darkness had prevented anything more than a quick look into the village itself where fires were found to be still burning.

On the morning of the 28th, the reconnaissance platoon of 44 Column, commanded by Captain K. M. Grant, and the Commanding Officer's party with the W.T. set, 2 signallers, the Regimental Sergeant-Major and batmen, followed by one platoon, left to occupy Phekekrima if possible. By 1.30 p.m. they were reporting themselves as in possession of the village, the last Japanese having apparently left during the night. Unfortunately they had to report finding bayoneted to death those believed wounded and missing in the earlier attacks.

Lieutenant-Colonel Walker subsequently forwarded to Brigade a report on the defences at Phekekrima in which he said:

"I have toured the Phekekrima defences and found it took two hours to walk round quickly. . . . The stronghold was much larger than expected. I consider it was meant for personal occupation by a garrison of at least three hundred. There is a central cookhouse and much rice stored in dugouts, and in the open awaiting dugouts to be constructed in all positions. . . .

"There are a great number of foxholes connected to bunkers and dugouts by trenches and fire-bays, and these in turn were also being connected to underground quarters. The whole defence was excellently sited, tactically. The only way to attack this place means either across two causeways with a sheer drop on either side or a climb of 2,000 feet through thick jungle ending in a 1/1 gradient. . . ."

As 44 Column occupied Phekekrima, a probing attack on the enemy position between the two columns cost 2 dead and 1 wounded for 4 Japanese killed and 1 wounded.

Lieutenant-Colonel Walker and Major Lovelace then arranged over R/T a plan of attack, whereby one platoon of 44 Column was to descend on the Japanese from Phekekrima, while three platoons of 56 Column attacked the position from the south.

The enemy, about 50 strong, had been located dug in, with L.M.G.s, in very thick jungle, and a first attack on the 29th April cost 56 Column 2 killed and 3 wounded. Lieutenant L. J. Bristow Jones of 44 Column was also wounded. Both platoons leading the attack found it impossible to advance more than a short distance, as the thickness of the undergrowth and elephant grass made it impossible to pin-point the enemy foxholes. Flame-throwers proved ineffective owing to the wet state of the undergrowth. Platoons were then ordered to withdraw and the area was thoroughly searched by mortar fire.

During this action the bodies of the 2 men of 56 Column killed on the previous day, the 28th April, were recovered, as was Private Hammond, the one man who had been wounded. The Japanese had found him and had bayoneted him five times, but he was still alive.

Plasma for the wounded was urgently required, and a signal was sent by 56 Column to Rear Brigade asking for it to be dropped by light aircraft. The plane was later heard overhead, but no drop was possible as low cloud was hanging over the area.

The next day, the 30th April, 44 Column had a successful supply drop at Chekrema, and during the drop made an arrow pointing to Gurkha Farm. Directing the aeroplane by this arrow and by wireless, the statichute containing plasma was successfully dropped near 56 Column R.A.P.

On the 30th April the enemy could not be located, but on the morning of the 1st May a Naga came to 56 Column bivouac area to report a party of Japanese lying up in a nullah. Major Lovelace then led a fighting patrol of 30 other ranks together with a medium machine gun to investigate.

Major Lovelace says, "So many times, back in India, we had practised ambushes when the column commander fired the first shot which threw the enemy into complete confusion, but alas! in actual practice it had so far seemed difficult to get just the right circumstances.

"In this case the Naga guide led us to a spot where with sweeping signs and pantomime he indicated how the platoon and the Vickers gun should be sited. We crept quietly behind the guide, who suddenly indicated that we were very close, and that he, armed only with a spear, would prefer not to be in front. A few more yards and then it was—the copy-book ambush."

Two of the column were slightly wounded by Japanese fire, but at least 11 of the enemy had been killed.

The Essex patrol broke off the engagement and disappeared once more into the jungle, a perfect example of the "hit-and-run" tactics for which they had been so carefully trained by General Wingate.

The enemy now being cleared from the Phekekrima area, arrangements were made to march to Keruma, but before going farther into this terrible country, it was necessary to evacuate the many malaria cases and wounded, particularly from 56 Column. For this Nagas acted as stretcher-bearers, carrying sick and wounded to the Car Post, a three-day march over very rough country. From the Car Post they were evacuated by M.T. to Dimapur.

On the 3rd May, 44 Column passed through 56 Column again to take the lead on the advance towards the Kohima area. The next objective was Keruma, which was found to be completely devoid of enemy and local inhabitants. 56 Column then moved up to join 44 Column. From the O.P. at Keruma it was possible to observe movement in the Zubza Valley and artillery firing at enemy positions from Kohima.

The next day 44 Column continued the advance to Cheswema, which it occupied on 5th May. A small skirmish occurred here that is worth recording. After 44 Reconnaissance Platoon had entered the right and higher part of the village unopposed and one platoon was nearing the village, the enemy entered the village from the other end.

A sharp clash ensued. The Company Commander, Captain Haynes, was at once wounded, being shot through the thigh. Lieutenant-Colonel Walker arrived and took over control. The Commanding Officer, his batman, and Sergeant G. H. Smith with one 3-inch mortar positioned themselves on a hillock in the centre of the village. Regimental Sergeant-Major G. Wildey took a party round the left and Captain Grant and an officer of the Royal Engineers took the Reconnaissance Platoon round the right. So the village was cleared. These Japanese were tall, well-built, and smartly dressed men. 44 Column suffered 2 men killed and 2 wounded in addition to the Company Commander.

On the 7th May casualties were again evacuated, this time through enemy territory to Zubza on the Kohima–Dimapur road. Zubza was at the time the headquarters of the 2nd Division, under whose orders 44 and 56 Columns were still operating.

56 Column now passed through 44 Column and took the advance a stage farther, to Thizama, which had been a considerable camp before the Japanese advance. The football ground was found to be an excellent area for a supply drop, and was in fact the only area found during the whole march which could have been converted into an airstrip for light aircraft.

Its suitability for a supply drop had been evident to the enemy, for as the third plane was finishing its drop, No. 4 platoon, in a defensive position south of the football field, saw a party of about 24 Japanese advancing along the road driving two bullocks in front of them. Fire was opened and another sharp clash ensued. About 6 of the enemy were killed or wounded while, of 56 Column, the R.A.F. officer attached to the column and 2 other ranks had been wounded. This was the only occasion that a supply drop was interfered with.

44 Column now joined up in Thizama, and during the 9th and 10th May active patrolling revealed that a strong enemy force was in position about a mile south of the village. This force sent patrols to shoot up the 1st Essex position by night, but without result.

The Battalion now took up a, considering the nature of the country, fairly good all-round defensive position. An enemy attack would have met with a very warm reception. He did not attack, but contented himself with throwing in grenades at night and shooting up some patrols. The Battalion was now fairly close up on the flank of the Kohima battle. It was a good view-point from which one could watch the guns and tanks firing.

E.R.—8

Life got a bit complicated at Thizama, as on the 10th May liaison officers arrived almost simultaneously from 2nd Division, 5th Infantry Brigade, and 33 Column with varying suggestions as to what to do next. Lieutenant-Colonel Walker now had three separate and conflicting orders. So 23 Brigade had to be asked to give the judgment of Solomon: should the Essex do an attack on the Kohima area and please both 5th Brigade and 2nd Division, or should it get on with its original role of long-range penetration?

The Brigade answer was that the Battalion was to act in the long-range penetration role for which it was trained and equipped. The Battalion was not to get involved in the set-piece Kohima battle, but to move to Nerhema, some five miles north, and relieve the 2nd Duke of Wellingtons.

The move from Thizama was carried out in three phases. First, the "soft" elements of both columns moved off about midday. Then 56 Column battle group moved off in the afternoon. Finally, 44 Column battle group, commanded by the Commanding Officer, moved out just as darkness was coming on. Before leaving, 44 Column laid good booby-traps which were later heard to go off. They also gave the nearest enemy locality a final shoot-up. Before 44 Column left, a terrific monsoon downpour set in which continued all night. 56 Column reached Nerhema during the night of the 11th May. 44 Column arrived next morning, having spent the night in some paddy-fields two feet deep in water, the only flat part of a 2,000-foot steep drop away from Thizama. The enemy were perhaps a minor worry compared with the water, mud, and incessant downpour.

Lieutenant-Colonel Walker says: "Neither column will ever forget that march. A real monsoon storm sprang up at about 4 p.m. 11th May, and lasted with torrential rains until about 8 a.m. 12th May. The 2,000-foot climb up a slippery mountain with wet packs was most exhausting. In addition to this, we were uncertain whether the Duke of Wellingtons had been warned of our coming and were somewhat doubtful of our reception."

In addition, there was the ever-present danger of a Japanese ambush. One platoon, No. 7 of 44 Column, commanded by Lieutenant S. M. Pitchford, was in fact ambushed, killing 4 of the enemy, but losing 3 killed and 3 wounded in driving off the ambush party.

Nerhema was a large village with a Christian community, but in a deplorable condition of sanitation. The following note applies equally to Nerhema and all Naga hill villages at this time.

"The most unsavoury aspect of these villages is the complete lack of sanitation. The Japanese in their advance had eaten the pigs which normally abound in the villages and which are excellent scavengers. With the pigs all sanitation had disappeared. There were myriads of flies, and the natives were much afflicted with dysentery and cholera. It is interesting to note that although they often performed 'puga' by sacrifice in order to obtain good health, the natives in the affected areas clamoured for inoculation against cholera."

Now followed a period of waiting. The battalion was ordered to hold Nerhema and prevent any enemy move north via Rekoma, Thizama, or Cheswema. The enemy were still located about a mile south of Nerhema, covering the main track running north to south. They were not much more than 50 strong, but their bunker positions were six feet in depth, with four layers of teak logs and earth on top: all well camouflaged. They were sited in thick jungle with fields of fire of only five to twenty yards.

Booby-traps were set on all tracks and possible approaches to the village, catching several Japanese. Twice the enemy put in probing attacks against the 1st Essex positions but without success, although in the second of the attacks Major Nelson and 2 other ranks were slightly injured by a grenade which landed on 56 Column's command-post trench.

In return, the Essex harassed the enemy daily with mortar and M.M.G. fire, and made, after reconnaissance, several attacks on the enemy positions. These were found to be on three small thickly wooded hills running north to south, and garrisoned by the very big and excellently turned out troops that the Essex had encountered earlier on.

In one of these attacks Major P. D. Comber, Company Sergeant-Major Sheppard, and Private Haynes of 44 Column were wounded, while in another raid Captain K. W. M. Mann, M.C., Sergeant E. Weakford, L/Sergeant S. Clarke, and Corporal Thoburn were killed and 6 wounded, all of 56 Column.

Unfortunately, in this latter attack the direct air support had been just off the target and the enemy bunker positions on the hill-top, the objective of Nos. 1 and 3 Platoons, were quite unaffected. The assaulting platoons were met with L.M.G. fire at about twenty-yards range. The enemy also withdrew the safety-pin from grenades, and then pushed them out of his fire slits to allow them to roll down the hill to the approaching infantry.

This enforced stay at Nerhema had a depressing effect on all ranks. The village filth upset everybody, and diarrhœa set in badly. There was also a fresh onset of malaria. But all this time each column was sending out very long-distance patrols, to lay booby-traps on tracks the Japanese were using.

However, at long last on the 4th June, 56 Column was released by Brigade to move east to Kidzemetuma, a three-day march. On the 7th June, 44 Column was also released from its task and started off to try to catch up 56 Column. The Battalion had orders to proceed to Phakekedzumi, where Advance Brigade H.Q. was located. This march, completed in seven days by each column respectively, was very stiff indeed, including climbs of 2,000 and 3,000 feet up and down extremely steep and slippery mountain sides. 44 Column collected 9 Japanese on the way. These were the only prisoners to be taken by the 23rd Infantry Brigade in these operations.

The general situation on the 23rd Brigade front was that by the 10th June the Jessami–Kohima track had been completely interrupted and a number of successful ambushes had been carried out here and elsewhere. During early June it was apparent that the enemy would be forced to withdraw from Kohima, and orders for the Brigade's future operations were "All on Ukhrul."

This plan envisaged the two Essex columns and the two R.A. columns sweeping round the left flank and to the south-east of the enemy, thereby cutting his minor L. of C. and working on to his main L. of C. south-east of Ukhrul. The corps plan was to invest Ukhrul by the 1st July. 56 Column was ordered to reach Saiyapaw by that date and Ongshim by the 8th July. Columns of 4th Border Regiment and 2nd Duke of Wellingtons were to proceed due south. In detail the intention was for the 1st Essex and gunners to go via Tusom Khulen–Somra–Fort Keary–Saiyapaw and block the eastern exits to Ukhrul. 4th Border Regiment to move via Kharasom and the Duke of Wellingtons to move via Chakyang to Ukhrul. Brigade Headquarters Defence Company and the section of 3·7-inch howitzers which had been allotted by 33 Indian Corps were to take over from 60 Column north of Kharasom Kuki.

This plan was unfolded to the 1st Essex on their arrival at Phakekedzumi. It was explained that, in the opinion of the local experts, it should be possible for men to get through, but that it was doubtful whether mules could do so in the monsoon. All reconnaissance reports stated that certain sectors of the track were impassable for mules, but

Lieutenant-Colonel Walker was told to get 44 and 56 Columns through at all costs.

56 Column, which was still three days ahead of 44 Column, was leading by the route Phakekedzumi–Jessami–Nungphung–Tusom Khulen–Somra–Ngacham (in the Kuki country and also in Burma)–Fort Keary–Tonghlang–Saiyapaw, and thence as circumstances directed.

Of this march Lieutenant-Colonel Walker says:

"This part of the operations will remain embedded in the minds of all ranks as the most exhausting feat we have ever been called upon to perform. The mountains and monsoon combined to make life hell. The long dreary slogging up and down in the incessant rain, the miles of deep mud, the stench of rotting Japs and their animals, the overhanging trees which shut out the sun, the packs heavier still now that everything was wet, all these and many other things beside made the march a supreme test of endurance."

The leading column (56) was additionally hampered by the fact that the Japanese, retreating about one day ahead, destroyed all the jungle bridges over the mountain torrents and ravines. These had to be rebuilt and the schedule of the advance adhered to.

44 Column having started off last was in the rear of the four columns. It soon became further delayed by a bridge built by 56 Column having been washed away by a 20-knot seventy-yards-wide river. They had to build a new bridge. 44 Column now had the additional hardship to contend with, that of ploughing along in the mud, filth, and stench of rotting Japs churned up by the three columns in front.

At Saiyapaw all four columns were together, owing to another bridge having to be built. 44 Column had to wait here three days to let the other columns get clear. Here 2 men of 44 who had been sick for days gave up and died. At Fort Keary a few days earlier 2 other sick men had wandered off into the jungle and died. Day after day the Column hoped for a supply drop, but owing to low cloud did not get one.

Some remarks from a contemporary record help to paint the picture. "Track from Tusom Khulen to Point 7946 (8,500 feet) was very steep and slippery, and along the ridge the track was knee-deep in mud and the jungle very wet. Skeletons and decomposing bodies of Jap troops were to be seen all along the route. Progress was very slow. Known to all ranks as Death Valley."

Captain P. P. S. Brownless of 44 Column says:

"This is certainly not the only Death Valley of the war. It is perhaps unique in being almost at the top of some enormous mountain ridges, and this elevated track received its name of valley from the fact that it ran round the inside curve of these ranges into which so much of the monsoon rains drained.

"The monsoon was at its height: the sky a lifeless white and the rain pouring in steady torrents, day after day, hour after hour. The weary column of men and mules which made up 44 Column plodded down and then up the slippery mountain tracks, waded through torrents, trudged for miles through thick mud.

"It was here that some began to suspect the extent of the defeat being inflicted on the Japanese army. An occasional corpse or the carcass of a dead pack pony had been a fairly common sight, but here the column was marching over corpses, corpses sunk in the mud, with a helmet or a piece of equipment or a limb showing, and past an almost continuous line of dead pack animals. . . .

"This continuous line of dead stretched for twenty to thirty miles.

"The extreme misery of the march is impossible to describe. The incessant rain, the monotonous drips from the trees were relieved very occasionally by the crash of some great tree falling in the jungle below. The men staggered through the mud and up the slopes, borne down by the weight of their great packs. All were tortured with exhaustion because all were sick. We were so upset that few could eat the already short rations. Many were marching with temperatures and tick typhus had begun to break out.

"We had been sodden for weeks, were covered with mud, and we stank. Hollow-eyed, wasted, hungry, and yet incapable of eating more than a minute meal, we talked of nothing else but food.

"Towards the end of the march the food supply became precarious and even a small ration difficult to maintain. Some tried to fill the aching void with stewed leaves. Two small monkeys were shot and a number shared them. A myten (buffalo-type animal) was shot and divided among the Column.

"Each afternoon for five days a supply drop had been arranged, and each afternoon a hungry battalion waited in position listening to the drone of the supply planes as they circled above the clouds, loaded with food and searching anxiously for a break in the heavy cloud.

"Food and food alone was the subject of all conversation."

Again from another report:

"Track from Ngacham very steep and passed through very wet jungle. The mud and stench of dead men and animals made this task a hard one. The mud was indescribable, being even nearly waist deep for miles on end and always knee-deep.

"Words, maps, even photographs cannot adequately describe the worst of this journey, which took us into Burma within twenty miles of the Chindwin River. Nor were matters improved by the low clouds which prevented many of our supply drops."

During the whole of this march, lasting from the 12th June to 1st July, and subsequently to the 8th July, 26 days, there was at no time any possibility of evacuation.

There is a medical note which tells the story as plainly as any words can do: "56 Column has had 3 deaths since leaving Phakekedzumi and 44 Column 2 other ranks died Saiyapaw. Pyrexial 10 fresh cases daily. Sickness mainly virulent malaria, and tick typhus, combined with persistent diarrhœa, reduces column efficiency to 50 per cent."

Thirty-seven mules and three ponies had died or had had to be destroyed since leaving Phakekedzumi.

From Saiyapaw the two columns moved to Ongshim, and the expedition ended for the 1st Essex with the establishment of ambushes on the main road from Ukhrul, south-east of Kamjong.

Several Jap parties were located. One of these fled before a numerically inferior patrol of 56 Column which inflicted casualties. In the main the Japanese succeeded in avoiding the ambushes, and on one occasion brought their field guns into action against one of 56 Column's blocks, but without results. Finally a patrol from 44 Column made contact with elements of the 4/1st Gurkhas advancing south-east.

After the capture of Ukhrul and other places to the west, the Battalion was ordered to cease operations and to march along the Imphal road via Ukhrul, a distance of some sixty miles. They found this a most unpleasant march owing to incessant rain and deep mud, and were glad to be lorried the last fourteen miles into Imphal, which was reached on the 23rd July. Here the Commander of the 33 Indian Corps, Lieutenant-General Montague Stopford, C.B., D.S.O., M.C., visited the columns and addressed the men, complimenting the Battalion on its achievement.

The Battalion then removed its three months' growth of beard, bathed, ate, and slept before moving with the rest of the 23rd Infantry Brigade to Dimapur.

Thus ended operations for 44 and 56 Columns, 1st Battalion The Essex Regiment. They had not killed hundreds of Japanese, but they had carried out a most difficult task, and had, by their operations on the flanks and rear of the enemy, largely contributed to his retreat from Assam.

They had killed a minimum of 95 Japanese, wounded 23, taking 9 prisoners. These figures do not include the many casualties caused by direct air support and by long-range mortar and machine-gun shoots. The Japanese always, if they get the time, dig huge pits in which to throw all their dead and dying. These pits they cover over with branches of trees in an endeavour to prevent the extent of their casualties being known. Owing to advanced decomposition, it was never possible to know the number of Japanese casualties. Many of these pits were found after engagements.

Main bodies of columns had marched:

Distance	Up	Down
44 Column 337 miles	62,900 feet	60,700 feet
56 Column 341 miles	65,400 feet	62,900 feet

These figures cover the movements of main bodies, and not patrols and reconnaissance parties, which covered many miles more.

Casualties had been:

Other Ranks		Officers
Killed in action . . 32	2	Captain K. W. M. Mann, M.C.
		Captain B. B. French
Died of wounds . . 5		
Died of sickness *en route* . 6		
Died in hospital . . 2		
Wounded evacuated . 28	3	Major P. D. Comber
		Captain R. J. Haynes
		Lieutenant L. J. Bristow-Jones
Wounded not evacuated . 9	2	

There were many congratulatory messages as the operations were brought to a close.

This was received by Brigadier Perowne from Lieutenant-General W. J. Slim, C.B., D.S.O., M.C., G.O.C.-in-C. Fourteenth Army:

"O. 2562(.) CONFIDENTIAL(.) SLIM to PEROWNE(.)

"On the successful conclusion of this phase of operations in this Imphal area I wish to convey to you and all ranks of 23 Brigade my high appreciation of the great contribution which you have made to the defeat of the Japanese. 23 Brigade was given a task which was a real test of its skill and determination and toughness, but never during the one thousand mile move of your columns over some of the most difficult country in the world was any difficulty, whether provided by nature or the enemy, too great for its Commanders and men to overcome.

"23 Brigade should be proud of the part it has played in the destruction of the Japanese Forces.

"You have more than sustained the reputation of the Special Force."

And this from Lieutenant-General M. Stopford, the 33rd Indian Corps Commander.

"H.Q. 33 INDIAN CORPS
"23rd July, 1944.
"To: BRIGADIER L. E. C. M. PEROWNE,
"Commanding 23 Infantry Brigade.

"Now that your task is completed, I wish to express to you and all ranks of 23 Infantry Brigade my warm appreciation of the manner in which the Brigade has carried out the role allotted to it in the operations which have terminated in opening the road Dimapur-Kohima-Imphal and the capture of Ukhrul.

"The task given to you was a dual one: firstly, of threatening and cutting the Japanese L. of C., thereby forcing him to withdraw; secondly, of protecting the left flank of the Corps during its advance southwards. This necessitated traversing many hundreds of miles of the most difficult country imaginable, in parts of which malaria and disease were rife, under severely trying climatic conditions and against a cunning ruthless enemy. I doubt if such a feat, demanding superb physical fitness, inexhaustible endurance, and unlimited determination, has ever been carried out by British troops in the history of the Army. Not only I, but units, brigades, and divisions in the corps followed your progress with the keenest interest and the knowledge that what you were accomplishing was the primary factor in forcing the enemy to withdraw and finally to crack on the remainder of the front.

"These operations have ended in the biggest defeat that the Japanese Army has yet suffered, and I wish to thank you for the magnificent part which you have played in it.

"I trust you will now have an opportunity for the rest and refitting that you so well deserve, and that when you are next ready for battle I may have the privilege of 23 Infantry Brigade serving with me again in 33 Indian Corps.

"(Sd.) M. STOPFORD,
"Lieut.-General."

By the 25th July the Battalion was concentrated at Dimapur, where it was to remain until the 14th August, and where it was visited by Field-Marshal Lord Wavell, the Viceroy of India, who congratulated all ranks on the very fine performance just accomplished.

On the 14th August transport to take the 1st Essex to a rehabilitation centre became available, and the Battalion entrained for Bangalore, which was reached eight days later. There it remained until the 21st October, when the period of rest and rehabilitation came to an end. At no time during these weeks did the strength of the Battalion in the station exceed 200. Some were on leave, but the great majority were in hospital.

Section XI

INDIA AND ENGLAND, 1944-48

On the 26th October, 1944, the Battalion moved to a training camp at Orcha, near Jhansi. Here it was brought up to establishment by the disbandment and absorption of the 51/69th Regiment R.A. The 1st Essex at this time had only some 30 or 40 Essex regulars in its ranks.

The Battalion soon became a properly reorganised and co-ordinated unit. Intensive training recommenced for the next operations, which were to be airborne. The Battalion quickly became efficient and tough. The final eight-day exercise—100 miles to be covered, including a 100-yards-wide river to cross—took place, but at the end there was a sad anti-climax. All commanding officers were summoned to meet General Sir Oliver Leese and told that Special Force was to cease to exist. It was too expensive. This news was a great blow to all ranks of the Battalion. All had grown to be very proud to belong to the famous 70th Division—Special Force. However, training continued in the hope of a reprieve or alternative role. This was not to happen, and on the 26th March, 1945, the 1st Essex left Jhansi for Dipetuli Camp near Ranchi, where Lieutenant-Colonel C. S. Mills took over from

Lieutenant-Colonel Walker, who had been repatriated to the United Kingdom.

The move from Orcha was more than a change in location. It was a change of atmosphere and role. The malarial rate continued to be high, which, together with the sudden easing of tension caused by ceasing to belong to Special Force, caused a sharp drop in morale. This was accelerated by a plan virtually to disband the battalions of the 23rd Brigade by taking commanding officers, seconds in command, adjutants, and quartermasters to form the nucleus of parachute battalions to be formed from volunteers from the three infantry battalions. The project was very clumsily handled, and the call for volunteers was badly worded and deeply resented, with the result that only some 18 men volunteered from the 1st Essex and about the same numbers from the other two battalions.

A further cause for the fall in morale was a widespread feeling that the honours lists submitted by Special Force had been harshly written down and that arduous service had been poorly rewarded.

It was not for a long time after the operations that the lists of honours and mentions included the following awards to the 1st Essex for gallant and distinguished service in Burma and on the Eastern Frontier of India 1943-44.

M.C.	Major A. Lovelace, M.B.E.
M.B.E.	Major (Quartermaster) F. Waddell.
Bar to M.M.	Sergeant G. T. H. Smith.
M.M.	Corporal R. Way.

Those mentioned in dispatches are listed in Appendix II to this history.

After a short stay in Dipetuli Camp, the Battalion was transferred to Barambe, a hutted camp in a sal forest some twenty-two miles east of Ranchi.

The 23rd Brigade now consisted of the 1st Queens and 1st Essex and three battalions of Gurkha Rifles. Training was based on the normal infantry role with mule transport augmented by a skeleton establishment of M.T.

The Battalion was so situated on V.E. Day. The V.E. Day Parade was held at Ranchi, where His Excellency the Maharaja of Bihar took the salute.

Whilst at Barambe, on the 19th May, Lieutenant-General Sir Geoffrey Howard, the Colonel of the Regiment, paid a literally flying visit to the Battalion. The first news of his impending visit was a telephone call saying that a senior officer of the Essex Regiment had been waiting on the airfield, some twenty miles away, for half an hour, and as Lieutenant-Colonel Mills says, "Quick work was required to prepare for his reception."

After seeing the Battalion, as he found it, without special preparations, the Colonel spoke highly of the morale and turn-out.

In June the Battalion left the 23rd Infantry Brigade with which it had served since the last months of 1941, and moved to join the 29th Infantry Brigade of the 36th British Division at Uruli Camp, some seventeen miles from Poona. Here was found the advance party which had left some weeks earlier, and a large draft, mostly men from anti-aircraft units of East Anglian origin. This was the second East Anglian if not Essex draft, and the composition of the unit was beginning to alter for the better.

The Battalion had at this time no specific task in view, and was called upon to supply officers and non-commissioned officers to administer marshalling camps for the forthcoming invasion of Japan.

Following the collapse of Japan in August 1945, preparations were quickly made for the formation of an occupation force consisting of the 2nd British Division, and for one week the 1st Essex was busy preparing for that role. Unluckily it was replaced by another battalion which had a record of long service in the Division, and so the 44th remained in Pashan Camp, some four miles from Poona. Here the Battalion was raised to a strength of over 1,100 by drafts of men in "Age and Service Groups" which made them eligible for early release, and a second difficult period set in. The new-comers had little interest in anything except repatriation—"Release happy" or "Boat happy" as the current expression ran—and their state of near insubordination was encouraged by certain shipping delays and other factors.

As a focus of interest it was decided to fire the annual classification course, and for this, before being ordered, the attached men volunteered to undertake the marking and camp fatigues, with the result that the morale rose again quickly. The repatriation of other age and service groups continued steadily, but it was not until April that the officer groups, which were lagging some ten groups behind, caught up.

On the 1st February, 1946, the Essex took part in the Victory Parade on the Poona Race-course, in which the salute of some 10,000 troops was taken by Major-General E. N. Goddard, commanding Poona Area. A *feu-de-joie*, assiduously practised, was successfully performed.

"Hardly anybody in the unit had ever heard of such a movement before, and certainly nobody had ever done anything so rash."

Then came the serious Bombay riots, the so-called Mutiny of the Royal Indian Navy.

During the winter, feelings were running high in India on account of the trials of those who had collaborated with the Japanese. Practice in duties in aid of the civil power was given a high priority. In February the Indian Navy mutinied, and the 2nd Leicesters, stationed at Colaba, was called out to deal with trouble in the Bombay Docks area. On the 21st February, when it appeared that the Royal Indian Navy shore installations were about to become implicated, the 1st Essex was moved at short notice to Kalyan, some twenty-five miles from Bombay.

When Battalion Headquarters (Lieutenant-Colonel D. E. Long Price) with "D" Company (Major B. J. Palmer) entered Bombay early on the 22nd, it was reported that the situation had changed. The 2nd Leicesters had the situation well in hand as regards the R.I.N., but serious civilian rioting had broken out in Bombay, the police had been badly mauled, and the Central Police-station was in immediate danger. In consequence the Battalion was ordered at once to relieve the Police Headquarters. If necessary it was to shoot its way in. There were in reality grave communal disorders within the personnel of the R.I.N., and these had spread in the familiar pattern to Hindu-Mohammedan riots in the city.

All three battalions of the 72nd Infantry Brigade—2nd Queens, 2nd Border Regiment, and 1st Essex—were moved into the city, with Lieutenant-Colonel C. S. Mills as Acting Brigadier. The Battalion was in Bombay for a week, during which the riots took the traditional form of any communal disturbance in the city—mill strikes, burning of trains on the G.I.P. and B.B.C.I. railways, shooting in Crauford Market and an almost complete calm in the European residential area of Colaba.

Fire had to be opened on rioters on a good many occasions, but by the 28th February the situation was under control and the Battalion returned to Pashan Camp. Here it was to remain until the 13th March, when a change of location to Ghorpuri Barracks, Poona, took place. This was a modern and well-equipped barrack block, until recently a base hospital. It was too good to last, said the rank and file, and they were right, for after about nine weeks the Battalion was transferred to Bangalore.

On the 15th May the 1st Essex Regiment was installed in a former hospital block at Jalahalli, and shortly afterwards visited by Lieutenant-General R. M. M. Lockhart, C.B., C.I.E., M.C., the G.O.C.-in-C. Southern Command. The accommodation at Jalahalli was compact and good, in fact better than at Ghorpuri, which perhaps was just as well, for the Battalion was to remain there for over a year. This was by far the longest stay in any station since the arrival in India early in 1942.

In November and December 1946 the Battalion took part in the 72nd Brigade Group training out on the borders of Mysore State and the Madras Presidency. To get to the training areas entailed a march of some one hundred and eighty miles, a fine start to some good training. It was a coincidence that the commander of the 72nd Brigade Group was now Brigadier L. E. C. M. Perowne, C.B.E., who had earlier commanded the 23rd Infantry Brigade in "Chindit" days.

Nineteen forty-seven was an important year, for on the 15th August, 1947, British rule over India ceased and the Dominions of India and Pakistan came into being. There was throughout 1947 a progressive run-down of the British Army in India, the army that had been represented in the country since 1754. Events were to make the 1st Essex one of the last British battalions to leave.

The impending changes did not directly affect the Battalion until later in the year, and the 1st Essex was to remain in the area of Bangalore and Madras until August. Here the Battalion was visited in February by the Commander-in-Chief, Field-Marshal Sir Claude Auchinleck, G.C.I.E., G.C.B., C.S.I., D.S.O., O.B.E., A.D.C., by the Adjutant-General to the Forces, General Sir Richard O'Connor, K.C.B., D.S.O., M.C., A.D.C., and by Major-General L. G. Whistler, C.B., D.S.O., the Major-General British Troops in India, who was to remain in close touch with the Battalion until the final evacuation.

Mid-1947 found the Battalion still based on Jalahalli, with two companies on detachment at Madras. One company was in Fort St. George and the other in a hutted camp at Saidapet. This had until recently been a married families transit camp, and was sited near the sea. Here such amusements as bathing, surf riding, and fishing could be easily obtained.

The Battalion Corps of Drums, started in 1947 for the first time since the war, had been re-formed in time to take part in an impressive and historic ceremony, the handing over of Fort St. George to the custody of the new Dominion of India.

In 1640 one Francis Day founded a small trading post on a strip of sandy beach on the west coast of the great sub-continent of India which became the stockade around which was built in 1673 Fort St. George, Madras. The whole early history of the British in India centres round this historic fort. A pivot in the early struggles with France for domination in India, it was from Fort St. George that Robert Clive, a writer in the service of the East India Company, took to arms, first against the French and then against the Rajah of Tanjore. The capture of Arcot followed and the establishment of British dominion over the whole of south India. Again, it was from Fort St. George that Clive set out in 1757 to recapture the British post at Calcutta and to avenge the victims of the "Black Hole of Calcutta." By his subsequent victory over Suraj-ud-Dowlah at Plassey, he was to win Bengal for the British and open the way to the conquest of the whole Ganges Valley.

There is probably no infantry regiment of the British Army that has not served its tour of duty in Fort St. George in the three hundred years since Francis Day first set up his trading post on that bare strand.

At midday on 2nd August, 1947, the guard on Fort St. George found by the 1st Essex "stood-to" as the Drums of the Battalion marched in the new guard, a Sikh guard from India. The guards changed, and then, headed by their Drums, the 1st Essex marched out, leaving that historic spot to the care of the new Dominion.

Handing over all responsibilities in Madras, the Battalion was moved to Nasik Road Camp, Deolali. Before leaving Madras the Battalion was presented with the Union Jack which had flown over Fort St. George and which on the evening of the 14th August, 1947, had been lowered for the last time.

At Deolali, the traditional "homeward bound" station of India, the Battalion was reduced to a cadre of approximately 200. All regular soldiers with unexpired colour service were posted to the 1st K.S.L.I. and other battalions remaining on the foreign service roster.

The stay at Deolali with the 29th Brigade Group (1st Lancashire Fusiliers, 1st South Staffords, and 1st Essex) was comparatively short, and by the middle of January 1948 the Battalion formed up for a farewell parade by Major-General L. G. Whistler. After his inspection he congratulated all ranks on the excellent way in which they had carried out their difficult tasks during the closing stages of British rule in India, and told them that their presence had materially assisted in the orderly withdrawal of British personnel.

A few days later, on the 20th January, the 1st Essex left Deolali and embarked with other troops of the 29th Brigade at Bombay in the *Empress of Scotland*, which sailed flying the Brigade flag at the masthead in recognition of the fact that she was carrying the last British brigade to leave India. So the long connection of the 1st Essex with India, dating back to 1822, was ended.

The Battalion disembarked at Liverpool on the 16th February, but owing to railway delays did not reach Colchester until 5 a.m. on the 17th February.

Here the 1st Essex Regiment was met by Brigadier G. H. Wilmer, D.S.O., M.C., the Colonel of the Regiment, but the civic reception and march through the town which had been arranged if the Battalion had arrived in daylight had to be postponed. It was carried out two days later in a snow-storm from Roman Way Camp, where the 1st Battalion was quartered alongside the 2nd Battalion.

On the 8th April, 1948, Lieutenant-Colonel C. S. Mills handed over the command he had held for nearly three years to Lieutenant-Colonel C. A. Southey, and temporarily took command of the 2nd Battalion.

In the early summer of 1948 the 1st Essex took over from the East Anglian Brigade Training Centre the duties of Group Basic Training Battalion to the East Anglian Brigade, becoming officially known as the 1st Battalion The Essex Regiment (East Anglian Group Training Battalion).

On the 3rd November, 1948, the 1st Battalion The Essex Regiment ceased to have a separate existence, and was amalgamated with due ceremony with the 2nd Battalion. The new Battalion thus formed was to be known as the 1st Battalion The Essex Regiment (44th and 56th). Its history to the end of 1950 is briefly chronicled in the last chapter of this book.

Chapter Three

THE 2ND BATTALION THE ESSEX REGIMENT, 1939-48

FOREWORD

by General Sir Evelyn H. Barker, K.B.E., C.B., D.S.O., M.C.,
Commander 49th (West Riding) Division, 1944-45

The history of the 2nd Battalion The Essex Regiment in World War II adds yet another eventful chapter to the conspicuous part played by the Regiment in the Service of our King and Country.

To the layman this story must appear a somewhat tedious account of modern battle. To the soldier, however, and in particular to those who took part in these stirring events, it is a record of courage and endurance of the English Infantry soldier and of splendid leadership by officers and non-commissioned officers—two essentials to success in battle.

I remember well how sad I felt at the disbandment of the 70th Brigade of my Division in August 1944 and its replacement by the 56th Independent Infantry Brigade. However, I was comforted by the fact that this new Brigade was composed of three regular battalions of renowned Regiments who had already proved themselves in battle.

I was not disappointed. The 2nd Battalion The Essex Regiment, with the other battalions of that Brigade, played a leading part in the Division's succeeding operations and in particular the capture of Le Havre.

I was proud to have them in my Division.

This history—factual though it must be—conceals many deeds of great heroism and devotion to duty of which those who took part may be justly proud.

It also serves as a fitting memorial to those who lost their lives serving in the 2nd Battalion.

6th June, 1951.

Section I
ENGLAND, FRANCE, AND BELGIUM, AUGUST 1939–APRIL 1940

THE 2nd Battalion The Essex Regiment, commanded by Lieutenant-Colonel A. H. Blest, was stationed in Warley Barracks, Brentwood, in that August of 1939 when war became, as in August 1914, almost inevitable, and the various measures of the "Precautionary Period" were put into effect.

The 2nd Essex, together with the 2nd Buffs and 1st H.L.I., had been warned for, and trained in, pioneer duties in the event of mobilisation, but there were other duties to perform even before mobilisation.

Perhaps the most pressing problem that confronted the British Government in those last weeks of peace was the state of readiness of the anti-aircraft defences of the country, for a great weight of opinion held that heavy air attack would precede or coincide with the declaration of war. So every effort was made to strengthen and augment Anti-Aircraft Command.

It was in accordance with this scheme that on the 24th August, 1939, the 2nd Battalion was ordered to deploy under orders of Anti-Aircraft Command and assist in the light anti-aircraft defence of London.

Detachments were spread far and wide, from Purfleet to Canada House, Brentford to Finchley. Their only weapons were Brens and Lewis guns. Their efficacy was problematical, but their efficiency was not, for their disciplined presence did much to sustain civilian morale, more perhaps than their weapons would have done to damage the enemy's had an attack been made. To the credit side must also be placed the fact that this period of detachment duty did much to weld platoons and sections brought up to peace establishment into that tight organisation from which fighting spirit springs in times of stress. This role ceased on mobilisation being ordered on the 1st September, 1939, and the Battalion reconcentrated at Warley.

Despite the fact that the Battalion had to quit barracks and move into billets to make room for the expansion of the Depot, everything went smoothly, and the hard work put in on the mobilisation scheme was to pay a handsome dividend. Five hundred and fifty strong on the 1st September, drafts of reservists and militia men raised the strength to 792 by the 4th September, and by the 6th Lieutenant-Colonel Blest could report mobilisation complete except for certain vehicles and equipment. In fact, he says, "Mobilisation went so smoothly that all ranks were given twenty-four hours' leave to fill in time."

The "Pompadours" were now at war establishment of 25 officers and 774 other ranks. The war-strength of vehicles and weapons was not attained until they had been in France for some considerable time, for sufficient stocks did not exist on mobilisation to complete all units to full war scale.

A war establishment of 25 officers may seem low to some, but it is to be remembered that in 1939 only one of the three platoons in each rifle company was commanded by a subaltern officer, the other two being commanded by warrant officers, Class III, platoon sergeant-majors.

With mobilisation went the business of safeguarding all regimental property, and Major C. L. Wilson, M.C., the Second-in-Command of the Battalion, says: "I recollect taking all the Regimental silver and plate to Lloyds Bank for safe custody. It was guarded *en route* by a guard of 6 men with fixed bayonets. Next day, when visiting the bank, I was horrified to see all the boxes being moved from the bank by one aged man and a Carter Paterson van. However, all's well that ends well, and the silver was duly restored to the Battalion after the war."

On the 10th September the advance party left under Major H. L. H. Boustead, and the Battalion followed three days later. The route of the rail journey was Warley–Cambridge–Oxford–Reading–Southampton, sufficiently circuitous completely to mislead the Battalion as to their destination, and—it is hoped—mystify the enemy.

On the morning of the 16th September, 1939, the 2nd Essex disembarked at Cherbourg from cross-channel steamers, and as they were forming up on the quay, Brigadier G. H. Wilmer, D.S.O., M.C., stepped off another ship. His delight at seeing the Battalion was only matched by their pleasure in seeing him.

A slow, roundabout, and bumpy train journey ended at Brest, where the Battalion was marched up a very steep hill to a disused wine storage and bottling factory. The buildings had been left indescribably filthy by the previous occupants.

The "Pompadours" were to remain in Brest until mid-October, carrying out unspectacular but essential work in the Base area, the unloading of M.T. ships and the carrying out of all the Dock and Base

Installation guards—a dull role, but one for which regular infantry battalions had had to be detached, there being no pioneer corps in the pre-war army.

On the 7th October the 2nd Essex was warned of a move to join the 2nd Corps. The route up was by Rouen, Amiens, and Arras to Lesquin near Lille, where they detrained. The remainder of the journey to Wattisard and Pont-à-Marcq was by road. The move was completed by the night 16th/17th October. On the journey up the Battalion was told that it was now part of G.H.Q. troops, had been lent to the 2nd Corps, and placed under the 3rd Division for work.

The task given by the Divisional Commander, Major-General B. L. Montgomery, C.B., D.S.O., was to convert the River Marcq into an anti-tank obstacle along the inter-corps boundary. A period of intensive work started. Tools and engineer equipment were short. The River Marcq, a small and narrow stream running approximately parallel to the Belgian frontier, rose in flood, and, overflowing its banks, destroyed much of the work done. This had been cutting the nearside bank so that it was vertical, and revetting it with stakes and fascines. The weather was extremely bad, and the "Pompadours" were glad to receive additional supplies of gum and thigh boots without which work in the flooded defence works was almost impossible. On the 26th October they were visited at work by Lieutenant-General Alan Brooke, the G.O.C. 2nd Corps.

This period in the Marcq valley was difficult and unpleasant, but the spirit of the Battalion did not suffer, particularly when, on the 31st October, a gift of 10,000 cigarettes was received from the Lord-Lieutenant and the High Sheriff of Essex.

An occasional week-end in Lille was a coveted reward for their hard work. Of "B" Company a Royal Engineer said, "If anyone deserves leave these chaps do: they are working up to their knees in mud and slush all the week, and if you meet them in Lille, they're the smartest men in the town."

On the 9th November, 1939, the Battalion was moved back to Gauchin Legal for work in the rail-head area. They were still there for the first wartime Christmas, a day very greatly appreciated by all ranks. Shortly afterwards they moved to Bruay.

In those last months of 1939, Lieutenant-Colonel Blest was disturbed by the possibility that the Battalion might become submerged in the flood of events and become pioneers for good. The Battalion was being denied periods of training although all fighting formations engaged in defence works were allowed such refresher periods. He was questioned as to a suitable war establishment for a pioneer battalion, and seemed to be more and more the hand-maiden of the Chief Engineer of Corps.

It was not a cheerful outlook for the "Pompadours," but Lieutenant-Colonel Blest's representations eventually bore fruit, and in December 1939 the Battalion was relieved off works for training. He had been fortunate in making his plea in that the Battalion was directly under 2nd Corps and so he could approach the Brigadier General Staff—Brigadier N. M. Ritchie, D.S.O., M.C.—direct, a great help, as he was an old friend of Lieutenant-Colonel Blest and of the Regiment.

Unfortunately, this training period coincided with some of the most severe winter weather on record and movement by road was almost impossible. It was bitterly cold, with the roads solid sheets of ice, and all ranks were glad that by then their slender resources of warm clothing had been greatly augmented by gifts from home, notably the Regimental Comforts Fund organised by Lady Howard. "Every man possessed several balaclava helmets, scarves, socks, mittens, and gloves—and they needed them." "The cold was so intense that bottles of beer froze solid and burst."

Everything possible was done to reinvigorate the infantry spirit in this training period. Turn-out and saluting were meticulous. The Drums beat Retreat on the Town Square at Bruay, and there were ceremonial Guard Mountings with the Drums on parade, the Drums also heading the Battalion on Church Parades. 2nd Corps expressed their pleasure in these activities.

January 1940 at Bruay was notable only for the weather. It was the first introduction for most to a Continental winter, for few remained who remembered the winters in France and Belgium in the First World War.

But collective training continued whenever the weather permitted, and individual training and administration was continuous. Nor was the social side neglected. On the 21st January one finds the officers entertaining their hosts in Bruay at a cocktail party in the officers' mess in the Cercles des Mines. These parties were very popular with the guests, and liaison with the local population was on a high level—at all levels.

On the 13th February the Battalion moved to Meurchin, not at first a popular change of station, for the reception was poor. "1230 hours. All Coys arrived in new areas. Majority of billets, especially officers, were bolted and barred in Meurchin, in spite of arrangements made by advance parties, and it wasn't until after dark that accommodation was finally secured. Men's billets were dirty and insanitary, and the attitude of the villagers, if not exactly hostile, was anything but enthusiastic. Weather throughout the day was extremely cold and light snow fell almost continuously." Conditions were made more intolerable by an acute coal shortage, and fires were almost non-existent. It must have been cold comfort to write:

"MEURCHIN. 15 Feb. 40. Continuous snow all day—warmer."

The Battalion remained with its Headquarters in Meurchin throughout March and into April. The role was still that of a pioneer unit, but, in anticipation of a return to infantry duties, every possible chance was taken to train, whilst leave and good welfare arrangements helped to keep morale at a high level. Football became possible as the countryside thawed out from that terrible winter, and matches were played with neighbouring units and also with French teams. There is little doubt that these matches, against French civilian sides, together with the "Pompadours'" impeccable discipline, did much to ease relationships at Meurchin, and these improved rapidly after the first frigid reception given to the Battalion.

During early April the Battalion was still employed on "works." "A" and "B" Companies were employed on road-making, "a monotonous and soul-destroying job," according to Captain R. H. A. Painter, commanding "B" Company. But even such a job had its better points, for Captain J. F. Cramphorn says of his company: " 'A' Company's task was making, or rather remaking, a road between Carvin and Carnin. The drill was to excavate by a diesel-driven road roller to a depth of eighteen inches or so, then fill up first with big stones, then smaller ones and finally roll in quite small ones with mud and water. The water was the attraction, as it was collected from the local brewery, and great was the competition to be on the water collection party. The brewer, a fine, well-built Alsatian, was very generous."

And then on the 23rd April, 1940, the scene changes. Brigadier A. H. Ramsden, commanding the 25th Infantry Brigade, came to Battalion Headquarters and told Lieutenant-Colonel Blest that they were to be relieved from pioneer duties and were to join the 1st Buffs and the 7th Queens in his newly formed 25th Infantry Brigade.

No news could have been better. Brigade training instructions followed, and a move to training areas was eagerly awaited. The executive order to move was, however, delayed, and companies had to resign themselves to road-making and other good works until early May. Only an advance party under Captain H. F. H. Jones had actually moved to the Brigade training area by the 10th May.

Section II

FRANCE AND BELGIUM, MAY–JUNE, 1940

The "Pompadours" had had no time to hand over their pioneer duties to a unit newly arrived from England before, on the morning of the 10th May, 1940, the Germans struck their long-awaited blow in the West. Holland and Belgium were invaded and the French frontier was crossed.

That morning the Battalion was awakened by bombs dropping some miles away and by continuous and heavy anti-aircraft fire. This was the first indication of anything unusual, for this was the first time that bombs had been dropped. There had been a leaflet raid on Meurchin on the 2nd April, the leaflets saying that Germany had no quarrel with France, but that was all until these bombs early on the 10th May.

Numerous aeroplanes were visible in the early morning light, and early risers heard the news of the German attack from the B.B.C. bulletin on the wireless. All local protection orders and measures were immediately put into effect. Air-raid alarms and "raiders past" signals were received in quick succession, but there was no signal ordering the move of the Battalion. All waited impatiently.

Rifle Company Commanders on the morning of the 10th May, 1940, were: "A" Company, Captain J. F. Cramphorn; "B" Company, 2/Lieutenant G. H. Watson, vice Captain Painter on leave in the U.K.; "C," Major T. O'C. Doherty; "D," Major H. F. Howell. During the morning the commanding officer of the battalion that was to take over the pioneer duties of the 2nd Essex came to see Lieutenant-Colonel Blest. Newly arrived in France, he knew little of the general situation or even of the neighbourhood, but it was not going to matter very much, for the picture was going to alter rapidly and almost continuously from now on. The position at the moment was that on the morning of the 10th May, 1940, "Plan D" had been put into effect. This was the strategical plan of the C.-in-C. Allied Forces, the French General Gamelin. It visualised the whole Allied forces leaving their prepared defended areas on the frontier and advancing as fast as possible into Belgium and Holland, there to meet the oncoming German army.

The French Seventh Army between the sea coast and Lille would advance into Holland. The B.E.F. from round Lille would advance to Brussels and Louvain. The French First and Ninth Armies, on the right of the B.E.F., would advance to the area of Namur and Dinant. These moves were in progress on the 10th and 11th May as the 2nd Essex sat impatiently in Meurchin. The move plan had of course been drawn up in advance, and the concentration of the newly formed 25th Infantry Brigade was delayed because of the necessity of not altering a long-prepared and most complicated march table. In the interests of security no reconnaissance had been possible before the German attack, and Lieutenant-Colonel Blest had been the only person to have a look at the route up to the Belgian frontier.

The 2nd Essex Regiment therefore moved in its original role of Corps Troops, the advanced billeting party, under Major C. L. Wilson, the Battalion Second-in-Command, leaving at 5 a.m. on the 12th May, followed by the Battalion on the night 12th/13th May.

Lieutenant-Colonel Blest led the column, followed by his Battalion command group. Various unit command groups came next, and then the "Pompadours," under Major T. O'C. Doherty. The column travelled all through the night through Lille, Tournai, Alost, and so towards Brussels. A diversion from the planned route had to be made because of heavy bombing of the roads at Alost. There was misdirection, probably deliberate by a fifth columnist, and finally Lieutenant-Colonel Blest's car crashed with a Belgian Citröen leaving the war at speed.

Unfortunately, Lieutenant-Colonel Blest had to be evacuated, as the Battalion heard when, about midday on the 13th May, it pulled in to its allotted billeting area of Sleeuhagen-Mollem-Bollebeke, nine miles north-west of Brussels. The move up had shown the effects of high-altitude and dive-bombing, for "towns such as Alost were not healthy, and we got the column through as quickly as possible in 'block,' reorganising on the far side, having dodged the next air sortie." It was experience to prove valuable later in the campaign.

In the new area Major Wilson assumed command vice Lieutenant-Colonel Blest.

The 2nd Essex was given operation orders that afternoon, when a Liaison Officer from Headquarters 2nd Corps reported to the Commanding Officer. He said the 2nd Essex was the only reserve left in the Corps Commander's hand, and that the Battalion might be used in one of two roles:

(a) To fill a wide gap of two to three miles between the left of the 4th Division and the right of the Belgian army south of Malines.

(b) To assist 2/7th Royal Northumberland Fusiliers in Brussels controlling refugees.

It was evident, from the Liaison Officer's report, that things weren't going too well.

Having assured himself that all measures for the local protection of the Battalion area were in hand, Major Wilson went forward after making telephone contact with 4th Division. His object was the reconnaissance of a battalion defensive position in order to fulfil role (a) should the Essex be called upon to carry out that task. Major Wilson says, "I had the greatest difficulty in moving forward to Louvain owing to the congestion of traffic, mainly cavalry, horsed guns, and other Belgian troops withdrawing. They were very intermixed and exhausted, but by no means in panic."

On reaching Headquarters 4th Division, Major Wilson was told that the gap referred to by the Corps Liaison Officer was too wide for any detailed reconnaissance to be possible, and that a general look-over the approaches to it was all that would be feasible. This Major Wilson did, and returned to the Battalion area, where he met Captain P. C. Hinde, the Adjutant, who had been up to Brussels and had gained touch with the 2/7th R.N.F., in case the Battalion was ordered to assist in the control of refugees—role (b).

No orders came in during the night 13th/14th May, and on the morning of the 14th, Lieutenant-Colonel Blest returned to duty and reassumed command. It was a day without a move, but with plenty of excitement. There were alarms of gas and alarms of parachutists. "A" Company saw some drop not far away. "Their drill was interesting. A lone aircraft came over with no opposition from us at about 1,500 feet. It dropped a bomb and immediately afterwards down came the parachutists. We immediately went to try to catch them, and there was great excitement until something white three or four fields away turned out to be a heap of lime." There was an attack by dive-bombers, too, which set alight a small pile of hardly acquired petrol tins, but there were no casualties. The 2nd Essex was thus the first unit to be dive-bombed, a fact that was officially reported in the Press later on in the war.

On the 15th May came move orders. The first out was No. 9 Platoon (2/Lieutenant P. J. Green), sent to assist the 2/7 R.N.F. in refugee control, a task of growing magnitude and a danger to the communications of the B.E.F. Then No. 16 Platoon (2/Lieutenant M. V. Foy) was ordered off to act as defence platoon to Headquarters 2nd Corps. It was not to rejoin the Battalion until after the return to England.

Next, at 10.50 a.m. a Corps Liaison Officer came with orders to the 2nd Essex to move to Berchem–St. Agatha (two miles west of Brussels), there to come under orders of the 4th Division for the defence of bridges over the Charleroi Canal. It was the first of a series of changes in command, and it is Captain G. N. H. Sheffield who writes, "What corps or division we were in from then on I can't remember, but I got fed up changing the vehicle signs every other day or so."

The "Pompadours" marched at 1 p.m., and arrived at their rendezvous three hours later. At 5 p.m., a reconnaissance of the bridges was made by company commanders, and on the following morning the Battalion was placed under command of the 11th Infantry Brigade. During the night the M.T. had moved to a rendezvous to the northeast of the city and no lights had been needed for that night drive owing to the glare of the fires in the town.

During the morning of the 16th, further reconnaissance of all bridges in the Anderlecht area of Brussels was carried out and selected defensive positions were taken up that evening. By then all the bridges had been prepared for demolition, and the authority to give the executive order for the actual blowing-up vested in the Company Commander in whose company area the bridge stood. Captain Cramphorn's "A" Company, on the right of the 2nd Essex, was in touch with the 1st Hampshire Regiment and had responsibility for two bridges. Major Howell's "D" Company came next with one bridge to look after, then "B" Company, commanded by 2/Lieutenant G. H. Watson, who was to hand over to Captain H. F. H. Jones on the 20th May, also with one bridge. "C" Company (Major Doherty), on the left of the Battalion position, had responsibility for two bridges. Barricades of furniture were erected in the streets and preparations made to wire up platoon localities for occupation immediately the bridges were blown.

During the 17th May all bridges were blown according to a time programme, the right (southern) bridge of "A" Company being the last to go at 4.25 p.m. Permission to blow had been given to Captain Cramphorn by the rear-guard commander of the 1st Division. Captain Cramphorn says, "2nd D.L.I. and 1st Grenadier Guards withdrew through the Company and took up positions behind us. In spite of the gruelling week they had had, they were in perfect order, and the bewilderment felt at seeing a withdrawal at such an early stage of the fighting was tempered by the obviously high morale of the troops engaged in it. . . ." (It was at this point that the rear-guard commander informed him that all the rear-guard was now across the river and he was therefore free to blow the bridges.) "With Henry Jones (Captain H. F. H. Jones), my second-in-command, I went to see to laying our mines in the road the other side, for a truck full of French mines had shortly before been given to 'A' Company. Work was proceeding well when suddenly we heard a rumble of trucks approaching. 'This is it,' we thought, and rapidly signalling to the platoon on the home side, prepared to do battle.

"To our relief a troop of the 4th Hussars who had been left behind approached and we hastily let them through. When they were over, we completed laying our mines and withdrew ourselves. After this, orders were received that only civilians vouched for by the Belgian police could cross to our side. Then followed some of those tragic sidelights of war—husbands sending their wives to safety and staying behind to join their units; parents sending their children to relations in the west of Belgium which, they thought, must be safe in this war."

The blowing of the bridges caused great damage in the confined spaces of the city, debris falling two or three hundred yards from the bridges. There was rubble and glass everywhere. Lock-gates had, according to orders and presumably because of the risk of flooding elsewhere on the front, been left intact. These provided crossing places for intrusive infantry to find and exploit. They were, of course, wired and covered by small-arms fire, and so when enemy attempts were made to cross on "A" Company's front about 11.30 p.m. that night they were easily stopped by fire from No. 7 Platoon.

A warning order for withdrawal was received at 9.30 p.m. from Headquarters 11th Infantry Brigade. The actual withdrawal started at 11.55 p.m., companies pulling out just as enemy shelling and mortaring was increasing considerably.

The ensuing march was a long one—twenty-five miles—before the 2nd Essex got to its next bivouac area at Aspeleares. The night had been without particular incident, and the withdrawal from the canal line effected without loss, except that "A" Company cooks'

30-cwt lorry was bogged down and had to be abandoned. Later, Captain Sheffield replaced this loss by salvaging one found by the roadside.

Once during the night the Essex column was fired on by a M.G. platoon of the Middlesex, but as soon as this opposition had been silenced by a verbal burst of unmistakable Essex, the march continued without incident. Two men had, however, been wounded.

Aspeleares was reached about midday the 18th May, and here the Battalion was joined by No. 9 Platoon (2/Lieutenant P. J. Green) from refugee duty in Brussels. This platoon claimed to have shot down one aircraft.

On the evening of 18th May Lieutenant-Colonel A. H. Blest, whose car accident injuries were now turning septic, had to be evacuated, and Major Wilson again assumed command. Major Doherty became Second-in-Command, and Major Newbold became O.C. "C" Company.

In the afternoon the Battalion was retransferred to the 25th Infantry Brigade with orders to march the night 18th/19th May to Lebeeke. On arrival it was to take up positions in reserve to the brigade which was then holding a defensive position on the west bank of the River Dendre at Ninove, about thirteen miles west of Brussels. At 6 p.m. that evening they marched as ordered, and took up positions with "D" and "B" Companies forward and "C" and "A" in reserve, with counter-attack roles to north and south of Ninove. Just before they moved, they were machine-gunned from the air whilst lying up in an orchard, and a little later had over their heads one of the biggest and longest concentrations of British artillery fire of this phase of the war. There was spasmodic enemy shelling and M.G. fire during the night, but no casualties were incurred.

At 3 a.m., the 19th May, after verbal orders from 25th Infantry Brigade, company commanders were given orders to withdraw at 8.30 a.m. A report at first light that enemy snipers or fifth columnists were firing into the rear area of the Battalion was investigated by a section of carriers under Sergeant Taylor. The house was located and a few grenades thrown, but finding no traces of enemy occupation the section then withdrew. At the same time as this fracas in the rear area, forward companies were signalling "enemy in sight," but no attack developed, and at 8.30 a.m. the withdrawal started as ordered. By 9.15 a.m. the rear elements of "B" and "D" Companies were successfully withdrawn in face of considerable shell fire on the forward areas.

The Battalion then had an unpleasant forced march of twelve miles back to Sottegen, being bombed and shelled for the greater part of the way, luckily, and almost incredibly, without casualties. "It was amazing that we had no casualties in this march," writes Captain H. F. H. Jones. "I saw the foreleg of a cart-horse removed by a shell within not many yards of the leading troops of the Battalion." During this march the carriers and Brigade Anti-Tank Company, under Captain A. J. M. Parry, formed the rear party to the 25th Brigade. At Sottegen the "Pompadours" were met by Brigadier Ramsden with a collection of troop-carrying vehicles, and having embussed at 1.30 p.m., moved off eventually to debus at Belleghem Bosche.

The original destination, believed to have been Sottegen Straat, was changed after the column was on the move. As a result of this and because of the congested state of the roads, the Battalion got badly dispersed, detachments reporting in at the final destination of Belleghem Bosche at varying times between 6 p.m. and midnight. Captain H. F. H. Jones says, "Not having heard of the new destination, I found myself in a village with Major Wilson, the Battalion office-truck, all the cooks' lorries, R.S.M. Sutton, and a few others. In the same village were the headquarters of a Royal West Kent Battalion who were preparing for a battle which seemed imminent. However, we reached Belleghem Bosche at about midnight, the rest of the Battalion having been found by Major Wilson, who guided us to the Battalion rendezvous."

The night was comparatively quiet, and the majority of the Battalion got some rest during the early hours while reconnaissances were being made to prepare Belleghem Wood for defence.

The orders for the morning of the 20th May allowed for two alternative roles: (a) a further withdrawal, (b) the formation of a strong-point which would be defended to the last round and the last man. This second role pleased everybody, for the "Pompadours" were tired of constant withdrawal before a somewhat nebulous enemy, and a chance to fight was eagerly awaited. But the opportunity was not to be given, and at 5 p.m. another withdrawal was ordered.

It was difficult at battalion level to know the whole picture and to appreciate the necessity for continual withdrawal when little was being seen of one's enemy. But on the larger canvas at divisional, corps, and army level the reason was clear. The sweep of the mass of the German armies through the Ardennes to Sedan, on to St. Quentin and the line of the River Somme and northwards to the Channel ports, was already becoming apparent. The B.E.F., if it delayed and stood to fight, might well be isolated from its Allies and cut off from its base ports. The extent of the German success did in fact become known to the Battalion that day. Private J. R. Treleaven noted, "On the 20th the incredible information was passed round that the enemy had occupied Arras."

And so, in accordance with orders, the Battalion embussed at 11 p.m., at Belleghem, and was routed via Aalbeke–Tournai–Lille–Seclin to Don, where it arrived at 6 a.m., the 21st May, after a tedious and much-intermixed journey. This series of night moves with no lights was by now placing a very heavy strain on the M.T. drivers, who were getting very tired.

At Don the 2nd Essex was at once ordered to take up defensive positions at the bridges over the L'Haute Deule and La Bassee Canals with Battalion Headquarters at Meurchin. The wheel had turned full circle, and the "Pompadours," greatly to their surprise, found themselves back to where they had started their advance into Belgium on the evening of the 12th May. The full seriousness of the situation was now realised by everyone.

The Battalion was allotted a sector of approximately four and a half miles with nine bridges to defend and "blow" when ordered. It was a very long frontage, and linear defence with no depth was the only solution. "A" Company (Captain J. F. Cramphorn) was on the right flank with a company frontage of approximately 2,000 yards and two bridges to defend. Its general area was Salome–Bauvin. Touch was gained with the 7th Queen's on the exposed flank. "D" Company (Major H. F. Howell), less one platoon under 2/Lieutenant M. V. Foy, had a frontage of about 1,000 yards and one bridge south of Bauvin. "B" Company (Captain H. F. H. Jones) had 2,000 yards and three bridges (two road and one railway) in the vicinity of Meurchin to defend, whilst "C" Company (Major L. A. Newbold) held the area Pont-à-Vendin–Esteuelles, with three bridges and 2,500 yards of front to look after.

To complicate matters, on the 21st May the supply system which had been becoming increasingly difficult finally broke down. The Battalion had to live on what could be commandeered locally and what could be obtained from the Quartermaster's (Lieutenant E. H. Crane) daily sweep round abandoned supply dumps, some of which were as far as seventy-five miles from the Battalion's position.

The 21st and 22nd May, 1940, were quiet, and there was as yet no sign of the enemy. Full advantage was taken of the time available to strengthen the platoon localities on the canal line and to store food, water, and ammunition with each section post.

The outlook for the defence improved when, during the 22nd May, the 162nd Battery R.A. (25-pounders) was placed under Battalion command. During the day, too, the French 12*ieme* Cuirassiers with some 75-mm. field guns withdrew over the bridges in the Battalion defence area and were incorporated into the defence plan.

During the 22nd May it had become evident that, although the bridges were to be destroyed, the barges lying in the canals at various points constituted a danger to the defence, offering as they did a potential means of crossing to the enemy. Steps were taken to burn and sink as many as possible, but as this was a long task and unlikely to be completed in the time available, the remainder were towed by carriers to the Essex bank of the canal and there secured.

Of this period Captain Cramphorn writes:

"We dug in fast. A battery of French 75s appeared commanded by a very fine type of French officer, very different to some French infantry who superimposed themselves on 'A' Company positions and who had no heart for fighting. They would insist, though, on firing their rifles at the least provocation, much to my annoyance, as we had been to considerable pains to conceal ourselves and only shot when there was something to shoot at.

"I was not alone, I know, in being worried about the pile up of barges in the canal. Even when the bridges should be blown, they would make crossing the canal very easy. We got permission finally to burn such of them as we could, and a rare old blaze they made, too, Lieutenant P. J. Green unfortunately burning himself in the process. In addition, a troop of 4·5 howitzers firing at point-blank range came in useful for the same purpose."

The shortage of rations did not immediately affect "A" Company, whose C.Q.M.S. (Bullemore) had found an abandoned N.A.A.F.I., and come back laden with good things. The Mayor of Berclin, who lived just across the main bridge in "A" Company area, gave Captain Cramphorn "fifty old hens which, tough as they were, made a very good and welcome dinner for the Company." "B" Company, too, had varying experience with the attached French troops, being full of praise for the Cuirassiers, but not so enthusiastic about a detachment of Moroccan machine-gunners who "were very trigger-happy and were a source of considerable anxiety to us. About the only time when they did not open up was when an enemy motor-cyclist appeared on the far bank of the canal."

At 2.10 a.m. on the 23rd May, 162 Battery opened up and brought down defensive fire, but it was a false alarm, as no S.O.S. signal had been made. The rest of the night passed peacefully, as did the following morning.

The enemy was, however, near. The civilian evacuation of the Battalion area started in the morning and the roads became jammed with refugees and their belongings. They did not know—nor did the 2nd Essex—that the way to the west was barred. Ten German armoured divisions, striking round the southern flank of the B.E.F., and then turning northwards, were already north of St. Pol, a bare thirty miles to the south-west of La Bassée. At the same time elements of the Sixth German Army advancing in the general direction of Lille from Brussels and Louvain were pressing against the B.E.F. from the east.

In the afternoon of the 23rd May, as the enemy approached, seven out of the nine bridges in the Battalion area were blown. Only the two main road bridges at Meurchin ("B" Company) and Pont-à-Vendin ("C" Company) were left for the moment for the passage of British, French, and Belgian rear-guards. The destruction of the bridges was successful except for one that remained passable by infantry, but not by tanks. Of this Captain Jones says:

"The railway bridge for which 'B' Company was responsible was to be blown by French sappers. Unfortunately, they had celebrated the success of their demolition before they had achieved it. When the order came to blow the bridge nothing happened, and the French sappers were much too far gone to take any effective action. A 4·5 howitzer was brought up and fired at point-blank range at this large steel bridge without the slightest effect. Some British engineers arrived and made a very fine job of demolishing it at short notice, but it was still passable to infantry, so we arranged the largest possible number of booby-traps with anti-tank mines."

At 6 p.m. that evening first contact with the enemy was gained when an enemy armoured car approached "A" Company posts on the right of the Battalion area, and opened fire from about 1,000 yards. It was a reconnaissance. Some of the vehicle crew dismounted and made their way towards the canal, but being brought under rifle-grenade fire in their observation post they were forced to withdraw. The A.F.V. then made off.

At 6.40 p.m., Battalion Headquarters and Headquarters Company in Meurchin were subjected to a dive-bombing attack, some fifteen to twenty bombs being dropped, causing casualties and damage. 2/Lieutenant A. J. Baines was killed and 9 other ranks wounded. The petrol dump, with 500 gallons of Captain Sheffield's hardly acquired petrol, went up, and one vehicle was damaged. It is of interest that cover from this attack was available in concrete shelters built by the Germans in 1914 and 1915 at the battles of La Bassée and Loos.

Shortly after this attack Pont-à-Vendin was dive-bombed and an ammunition train set on fire, but that was the end of activity for the evening. There is little doubt that many of these attacks were based on information supplied by fifth columnists and other spies. About this time the Battalion Intelligence Officer, 2/Lieutenant G. C. Meares, had a record bag of 10 suspected priests before breakfast. How many were genuine was never proved.

Just before dark on the evening of the 23rd May, Battalion Headquarters was visited by a liaison officer from a six-vehicle French armoured-car unit which was patrolling the Battalion front from across the canal. The "French officer was confident, efficient, and practical."

On the morning of the 24th May the two remaining bridges were successfully blown, and by the afternoon many refugees had assembled on the far banks of the canal. Some attempted to cross by raft, and all formed a serious obstacle to the efficient fire of the forward defences. Soon after the road bridge at Meurchin had been blown, a field park company of Royal Engineers arrived on the far side. They ferried their light transport across, and "A" Company then crossed to investigate the abandoned heavy vehicles, handsomely augmenting their rations and obtaining a supply of new boots. Steps were taken to demolish the vehicles, but before this could be done effectively an enemy motor-cyclist, followed shortly afterwards by two armoured cars, arrived on the canal line. These were engaged with small-arms fire and anti-tank rifles, but the armoured cars withdrew without visible damage.

At about 6 p.m., the enemy reconnaissance of "A" Company's sector was repeated, but the A.F.V. was engaged by the anti-tank platoon under 2/Lieutenant D. G. Calvert, who reported that it burst into flames after the third shot from the 25-mm. gun. Several enemy motor-cyclists were hit, their machines damaged, and the crews forced to take cover in the woods. Covered by fire from one of his platoon posts, 2/Lieutenant A. S. Irwin, accompanied by Private C. T. V. Clarke, then crossed the canal by rowing boat and made his way up to the damaged motor bicycles to return with two maps and a machine gun. Shortly afterwards several armoured cars appeared and were engaged, one car being put out of action. For this operation 2/Lieutenant Irwin was awarded the Military Cross and Private Clarke the Military Medal.

Later that night a private of the 2nd Cameronians came in through a "C" Company post. He had been captured near Vimy and had escaped when the armoured cars came under fire. He had been wounded by the Essex fire, but nevertheless managed to swim the canal to give much valuable information.

During the 25th May the enemy continued the same procedure, sending armoured cars at intervals to reconnoitre the canal. But the "Pompadours" were not to give battle on La Bassée Canal line. After virtually getting no sleep at all since leaving Brussels over a week before, they were relieved during the afternoon of the 25th May by the 2/5th Leicesters.

After a short period in bivouac they marched through the evening and night to Camphin and on to reach Fromelles about midday on the 26th. During this march Private Treleaven says that Lieutenant Abbay, infuriated at the apparent immunity of the enemy aircraft, "took a shot with a rifle at a receding bomber. He might as well have used a pea shooter, though it probably eased his feelings." Most probably the main idea was to make the platoon laugh and give them something to talk about, for men were getting very tired, and there was increasing bewilderment at the constant retreat under bombing and shell fire with never a chance to retaliate.

At Fromelles the Battalion had a short rest that afternoon, but there was little for the officers. The 2nd Essex had been given a counter-attack role and reconnaissances had to be made. The Battalion task was to counter-attack to assist the withdrawal of the 1st Royal Scots from round Le Paradis (south of Merville) or that of a battalion of the Norfolk Regiment from Neuve Chapelle.

On the 27th May the shape of things to come was apparent. The Germans had reached the Channel, and Calais and Boulogne were invested. Other German forces had turned north-east, and were pressing in towards Gravelines, Cassel, Merville, La Bassée, and Lille. The escape of the B.E.F. hung in the balance.

At 4 a.m., the 27th May, 1940, 6 officers, 1 warrant officer, and 1 non-commissioned officer left for Dunkirk by truck for evacuation to England. Among those who were sent were Major Doherty, Captain Parry, Lieutenant Abbay, and 2/Lieutenant Irwin. They were in general the "seconds-in-command." Their role was to form the nucleus of a new 2nd Battalion The Essex Regiment should the enemy's will prevail. The more senior officers remained to lead the Battalion in the heavy fighting that was expected. The Quartermaster, Lieutenant E. H. Crane, was also detailed for the cadre party but was held up and did not get away. Orderly Room Quartermaster-Sergeant G. Reeman went with the party.

At 9 a.m. the 2nd Essex was ordered to move by M.T., and route march to Vierhouck (four miles north of Merville) and take up a defensive position facing the Forêt de Nieppe. As the Battalion was concentrating in Fromelles before the start of the move, an artillery column, jammed in the village street, was dive-bombed. Bombs fell on part of the Battalion transport, destroying three Bren carriers, two 15-cwt. trucks, and a lorry. However, the loss in vehicles was not unduly serious, as Captain Sheffield had specialised in collecting abandoned vehicles during the retreat and at the moment had eight surplus to establishment in the M.T. column.

At 4.30 p.m., the 27th May, the Battalion debussed near Vierhouck, having been continuously attacked *en route* by low-flying aircraft. But their luck had held good and only 3 other ranks had been wounded. As they debussed, companies took up defensive positions in the area of the village of L'Epinette, in touch with the 1st Royal Berkshires on the right. Moving into their positions, "A" and "B" Companies were soon attacked by enemy armoured cars which debouched from the Forêt de Nieppe. Their orders had been to seize and hold L'Epinette cross-roads, and the German A.F.V.s must have had the same orders, for they arrived almost simultaneously. There was a sharp action, in which 2/Lieutenant Jennings and 3 other ranks were wounded. Despite the fact that small arms and anti-tank rifles seemingly had no effect, they must have been some deterrent, for the armoured cars withdrew, whereupon "A" and "B" Companies proceeded to dig in as quickly as possible and put the hamlet into a state of all-round defence.

Captain Jones speaks of the action when he says:

"'B' Company had debussed, and I had gone forward to see Captain Cramphorn, whom I found in the village, when the A.F.V.s arrived and opened fire. 'A' Company opened up with all Bren guns, but I do not remember that their anti-tank rifles were in action. On John Cramphorn's orders I personally ran back to my own company, picked up an anti-tank rifle, and was able to get into position in a farmyard facing the A.F.V.s, which was not a very good direction from which to fire at them, and rested the rifle on the top of a car standing in the farmyard. Sergeant Bradford of 'A' Company was in the farmyard at the time. A private from 'B' Company who was carrying ammunition and running behind me was shot so I had to use ammunition from 'A' Company, and after a few minutes the A.F.V.s turned round and withdrew. I doubt whether my personal efforts had any effect at all. I think it was probably the hail of Bren-gun fire which checked them."

The whole Battalion was now under continuous long-range artillery and machine-gun fire. During the late evening the 8th King's Own Royal Regiment withdrew through the left of the Essex positions. It was an eerie night, for the enemy were all around in the darkness, which was lit only by the glare of numerous fires burning in villages and towns at all points of the compass. The front was fluid, and "A" Company, over a quarter of a mile from "B" Company, felt somewhat isolated.

At 12.30 a.m., the 28th May, the 2nd Essex was ordered to withdraw immediately, an order that gave a small qualm of anxiety to Lieutenant-Colonel Wilson, for the "Pompadours" had outmarched their supply of official maps, and only a Michelin motorists' road map remained to guide the Battalion on the last stages of the withdrawal. There were some nasty moments in companies before platoons got to their rendezvous and the withdrawal could start. They were now heading for Le Doulieu, where a fresh defensive position was to be taken up in touch with the 2/7th Queens. The line was by now facing almost due south, with Dunkirk and the coast some thirty or more miles to the north.

At first light on the 28th May, "I was marching with 'B' Company to rejoin the rest of the battalion," says Captain Jones, "with 'A' Company not far behind, and met Brigadier Ramsden in pouring rain. He looked very damp and depressed, but when I told him we were 'A' and 'B' Companies, 2nd Essex, he immediately cheered up and said, 'Good. Now we've got some troops we'll make a plan. I wasn't sure that I should be seeing you again.'"

With daylight came signs of real retreat—hospitals being evacuated, numerous abandoned vehicles, fires, and stragglers. The morning wireless gave the news of the capitulation of Belgium. The "Pompadours" were hardly into their defence position at Le Doulieu before they were ordered out. This time they were to form the rear-guard to the 25th Brigade on the march to Watou, where the brigade would hold a defensive line Watou-Poperinghe facing south.

It was the beginning of the end. Enemy armoured vehicles were reported at Meteren, and the Battalion deployed for local defence. There was no attack, but a portion of the Battalion "A" Echelon transport here had to be abandoned, for it was impossible to get it on the move again, such was the congestion on the roads. The vehicles were set on fire and completely destroyed.

At Berthen, a few miles farther on, other vehicles were destroyed, as enemy action had blocked all roads. Captain Sheffield was here told to get his truck, the Battalion water-carts, and the ration truck to the beaches if humanly possible. "I think Wilson knew this order was safe," he says, "as I hate walking. Anyway, we got them there after driving over fields and anywhere to get them round bombed villages and shelled roads.

"I passed Henry Boustead (Major H. L. H. Boustead) and offered him a lift which he refused. He was now dressed in his riding boots, breeches, serge jacket, and Sam Browne belt, having changed and left his battledress for the Germans." (Major Boustead was at the time attached to Headquarters 2nd Corps, and was withdrawing as part of that formation headquarters.)

By 2 a.m., the 29th May, the "Pompadours" reached Watou. They were now extremely tired and very foot-weary, but still in great heart. Here took place the tragic episode of burning the Drums to prevent them falling into enemy hands. The last of the secret and important documents were also burned.

At 6 a.m., the 29th, fresh orders were issued. The 2nd Essex was to march to Dunkirk by way of Houtkerque, Oustcappel, and Bergues. No halts were to be permitted, and the Battalion, marching in rearguard order, was to get to the beaches as best it could. A state of confusion existed. A whole French horse-drawn artillery regiment had turned its horses loose and spiked its guns by the road-side. French and British stragglers were everywhere; thus the Battalion became very intermixed with other units and drawn out. Each man had been given a tin of bully beef and a packet of biscuits for that last twenty-four hours, and it just kept them going.

Between noon and 4 p.m. on the 29th May the main body of the

"Pompadours" had reached the Dunkirk Beaches. A roll-call showed that 11 officers and 430 other ranks were present. Most had retained their personal arms and equipment, and those without were easily fitted from cast-off equipment and arms.

This bald statement can only give the plain facts. It cannot hope to depict the chaotic last hours of retreat, during which time platoon got separated from company and section from platoon under the relentless pressure of the retreating thousands, all squeezed together by constant A.F.V. activity on the flanks and under threat of attack from the air. Nor can it hope to paint that epic of battalion pride when, on the very beaches of Dunkirk, the temporarily scattered "Pompadours" regathered to stand, aloof from the tens of thousands around them, to wait as on a battalion parade-ground for the shout of "Right Markers," and then to fall in, to stand once more "The 'Pompadours.' Present and correct."

We are fortunate in having three first-hand accounts of these hours. First, from Captain G. N. H. Sheffield, who, with his surviving M.T. party, reached the beaches some twenty-four hours ahead of the Battalion, then from Captain J. F. Cramphorn, who came to the beaches with "A" Company and the Battalion main body, and finally from Captain H. F. H. Jones, who brought "B" Company to the seashore.

Captain Sheffield with the M.T. was at Dunkirk ahead of the marching columns. "Having arrived at Dunkirk we were ordered to destroy our vehicles (thank God they were not horses) and then proceed to the sands, where every officer had to collect a party of 50 other ranks of any regiment, form up in the queue, and move towards the harbour. To my amazement 2 of my drivers who had been missing since they took back the cadre party from Fromelles turned up. They had been looking for me for four days.

"We had been there about twenty-four hours when Wilson turned up! He then got hold of all Essex officers he could find. We were warned to find as many Essex men as possible and rendezvous on the Dunes above the Beaches. This was not too popular in some cases, as some were by now well up the embarkation queues.

"Eventually we collected about 400. We then called 'Right Markers' (my first and last time as Adjutant of the 'Pompadours'); we held a roll-call to the best of our ability, and maintained them all together until we embarked——"

Captain Cramphorn, too: "I was told by a strange Brigadier to collect 50 men—the first 50 I came across—and take them to the end of the queue, which by that time was some miles long. So 'A' Company Headquarters, with 50 strange soldiers of many regiments, took its place in the mass of humanity waiting for ships. And then a thing happened which was almost unbelievable. Among those tens of thousands, No. 9 Section, complete with all its arms, clean and in good order, reported, closely followed by the rest of 9 Platoon. Then came the rest of the Company, by sections and by ones and twos, and so in no time we were nearly complete again. Later in the afternoon 'B' Company was there, and before nightfall the Battalion, almost to a man, was there."

Captain Jones carries on the narrative:

"I can confirm the complete confusion on the roads on the 29th May. I did my best to keep "B" Company together, but we became inextricably mixed with other troops. Eventually John Watson, my Second-in-Command, found an old bicycle, and I asked him to go on ahead to the beaches and to try to form a rallying point and to get the Company together. This he did, and I found myself on the beach eventually with about 50 men of the Company, and quite a number of men from other companies. The bombing was very heavy and every ship which appeared in sight was hit by dive-bombers. Some were sunk, and I remember seeing a destroyer in smoke and flame making its way over the horizon."

Meals during those last days on the beaches were mainly composed of hard biscuit, bully, condensed milk, and chocolate foraged from abandoned N.A.A.F.I. stores. Lieutenant-Colonel Wilson remarks that he was astonished to see the Officers' Mess Corporal, L/Corporal Dyer, appear with the Officers' Mess truck on the beach. How he had got it there only L/Corporal Dyer can tell, but unfortunately the officers could not take a meal from the truck, as would have been a fitting end to such an Odyssey.

That evening heavy and sustained dive-bombing attacks were made on ships and beaches. The men were very steady, although bombs fell all round the areas where the Battalion was lying, Private Gridley being killed. The night was chill but uneventful, except for the frequent moves along the beach towards the Mole as troops ahead were taken on board.

On the morning of the 30th May the 2nd Essex was allotted a serial number for embarkation. Rolls were called, arms and equipment checked, and water-bottles filled from houses nearby.

About 3 p.m., that afternoon, the 2nd Essex embarked from Dunkirk

Mole in the destroyer *Whitehall*. Movement along the Mole was at the double, and anti-aircraft Brens were manned the minute the unit was on board. Sailing immediately, *Whitehall* was subjected to frequent bombing from about 4 p.m. to 6 p.m. She was not hit, and about 8 p.m., the 30th May, 1940, entered Dover Harbour.

The "Pompadours" were home.

They had retained their identity all through the rigours and difficulties of the retreat. They landed in England each man armed and equipped. It was not until they were taken in detachments by various trains to different destinations in England and Scotland that the 2nd Essex lost identity.

They had had 1 officer and 1 other rank killed, 1 officer and 18 other ranks wounded, and 53 other ranks missing. The small casualty list is a tribute to the discipline and cohesion of the Battalion, which had kept together as a unit through all the difficulties of a long retreat. Had discipline and battalion spirit been less strong, the casualty list might well have been much longer.

A short paragraph must suffice to record the adventures of No. 16 Platoon which, it will be remembered, left the Battalion on the morning of the 15th May under 2/Lieutenant M. V. Foy, to act as defence platoon at 2nd Corps Headquarters.

The platoon joined Corps Headquarters near the site of the Brussels Exhibition, and early on the morning of the 16th May hit with Brengun fire one of the engines of a low-flying German bomber which came down about one and a half miles away. Another bomber was claimed by the platoon the following day at Terlingden.

By the 20th May the withdrawal had taken the platoon back to Armentières, where Corps Headquarters was heavily bombed, and then on to Abeele by the 24th May.

From Abeele, on the 25th May, the platoon was moved to Vinckem, where it was sent to guard stores being washed up on the shore near Nieuport. For three days food and water were extremely scarce, and at one time German patrols, penetrating to the coast, isolated the platoon from the nearest British troops at La Panne.

The period 28th–31st May was spent at La Panne engaged in A.A. defence, a long three days which terminated when, on the 1st June, No. 16 Platoon was ordered to march to Le Bray. Here, at 10 p.m. that evening, it was embarked in the cross-Channel steamer *Princess Elizabeth* and landed during the night 1st/2nd June on Margate Pier.

A short narrative must also suffice to remember those of the "Pompadours" who in formed bodies or as individuals made their way to England after the evacuation from Dunkirk had ended.

There was, for example, the Reinforcement Company, 2nd Essex, left in Brest in October 1939 when the Battalion moved up to the Belgian frontier, and which moved in April to the Rouen Infantry base depot.

In mid-May, when it became clear that reinforcements could no longer reach units withdrawing through Belgium, this Company, now under Major D. R. Gahagan, was sent first fifty miles by road to Bernay, and then by train to La Hutte.

The march to Bernay was completed between the morning of the 21st May and the evening of the 22nd. The march was difficult because of the movement of much transport, numerous stragglers, and general chaos. Despite all difficulties there was not one straggler from the "Pompadours" Company which marched, in perfect order, into Bernay to receive much congratulation from commanders and staffs for the example of discipline they had set the thousands of troops withdrawing from Rouen.

At La Hutte the Company became part of a mixed battalion ("Syme" Battalion) which joined Beauman Division. This, to quote Winston S. Churchill's *The Second World War* (Vol. II, "Their Finest Hour"), was a composite force "scraped together from the bases and lines of communication in France. It consisted of nine improvised infantry battalions. Armed mainly with rifles, and very few anti-tank weapons, it had neither transport nor signals."

Major Gahagan became Second-in-Command of "Syme" Battalion. "A" (Essex) Company was officered by Captain R. H. A. Painter, Lieutenant D. W. Browne, and 2/Lieutenant H. J. B. Petit-Dann.

On the 7th June "Syme" Battalion was in action astride the road Rouen–Forges in the area of Le Bourguet, some five kilometres north of Rouen. The German advance was checked, but not halted. During the 8th June "Syme" Battalion was withdrawn west of the River Seine. Complete chaos was experienced at the bridges, but by the night 8th/9th June the bulk of the Battalion had reached a rendezvous to the south-east of Rouen. The Essex Company was now without officers as Captain Painter and 2/Lieutenant Petit-Dann had been forced to cross the Seine by the lower of the two bridges in Rouen, and had lost touch with the Company. Lieutenant Browne was still east of the river when the bridges were blown. It was the 13th June before he rejoined. In the interval he had carried out valuable reconnaissance work for elements of the 1st Armoured Division.

APPOINTMENTS 2ND ESSEX,

Appointment	Mobilisation	Operations Culminating at Dunkirk
Commanding Officer	Lieutenant-Colonel A. H. Blest	A/Lieutenant-Colonel C. L. Wilson, M.C.
Second-in-Command	Major C. L. Wilson, M.C.	Major T. O.'C. Doherty
Adjutant	Captain T. L. G. Charles	Captain P. C. Hinde
Quartermaster	Lieutenant E. H. Crane	Lieutenant E. H. Crane
I.O.	2/Lieutenant G. C. Meares	2/Lieutenant G. C. Meares
R.S.M.	R.S.M. A. F. Sutton	R.S.M. A. F. Sutton
R.Q.M.S.	R.Q.M.S. J. Bathurst	R.Q.M.S. T. Gagen
O.C. H.Q. Company	Major H. L. H. Boustead	Captain G. N. H. Sheffield
M.T. Officer	Captain G. N. H. Sheffield	Captain G. N. H. Sheffield
Signal Officer	Lieutenant G. M. M. L. Petre	Lieutenant G. L. M. Petre
		2/Lieutenant D. E. Long-Price (Battalion Liaison Officer)
O.C. "A" Company	Captain E. C. Vander Kiste	Captain J. F. Cramphorn
	Lieutenant H. F. H. Jones	
O.C. "B" Company	Major T. E. Hearn	2/Lieutenant G. H. Watson
	Captain P. C. Hinde	Captain H. F. H. Jones
	2/Lieutenant G. H. Watson	
O.C. "C" Company	Major T. O'C. Doherty	Major T. O'C. Doherty
	Captain R. H. A. Painter	Major L. A. Newbold
	2/Lieutenant A. S. Irwin	
O.C. "D" Company	Major H. F. Howell	Major H. F. Howell
	Lieutenant R. L. Fountain	Lieutenant R. L. Fountain
	2/Lieutenant M. V. Foy	2/Lieutenant M. V. Foy
		2/Lieutenant P. J. Green
		2/Lieutenant G. H. Watson
		2/Lieutenant A. S. Irwin
		2/Lieutenant D. B. Jennings
		2/Lieutenant D. G. Calvert
		2/Lieutenant P. R. Barrass
	First Reinforcement Company	Major D. R. Gahagan
		2/Lieutenant D. W. Browne
		2/Lieutenant H. J. B. Petit-Dann

SEPTEMBER 1939–MAY 1940

Remarks

Vice *Lieutenant-Colonel Blest*, evacuated sick, 18th May, 1940.

Vice *Major Wilson*, to Commanding Officer, 18th May, 1940.
Vice *Captain Charles*, to Staff Course, January 1940.

—
—

Vice *R.Q.M.S. Bathurst*, to Headquarters 2nd Corps, 9th December, 1939.
Vice *Major Boustead*, detached for duty Headquarters 2nd Corps.
—
Sent to U.K. with cadre party, 27th May, 1940.

Vice *Major Vander Kiste*, to U.K., January 1940.

Major Hearn to U.K. (sick), September 1939. *Captain R. H. A. Painter*, O.C. "B" Company, but absent U.K. on leave on 19th May, 1940, and unable to rejoin. *2/Lieutenant Watson*, O.C. "B" Company, 10th–19th May, 1940. *Captain Jones*, O.C. "B" Company, 20th–30th May, 1940.

Captain Painter to O.C. "B" Company, September 1939. *Major Doherty*, O.C. "C" Company, to 18th May, 1940, when he became Second-in-Command; went to U.K. with cadre party, 27th May, 1940. *Major Newbold* became O.C. "C" Company, 18th May, 1940. *2/Lieutenant Irwin*, to U.K. with cadre party, 27th May, 1940.

Major Howell remained O.C. "D" Company until 27th May, 1940, when he became Battalion Second-in-Command vice *Major Doherty* to U.K. *Lieutenant Fountain* took command 28th–30th May, 1940. *2/Lieutenant Foy* to Headquarters 2nd Corps as defence platoon Commander 15th May, 1940.

"Syme" Battalion withdrew from defensive positions along the River Risle near Pont Audemer through Pont L'Eveque, Caen, Bayeux, to reach Cherbourg on the 16th June. From Cherbourg the Battalion was embarked to reach Southampton on the 18th June.

The 2nd Battalion was to be awarded for these operations one Military Cross (2/Lieutenant A. S. Irwin), one M.B.E. (Captain G. N. H. Sheffield), one D.C.M. (Regimental Sergeant-Major A. F. Sutton), and three Military Medals (L/Corporal C. T. V. Clarke, Sergeant L. J. Head, and Private P. P. Lorraine). Private G. Andrews, Lieutenant-Colonel A. H. Blest, 2/Lieutenant D. W. Browne, Private S. H. Coffee, Captain J. F. Cramphorn, Company Sergeant-Major W. Green, Company Sergeant-Major R. Lewis, Captain W. S. Smith, and Major C. L. Wilson, M.C., were all mentioned in dispatches for distinguished services.

Section III

HOME DEFENCE AND PREPARATION FOR THE COUNTER-OFFENSIVE, JUNE 1940–JUNE 1944

It is not proposed to tell in great detail the story of the 2nd Essex in the period that lay between the withdrawal from Dunkirk and the landings in Normandy four years later. The story is that of every unit in the home base. Re-equipment and slow rearmament; the Battle of Britain; the threat of invasion; beach defence, coast defence, aerodrome defence, and defence of every kind of vital areas from seashore to far inland. Then the swing-over from defence to offence. Battle-schools and battle-drills, schools and courses, Exercise "Bumper," Exercise "Bulldog," Exercise "This" and Exercise "That," culminating in the strains and hardships of Exercise "Eagle."

And then at last—Operation "Overlord," the landings in Normandy.

It is, however, necessary to tell in outline the story of those years, for they belong to history. And the history of the 2nd Battalion in those years must also be recorded.

On its arrival at Dover, the Battalion had been dispersed to reception stations all over the country from Aberdeen to Bulford. On the 3rd June, 1940, the Headquarters of the 2nd Essex reopened at Tatton Park Camp, Knutsford, a camp set up for the reception and re-establishment of the 50th Division, to which the 25th Infantry Brigade was now temporarily to belong. From here all ranks as they reported were

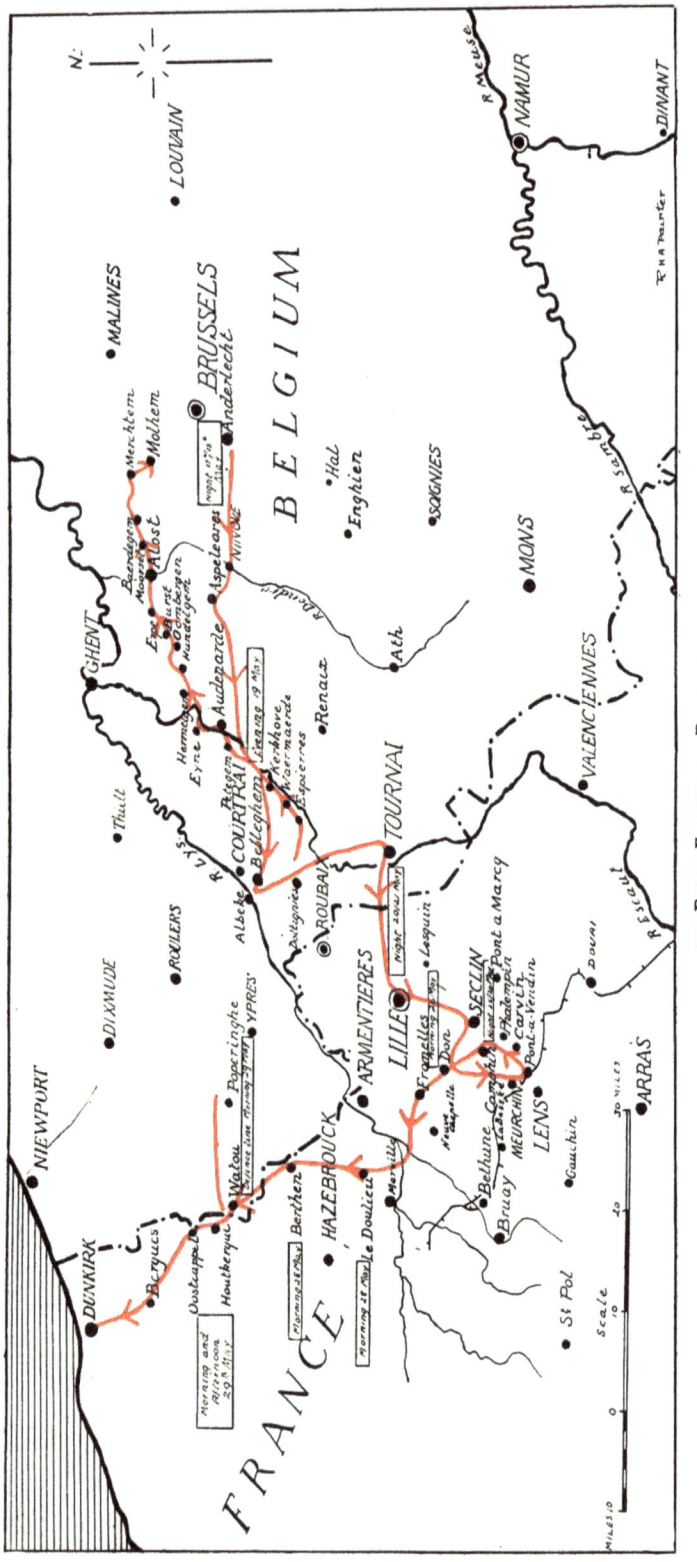

2ND ESSEX. FRANCE AND BELGIUM. 1940.

sent on disembarkation leave, with orders to return to Keele Hall, Newcastle-under-Lyme, where the 25th Infantry Brigade camp was to be established.

Here, on the 10th June, 1940, the 2nd Essex, again under command of Lieutenant-Colonel A. H. Blest, began to re-form. The strength was 3 officers and 37 other ranks. But by the 27th June, returning leave parties and fresh drafts had brought the strength to 23 officers and 895 other ranks.

It was not until the 29th June that any re-equipping of the Battalion was possible. Although each man had brought home his rifle from the Low Countries, it had not proved possible to save all Brens, mortars, and anti-tank rifles. So short were supplies that the first allocation over four weeks after landing in England was only to be ten Bren guns and three anti-tank rifles. Men in those days were more easily obtained than the weapons with which to arm them.

On the 3rd July, 1940, the first of that long series of moves that was to mark the years at home took place, a move to Kington, Herefordshire, with other units of the 25th Infantry Brigade. The work was unceasing, its nature dictated by the needs of the moment. Physical fitness, practice in tank-hunting, dealing with parachute troops, and instruction for the Home Guard were all sandwiched between battalion, brigade, and divisional exercises. Invasion was possible and everyone was at high pressure.

In common with every other unit in the British Isles, the 2nd Essex received the signal "Cromwell"—invasion imminent—on the evening of 7th September, 1940. Placed at a quarter-hour's notice to move, the Battalion stood-to, until the first drastic restrictions were removed and the more modified routine of a 10 p.m. curfew, and a ban on moving off duty more than three miles from unit headquarters was imposed. Those were stimulating days, and all ranks were on their toes ready for any emergency that might come.

With the onset of winter and the decreased risk of invasion, those restrictions were gradually lifted, but not the pressure of training. This was continuous, and it was a very fit and well-trained Battalion that moved first to Leominster and then to Worthing in the spring of 1941, where the "Pompadours" had their fill of beach protection and coast defence. At Worthing, too, on the 17th April, 1941, Lieutenant-Colonel L. W. W. Marriott took over command from Lieutenant-Colonel A. H. Blest, who had been appointed to command the 25th Infantry Brigade in succession to Brigadier E. T. L. Gurdon, M.C., injured by a beach mine which killed the Divisional Commander, Major-General C. C. Malden.

The 25th Brigade, in which the 2nd Essex still served, was now part of the 47th (London) Infantry Division, under the command of Major-General J. E. Utterson-Kelso, C.B.E., D.S.O., M.C.

At the end of June 1941, the 2nd Essex was relieved on beach defence by the 10th Royal Welch Fusiliers, and moved from Worthing back to Borde Hill Camp, Haywards Heath, for training. That this training was not without difficulties is shown by the plaintive entry in Battalion records for 19th July, 1941: "Dress rehearsal for demonstration of tank and infantry co-operation on the Downs north of Seaford completely ruined by a military policeman, who appeared on the skyline at zero hour, when the field artillery was about to fire. Rehearsal was then cancelled." However, all's well that ends well, and when the actual demonstration was given two days later, it went without a hitch, the "Pompadours" being congratulated by Lieutenant-General B. C. T. Paget, C.B., D.S.O., M.C., and by Major-General Utterson Kelso. General Paget was at the time the G.O.C.-in-C. South-eastern Command, and was shortly to become Commander-in-Chief Home Forces.

The Battalion remained hidden for months in the woods of Borde Hill, first under canvas and then in huts. But they were not to winter on Borde Hill, for just as the hutted camp was nearing completion, the 2nd Essex was relieved by the Regina Rifle Regiment of the 3rd Canadian Division, and went to Cosham, near Portsmouth, where it was quartered in Fort Widley and Fort Southwick.

Nineteen forty-one had been a year of hard training, and it was hoped to be able to note in this history some relaxation at Christmas, but Battalion records merely report coldly: "25.12.41. Commencement of 5th Corps Salvage Week."

The stay in Cosham was short, the Battalion moving, on the 5th January, 1942, to the Isle of Wight to join, on temporary loan, the 214th Infantry Brigade (Brigadier J. O. Carpenter, M.C.) and to take over the Southern Sector from the 20th Royal Welch Fusiliers. It was a difficult sector, with a frontage of fifteen miles to be held with three companies forward and one in reserve. Throughout the tour on this sector, duty platoons in forward companies were at ten minutes' notice by night. Brigadier Carpenter wrote an extremely appreciative letter to Lieutenant-Colonel Marriott when his Battalion left the 214th Brigade.

There was no relaxation of work, despite severe winter conditions, and as the length of the Battalion frontage dictated the maximum use of obstacles, the erection of tubular scaffolding beach defences was the first priority of work. A relief on the 10th March, 1942, by the 6th Oxford and Bucks Light Infantry only took the 2nd Essex to Cowes, where the role was that of mobile reserve to the forward sector. As a change, the Battalion moved across the Solent on the 17th March to take part in Exercise "Yorker," and when it returned five days later, it had covered over 400 miles. The director was Lieutenant-General C. W. Allfrey, C.B.E., M.C., who was now in command of the 5th Corps. The standard of M.T. discipline and maintenance was severely tested during the exercise, and the Battalion came through with flying colours.

Whilst at Cowes the "Pompadours" were visited by Lieutenant-General H. C. Lloyd, C.B., D.S.O., M.C., the G.O.C.-in-C. Southern Command.

They next moved to Whitwell (I.O.W.) and then, on the 6th April, to Southampton, where they were visited by Major-General G. W. R. Templer, D.S.O., O.B.E., who by now was commanding the 47th Division. The next transfer, in July 1942, was to Fairthorn Camp, Botley, followed in October by a move to New Arlesford, and there the close of 1942 was still to find them part of the 25th Infantry Brigade and the 47th (London) Division. However, by early February 1943 they were off again, this time to Barton Stacey. This was the thirteenth major move since the reassembly of the Battalion after Dunkirk. Only staying six weeks, they next went to New Milton, but by the end of May were back at Whitwell (I.O.W.) which they had left a year before.

On this tour "S" Company in the Niton area was raided by four M.E. 109s shortly after the Battalion's arrival. The Company offices and mess building were completely destroyed and 2 other ranks killed and 3 injured.

In mid-June the Battalion went to Haverfordwest and later to Tenby in Pembrokeshire, on a six weeks' visit in order to take part in Operation "Jantzen." This was a big-scale exercise for which a considerable administrative staff was necessary, the duties falling to the 2nd Essex, augmented by companies from the 31st R.W.F., and 8th Black Watch. At the conclusion of the exercise the Battalion was inspected by Major-General J. G. Halsted, who complimented all ranks on their high standard of discipline and the manner in which their administrative duties had been performed.

Towards the end of August 1943, the Battalion was once more back in the Isle of Wight, this time with headquarters at Freshwater. From there to Shanklin and back again to Freshwater by the end of September. Despite all these peregrinations, the 2nd Essex still remained part of the 25th Infantry Brigade and the 47th Division.

In December 1943 a move from Freshwater to Bournemouth proved to be the end of the series of trips to and fro across the Solent. In January 1944 the Battalion at last got away from the South Coast. The transfer took the 2nd Essex to Durham, and then to camp at Fimber to take part in Exercise "Eagle," in which the 47th (London) Division formed part of a corps representing German forces in defence which would be attacked by the 8th Corps. It was an exacting exercise in a typical North Country February, and it is understating matters to say: "Exercise Eagle gave all ranks invaluable experience under most realistic conditions."

From the training areas the Battalion returned to Durham, and then moved to Clacton to join the 56th Independent Infantry Brigade. The move severed the long connection with the 47th (London) Division. The "Bow Bells" had been the divisional sign for three years and more, and Major-General A. E. Robinson, the Divisional Commander, said a personal good-bye to the "Pompadours" at their entraining station.

Headquarters 56th Independent Infantry Brigade was at Frinton. It was commanded by Brigadier E. C. Pepper, C.B.E., and was affiliated to the 50th (Northumbrian) Division under Major-General D. A. H. Graham, C.B.E., D.S.O., M.C. The 50th Division and the 56th Independent Infantry Brigade were now part of the 21st Army Group, and they were to take part in Operation "Overlord."

Major-General Graham visited the "Pompadours" at Clacton, and while talking to some of the men he said to Corporal W. Ankrett, "And what do you think about going to the battle again?" "Well, sir," replied Ankrett, "the perishers chased me across France in 1940, and I shall be only too glad to chase them back again."

As he turned away, General Graham said to Lieutenant-Colonel Marriott, "I like the spirit and bearing of these men of yours."

One day when he was over at Brigade Headquarters Lieutenant-Colonel Marriott was asked by Brigadier Pepper for any ideas as to a brigade sign—a pepper pot had been one idea. Lieutenant-Colonel Marriott suggested a sphinx, as this was part of the badge of the Essex Regiment, the Gloucestershire Regiment, and the South Wales

Borderers. The Second Battalions of these Regiments formed the 56th Independent Infantry Brigade. The sphinx was adopted.

At Clacton, on the 15th March, 1944, the re-mobilisation of the Battalion was ordered, and a replacement of all fighting and transport vehicles took place, the unit being completed to war establishment in men and vehicles.

Then, on the 25th March, a move to Inveraray for ten days' special training in combined operations, the training of an infantry battalion of an assault brigade. The "Pompadours" had now no doubt of what lay before them.

At Inveraray the Battalion was extremely sorry to say good-bye to Lieutenant-Colonel L. W. W. Marriott who had commanded for the past three years, his place being taken by Lieutenant-Colonel J. F. Higson, M.C. A contemporary record says: "The loss of Lieutenant-Colonel Marriott, who has spent the greater part of his service with the Battalion, was deeply regretted by all ranks. His untiring efforts, together with his vast experience, have done much to maintain a high standard within the unit. His fairness and tact in all his dealings have contributed much to the good feeling within the unit."

From Inveraray the 2nd Essex moved to Christchurch, where Major G. G. Elliott, the Queen's Own Royal West Kent Regiment, joined as Second-in-Command. Here the tempo of training steadily quickened, and Exercises "Smash," "Bounder," and "Fabius" took place in quick succession. "Fabius," an amphibious exercise to test the embarkation machinery, took place in early May, and was marred for the Battalion by the death, through drowning at sea, of Major N. E. Ayres and 6 other ranks. It was the last big exercise. By mid-May the "Pompadours" were in their concentration area, where they were visited by Lieutenant-General A. H. Bucknell, C.B.E., D.S.O., M.C., the 30th Corps Commander. In the concentration area there was no relaxation in training for the battle to come. Street fighting, mine laying, and mine lifting were all practised, as best could be in the restricted space available. There were extensive night operations and much physical training to bring everyone to the last pitch of physical fitness and mental alertness.

The 1st June, 1944, found the "Pompadours" fully trained and eager to end the days of waiting. They had been behind the wire of Camp B3, at Beaulieu, since 19th May, 1944. They had not much longer to wait.

Section IV

OPERATIONS IN NORTH-WEST EUROPE, JUNE 1944–MAY 1945

Once in the concentration area the "Pompadours" began to know the details of the task that lay before them. Briefing was most thorough but closely cloaked by security measures in case a last-minute leakage of information would jeopardise the whole operation.

As D-Day approached, Lieutenant-Colonel Higson, himself now thoroughly briefed, was permitted to explain the last details to company commanders. They, in turn, briefed all ranks under their command. A briefing tent, complete with large-scale models, air photographs, maps, and a complete picture of the enemy order of battle, was set up in the camp and placed at the disposal of company commanders. Even now the secret of the actual area of operations was not disclosed below company commander level. Maps with code instead of actual names were used to brief all other officers and men. Thus, to the very last moment, the exact area of assault was unknown, although its smallest topographical detail and the size and nature of each enemy garrison were clearly understood by all ranks.

In short, the plan was as follows. The 56th Independent Infantry Brigade (Brigadier E. C. Pepper, C.B.E.) was to be attached to the 50th (Northumbrian) Division. This division, as part of 30th Corps, would assault at Arromanches, some six miles north of Bayeux, and secure a beach-head. Then the 56th Independent Infantry Brigade, landing some three to four hours after the initial assault, was to pass through the beach-head and seize the high ground to the south of Bayeux, thus extending the initial covering position. It was in furtherance of this plan that the 2nd Essex, under Lieutenant-Colonel J. F. Higson, M.C., left Pennerley Camp B3 on the 3rd June, 1944.

Major G. G. Elliott (Royal West Kent) was Second-in-Command, and Captain J. Townrow was Adjutant. Major M. W. Holme commanded "A" Company, Major E. I. Watson "B," Major P. R. Barrass "C," and Major G. M. M. L. Petre "D." Captain P. J. Chell commanded Headquarter Company and Major P. J. Wilkins the Support Company.

At Lymington the Battalion was embarked on to landing-craft infantry (large), American and Canadian vessels built specially for invasion duties. They were of light steel and manned by crews who made up in enthusiasm for their inexperience. Each L.C.I. held approximately 180 men, or approximately one and a half companies. There were four holds for the troops and a small cabin to hold 8 officers, but the latter were little used, the majority of officers being with their companies in the troop decks. On the poop deck in some vessels were stored landing rations in vast quantities and some airborne bicycles for the advanced guard.

Embarked, the Battalion moved down to Southampton Docks. It had been a short but rough passage, which tested the efficacy of "bags, vomit," and "pills, seasickness, remedial." Altogether it was not a complete surprise to hear in the dock area that the operation had been put back for twenty-four hours because of the unfavourable weather. Troops could land on to the quays to visit canteens, but otherwise were confined to their landing craft. It was an almost interminable forty-eight hours before the L.C.I.s carrying the three infantry battalions of the 56th Brigade slipped their moorings on the quayside at about 5 p.m. on the 5th June, 1944, and moved down Southampton Water to take up position in the vast armada of landing craft and warships now heading out into the English Channel.

The evening was dull and overcast, with a heavy swell running, but the crossing was to be quiet and free from enemy action, despite the fact that bombs or torpedoes could hardly fail to hit the closely ranked assault craft. Packed like sardines, the "Pompadours" drank their tins of self-heating cocoa or kidney soup, gambled or grumbled awhile, or even quietly read a paper-backed thriller, and then tried to get a few hours' sleep before the strains and excitements of the coming day.

"D" Day and the Capture of Bayeux

"We slept well that night without a worry," remarks Captain A. A. Vince, "but the morning light of the 6th June, 1944, found us very shaken by the rolling and pitching of our ship. Many of us were violently seasick...." For it was very rough in mid-Channel away from the shelter of the land, while Lightnings and Spitfires patrolled over the convoy which crawled and circled towards the shore.

Ahead, "clouds of smoke could be seen billowing upwards from the land, and battleships and cruisers, destroyers and rocket-firing craft were still pouring fire into the defences and lines of approach."

Presently the empty L.C.I.s of the assault brigade—231st Infantry

Brigade on this sector—were seen, as was the debris of the assault floating by the slowly moving landing craft.

Towards midday the message was passed back from Headquarters 50th Division telling the 56th Brigade to land, and the landing-craft began pressing into the coast-line. There was "akin to consternation when it was found that the coast-line could not be reconciled with the topography so carefully studied and memorised in Camp B3."

At 12.30 p.m. the 6th June, 1944, the "Pompadours," wearing "Mae Wests" in addition to their fighting equipment and carrying two twenty-four hours' ration packs and tommy cookers, landed without casualties on the coast of France just to the east of Le Hamel. This landing was $2\frac{1}{2}$ hours later than the plan intended, and was on the wrong beach. The Battalion assembly area had been selected, from maps and air photos, in the orchards just west of the road between Buhot and Ryes, and the Battalion should have been landed, if the original plan could have been adhered to, at 10 a.m. at Le Hamel. In actual fact the landing was some 1,500 yards east of Le Hamel, because the enemy were still holding out in the pre-selected area.

Major G. G. Elliott says: "The sea was choppy, the tide was right up to the sea wall; there was difficulty and confusion on all sides. Battalion Headquarters was, of course, divided. My L.C.I., with one half H.Q. and a company of infantry and other detachments, found a gap, and we went in successfully, though in deep water. Other craft spent some time trying to find their way into a place from which infantry and vehicles could struggle ashore."

Pressing through the debris on the beaches, the Battalion, party by party as they came ashore, made their way through the minefields to the prearranged assembly area between Buhot and Ryes, coming under some artillery and mortar fire on the way.

Major Elliott gives the story of the first four hours in Normandy when he says: "On landing we at once started off west towards Le Hamel, making our way through the rear elements of the leading brigade and various other troops and then turned inland towards Meavaines.

"50th Division had assaulted with two brigades and some commandos at about 8 a.m. Their objective was about 3,000–4,000 yards inland, incidentally to include our assembly area. 56th Infantry Brigade landed on the right, behind the right assaulting brigade, with the prime task of seizing the important town and communications centre of Bayeux that evening if possible, but in any case by next morning.

"As already stated, Le Hamel held firm, which set back the whole programme. Moreover, the initial bridge-head did not reach far enough to include our assembly area, though this was not apparent until afterwards. However, our orders were to push on regardless of anyone else. We quickly reached Meavaines and joined up with more of the Battalion. We paused here to allow stragglers to catch up, and the Commanding Officer and his shipload fortunately arrived here shortly after. There was fighting in progress on the ridge a few hundred yards to the east, and we could see Sherman tanks advancing with infantry and firing and also detachments of enemy moving about. There was some shelling and mortaring, but this was ineffective.

"From Meavaines we again turned west, and, having gone behind the fighting still continuing in Le Hamel, reached the orchard area south of Buhot. The situation was obscure. There was fighting behind us, and on our right flank. I saw enemy detachments moving about to our front, in fact, one approached the assembly area, but made off when our tanks came up. By mid-afternoon the Battalion was complete except for three vehicles 'drowned,' and at about 4 p.m. we started for Bayeux."

"A" Company (Major M. W. Holme) led the advance with energy. No. 9 Platoon was in the van mounted on Bren carriers, and Nos. 7 and 8 Platoons followed on bicycles. The advance was supported by some tanks which blasted at anything which moved in front. There were a few enemy about, but they were still disorganised, and the speed of the advance and "the indiscriminate but nevertheless effective policy of shooting first and reconnoitring afterwards brushed aside any opposition."

From Ryes the Battalion took a small road to St. Sulpice, the first objective, or rather firm base. The cross-roads at St. Sulpice was occupied at 9.30 p.m.

On the Essex right the 2nd South Wales Borderers were having quite a battle round Vaux-sur-Aure. It was now getting too late to mount a major attack, should it be necessary, that evening, and the Battalion therefore dug-in, pushing patrols down to Bayeux. These were fired on.

Bayeux, now only about one and a half miles ahead, had some efficient infantry and anti-tank defences, and a head-on attack with only one battalion and few supporting arms was not attractive.

Lieutenant-Colonel Higson remarks: "It is interesting to note that the detailed positions occupied by the Battalion on the evening of

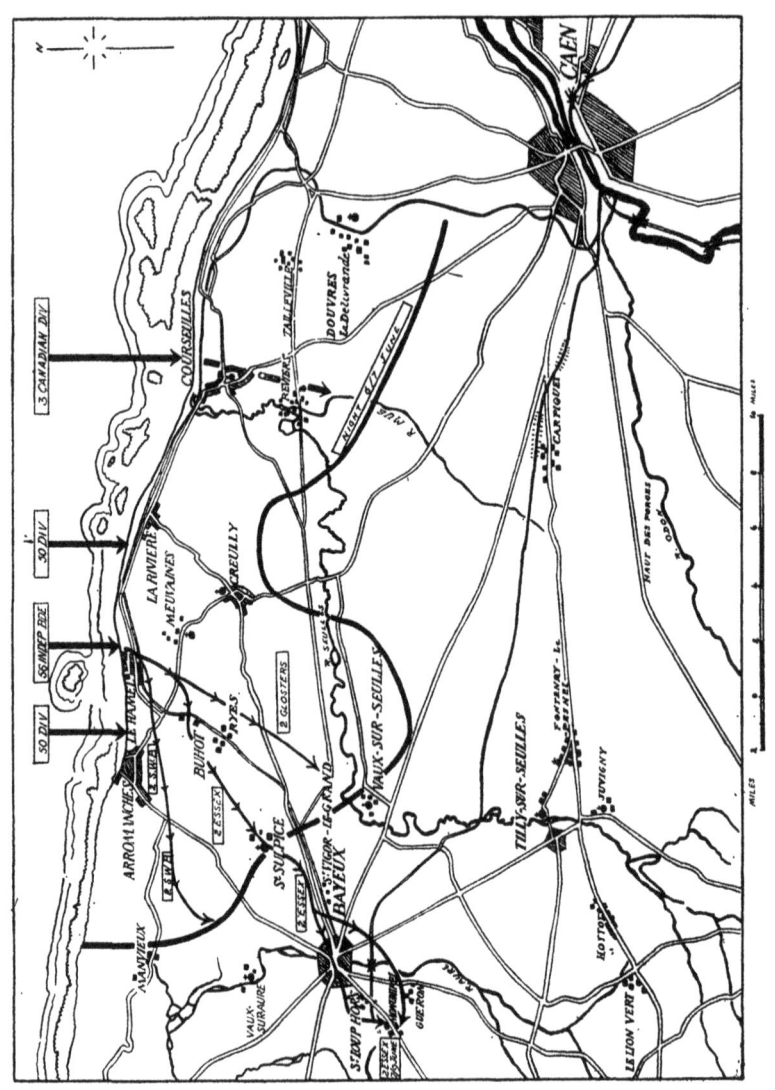

2ND ESSEX, NORMANDY, THE INITIAL BREAK-IN, 6TH-9TH JUNE, 1944.

D-Day were in fact those selected from a study of the excellent air photographs provided in the concentration area. These air photographs even made it possible for the individual anti-tank gun positions to be pre-selected."

It had been a satisfactory day, for the Battalion was now approximately four and a half miles deep into Normandy and with flanks secure, for the 2nd Glosters and 2nd S.W.B. had progressed equally well. The 2nd Essex had been lucky, for there had been only 4 men wounded by snipers during the whole day's operation.

Patrolling continued throughout the night, but any approach to the formidable anti-tank ditch surrounding Bayeux brought immediate fire from the defenders. It was therefore decided to avoid the more direct approaches to the town and use a subsidiary track as the axis of advance for the 7th June.

At 10.30 a.m. the forward body of the 2nd Essex Regiment, supported by tanks of the "Sherwood Rangers," advanced on Bayeux but instead of the expected resistance, the town was entered without opposition. The enemy had withdrawn earlier that morning. Whether the enemy intended to abandon Bayeux or whether the unexpected approach from the east through the suburb of St. Vigor–Le-Grand surprised him sufficiently to induce him to leave is not known, but as the 2nd Essex entered he was just clear of the southern side of the town. The first phase of the advance inland had now been successfully accomplished and the first big town in Normandy had been liberated.

During the advance and entrance into the town, the inhabitants remained indoors, and apparently showed little interest in the proceedings. When it became apparent that Bayeux had been liberated without bloodshed, they threw off their reserve and the tricolour was soon flying from many houses, whilst many a bottle of wine and fiery Calvados were brought out.

Quickly searching the town and rounding up the odd German straggler who still remained, the 2nd Essex pushed on. After considerable delay, owing to a blown bridge at St. Loup Hors which necessitated a complicated diversion, the Battalion reached by nightfall its final objective for the day, the ring contour round the hamlet of Monunirel, two miles south-west of Bayeux. This was, at the time, referred to as the Gueron feature, Gueron being a village about a mile to the east. Here they "firm-based" and awaited the expected counter-attack which did not come.

During the day the Battalion Signal Officer, Captain Hearne, was wounded and evacuated when the carrier in which he was travelling was blown up by a mine in the roadway. Corporal B. Downs, the carrier driver, was also injured. Lieutenant H. J. Fradin became Signal Officer.

Extensive patrol activities were carried out to the south-east, but the enemy had pulled away back and there was no contact. Patrols and civilians gave indications that the 1/916th Grenadier Battalion of the German 352nd Division was ahead, but the enemy seemed disorganised and ignorant of where the front actually lay, for first a motor-cycle combination carrying 3 men and then a German Press correspondent came into the 2nd Essex lines. In the first encounter the motor-cyclist was killed and his two passengers captured. The Press correspondent was also taken prisoner. The 2nd Essex had 1 man killed.

Operations with 7th Armoured Division 9th/12th June 1944 (Juaye Mondaye—"Essex" Wood).

The 2nd Essex used the pause of the 8th/9th June to check and clean up. The balance of the Battalion transport also reported. The "Pompadours" were then complete and ready for the next stage. On the evening of the 9th June they were relieved at Monunirel by the 1st Hampshires and moved back to the St. Loup Hors suburb of Bayeux, where they spent a wet and miserable night.

Although the 56th Infantry Brigade had landed as part of the assaulting 50th Division, it had plans to join the 7th Armoured Division (the Desert Rats) for a thrust to the south as soon as Bayeux had been captured and the beach-head area properly cleared of the enemy.

The Queen's Brigade, the lorried infantry of the 7th Armoured Division, had not yet arrived from the beaches, and the 56th Infantry Brigade was detailed to take its place.

Early on the 10th June the Armoured Brigade, with the 2nd Essex under command, headed south from Bayeux on the axis La Senaudière cross-roads–point 7868–Le Lion Vert, whilst the 56th Infantry Brigade (less 2nd Essex) with some armour attached headed south-east towards Tilly-sur-Seulles.

The Battalion moved in rear of the Armoured Brigade, reaching the village of Ellon at about noon. At this time the leading elements of the 7th Armoured Division were engaged in confused fighting with the leading elements of the Panzer Lehr Division, just arriving from the south and presumably headed for Bayeux. Little or no information reached the Battalion, but there were sounds of battle and rumours of enemy tanks to the front. By now they were in typical bocage country—"small fields with extremely thick hedges, scattered woods and sunken roads and footpaths, with everything in favour of the defender and nothing to help the attacker, who must crash through all the obstacles and never see the enemy who waits until he cannot miss."

Late in the afternoon the 2nd Essex was ordered to attack and clear out the enemy holding the large monastery and farm building of Juaye Mondaye and capture the Butte Du Gros Orme just to the south.

The thick country made reconnaissance impossible, but nevertheless at 6 p.m.—the ordered time of advance—the Battalion moved off on a two-company front under artillery concentrations.

"D" Company (Major G. M. M. L. Petre) and "A" Company (Major M. W. Holme) pushed in their attack, and there was some confused small-arms fire by both sides, but by last light the enemy opposition had been overcome, and the Monastery captured. Prisoners had been taken and more were taken next morning, still lurking in the thick country in rear of the forward companies. It was the Battalion's first full-scale attack, and their first experience of the difficulties of control and movement in the thick bocage country which they were now entering.

Early on the morning of Sunday, the 11th June, the Commanding Officer was summoned to Brigade Headquarters, and the Second-in-Command was ordered to hand over the position held at Butte Du Gros Orme and the Monastery to elements of a reconnaissance regiment and to take the Battalion forward to Bernières-Bocage.

Information about the enemy was still confused or not forthcoming, though sounds of battle still continued from the south. It is probable that the Panzer Lehr Division met 7th Armoured Division head on just north of the east-west highway, Tilly-sur-Seulles to La Belle Epine, and was at this time organising a defence along that general line.

The 2nd Glosters with 56th Infantry Brigade actually entered Tilly-sur-Seulles, but were quickly driven out of it. The armoured brigade which the 2nd Essex was supporting found it impossible to advance, and had suffered casualties from enemy infantry anti-tank weapons, though the latter were comparatively thin on the ground. There was another factor: the Panzer Lehr Division were equipped with Panther and Mark IV special tanks which outmatched the 7th Armoured Division cruiser-type tanks.

During the early morning Lieutenant-Colonel Higson returned from Brigade with orders for a full-scale attack to capture the orchard-type woods some 500 yards to the north of Lingevres and just west of the hamlet of Verrières.

Major G. G. Elliott says:

"The Battalion 'Order' Group drove hurriedly in jeeps to some higher ground just outside Folliot, but the view was not worth the drive: the tops of all woods and orchards look alike in this country at a distance of a mile, and in this particular case the line of orchards to our south were on a slight reverse slope: we could only see tree-tops. In fact, the terrain to the south and east of Bernières Bocage across which we were about to attack was comparatively open, and consisted of cornfields and other low crops: the only comparatively open country for many miles around."

Lieutenant-Colonel Higson's appreciation follows: "This was a formidable task, because 1,500 yards of flat open country which lay between the Battalion and its objective provided the enemy with an ideal killing ground and was, moreover, especially suitable for the enemy tanks which had been observed in Verrières Wood. It was therefore necessary to arrange for the maximum fire support to cover the Battalion over this long advance, and to include artillery of sufficient weight to dislodge the enemy tanks. In these respects the Battalion was well served, and it was decided to subject the objective to a concentration of medium artillery and to support the advancing infantry with a moving barrage of 25-pounders."

The Battalion formed up under difficulties, despite tapes, in the orchards and fields around the south fringe of Bernières Bocage, with "C" Company (Major P. R. Barrass) on the right and "A" Company (Major M. W. Holme) on the left in the lead. "D" Company (Major G. M. M. L. Petre) on the right and "B" (Major E. I. Watson) on the left were in rear. The Commanding Officer went forward with the two leading companies, with the Battalion Second-in-Command following between the two rear companies. The country was so confusing that leading companies were forced to advance on a compass bearing.

Major Elliott says: "It was understood that tanks would follow us up as soon as we had cleared the orchards of the enemy infantry. I am unable to recall what orders were given to our own anti-tank guns

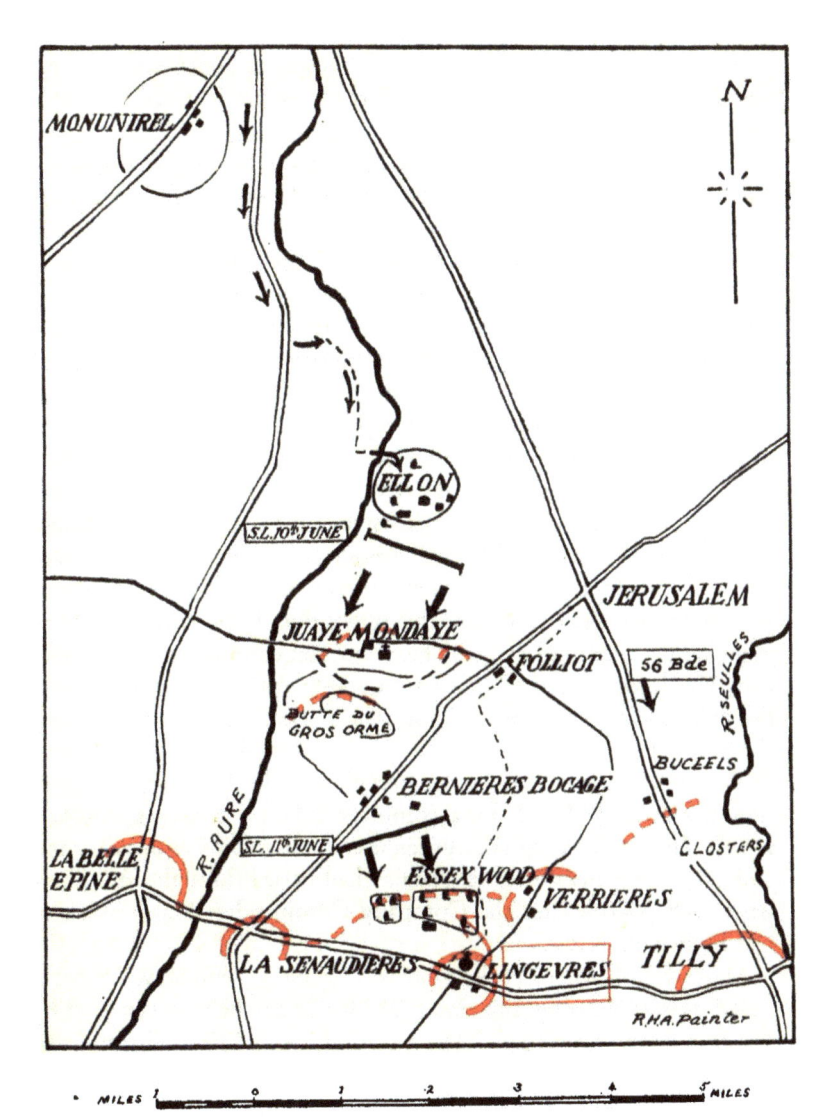

2ND ESSEX, JUAYE MONDAYE AND VERRIÈRES (ESSEX) WOOD, 10/11TH JUNE, 1944.

and mortars, but there was some initial and natural reluctance to move those vehicles close behind the infantry across the open country and under the enemy's observation until the situation in front had been cleared up."

At 6 p.m., the Battalion crossed the start-line on a two-company front, at a rate of advance of 100 yards per two minutes. The two leading companies "A" (Major Holme) and "C" (Major Barrass) advanced steadily and in perfect formation through the standing corn to the accompaniment of the continuous whine and explosion of our own shells as they pounded the enemy. It was not until the leading platoons were within 500 yards of the objective that the enemy opened fire with artillery, mortars, and small arms.

Despite casualties, the leading companies still moved forward at a steady rate until, with only a hundred yards to go, they opened fire with their small arms. The objective was quickly cleared, and the Battalion was soon in a square defensive box based on the north side of Verrières Wood. The left of the position was held up to spandau fire from the direction of Verrières and "D" Company (Major Petre) was sent round the left to clear this opposition, but before the movement started met misfortune. A heavy mortar concentration hit Company Headquarters and 2/Lieutenant Cannon's platoon, causing casualties in killed and wounded. 2/Lieutenant T. G. L. Cannon was among the killed.

This was followed, before the Battalion could dig in on the north side of Verrières Wood, by a combined infantry and tank counter-attack. There was no sign of our tanks or the Battalion anti-tank guns, and "B" Company on the left, which had passed through "A" Company, was overrun after the Company Commander, Major Watson, had been wounded.

Major G. M. M. L. Petre, who was trying to reorganise his command, was killed about this time, "D" Company being taken over by Captain F. R. Alexander. "The situation," says Major Elliott, "was critical on the left flank. Most of the wireless sets were out of action from damage, and by nightfall the sole means of reliable communication was through the artillery forward observation officer."

Lieutenant-Colonel Higson says: "In spite of gallant efforts with the Piat, the situation soon became critical. The enemy tanks, working in pairs, blasted the section positions at point-blank range, and very heavy casualties were sustained, including two platoons of "B" Company which were rounded up and taken prisoner. Nevertheless, the Battalion held its ground, and as night began to fall, the enemy tanks withdrew."

The night, however, was by no means a peaceful one. Soon after midnight a sudden infantry counter-attack supported by flame-throwers was put in. "By using this rather terrifying weapon the enemy made serious penetration into the Battalion position," the flame-throwers being operated from armoured half-track vehicles. The attack was stopped at Battalion Headquarters, mainly by Lieutenant C. Price using a combination of fire from a 2-inch mortar and a Piat. A half-track was burnt out, and the enemy withdrew from the vicinity.

So serious was the general position that the Commanding Officer decided to call for artillery fire on to the Battalion location, on the assumption that our own troops would be relatively immune in their slit trenches. This critical action was successful, and the artillery concentration which followed proved too much for the enemy, who withdrew.

But the Battalion was still completely out of touch with the headquarters of the Armoured Brigade and with the Battalion rear link itself. The situation was grave and the outlook for the morning gloomy. At about 1 a.m., on the 12th June, Lieutenant-Colonel Higson instructed Major Elliott to make his way across country to the Armoured Brigade Headquarters and to request some tank or S.P. anti-tank support by first light. Unfortunately, that Headquarters had moved from their reported location at Jerusalem, and Major Elliott, after contacting the Battalion rear link at Bernières Bocage, went next to Headquarters 56th Infantry Brigade. Before leaving rear headquarters Captain J. Townrow told him the Battalion anti-tank guns were on their way up to the forward area and had, in fact, started immediately after dark.

Major Elliott, of his visit to 56th Infantry Brigade Headquarters, says: "I . . . called on Brigadier Pepper in his caravan. As soon as he heard the situation he called the Divisional Commander, and requested that either tanks or self-propelled anti-tank guns be sent up by first light as a matter of urgency. This was done and thereafter matters improved."

With the arrival of the Battalion anti-tank guns and tank support, the Battalion position was reorganised and the wounded evacuated by carriers. So ended a memorable battle. The casualties had been severe, but Verrières Wood (better known as Essex Wood) remained firmly in the hands of the 2nd Essex.

During this action there were many deeds of bravery, but perhaps the most outstanding was that of the Battalion Chaplain, the Reverend F. Thomas. He remained with the forward platoons throughout the battle, shielding the bodies of the wounded with his own and entirely disregarding his own safety, gallantry for which he was given an immediate award of the Military Cross.

An officer writes: " Much of the success of the battle and the retention of Verrières Wood was due to the bravery and example of Major M. W. Holme, who was here, there, and everywhere constantly guiding and encouraging everyone." Major Holme himself says: "How well I remember, when, in the middle of trying to sort out my company, the air was pierced by groans and shouts from one of our wounded lying about 100 yards in front of our positions, having got left behind unnoticed in the confusion and darkness. Just as I was wondering what to do, up came the C.O., John Higson, and said, 'I'm going to get that man,' and off he went, with myself a rather badly placed second, straight into the unknown, picked the man up and carried him safely back."

During the morning of the 12th June the position was organised to get more depth and the anti-tank guns were sited properly. "C" Company (Major P. R. Barrass) was intact on the right, and Major M. W. Holme formed one composite company of four or five platoons of the remainder of the rifle companies.

The Battalion now felt secure and ready for anything. Tanks could still be heard moving about to the front and flanks, and there was some indiscriminate shelling by both sides. Otherwise all was quiet, and the four Mark X self-propelled guns that had reinforced the Battalion's own 6-pounder anti-tank guns gave added depth to the anti-tank defence.

During the morning Major G. G. Elliott assumed command of the Battalion. "That afternoon," he says, "I was somewhat surprised to be told to withdraw into reserve at Folliott, the timing to be at my discretion depending on the situation. This, of necessity, was conducted after dark, and was carried out as a normal withdrawal operation in the face of the enemy. The precautions proved unnecessary, and we came back without any hindrance. Two days later another unit attacked the same area and suffered severely. The enemy had reoccupied the ground which we had gained and kept at such cost. This was the only withdrawal operation carried out by the Battalion in Normandy."

Buceels–Tilly-sur-Seulles, 16th–20th June, 1944

The Battalion had a quiet day on 13th June, but on the 14th, although Battalion Headquarters and "D" Company remained at Folliott, "A", "B," and "C" Companies had to be moved east of Bernières Bocage to relieve a D.L.I. battalion which was required to move forward for a drive towards Verrières Wood.

Company Commanders now were: "A," Major M. W. Holme; "B," Captain D. W. Browne; "C," Major P. R. Barrass, "D," Captain F. R. Alexander, and "S" Company, Major P. J. Wilkins.

Captain Vince says: "The line was thinly held, and although officially in reserve, we were merely echeloned back to give depth to the defence and Bosche 88s and even rifle fire continued to annoy us. However, we snatched a little badly needed sleep, food became more regular. . . ."

On the 15th June the 2nd Essex came temporarily under command of the 151st Infantry Brigade and took over the village of Buceels from the 2nd S.W.B. who had been in close combat with the enemy for some days. Some of the enemy having been reported at Pont-de-la-Guillette, the Battalion snipers were posted to watch all covered approaches and vigorous patrolling was carried out.

On the night 15th/16th June, reconnaissance patrols were pushed out to Tilly-sur-Seulles, where contact was gained with the enemy, Lieutenant N. M. Murphy being wounded. The enemy was thus proved to be holding Tilly-sur-Seulles in strength, with outposts in the area Pont-de-la-Guillette, but the situation on the eastern flank was obscure. Of this Lieutenant-Colonel Elliott says: "49th Infantry Division had admittedly come up at about this time and were in action somewhere across the valley of the River Seulles, the inter-division boundary.

"During the defensive phase at Buceels, and even more so during the attack on Tilly, we had trouble from the east flank, as 49th Division had not cleared Saint Pierre of enemy snipers and observers, and we were somewhat vulnerable on this flank."

The Battalion was disposed four-square round Buceels, and there were considerable patrol activity and shelling. Battalion Headquarters, in an orchard in the south-east section of the village, received several direct hits which caused many casualties, including the death of Lieutenant H. J. Fradin, the Battalion Signal Officer, and the wounding of the Brigadier commanding 151st Infantry Brigade. Lieutenant J. L. Spencer became Signal Officer.

The Brigade Commander's visit had been to co-ordinate arrangements for an attack on Tilly-sur-Seulles, which the 2nd Essex was ordered to capture on the 17th June. This pretty little village in rolling country almost due south of, and about six miles from, Bayeux was a focal point on the front of 30th Corps. The intention was to thrust south through Tilly-sur-Seulles towards Villers Bocage, "thereby developing a southern pincer movement towards Caen by 30th Corps, while 1st Corps maintained steady pressure on the mounting enemy forces grouped round the town."[1]

While the 2nd Essex had been engaged at Verrières Wood on the 11th June, Tilly-sur-Seulles had been occupied by the 2nd Glosters and elements of 7th Armoured Division, but they had been quickly driven out by a very heavy counter-attack, and repeated efforts by other units to retake Tilly-sur-Seulles after the 11th June had failed.

The new plan for 30th Corps was for 7th Armoured Division to thrust towards Villers Bocage from the right front of the Corps area, while elements of 50th Division and attached troops attacked Tilly-sur-Seulles southwards across to the Balleroy–Tilly road.

To the 2nd Essex fell the task of taking Tilly-sur-Seulles itself, which had now resisted all attempts for its capture for almost a week. On the night of the 16th/17th June, patrols were again sent towards Tilly-sur-Seulles to find out what could be learnt of the enemy dispositions, and at 4 p.m., the 17th June, the Battalion passed over to the attack. It was a stiff fight forward, with the main Bayeux–Tilly road as a directional guide to the two forward companies advancing astride it through the thick bocage country.

Again the enemy observation points had been well selected, and soon artillery support was necessary to help "A" and "D" Companies forward. Snipers, spandaus, artillery, and booby-traps in ditches and hedges all hindered but did not stop the "Pompadours'" advance, until right in front of the main defences the advance slowed and finally lost momentum. At 10.30 p.m., the 17th June, the forward companies were still about 800 yards short of the centre of the village. Here they were ordered to hold and consolidate, Battalion Headquarters being established in an orchard about 500 yards south-east of Pont-de-la-Guillette.

During the 18th June little progress was found possible either by

[1] *Normandy to the Baltic*, Montgomery, p. 71.

the 10th D.L.I. on the right or by the 2nd Essex themselves round the left flank, for any advance immediately came under heavy shell fire. Furthermore, the only approach into the town from this side was found to be blocked by an Armoured Vehicle, Royal Engineers, which had blown up on a mine during some previous attack.

Altogether, 27 other ranks had been wounded, and Lieutenant D. T. Whitley ("C" Company) had been killed, as had Captain N. F. Harrison (the carrier platoon commander). There was much gallantry in these thirty-six hours of probing and attack. Lieutenant J. Cooper stoutly completed a patrol after being wounded, action which gained him the Military Cross. Private J. R. Giles won the Military Medal for escaping, after capture, with a marked map of German dispositions. Lance-Corporal W. A. Worwood, too, was awarded the M.M. for his actions as stretcher-bearer.

The morning of the 19th June brought torrential rain as the Battalion was ordered once more to attack. Lieutenant-Colonel Elliott knew that the 10th D.L.I. was due to attack a ridge that morning to the south-west of Tilly, passing round the western edge of the strong and stoutly defended village. He accordingly ordered "A" Company to follow up the D.L.I. attack, and when in rear of Tilly to turn inwards and reach the central square as quickly as possible. The remainder of the Battalion was held ready to exploit the flanking move if successful.

In the area of the 10th D.L.I., and on the line of advance towards Tilly, there was much evidence of the severity of the long-drawn-out fight for the village. Knocked-out Shermans and Cromwells and wrecked German tanks seemed to be everywhere.

"A" Company got forward comparatively easily, the enemy being outmanœuvred by this right flanking move. After some defensive mortar fire and shelling, the enemy pulled back to Juvigny. And so Tilly-sur-Seulles was finally taken, the last advance into the village being at the cost of 8 ranks wounded. The village and all roads leading to it had been most thoroughly mined and booby-trapped, and its entry and occupation were extremely hazardous. Further casualties were caused in the village by the numerous "Tellermines."

All through the 19th the Battalion was subjected to very heavy artillery fire, German 88-mm. guns firing air-bursts in some of the most brilliantly accurate shooting experienced during the whole campaign. On the 20th the 2nd Essex, relieved by elements of the 9th and 10th D.L.I., was withdrawn to Ellon for rest. The relief was not with-

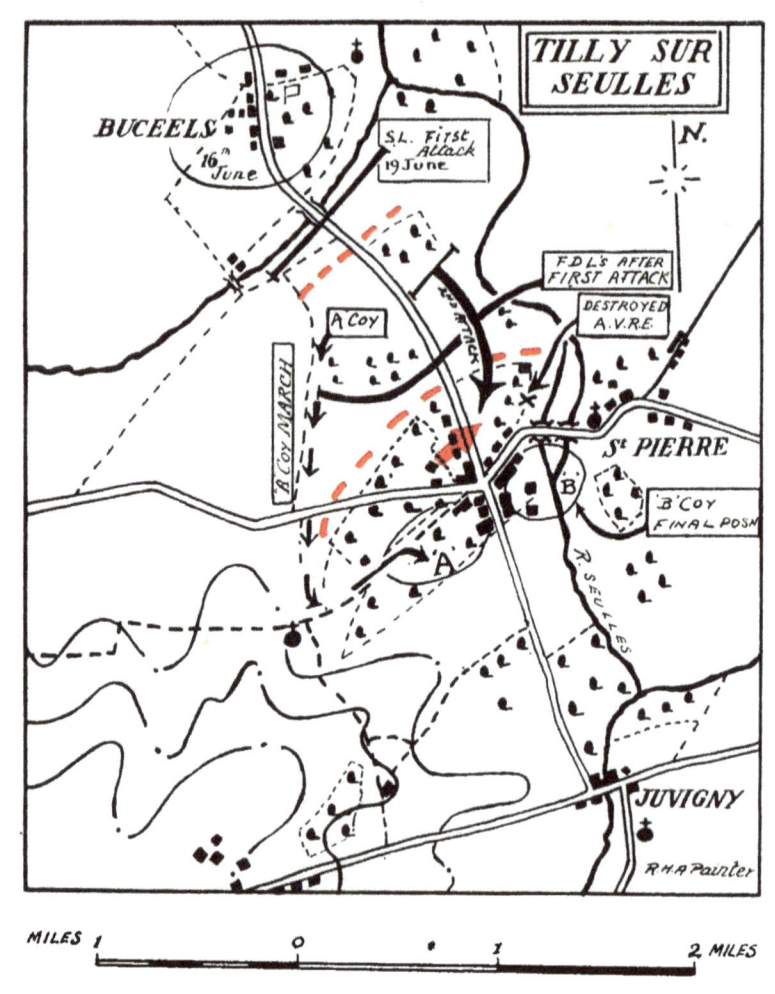

2ND ESSEX, TILLY-SUR-SEULLES, 16TH–20TH JUNE, 1944.

out difficulty, as shell fire was heavy. "B" Company (Major D. W. Browne), down at the Château, had to stay in position until after dark, when it was successfully withdrawn to Ellon.

Thus ended fourteen days of practically unbroken action with very little sleep. There had been cases of battle exhaustion in the ranks, and over one-third of those who had landed on D-Day a fortnight earlier had been killed, wounded, or reported missing. The "Pompadours" had played their full part in the enlargement of the bridge-head.

On the 21st June, 1944, Brigadier E. C. Pepper visited them and complimented all ranks on their splended achievements, with special mention of their first entry into Bayeux and the capture of Tilly-sur-Seulles.

They were to remain at Ellon from the 20th to 28th June, eating, sleeping, and bathing. It was when back in Bayeux for baths that the Commander-in-Chief, General Montgomery, came up to a group of men standing in the street and said, "I've been wanting to meet you Essex chaps—I've heard how awfully well you've been doing—the whole thing is going well and we're right on tóp. Any of you chaps smoke? I've got a few cigarettes here——"

Major M. W. Holme, who gives this picture, admits these are not the exact words of the Commander-in-Chief, but convey the meaning. It was a nice touch of recognition for excellent service which was appreciated by all ranks.

Received during this period out of the line was a reinforcement draft of 5 officers and 131 other ranks, a welcome addition to the fighting strength.

Les Orailles–Bois de St. Germain

Even whilst resting at Ellon the Commanding Officer was instructed to take notice of the area around Granville and the Bois de St. Germain, as the Brigade was possibly to be moved to this flank in the near future.

In brief, for the future course of operations, General Montgomery planned to use the 8th Corps, on the left of 30th Corps, to establish a bridge-head over the River Odon as a preliminary to the capture of Caen. 30th Corps was to start the operation by an advance of the 49th Division towards Noyers. Then at such time as the 7th Armoured Division could successfully exploit any weakening of the enemy by this advance, 50th Division, with the 56th Brigade on the extreme right and joining the United States 6th Corps, was to advance towards Villers Bocage.

This then was the plan of the operation to which the 2nd Essex was next committed. The Battalion's role was no spectacular move nor brilliant break-through. Those days still lay ahead, and for the moment every infantry battalion of 30th Corps had the same role—that of relentless pressure against the enemy attempting to contain the slowly expanding bridge-head, attacks in which the capture of every village, every road junction and every river crossing was a victory and a means to the end—the break-out. But the break-out was still an event of the future, and for the present every thousand-yard advance was a substantial gain.

The first step in the new operation was for the 2nd Essex to send night patrols forward from a patrol base at Quesnay Guesnon. These soon established the fact that the enemy was holding the Granville area in some strength. Next, on the morning of the 28th June, the Battalion left Ellon and took over from the 7th Green Howards in the area Les Orailles–Les Landes. The 2nd S.W.B. came up on the 2nd Essex right around La Butte and the 2nd Glosters even farther away (with a large gap between themselves and 2nd S.W.B.) at Parfouru L'Eclin.

The positions were in typical bocage country. A little over a mile to the south was the Bois de St. Germain, with the small village of Granville to the right, and with the Tilly–Hottot–La Chapelle lateral road to the front. This, the German Seventh Army was still defending fiercely.

The 56th Infantry Brigade was now on the extreme right of the British line. There the Battalion stayed through eight days of indifferent weather before the general situation became favourable for the plan to advance on the right of 30th Corps area.

Of this period round Les Orailles–Les Landes, Lieutenant-Colonel G. G. Elliott writes:

"Although activity in this particular front was negligible, the position we had taken over was unsatisfactory; it was too cramped and afforded poor fields of fire. We rectified this by pushing forward and to our flank by some hundreds of yards, and eventually had the best defensive position ever occupied during the whole campaign.

"We had outposts on the crest of the ridge, and the rifle companies and anti-tank weapons sited on the gentle reverse slope between the top of the ridge and the main road, all with good fields of fire. At one time it was thought the enemy might attack down the international boundary which was close to our flank. We should have been ready for them in this position.

"Despite some attention to the defensive layout, most of the time was given up to patrolling and the training of patrols. For the first time the Second-in-Command was made responsible for this activity with the Intelligence Officer as his deputy. This arrangement worked well, and our patrols began to get results instead of nothing but casualties." (Major G. Lance, D.S.O.[1] was Second-in-Command at this period. He shortly went to command a battalion in the 3rd Division, where soon afterwards he was killed.)

"He was succeeded, about mid-July, by Major Pallot,[2] also a most energetic, pleasant, and efficient officer. We had many 'attachments' from other regiments, including Canadians,[3] all of whom were quickly assimilated into the Battalion. Although casualties were heavy, we were undoubtedly more than lucky in the fact that after 'Essex Wood' we had comparatively few casualties amongst the Company Commanders and specialists."

On the 7th July, 1944, the 2nd Essex received orders to secure the road Tilly-Hottot-La Chapelle on the Battalion front, also the surrounding woods forming part of the Bois de St. Germain. On the right, 2nd S.W.B. would capture Granville.

Battalion records for the period give little detail. There are two notes:

"7th July, 6 p.m.   The Battalion prepares cheerfully for battle and all appear very calm and normal at eventide.
"11th July.   A rest day and conclusion of battle. Battalion get its breath back."

Magnificent reporting, but little good to one in search of detail. Luckily, Lieutenant-Colonel Elliott was able to fill in any small gaps.

"On 8th July we went over to the offensive and attacked at Bois de St. Germain. 2nd S.W.B. on the right were charged with capturing Granville and the crossroads at La Chapelle, whilst we on the left were ordered to cut the main road around La Croix des Landes. This plan presented a difficult tactical problem, as it left out the Bois de St. Germain, known to be strongly occupied, between the two attacking battalions. Eventually, Brigade directed that I send one platoon of 'C' Company through the wood as a 'fighting patrol,' but this was

[1] Major G. C. P. Lance, D.S.O. (Somerset L.I.).
[2] Major M. G. St. G. Pallot (Leicesters).
[3] For example, "D" Company at this time was commanded by Captain F. R. Alexander who, except for Lieutenant R. E. Miller, was the only British officer in the Company, Captain D. J. Selvage and Lieutenants Irwin and J. N. Orr being Canadians.

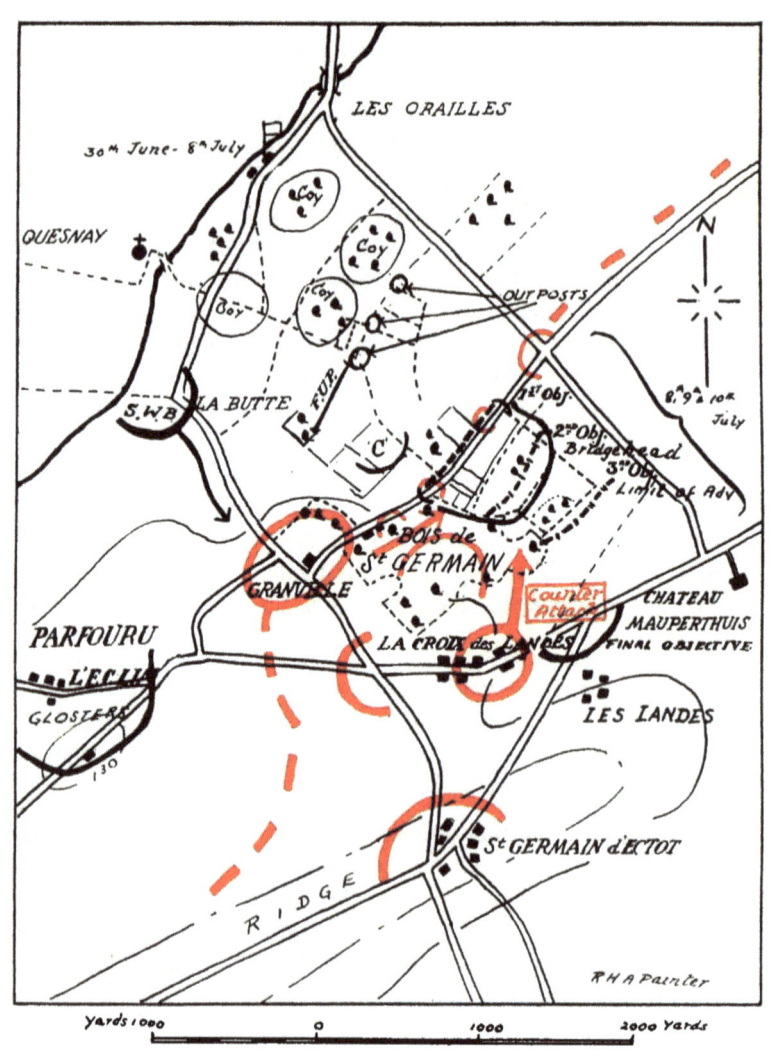

2ND ESSEX, LES ORAILLES–BOIS DE ST. GERMAIN, 28TH JUNE–10TH JULY, 1944.

still not satisfactory unless the opposition in the end proved less effective than patrolling had indicated.

"There was sufficient time to plan for this attack, which was as well, as there were a large number of details to be worked out, and many and various sub-units under command, including for the first time Churchill's 'Crocodiles' (flame-throwing tanks).

"We formed up on tapes in the fields to the right of the position we had been occupying, and started off on time.

"In view of the very thick nature of the country, the small size of the fields, and the threat of trouble from the Bois on our right, we attacked on a one-company front, led by 'A' Company (Major M. W. Holme).

"'A' Company was given the Battalion first objective, the road 800 yards from our start line, with orders to hold the shoulders of the 'break in' at all costs—which they did. 'B' then passed through to the second objective, a convenient line of hedgerows, some 500 yards on, and dug in, with half their attention on the Bois on their right. 'D' then passed through 'B' to the third objective, about 300 yards on. 'C' Company (less the one platoon which was to go through the Bois —it got out of control in the thick woods, and was lost for a time) was held in reserve on the high ground north-west of the first objective, ready to exploit through 'D' Company, or to hold off any counter-attack from Granville.

"This on paper appears to be a slow and methodical attack. Even without an enemy manœuvre was difficult in this country. In this particular attack we were asked to advance more than 2,000 yards through the thickest 'bocage' imaginable—some of the fields were no larger than tennis courts, and all banked and ditched with thick hedges interspersed with large trees. Armoured 'bulldozers' were an essential to wheeled movement. Even the very accurate 1:25,000 map could not indicate the real nature of the 'going,' and all plans and orders were based on air photos, not only in this but in most other battles. 'A' Company, however, jumped off at 8 a.m., and captured their objective without difficulty. 'B' and 'D' in turn passed through 'A.' Although progress was necessarily slow, the enemy reaction was slow also; but not so on our right, where the 2nd S.W.B. met heavy opposition and failed to reach their first objective: they were held up all day. There were also signs of something 'brewing up' on our front, and on our right and left flanks.

"We were by now (about 11 a.m.) in a salient, with the enemy, who were by now obviously in some strength, able to counter-attack from three directions, and especially easily from the Bois. We were exposed to observation from the high ground to our left, about Hottot, though the hedgerows gave a large measure of cover.

"It appears that the enemy 277 Infantry Regiment (three battalions supported by tanks of the 2nd Panzer Division) was due to attack on our front at 12 midday, and our attack forestalled them by a few hours. In view of the increased and obvious activity around us, I halted the advance, and on the recommendation of the Company Commander actually pulled back 'D' Company a hundred yards or so, to obtain a more co-ordinated position with 'B' Company, and better fields of fire. This proved fortunate, as their original position out in front was heavily mortared and shelled soon afterwards, and before they could dig in. However, the enemy did little but probe the position that day with strong fighting patrols. Our troop of tanks withdrew that night, promising to appear again next morning by first light. They were, however, a little late, as three Mark IV Specials with infantry support managed somehow to drive down some tracks in the Bois, and as dawn broke on the 9th July appeared in the right rear of our position, in the neighbourhood of Lieutenant Filby's right-hand platoon of 'A' Company.

"Then the battle began in earnest. Lieutenant R. G. Filby was responsible for knocking out two of the tanks with a Piat (for some reason a 17-pounder which was sited to cover this particular eventuality did not fire—the reason alleged was lack of visibility through ground mist). One of the two tanks was captured intact with radio still switched on, and was later driven back proudly by one of our tank drivers.

"The infantry companies were having a really hot fight at close range. All the communications were working perfectly, the tanks had arrived up, and, with artillery, mortars, and machine guns, we 'stonked' the enemy unmercifully both when he was attacking and when withdrawing to reorganise for other attempts. Typhoons also attacked the rear areas.

"We slew a large number of the enemy on that day, and took many prisoners, as there were repeated counter-attacks which were pressed in bravely.

"The last main attack came in during the evening, and was broken up by 'Crocodiles,' directed by Major Browne of 'B' Company, all three of which were hit or holed by enemy fire. Major Browne all through this battle, and in particular during this last phase, displayed the greatest courage and leadership." (Major D. W. Browne was awarded the M.C. for his skill and gallantry in this action.)

"Except for a few patrols which later tried to probe for weak places, the battle was over. Our casualties were not light, but those inflicted on the enemy must have been extraordinary, and included about 100 prisoners.

"Although we had not succeeded in gaining our objective—a difficult undertaking under the circumstances—the Battalion had succeeded in crippling a force three times its size. Interrogation of prisoners left no doubt about this fact."

The 10th July saw a cold, wet, tired but victorious Battalion being relieved by the 6th Green Howards and moving back to its original starting-line position.

The Brigade Commander quickly congratulated them on the information given by prisoners, which showed the German 276th Division to be very badly shaken by the 2nd Essex attacks. One prisoner said, "Our officer told our General it was terrible, and we will not attack again," a nice tribute to the offensive spirit of the "Pompadours."

Parfouru L'Eclin–Launay Ridge, 11th July–1st August

On the day after the Battle of St. Germain the 2nd Essex relieved the 2nd Glosters on the 130-metre ring contour just south of Parfouru L'Eclin. "They seemed happy to leave, which was an ominous sign," said Lieutenant-Colonel Elliott.

The Battalion was to spend three weeks in and around Parfouru L'Eclin and Pont Mulot, three weeks of active patrolling, shelling, and mortaring. Throughout the enemy, at first the 2nd Panzer Division, retaliated in good measure.

A quotation from a Battalion "anniversary memoir" published in July 1945 typifies this period:

". . . We were pursuing a policy known as 'leaning on the enemy,' and damned uncomfortable it was! We did, however, have the occasional consolation of a bath at Brigade and that most forward of all cinemas, the 'Sphinx' at La Belle Epine. But life was very tiring, and nobody got much sleep and explosions were pretty frequent. How well one remembers a plaintive 'phone message from 'A' Company Commander in the middle of the night to the effect that he could stand shells, mortars, and nebelwerfers—but when it came to sea-mines . . .!! One of the few German planes that came over dropped one in 'A' Company area, evidently thinking it was the coast. The Hun's shelling was pretty regular on the whole, however, and we always knew that we could rely on the dinner-time 'stonk' at 12.45 p.m. and accordingly changed the time of feeding.

"Our opponents were the famous 2nd Panzer Division for the first fortnight. Night after night our patrols used to come back at 3 a.m. after nerve-racking hours round La Couarde and even sometimes down to the St. Germain d'Ectot road. Very often patrols used to pass each other, for La Couarde and Torteval were very frequently patrolled by both sides."

The "Pompadours" were now on the extreme right of the British line and alongside the 3/41st U.S. Battalion from Texas, a unit of the 2nd U.S. Armoured Division under the command of Brigadier-General Rose, "who," says Lieutenant-Colonel Elliott, "was always most co-operative and had already helped us with some of his artillery battalions in support of our previous activities in front of the Bois de St. Germain. On one occasion Lieutenant Miller's platoon carried out a raid under a box barrage fired by our divisional artillery and six battalions of American guns; but without success."

Battalion Headquarters was in an orchard at the end Pont Mulot. There was a little café between Battalion Headquarters and the forward companies, a café which kept open despite shell and rifle fire and where freshly killed pork, raw cider, or even fiery Calvados could often be bought.

Then at the end of July came the break-out. On the right, the U.S. Army was through to St. Lo, whilst on the left the British and Canadians were approaching Falaise.

On the right of the 2nd Essex the 43rd (Wessex) Division, which had joined 30th Corps, had, by the 30th July, come up and taken over from the Americans, thereby freeing the American 5th Corps for the break-through advance. The British 8th Corps had come up, too, on the right of the 43rd Division, thereby extending the British line through Caumont westwards along the River Drome. General Montgomery's plan was to attack on the 30th July, the main weight being developed by 8th and 30th Corps on a narrow front. 30th Corps was to wheel to the line Villers Bocage–Aunay-Sur-Odon, while the 8th Corps swept wider to the right. The initial objective was the general area St. Martin des Besacres–Le Beny Bocage–Forêt L'Eveque.

On the 29th July the frontage of the 2nd Essex was extended to free the 2nd Glosters for an attack to be made in conjunction with the 2nd

S.W.B. on the following day. The 2nd Essex was to be in Brigade reserve.

Lieutenant-Colonel Elliott's account of the Battle of Launay Ridge is as follows:

"On 29th July the Brigade went over to the offensive in general

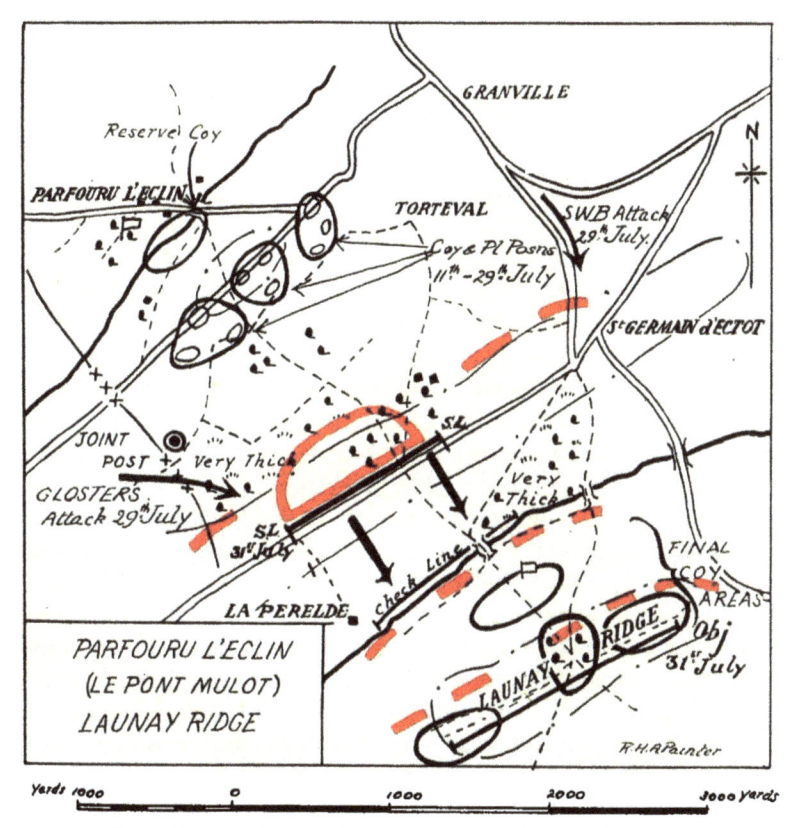

2ND ESSEX, PARFOURU L'ECLIN–LAUNAY RIDGE, 11TH JULY–1ST AUGUST, 1944.

support of the major operations which were soon to end in the Falaise Gap.

"The 2nd Glosters attacked from our right, to seize a strong-point on the St. Germain d'Ectot ridge immediately to our front, whilst the 2nd S.W.B. came in from the left at Granville. We were held in reserve, on a wide four-company front, covering the whole Brigade, not an easy position from which to concentrate quickly. I had appreciated that Launay Ridge might be our objective, and we had already carried out a reconnaissance and decided to attack from the north-west, to avoid the mines and wire which were so liberally laid around the 'strong-point' to our immediate front. The Glosters and S.W.B. made heavy going, but by the 30th were either on the d'Ectot ridge or very close to it.

" 'B' Company, led by Major M. St. G. Pallot, tried to help the Glosters on this day, but it was still impossible to cross the line of the ridge without drawing heavy fire.

"At about 4 p.m. on 31st July I was summoned to Brigade Headquarters, where I met the Brigadier and Commander, Royal Artillery, and received orders to capture Launay Ridge that evening, starting at 6 p.m. This was a little too quick in my opinion, and after some discussion H-Hour was finally arranged for 8 p.m. Even then 'C' Company, some miles away on the extreme right of the line, barely had time to close and march in to the forming-up place. The supporting arms, tanks, bulldozers, etc., were on their way to my Headquarters and also arrived just in time. The artillery fire plan, a heavy barrage at 200-yard intervals, lifting in succession before the infantry, had already been arranged, and we had no alternative but to do a 'straight on' attack, starting amongst the enemy minefields which I had hoped to avoid. The pioneer platoons of the other two battalions came to our help in clearing lanes, and the infantry initially and until they had crossed the start-line—the line of the road along the ridge—followed in the tracks of tanks. In the end we only had one known casualty from anti-personnel mines before crossing the start-line: one man lost a foot.

"We jumped off just, but only just, on time. The tanks gave magnificent support, the leading waves really 'leaned into' the barrage, with the result that, although there were a few casualties from our own fire, there were very few from the enemy, as the infantry were right on top of them before they could recover from the shock of the barrage. Typhoons also attacked the ridge in front.

"So energetic were the two leading companies ('A' and 'B') that they advanced about 200 yards too far beyond the one check line, where they should have paused for five minutes. I suddenly realised that the whole of our artillery would shortly reopen on our leading sections. We could try to pull them back, but this might be difficult, and might indeed disorganise the further advance. Artillery are loath to make any changes in the middle of a timed and complicated barrage —there are so many chances of error—but in this case the battery commander gave an urgent order to cancel fire on the reopening line, and to continue on the next line according to previous timing. Happily, it worked. The two companies remained lying down. As soon as the barrage reopened in front of them, they jumped up and moved up to it.

"We captured a large amount of equipment and some prisoners. The enemy were obviously on the point of pulling back, and had probably already thinned out. Nevertheless, this was a very well executed attack, and would have succeeded against even strong opposition.

"By the time the leading companies reached their objective, the line of road along the Launay Ridge, it was dark. Luckily the moon rose early, and it was possible to move about without confusion, and to send forward patrols.

"Next morning we had our reward—at long last a long view of several miles' extent, a pleasant change from the next orchard and hedgerow a few yards in front."

There is no doubt that this was one of the most brilliant attacks of the campaign. Major M. W. Holme says: "Senior gunner and tank officers who watched from a hill in rear described it as a perfect attack. I can only speak from my own company, but that was a most exhilarating experience—the whole thing was brilliant—the Commanding Officer warned only about three hours before H-Hour, orders given out, tanks and artillery worked into the plan, etc., etc.—the depth of the attack quite 2,500 yards and no time to look at the ground. The enemy on the next hill with a large valley in between. Everything went exactly according to plan—artillery perfect, tanks superb, and the enemy (one battalion plus) turned and ran."

Captain A. A. Vince wrote: "The attack was an incredible sight. We walked slowly twenty yards behind the barrage. Not a man even ducked or took cover for a second. Bullets and shrapnel all over the place, but we had wonderful luck and few casualties. Major Holme and Major Browne walked calmly in front of the troops as if on a picnic."

It had been a copy-book battle.

It was to be the last action of the 2nd Essex with the 50th (Northumbrian) Division, and it was fitting that it should have been a resounding success. The enemy withdrew after the battle for a distance of from six to ten kilometres, and as 50th Division moved forward to follow up the 2nd Essex success, the 69th and 231st Infantry Brigades passed round the 56th Infantry Brigade and so squeezed it out from the battle. Thus the "Pompadours" were withdrawn on the 2nd August, 1944, to rest at Buceels.

They had six carefree days: days of sleeping, bathing, eating, and sun-bathing, with E.N.S.A. concerts and Battalion concert-party shows. A Drumhead Church Service, too, was held at which the Brigade Commander expressed his admiration for the fine work of all three battalions in the 56th Infantry Brigade.

It was to be the last few hours of life for the 56th Brigade as an independent formation, for on the 7th August, 1944, it became part of the 59th Division. This Division had for some time past been operating on the left of the 50th Division, and the 56th Infantry Brigade was transferred to replace units which were being broken up owing to the shortage of man-power.

With the 59th Division. Crossing the Orne–Forge-à-Cambro–Bas Breuil Wood

The 56th Infantry Brigade officially joined 59th Division on the 2nd August, but there was no physical transfer until after the rest period at Buceels, of which Lieutenant-Colonel Elliott says:

"Although the rest did much to restore the health and spirits of the men, there had been so many casualties that the standard of training of the Battalion had fallen. We were now a strange collection of many regiments (by complete platoons as far as possible) and many still wearing their own badges."

The general situation at the beginning of August 1944 was, very briefly: following the break-out by the American Army and the corresponding drive southwards towards Le Beny Bocage by the 8th Corps, General Montgomery had directed the Second British Army to pivot on 12th Corps, thus swinging part of that Corps and all 30th Corps down towards Thury Harcourt, Condé, and Fliers. It was a preliminary move towards the formation of the northern side of the Falaise pocket that was soon to prove so disastrous to German arms.

This swing brought the 59th Division to the River Orne just when the 2nd Essex, as part of 56th Infantry Brigade, was transferred to that Division. The Brigade was moved straight up in relief of another brigade of 59th Division. The 2nd Essex was ordered to move by La Feterie and La Caine to the west bank of the Orne, opposite the Forêt de Grimbosq, and to bivouac the night of 8th/9th August around the village of Ouffières.

The same night a battalion of the Royal Warwickshires (59th Division) secured a crossing over the River Orne at Brieux, and managed to hold on to its bridge-head in spite of vicious counter-attacks by German Panzer units.

On the 9th August the 2nd Essex, in a new and strange division, not properly re-equipped after earlier battles and with many of the men in tattered uniforms, reconnoitred from the high west bank of the river the ground east of the Orne with special reference to the routes leading south from the bridge-head.

All through the 9th the Royal Warwickshire bridge-head held firm and the enemy counter-attacks began to die down. That evening the Brigadier 56th Infantry Brigade gave out orders. The 2nd Essex on the right with 2nd Glosters on the left were to advance that night, 9th/10th August, out of the bridge-head, take the secondary road leading south from La Bagotière and capture Forge-à-Cambro by a coup-de-main. 2nd S.W.B. and Brigade Headquarters would remain on the west bank. "Artillery and tanks," remarks Lieutenant-Colonel Elliott, "would catch up with us when they could do so in the morning."

Lieutenant-Colonel Elliott continues the story:

"Lieutenant-Colonel Biddulph, of the Glosters, and myself were a little anxious about our right of way over the one narrow bridge. We were told, however, that it would be allotted to us for two hours, from (I think) 10 p.m. to midnight. In the event we met a tank brigade and other vehicles returning from the bridge-head: there was complete chaos and apparently no proper traffic control. However, we filtered the infantry across in single file, and started off into the night, and into enemy territory, without a single vehicle or anti-tank gun between us. We were delayed some hours by this example of poor staff work.

"It was an extraordinary operation of war: two battalions of infantry marching side-by-side down a narrow road at night, with some moonlight luckily, but with no idea of the enemy's whereabouts and with no supporting arms. Our plan was simple. We had a 'joint' advanced guard, etc., and we two C.O.s walked together. If we met trouble the Essex would deploy to the right, and the Glosters to the left.

"During the night a few jeeps managed to catch up with us—as we were held up by mines and other obstacles.

"About an hour before first light on the 10th August we were up to the village of Courmeron 9649, an advance of only about three miles from the bridge, which gives some idea of the delay caused by the block on the bridge and the mines on the road. The C.O. of the Glosters and I decided to get into some form of position before first light, as we had no intention of being caught by Panzer units with two battalions of infantry strung out along two miles of road in broad daylight, with no proper anti-tank weapons.

"The Glosters deployed to the left on the ridge by Le Mesnil. I pushed on up to the advance guard (Major Holme's 'A' Company), which had by now reached an orchard at a track junction about 300 yards north of Forge-à-Cambro. They were halted.

"We could hear distinctly the sounds of digging and voices just over the crest. 'D' Company quietly deployed to the right, and 'B' to the left, whilst 'A' held the road. I warned 'C' Company to be ready for anything in the morning. We were on the reverse slope, and I doubt whether the enemy realised that we had arrived in any strength.

"Battalion Headquarters was in Courmeron, whence incidentally we routed out some sleeping Germans next morning.

"As day broke the Bosche, probably from the high ground of Point 174 just west of Forge, perceived the Glosters Battalion Headquarters on the ridge to our rear and the first of the arriving tanks. At this stage we were still unmolested, but the Glosters got shelled heavily over our heads, and unfortunately Lieutenant-Colonel Biddulph was the first to be wounded.

"Our squadron of Churchills (our first experience with this excellent tank) arrived up and tried to work around the left flank, but got heavily shelled and withdrew. Our artillery battery commander and one or two F.O.O.s reached us about this time.

"We arranged a simple attack. 'C' Company, supported by the tanks, were to advance straight over the crest, supported by artillery concentrations, first on the orchards on the north edge of Forge, lifting to beyond the main road, and then 'at call.'

" 'C' Company disappeared over the crest, and except for the noises of battle, nothing happened for about forty-five minutes (it seemed longer). The wireless was working, but the operator had lost Major Barrass, the Company Commander, who was particularly active to the front and neglectful of his rear on this day; and no news came back. I was going up to see for myself whether the battle had been won or lost, when I met over 120 German prisoners marching down the road, escorted by 2 men of 'C' Company."

And so Forge-à-Cambro was captured. But the end was not yet.

The enemy reacted violently, and although he did not counter-attack, he brought up a considerable amount of artillery and nebelwerfers. That day and succeeding days the 2nd Essex area was shelled heavily. Battalion Headquarters appeared to be the main target, though "D" Company alone lost some 15 men in killed and wounded, despite being well dug in.

On the evening of the 10th August the 2nd Essex was ordered to carry out another of these unreconnoitred night advances, this time with the 2nd S.W.B. as partner. The order was not appreciated, as the march of the night before had been a very heavy strain and the day had given neither relief nor rest. The 2nd Essex objective was the main road from Thury-Harcourt to the south-east at Haute Breuil, that of the 2nd S.W.B., the ridge at Point 161.

Lieutenant-Colonel Elliott continues his story of this quite extraordinary operation of war: "During the day I drove down the forward slope from Forge in a jeep and had a look from the orchard at 9647. The country in front looked impenetrable. Air photos disclosed some 'rides' in the woods, though very indistinctly, and the map showed a narrow track leading from the main road south into the ravine which runs east and west just north of the Forêt de Bas Breuil. The track down into the ravine, on the north side, indicated a drop of fifty metres in the last 200 yards.

"Lieutenant-Colonel F. S. Barlow, C.O. of the 2nd S.W.B., and I conferred on the best way of getting our two battalions down that narrow track during darkness and maintaining them there next day. Incidentally, we were all very hungry by this time. The Division had not issued us with 'Compo' rations. Brigade Headquarters and the Services were still, so far as I know, west of the Orne, and no victuals had come up. (I believe Brigade Headquarters crossed the night 10th/11th and went to the Château de Villerei). There were two other factors: the open slope down from the main road, which was in full view of numerous German batteries and 'nebels' (neither of us intended to be caught out there in daylight) and the state of training of the Battalion, or of any battalion for that matter, which made the prospect of a night attack in very thick and unreconnoitred woodland uninviting.

"The 2nd S.W.B. had the easier task once we had surmounted the problem of the narrow track. The 2nd S.W.B. therefore led off with one advance guard company. Next followed a composite company of 2nd Essex formed out of our four best platoons, from various companies, in fact, four strong fighting patrols, each of which had a definite objective in the wood, selected from air photos. Major Pallot, the Second-in-Command, commanded this 'forward body.' Then followed the remainder of 2nd S.W.B., and finally 2nd Essex less one company, which was to remain as a reserve at Forge. If daylight came before the whole force was across, we would stop infantry movement down the exposed and lengthy slope, and expect the units that were over the obstacle to hold out in the woods; and then complete the move next night.

"On reflection it was not a good plan, but the best that seemed possible at that time. It would have worked well if only the little track down to the ravine had been passable to carriers. In the event even jeeps had the greatest difficulty in getting down, and to anticipate, when later we sent a bulldozer, its blade could not operate, as the way down resembled a dry rocky water-course rather than a track: it was cut into solid rock.

"At last light on the 10th August the advance started. On reaching the track down into the ravine, the troubles started. I went down early with Lieutenant Barrett-Lennard, the I.O., stepping over the waiting bodies of 2nd S.W.B. and our platoons. They were held up by the leading files who were feeling their way down the overgrown track (it had obviously been disused for years) in pitch darkness. On reaching the bottom we could just see the loom of the dark wood on our right and the high ground (the 2nd S.W.B. objective) on the left. The 2nd S.W.B. company was sorting itself out, preparatory to starting off up the hill. Major Pallot, the I.O., and I went forward with our leading platoon to the bridge over the stream. At that moment a spandau opened from our left, the fire coming unpleasantly close.

"However, the 2nd S.W.B. company did not falter, and charged straight up the hill. Our 'fighting patrols' disappeared into the darkness of the wood. We returned up the track where we met Major Holme, who had come down with us. We waited at the top of the track on the open hillside. The night was absolutely still and misty. Every sound carried across the ravine as distinctly as though from a few yards away. The 2nd S.W.B. were having a fight working up their steep hillside. One could see the flashes, and hear the words of command quite clearly; the German fire orders and shouting, and the screams of some wounded men.

"The 2nd S.W.B. finally captured their ridge, but the delay in the sunken track had been such that their final company was only just clear of the open hillside by first light. I halted the remainder of the Battalion as arranged on the Forge feature. Our four platoons had considerable difficulty in finding their way through the thick forest, but they reached their positions without opposition. Major Pallot established his headquarters about 100 yards to the west of where the downward track debouched from the wood ravine.

"Next morning I went down, with one sniper as escort, and scrambled down through the wooded slope to the north of the ravine, approaching our right-hand outpost from Thury-Harcourt. Everything was absolutely still, and things looked promising for the final stage that night.

"However, later that day there was some exchange of fire in the wood between patrols, and thereafter the pace quickened.

"That night 'C' Company, under Captain P. J. Chell, came down and reinforced the four platoons in the wood. We tried desperately to get the track opened for carriers and anti-tank guns, but in vain. With the 2nd S.W.B. using it also, I considered it injudicious to throw more troops into the wood until they could be maintained properly. An advance into the open beyond the wood seemed out of the question without any anti-tank guns, and with the enemy reacting so strongly."

There were many deeds of gallantry in this battle, only a few of which were seen and recorded owing to the thickness of the wood. There was for example Corporal W. J. Skittrall who was seen to dash and then crawl forward almost up to the enemy to retrieve a wounded private and then walk back bareheaded with the man over his shoulder. The whole area was at the time flooded with small-arms fire. He later carried the wounded man back to Company Headquarters through enemy positions and then returned to the forward platoon carrying ammunition which was at the time very short. Corporal Skittrall was later awarded the D.C.M. and the Croix-de-Guerre.

Early on the 12th August, No. 7 Platoon (Lieutenant R. G. Filby), the forward platoon, was attacked by three fighting patrols. Outnumbered and outgunned, it hung on until finally forced back—not by the enemy, although attacked from all sides—but by fires set alight by the enemy nebelwerfers. It then joined up with No. 9 Platoon (Lieutenant A. A. Vince), the second forward platoon, which controlled the rides in the middle of the forest.

At 4 p.m., another strong attack developed, this time against "C" Company on the Battalion right flank. There was a sharp engagement,

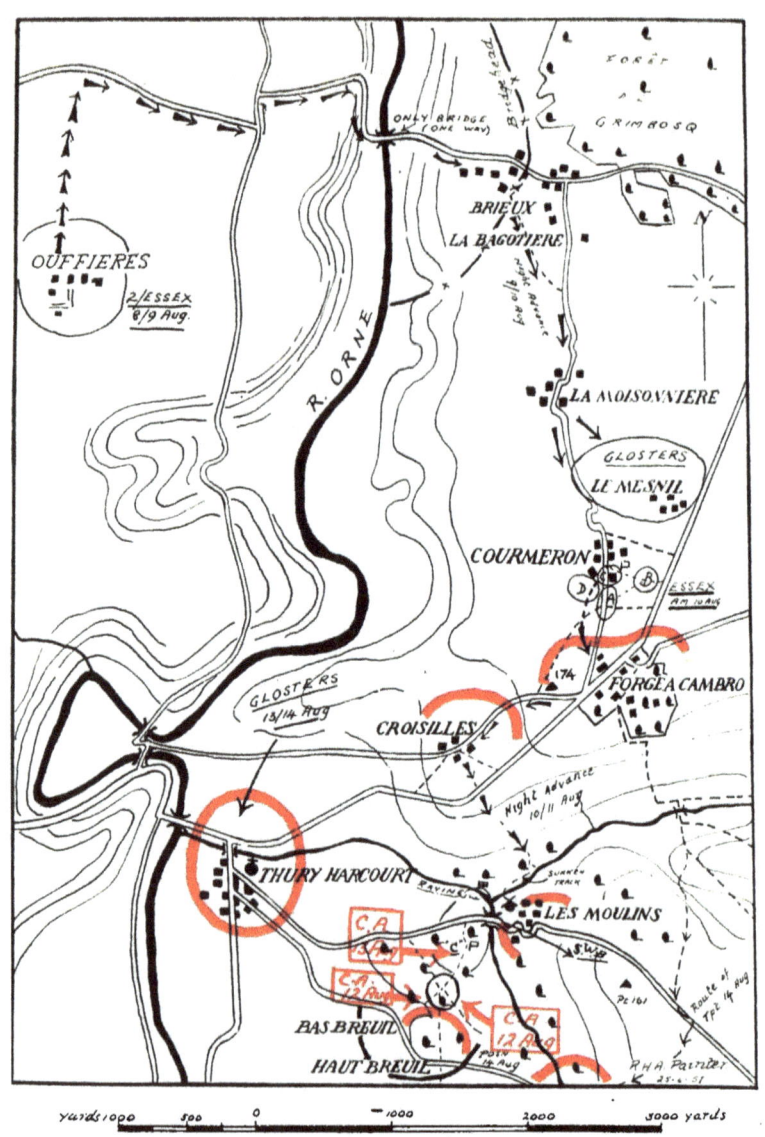

2ND ESSEX, CROSSING OF THE ORNE-FORGE À CAMBRO-BAS BREUIL-ESSON,
8TH-17TH AUGUST, 1944.

in the course of which No. 13 Platoon was overrun and "C" Company Headquarters attacked. Captain Peter Chell was killed in this close-range fighting, gallantly defending his Company Headquarters. It was most difficult to control the supporting artillery fire, owing to lack of observation, but nevertheless the fire of three regiments of 25-pounders and some 4·2 inch mortars was brought down and the enemy finally withdrew after suffering many casualties.

On the 13th Thury-Harcourt fell to the 2nd Glosters, and the pressure on the 2nd Essex eased off.

On the 13th the Battalion again advanced, the infantry through the woods and the vehicles by a circuitous and difficult route, via Rue Gournay. That night the 2nd Essex was in Esson, with leading elements on the high ground round Caumont. The Battalion had been much delayed by mines and there was some shelling but otherwise the battle or series of battles was over.

It had been a most unpleasant operation. It had involved a great strain on the troops taking part, as in most places visibility was between three and five yards, and the whole area had been under heavy and continuous shell and mortar fire for forty-eight hours. Atmospheric difficulties had been intense, and from every angle the 2nd Essex was extremely glad to have the 15th and 16th August as quiet days. All were tired, dirty, hungry, and in need of rest. The lazy days, bathing in the lovely River Orne and being welcomed by the civilians who had remained through the battle, long remained a memory. So much so that when in August 1947 the village of Esson held a Thanksgiving Service on the third anniversary of their liberation from the German occupation, a party of the Essex Regiment was invited by the Mayor and Curé to attend. The invitation was gladly accepted. The party officially representing the Regiment consisted of Captain M. W. Holme, M.C., Sergeant W. Ankrett, and Sergeant P. Bidwell from the Depot, while Major P. R. Barrass, Captain A. A. Vince, M.C., and Captain H. Barrett-Lennard also attended. Unfortunately, a party from the "Pompadours," then in Mestre, North Italy, was unable to get through to Esson in time for the reunion and the Thanksgiving Service.

On the 17th August the 2nd Essex moved to Trepal near Falaise, the move being part of the relief of the 168th Infantry Brigade by the 56th Infantry Brigade. Here the Battalion was in reserve and not employed in the final stages of the destruction of the German army in the Falaise pocket.

Transfer to the 49th (West Riding) Division

The "Pompadours" had been with the 59th Division only twelve days when they, with the 56th Infantry Brigade, were ordered to move and join the 49th (West Riding) Division—Major-General Evelyn Barker's "Polar Bears."

The 59th Division had done its task and was to be disbanded. Losses in the break-out of the Normandy bridge-head had been heavy and it was proposed to reduce the number of British divisions to be employed after the break-out. The fall in British man-power was, of course, more than balanced by the now rapidly increasing Allied strength. American divisions were landing almost continuously at Cherbourg and Brest direct from the United States.

With the transfer to the 49th Division, the 2nd Essex left the 30th Corps and the Second British Army to come under the command of 1st British Corps now part of the First Canadian Army.

On arrival in the 1st Corps area, after a confused move (the Battalion was misdirected to an area north of Caen when the 49th Division had already moved many miles east), the "Pompadours" billeted at Pedouze. Here they were, for the first time since D-Day, properly re-equipped by the efficient and helpful Divisional A/Q. Staff and services, and visited, too, by the Divisional Commander.

It should be stressed that since D-Day the 2nd Essex—and indeed all 56th Infantry Brigade—had been administered by and fought with the 50th and 59th Divisions and had fought with the 7th Armoured Division as well. With the efficient 50th Division it was, if not the fifth wheel in the coach, the fourth infantry brigade where the administrative machine was designed for three, and in the 59th Division the 56th Infantry Brigade was administratively hardly noticed before the Division was disbanded. And so it was with some feeling of relief that the "Pompadours" joined a division in which they were immediately and properly cared for and made to feel "they belonged." This change of command was to be the final one, for "V.E.-Day" was to find the 2nd Essex still one of General Barker's "Polar Bears." [1]

Pedouze and the new divisional area were to the south and east of Caen. Here the First Canadian Army was moving east with the 2nd Canadian Corps directed on Rouen and the 1st British Corps on the lower reaches of the River Seine.

[1] The 49th (West Riding) Division took a polar bear for the divisional sign by reason of its service in Iceland in 1940-41.

The Germans on this front had not been involved in the Falaise debacle, and were conducting an orderly withdrawal to the river line. It was as Lieutenant-Colonel Elliott says, "An alternate series of halts, advances, and quickly planned attacks against enemy rear-guards on successive obstacles."

Cormeilles

During the afternoon of the 24th August the Battalion, preceded by the Divisional Reconnaissance Regiment, crossed the River Tuoques by an engineer bridge at Le Breuil-en-Ange, and advanced via Blangy-le-Château towards Cormeilles, a small town set in picturesque wooded country bisected by a number of small streams and rivers.

On approaching from the west, it was found that the enemy was holding the town and the line of the River La Calonne, and that the reconnaissance regiment had not succeeded in finding a way in or around.

Lieutenant-Colonel Elliott went forward with the Battalion "R" Group to the high ground overlooking the town, but owing to the dense woods, it was impossible to see anything useful. It was raining.

Cormeilles lies mostly on the eastern slope of a narrow steep valley, and at 8.30 p.m., two companies, supported by artillery, and tank fire from the right flank, attacked from the west.

"B" Company (Major D. W. Browne) led and quickly seized the western half of the town, and "A" Company (Major P. J. Wilkins) passing through, entered the main square. There was little or no opposition, and the enemy fled out of the east end of the town as the "Pompadours" came through from the west. "C" Company (Major P. R. Barrass) was quickly pushed through on to the high ground to the east and north-east, and the place was further secured by patrols from all three companies moving out in all directions. (The Battalion was at the moment operating with only three rifle companies, "D" Company having been temporarily disbanded owing to heavy casualties not yet replaced.)

The 25th August was a gala day, with everything free, the Battalion being fêted for the few hours it was in Cormeilles. Many R.A.F. personnel shot down over France and hidden up by French patriots in or near Cormeilles were found in the area.

Pont Audemer

On the 26th August the eastward movement of the 1st Corps took the 2nd Essex to Pont Audemer, the western part of which was found

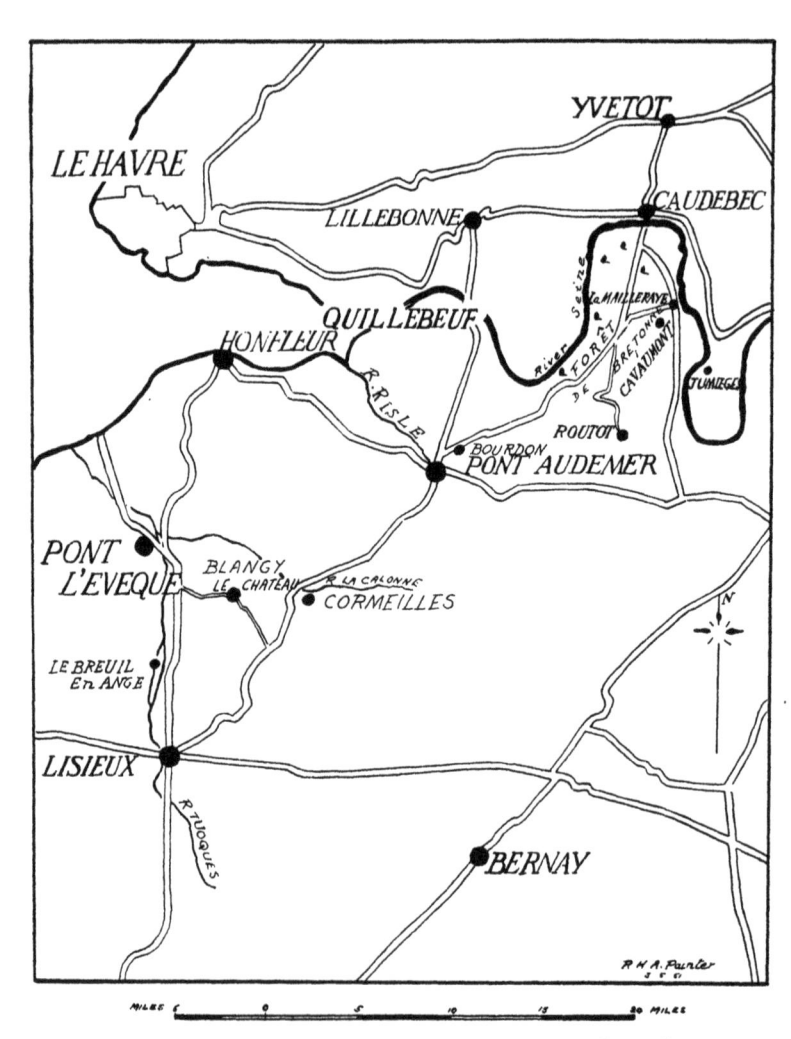

2ND ESSEX, THE ADVANCE TO AND CROSSING OF THE RIVER SEINE,
24TH AUGUST–2ND SEPTEMBER, 1944.

to be held by elements of the 6th Airborne Division. By strange chance, one of the first members of the 5th Parachute Brigade to see the arrival of the 2nd Essex was Major J. F. Cramphorn, who remarks that just as his battalion had reached the edge of the river he was delighted to see a strange jeep arrive with an officer wearing the Essex badge. Unfortunately his unit was ordered to move before he could contact his old battalion.

Pont Audemer, a fair-sized town, lies in a valley about a mile or so wide, mainly on the west side of the River Risle, but close up to the predominant and steep east bank, or rather escarpment. The enemy were holding the escarpment and east bank in some strength. All bridges were blown. There could be no delay, as a bridge-head was an urgent necessity to allow the subsequent construction of bridges to carry the 1st Corps forward in their effort to liquidate the German army still west of the Seine.

There was some intermittent shelling and mortaring, directed at the town. Brigade ordered a crossing that night, 2nd Essex on the right (i.e. to the south-east of the town) and 2nd S.W.B. opposite the town itself. The 2nd Essex objective was the line of orchards on the edge of the plateau above the escarpment.

It was impossible to get down to reconnoitre the river by daylight, as the open fields on the flat valley were in full view of the enemy on the escarpment opposite, but the Risle could be seen as a fast clear stream, not easy to cross even by boat. Local F.F.I. (French Forces of the Interior, or the Resistance Army) gave information, some true, some proved later to be inaccurate.

Lieutenant-Colonel Elliott had, at this time, been joined by Lieutenant-Colonel R. C. Stockley, Royal Northumberland Fusiliers, lately G.S.O.I. (Air) Second Army, an old friend, who had come for some practical experience prior to taking command of a battalion.

Lieutenant-Colonel Elliott gives his account of the action:

"We had been provided with four folding boats. From the map and from the photos, I decided to cross in two places: on the right at Les Baquets, and on the left at 778088, opposite a track leading from the main road.

"Lieutenant-Colonel Stockley led the right-hand two companies, and I went down with the two left companies.

"After dark I preceded the taping parties, with one sniper, and actually walked along our side of the bank at the left crossing site. There was no sound from the enemy side, and the affair looked hopeful.

"At about 11.30 p.m. the boat parties started to arrive, making considerable noise. The wire fences round the fields were not of the usual round-wire variety, but constructed of steel 'tape,' which was too

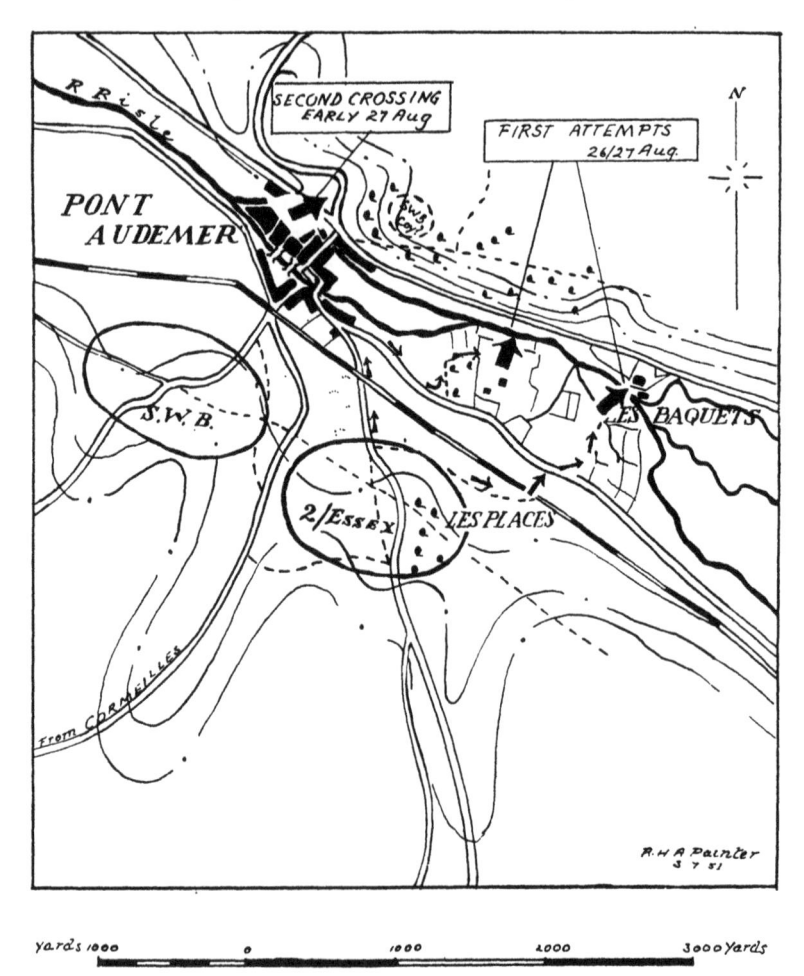

2ND ESSEX, PONT AUDEMER, 26TH/27TH AUGUST, 1944.

tough for the ordinary wire-cutters. As the leading platoon crept down to the river, to take up positions to cover the move-up of the boats and the launching, several spandaus opened at point-blank range from the far bank. It was most uncomfortable, as the tracers were sweeping the flat fields, and there was no cover.

"The leading platoon suffered casualties, and became disorganised. 'A' Company from the left, near the end of the track, now opened up with Piats at the enemy positions. Although we won the fire fight, we had not crossed the river.

"The two companies on the right also received a similar reception, their F.F.I. guide, who had been so certain of getting across undiscovered, being killed.

"At about this time a company of the 2nd S.W.B. managed to cross undetected, in the town, and reached the edge of the escarpment, where they remained cut off for some hours.

"The first attempt having failed, we were ordered to try to get over in the town, to reinforce the one company of the 2nd S.W.B., though their position and condition were not known.

"A" Company attempted the obvious, and tried to cross, by wading, by the demolished main-road bridge. One section succeeded, but then the enemy 'came to' with alacrity, and further movement was impossible. This section held out most of next day, until the enemy pulled back. This battle only served to prove the well-known fact that a river crossing by night without adequate reconnaissance and preparation, and without adequate unit training, is a very hazardous operation: under these conditions it has very little chance of success."

The section referred to by Lieutenant-Colonel Elliott was one and one-half sections of No. 9 Platoon (Lieutenant A. A. Vince). They were at dawn in a couple of wrecked buildings completely encircled by the enemy, who frequently and unsuccessfully called upon them to surrender. The stalemate continued until the early afternoon when the Germans withdrew.

Forêt de Bretonne

At 3 p.m., the 27th August, the remainder of the Battalion crossed the Risle and the eastward march was continued.

On the 28th, the 56th Infantry Brigade was given the task of clearing the Forêt de Bretonne, a large wooded area running down to the bank of the River Seine, and the only area on the sector of the front that the enemy still held west of that river. It was known to be full of men, horses, and material; in fact, the residue of the German Seventh Army which still hoped for evacuation eastward across the river.

That day, the 28th August, the 2nd Essex Regiment closed upon the south side of the Forêt de Bretonne with the enemy holding the southern entrances to the forest. They were not in strength, but still fought with gallantry to hold off the Brigade advance whilst their main bodies were crossing the Seine in confusion. The Battalion had been on the move or fighting with little sleep for a week and all ranks were very exhausted by this time.

The advance guard first engaged the enemy among the orchards around the hamlet of Le Bourdonne, a few miles north of Routot. Efforts of infiltration were thwarted by well-sited enemy machine guns, which were most difficult to locate in the thick hedgerows.

The 2nd S.W.B., on the 2nd Essex left, astride the one main road through the forest (Routot to the Caudebec-en-Caux Ferry) was also held up. The plan for the 29th August was for the 2nd Essex to patrol up to the edge of the forest and then go forward, by limited attack, to areas where the enemy was reported.

"We put in a one-company attack, which failed," says Colonel Elliott. "Sergeant J. Pullen, one of our best men who had been with the Battalion throughout, was killed in this attack. Sergeant B. Burton, the medical sergeant, was also killed about now by a small splinter of glass when his rear driving mirror was hit. The splinter entered his neck and left hardly any mark to show for it."

On the 30th the whole front loosened up. The 2nd S.W.B. moved fast up their main road and reached the river. The 2nd Essex, entering the forest, drove the stragglers before them into the waiting arms of the 2nd S.W.B. The forest was found to be full of abandoned enemy equipment all most thoroughly burnt or destroyed.

There was considerable trouble with mines. Lieutenant D. W. Grigg was killed later, whilst on a "count" of enemy material, ordered by Brigade, when his jeep was blown up. Many thousands of horses were there for the rounding up; indeed, many "Pompadours" chose their mounts, and for the following two rest days at Cavaumont and La Mailleraye-sur-Seine the Battalion was to all intents and purposes mounted infantry.

On the 2nd September the Battalion crossed the Seine. The infantry in raft, assault boat, and amphibious craft had a somewhat dangerous crossing owing to the "chop" on the water. "A" Echelon crossed by ferry opposite Jumiéges, and "B" Echelon crossed by a broken bridge and under divisional arrangements many miles away to the south-east. On this day the Battalion was, in fact, spread over about fifty miles of country.

The Attack on Le Havre—Operation "Astonia"

After crossing the Seine, the Battalion concentrated at Alliquerville some twenty miles from the outskirts of Le Havre. The march from the Seine was expedited by the use of three captured German diesel-engined buses.

At this time the British Second Army was advancing rapidly towards Arras and Belgium, whilst First Canadian Army was given the task of clearing the heavily defended Channel ports. Le Havre was top priority, as this port and Rouen were urgently required for maintenance of the British, Canadian, and American armies. The capture of Le Havre was allotted to 1st British Corps, consisting of 51st (Highland) Division on the right and 49th Division on the left.

On the 3rd September the Battalion moved forward at first light, and took over from the 49th Divisional Reconnaissance Regiment on the high ground just south-east of Montivilliers.

The outline plan was as follows: *Phase I*, the 49th Division, supported by a heavy weight of armour and artillery to breach the obstacles just west of Montivilliers and capture the northern plateau. *Phase II*, the 49th Division to capture the southern plateau and the 51st Division to widen the original breach and secure a base north of the Forêt de Montgeon. *Phase III*, the 51st Division to attack north-east to Octville. *Phase IV*, both divisions to exploit into the town.

From here on we are only concerned with Phase I, as the 56th Infantry Brigade was given the honour of opening the attack and breaching the obstacle.

The 56th Brigade plan was as follows: two squadrons of "flail" tanks (22nd Dragoons), supported by two squadrons of "gun" tanks (7th Battalion Royal Tanks), and various armoured engineer detachments were to breach the obstacles and make nine lanes. Next, the 2nd S.W.B. on the right, and the 2nd Glosters on the left, supported by "gun" and "flame" tanks, were to pass through and clear strongpoints numbers one to seven. Thereafter the 2nd Essex, mounted in "kangaroos" and supported by one squadron of "gun" tanks and one troop of A.V.R.E. (armoured vehicles, Royal Engineers), were to pass through, capture strong-points numbers 9, 9a and 10, seize two bridges over the River Fontaine, and then establish a footing on the escarpment on the southern plateau.

Lieutenant-Colonel Elliott continues:

"Now began a period of extensive patrolling and preparation. Except for the initial assault on the beaches, this was the most thoroughly organised attack of the campaign. It had to be, because the enemy defences were formidable indeed, having been constructed over years to deal with just such an attack as we were now preparing. However, enemy morale, with the exception of a few units, was reported to be low. On the 5th September the Battalion moved across to Le Tot. Here the final touches were made, e.g. practising loading and quick dismounting from our 'kangaroos.'

"D-Day had been fixed for the 9th September, but heavy rain fell, and the operation was delayed until the 10th. The ground became water-logged, and we had misgivings, later justified, that our wheeled and half-tracked vehicles would have trouble off the roads.

"Our route down to our forward assembly area at Fontenay 545337 had been cleared and taped. Owing to the weight of air bombardment we could not move down to this area until just prior to the attack. Major Barrass was in charge of the forward assembly area, and made certain that the various infantry, tank, and other sub-units were 'married up' with their various groups and teams. For example, both leading companies, 'A' on the right, and 'B' on the left, were 'grouped' as follows:

" 'A' (or 'B') Company.
One section carrier platoon.
One section pioneer platoon.
Forward Observation Officer, 185 Field Regiment.
Forward fire controller, mortar platoon.
Two troops 'A' Squadron 7th Royal Tanks.
Half-troop 617 A.V.R.E.

"On orders from Brigade, we were to drive through whichever gaps were open straight to our objectives. 'A' Company were allotted strong-points 9 and 9a (the latter discovered later by reconnaissance and air photographs) and the two bridges. 'B' Company strong-point 10, then into reserve ready to move to the escarpment; 'C' Company, to follow in rear to just north of strong-point 3, ready for the last phase."

The assault started at 5.45 p.m. on the 10th September, preceded by bombing by "heavies" of Bomber Command. These and the artillery bombardments succeeded in "softening up" the enemy in no mean fashion, but they had one other effect also; the ground was so dis-

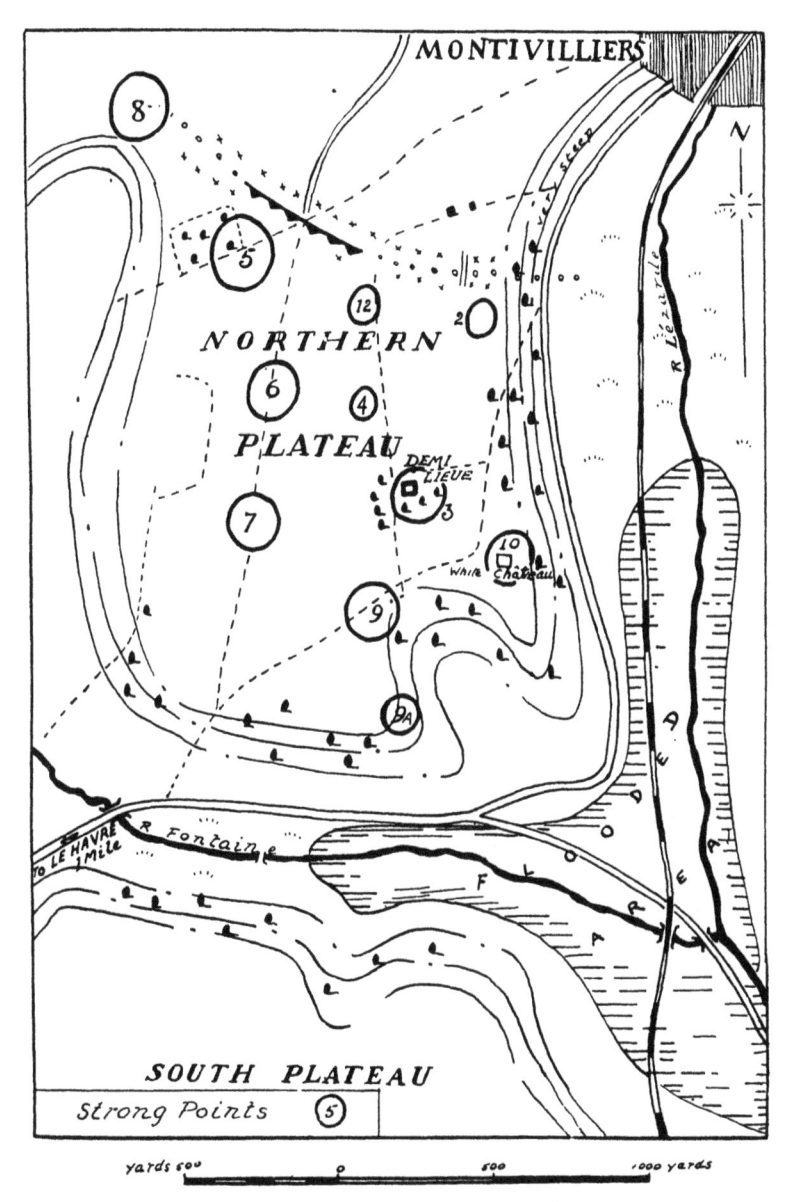

2ND ESSEX, THE CAPTURE OF LE HAVRE, 3RD–12TH SEPTEMBER, 1944.

turbed and the trees were so destroyed and cut up that movement either by foot or vehicle became a major problem. The woods became an absolute tangle, and even with the help of artificial moonlight[1] it was most difficult to advance.

The air preparation culminated in a mighty ninety-minute attack before H-Hour, in which nearly 5,000 tons of bombs were dropped. To this attack and to the earlier "softening-up" raids must be attributed much of the credit for the great success of the assault.

"The men were lying down waiting for the assault when Bomber Command appeared," says Major M. W. Holme, "but everyone was too enthralled to think of the enemy and promptly stood up to watch. Several thousand tons of bombs were dropped, the closest about 1,500–2,000 yards from us. After that it wasn't a battle—it was a question of finding the Boche at the bottom of his shelters and some of them were forty feet deep. I am told the Corps Commander watched the air attack and said, "This isn't war, it's murder."

The two leading battalions, 2nd S.W.B. (right) and 2nd Glosters (left), had been withdrawn 3,000 yards and the armour 2,000 yards from the bombed area for safety reasons. At 5.45 p.m., the leading infantry crossed the 35° northing, and the flailing of the nine lanes through the minefield started about 6.30 p.m.

About the same time the 2nd Essex moved down to the forward assembly area under the second-in-command (Major C. L. Sayers) and Lieutenant-Colonel Elliott reported to Brigade Headquarters at Bertrand.

"The commander of the tank brigade also had his report centre here," says Colonel Elliott, "and we had a clear view of the battlefield though from afar. The flail tanks seemed to be hardly moving at this distance. Shelling was intense, and in rear of the 'flails' the gun tanks kept up rapid fire. Every now and then one could see a puff of earth and smoke as the mines were exploded. Owing to the long grass and wet ground, flailing was not as effective as usual, and several mines exploded under the tanks, knocking them out.

"To complete the story of the gapping, and in one instance the bridging of the ditch, three lanes were completed initially on the right (Laura 4, 5b and 6) none in the centre (Hazel 7–9) and one on the extreme right (Mary 11). However, such was the state of the ground that at no time could one guarantee a passage, as infantry and other

---

[1] Searchlight reflections from the sky arranged at the most suitable angle dependent on the operational requirement.

vehicles were continually bogging down and blocking the few lanes open. Also, mines, which had been passed over or missed by the flails, continued to take their toll. At 8.15 a.m. on the 11th, only two lanes remained open, one for wheels, one for tanks. Twenty-nine flail tanks, two command tanks, and six A.V.R.E.s were knocked out, the majority due to mines but some to anti-tank fire. This gives some idea of the conditions.

"Tanks of the 7th Royal Tank Regiment, which had been supporting the gapping or first phase, started to pass through about 7.30 p.m., thirty minutes behind schedule. I saw four tanks 'go up' on mines almost simultaneously. The 'crocodiles' and infantry followed hard after. Despite the awful effect of the flame-throwers (they annihilated one German platoon, which was either counter-attacking or withdrawing—it was not clear which, but they were in the open), the 2nd S.W.B. had considerable trouble, suffering 60 casualties in their second company, directed on strong-point 6. Most of this fire came from strong-point 8, which had not been included as an objective, though saturated by preliminary artillery concentrations and 800 rounds of 3-inch and 1,400 rounds of 4·2-inch mortar fire. Unfortunately, the 2nd S.W.B.'s forward observation officer on this flank was taken prisoner, and after the initial bombardment no artillery fire was directed on to strong-point 8.

"The 2nd Glosters on the left made slow but steady progress and captured their objectives by about 9.15 p.m.

"It was now getting dark. At about 10 p.m. the exact position was obscure, but the Brigadier told me to go. I dashed down to the forward assembly area, where the 'Order group' was waiting under cover. In view of the state of the gaps, of the going and of the light, I ordered the Battalion to dismount and take off on foot. I ordered the squadron of tanks to move at once and independently to a rendezvous just north of strong-point 3 at Demi-Lieue, where the infantry would catch up. Realising that the half-track (rear link) might not get through, I kept one 'kangaroo' only as command vehicle. I gave the Adjutant a rendezvous for the morning. 'Mary' seemed to be the most reliable gap, and we headed for there. Carriers were quite useless and simply 'bellied' between the deep tank tracks.

"Although slowly, everything went according to plan. As anticipated, the rear-link half-track could not get through. Fortunately, the 2nd Glosters' half-track did so, and for the remainder of that night we used their rear link for messages back to Brigade. In any case, there were so many armoured units on the air that radio communications were more often than not ineffective.

"About 11.30 p.m., 'B' Company with a troop of tanks (the latter were more useful for bashing through the tangled trees and undergrowth than for fire support) captured strong-point 10 and 'A' Company strong-point 9 and later 9a. About 40 prisoners and 2 female camp followers were taken. Both companies then cleared the south end of the northern plateau and 'A' Company seized the bridge intact over the River Fontaine, which a patrol had reported as intact, and which might serve as an approach for any possible counter-attack in the morning. (It had been reported that the Germans had one good battalion available as a reserve.)

"At about 2 a.m., not having heard from 'B' Company, I went forward with difficulty to visit the 'White' Château, strong-point 10. It was difficult going, and at times one had to crawl under and climb over the fallen trees. I found Major Browne and his Headquarters comfortably established in the cellars of the ruined château sampling the captured victuals. His company were all out on various tasks, e.g. supporting the A.V.R.E.s, which were trying to clear the main road below the escarpment, and it was obviously too late to launch an attack on the escarpment of the southern plateau.

"Having cleared the northern plateau and seized three bridges intact, I considered that we had done enough for the night, and therefore stood fast to see what daylight might bring.

"*En route* back to 'Tac.' Battalion Headquarters at Demi-Lieue, I discovered the entrance to a dugout which led to an O.P. which we had suspected but never identified reliably from air photos. The contents were valuable, so I immediately sent back to Major Browne and told him to place a guard on it. This was as well, as next morning various staff and service representatives came up as usual from the rear on a searching expedition, but were turned away from our legitimate spoils (which later gave good cheer to the various messes) at the point of the bayonet.

"There is not much more to say about the Battle of Le Havre. We only had 9 casualties, but it was nevertheless an exciting experience, and the companies did very well considering the difficult conditions.

"We spent the night of the 11th on the outskirts (other battalions having passed through), and next morning entered the town, with the responsibility of clearing one sector of it. During the morning an agitated F.F.I. 'major' informed us that the local gaol was being held by Gestapo and collaborators. There was a good deal of indiscriminate shooting. After considerable persuasion we cleared the armed civilians away—they were very dangerous, many youths being armed literally to the teeth, with rifles, revolvers, grenades, and other captured weapons—and surrounded the building. A Sherman tank then blasted down the gates, and we entered warily. The birds had flown."

The Intelligence Officer gives a short picture of the final stage: "1158 hours. 2 Glosters report capture of C.R.A. and staff—all enemy guns silent. By tea-time the job is finished and we are waiting for the cafés to open. During the whole operation the Essex lost 1 killed and 8 wounded, against which we contributed over 1,000 prisoners to the Brigade score of 2,901." In all, over 12,000 prisoners were taken, and one of the strongest fortresses of the Western or Atlantic Wall had fallen after only forty-eight hours' fighting.

The 2nd Essex only stayed one more night in Le Havre, moving to Lillebonne on the 13th September to refit and rest. "This," says Captain A. A. Vince, "was a great pity, as there were untold stocks of wines and spirits in the German stores, and most of it had to be left for the fellows who had not fought for it." However, that "most of it" leaves one to suppose at least some of it went with the Essex to Lillebonne, to cheer their five-day rest. Here reinforcements were received, and "D" Company, disbanded through casualties, was reformed as a training company, command being taken by Captain W. F. McMichael, M.C.

On the 18th September, the Battalion was moved to Avesnes-en-Val, near Dieppe, to continue training and recuperation. But on the 22nd the rest period ended, and the 2nd Essex embussed in divisional transport vehicles of varying natures for the move-up to the battle front in Belgium. It will be remembered that while the 1st Corps was reducing the fortress of Le Havre, the remainder of the British and Canadian armies had swept forward into Belgium and almost to the Rhine itself.

And so on the 22nd and 23rd September the Battalion moved forward to Helleburg, near Lierre, staying *en route* at Phalempin, near Carvin, where the "Pompadours" had been temporarily quartered in 1939–40. It was a two-hundred-mile progression through flag-waving, cheering crowds. The convoy was showered with fruit, wine, and flowers. It was an experience never to be forgotten and some compensation for the hard days that had gone before.

Ryckevorsel, 25th/26th September, 1944.

At Helleburg the 2nd Essex rested for two days in various châteaux and farmhouses in the neighbourhood.

At this time the leading elements of the 49th Division were attempting to cross the Turnhout-Antwerp Canal to the north, and on the 25th September the 2nd Essex moved forward to a position of readiness at Oosmalle.

The situation was rather obscure. The 4th Lincolns, of the 146th Infantry Brigade, had seized a bridge over a lock by the brickworks which are shown on the sketch-map of the Ryckevorsel area, and were alleged to be holding Ryckevorsel itself.

The 2nd Essex was, on the 25th September, ordered to relieve this battalion.

As Lieutenant-Colonel Elliott says:

"I drove up in the jeep, and joined their C.O. (and also his Brigadier) at the road junction a few hundred yards south-east of the town. There was a stiff battle in progress, and the Lincolns were only then entering the fringe of the town, and meeting considerable opposition. It hardly seemed the right time to arrange relief, but we were completely out of touch with both brigade and division, so we carried on.

" 'A' Company on the right and 'B' on the left took over somewhat untidily after dark in the southern parts of the town, with enemy in close contact. It was impractical to pull out the other battalions' anti-tank guns, and they remained with us until the next night, when the situation was more settled.

"I kept 'C' Company in reserve, around the road junction, as we were very exposed from the flanks and left rear.

"Next morning we were heavily shelled and then counter-attacked by large numbers of infantry. The forward platoons fought back magnificently, but even so, elements of 'B' Company got surrounded, but held on. However, the enemy were working around our left rear (south of the 'windmill'—see sketch-map) and were nearing our approach road. Bullets were smacking into Battalion Headquarters with unpleasant frequency. The 2nd S.W.B. were reported to be holding the bridge and the ground to the east and west of it, but there was a large gap between us.

"Someone reported that a squadron of Canadian Sherman tanks had crossed the bridge, and were lying up in preparation for some subsequent operations by a Canadian division. I sent the I.O. back

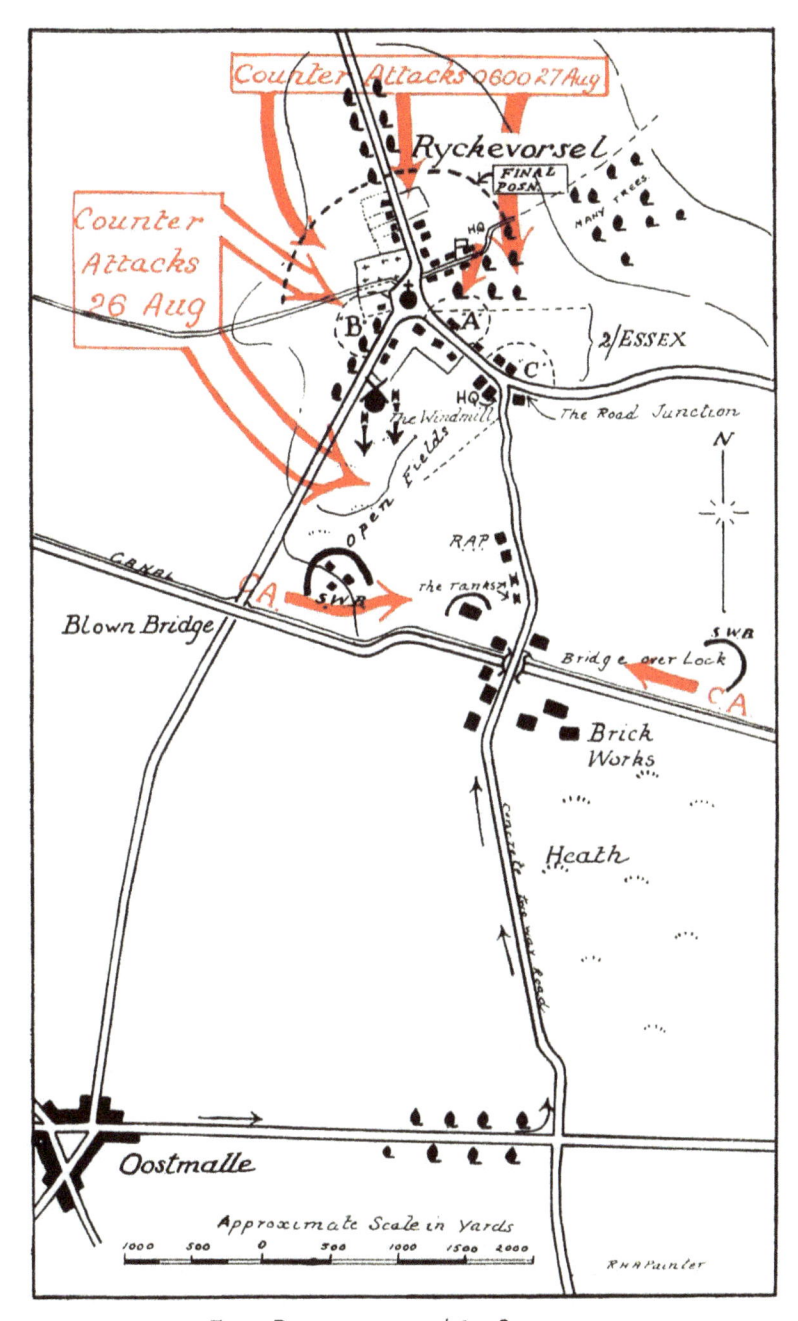

2ND ESSEX, RYCKEVORSEL, 25TH/26TH SEPTEMBER, 1944.

with an invitation to the squadron commander that he helped us out with the loan of three or four tanks. He responded with alacrity, and shortly after (it must have been about midday on the 25th September by this time) a young subaltern reported to Battalion Headquarters with a troop of tanks. I told him that if he would risk driving into the village square, and turning sharp left for the windmill he would take the equivalent of at least one enemy infantry battalion in flank, and out in the open.

"He drove off, and although sniped at *en route*, duly reached the windmill, where, in his own words afterwards, 'he had the best shooting of his career.' This tank manœuvre completely broke up the attack, though shelling and mortaring, and some attention from an S.P. gun (alleged to be a 'Tiger' tank, as usual) and some 20-mm. cannon, continued throughout the day and night. (Incidentally, the 2nd S.W.B. nearly lost the bridge during the night, as the enemy came down the canal banks in some strength.)

"Early next morning the second and stronger counter-attack developed, this time a frontal attack with the equivalent of six infantry battalions. We were first shelled very heavily (as heavily as at any time during the campaign), especially round the road junction and Battalion Headquarters. It was a miracle that no one was hit.

"Again I sent back for the tanks, and up they came without hesitation (and contrary to their orders: the squadron commander had been rebuked for supporting troops of another division on the previous day without higher authority). This time they went into a supporting position in rear of 'A' Company on the right, but the leading platoons held out.

"After this battle the enemy dead lay out in rows in the fields in front of our positions. Burial was a major problem.

"As the enemy recoiled, we went forward and occupied the northern half of the village. Except for shelling and fighting patrols, the battle was over, and they did not try us again.

"Our main problem after the battle was the feeding of the many hundreds of civilians who had spent the two days crouching in their cellars. Milk for children was particularly difficult. However, the Belgian Red Cross (or some equivalent organisation) quickly came to our assistance, and were most efficient and co-operative."

The "Pompadours" remained in the line near Ryckevorsel until the morning of the 7th October, almost ten days of continuous deep patrolling and under constant shell fire. The front was wide and the

Battalion so thinly spread over the ground that "S" Company (Captain W. J. Barry), in addition to its normal commitments with rifle companies, formed a composite company to hold a part of the line, flanked by another force made up from the M.T.

On the 1st October the Battalion was extremely sorry to part with Lieutenant-Colonel G. G. Elliott, who had been in command since the 10th June, 1944, a distinguished period of command for which he was later awarded the D.S.O.

Writing to Lieutenant-General Sir Geoffrey Howard, Colonel Elliott said: "We have had many casualties. But the Battalion never failed to acquit itself well and they remained happy and cheerful."

Writing of Lieutenant-Colonel Elliott, Captain J. Townrow, his Adjutant, says:

"He used to make full use of the magnificent artillery support we invariably had available. When an enemy counter-attack was impending or had actually started, he would listen to sounds of the battle, and together with company reports and a careful study of the map and accurate appreciation he would call for artillery support, usually to great advantage. No doubt there is nothing new in this, but the fact that he remained calm and could make a good appreciation quickly was I think a great help (and comfort) to forward companies. This worked particularly well at the Bois de St. Germain, when it looked impossible for our companies to hold the Boche onslaughts and it appeared we must be overwhelmed."

The new Commanding Officer was Lieutenant-Colonel N. W. Finlinson, D.S.O. (The South Staffordshire Regiment). Major C. L. Sayers was now Second-in-Command. Captain J. Townrow was Adjutant, and Captain A. A. Vince Intelligence Officer. Headquarter Company was commanded by Captain P. E. Butler, "A" Company by Major M. W. Holme, "B" by Major D. W. Browne, M.C., "C" by Major P. J. Wilkins, "D" by Captain W. F. McMichael, M.C., and "S" Company by Captain W. J. Barry.

On the 7th October the 2nd Essex was relieved in Ryckevorsel by a composite group—"Bobforce," comprised of light anti-aircraft and anti-tank units fighting as infantry—and spent that night near the small town of Poppel.

Here the Battalion dug in and held the front north of Poppel for ten days, as conditions became temporarily static on this sector. It was to be ten days of rain, with slit trenches at all times over ankle deep in mud, days in which movement was impossible with an alert enemy only a few hundred yards away, and nights of endless patrolling. There was never-ending shelling and mortaring, and some 20 casualties were incurred with another 40 sick. It was not an inviting period; and sitting in their isolated positions in the woods round the town, the "Pompadours" began to wonder if they were dug in for the winter. The one bright spot was the possibility for a few of forty-eight hours' leave in Turnhout, provided they were able to catch the train which ran daily between Poppel and Turnhout despite enemy shelling.

However, the period of waiting came to an end on the 18th October, when the 2nd Essex was relieved by an infantry unit of the Polish Armoured Division, and concentrated the following day in the small town of St. Leonard preparatory to the next attack.

St. Leonard-Leonhout, 20th/21st October, 1944

This was to be an attack by 49th Division in company with the 4th Canadian Armoured Division and the Polish Armoured Division to clear south-west Holland towards the River Maas. The attack was complementary to the operations of the Canadian Army on the south bank of the River Scheldt, for by now the Allied need of Antwerp was imperative. The long carry from the bases in Normandy was exercising an increasing drag on the administrative machine and operations were being slowed up. Indeed, at this time, the situation was so grave that General Montgomery had been forced to shut down all offensive operations in the 21st Army Group and devote all his resources to getting the Scheldt estuary cleared of the enemy and the port of Antwerp working to capacity.

In the sector to which the 2nd Essex was now allotted north of St. Leonard the Germans, firmly dug in on marshy ground favouring the defence and well supported by artillery and S.P. guns, were holding a position in depth about two miles south of the small town of Leonhout, with the forward position about two miles north of the 2nd Essex position near St. Leonard.

Everything had to be done quickly. The attack was planned for 7.30 a.m., on the 20th October, exactly twenty-four hours after the Battalion had been ordered to the St. Leonard concentration area. But they were equal to the task. "Maps, air photos, admin. plans, artillery, mortars, tanks, flame-throwers all have to be organised, and we surprised ourselves by doing all this and still having a good night's sleep." So said the Intelligence Officer on the 19th October.

At 7.28 a.m., the 20th October, four field regiments (25-pounders) and three medium regiments (5.5-inch), together with all available 3-inch and 4.2-inch mortars, opened up, and two minutes later tanks, "crocodiles," and infantry crossed the taped start-line. It was a two-battalion attack, the 2nd Essex being directed on Leonhout, with 2nd Glosters on their right, while the 2nd S.W.B. were to make tentative thrusts, or worrying efforts, from their base at Brecht towards Beekhoven.

The 2nd Glosters reported their first objective taken at 7.43 a.m. Similarly, Major Browne's "B" Company only took thirteen minutes to gain its initial objective, but "C" Company (Major Wilkins), the left forward company, ran into very strong enemy opposition in the small village of Stapelheide, which had been little affected by the artillery concentrations. This defended locality was held by at least one company of infantry in well-sited weapon positions, and despite support from two troops of tanks and one troop of "crocodiles," "C" Company was unable to get on. For eight hours the Company had to fight from ditch to ditch, supported by the flame-throwing "crocodiles" and tanks.

As it appeared that the insecure left flank might delay the whole operation, Lieutenant-Colonel Finlinson decided to send "A" Company to reinforce the success of "B" Company. With tank support these two companies drove forward in the late afternoon, and by nightfall were holding an area south-east of Leonhout. As they had arrived in the vicinity of the town well after dark, it was decided not to attempt to take the town until daybreak. All the haystacks and most of the farm buildings in the vicinity were ablaze.

By nightfall "C" Company had overcome the enemy resistance and had occupied Stapelheide.

The day's operations cost the 2nd Essex 5 killed and 15 wounded, the majority from "C" Company. In addition, a complete troop of the supporting tanks had been knocked out by the garrison of Stapelheide. As a counter to these casualties was a tally of over 300 prisoners into the 2nd Essex P.W. cage.

At 7.30 a.m. on the 21st October the capture of Leonhout was completed and another 45 prisoners taken.

The 2nd Essex remained in Leonhout under intermittent shell and mortar fire until, on the afternoon of the 23rd October, it was relieved by elements of the 104th U.S. Infantry Division, a formation being put into the line for the first time, and very anxious to learn what they could from the battle-experienced 56th Infantry Brigade.

Hopes had been cherished that on relief there would be sufficient time to have a long-overdue bath, but these were quickly dashed when the Battalion was told to concentrate at St. Leonard and be available almost immediately for another operation.

Esschen and Nispen, 25th–27th October, 1944

Back in St. Leonard at 4.30 a.m. the 24th October, the Battalion got a few hours of sleep before at midday it was moved to Esschen, where positions were taken over from an infantry battalion of the 4th Canadian Armoured Division.

Esschen is a long straggly town astride the Dutch-Belgian frontier. The Canadians had been fighting very hard and, with Esschen already badly damaged, heavy shelling was still proceeding as the 2nd Essex and the other units of the 56th Infantry Brigade took over. Perhaps they experienced as heavy shelling in Esschen and in the operations therefrom as at any stage in the whole campaign.

On the morning of the 25th October orders were issued for an attack on Nispen, some 2,000 yards north of the 2nd Essex positions.

The operation was to start with the 2nd S.W.B. infiltrating northwest of Esschen in the early hours of the 26th. Then the 2nd Essex were to move through the 2nd S.W.B. and establish a firm base in the woods astride the road north-west of Nispen. Finally, the 2nd Glosters were to clear Nispen itself. In support of the 2nd Essex would be "B" Squadron 9th R.T.R. and a "crocodile" troop from the 1st Fife and Forfar Yeomanry.

In the event, the 2nd S.W.B. had little success in their infiltration role. They had had the use of artificial moonlight for their attack before it was light, but as there was a moon, it was found that the artificial moonlight had to be turned down, and in the end turned out altogether.

When the barrage opened at 6.30 a.m., the position was that the 2nd Essex had to fight its way forward from the very beginning of the advance.

"A" and "B" Companies crossed the start line at 7 a.m., "A" on the right and "B" on the left, each company supported by a troop of tanks. "B" Company had, in addition, the troop of "crocodiles." The tanks, "crocodiles," and Essex infantry all fought magnificently and in perfect co-operation, and by 8.34 a.m. the two rifle companies had completed their 2,000 yards advance and were digging in as fast as possible in the face of extremely heavy enemy retaliatory shelling.

"D" Company, since the 13th October once more a fighting rifle company, in an effort to cut off the enemy in Nispen, was pushed through "A" Company to gain the road bridge over the canal north of the village, but enemy resistance here was still strong. Many of No. 17 Platoon became casualties from small-arms and 88-mm. fire as they crossed the open ground in front of their objective.

Lieutenant-Colonel Finlinson had moved his headquarters up behind the attack, and by 9.15 a.m. it had been re-located, while the Battalion quickly reorganised to provide the firm base necessary for the attack on Nispen by the 2nd Glosters. This was soon accomplished and the whole operation well concluded.

Casualties were not light—12 killed, including 1 officer, and 21 wounded—but 167 prisoners passed through the brigade cage, the 2nd Essex accounting for 106.

Heavy shelling was experienced throughout the 26th. Battalion Headquarters was temporarily established in the cottage of a smallholder, and as in all smallholder cottages in Holland, the barn where all the animals were kept was part of the cottage. Shelling was at one time very heavy and all were taking cover. When the shelling finished, "somebody," says Captain Townrow, "shouted for L/Corporal Rosier, the sanitary corporal, and one of the most conscientious men we had, and two heads popped up side by side over the side of a loose-box in the barn. One was Rosier's and the other that of a large goat. They both looked so serious."

The attack on Nispen was a most successful operation, and— "The highlight was the perfect co-operation of tanks and infantry, and it indicated how much better results may be obtained if these two arms can be blended together by personal contact before the attack."

The 2nd Essex parted with real regret from the 9th R.T.R. and the Fife and Forfar Yeomanry.

As October 1944 drew to a close, it became apparent that the German retreat to the River Maas was quickening, and that an entry by the 49th Division into Roosendaal would not be opposed in any great strength. Consequently 146th and 147th Infantry Brigades were ordered to cross the anti-tank ditch at the south of the town. There was no opposition to the advance nor to the advance of 56th Infantry Brigade which entered, 2nd Glosters leading, the eastern side of the town. So on the 30th October fell Roosendaal, a large rail and manufacturing town little more than ten miles from the estuary of the River Maas.

Operations up to the River Mark

There was, however, still plenty to be done in south Holland. The enemy was now holding the line of the River Mark, which runs approximately from west to east half-way between Roosendaal and the Maas. This was an attempt to form one last line south of the Maas. It was decided to frustrate this by effecting a crossing over the Mark as soon as possible.

Orders for the crossing were given out at Brigade Headquarters on the morning of the 2nd November. Late that afternoon the 2nd Essex moved forward to Meer-en-Stoof preparatory to a silent crossing that night just south of the little village of Barlaque.

The operation started at 8.30 p.m. with the 2nd Glosters attacking Stampersgat on the left and the 104th U.S. Division forcing a crossing over the Mark at Standdaarbuiten. Both these efforts were supported by heavy artillery preparation in contrast to the silent crossing to be made by the 2nd Essex.

"A" Company (Major M. W. Holme), which provided the boat-carrying, launching, and local-protection parties, crossed the start-line at 8.30 p.m., and at 9 p.m. reported everything ready, when "C" Company (Major Wilkins) moved forward and started the crossing. Major Holme and Major Wilkins were both to be awarded the M.C. for this operation.

A certain amount of spent small-arms fire from the other sectors was the only thing that worried the Battalion in the early stages, but this good luck could not last, and before "C" Company had completed their crossing, the operation was discovered and heavy defensive fire came down on the crossing-point, and on the long line of approach to the river.

The assault continued, despite mounting casualties, and by 11.30 p.m. "C" Company, having crossed the Mark, had pushed inland to Barlaque. Finding this empty, they thereupon swung right-handed and seized an important bridge over a canal. "C" Company was now well in position, and shortly after midnight "B" and then "D" Companies were put across together with two anti-tank 6-pounders and a jeep. They were unable to make much progress, for heavy fire from Kade held up "D" Company, while "B" could make little headway with their patrols to the west along the two dykes north of the river.

Shortly after dawn the Germans put in heavy counter-attacks to destroy the bridge-head, but the "Pompadours" stood firm, and at 8.58 a.m. "C" Company was able to report that the enemy were retreating to the north-west. Heavy artillery and mortar fire continued, but despite casualties the positions were held. In the late afternoon the 2nd Glosters were successful in their attempt to destroy the German bridge-head south of the river, and the American 104th Division, having crossed the River Mark during the night, finished the construction of a class 40 bridge at Standdaarbuiten. The battle was now almost over, but it was not until the 4th November that, after forty-eight gruelling hours, the 2nd Essex was withdrawn and returned to Roosendaal. The Battalion had had 5 killed and 31 (including 4 officers) wounded in the operation.

The 2nd Essex now had had almost six weeks in the line without a break, six weeks in close contact with the enemy under most adverse weather conditions, during which time they had had 14 officer casualties (1 killed and 13 wounded) and 150 other ranks casualties (21 killed, 112 wounded, and 17 missing). In addition, 2 officers and 112 other ranks had been evacuated sick. These figures are indicative of the strain under which the Battalion was operating.

However, the "Pompadours" were now promised a rest after one more operation and put back to Roosendaal. Back in Roosendaal on the 4th November they were only given two quiet days before being put in, at one hour's notice, this time to relieve the 414th Regimental Combat Team of the 104th U.S. Division, near Moerdijk.

This river port was one of the two remaining enemy pockets south of the Maas. The 2nd Essex took over in the line on the evening of the 7th November. Now holding a small barren area south-west of Moerdijk, their time was more unpleasant because of bad conditions than because of enemy activity. "With flooded fields and wrecked farmhouses, one could only live in the banks beside the roads, and the roads were regularly shelled by heavy guns from the North Bank," says Captain Vince. By the evening of the 8th November it was apparent that resistance in Moerdijk was crumbling under pressure from the Polish Armoured Division and that the 2nd Essex would have no active role to fulfil. On the 9th November the Battalion was released and returned once more to Roosendaal, where it spent the next six days resting, cleaning, drilling, and refitting. There was leave, too, for a few, who got forty-eight hours in Ghent, Antwerp, or Brussels, for a system of local leave in these towns had just been inaugurated.

On the 15th November, the Battalion moved to Lille St. Hubert, and with the rest of the 49th Division, temporarily left 1st Corps to become part of the 12th Corps.

In the new area preparations were put in hand for the next operation, which was to be the clearing of the enemy pocket still remaining on the west bank of the Meuse in the area of Venlo and Roermond. These preparations included thorough liaison with the 3rd Sharpshooters, the Royal Armoured Corps unit with whom the 2nd Essex was to co-operate when next in action. Demonstrations were given in the use of "kangaroos" for those who had joined the Battalion since the battle for Le Havre, the last occasion on which "kangaroos" had been allotted to the Battalion. These armoured troop carriers were very well thought of by the troops, to whom was given a great sense of security in the approach to battle.

On the 20th the 2nd Essex left Lille-St. Hubert for Weert, a move eastwards and a step towards a new concentration area for the next operation. On the 21st, another move eastwards took the Battalion to Panningen, whence it was to advance on the following day for the capture of Korteheide.

On the 21st November there was another change in command. Lieutenant-Colonel N. W. Finlinson, D.S.O., left the Battalion to take up another appointment, and Major C. L. Sayers temporarily took command.

At 7 a.m. the 22nd November the Battalion moved forward from Panningen to Kasteel and at 8.30 a.m. "A" (Major Holme) and "C" (Major Wilkins) Companies crossed the start-line for the capture of Korteheide. Little was known of the enemy's strength, dispositions, or intentions, and accordingly a minimum of artillery support was laid on. This diagnosis was correct, for there was practically no opposition, and by 10.23 a.m. Korteheide was captured. In the afternoon a further advance to exploit success was made and Langeheide occupied. There was plenty of enemy artillery in action in the latter part of the day but no infantry. The only enemy seen was one German air-force officer who when captured stated that half his platoon had been withdrawn and the balance had either been wounded or had disappeared.

A further advance during the 23rd still only led to hostile artillery and mortar fire which caused some casualties. Late in the day the 2nd Glosters passed through the 2nd Essex, which was withdrawn to Korteheide for a night under cover. The weather was now very bad and winter was rapidly approaching.

At Korteheide a squadron of "kangaroos" was allotted to the Battalion for the next operation, which was to move to positions to the north of Blerick. Once again there was no opposition during the advance, and by 11.51 a.m., 25th November, they were in position a few hundred yards from Blerick, a suburb of Venlo.

The situation was obscure, and so no time was lost in establishing observation posts and sending out patrols. Patrols sent by night towards Blerick quickly drew small-arms fire from the outskirts of the town. Heavy enemy shelling and mortaring developed during the night, but during the 25th and 27th November the enemy dispositions became pin-pointed. The British were now able effectively to retaliate, some twelve hundred 3-inch mortar bombs being fired on the 26th, whilst on the 27th it could be said, "we now have excellent O.P.s and any enemy movement is severely dealt with."

As things turned out, the 2nd Essex was not committed to an attack on Blerick. During the 28th November it was relieved by the 49th Reconnaissance Regiment and withdrawn to the area of Sevenum there to harbour the night 28th/29th November preparatory to moving with other units of the 49th Division to relieve the 50th Division in the Arnhem area.

This move brought the Division once more under command of the First Canadian Army, the formation which it had temporarily left on the 15th November to come under command of the 12th Corps (British Second Army) for the operation to clear the western side of the River Maas round Venlo.

On the 28th November Lieutenant-Colonel M. A. H. Butler, M.C., The South Lancashire Regiment (The Prince of Wales's Volunteers), took over command from Major C. L. Sayers. He arrived wearing an old jeep coat showing no badges or rank, and quite unknown walked round to judge the form, standing to watch an anti-tank gun crew cleaning their gun. After a few minutes he asked a question to which the N.C.O. replied rather shortly; he still stood there, whereupon Sergeant Jago turned round and said "Just —— will you, as we're busy cleaning up for the new C.O.," whereupon Colonel Butler went off without another word. But nevertheless this and other impressions gave him an idea of the spirit of the Battalion. Lieutenant-Colonel Butler himself says: ". . . Within a few hours of my arrival I was able to sense with a feeling of relief that the spirit of the Battalion was good. This was due to the fact that, firstly, a comparatively high proportion of company commanders and specialist officers had been together with the Battalion since well before D-Day. These officers got on well together, and, with the men, were intensely proud of the Battalion."

The Final Phase (The Island)

The operations between the 12th October and the 30th November by the 8th and 12th British Corps had brought them up to the line of the River Maas.

General Montgomery was now principally concerned with clearing the area between the Rhine and the Meuse, the establishment of a bridge-head north of the Ruhr, and the eventual crossing of the Rhine. The 2nd Essex and the 49th Division were not to take part in this operation and the advance through Germany to the Baltic, but were destined to remain in Holland.

There was little time at Sevenum for the new Commanding Officer to get to know the Battalion, for on the 30th November, 1944, the 2nd Essex moved into Nijmegen and marched to an assembly area at Elst.

As the "Pompadours" moved across the River Waal they crossed on to the "Island" that was to be the centre of their interest and existence for the next six months. Nijmegen itself had obviously suffered heavy air bombardment, and as the Battalion came through to the river bridge, a large notice greeted it, a notice placed there by the Canadians: "Spend your holidays in the Nijmegen Salient. Hot and cold water—mostly cold. Boating. Shooting both ways, Boche hunting in the woods."

The bridge on to the Island had been partly destroyed, and over the gap had been slung a Bailey bridge. Few drivers will ever forget that bridge with its sloping steel ramps at each end. Certainly nobody took it twice at any speed.

The Island itself was still green, although by now trees were leafless. It was a stretch of land about fifteen miles long by ten miles wide, garrisoned at the end of November 1944 by the 50th Division and the 51st (Highland) Division. The 49th Division came in relief of the 50th Division. Villages were all badly damaged, particularly churches which had been singled out for shelling because of their value as observation points over an otherwise extremely flat expanse of country.

Well below sea-level, no digging was possible, and so there had been recourse to fortified houses. It was not a prepossessing sector for which to become responsible at the onset of a Continental winter, and

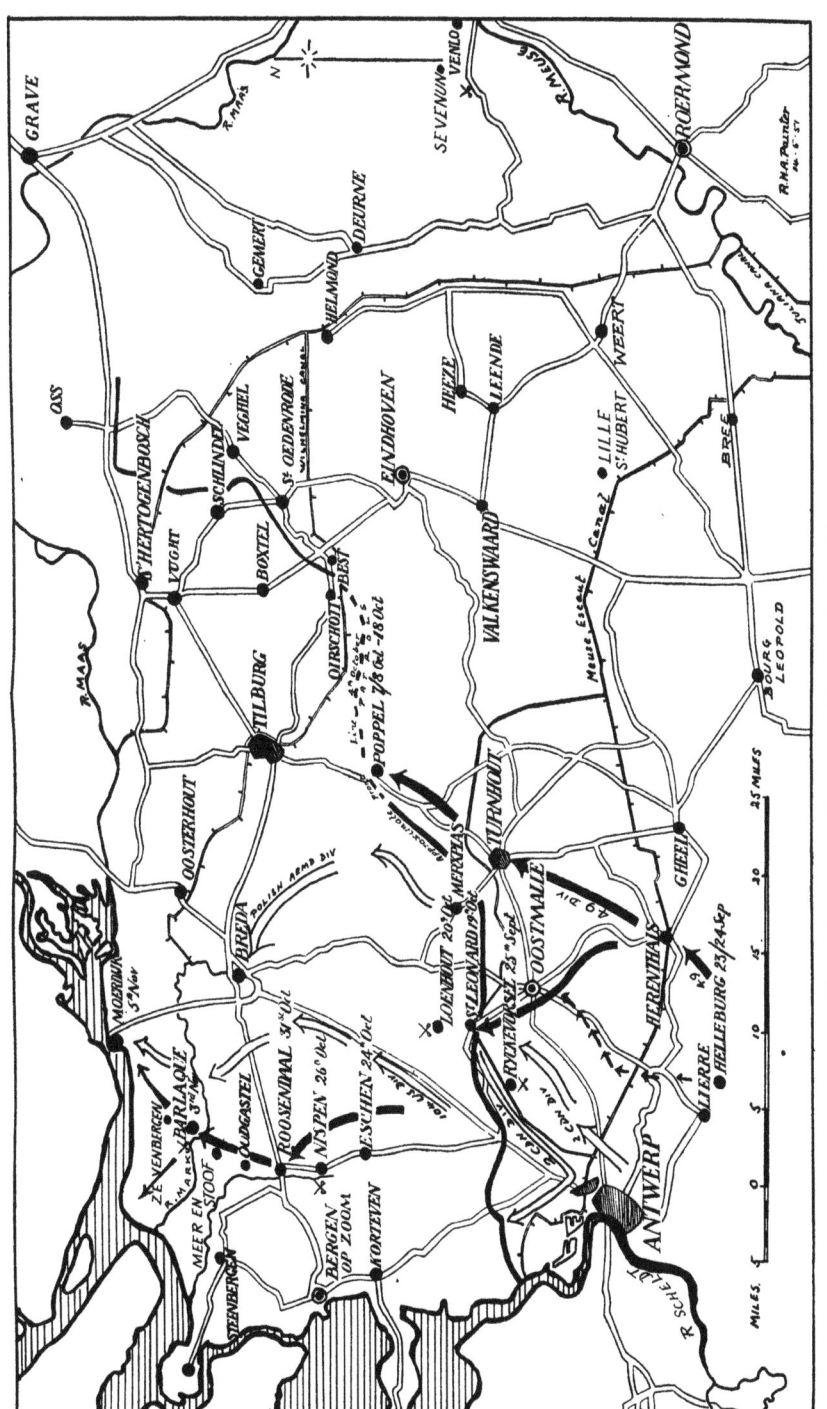

2ND ESSEX. OPERATIONS IN SOUTH-WEST HOLLAND. OCTOBER–NOVEMBER 1944.

leather jerkins and "boots, rubber knee" or "boots, rubber thigh" were found to be the official dress.

Arriving at Elst, the take-over from the 6th D.L.I. started at 2 p.m., but it was necessary to wait until dark to relieve the forward elements, as contact was close and the country extremely flat. However, command passed at 6.25 p.m., and the 2nd Essex was left holding a new sector which certainly had unusual features and many possibilities. They had not very long to wait for the first novelty.

Twelve miles to the north was Arnhem, on the far bank of the Neder Rijn. On the left of the 2nd Essex positions lay units of the 51st Division, whose line swung northwards to reach the Neder Rijn at Heteren and Randwijk. On the right was the 49th Divisional front stretching down to the River Waal at Haalderen, leaving a large stretch of swampy ground, including the villages of Elden, Huissen, and Angeren, to the enemy.

On the afternoon of the 2nd December a loud explosion was heard to the front and well behind the enemy lines. Rising water soon made it clear that the enemy had breached the dykes on the southern bank of the Neder Rijn west of Arnhem, and that the river water was flowing across the countryside.

This contingency had been anticipated and the necessary orders drawn up—christened, needless to say, by the code word "Operation Noah."

Nevertheless, there was an element of uncertainty as to how it was all going to end, as the low-lying ground to the south of Arnhem was quickly flooded as far as the railway running west from Elst. The 2nd Essex positions themselves became flooded early on the morning of the 3rd December. Throughout the day a gradual and planned withdrawal was carried out, but no vehicles or equipment were lost. Towards the end of the day the rate of rise of the water-level became very slow. At last light "C" and "D" Companies were still well forward of Elst, and although almost surrounded by water, quite happy. No ground had been given until the water was knee deep.

The enemy action had failed to deprive the British of a bridge-head adequate to cover the Waal bridges, but General Montgomery had in fact been denied any possibility of attacking north to secure the high ground between Arnhem and Apeldoorn. In consequence the Island sector became more certainly static than before the flooding.

All commanding officers like to have a pause on taking over so that they can get the whole machinery of the Battalion working in the way they consider best, and Lieutenant-Colonel Butler says: "I was extremely fortunate as, although we moved within a few hours of my taking over and had to withdraw in the face of flood waters within a short time of occupying the new positions, we did spend a quiet December and early January, and I was able to get to know the Battalion and become extremely fond of it."

During the 4th and 5th December the Battalion made the minor adjustments to its positions necessitated by the new conditions, "A" and "B" Companies guarding the left flank of Elst, with "C" and "D" Companies well forward of the village. The 2nd S.W.B. held the eastern half of Elst, whilst on the extreme right of the 2nd Essex positions lay a battalion of the Duke of Wellington's Regiment.

Despite the fact that by the 5th December three companies were completely surrounded by water, it was reported that "the troops are in high spirits and living reasonably comfortably in fortified houses." Having accustomed themselves to these strange conditions, it was not long before the "Pompadour" offensive spirit showed itself, and by the 7th December patrols in assault boats and amphibious "weasels" (tracked carrier-type vehicles) had been organised, whilst observation posts were set up and snipers began to work. It says much for the discipline and man-management of company and platoon commanders that there were no cases of trench-feet or similar complaints during this period.

The enemy dispositions on the 2nd Essex front were obscure, and with a three-mile lake ahead and the bulk of the Battalion surrounded by water, it was necessary to patrol far "out to sea" to discover his dispositions and intentions.

During this first spell in the line, Lieutenant-Colonel Butler had appreciated that the 49th Division was likely to spend some time on that cold, wet island, and that his battalion would defend various watery posts in discomfort until either the division moved or the waters subsided. "I was anxious lest we became too defensive in attitude, since it was pretty certain that all of a sudden, probably when least expected, we should be required to take part in a really tough battle which would call for a high standard of battle-worthiness from all of us. Training whilst in the line, on other than new and interesting techniques or weapons is more likely to tire already tired troops than do any real good—it is almost impossible to organise properly, and unless it has to do with something connected with a present or a near-future operation is nearly always a waste of tired men's resting time.

"Patrolling has always seemed to me to be the finest training for all infantry soldiers. Troops going on patrol will take every opportunity to know and practise with their weapons: if therefore a battalion does a lot of patrolling which is properly run and co-ordinated, it should maintain a high standard of training. Thus I resolved we would carry out as much patrolling as possible, not merely to obtain the training value, but to prevent us from becoming defensively minded and to dominate the area between us and the Germans."

The Battalion carried out an average of three patrols each night whenever in the line. It has to be remembered these patrols were by no means normal, being carried out mostly in boats, since the flood waters were high throughout December. In the normal land patrol the formation gives all-round protection, all can make best use of their weapons, and every precaution can be taken against surprise. "Patrolling by boat on land covered by a few feet of water is, to say the least, nerve-racking. The whole patrol is in one unarmoured, old, and generally battered boat. The splash of oars to those in the boat seems as though it must carry for ten miles. A boat is a big target. The patrol formation cannot possibly be changed, and it is impossible for more than a few members of the patrol to use their weapons at one time. Yet to obtain information these boat patrols had to visit the many partially submerged houses in the area, knowing that to the enemy within they were an easier target than any sitting duck." (The description is Lieutenant-Colonel Butler's.)

On the right the 2nd Glosters were able to raid down a road that was still above water, killing 34 of the enemy, and to pin-point his positions, but for the 2nd Essex it was not so easy. There was a stiff westerly current which made the propulsion of assault boats extremely hard, and it was recorded that "the troops deserve the highest praise for their efforts."

Assault-boat patrols were sent out two thousand yards or more to the north, and the whole battalion front kept constantly under observation and patrol. For the highest degree of vigilance was necessary at all times to prevent enemy infiltration of the thinly held flooded front, and the "mopping up" of one or more of the isolated fortified houses.

On the 14th December the 2nd Essex was withdrawn to rest in Nijmegen on relief by the 2nd S.W.B. The Battalion was not due to return to the Island until the 24th December, and so Christmas preparations were put in hand. The idea was to hold "Christmas Dinners" and generally celebrate Christmas on the 22nd and 23rd December.

But as so often happened, the unexpected intervened and the period of rest was curtailed. The Battle of the Ardennes, the great German counter-offensive, had now opened, and the penetration of the American lines offered a threat to Brussels and even to Antwerp. This threat necessitated the formation of a strong force to counter it. Included by General Montgomery in the 30th Corps for the operation was the 51st Division, which was to move forthwith from "the Island" to its new Corps concentration area. The 49th Division had therefore to extend its front.

So on the 20th December plans for Christmas celebrations had to be postponed, as the 2nd Essex moved into the line near Valburg and relieved the 5th Camerons. The positions taken over did not attract favourable comment, and the next few days were spent in "getting things sorted out to our own satisfaction."

Christmas Day, 1944. "Christmas is just another day to us in which further to improve our position, lay wire and trip flares, mines and booby traps. However, the men are in very good heart, despite the extreme cold. A 'weasel' patrol, led by the Commanding Officer himself, went out to locate a standing patrol which had failed to return the previous evening. They were discovered hacking a way through the ice and still in excellent spirits despite lack of food and sleep."

Such a contemporary comment—and there are many similar—shows clearly the high morale of the "Pompadours." Captain A. A. Vince speaks of this incident when he says; "Half-frozen, tired and hungry, they had already made 2,000 yards chest deep in water and ice, covering barely 100 yards an hour. Even that could not take the grin off their faces."

As the German offensive in the Ardennes was first slowed down and then halted, so the possibility of large-scale airborne operations against the thinly held front of the 49th Division faded and tension lessened.

January 1945 found the 2nd Essex still on the Island front. As the winter deepened, patrol conditions became terrible, involving as they did long treks with all ranks wading through icy water or crashing over crunchy ice which gave their approach away to any enemy in the neighbourhood. They were very disappointing days for patrol or sniper, for rarely was there any tangible result in a number of enemy dead to cheer their long and cold hours of duty.

"However," says Captain Townrow, "Colonel Butler appeared to enjoy life as if he were back at school again. He revelled in being up with the forward companies, and on one occasion, when Battalion

Headquarters was at Valburg, we visited a forward company and then walked on up the road into no-man's-land. The country was all flooded around us, but the road was just above water-level. The Commanding Officer just wanted to 'have a jimmy Dekko.' Four hundred to five hundred yards out he saw a cat which must have been stranded on a tiny piece of high ground when the Boche flooded the Island. The war was temporarily forgotten, and rafts were floated out to rescue the unfortunate animal. After a few unsuccessful attempts, we managed to rescue the cat and the party then returned back to our own lines."

The Battalion remained in the Valburg sector until the 6th January, 1945, when, on relief by the 11th Royal Scots Fusiliers, it returned to Nijmegen to rest and train. No fewer than sixty offensive and reconnaissance patrols had been carried out during the nineteen days of appalling weather conditions spent by the 2nd Essex in the Valburg sector. Both the Divisional and the Brigade Commander visited the Battalion in Nijmegen and complimented it on its efforts.

But Lieutenant-Colonel Butler did not think these efforts enough. In his training directive for the Nijmegen rest period he said: "For the past six weeks the Battalion has been standing away from the enemy separated from him by water or ice. This has had an adverse effect on alertness. At Haalderen (the next sector), a sector which we have especially asked to take over for obvious reasons—the forward defended localities will be between 150 to 300 yards from enemy F.D.L.s . . . We will dominate the enemy by offensive patrolling and sniping, so that he is kept within his own limits in a state of mental anxiety and given as much hell as possible during our fourteen days in fairly close contact."

Brigadier R. H. Senior, D.S.O., T.D., who took over command of the 56th Infantry Brigade in January 1945, wrote of these winter patrols, saying: "Activity was mainly confined to intensive patrolling and artillery action, but I found the keenness of 2nd Essex under their Commanding Officer, Lieutenant-Colonel Butler, of the highest order. Their patrols were invariably excellent, and they almost always managed to bring back the answers to the questions their patrols were asked to solve. The reputation of the Battalion was very high."

The success of patrols from the Battalion was largely due to the institution of a series of patrol bases ahead of the foremost defended localities on which were based anything up to a platoon and a half and from which patrols moved out by night. "These bases did, I am sure," says Lieutenant-Colonel Butler, "contribute a great deal to the fact that in dominating no-man's-land and water we had very few casualties. The bases were chosen to give good observation, and by day observation posts would study any enemy activity, and from these O.P.s patrols would be briefed. They gave patrols a big start and enabled them often to reach their destinations more quickly than the enemy believed possible."

However, the projected move to Haalderen did not take place, for on the 19th January, 1945, the 2nd Essex was placed at half an hour's notice to move because of German attacks on the villages of Hemmen and Zetten to the west of Valburg.

The Battle of Zetten, 19th–22nd January, 1945

The attacks were directed towards Nijmegen with the object of securing the bridge there and isolating the Island. They were in about regimental strength (three battalions) and being resolutely led were able to capture the whole of Zetten and much of the surrounding area. The initial assault of the German parachute troops was held temporarily on the southern edge of Zetten, where a battalion of the Leicestershires, assisted by the 2nd Glosters, was holding a precarious line.

Despite the fact that the Battalion was at short notice to move, nothing transpired until about midday the 19th January, when battalion reconnaissance groups were ordered to carry out reconnaissances forward with a view to counter-attacking on the 20th. Information was very sketchy, and owing to the flatness of the ground it was not possible to see the objective, the town of Zetten, at all clearly. However, the various reconnaissances were carried out in so far as was possible, and in the morning the 2nd Essex moved up in transport to a small village about three miles from Zetten.

The plan, dictated entirely by the ground, had to be simple and flexible, since little information was available about the enemy.

The ground was covered in several inches of snow. On either flank of Zetten, the fields were flooded or intersected every few yards by ditches which were not sufficiently frozen to carry a man's weight. It was not possible therefore to by-pass even portions of Zetten which were likely to be extremely well defended.

The town itself was quite small, not much more than half a mile long from north to south, and consisted of the usual Dutch houses with cellars, outhouses, and gardens, with several outlying farm buildings.

The 2nd Essex was to attack through the Leicesters at 8 a.m. the

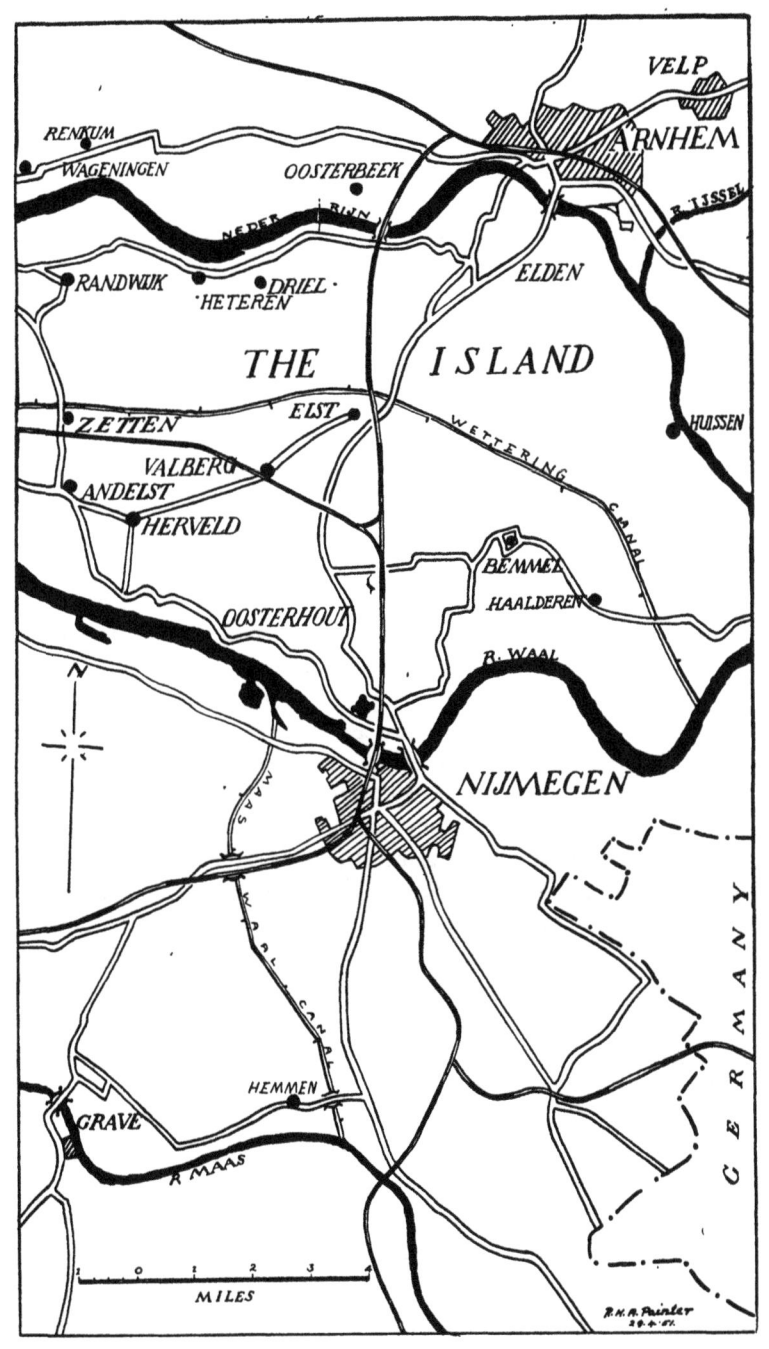

2ND ESSEX, NIJMEGEN AND THE ISLAND, 30TH NOVEMBER, 1944–12TH APRIL, 1945

20th January. The 2nd S.W.B. to the 2nd Essex left were to carry out a similar but separate attack some miles to the west of Zetten.

Lieutenant-Colonel Butler continues: "My plan was firstly to move up two sections of the carrier platoon (dismounted) to make quite certain of the Battalion start-line, which was a road running at right angles to the main road into Zetten. This start-line was some 200 yards south of the entrance to the town, and was supposed to be held by the remnants of the Leicesters through whom we were to attack. Tactical Battalion Headquarters was to move into a farmhouse some 200 yards south of the start-line.

"Secondly, 'A' Company (Major M. W. Holme, M.C.) was to attack astride the main road to get a grip on the first few streets. It was to be supported by one troop of 'B' Squadron 6th Canadian Armoured Regiment, who were to assist in 'shooting in' the company by blasting enemy defences in buildings. Subsequent action was to depend on the strength and type of opposition, but 'C' and 'D' Companies were to be held ready to go through 'A' Company. The artillery support available was much more meagre than people had become accustomed to by this time of the war.

"The fire plan was due to start at 7.50 a.m., and 'A' was to assault at 8 a.m. However, the enemy had avoided the Leicesters supposed to be holding our start-line and sent several strong fighting patrols well to the south. One of these nearly captured the signal officer (Captain Spencer). Several small actions were fought during the advance to the start-line, and it soon became clear that the attack could not go in at 8 a.m. I put off the fire plan and left it to be called for, and meanwhile I stopped Major Holme's 'A' Company and used 'C' Company (Captain W. F. McMichael) to right hook so as to clear the various woods and a cemetery as far as the start-line. 'C' Company did this with magnificent dash, and by 8.45 a.m. the start-line was in our hands, together with 1 officer and 25 German parachutists, whilst many more had been killed or wounded.

"It is interesting to ponder," continues Colonel Butler, "that although at the time it was most irritating to have to fight our way to our so-called secure start-line, put off the main attack and suffer the delay, the fact that this enemy company had caught us moving up meant that we were able to annihilate it entirely in the open: this company, had it remained in its defences in Zetten until the attack, would without doubt have made the task of the Battalion even harder than in fact it turned out to be."

At 9.40 a.m. "A" Company with a troop of tanks started the attack to gain a footing in the town. The fighting was extremely tough. Every room, cellar, and outhouse had to be cleared in fierce close fighting. Every garden, street, and lane was covered by fire, and it was a slow and costly business. "A" Company suffered fairly heavy casualties, including the Company Commander, Major Holme, who was wounded. Lieutenant R. G. Filby took over the company, and led it with great dash for the rest of the battle, showing leadership and personal gallantry which earned him the Military Cross.

After two hours of hard fighting a footing had been gained and room made for the deployment of more of the Battalion. Lieutenant-Colonel Butler put in "C" Company (Captain W. F. McMichael) on the left of "A" Company to clear up the western outskirts of the town. At first the fighting was very bitter, but by about 1.30 p.m. (after four hours of room to room fighting) "A" and "C" Companies had reached the centre of the built-up area. "D" Company (Major Ferrier) was then launched through "A" and "C", and made good headway despite receiving several casualties on its start-line from mortaring. Major Ferrier was among those wounded. Throughout the afternoon "D" Company fought its way forward, while "A" and "C" Companies mopped up and gradually took over more of the town.

Before darkness "B" Company (Captain J. A. Boucher) was moved up to take over portions of the area won by "D" Company.

"It was now fairly clear," says Colonel Butler, "that the crisis of the battle, anyway for the moment, was over, and I felt that the enemy might withdraw out of the rest of the town and across the Wettering Canal to the north during darkness. Several patrols therefore were used to keep touch. However, patrolling in a town is difficult, and the exact moment when the main body of the enemy pulled out was missed.

"Nevertheless, 'B' Company was moved up to complete the securing of the town well before first light, and due to taking advantage of patrol information was able to take its objective without casualties."

During early morning the 21st January, "C" Company was moved through "B" Company to clear a wooded area due east of the main part of Zetten itself from which desultory sniping had been carried out.

"The area to be cleared," goes on Colonel Butler, "was also close—thereby ideal for an enemy to form up—and dominated the only remaining bridge over the Wettering Canal. We were told that the enemy were about to attack again in considerable strength with a good deal of armour, and that every effort should be made to blow up the bridge. Despite heavy sniping and accurate fire from the north of the canal, 'C' Company managed to secure the area dominating the bridge, and Captain McMichael personally led a small party which, under fire from very short range, succeeded in almost completely demolishing the bridge. For this and his outstanding leadership and example to his company, Captain McMichael won a bar to his Military Cross."

While the 2nd Essex had been engaged in Zetten, the 2nd Glosters had eased forward on the right flank and the 2nd S.W.B. on the left. Now these two battalions came forward, and the southern side of the Wettering Canal was largely cleared of the enemy.

The Essex losses had been 8 killed and 52 wounded. The enemy lost 387 as prisoners of war and a very large number of killed and wounded. On the Essex front there were 25 enemy dead in various buildings alone and an uncounted number in fields and orchards. A contemporary estimate is a total of 700 killed, wounded, and taken prisoner, and of these a very large proportion can be attributed to the actions of the 2nd Essex.

There were many acts of gallantry and many examples of fine leadership. Lieutenant-Colonel Butler was awarded the D.S.O., while Captain W. F. McMichael gained a bar to the M.C. and Lieutenant H. A. S. Cooper and Lieutenant R. G. Filby the Military Cross. Several awards were also made to other ranks, but unfortunately the records for this battle are not to hand.

On the 22nd January the 2nd Essex was once more relieved and returned to Nijmegen to complete the interrupted period of rest.

By the 25th the "Pompadours" were once more back in the line, the Haalderen sector being taken over from the Hallamshire Battalion (York and Lancasters). Here the enemy front was between 100 and 400 yards away. Both "B" and "D" Companies were unable to move by day despite white suits as camouflage against the snow background.

Captain Vince says of this sector:

"Haalderen sector derived its name from the small village in the centre, and as time went by we agreed it was the worst sector to look after. On the right ran the River Waal well above ground-level and contained by a bund. The only road was under small-arms fire, and approach had to be made by the 'jeep track,' which was made out of the rubble from the destroyed houses. Whether the ground was frozen or feet deep in black mud, it was impossible to dig, and one had to fight from the ruins of buildings and from cellars. Not a house remained whole, and almost every room was fortified with sandbags and chests filled with dirt: in the small slits where windows used to be there was a weapon of some kind with the safety catch permanently at fire and a finger always on the trigger. The few houses not defended were mined, and the unwary patrol from either side rarely left such a building in one piece. Contact with the enemy was as little as 100 yards, and the whole Battalion area could be and was swept by spandaus and other weapons."

The 2nd Essex stayed in the line under these unpleasant conditions until relieved on the 24th February, 1945. Even then they were not withdrawn right back to Nijmegen, but remained on the Island as divisional immediate reserve battalion, with Headquarters at Oosterhout. From there companies were sent in turn to Nijmegen for a day, where baths, cinemas, and E.N.S.A. shows were available.

All through February the 49th Division hoped and expected to be called in to take their part in the offensives by the First Canadian Army and the Ninth U.S. Army towards the Rhine. But by early March it was clear that so well had the offensive gone that little likelihood remained of a call upon the 49th Division. The "Pompadours" therefore resigned themselves to their static task of containing the German garrison of the Island. They stayed at Oosterhout until the 11th March, 1945, when they again found themselves holding the Valburg sector in relief of the 4th Lincolns.

The sands of time were now fast running out. By the 29th March, 1945, when the Battalion moved once more to Haalderen, the British and American armies were across the Rhine. 30th Corps had on crossing turned left-handed, and the 3rd Canadian Division reaching Emmerich had continued to push down the west bank, meeting little opposition. Although patrols established the fact that there had been no withdrawal from the front of the 49th Division, the general strategic situation was now favourable for a clearance of the enemy from the Island.

Broadly, this operation was part of the main operation to clear Holland. The 2nd Canadian Corps, having captured Emmerich, struck northwards to Doesberg and Zurpen and thence across the River Ems. The 1st Canadian Corps attacked to clear Arnhem. By the 5th April, 1945, the area between Nijmegen and the Neder

Rijn had been occupied. Instead of attempting a frontal attack on Arnhem across the river, it was decided to seize the town by a right hook. While the 5th Canadian Armoured Division and the 1st Canadian Division demonstrated to the south of the town, the 49th Division was to make a surprise crossing of the Neder Rijn on the night of the 12th April and drive west on Arnhem.

This was the strategic plan on the higher level. On the lower level of the Company Commander the picture was not nearly so clear-cut during the ten days that elapsed between the first advance by the 146th and 147th Infantry Brigades on the 2nd April and the entry of the 2nd Essex into Arnhem on the 12th April.

The initial attack by 146th and 147th Infantry Brigades went well, and almost all the Island salient was cleared with light casualties. Then the 2nd Essex was warned that 56th Infantry Brigade would capture Arnhem on the 4th April, using "buffaloes," L.C.M.s, L.C.A.s, and other craft.

Twenty-four hours later this order was cancelled and instructions to concentrate on Nijmegen issued. This in turn was superseded by other orders, and so it went on, plan after plan for the recapture of Arnhem and the liberation of north-west Holland.

Finally, in the darkness of the 12th/13th April the 2nd Glosters made the initial assault on Arnhem from the east, crossing the Ijssel River in "buffaloes" and assault craft. The subsequent landing was difficult owing to mines and defence works, but the men defending them were in poor heart. After an initial hard fight for the bridgehead, the 2nd S.W.B., and 2nd Essex who passed westwards into the heart of the town, met practically no opposition.

But even now the Germans, still some distance from the assaulting infantry on the high ground outside the town, manned the guns and mortars, and had little difficulty in causing casualties, including the Officer Commanding Headquarter Company, Captain P. E. Butler, who subsequently died from his wounds.

Of this operation Lieutenant-Colonel Butler says: "Once again it was street fighting, but this time the opposition was nothing comparable to that met with in Zetten, except that the shelling by the enemy was a little more violent, being directed from overlooking ground to the north of our advance and delivered by medium and heavy artillery. In this battle we were supported by 'Funnies' of 79th Armoured Division (flails, 'crocodiles,' and petard tanks), and they proved themselves to be of exceptional value in town fighting. They were used in a similar manner to the way a golfer uses different clubs for different shots. They operated in mixed troops during certain phases of the battle, and the combination of a petard to knock holes in buildings, gun tanks using their main armament, and 'crocodiles' administering the *coup-de-grace* with flame was more than many of the enemy defended posts could take. Fortunately, our casualties in this battle were light, but amongst them we lost one of the most popular, loyal, and conscientious officers of the Battalion—Peter Butler. He had been with the unit so long and had done so much for it that his death cast a gloom over the whole Battalion."

The clearing up was completed by the evening of the 14th April, and as soon as the Battalion had emerged on the west of Arnhem, where the 1st Airborne Division had, by their incredible gallantry, made history, the "Pompadours" were ordered to retrace their steps and attack in a few hours a village north-east of Arnhem, called Velp.

"This," says Colonel Butler, "was a lovely village which for some unknown reason was thought to be strongly held and thus we were given formidable artillery support for the assault. In the event the opposition was slight, and most of the supporting fire knocked down portions of a lovely village. At the time we all felt irritated that this should have happened, especially since the local Dutch gave us a really warm welcome. It is easy, however, to be wise after the event, and the fact that some houses, no matter how lovely, were saved, could never have compensated for the loss of one soldier of the Battalion."

Disorganised, dispirited, and lacking in any order, the German garrison of about 100 or more men offered not the slightest resistance to the 2nd Essex as they swept through the town. All were taken prisoner without a single Essex casualty.

The Battalion returned to Arnhem, and embarking in landing craft moved down the Neder Rijn to Renkum.

In this completely ruined village they disembarked and marched into Wageningem, about twenty miles west of Arnhem. Here was found a laboratory where the Germans tested one-man submarines.

At this point Lieutenant-Colonel Butler left the Battalion. He went to command a battalion of South Lancashires, and as an officer writes, "His departure left a sense of great personal loss to every man in the Battalion." He was succeeded in command of the "Pompadours" by Major E. S. Scott, M.B.E. (The Buffs), who had been Battalion Second-in-Command since early in the New Year.

Between the new British positions and the enemy's ran the line of the Rivers Grebbe and Eem. Once more the front became static, with extensive patrolling by both sides, in which the enemy suffered far more heavily than did the British.

The Allies had by this time cut off northern Holland, and therefore the whole of the German forces in this country could not get back to join with the main armies now well back into Germany, nor yet could they be supplied. They therefore continued to plunder the Dutch to keep themselves fed, and there was thus a serious shortage of food for the Dutch people.

But the end could not now be long delayed, and General Montgomery ordered the 1st Canadian Army, in which the 49th Division still served, to halt its offensive operations against "Fortress Holland." On the 25th April, 1945, a truce between the opposing forces began to operate, and measures were taken to transport supplies into enemy-held Holland for the relief of the semi-starving population.

Lieutenant-Colonel Scott says: "The route of these lorries was through our village of Wageningem, and we had to allow a few German officers to come over under a white flag to this village to arrange details of the truce. Prince Bernhard of the Netherlands came with the Allied officers, and a meeting took place in the village hall. After the details of the truce and safe conduct of the lorries had been arranged, the German officers had to be returned to their own lines.

"The A.P.M., 49th Division was one of the conducting British officers, and he invited me to travel in his jeep through the Boche lines. This gave me a somewhat unauthorised look at the German position on our part of the front (and incidentally the poor state of the German troops) in case the need should arise of having to attack them."

At Wageningem, too, where the Battalion "front" was very roughly demarcated by a road running from north to south, one night a "party" was reported approaching from the north down the road. It had refused to halt, and had been fired on without success. As this "party" or another had already been reported farther to the front, the company called for defensive fire, which was duly put down and added to the general confusion and noise.

Lieutenant-Colonel Scott says of all this:

"... By now the 'party' had been identified as a lone cyclist pedalling 'flat-out' towards the river. The road ended at a T-junction, where a platoon of the left-hand company was ordered to stop this cyclist at all costs. The Platoon Commander lined himself up in the middle of the road and prepared for a rugger tackle, but somehow failed to stop the intruder. The Company Commander of the left-hand company, Major Perry Wilkins, then led a hunt round the houses, and eventually found the cyclist standing forlornly at a corner, very lost.

He was a German in full marching order and complete with food panniers on his bicycle. When asked how he came there, he said he was cycling back to Germany. He had no idea where the Allied troops were. He had crossed the Neder Rijn from the south when that part of Holland had been liberated, and had somehow bicycled through his own front line on the north side of the river, and had lost his way to Germany. So for the "Pompadours" the war in Europe drew to a close in conditions not unsimilar to those immediately after the "break-in" north of Bayeux on the 6th/7th June, 1944, when forlorn, lost, and isolated Germans came bumping into the Essex positions.

On the 5th May, 1945, the German Army in Holland surrendered unconditionally, and the 49th Division prepared to march into the occupied part of the country.

On the 7th May, 1945, the move-up took place, the area allotted to the Division being Utrecht–Milerson–Amersfoort. The Divisional Reconnaissance Regiment passed the starting-point, which was just west of Wageningem, at 9 a.m., the harbour party of the 2nd Essex taking its place in the column at 10.30 a.m. The Battalion followed at 1.45 p.m., and was given a most tumultuous welcome by the liberated and nearly starving population.

By 5 p.m. the Battalion was concentrated in the area of Ziest.

The final surrender of all German forces had been signed at 2.41 a.m. that morning, and so, with the move into Ziest, another phase in the long history of the 2nd Battalion The Essex Regiment (the "Pompadours") came to an end.

The way had not been easy and the price paid not light. In the period 6th June, 1944, to 5th May, 1945, the "Pompadours" had had 10 officers and 146 other ranks killed in action, while 35 officers and 526 other ranks had been wounded and 2 officers and 85 other ranks had been reported as missing. This total of 804 casualties takes no account of the many who were evacuated through battle exhaustion and sickness. Denied the more spectacular service that was the lot of those units and formations which took part in the advance through Belgium, the crossing of the Rhine and the approach to the Elbe and even to the Baltic Sea, the "Pompadours" took part in battles which in severity and hardship were second to none in the whole campaign. The 2nd Battalion had throughout the campaign, in battle and rest, maintained a standard that was in the highest traditions of the Essex Regiment.

During the campaign in North-west Europe, the 2nd Battalion The Essex Regiment was awarded two D.S.O.s, one M.B.E., two D.C.M.s, fourteen M.C.s, thirteen M.M.s and two Croix de Guerre, while over twenty-four were mentioned in dispatches or were awarded Commander-in-Chief's Certificates.

Section V
GERMANY, ITALY, AND ENGLAND, 1945-48

As the column moved into Ziest that 7th May, orders were given that made the 2nd Essex, together with the 2nd Glosters, responsible for the concentration and disarmament of the German 346th Infantry Division, some 9,700 troops strong.

These duties took the "Pompadours" to Amersfoort, where, a few days later, it became known that the 49th Division was going to be relieved in Holland by the 3rd Canadian Division and was to move up into Germany as part of the 2nd Army.

The 2nd Essex had had a long spell in Holland and was glad to move on, but before leaving, a representative party, nearly 200 strong, was sent to take part, on the 21st May, in the 1st Canadian Corps Victory Parade in The Hague, a ceremony somewhat marred by unceasing and heavy rain.

Unna, 1945

On the 4th June the 2nd Essex moved into Unna, near Dortmund, in relief of the 1/313rd U.S. Infantry Regiment, and took over an area of responsibility extending over fifty square miles just east of the Ruhr and honeycombed with P.W. camps and, worse still, camps for displaced persons.

Life was not easy, for many of these D.P. camps were filled with Russians, to the terror of the local inhabitants. There were rape, murder, and looting by the Russians, and counter-action by the Germans. One of the very first notes in Battalion records for this period reads: "For the second day running bread delivered by the Germans to the camps is found to contain powdered glass. The excuse is bomb damage in the mills."

Appropriate action by the Commanding Officer with the Bur-

(Imperial War Museum)
2ND BATTALION THE ESSEX REGIMENT. PERSONNEL PASS A KNOCKED-OUT GERMAN PANTHER TANK NEAR TILLY-SUR-SUELLES. 19TH JUNE, 1944.

(Imperial War Museum)
2ND BATTALION THE ESSEX REGIMENT. TILLY-SUR-SEULLES IMMEDIATELY AFTER ITS CAPTURE BY THE BATTALION. 19TH JUNE, 1944.

(Imperial War Museum)
2ND BATTALION THE ESSEX REGIMENT IN ZETTEN AFTER ITS CAPTURE. 22ND JANUARY, 1945.

(Imperial War Museum.)
2ND BATTALION THE ESSEX REGIMENT ON THE NEDER RIJN IN THE SECOND BATTLE OF ARNHEM. 14TH APRIL, 1945.

gomaster to ensure no repetition was resented. In fact British insistence on fair play for both sides led not only to resentment but to open acts of disrespect as the following record shows: "As the result of a Boche being seen to spit on passing the Union Jack at B.H.Q., the Burgomaster is ordered to decree that in future males will doff hats on passing. Largely the Germans now go hatless."

Raids and shootings now reached such a scale that on one occasion the carrier platoon had to be turned out to lay an ambush and a running battle ensued. Shooting affrays were mixed with such episodes as when the Russian D.P.s distilled petrol they had stolen and drank the result. Fifteen died.

Altogether the Battalion was relieved to see the original total of 10,000 Russian D.P.s gradually dwindling, as these turbulent people were packed into repatriation trains. A quiet day was an event to be recorded. "2nd July. A singularly quiet twenty-four hours, possibly attributable to the dampening effect of heavy and continuous rain."

The British soldier's ambassador spirit was evident when "C" Company induced the D.P. camp they were administering to play football in a match, Company versus Camp. "C" Company won by an odd goal, but the match was remarkable perhaps in that the Russian referee favoured a hunting-horn rather than the customary whistle.

Altogether, one is led to suspect that Lieutenant-Colonel E. S. Scott, M.B.E., cannot have been sorry when, on the 25th July, 1945, he handed over command to Lieutenant-Colonel V. C. Magill-Cuerdon. Battle must have been child's play compared to the hazards of Unna.

But Unna had a brighter and lighter side. Life wasn't all shepherding recalcitrant D.P.s or re-educating Nazi Germany. There was the 2nd Battalion band on tour from Warley and the periodical shows put on by the "Pompadour Prunes"—an expression that must remind many who served with the Battalion in that last winter of war of Lieutenant-Colonel Butler. Also there was "Essex College," the first unit educational establishment in the B.L.A., which served over 250 students before they returned to civil life.

Essex College attracted much notice, and visits by the Corps and Divisional Commanders were frequent, as were the visits by the new Brigade Commander, Brigadier K. G. Exham, D.S.O., who had taken over from Brigadier R. H. Senior. Brigadier Exham also attended, and appreciated, the performances of the "Pompadour Prunes."

Unna, too, saw the liaison visit to the Regiment of a party from the 1st Battalion Essex Scottish Regiment of Canada complete with pipe band. It was a great success, as was the return visit to the Essex Scottish. The Essex Regiment was one of very few which managed such liaison visits to sister regiments of the Dominions.

Berlin, 1945-46

In November 1945, the Battalion left Unna, and the 56th Infantry Brigade, with whom it had served since March 1944, and went to Berlin to join the 131st Lorried Infantry Brigade of the 7th Armoured Division (the Desert Rats).

Major-General L. O. Lyne, the Divisional Commander, was quick to remind the Battalion of its spell under the 7th Armoured Division's command earlier in the campaign, saying how glad he was to have them under command once more.

The Battalion had come into Berlin by the great autobahn that stretched from Cologne to Berlin, with the last 150 miles running through the Soviet zone of occupation. The city was under four-Power occupation, with the British occupying the western districts of Spandau, Charlottenberg, Tiergarten, Wilmersdorf, and Schmargendorf.

Once in the city the Battalion was put to training, for the 7th Armoured Division had an operational rather than an occupation task. Despite the calls of guards and garrison duties, some useful platoon and company training was accomplished.

In Berlin, Headquarter Company, 2nd Essex, won the British Troops, Berlin, Small-bore Championship, beating "A" Squadron the 11th Hussars by 345 to 297 in the final shoot. The "possible" was 360. The "Pompadours" team was Captain (Q.M.) P. Hale, Captain A. A. Vince, Captain F. R. Alexander, Regimental Sergeant-Major J. R. Gulliver, L/Corporal Hodges, and Private Crouch.

On the 23rd December Lieutenant-Colonel G. H. Walker took over command, just in time for the Battalion's first peace-time Christmas for six years. This was celebrated in "Pompadour" style, a high-light being the traditional football match of officers versus sergeants. This, according to one report, "was indeed comical and amusing, but left the local population amazed at our sense of humour."

Einbeck, 1946

The stay in Berlin was neither long nor exciting, for life had been found somewhat quiet after the hazards of Unna. Indeed, what were most missed on transfer to Einbeck were the many excellent welfare institutions that had been set up in Berlin.

It was March 1946 when the 2nd Essex left Berlin and the 7th Armoured Division to move to Einbeck, there to join the 5th Infantry Division ("The Globetrotters") as part of the 13th Infantry Brigade.

The Essex Regiment was no stranger to the 13th Infantry Brigade. The 1st Essex had served with it at Catterick and in the Saar in 1934 and 1935, while the 5th Battalion had been in the Brigade since July 1944. The 2nd Essex, too, was not a stranger in the 5th Division, for it had formed part of the formation whilst in Egypt in 1935 and 1936, and again had served under 5th Divisional command for a short time during the withdrawal to Dunkirk in May 1940.

Einbeck, a small town in the Harz Mountains, some 68 kilometres from Hanover and 38 kilometres from Göttingen, is extremely old and attractive and very famous for its beer.

Once settled and largely free from occupational duties, the Battalion pressed on with training. This was urgent, for the release scheme had taken heavy toll of all ranks and few remained who had fought with the Battalion in 1944–45. Indeed, all that remained of the pre-war "Pompadours" were R.S.M. J. R. Gulliver and Private W. Gant, both of whom had served with the Battalion almost continuously for over twenty years.

On the 30th May, 1946, Lieutenant-Colonel T. L. G. Charles, D.S.O., returned to the Battalion and took command.

A high standard of training was very necessary, for in 1946 the 5th Division formed part of the Imperial strategic reserve and was expected to be ready for service in any part of the globe. The summer was thus spent in training, full use being made of the Rhine Army Training Centre at Paderborn, to which companies were sent in rotation for 10–14 days' strenuous training.

Trieste and Mestre

In September 1946 the 13th Infantry Brigade (1st Worcesters, 2nd Oxford and Bucks L.I., and 2nd Essex) was transferred to form part of the international force in occupation of the much-disputed town of Trieste, a seaport on the Adriatic, some seventy miles east-north-east of Venice.

Trieste was eagerly coveted by Jugoslavia, and to prevent any one-sided action, the city and its immediate precincts were guarded by British and American forces. The so-called Morgan line divided the Allied territory from that held by Jugoslavia.

It was to join this force that the 2nd Essex left Einbeck on the 11th September, 1946. After a five-day journey, first westward to Calais and then south through Salzberg, Villach, and Udine, they arrived to be quartered at Lazaretto, near Trieste. They found a lovely city, with shops filled with foodstuffs and luxury goods at not exceptionally high prices, an astonishing sight to those who since 1940 had only served at home or in North-west Europe.

Very soon after their arrival, Lieutenant-General Sir John Harding, K.C.B., C.B.E., D.S.O., M.C., Commander 13th Corps, accompanied by the Commander of the 1st Armoured Division and Brigadier R. M. W. De Winton, D.S.O. (Commander 13th Infantry Brigade), came to see the Battalion and welcomed it to the C.M.F.

Unfortunately, the move down to Trieste in September had prevented the "Pompadours" from sending a representative detachment to attend the ceremony of unveiling and dedicating the 56th Infantry Brigade war memorial which was held in Bayeux Cathedral on the 28th September, 1946. The memorial is a bronze plaque surmounted by the Brigade Sphinx and title. Below the Sphinx are the Regimental crests of the three battalions which served in the Brigade during the campaign in North-western Europe. Below the Regimental crests, which are in line, is the following inscription:

"To the memory of all ranks of 56th Infantry Brigade who died in the campaign for the liberation of North-western Europe, June 1944–May 1945.
"Erected by their Comrades."

Brigadier K. G. Exham, D.S.O., then commanding the 56th Infantry Brigade, was representative brigadier, while the O.C. Troops on parade was Major J. F. Higson, M.C., Brigade Major 56th Infantry Brigade. Major Higson represented the 2nd Essex at this ceremony. The 2nd S.W.B. and 2nd Glosters still serving in the theatre were represented by detachments, all 9 officers and 92 other ranks on parade having landed with the Brigade on D-Day on Arromanches beaches.

> *"The tumult and the shouting dies:*
> *The Captains and the Kings depart:*
> *Still stands thine ancient sacrifice,*
> *An humble and a contrite heart.*
> *Lord God of Hosts, be with us yet:*
> *Lest we forget—Lest we forget."*

In January 1947 the Battalion was transferred to Mestre, a town on the mainland of Italy opposite Venice. Here they found heavy guard duties awaiting them, duties so onerous that little training was possible. With the run-down of the C.M.F., there were vast accumulations of stores to be collected and shipped out of the country. And anyone who served in Italy will know that to leave anything unguarded for five minutes, luggage or locomotive, was to say good-bye to it for ever.

However, time was found to make history in two directions. First, when on the 3rd February five inexperienced skiers set off for Cortina D'Ampezzo, the Italian winter sports centre in the Dolomites, to take part in the C.M.F. ski championships. Lieutenant-Colonel Charles's team did not win—that was not expected, for ski-ing championships do not fall to the inexperienced—but they were not disgraced, and it was a great effort.

The second historic event was when the 2nd Battalion Corps of Drums, only recently re-formed after the war, beat Retreat at the invitation of the Sindaco of Venice in the Piazza San Marco. This event was quite unparalleled, and received great publicity in the C.M.F. newspaper *Union Jack* as elsewhere. As indeed it should, for St. Mark's Square is known the world over and the sight of the Corps of Drums of a British infantry battalion beating Retreat before a crowd of at least five thousand in that historic square for the first time in history was indeed news.

At Mestre the 2nd Battalion heard it was to go almost immediately into suspended animation, a very great blow indeed. This unpleasant fate was fortunately postponed for nearly a year, as it became evident that the peace treaty with Italy would not be finally ratified until late in 1947, and that the Battalion would be required for duty in Italy until the final evacuation.

It was thus decided that Lieutenant-Colonel C. A. Southey should come out and take over command, for Lieutenant-Colonel Charles had left in April 1947 to take up an appointment as G.S.O.I. of the 5th Division in B.A.O.R.

So in the end the Battalion remained at Mestre throughout the greater part of 1947 as the C.M.F. grew smaller and smaller, till only 86 Area under Brigadier R. A. T. Eve remained out of all the hundreds of thousands who had once fought from Taranto northwards to Austrian Villach.

Then, too, 86 Area troops began to move, until by early December only the 2nd Essex remained. The Battalion evacuated Mestre on the 5th December, 1947, to embark in the *Taos Victory* and to sail from Venice three days later.

Colchester, 1948

As it arrived at Southampton on the 16th December, 1947, the Battalion was greeted by Brigadier G. H. Wilmer, D.S.O., M.C., Colonel of the Regiment, by many members of the Regiment past and present, and by the Regimental band.

Disembarked so as to reach Colchester the following day (the L.N.E. railway engine "The Essex Regiment" pulling the train over the London and North-Eastern Railway portion of the route), the Battalion marched through the town with bayonets fixed, colours flying, drums beating, and bands playing, thus exercising the privileges granted to the Essex Regiment in May 1946. They were quartered in Roman Way Camp, which seemed to many a poor exchange for sunny Italy.

There is little more to tell, and it is not proposed to dwell on the final months of life of this fine Battalion, months in which numbers grew smaller and smaller and duties more and more irksome. Just let it be recorded that sporting spirit and prowess remained to the end, the 2nd Essex winning the East Anglian District Cricket Cup by beating the Military Provost Corps at Colchester on the 18th August, 1948.

On the 3rd November, 1948, at Meeanee Barracks, Colchester, the ceremony of the amalgamation of the 1st and 2nd Battalions The Essex Regiment (44th and 56th) was held, and the 2nd Battalion The Essex Regiment (the "Pompadours") ceased to have a separate entity.

Chapter Four

THE 1/4TH BATTALION THE ESSEX REGIMENT, 1939-46

FOREWORD

by Lieutenant-General Sir Francis Tuker, K.C.I.E., C.B., D.S.O., O.B.E., Commander 4th Indian Division, 1941-1944.

Any soldier who knew this distinguished Battalion in its war years would welcome the opportunity of writing a foreword to its history.

The Battalion came to me, as Commander of the 4th Indian Division, when that Division was refitting in Egypt in the spring of 1942 after the strenuous operations of the winter. From then onwards, until March 1944, they and I were in constant and close contact; for me it was always a pleasant experience to visit them—smart, soldierly, with an intense esprit de corps and a high fighting spirit. Efficient and devoted officers made a first-class team of as fine a body of men as one could wish to lead into battle.

This, then, is one of the greatest infantry battalions of the Second World War.

The story told here will speak for itself. A grateful Divisional Commander will never forget their endurance, week after week, in the early days of the defence of the Ruweisat Ridge; their skill and boldness at Akarit, at Garci, and on the Medjerda; and their staunchness among the shambles of Cassino. It was battalions such as this that made the name of the 4th Indian Division.

The record is one that has added lustre to the Essex Regiment that the Battalion holds so dear, to our Territorial Army, and to our matchless British Infantry.

3rd May, 1951.

Section I
HOME DEFENCE, 1939-40

THE 1/4th Battalion The Essex Regiment returned from annual camp in the first half of August 1939, and all ranks dispersed to their homes from their drill halls. They were not to remain scattered for long.

By the 25th August, 1939, code words putting the "Preparatory Period" into force and foreshadowing the embodiment of the Territorial Army had been received at Battalion Headquarters at Ilford. "Key" parties were called out, and on the 1st September the order for general mobilisation was issued.

On embodiment the Battalion, commanded by Lieutenant-Colonel G. M. Gibson, T.D., formed part of the 161st Infantry Brigade, under command of Brigadier H. Pawle, but it was to be temporarily in the London area and under command of the London Division.

Mobilisation had gone well, men reporting quickly at Ilford (H.Q.), Dagenham ("A" Company), Burnham ("B" Company), Epping ("C" Company), and Manor Park ("D" Company).

The initial task was security duty in East London, but this role did not last long. On the 1st October, 1939, the Battalion ceased to be under the London Division, and reverted to the command of 54th (East Anglian) Division.

At this time the 1/4th Essex was ordered by the 161st Infantry Brigade to prepare to concentrate in billets in Epping. The move took place on the 10th October, the Battalion entering the town headed by the band and drums.

Whilst at Epping the Battalion received its first intake of Army Class, approximately 100 strong, who were formed into a training company known as "T" Company. They were all twenty-three to twenty-four years old, and a very good lot, many of whom later became N.C.O.s and key personnel.

At Epping the first of a long series of orders to provide drafts for overseas was received. This was for Egypt, presumably to join the 1st Battalion, and the call was quickly filled with volunteers anxious to get overseas as soon as possible.

At Epping, too, a photograph was taken of all ranks serving in possession of the Mons Star, denoting service in France in the 1914-18

War previous to December 1914. There were only six: Lieutenant-Colonel G. M. Gibson, T.D., Lieutenant (Quartermaster) H. Pouch, Company Sergeant-Major H. M. Strong, Sergeant G. W. Vince, Sergeant R. Smith, and L/Corporal L. Wood.

Hardly had the 1/4th Essex settled in Epping than it was on the move again, this time to the area of Kelvedon and Witham, where it arrived on the 2nd December. Here training was to start in real earnest, and the soundness of that basic training is proved by the success achieved in battle in the succeeding years.

Before Christmas 1939 the 1/4 Essex had been seen by a number of distinguished visitors, which included Major-General J. H. T. Priestman, C.B., C.B.E., D.S.O., M.C. (Commander 54th (East Anglian) Division); Colonel Sir Francis Whitmore, K.C.B., C.M.G., D.S.O. (the Lord-Lieutenant of Essex); Brigadier-General J. T. Wigan, C.B., C.M.G., D.S.O., T.D. (the Honorary Colonel of the Battalion), and Lieutenant-General Sir Guy Williams, K.C.B., C.M.G., D.S.O. (the G.O.C.-in-C. Eastern Command). There were also many visits from Brigadier J. W. L. S. Hobart, D.S.O., M.C., now in command of the 161st (Essex) Infantry Brigade.

By the New Year of 1940, although Battalion Headquarters remained at Witham, the unit was once again split up, with companies at Maldon, North Weald, and Hornchurch. The dispersion was caused by the role of the Battalion—defence of a sector of the East Coast—which included aerodrome defence as well as coast watching. This was to continue into the spring of 1940.

In spite of a busy life, time was always spared to remember great events of the past, and it is pleasant to read that on the 26th March, 1940, the 1/4th did not forget those who had fallen at the Battle of Gaza in 1917. At the Commemoration Service, the Reverend A. D. Johnson, M.C., Chaplain of the Essex Infantry Brigade at the Battle of Gaza, conducted the Service, which was attended by Lieutenant-General Sir Geoffrey Howard, K.C.B., C.M.G., D.S.O., the Colonel of the Essex Regiment, who afterwards inspected the Battalion on parade and took the salute at a march past.

Whilst stationed at Witham, the Battalion had to say good-bye to their "Immatures," which was a sad loss, as they were all very keen. A few rejoined later when old enough for foreign service, but most of them remained permanently with anti-aircraft units. At about the same time the Battalion received its second intake ("M" Company), also good material, and the arrival of this second large draft coincided with the posting of some very good regular reservist non-commissioned officers. The 1/4th Essex was now changing its material make-up very quickly, as just before leaving Witham the third (and last) intake was also received.

By the end of March 1940 the Battalion had received warning orders for a move to Northumberland. Before leaving Witham, the 1/4th Essex was given a silver bugle by the Great Totham and Wickham Bishops Branch of the British Legion to commemorate the stay in the area. All were very sorry to leave a district in which they had been received so well, and where they had done so much that redounded to the credit of the Essex Regiment.

On the 16th April, 1940, the 1/4th Essex arrived at Wooler, in the heart of Northumberland. Companies were scattered under canvas and in none too good billets in a radius of some three to six miles from Wooler itself. Not far away lay the 1/5th and 2/5th Essex.

The move to the North of England took place at a time when it was becoming clear that the period of inaction was drawing to a close. British troops were engaged with the enemy in Norway, and on the 20th April, 1940, Lieutenant-Colonel Gibson was asked by the Divisional Commander to provide 2 officers and 24 other ranks for a hand-picked composite company which was being formed for surprise landings along the Norwegian seaboard. The 54th (East Anglian) Division Composite Company became "No. 3 Independent Company," and sailed on the 3rd May, 1940, for an unknown destination. The O.C. of this Independent Company was Major A. C. Newman (Colonel A. C. Newman, V.C.), and those other ranks which the Commanding Officer selected from the large number of volunteers were the pick of the Battalion. They included several of the unit boxing team. Many of these men afterwards served very gallantly in Commandos.

The 10th May, 1940, and the invasion of the Low Countries brought added urgency to the preparation for war in this country. There was now a possibility that an attack against the British Isles might be added to the list of German attacks elsewhere. Mobile columns were prepared and made ready to move at very short notice. The 1/4th Essex was the unit in the 161st Infantry Brigade selected for this role. It was brought up to war establishment by the loan of transport from the 1/5th and 2/5th Essex and other units.

As the withdrawals from Dunkirk and the Battle of France marched steadily to a climax, so invasion risks increased. The 1/4th Essex was kept on its toes by such messages as this received from the Headquarters 54th Division: "Special vigilance is necessary during the hours of darkness. Defences will be manned. An attack is expected by air and sea." The coast of Northumberland, the defence of which was the responsibility of the 161st Infantry Brigade, was an obvious target for any such attack. But there was no attack, and fully engaged in training and on defence works in those strenuous days of the summer of Dunkirk, the 1/4th Essex knew no threat, alarm, or physical exercise that was not shared by all units guarding this island fortress.

And so on through the air raids, the alarms, the orders, and counter-orders that filled those days, on to the 10th June, 1940, the fall of France and the entry of Italy into the war. That same day came orders for almost immediate embarkation to twelve picked battalions, of which the 1/4th Essex was one, to proceed to an unknown tropical destination. Was it Egypt or French West Africa? Nobody knew. There was no time to conjecture, and by the 20th June arrangements for embarkation were complete.

The Battalion was now the only unit left in the former brigade area, for the remainder of the 161st Infantry Brigade had moved to the Hexham (Newcastle) area. But on the 20th June a telephone message from Headquarters 54th Division said, "Your move is off. All of your equipment and vehicles are to be returned immediately." This was followed on the 22nd June by orders to establish advance Headquarters at Belford Hall, there to come under command of the 162nd Infantry Brigade. The role, coast defence.

On the 1st July the Battalion moved back to Wooler and reverted to the command of the 161st Infantry Brigade, and here, on the 19th July, warning orders were received that the 1/4th Essex might again be removed from command of the 54th Division and placed under War Office control. Some days of uncertainty followed, and it was not until the 23rd July that written orders were received to confirm the fact that the Battalion was under War Office control to mobilise for service overseas, mobilisation to be completed by midnight of the 31st July/1st August, 1940. It was to be a move to a tropical country.

Section II

WEST AFRICA, 1940-41

The almost impossible task was completed to time, and, after farewell visits from Major-General J. H. T. Priestman and Brigadier J. W. L. S. Hobart, the Battalion entrained at Wooler station on the evening of the 4th August, 1940. The trains arrived at Liverpool on the morning of the 5th August, and the Battalion embarked immediately in the troopship *Monarch of Bermuda*.

The strength of the Battalion on embarkation was 32 officers and 741 other ranks. Six officers and 148 other ranks formed the "First Reinforcements." Officers who embarked with the Battalion were Lieutenant-Colonel G. M. Gibson, T. D., Majors R. M. Doyle, E. J. Sheldrake, A. Noble, Captains L. W. A. Chappell, D. J. M. Smith, E. A. Hawkins, H. E. Heard, T. W. L. Lewsey, A. G. Fowler, Lieutenants R. M. Creese, D. S. Farr, and 2/Lieutenants E. J. C. Williams, C. J. A. Foote, H. C. Gregory, D. G. Counsell, R. A. Plackett, N. Reeves, H. J. Young, D. A. Beckett, T. W. Grist, A. Beckett, J. Watt, T. G. Graves, D. J. V. Fisher, C. N. Bolton, A. W. Bunch, and S. Banks. Lieutenant H. R. Pouch was Quartermaster; Lieutenant T. W. G. Atkins, R.A.M.C., was Regimental Medical Officer, and Captain the Reverend E. G. Moreton was Chaplain. Lieutenant-Colonel Gibson was O.C. Troops, which consisted of his battalion, a Field Company R.E., and a General Hospital, plus details. The first reinforcement party under Captain J. F. B. Fadden sailed at the same time in a slow convoy.

On the evening of the 5th August, 1940, the *Monarch of Bermuda* sailed, and after two days in company with slower ships, a fast convoy was formed consisting of the *Monarch of Bermuda*, *Empress of Britain*, *Empress of Canada*, *Strathaird*, *Stratheden*, *Andes*, and *Batory*. Those who have seen a big ship convoy at sea under war-time conditions with an escort from the Royal Navy can never again be in doubt of the meaning of "Sea Power," the ability of a nation to move its ships across the seas and deny such facilities to an enemy.

At sea the destination of the 1/4th Essex was disclosed—Freetown, Sierra Leone. This magnificent natural harbour and defended port became of added importance after the entry of Italy into the war had denied the Mediterranean to British and Allied shipping. It was the first refuelling port on the route round the Cape of Good Hope to the Middle and Far East, and it was the marshalling point for homeward-bound convoys on their way from the Cape and from South America.

Freetown was, however, not free from danger. The British colonies of Sierra Leone and the Gambia are adjacent to French West Africa. Large garrisons were maintained in Senegal, the French Sudan, and French Guinea. All these had declared for Vichy France and Marshal Petain rather than for Free France and General de Gaulle. A reinforcement of garrisons in British West Africa, including Freetown, was therefore essential.

On the 14th August, 1940, the *Monarch of Bermuda* lay off Freetown, but it was not until the 31st August that the 1/4th Essex disembarked, as Wilberforce Barracks, Freetown, were not ready for occupation.

The march of the Battalion from ship to barracks through the streets of Freetown, headed by the band and drums (which at War Office suggestion had been taken overseas with the Battalion), was quite an event both for Europeans and natives, especially the latter, who had never before seen British infantry. Much less had they seen or heard music played by marching white soldiers. They crowded the streets amid tense excitement, for this was the first time in history that a British infantry battalion had formed part of the garrison. That night the Battalion signallers exchanged messages by morse lamp with the *Monarch of Bermuda* as she left harbour.

Brigadier M. A. Green, O.B.E., M.C., the Garrison Commander, soon visited the Battalion. He was followed, on the 16th September, by Lieutenant-General G. J. Giffard, C.B., D.S.O., the G.O.C.-in-C. West Africa.

General Giffard inspected the beach defences which were sited in front of a malarial swamp, and ordered the Battalion to occupy them forthwith with one company by night. The sole shelter for the men on this duty consisted of huts recently occupied by African troops and quite unsuitable for British troops. As a direct result of this duty, the sickness from malaria started, and in the eleven months that the Battalion was stationed in Freetown, nearly 300 of its effectives were admitted to hospital with malaria.

The Battalion medical officer, Captain T. W. G. Atkins, R.A.M.C., worked incessantly to reduce the incidence of the disease, as did Major Jameson Carr, R.A.M.C., a specialist in tropical medicine and an old friend of the Regiment.

The order to man the defences despite the very evident danger from malarial infection was a risk that had to be run. A decision at Cabinet level to attack Dakar, the French naval base in West Africa, had been taken, and the necessary forces were assembling. A French counter-stroke against Freetown was possible and precautionary measures essential.

On the 22nd September, 1940, the fleets of naval vessels and transports that for the past few days had been assembling in Freetown Harbour sailed, and it was known that Dakar was the objective. On the 24th September the 1/4th Essex was warned that operations were obscure, and that, if reinforcements were required, they would be moved at twelve hours' notice. However, the naval attack was repulsed, and in consequence the army landing did not go in, and on the 26th September the Allied force withdrew.

The Dakar Force was dispersed from Freetown, and before departure its Commander, Major-General N. S. Irwin, C.B., D.S.O., M.C., visited the 1/4th Battalion of his old Regiment. Two battalions of Royal Marines remained as part of the Freetown garrison for three months, and a great liaison both at work and play was established between the Royal Marine units and the 1/4th Essex. Athletic sports meetings, football, and boxing were arranged, with varied fortunes to the three contestants.

Despite all distractions, training went on at top pressure and morale remained at a very high level, for the now heavy sick rate did not affect the spirit of the Battalion.

By early October the full price the Battalion had to pay for manning the beach defences after 17th September was apparent: 155 in hospital or excused duty—15½ per cent. of the Battalion. Remedial measures, such as the issue of anti-malarial ointment to deter mosquitoes, were made too late, the first issue being made on the 11th October, by which time over 100 men had become infected.

But with its drawbacks, malaria, high rainfall and excessive humidity, snakes, and delayed mails from home, Freetown had its good points. Facilities for games generally were good, football, cricket, hockey, and boxing predominating, in all of which the Battalion did well. The very large parade ground at Wilberforce Barracks provided for most sports, not to mention the Commanding Officer's parade held on it every Saturday morning throughout the Battalion's stay. Bathing at Lumley Beach—some of the finest surf-bathing in the world—shooting guinea-fowl in the bush, and other relaxations from training and barrack life were there for the asking.

With the oncoming of the winter season the rains decreased, until in December the *harmattan*, hot, parched winds from the Sahara Desert, brought dry fine weather. Training endeavours were intensified with the finer weather, and many arduous schemes were undertaken in the Bush. These schemes were often watched by Brigadier M. A. Green and by the Area Commander, Major-General C. G. Woolner, M.C. Meanwhile, the calls upon the Battalion were very numerous. The whole of the regimental transport was pooled under Area Headquarters. The Battalion was ordered to run the area transit camp and the local detention rooms as well as to find all the military police for Freetown. In addition, there were large permanent guard duties as well as many sudden calls for armed parties (frequently officer guards) to go on board captured ships brought into harbour. These duties often lasted for weeks. Once the Battalion was ordered to find 3 officers and 100 other ranks as guard on a prison ship going to Kingston, Jamaica. This party did not return to the Battalion for three months, and Lieutenant-Colonel Gibson received letters of congratulation on the fine impression they made while in Jamaica.

On Christmas Eve, 1940, a ceremonial guard changing at Government House was carried out before an audience of European and African notabilities. The band and drums were on parade, and as nearly as possible Buckingham Palace procedure was adhered to. It was a great success. So too was the Battalion Christmas dinner on Christmas Day. It takes more than the West African climate to curtail an Essex Christmas dinner: "A good meal of roast beef, roast potatoes, Yorkshire pudding, and brussels sprouts, followed by Christmas pudding and custard, beer, and cigarettes." In the evening of Christmas Day a serious fire broke out in Freetown, involving a large portion of the town. Anticipating orders, the Commanding Officer immediately sent two companies to the scene, whose enthusiastic intervention saved the town and earned high praise from civil and military authorities.

In December 1940 Lieutenant-Colonel Gibson was warned of the forthcoming arrival in Sierra Leone of Headquarters 161st Infantry Brigade, the 2/5th Essex, and certain other units. The 1/4th was to remain at Wilberforce and the 2/5th to go to Benguema Camp. Thus, on 11th January, 1941, the 1/4th Essex reverted to command of 161st Infantry Brigade, still under Brigadier Hobart. On the 26th March the Battalion "Trooped the Colour" before the Brigade Commander and a large crowd to commemorate the anniversary of Gaza Day.

So the early months of 1941 passed by. There was fresh interest as the news from home brought by the 2/5th Essex spread through the ranks, and there was a new interest in training, too, now the 1/4th Essex was a brigaded unit once more. Training continued unabated until April, when with the onset of the rainy season the weather took charge and curtailed operations.

An added interest was that the Battalion, together with the 2/5th Essex, was detailed for Operation Shrapnel, a top-secret plan which involved close co-operation and training with the Royal Navy. It has since been disclosed in Winston Churchill's book, *The Second World War* (vol. 2, "Their Finest Hour," page 552), as being a plan to occupy the Cape Verde Islands, and to set up air and refuelling bases to maintain naval control of the critical stretch of the sea route round the Cape.

But there were not to be many more weeks in Freetown. The first tornado blew on the 27th April, and by mid-May the Commanding Officer knew his Battalion would soon be on the move once more.

On the 13th June, 1941, Wilberforce Barracks were handed over to the 4th Nigeria Regiment, a unit of the incoming 6th (West Africa) Infantry Brigade, which was to take over from the 161st Infantry Brigade. By the 16th, the 1/4th Essex was on board the *Bergensfjord*, as, soon, were the 2/5th Essex and the Headquarters of the Brigade. The ship sailed on the 20th June, 1941, *en route* for the Middle East. Disembarked at Durban, the Essex Brigade re-embarked on the *Ile de France*, and sailed on the 11th July for Suez, disembarking on 27th July, 1941.

Section III

EGYPT, CYPRUS, AND PALESTINE, 1941-42

The disembarkation strength of the 1/4th Essex was 38 officers and 837 other ranks. As they moved into El Tahag Camp they were warned to expect a move forward to Mersa Matruh soon after the 1st August.

The strategical and tactical situation in the Western Desert at the time the 1/4th Essex landed in Egypt was not favourable. General Wavell's offensive in the winter of 1940/41 had taken the Desert Corps to Benghazi; but weakened by calls upon it to provide troops to fight in Greece, it had been attacked by General Rommel and his newly formed Afrika Korps, and by the end of April 1941 forced back to the frontier of Egypt. Tobruk, however, had been held.

(*Imperial War Museum.*)
1 4TH BATTALION THE ESSEX REGIMENT IN CO-OPERATION WITH CHURCHILL TANKS (145TH REGIMENT R.A.C.) MOVE INTO THE ATTACK. MEDJEZ-EL-BAB. 6TH MAY, 1943.

(*Imperial War Museum*)
H.R H THE DUKE OF GLOUCESTER INSPECTS THE 1/5TH BATTALION THE ESSEX REGIMENT. MOSUL. MAY 1942.

Lieutenant-Colonel A. Noble outside Battalion Headquarters, Point 62, Ruweisat Ridge. July 1942.

El Alamein Railway Station.

The Track Junction known as "Knightsbridge."

Battalion Headquarters in the "Playground." June 1942.

1/4TH BATTALION THE ESSEX REGIMENT IN THE WESTERN DESERT. 1942.

On the 1st July, 1941, General Wavell had been transferred and General Auchinleck succeeded him as Commander-in-Chief the Middle East, but before he handed over command, General Wavell had tried to drive back the Germans and relieve Tobruk. He had not succeeded, and the Germans were still on the frontier of Egypt.

On the 5th August, 1941, the 1/4th Essex left El Tahag Camp by train for Maaten Bagush, some sixty miles west of El Alamein. Here it came under the 11th Indian Infantry Brigade of the 4th Indian Division for operations and under 161st Infantry Brigade for training. At this time defensive positions in desert warfare were held in what were called "boxes," and like many other desert positions, Bagush had its defensive box. The 1/4th Essex held the eastern face of the box with the 2/5th Essex on their left and the 2/5th Mahrattas on their right.

The Battalion rapidly absorbed the atmosphere of the Western Desert, and training in desert warfare was undertaken with enthusiasm and determination. Major-General F. W. Messervy, the G.O.C. 4th Indian Division, came to visit them, as also did Lieutenant-General Sir Noel Beresford-Peirse, K.B.E., D.S.O., then in command in the Western Desert. He was accompanied by Brigadier John Harding, his principal staff officer. Brigadier Harding knew the Battalion of old, for he had commanded the machine-gun company of the 161st (Essex) Infantry Brigade in the First World War. General Beresford-Peirse was impressed with the fitness of the 1/4th Essex, but said he felt they should undergo a period of strenuous training in preparation for the future, which was exactly what Lieutenant-Colonel Gibson had hoped to do.

During this period Major A. Noble was attached for three weeks to the Support Group of 7th Armoured Division, then commanded by Brigadier W. H. E. Gott, D.S.O., M.C. ("Straffer" Gott), and learnt many lessons of desert fighting, lessons that he was able to apply later in the campaign.

On the 13th September it was learnt that the Battalion would take over the anti-aircraft defences of landing grounds in the Sidi Barrani area. The 1/5th Essex (who had a few weeks before arrived from the United Kingdom to complete the 161st Infantry Brigade) and 2/5th Essex had similar commitments. All posts were also equipped for ground defence in case of sudden attack by the enemy. The Battalion came directly under the command of 13th Corps, being attached for operations to the 12th A.A. Brigade R.A. These duties continued until 22nd October, when they were taken over by the 1st Buffs, the 1/4th Essex concentrating at Sidi Haneish, where it remained until the 1st November. The Battalion then left Sidi Haneish under the impression it was on its way to Haifa.

The 161st Infantry Brigade had now changed its composition. Both the 1/5th and 2/5th Essex had left, their places in the Brigade being taken by the 3/7th Rajput Regiment and the 4/7th Rajput Regiment. Brigadier Hobart was soon to go, being appointed Brigadier-General Staff the Sudan, and his place as brigade commander was to be taken by Brigadier W. D. Stamer, C.B.E., D.S.O., M.C. The Brigade was now to form part of the 5th Indian Division.

At Alexandria, on the 2nd November *en route* for Haifa, the Battalion advance party and that of the 4/7th Rajputs together with parties from 7/66th Battery 4th Field Regiment were embarked in the destroyer *Hasty*, which almost immediately sailed at 30 knots for Cyprus. This change of destination was not known till after sailing. The main party moved by train to Haifa, and from there was transferred by flights of destroyers to Cyprus. Disembarkation was at Famagusta. Cyprus was now of high strategical importance. The object of its greatly augmented garrison was the creation of an island fortress as outpost of the Middle East Command nearest to occupied Europe. At all costs another "Crete" was to be avoided.

The Commander of the 5th Indian Division, Major-General A. G. O. M. Mayne, C.B., D.S.O., soon visited the Battalion, and met Lieutenant-Colonel Gibson.

But Lieutenant-Colonel Gibson was no longer to remain in command of the Battalion. On the 22nd November, 1941, he heard he was to leave the Essex Regiment on promotion to colonel as Commander Port Sudan Sub-Area. This was a great blow to the Battalion, for Lieutenant-Colonel Gibson had been connected with the 4th Essex for twenty-five years, of which five and a half years had been in command. He left a battalion fit and ready for battle, and Lieutenant-Colonel A. Noble, who had been commissioned with the 4th Essex in 1927, took command.

There is little to tell of the winter months 1941-42 spent in Cyprus, or of the short stay in Egypt which followed in the spring of 1942. But the time in Cyprus was not wasted. In the event of invasion of the island, the Battalion had the role of a mobile task force to destroy enemy seaborne or airborne landings. For this they were organised into company groups of all arms, which would operate separately or collectively. The thorough and intense training carried out gave all concerned considerable experience in working with field artillery and engineers under command. Several full-scale invasion exercises were carried out and contact with battle-experienced troops was of great value to all ranks of the Battalion, who had, as yet, seen no action.

At the end of April the 1/4th Essex was moved up into Palestine and established in camp at Karkur. Here the Battalion joined the 5th Indian Infantry Brigade. On the 1st May their new brigade commander, Brigadier D. Russell, O.B.E., M.C., visited the camp to discuss future policy with Lieutenant-Colonel Noble.

The 5th Indian Infantry Brigade (1/4th Essex, 4/6th Rajputana Rifles, and 3/10th Baluch Regiment) was part of the 4th Indian Division (Major-General F. I. S. Tuker, C.B., D.S.O., O.B.E.), a formation with a distinguished fighting record since the day it was first committed to battle at Sidi Barrani in December 1940.

One of the early tasks given to the 1/4th Essex was siting the defences of two sub-sectors (Jenin and Nablus) of the Palestine Keep. This was to be done by the Commanding Officer and five other officers, an important task, for there was great need for a barrier against the potential threat of a German irruption through Turkey and Asia Minor.

On the 17th May the Battalion was inspected by H.R.H. the Duke of Gloucester, who complimented the Commanding Officer on the smartness of the parade.

One of the features of this month in Palestine is the emphasis that was laid on liaison within the 5th Indian Infantry Brigade. The Brigadier became known personally to every officer, warrant officer, and senior N.C.O. He and his staff dined in the officers' mess. Every possible opportunity was taken by the officers of the 1/4th Essex to get to know the British and Indian officers of the Rajputana Rifles and the Baluch Regiment. It was a policy that was to pay handsome dividends in battle, where knowledge of personalities is sometimes of incalculable value.

Section IV

THE WESTERN DESERT, JUNE TO OCTOBER 1942

The 1/4th Essex did not remain long in Palestine. In May, as the Battalion joined the 5th Indian Brigade, the situation in Cyrenaica was that the German and Italian forces under Rommel lay west of Gazala, while the Eighth Army, under Lieutenant-General N. M. Ritchie, countered the Axis forces from a series of defended areas or "boxes" running from Gazala to Bir Hacheim. The 13th and 30th Corps were commanded by Lieutenant-Generals W. H. E. Gott and Sir Willoughby Norrie respectively.

General Ritchie had planned to attack early in June, but was forestalled by Rommel, who attacked on the 27th May, and who by the 4th June had reached the neighbourhood of El Adem and "Knightsbridge." On the 4th June a counter-attack by General Ritchie failed, and Rommel moved in to invest Bir Hacheim. It was at this stage that the 5th Indian Infantry Brigade was ordered westwards.

About the 1st June the 1/4th Essex had been placed at short notice to move, and while preparations were being made Lieutenant-Colonel Noble, with his siting team, devoted most of the time remaining in an endeavour to get the Nablus and Jenin defended localities marked down to section posts. On the 8th June a complete record of the siting in map form, together with the Commanding Officer's written defence plan, was passed to Brigade.

On the 7th June move orders were received, and on the 9th the road party under Captain T. W. Grist left for Amriya. The main body left by rail from Hadera station on the morning of the 11th June. At Amriya Captain Grist came to tell the Commanding Officer that the road party was already under orders to proceed to Mersa Matruh.

On the evening of the 11th June the 1/4th Essex moved into the Western Desert for the second time during its tour in the Middle East. On the 12th June the Battalion detrained at Mersa Matruh and re-entrained in box wagons to continue the rail journey into the desert. Mishiefa was reached at 6 p.m. that night, and there the 5th Indian Infantry Brigade Group remained for twenty-four hours. On the evening of the 14th June orders were received that the brigade group would move the following day and occupy the "Kennels."

By now the Free French garrison in Bir Hacheim had been withdrawn, as had the Guards Brigade from "Knightsbridge." As this left the Gazala position exposed its garrison was also ordered to withdraw. The Eighth Army was in retreat.

This, then, was the position when, on the 15th June, 1942, the 5th Indian Infantry Brigade, now temporarily under command of the 5th Indian Division (Major-General H. R. Briggs, D.S.O.), left to occupy the "Kennels." The 1/4th Essex and 3/10th Baluch Regiment occupied the west face of the box and the 4/6th Rajputana Rifles the east face. There were three of these divisional boxes in this area of the Libyan border—"Kennels," "Warren," and "Playground"—and their names are misleading. They were uncomfortable, short of water, and, in view of what had happened at Bir Hacheim, "Knightsbridge," and elsewhere, of dubious tactical value.

The 1/4th Essex did not stay long in the "Kennels," for during the 17th June the positions were taken over by the 1st South African Division withdrawing from the forward areas. The 5th Indian Brigade Group moved to the "Playground."

Here the administrative situation of the Battalion was improved by the return of Captain H. C. Gregory from the N.A.A.F.I. at Fort Capuzzo. After purchasing and paying for some two hundred pounds' worth of stock, he was told by the manager to help himself, as the depot was about to be destroyed to prevent it falling into enemy hands. Captain Gregory doubled his original bid, and arrived back in the Battalion area with somewhat overladen trucks. He was well received, as the men had been without beer or cigarettes since leaving the Delta a week earlier.

Fortified by this distribution, the 1/4th Essex took calmly the order to leave the "Playground" forthwith—they had only arrived that morning—and to proceed to Sollum and come under the orders of the 10th Indian Division.

Since the 1st June, the 1/4th Essex had belonged to the 4th, 5th, and 10th Indian Divisions in rapid succession, an indication of the difficulties experienced as General Rommel advanced upon Egypt.

At Sollum the 1/4th Essex relieved troops of the 2nd Free French Brigade in the south sector of the Halfaya Box. The enemy that day—the 20th June—gained contact with the north sector, and the area was being shelled spasmodically as the Essex took over.

The general situation had deteriorated very rapidly in the last few days. The withdrawals from Gazala, Bir Hacheim, and "Knightsbridge" had been closely followed up. General Auchinleck, the G.O.C.-in-C. Middle East, had taken over in person the command of the Eighth Army, and had ordered Tobruk to be held as it had been in 1941. But it was not to be. On the 21st June, 1942, Tobruk fell, and the way across the frontier into Egypt was wide open. Thus any idea of holding the enemy on the frontier had to be abandoned, and a decision was made to evacuate Sollum and Halfaya during the night 22nd/23rd June.

Withdrawal orders for the 1/4th Essex were issued at 4.30 p.m. The necessary lifting transport arrived in the Battalion area at dusk. Thinning out of the forward localities started about 9.15 p.m., and the Halfaya Box positions were finally abandoned at 10 p.m. Companies assembled in rear of their positions, and when embussed moved off to the column rendezvous about two miles east of the perimeter wire. From the rendezvous the Battalion column moved off in three echelons to Sidi Sulieman, where arrangements had been made to link up with "L" Battery 2nd R.H.A. The column continued moving till first light, with occasional halts to enable stragglers to catch up. Though there was no contact with the enemy, he was known to be close, for his advance troops had crossed the Egyptian frontier that night. Contact was maintained with Brigade by radio-telephone, and orders were received that there would be no halt until the column was south of the 30 grid line. So passing round the "Kennels," they proceeded to Khamsa, where leaguer was made for the night.

At 6 a.m., the 24th June, the Brigade columns continued their way eastwards to reach the Siwa track south of Mersa Matruh, where they turned north and assembled south of "Charing Cross." Orders were here received to proceed to the escarpment south of Sidi Haneish, and Lieutenant-Colonel Noble moved his Battalion column on to that axis and then leaguered for the night.

On the morning of the 25th the Battalion, still with "L" Battery 2nd R.H.A., reached the Sidi Haneish rendezvous. Here the battery left to join a battle group and the 1/4th Essex was ordered to proceed forthwith to Mersa Matruh by the coast road. The Battalion arrived in Matruh at about 4 p.m. and moved straightway to a sector on the south side of the box, where it relieved the 23rd N.Z. Battalion.

Mersa Matruh was full of units straightening themselves out after withdrawal. There were units of the 50th Division, the 2nd N.Z. Division, and the 10th Indian Division to be sorted and organised for defence, but by nightfall the 5th Indian Infantry Brigade was holding the south side of the box, 1/4th Essex in the centre, with the 4/6th Rajputana Rifles on the left and the 3/10th Baluch Regiment on the right.

During the morning of the 26th June a column consisting of "B" Company 1/4th Essex, one section of Essex carriers, one troop of 121st Field Regiment R.A., a troop of anti-tank guns, an ambulance car, and a wireless link was formed under command of Major D. J. M. Smith. This column was known as "Smithcol." Its tasks were: (a) To patrol the minefields south of Matruh and prevent penetration or interference by the enemy; (b) to harass or destroy any enemy formations attempting to breach the minefields, and (c) to establish contact with 29th Infantry Brigade and 50th Division.

At 4.30 p.m. the column moved off out of the Matruh Box along the main Siwa road to find that the main gap in the minefields was already in the hands of the enemy, who was busily moving columns east of Matruh.

"Smithcol" came under artillery and M.M.G. fire and turned north. Moving round to the east side of the minefields, it passed Matruh along the south face of the box. At 7.30 p.m. the column was attacked from the air by M.E. 109 F.s, at the same time coming under mortar fire, the latter being silenced by the guns of the column.

After dark two enemy leaguers were encountered. One was identified by a bold carrier patrol led by Sergeant E. K. Chapman, who captured an enemy officer. Sergeant Chapman, who was later to be awarded the Distinguished Conduct Medal for these actions, also located an enemy advanced landing ground and destroyed two enemy aircraft.

Meanwhile, during the 26th June in the Matruh box the Battalion was busily improving positions and preparing for a fight when at 2.30 p.m. the Commanding Officer was called to Brigade Headquarters and told that the 5th Indian Brigade was to move out of the box and occupy a position to the east of the minefields south of Matruh. The 1/4th Essex and the 121st Field Regiment (less a troop with "Smithcol") were to move out that night, the 26th/27th June, and form a pivot where they would be joined by the remainder of the Brigade in the morning. Matruh was not to be held, and the operation the 1/4th Essex was now to carry out was part of the withdrawal plan.

At 4.30 p.m., as the Battalion was preparing to leave the box, Captain F. J. Ketteley was ordered to reconnoitre a suitable area fifteen miles to the south of Matruh where the column could leaguer that night. He was quickly back with the information that the enemy was moving east in strength, and had already occupied the suggested leaguer area. The Brigade Commander immediately ordered the 1/4th Essex out of the box to establish contact with the enemy at first light when the remainder of the brigade group would join up.

At 10.30 p.m. the 1/4th Essex moved out in company with the 121st Field Regiment, "C" Company, under Major L. W. A. Chappell, being detached from the Battalion with orders to travel by the coast road back to Amiriya in the Nile Delta, there to become the nucleus of a new battalion should the original 1/4th Essex be overwhelmed by the enemy, as indeed seemed possible.

Before first light, the 27th June, the 1/4th Essex, the 121st Field Regiment, and a weak battery from the 2nd Indian Field Regiment began to move south. The carrier screen soon established contact with the enemy. A reconnaissance by Lieutenant-Colonel Noble and his "R" (Reconnaissance) Group found a large leaguer some 5,000 yards to the west. This was confirmed as hostile by a reconnaissance made by Captain J. Watt, who drove his carrier to within 200 yards of the enemy position. The field regiment was ordered to engage and the leaguer was quickly dispersed. During the action the rest of the brigade group linked up, and after a personal reconnaissance Brigadier Russell gave orders for a general advance. The Brigade moved forward about 11 a.m.

The carriers were soon once more in contact, receiving casualties, and the Essex column was unable to advance. The 3/10th Baluch Regiment on the 1/4th Essex left was similarly held up. The British positions were shelled spasmodically during the day, and any attempt to move forward was at once checked by tanks and armoured cars in hull-down positions. Orders were then received that the Baluch Regiment and the Essex were to try to advance by night and establish a position on the escarpment about three miles to the south. The 50th Division was to act in a similar manner.

Meanwhile, "Smithcol" had had further contact with the enemy before dawn on the 27th June without casualties, and at 5.15 a.m. contacted the N.Z. Division twenty miles to the south of Matruh. "B" Company and the carrier section came under command of the 19th N.Z. Battalion (Lieutenant-Colonel S. Hartnell), the guns under the Commander Royal Artillery, and the column broke up. During the day the New Zealand Division beat off an attack by some thirty tanks and about 200 trucks of lorried infantry.

To revert once more to the main column. Late on the evening of the 27th June, "D" Company, with a No. 18 wireless set, had moved out towards the escarpment with orders to report if they were able to establish themselves on the escarpment. As there had been no signal back by midnight, the 27th/28th, 2/Lieutenant D. Beech was sent with a platoon of "A" Company to contact "D" Company and to signal with three red Very lights if all was clear for the guns to be brought forward.

At 1.15 a.m. three red Very lights were seen, and Lieutenant-Colonel Noble ordered the column forward, but just as it was about to move 2/Lieutenant Beech returned with his patrol to say the enemy was in strength at the foot of the escarpment and he had failed to contact "D" Company. He had not given the Very light signal. The move to the escarpment was therefore cancelled. At first light, the 28th June, the 5th Brigade Group was roughly in the same positions as on the evening before, and those positions were clearly ringed in to the south and west by the enemy in some strength. About 6 a.m. "D" Company rejoined. Appreciating his liability to be surrounded, Captain R. A. Plackett had made a skilful detour, and so was able to join up once more.

During the afternoon and evening, it appeared evident that the position held by the 5th Indian Brigade Group was going to be attacked late in the evening or after dark. Lorried infantry were seen to be moving up and tanks and armoured cars were operating on the west flank.

At 6 p.m. Lieutenant-Colonel Noble received orders through a liaison officer that the Brigade would attempt to break out at 9.30 p.m. that night, as the situation was desperate. The column, if broken up by enemy action, was to proceed by groups of vehicles and rally at Fuka, some eighty miles to the east. Lieutenant-Colonel Noble did not issue his orders until the last possible minute to avoid unnecessary alarm.

At 9.30 p.m. the break-out was made. The column came under heavy fire of all types about three miles south of the position. There was difficult country to negotiate, and several vehicles were soon hit. Control became impossible. Groups of vehicles moved independently. "The flames from the burning vehicles lit up the racing column," said

Captain D. A. Beckett, who was then the anti-tank platoon commander and who had the duty of Officer Commanding rear-guard in this operation. He goes on: "By the time I moved, light shells and M.G. fire were being felt all over the old area, and every type of fire was being directed on the wadi some 800 yards south of the position. My 15-cwt. truck was soon knocked out.

"Somehow, despite the terrific pounding it received, the bulk of the column got through," to approach Fuka early on the 29th. Fuka was found to be in enemy hands, and Lieutenant-Colonel Noble decided to proceed towards El Alamein.

The 5th Indian Brigade rallied during the 29th June on the Deir El Abyad track, and moved in the evening to a position north of the Ruweisat Ridge. During the day many of the 1/4th Essex had pulled back through the defensive position then being prepared by the 2/5th Essex at Deir-el-Shein.

On Ruweisat Ridge, during the 29th and 30th, parties continued to join the Battalion. Among them were "B" Company and the other detachments from "Smithcol" which had joined up with the 19th N.Z. Battalion in the Minqa Qaim area, and which on the 28th June had taken part in a spirited bayonet charge with the New Zealanders to secure their break-out.

Of this, Major H. J. Young, M.C., then Officer Commanding "B" Company, says:

"'B' Company's introduction to battle on the 27th and 28th June, 1942, was about as thorough and complete as it could have been.

"After a very active night's patrolling with 'Smithcol' on the 26th/27th, the Company came under command the 19th N.Z. Battalion and was heavily shelled and mortared during the German attacks on the Minqa Qaim feature throughout the 28th. These attacks were repulsed at some loss, including 'B' Company's first casualties. During the afternoon General Freyburg (who was also wounded that day) decided that the New Zealand Division should break out through the German lines during the night.

"This was a considerable task, as by nightfall the enemy had the whole of his 21st Panzer Division to the north and east of the feature, and our only way out was to bust straight through it.

"Shortly before midnight the Commanding Officer 19th Battalion (Lieutenant-Colonel Hartnell) called his 'O' (Order) Group, and issued what seemed to be the simplest of orders! The 4th Brigade was to make the gap for the Division, and the 19th Battalion was to lead the 4th Brigade, and all we had to do was to form up in 'assault formation' shortly after midnight, advance silently for about 1,000 yards to the German positions, and fight our way through with 'butt and bayonet.'

"This 'assault formation' seemed to be quite a normal drill with the Kiwis who, it appeared, were in the habit of breaking through the German lines quite frequently, and it simply consisted of forming up the battalions as a square, two companies forward and two in rear, in extended order of platoons, and advancing.

"Anyway, it all worked very well, in spite of half an hour's delay on the start-line, until we were within about 300 yards of the enemy. From then on the scene was like a thousand Brock's Benefits rolled into one. The Germans fired and went on firing every weapon they had, and seemed especially strong in machine guns firing tracer on fixed lines. This tracer was all to the good, as we could see the line of fire, and could get across it when firing ceased for magazine changing, etc.—thus saving ourselves many casualties.

"Once amongst the enemy, the fighting really became rough, and it was very evident that he had the greatest dislike of close fighting with the bayonet and grenade. By this time, of course, transport was on fire all around, and one could see well enough to distinguish between enemy and 'us.'

"After getting through the enemy line, it was possible to get most of the company together and put them on the transport which the staff had very cleverly got to the right place at the right time, and to check up on casualties. It was about this time, as we were actually waiting for the transport to move off, that we heard that Private Cooper had gone half a mile back into the enemy lines to fetch his friend Petticrow who had been severely wounded. This was a very brave action indeed, since Petticrow was half as big again as Cooper, but in spite of this, Cooper brought him out and got him on the ambulance, where he died later in the night.

"It may be recorded here that 'B' Company brought out from this action every one of its wounded with the exception of Private Wiltcher, who insisted on being left behind because he believed himself to be mortally wounded. In fact, Wiltcher was taken prisoner and later recovered in an enemy hospital.

"It may be remembered that the rough handling of the Germans during this break-out resulted in a tirade from Hitler on the German radio, and generally caused quite a storm at the time. The whole action has since been recognised as a most valuable one in the delaying of the German advance to Alamein, both on account of the delay imposed on him during the day of 27th June and on account of the severe casualties inflicted on the Panzer Division during the night action. Minqa Qaim has always been recognised by the New Zealand Division as one of their most important actions, and one of which they are exceedingly proud."

This action of "B" Company was the subject of a letter to Lieutenant-Colonel Noble from Brigadier J. J. Burrows, Commander of the 4th New Zealand Infantry Brigade. Dated the 4th August, 1942, it read: "I wish to say how much I admired the conduct and bearing of your men who were attached to us, particularly on the night of the 27th/28th June, when the Brigade cleared a path through the German lines with the bayonet. Their behaviour was first-class and their determination and dash all that could be desired. I want you to know their presence and assistance were of considerable value to us, and our men speak very highly indeed of their actions. I wish you and your Battalion the best of luck in future operations."

The 1/4th Essex had escaped from the enemy encirclements, but the price had not been light. Four officers and 138 other ranks were casualties. Among those taken prisoner were Captain T. W. G. Atkins, R.A.M.C., and the Reverend S. Day, C.F., two officers who were sadly missed in the difficult days that followed. Captain Atkins, an Australian, had joined the Battalion in England shortly before the move to West Africa, and all ranks had learnt to have the highest opinion of his judgment and ability.

The situation was now critical. The present British line from Alamein in the north round towards the Qattara Depression thirty-six miles to the south was the last defensible position before the Nile Delta and the rich prize of Alexandria, Cairo, and the Suez Canal. The first few days of July would show whether the British could hold the German attack or not.

On the 1st July a reorganisation of the Battalion started, the object being the formation of two companies for operation with an independent column. "B" were to form one company and the remnants of "A" and "D" the second; all Bren carriers were to be used under Captain J. Watt. Re-equipping was carried out by taking transport, weapons, and stores from the 4/6th Rajputana Rifles and the 3/10th Baluch Regiment, and having handed over to the 1/4th Essex what they required, the 5th Indian Infantry Brigade was then withdrawn to the Delta to reorganise, leaving the Essex in the line.

"C" Company at this stage rejoined the Battalion from the Delta. As Major L. W. A. Chappell reported his company ready for action, a decision was made to add his company to the mobile column forming under Brigadier R. B. Waller, D.S.O., M.C.

Brigadier Waller had decided that, in view of the situation, the column—to be known as "Robcol"—must move that evening, the 1st July. As the first two Essex companies were not yet re-equipped and rationed, it moved off with "C" Company and the 11th Field Regiment R.A. The remaining two companies, under Lieutenant-Colonel A. Noble, joined "Robcol" during battle on the afternoon of the 2nd July.

At the moment of their joining, "Robcol" was under heavy shell fire, fire that increased in intensity throughout the evening as enemy tanks attempted to overrun the forward troop of the 11th Field Regiment. This troop, with No. 13 Platoon of "C" Company, stood its ground magnificently, and gave back as much as it received, if not more.

At last light Brigadier Waller ordered closer leaguer to be formed seven miles to the east. Batteries moved back independently with their respective companies after all wounded had been collected and damaged guns and vehicles destroyed. Six field guns and their crews were lost during this action. The 1/4th Essex suffered 2 killed and 18 wounded.

This was the opening action of "Robcol" which, with two similar formations and a depleted tank force, was the 1st Armoured Division to which the official Ministry of Information version of the battle pays high tribute. "On the 2nd July, in an attempt to enlarge the gap (made by the overrunning of an Indian Brigade), Rommel flung the 90th Light Division, most of his Italian infantry, and three armoured divisions at the 1st Armoured and South African Division. The battle ebbed and flowed throughout the day, and the 1st Armoured Division received the special congratulations of General Auchinleck for its superb work."

At first light on the 3rd July "Robcol" replenished and prepared to move forward once more. It was under direct command of the 1st Armoured Division, and had been joined by a weak battery of the 11th R.H.A. (H.A.C.). This battery and "C" Company 1/4th Essex were in action all day, withdrawing late in the afternoon to a position

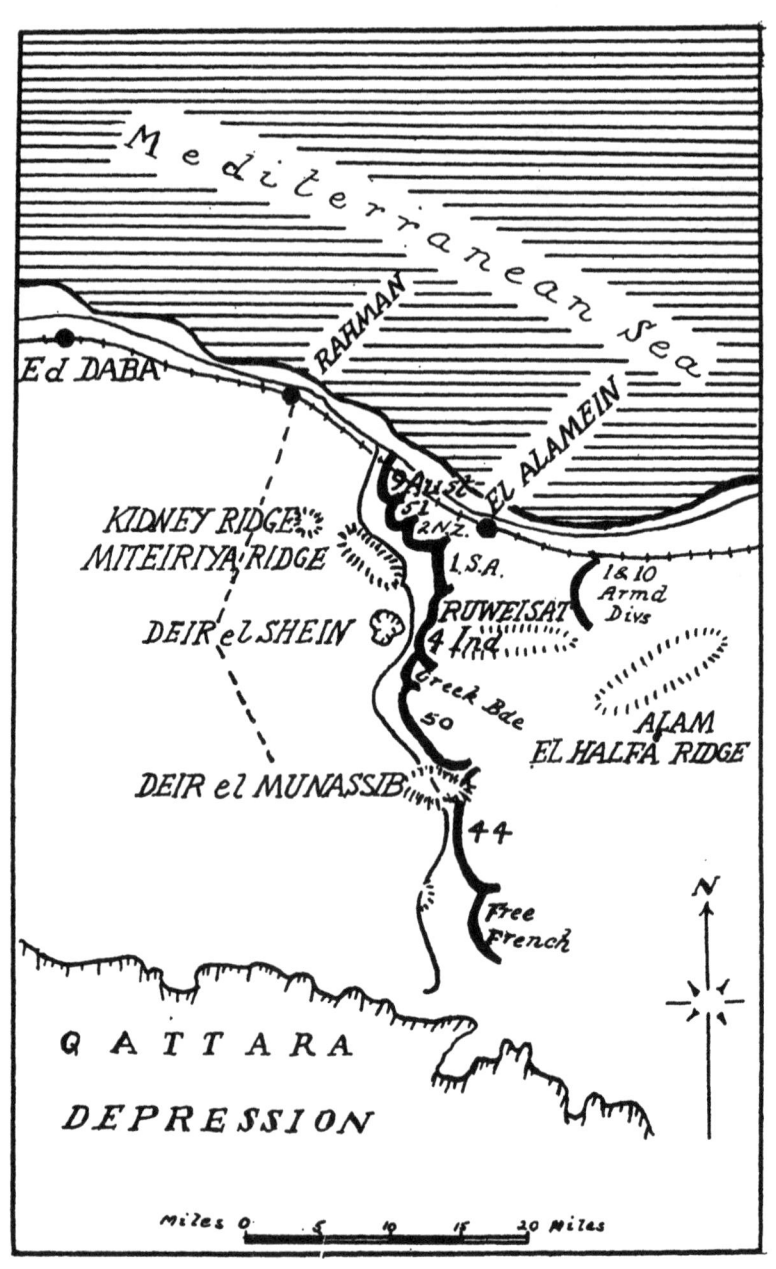

1/4 Essex, Operations on the El Alamein Position, July–October 1942.
Note. The British dispositions are those at the eve of Alamein, 23rd October, 1942.

not under observation by the enemy. From here they watched a large-scale tank battle develop at dusk about 1,000 yards out from the British position. The action was successful, the enemy tanks withdrawing, so that the night 3rd/4th July passed without incident. On the next morning the tank battle was resumed, and once more "Robcol" was in action all day.

By this time the chances of a German break-through to the Nile Delta were fading, for it was clear that the Germans were more exhausted than the British. To quote again the Ministry of Information account: "They were thrown back by wearied troops, who, in spite of their bewilderment at their earlier defeat, had found the strength to hold the last ditch."

As Major Beckett says: "The particular bit of that last ditch assigned to the Battalion was a low ridge, running from east to west, a little to the south of Ruweisat. In the course of the next few days it came to be known locally as Essex Ridge, and was the scene of some heavy fighting, during which for a time the Battalion had the unique experience of being supported by guns of the Essex Yeomanry."

The 1/4th Essex operated with "Robcol" from Essex Ridge continuously throughout the first half of July. Casualties were not light, but the Battalion played a great part in keeping the enemy under control and preventing any further infiltration eastwards.

On the 5th July it was decided to raid the enemy lines, and the following night "C" Company was ordered to capture or destroy a number of posts along a ridge to the north of a feature known locally as "Barrel Hill."

Major L. W. A. Chappell, in command of "C" Company at the time, gives his account of the night's activities:

"The enemy position to be attacked was on the front of the 60th Rifles, and during the afternoon before the raid, the Officer Commanding 'C' Company and the Battalion Intelligence Officer went up to the 60th positions for a reconnaissance. This was carried out with the Company Commander on the spot in his jeep, by driving westward and then turning north up rising ground until enemy fire was drawn, when bearings were taken on the position. There was a gunner observation post in a Honey tank nearby, which was to stop in position until last light and would help our navigation.

"In the early evening the patrol, which consisted of all available members of 'C' Company (the patrol went at full strength for experience), moved up to the forward area and arrived near the O.P. just before this tank left its position. The object was to attack the enemy position and take prisoners, and if possible to bring away vehicles which might be fit for our own use. A 3-ton lorry was, therefore, brought up to the O.P., which became our starting-point, in case this was required for towing purposes. As the light faded the patrol moved forward with a section ahead as an advance guard under the Battalion I.O., Lieutenant D. J. Fisher, closely followed by the main body. Shortly after darkness fell, the patrol heard a vehicle moving slowly, across its front, and a detachment under Lieutenant K. D. Edrupt (who was later killed in Italy) was detailed to stop and capture this vehicle. It turned out to be a British 'Quad' or artillery tractor driven by a German soldier and accompanied by an officer, and Lieutenant Edrupt with 2 men was ordered to return to our own lines with this vehicle and its occupants. However, they lost direction on the way back, and were recaptured by an Italian unit, from which Lieutenant Edrupt escaped and returned to our lines some fortnight later after an exciting time.

"The patrol then continued on the bearing, and after a short time heard a great deal of noise from a German leaguer which was forming up for the night on the position which had been reconnoitred during the day. The patrol approached to within about fifty yards of the leaguer, which consisted of 8/10 vehicles and approximately 40 men, and then laid down and waited for quietness. The plan was then made that the main body of the patrol would attack the leaguer with bayonet, grenade, and tommy gun, whilst a secondary leaguer, which had formed up some 100 yards away, was neutralised by a detachment with Bren guns under Sergeant Wynn. The assault party was told off for individual objectives.

"The night was clear and starlit, and although our desert navigation had not then reached the practised condition which later obtained, it was possible to instruct the men to find their way back to the S.P., which was to be used as a rendezvous, by following the Milky Way. A batman (Private Bacon) had been detailed to fire green Very lights at intervals from the R.V., and the Battalion I.O. remained in the position where the patrol then lay, with instructions to fire red Very lights as he returned to the S.P. The Germans took a long time to settle, and it was not until after midnight that it was thought proper to put in the attack. Incidentally, at this stage we were not equipped with desert boots, and as the surface was of a hard gravel nature, we had wound puttees and extra socks round our boots, but they had mostly worn through by this stage and consequently, as we ran in, there was a good deal of noise. However, the Germans took fright and did not attempt to fight. Some were killed in their lorries where they slept and several prisoners were taken. There was immediately a lot of wild firing from other leaguers in the vicinity, and it was not possible to control the situation sufficiently to drive away any of the enemy vehicles. However, three of these were set on fire and a grenade thrown by Private Jackson (who later won the D.C.M. as a stretcher-bearer and was killed in Italy) into a pit which contained a small gun (probably A.A.) caused a very heavy explosion, which killed or wounded the enemy occupying this. The patrol then withdrew at a whistle signal, and commenced the return to the S.P. Several of the prisoners attempted to escape, and had to be killed in so doing, but two were safely brought back to our lines. The scene was visited some months after the action, and there was a large grave, probably the gun-pit, which had five or six crosses stuck in it, and another some distance off, with two crosses, so it seemed likely that our original estimate of 9 or 10 enemy killed was right.

"The plan for the withdrawal did not work out particularly well, as the effect of the red Very lights fired by Lieutenant Fisher was to draw all the enemy fire in the neighbourhood, so that it was difficult for the patrol to reassemble there. However, the patrol returned to our own lines with no casualties whatever. The two prisoners were brought back, one by Company Sergeant-Major C. Rose (later Regimental Sergeant-Major C. Rose, D.C.M.) and another by Sergeant T. King (later wounded at El Alamein). The Very lights fired by Private Bacon were of very little help, because by this time the sky was full of lights of all colours, but the Milky Way was of great value and enabled everyone to get back. A number of valuable lessons had been learnt."

Major L. W. A. Chappell was awarded the M.C. for this operation.

By the night of the 14th July the re-equipped 5th Indian Infantry Brigade was back in the forward areas and ready to attack Ruweisat Ridge with the two Indian battalions. The 1/4th Essex was to revert to brigade control from the time of the attack.

By the morning of the 15th July the attack by these battalions and that of the New Zealand Division had gone successfully, but by about midday it became clear that the 4/6th Rajputana Rifles were held up by a ridge known as Point 64 and that the 3/10th Baluch Regiment was unable to advance beyond its first objective because of heavy mortar fire from that same feature.

The 1/4th Essex, warned for attack, was given two objectives. The first assault would be on an enemy strong-point 2,000 yards south of Point 64. The attack was then to continue to Point 64 itself, but just before the attack went in the Rajputanas managed to get to Point 64, thus leaving the Essex with only the capture of the strong-point. Even this effort was not required, as it became known that the strong-point had been taken by the New Zealanders.

The 1/4th Essex was left in position on Point 64 during the 15th/16th July. Two companies, one a composite company under Captain T. W. Grist, consisting of drivers, cooks, and storemen, and "B" Company under Captain H. J. Young, were the garrison. They held their position through a very determined German counter-attack on the evening of the 16th, repulsing all attacks with the aid of the 2nd Armoured Brigade. During this engagement the enemy lost thirty-five tanks, but the Essex losses were light. The night of the 16th/17th July was quiet except for German attempts with tanks and infantry to recover the armoured vehicles lost in the battle of the previous evening.

During the 17th there were spasmodic attempts by enemy tanks and infantry to recover Point 64, but all were repulsed. That evening Lieutenant-Colonel Noble learnt that it was intended to extend the hold gained on Ruweisat westwards to Point 63. The attack was to be made by the 2nd West Yorks, with the 1/4th Essex passing through to consolidate the ground won.

On the morning of the 18th this plan was altered, and the objective limited, so that the 1/4th Essex was not required. Accordingly, the Commanding Officer got Brigade permission to relieve "B" Company immediately with "C" Company on Point 64.

On the 19th, Brigade Headquarters said the 1/4th Essex would be called upon to relieve the 2nd West Yorks on Point 62 the following evening, and would remain there for approximately forty-eight hours. It was planned the 161st Indian Motorised Brigade would then pass through to attack on the night 21st/22nd July, and in the event of the attack proving successful, the Essex would be withdrawn. This was the old 161st Brigade which the 1/4th Essex had left in Cyprus, and which had now been replaced by an Indian Battalion.

The relief of the 2nd West Yorks was carried through successfully and completed by about 11 p.m. on the 20th June. The night was quiet, but at 7 a.m., the 21st, shelling started and continued all through the day, being particularly heavy at times. During the evening of the 21st the 1/1st Punjab Regiment and 3/7th Rajputs of the 161st Indian Brigade came up, and about 8.30 p.m. went forward to the attack. Immediately very heavy counter-preparation fire came down all over the area of the 1/4th Essex, and both Indian battalions were unable to get forward. At first light, the 1/1st Punjab Regiment having been withdrawn, the 1/2nd Punjab Regiment was put through to attack Point 63. They were driven off later in the morning.

The 161st Brigade attack having proved unsuccessful, the 1/4th Essex could not be withdrawn, but was placed temporarily under command of the Brigade. It remained there in conditions of some uncertainty until, on the morning of the 29th July, the 5th Indian Infantry Brigade came up in relief of the 161st Indian Motorised Brigade. The 1/4th Essex then reverted to command of its own Brigade, being relieved by the 4/6th Rajputana Rifles, and withdrawn to a position in rear of Ruweisat Ridge. Here the Battalion had a dual role: first, to counter-attack the ridge in the event of enemy attack, and, second, to maintain contact and dominate the area between the ridge and the 2nd South African Brigade.

The 1/4th Essex had been continually in action since first being committed in the Halfaya Box on the 20th June. The days on Ruweisat Ridge had been particularly unpleasant. There had been little cover either from the enemy or from the sun. There was dust everywhere, and every vehicle that entered the area raised more. Water was scarce and cooking almost impossible. But the greatest trial had been the crawling beastliness of the myriads of flies that were everywhere from sunrise to sunset.

The fighting strength of the 1/4th Essex on withdrawal from the line was about 230 all ranks. They had come into Egypt a year ago 875 strong.

Section V

EL ALAMEIN AND THE ADVANCE TO TUNIS, 1942-43

It will be remembered that when the 1/4th Essex, with the remainder of the 5th Indian Infantry Brigade, moved from Palestine into the "Kennels" position on the 15th June, they had come under the command of the 5th Indian Division, and had remained, except for a short attachment to the 10th Indian Division, with that formation.

This formation had been part of the 13th Corps (General Gott), but now on the 1st August, 1942, command of the 5th Indian Division passed to the 30th Corps.

Nearly all August the Battalion remained in reserve behind the Ruweisat Ridge, preparing defences and training. It was not an easy period. Shelling and dive-bombing took a steady toll without opportunity to hit back, and tempers were often strained. There was no shelter from the pitiless sun, the area was littered with the debris of battle, and the millions of flies brought with them discomfort and dysentery.

Early in August the Battalion was delighted to hear the following extract from the B.B.C. African Service nine o'clock news:

> "During the recent operations in the Central Sector, a Territorial battalion of the Essex Regiment gave such a good account of themselves that a ridge has been named after them, Essex Ridge. Later, they stood for two days and held their ground against repeated dive-bombing attacks and concentrated fire from enemy artillery and armoured forces, making it possible for us to hold the important gains in this sector."

On the 13th August, 1942, command in the Middle East passed to General the Hon. Sir Harold Alexander, K.C.B., C.S.I., D.S.O., M.C., and that of the Eighth Army to Lieutenant-General B. L. Montgomery, C.B., D.S.O.

The 1/4th Essex Regiment received a visit from General Alexander on the 24th August. The G.O.C.-in-C. was interested to learn that the Regimental Sergeant-Major, Mr. D. Canty, had served under his command in a battalion of the Irish Guards.

The Battle of Alam-Halfa, August–September 1942

That same day all leave was suddenly cancelled and warning given that a further German offensive was imminent. The role of the 1/4th Essex was to recapture Point 62 or 64 on Ruweisat Ridge should either fall to the enemy in his initial advance.

Rommel passed to the offensive on the 31st August, but although heavily reinforced and with a superiority in tanks, his effort was too late. The Eighth Army, too, had been reinforced in men, material, and morale. The new commander had already made his mark on the army under his command. The Eighth Army, always a fine army, now had the leadership it deserved.

The German attack came in on the north, centre, and south of the

British positions. The main thrust was to the south and directed towards Alam-el-Halfa Ridge to the south-east of Ruweisat. This main attack passed to the south of the New Zealand Division which was on the left of the 5th Indian Division, while the latter had to deal with an attack by the Italian Bologna Division, supported by elements of the German Afrika Korps.

Early on the 31st August elements of the Bologna Division attacked against the New Zealand Division, but losing direction in the darkness came against the 9th Indian Infantry Brigade, and overran the forward companies of the 2nd West Yorks.

At 4.30 a.m. the 1/4th Essex received a signal to say that the 2nd West Yorks position on Point 62 had been overrun. Lieutenant-Colonel Noble then spoke to the Divisional Commander over the telephone, and received orders to proceed forthwith to the forming-up place for the immediate counter-attack. The Battalion was to come under the 9th Indian Infantry Brigade for the operations.

At 5.20 a.m. "A" Company crossed the gap in the minefield. Lieutenant-Colonel Noble went forward to 9th Brigade Headquarters with the Officer Commanding "C" Squadron 46th Royal Tank Regiment and the Officer Commanding 14/66th Battery Royal Artillery.

At 5.45 a.m. he was back and gave his orders to his "Order" Group. "A" Company was to re-establish the rear company position in the West Yorks area, and "D" to pass through and restore the forward position. "C" Squadron 46th Royal Tank Regiment would support the first phase with all tanks, and one troop would support the second phase. Zero was to be 6 a.m.

During the advance Lieutenant-Colonel Noble met the Commanding Officer of the 2nd West Yorks and learnt that the real situation was that only his forward company had been overrun and there was a chance the enemy might have withdrawn. Lieutenant-Colonel Noble accordingly altered the plans by ordering that there would be no movement of tanks west of Point 64 without his orders, and that "A" Company would re-establish the forward company position, while "D" Company would remain in the reserve area of the tanks. This was all ordered while sub-units were on the move and was successfully carried out. By 7.30 a.m. "A" Company had reorganised in the objective area.

At 8.45 a.m. the Commanding Officer ordered the Intelligence Officer to explain the situation to Headquarters 9th Infantry Brigade.

The Brigadier decided that "A" Company would remain temporarily at Point 62 and under command of the 2nd West Yorks, while the rest of the 1/4th Essex returned to its leaguer area. During the evening preceding this counter-attack, a new chaplain had arrived with the Battalion, the Reverend H. B. Evans. After the attack the Commanding Officer was somewhat surprised to find the new padre critically discussing the operation. Padre Evans had at once followed his new battalion into battle, a spontaneous act of one who was to see many months of toil and battle, a chaplain who earned the deep respect of all ranks.

The next day the whole of the 5th Indian Infantry Brigade was moved from the reserve area to forward positions two miles south of Ruweisat Ridge in relief of the 6th New Zealand Infantry Brigade which was to attack elsewhere in the New Zealand divisional area. The 1/4th Essex lay under considerable shell fire, but no attacks materialised. With the failure of his southerly flanking drive on Alam-el-Halfa, the enemy refrained from any further frontal attacks on the central sector. The battle was in fact already won.

The 5th Indian Infantry Brigade remained under command of the New Zealand Division until the afternoon of the 4th September.

This had been General Montgomery's first battle with the Eighth Army. It was an admirably fought defensive action which inflicted a defeat upon Rommel and greatly heartened the Eighth Army. The rest of September was spent improving defensive positions and probing the enemy defences by patrolling action.

The 1/4th Essex, with 5th Indian Infantry Brigade, now once again formed part of the 4th Indian Division under Major-General F. I. S. Tuker, C.B., D.S.O., O.B.E. They still formed part of the 30th Corps, now under command of Lieutenant-General Sir Oliver Leese.

On the 30th September the Battalion was withdrawn to train and rest. But before this particular period is ended, it may be of interest to quote a report made by Captain H. C. Gregory on an incident that occurred on the 2nd September whilst "A" Company was holding a position with the 2nd West Yorks after the Company's counter-attack on Ruweisat Ridge. "On 2-9-42 at about 3.30 p.m. two men were seen approaching our line under a white flag. They turned out to be Lieutenant Withelm and an N.C.O., who, when brought to my Company H.Q., called upon me to surrender. His words as near as I can remember were:

"'I am Lieutenant Withelm, and my commanding officer has sent me to call upon you to surrender. Rommel is behind you and you cannot get away. If you do not surrender the Stukas are standing by to blow you to Heaven and to Hell.

" 'My C.O. is a kind man and does not want to cause unnecessary bloodshed, and is giving you this chance to surrender.' "

Captain Gregory goes on to say that he thought the German really expected him to surrender on the spot. However, the delegation was escorted to the Headquarters of the 2nd West Yorks and thence to 30th Corps, from where they were to be returned to the German lines at a later date.

The Battle of El Alamein, October–November 1942

Through October preparations were being made for the Battle of El Alamein and the advance to Tunis, an historic time, a time perhaps when the names of the officers serving with the Battalion should be recorded, as far as can be traced.

They were: Lieutenant-Colonel A. Noble, Major D. J. M. Smith, Major E. A. Hawkins, Captains H. J. Young, H. C. Gregory, D. C. Counsell, F. J. Ketteley, D. A. Beckett, D. J. V. Fisher, J. A. Porter, T. W. Grist, J. Watt, Lieutenants J. R. Cooper, W. A. Matthews, N. H. Dear, P. H. Smith, C. Hailes, S. G. Banks, K. D. Edrupt, T. K. Perton, J. R. Rose, T. H. Pattle, D. J. Beech, S. F. Davies, J. R. Evans, I. W. Thulborn, E. R. Mayer, R. A. Ulph, H. B. Dean, A. M. Edwards, H. R. Simpson, and Lieutenant (QM.) S. G. Mason. Captain the Reverend H. B. Evans was Chaplain, and Captain J. G. Clay, R.A.M.C., the R.M.O. Major L. W. A. Chappell was evacuated sick on the 10th October, returning to duty on the 10th November.

The early part of October had been occupied by large-scale exercises in rear of the El Alamein position, but it was not until the 23rd October that it became generally known that these were in fact rehearsals and training for the coming offensive.

Earlier in the month Lieutenant-Colonel Noble had attended a briefing conference by General Montgomery, and had learnt the Army Commander's detailed plan for the coming battle. But it was not until the morning of the 23rd October that the Commanding Officer was allowed to explain the plan to the Battalion. This he did by talking to each company in turn. All ranks were very pleased to learn of the coming offensive.

The 5th Indian Brigade was detached from the Division at the beginning of the operation to form a reserve for the 30th Corps, and on the night of the 23rd/24th October the 1/4th Essex moved to a reserve position east of the Miteiriya Ridge. That night, on the sector between the sea and the area held by the 4th Indian Division, the El Alamein offensive started. An augmented 30th Corps (9th Australian Division, 51st Highland, 2nd New Zealand Division, and 1st South African Division with the 9th Armoured Brigade) was the attacking force. The 1st and 10th Armoured Divisions were echeloned in rear ready to exploit the break-through.

To the south of the 30th Corps lay the 4th Indian Division (less 5th Brigade), which would carry out limited attacks from the area of the Ruweisat Ridge. To the south again lay the 50th and 44th Divisions and other formations of the 13th Corps.

By midnight of the 23rd/24th October the 1/4th Essex was in its new positions taken over from the South Africans. Notification had been received from 5th Indian Brigade Headquarters that the Brigadier had gone to 30th Corps Headquarters, where he would remain while his brigade stayed as Corps reserve.

During the 24th–26th October the Battalion remained in reserve while the main battle was being fought to the north. The battalion area was dive-bombed by Stukas during the 25th, 2 men being killed and 2 wounded, but otherwise there was no activity, and only noise as a constant reminder of the major battle to the north.

On the night of the 27th/28th the 1/4th Essex moved, as part of the 5th Indian Infantry Brigade, forward to take over positions from the South Africans on Miteiriya Ridge, with "B" Company disposed in low ground forward of the ridge. Here movement was very restricted, and meals had to be cooked north of the ridge and brought forward to the company after dark.

The 5th Indian Brigade had taken over a two-brigade position, and so the 1/4th Essex and 4/6th Rajputanas were each holding a two-battalion front with the 3/10th Baluch in reserve.

The Battalion was now in very close contact with the enemy and experienced heavy mortaring, attempted raids (on "B" Company), and Stuka attacks from the 28th October until the 2nd November. On that day the Army Commander decided that his attacks on the northern part of the enemy position had made the enemy draw in the 21st Panzer Division from the southern sector, thus weakening that portion of the front.

It was what General Montgomery had been waiting for, and he now planned a very heavy attack on that weakened southern portion of the front with a break-out in view. This was to be known as Operation "Supercharge," and it was the role of the 4th Indian Division, following the 51st (Highland) Division, to force back the anti-tank screen, widen the gap, and allow the British armour through.

Major D. J. M. Smith was now commanding the 1/4th Essex, for Lieutenant-Colonel Noble had been evacuated with jaundice on the evening of the 29th October. He was called to 5th Indian Brigade H.Q. on the morning of the 3rd November, where he was told that the Brigade was now under command of the 51st Division, elements of which were putting in an attack that evening, and that the 5th Indian Brigade would attack that night. Passing through the objectives taken by the 51st Division, they would advance a further 5,000 yards to clear the enemy from, and hold against counter-attack, an area given to Major Smith off the map.

At 7.15 p.m. Major Smith gave his final orders, which were, in condensed form, as follows: the 5th Indian Brigade would attack, the 1/4th Essex right forward battalion, the 3/10th Baluch Regiment left forward battalion, with the 4/6th Rajputana Rifles following the left rear. The 1/4th Essex would go forward in a box formation, "A" and "C" Companies forward, with "B" and "D" in rear. Only essential transport would be taken, and this would be in three columns following Battalion Headquarters, which would be moving in the centre of the box.

The Battalion moved to its forming-up areas, and was in position and ready to move before midnight. This had meant an approach march of some twelve miles over unknown country, followed by an advance over the battle area of some miles more. By 1 a.m., the 4th November, it was clear that, except for the 1/4th Essex, the Brigade was not ready. The attack was therefore postponed for one hour.

At 2.30 a.m. the Battalion left its forming-up place, and began the long advance, the start-line being crossed on schedule. The going was terrible, every vehicle except carriers getting stuck in the soft sand, and so about 3 a.m. it was decided to leave the transport to advance as best it could after first light.

At 3 a.m. "A" Company was held up by medium machine-gun fire. A patrol was sent out under Lieutenant D. J. Beech which destroyed two M.M.G. posts, killing the crews. By 5 a.m. visibility was less than ten yards owing to cordite fumes and occasional smoke shells, but the Essex advance was resolutely continued, many posts being

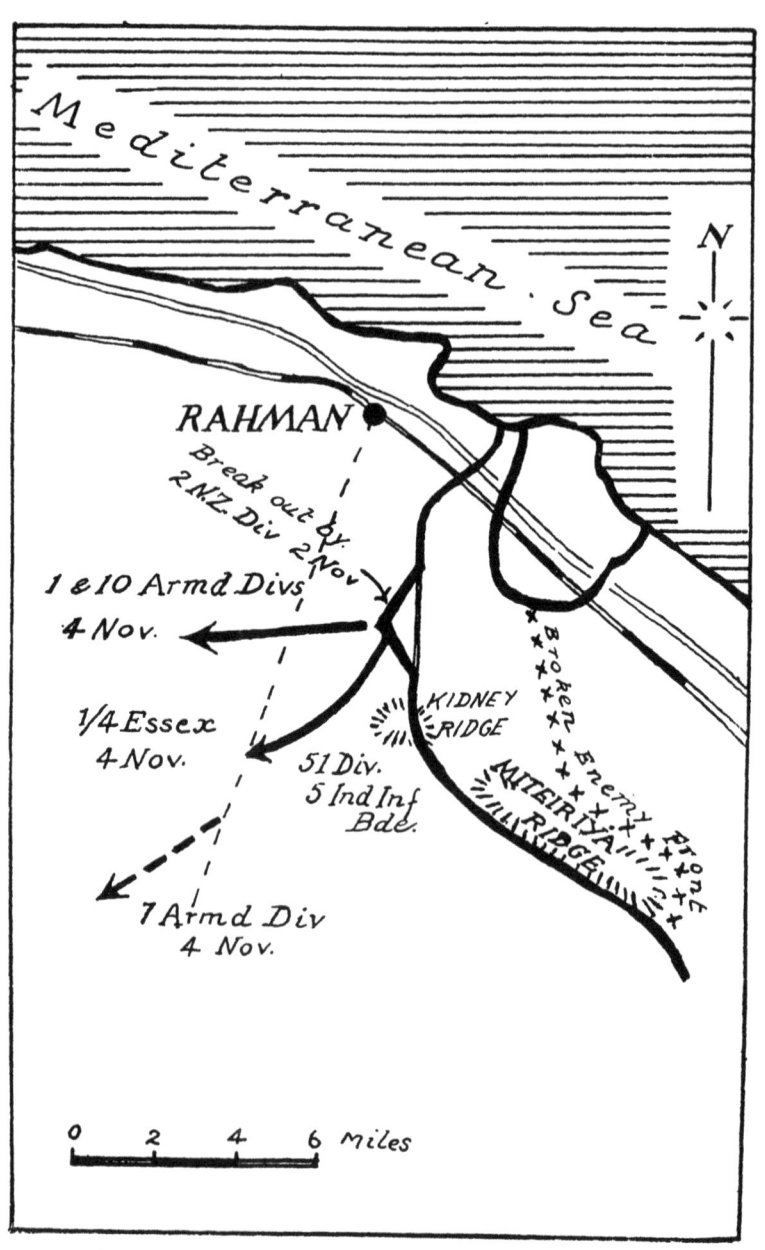

1/4TH ESSEX, EL ALAMEIN (OPERATION "SUPERCHARGE"), 2ND–4TH NOVEMBER, 1942.

overrun and over 100 prisoners, all Panzer Grenadiers, taken. At 7 a.m. the objective was captured and consolidated by pushing out a carrier patrol under Lieutenant C. J. Kenrick, which took another 50 prisoners. Lieutenant Kenrick had joined the Battalion as a reinforcement only the previous day. This was his first experience of action. He had not even had time to know the names of his men.

A glance round showed that only the 1/4th Essex and two companies of the 4/6th Rajputana Rifles had succeeded in gaining the objective. But the task had been accomplished and the armour was through. The Battle of El Alamein was won.

In the course of this break-through, the 5th Indian Brigade took 351 prisoners, of which the 1/4th Essex had taken 237, mostly Panzer Grenadiers, as well as numerous anti-tank guns.

The action of the 1/4th Essex with the 5th Indian Brigade had been decisive and was the subject of much congratulation. Among complimentary letters received by the Battalion was one from the Brigade Commander, who said he had been asked by the Commander of 30th Corps to inform all ranks that he congratulated them on their excellent night attack on the 3rd/4th November carried out in exceptionally difficult circumstances. The Corps Commander said: "It was the deep penetration made and the loosening up of the enemy defences thereby which made it possible to pass the armour through in force. The importance of this success is obvious to all."

Major-General F. I. S. Tuker, the 4th Indian Divisional Commander, had a semi-official letter from the Corps Commander. It said: " . . . Your 5th Bde did a magnificent attack the night before last. . . . It was a tremendous achievement to move such a distance at night, and the Army Commander tells me that the captured Commander of the German Afrika Korps (General Thoma) stated that one of the reasons for the success of our armoured battle on the following day was that all the Italians on the front of the break-through had been captured by your 5th Brigade; thus, no information of the advance of the break-through of the armour reached Corps Headquarters."

This was high praise indeed.

With the break-through, the tide of battle flowed rapidly westwards, and although Major-General Tuker was quick to organise his brigades for pursuit, they were not called upon.

The first consideration in the pursuit was the maintenance of mobility, and so care was taken not to strain long lines of communication with one unit more than was needed. Thus, some formations were left static on the battlefield, only being called forward into Cyrenaica as the administrative machine permitted.

The 4th Indian Division was one of the formations so left to caretake and act as maid-of-all-work on the field of battle.

On the 20th November Lieutenant-Colonel Noble returned from convalescence and reassumed command.

First the 51st Division, and next the 50th Division, moved forward, and then on the 2nd December came orders for the 4th Indian Division to start moving to the Tobruk area on the 10th of the month.

The 1/4th Essex spent Christmas 1942 at El Adem, close to Ed Duda, the site of an historic fight by the 1st Essex exactly a year before. "It was the least pleasant of all wartime Christmases," said Major Beckett, "owing to a shortage of N.A.A.F.I. supplies." But this was only one of many causes. All felt disappointed to be lying inactive instead of taking part in the pursuit to Benghazi and beyond, and there was all the discomfort of a battle area without the moral stimulus of actual battle. "It was bitterly cold (even with five blankets if one could get them), water was extremely short, and the half-bottle of beer a head as the Christmas ration came as the final straw."

On Christmas Day Church parade, the Brigade Commander, Brigadier R. Russell, O.B.E., M.C., addressed the Battalion, and congratulated them on their work in the past. He also congratulated Major D. J. M. Smith, D.S.O., Captain H. C. Gregory, M.C., Lieutenant D. J. Beech, M.C., and Sergeant T. Horne, M.M., on their recent awards.

Moving forward to Benghazi in the first week of January 1943, the 1/4th Essex learnt that the 4th Indian Division was now to come under the 10th Corps, commanded by Lieutenant-General B. J. Horrocks.

Brigade command also changed at this time, Brigadier D. R. E. R. Bateman, D.S.O., O.B.E., taking over the 5th Indian Infantry Brigade from Brigadier Russell, who went to command the 8th Indian Division.

Both General Horrocks and Brigadier Bateman visited the Battalion very shortly after its arrival in Benghazi.

The 10th Corps was now in reserve, and divisions utilised every opportunity to train for tasks that lay ahead, for all realised that desert fighting would not last very much longer. And so street fighting, mountain and hill warfare, and river crossings were all studied and practised. The 1/4th Essex gave a demonstration of street fighting which was attended both by Lieutenant-General Horrocks and by Major-General J. S. Nichols, D.S.O., M.C., the Commander of the 50th Northumbrian Division (and until a year before the Commanding Officer of the 1st Essex). All the brigade commanders of the 50th and 4th Indian Divisions were also present.

On the 8th March, 1943, the 4th Indian Division left Benghazi. Again it was part of the 30th Corps, and on its way to battle and fresh honour.

The Eighth Army was now past Tripoli, and at the borders of Tunisia. At the beginning of March 1943 it was in contact with Rommel's rear-guard south-east of the Mareth Line.

It was clear to the Essex as they moved forward from Benghazi into Tripolitania that they were at last coming out of the desert. There was a touch of green on the dunes and in the marshes, and the wadis sometimes held water. Farms, fields, and orchards began to appear as Tripoli was neared.

On the 6th March the Eighth Army was attacked at Medenine, but the enemy was beaten off, losing much of his now very precious armour. It was now General Montgomery's chance to resume the offensive.

The Battle of Mareth–El Hamma, 26th–29th March, 1943

In dealing with this battle, it is proposed to quote from a letter written very shortly after the battle by Brigadier Bateman, Commander 5th Indian Infantry Brigade, to Lieutenant-General Sir Geoffrey W. Howard, Colonel of the Essex Regiment:

"The Mareth Line had been constructed by the French prior to the war and is a strong natural position. There is a coastal strip covered by a difficult wadi—the Zigau—of some fifteen to twenty miles, and here the defences consisted of a series of strong-points in depth with minefields. Near the sea itself there were areas of very bad going almost impassable to vehicles. The southern part of the position was extended in the Matmata Hills, entry to which was by a few passes, which again had been mined, and which were initially held by the enemy. During the first contact, the Eighth Army secured the southernmost of these passes, but the ground to the west of them was considered by the French, and presumably by the enemy, impassable for large forces. Altogether the enemy must have felt himself fairly secure here, and undoubtedly hoped we would be delayed considerably.

"The initial plan of the Army Commander was to carry out an

infantry attack on the north or coastal sector of the position, and roll up the defences from this direction. At the same time a powerful armoured and mobile force—under General Freyberg—was to carry out a wide out-flanking movement round the Matmata Hills, and come in on the enemy rear about El Hamma–Gabes.

"The infantry attack was to be carried out by the 50th Division initially, and once they had secured a bridge-head into the defences, our Division was to pass through and exploit. The attack started on the night of the 20th/21st March, 1943, and we moved up prepared to pass through the leading infantry.

"In the first attack a footing was secured in the enemy defence, but owing to the difficulties of getting crossings over the Wadi Zigau, the bridge-head could not be widened sufficiently to let us pass through. Fierce fighting continued the next two days, and on the 22nd the enemy counter-attacked with his main reserves and dislodged the footing our leading infantry had gained. Having examined the position subsequently, I am very glad we were not committed to this operation in which we could not have avoided heavy casualties.

"Meanwhile, General Freyberg's force had made excellent progress, and was beginning to threaten the enemy rear, so now the Army Commander decided to reinforce this movement with more armour, and at the same time use our Division to move into the Matmata Hills: so reducing the L. of C. to General Freyberg by some 150 miles and turning the Mareth Line much nearer home. Our Brigade was on the inside of the wheel of the Division, and by morning of the 25th had secured the Halouf Pass into the Hills. The enemy had relied on mines and demolitions to hold us up, but these had been cleared within twenty-four hours, and we then passed through with the 1/4th Essex as leading battalion."

As the 1/4th Essex passed through on the morning of the 26th March, "D" Company led the advance, followed by the Commanding Officer with Battalion Tactical Headquarters. Progress was slow owing to the uneven road and the mines that were still being lifted by the sappers and miners, but at 10.40 a.m. first contact was made with the enemy, a party in a defensive position at a cross-road. "D" Company deployed, sending two platoons to the right, and the carriers under company command to the left. At the same time M.M.G. fire was brought to bear on the enemy forward positions. This first engagement was short, and 12 prisoners had been taken by 11 a.m.

The artillery then opened fire, while "D" Company continued to

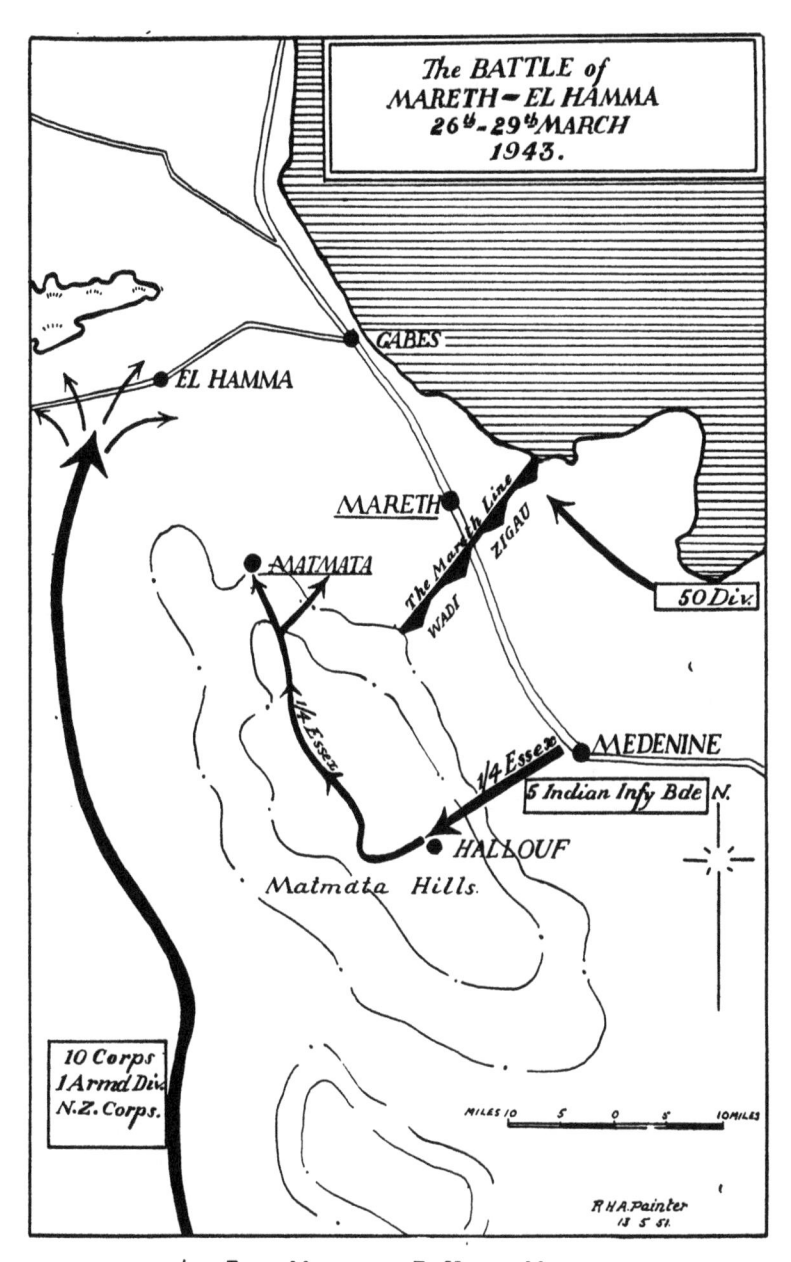

1/4TH ESSEX, MARETH AND EL HAMMA, MARCH 1943.

advance round the features occupied by the enemy, and by 11.30 a.m. the company had reported a further 15 prisoners. Shortly after this enemy resistance was overcome, and the number of prisoners was raised to 80. At 1 p.m. the column was able to continue its advance, but the advance was still slow owing to the number of mines that had to be lifted. Prisoners taken proved to be from the Italian Pistoia Division.

By 4 p.m. the column had reached a point known as "Hardy" on the crest of the Matmata Hills, where it came under heavy artillery fire. Lieutenant-Colonel Noble went forward to reconnoitre the situation. It was clear that the main position of the enemy rear-guard had now been encountered. While patrols and engineer patrols went forward to find the enemy position and any possible demolitions, the Battalion deployed and took up defensive positions.

The patrols returned early on the morning of the 27th March, without having contacted the enemy or finding any further demolition for approximately 4,000 yards ahead of the Essex position. This was explained to the Brigade Commander when he visited Battalion Headquarters at 7.30 a.m.

Lieutenant-Colonel Noble then ordered "A" Company (Major H. C. Gregory, M.C.) to secure "Hardy," with "C" Company holding a firm base in the rear. "B" and "D" Companies were to follow in column, and be prepared to pass through once "Hardy" had been captured, and make for two further objectives—"Swan" and "Edgar."

The Battalion advanced at 8 a.m., and forward companies soon came under heavy shell fire, as did the road up which the column was advancing. "A" Company's 15-cwt. truck and the 3-tonner loaded with the company stores, rations, and reserve ammunition were both hit.

By 3 p.m. "Hardy" had been reached, and an initial 80 prisoners taken. The day's total was to exceed 200, at the cost of 9 Essex casualties, the majority of whom had been wounded from unmarked enemy minefields.

"The last stage of the advance," says Brigadier Bateman, "was a difficult night movement over narrow hill roads, in which the leading companies showed commendable skill and dash, and by the morning of the 28th had secured Toujane and Techin, the main centres of communication." The Mareth Line had now been definitely turned. "What struck me in this operation," adds the Brigadier, "was the skill and initiative shown by young company commanders in a type of warfare which was quite new to them. I am glad to say that two of them—Watt and Ketteley—were given immediate awards of M.C.s for it." (Captain F. J. Ketteley and Captain J. Watt.)

Having been turned out of the Mareth position, the enemy withdrew to a naturally strong position on the Wadi Akarit. This position covered the Gabes Gap, and prevented the final junction of the Eighth Army with the Americans and the First Army via Gafsa. To this area the 1/4th Essex moved on the 1st April, 1943.

The Wadi Akarit and Djebel Garci, April 1943

There was no way round the Akarit position, and to attack it the Army Commander planned to use the 51st Highland Division on the right, the 50th Northumbrian Division in the centre, and the 4th Indian Division on the left.

Brigadier Bateman, in his letter to the Colonel of the Regiment, says: "Our Division (was) to secure the Fatnassa Hills by an attack by night prior to the main attack, and so secure the 50th Division's left flank, and protect that flank of the armour break-through. Prior to this attack, 1/4th Essex carried out some excellent patrolling, one patrol particularly, commanded by Lieutenant Hailes" (Lieutenant C. Hailes, M.C.), "penetrating the enemy position and bringing back valuable information. In the initial plan of attack, the 1/4th Essex were detached from the Brigade under direct command of Division."

On the evening of the 5th April the Commanding Officer issued orders for the attack which was to be launched during the night of the 5th/6th. The 4th Indian Division, less the 1/4th Essex, on the left of the Eighth Army attack, was to secure selected high features. The 1/4th Essex, with the 11th Field Regiment, 513th Battery Anti-Tank Regiment and other supporting arms under command, was alone responsible for attacking frontally and securing part of a bridge-head over the Wadi Akarit to ensure that the Divisional "F" Echelon would get across the obstacle. The main bridge-head was to be made by the 69th Infantry Brigade of the 50th Division.

By 6 a.m. the 6th April, "A" Company had reached the first bound, but then came under heavy artillery fire. By 7 a.m. the entire Battalion axis was under heavy shell fire. The advance continued slowly, and though the 7th Indian Infantry Brigade on the left seemed to be progressing satisfactorily, as did the storming of the Roumana feature by the 51st Division on the right, the issue forward of the Battalion appeared obscure.

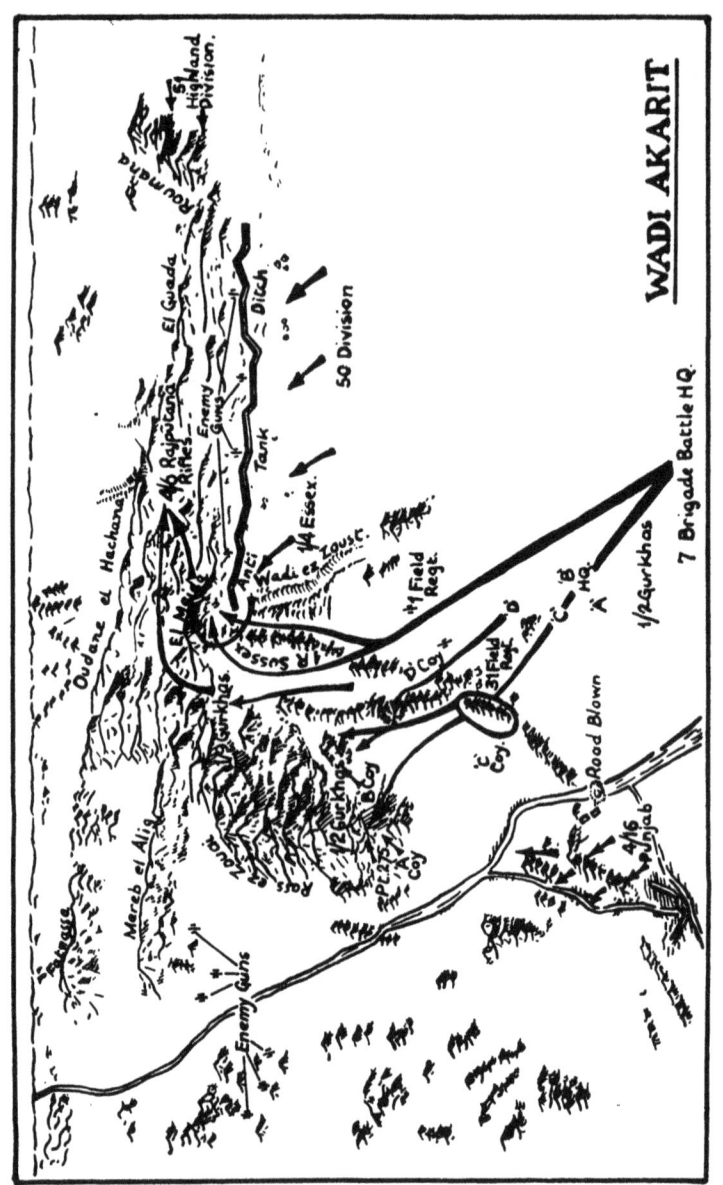

1/4TH ESSEX, THE WADI AKARIT, MARCH 1943.

On making his way forward to "A" Company, Lieutenant-Colonel Noble found that the 50th Division had failed to get a bridge-head, and he was planning a battalion bridge-head operation at the time he received orders from Division over the R/T to the effect that the 1/4th Essex was to switch to the 7th Indian Brigade axis and follow up behind the 5th Indian Brigade.

This change of axis was successfully carried out under heavy fire, and the Commanding Officer went forward to contact the 5th Indian Brigade Tactical ("Tac") Headquarters with "D," "B," and "C" Companies following. The support group, under Major L. W. A Chappell, was left at the foot of the hills, with "A" Company for protection, and was to be available for porterage.

On his arrival at "Tac" Headquarters, Lieutenant-Colonel Noble was ordered to secure the Ouidane feature and to exploit forward. Contacting the 4/6th Rajputana Rifles, a plan was made for securing Ouidane and for reorganisation of the brigade objective area. This was immediately put into effect. But by now the battle of Wadi Akarit had been won, and the advance elements were over the bridge-head and into the open country beyond very soon after midday. Over 9,000 prisoners had been taken. Battalion casualties had been Lieutenant G. R. Single and 8 other ranks killed, and 25 wounded.

Of the difficult move from the 7th Brigade axis to that of the 5th Brigade, the official history of the 4th Indian Division says: "They moved to the west through the midst of the battle and only a few hundred yards behind the firing line. The Royal Sussex and Gurkhas on the high ground watched them coming, and observed their steady bearing under fire."

On the 7th April junction was made by the Eighth Army with the Americans near Gafsa, and the fate of Tunisia was sealed. Taking the coastal towns in quick succession, the Eighth Army reached the area of Enfidaville a week later.

Left behind at Akarit for a few days, the 1/4th Essex moved on the 13th April to Sfax and then on the 15th a further 100 miles to a position ten miles south-west of Enfidaville. Here the Battalion was briefed for the next attack, which was to start on the night of the 19th/20th April.

Djebel Garci and Enfidaville, April 1943

The Eighth Army attacked with the intention of clearing Enfidaville itself and capturing the first series of hills on the way to Cape

Bon. The 5th Indian Brigade objective was a very formidable and broken series of features called the Djebel Garci. Its capture would secure the flank of the New Zealand Division's attack on the right of the 4th Indian Division. On the left of the 5th Brigade the Fighting French Forces under General Le Clerc were to operate.

Brigadier Bateman, in his account of the battle to Lieutenant-General Howard, says, "Preparatory to our attack, each battalion sent forward a strong fighting patrol with the idea of penetrating right into the enemy positions and creating diversions in their rear. That of 1/4th Essex, under Lieutenant Hailes, particularly distinguished itself. Unfortunately, by daylight they were discovered after they had fought their way well in. Hailes himself was badly wounded and had to be left— we have just heard much to everyone's relief that he was recaptured after the final surrender. The patrol then found its way back very gallantly and well. Private Jackson (Private George Jackson) has just got an immediate D.C.M. for what was a very fine show on it— almost a V.C. act, and I hope other awards will follow."

The actions for which Private G. Jackson was awarded an immediate D.C.M. included making four journeys across fifty yards of ground swept by intense cross machine-gun fire in full view of the enemy. "He appeared each journey to face certain death, and it was a miracle that he survived."

A report on this patrol, by Corporal H. Thompson, is given as Appendix C to this chapter.

Brigadier Bateman goes on:

"The main brigade attack started at 8.15 p.m. on a one-battalion front. The Essex were to be in reserve, but subsidiary to the main attack had sent forward 'D' Company under Captain Watt to secure a feature to the right of our attack, held by the enemy. This Company did most excellently. In spite of the darkness, difficult going, and the feature being more extensive than was at first thought, the Company fought its way forward and secured its objective by dawn, taking some hundred prisoners and killing many more. The commanding officer of the Gurkha battalion which relieved the Company in the morning, said he would not have liked to do what they did with less than a battalion."

The feature referred to in the Brigadier's letter was El Blida, a subsidiary of the Djebel Garci towering over 1,000 feet above the plains below, and just to the north of Rahman village.

The attack was laid on with great care. On the 17th April, Captain

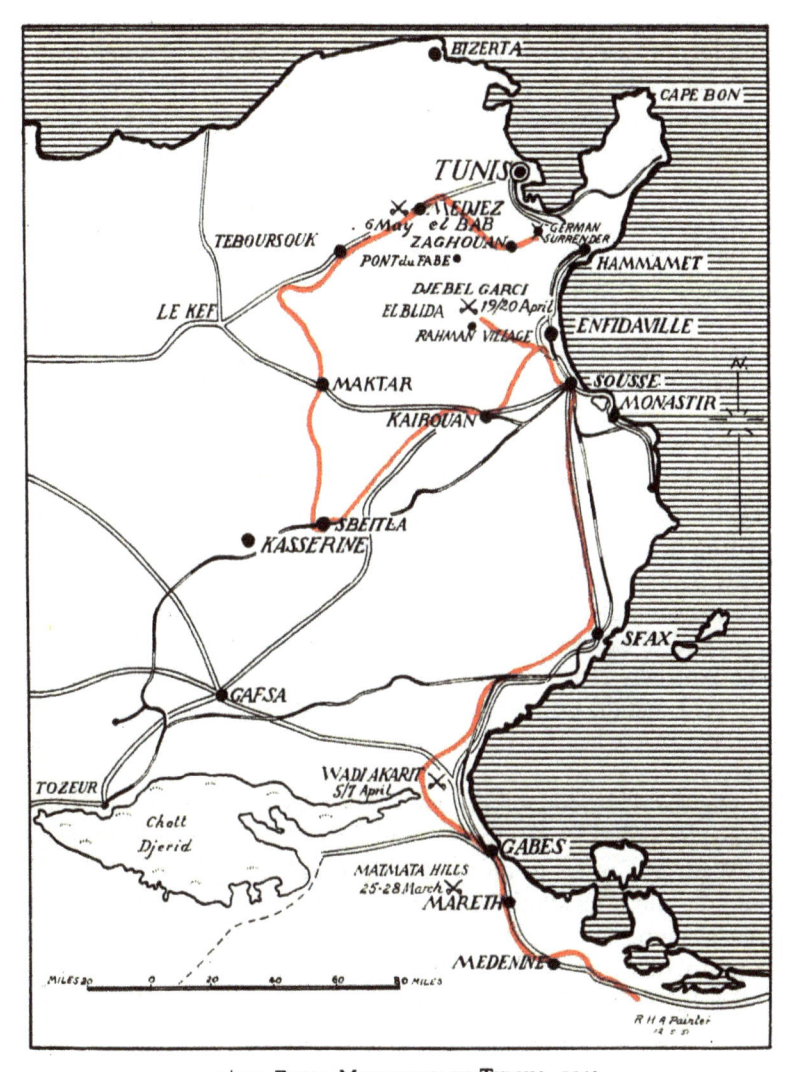

1/4TH ESSEX, MOVEMENTS IN TUNISIA, 1943.

C. J. Kenrick, the Battalion carrier platoon commander, went forward with a section of carriers on a daylight reconnaissance. Despite the loss of one carrier from enemy fire and another through overturning into a wadi whilst "jinking" to avoid enemy fire, the patrol was boldly carried through right under the enemy positions on Blida. That night Lieutenant S. F. Davies led another patrol, which brought in much useful information.

The next night Lieutenant G. Summers, with Captain K. D. Edrupt, Brigade patrol master, led a fighting patrol of "A" Company against the enemy, returning with information and some Italian prisoners.

Intelligence reports had given the enemy facing the Brigade as the German 164th Division. The Brigade plan was for the 1/4th Essex to capture the El Blida feature as a preliminary move in the Brigade attack. Captain Kenrick's carrier patrol on the 17th had drawn fire which was identified as Italian, and Lieutenant Summer's fighting patrol had confirmed that the forward positions on Blida were held by Italians. On this positive information it was deduced that the Italians holding Blida were probably bait in front of a strong German-held position deeper in the hills, a trick that had been met before. Lieutenant-Colonel Noble told the Brigade Commander that he was prepared to capture Blida with a company, making the remainder of the Battalion available as a brigade reserve. This change of plan was adopted, and the Commanding Officer's appreciation that the forward positions were held by Italians with Germans behind was found to be correct.

On the afternoon of the 19th April Lieutenant-Colonel Noble issued his orders for the forthcoming battle. "D" Company (Captain J. Watt, M.C.) was to capture El Blida, and so obtain a bridge-head into the hills. This attack was to precede the main Brigade attack. On this phase being completed, the 4/6th Rajputana Rifles and the 1/9th Gurkha Rifles would secure tactical points north of Blida, with the 1/4th Essex (less "D" Company) in brigade reserve.

"D" Company thus led off at 6.45 p.m. that evening, and at 8.15 p.m. crossed the start-line exactly seventy-five minutes before zero hour for the Corps attack. Advancing with the prominent white mosque in the village of Rahman as landmark, they entered the village, which was found unoccupied. Passing on up El Blida, very stiff opposition was met, but by brilliant leadership Captain Watt got his company forward and El Blida was captured, 50 prisoners being taken. At 8.15 p.m. the main attack started, the 5th Indian Brigade going forward with the 4/6th Rajputana Rifles and the 1/9th Gurkha Rifles leading.

By 3.45 a.m., the 20th April, it was learnt that the 4/6th Rajputana Rifles were held up short of their objective, and Lieutenant-Colonel Noble was ordered to commit his battalion to assist.

Only "A" and "B" Companies were available. "D" was already committed on El Blida and "C" and "S" Companies were being used for porterage in advance of road- (or jeep) head. Owing to the mountainous country, forward companies were entirely dependent on "porters" for all supplies, whether ammunition, rations, or water.

The Commanding Officer immediately went forward to see Lieutenant-Colonel Scott, 4/6th Rajputana Rifles, and to make an appreciation of the situation, leaving "A" and "B" Companies in the village area at the foot of Djebel Garci.

At 7.30 a.m., the 20th April, "B" Company was ordered forward to secure a high feature in front of 1/9th Gurkha Rifles and the 4/6th Rajputana Rifles to the north of El Blida. One platoon (No. 10) was given the task, while another (No. 12) was to take two smaller features to the west. This would allow "A" Company to advance through "B" Company and secure the objectives of the 4/6th Rajputana Rifles.

"B" Company (Captain F. J. Ketteley) advanced well, taking advantage of the low ground round the western edge of El Blida. Both platoons secured their objectives, taking about 30 prisoners, but immediately on capturing its objective, No. 10 Platoon came under extremely heavy artillery, mortar, and small-arms fire. Their position on the objective was unsuitable for defence from the south owing to the convex slope, which necessitated men standing erect to enable them to direct accurate fire on the enemy. This was done without hesitation in the face of extreme enemy fire of all kinds. Eventually the platoon was forced to withdraw slightly, having lost 3 killed and 6 wounded. L/Corporal J. J. Glibbery, stretcher-bearer with "B" Company, did magnificent work in evacuating these wounded, and was subsequently awarded the Military Medal, as was L/Sergeant A. Marjoram. During the action No. 11 Platoon moved up to strengthen No. 12 Platoon, which it did successfully, and by 10.30 a.m. "B" Company was fairly established on its objective.

With "B" Company on the position that had been holding up the Gurkhas, the Commanding Officer decided to employ "A" Company (Major H. C. Gregory) to capture the objective of the 4/6th Rajputana

Rifles, but before the attack could be put on, a strong enemy counter-attack dislodged "B" Company from vital ground in their objective area.

It was evident that enemy resistance was thickening very rapidly,

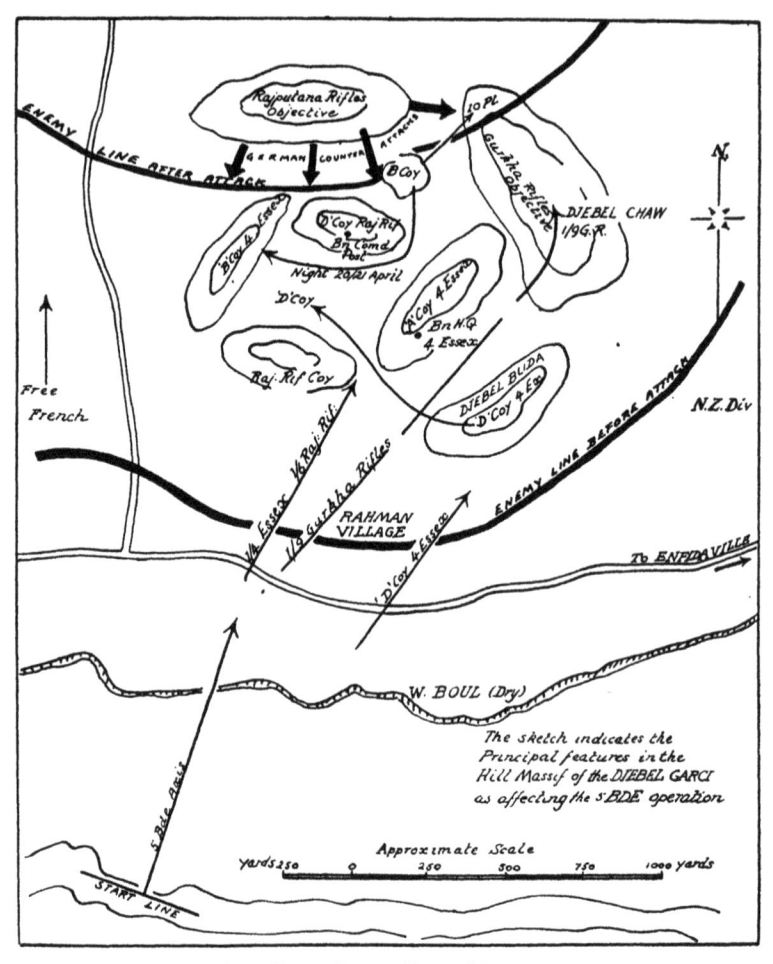

1/4TH ESSEX, DJEBEL GARCI, MARCH 1943.

and a warning from Brigade told the Essex to expect counter-attacks in strength. Lieutenant-Colonel Noble therefore made a careful reconnaissance with Lieutenant-Colonel Scott, and decided that the whole position must be thoroughly reorganised and prepared for counter-attack before any further advance could be considered.

Consequently, "B" Company was ordered to hold the ground it still held, and "A" Company was brought forward and placed on vital ground in advance of the position of the 4/6th Rajputana Rifles. The area was thus secured by a series of strong Rajputana and Essex Company localities. As the situation seemed to call for sector rather than battalion control, Lieutenant-Colonel Noble took command of the forward sector ("A" and "B" Companies 1/4th Essex and "D" Company 4/6th Rajputana Rifles) and Lieutenant-Colonel Scott took over the rear sector.

Throughout the rest of the 20th April the 1/4th Essex held on to all points gained, the enemy making continuous attempts to dislodge them with almost continuous sweeps of artillery and multiple mortar (nebelwerfer) fire.

During the afternoon, the 1/4th was ordered to be prepared to take the original objectives of the 4/6th Rajputana Rifles the next morning. Lieutenant-Colonel Noble represented on the phone to Brigadier Bateman that it was more than a one-battalion task, and in any case the recapture of vital ground where "B" Company had been was an essential preliminary operation. He further said that to extend still further the hard-tried 5th Brigade was to court disaster. This view was put forward to Major-General Tuker, and it was finally decided that the Brigade was too extended to attack further.

Later that afternoon the 4/16th Punjab Regiment from the 7th Indian Brigade came under command of the 5th Indian Brigade, and was employed on the right of the 1/9th Gurkhas. For forty-eight hours efforts were made to regain the feature which "B" Company had held and lost, but without success.

There were heavy enemy counter-attacks throughout the evening of the 20th April, but these failed to make any progress. Major L. W. A. Chappell, M.C., Captain F. J. Ketteley, M.C., and Lieutenants H. Andrews and S. C. Spicer had been wounded, as had Lieutenant-Colonel J. L. Spencer, the Commanding Officer of the 1st Hampshires, who had been accompanying Lieutenant-Colonel Noble throughout the day's operations. The tally of killed and wounded other ranks was also mounting.

Lieutenant-Colonel Noble had decided that the position occupied by "B" Company could not be further held against determined counter-attack by daylight, since the vital ground in the locality had been regained by the Germans. During the night 20th/21st April he therefore moved "B" Company to an important feature on the left of "D" Company of the Rajputana Rifles, in order to secure the flank of the forward sector. "D" Company of the 1/4th Essex was also brought forward from the Blida feature to form a reserve for the forward sector to counter-attack the centre position if lost.

More attacks during the 21st and 22nd April still failed to bring the enemy any success, for the 1/4th Essex and the three Indian battalions stood the heavy artillery and mortar bombardments magnificently. Very heavy losses were inflicted on the enemy for all his attempts to advance.

On the night of the 22nd/23rd April the 153rd Infantry Brigade came in to relieve the 5th Indian Brigade, the 1/4th Essex being replaced on the hill-tops by the 5th Black Watch.

"The battered but indomitable Essex, Rajputana Rifles, and Gurkhas" (Official History, 4th Indian Division) then moved to a reserve area near Enfidaville.

The 1/4th Essex had been continuously in action for the past four days, and had had 12 men killed and 5 officers and 71 men wounded.

As they came out of the line to rest and refit, Lieutenant-Colonel Noble received a personal letter from Major-General Tuker which said: "I have only just heard of the exploits of your men on Garci. I do wish to congratulate them on what they did. For a Battalion that has seen so little of the hills to do what they did, and at night, is really wonderful—particularly, the Company that took Blida was, if anything, outstanding."

Among the awards granted to the 1/4th Essex for this action was the D.S.O. to Lieutenant-Colonel A. Noble and the M.C. to his adjutant, Captain H. J. Young.

In the new area near Enfidaville preparations were put in hand for the next attack, which was planned for the beginning of May with the object of clearing the coast road.

However, this plan was changed and a new role allotted to the 4th Indian Division, which, with the 7th Armoured Division and the 201st Guards Brigade, was ordered to stand by to leave the Eighth Army and transfer to the First Army near Medjez-el-Bab.

On the 30th April the 1/4th Essex embussed and formed part of an endless column that moved night and day, with only an occasional halt for a "brew-up" until it arrived in the new area on the 2nd May.

The contrast between the two British armies was extreme: the

First Army, with comparatively new vehicles all painted and camouflaged to meet northern or European requirements, contrasting with the old battle wagons of the Eighth Army, sandy grey, dust covered, and showing all the scars of their 2,000-mile journey under most adverse conditions.

In the area west of Medjez, the Battalion heard the preliminary plans for the new operation in the hills east of Medjez, where the First Army had been contained since December 1942. The 4th Indian Division was to be part of the 9th Corps, now taken over by Lieutenant-General Brian Horrocks. The Corps was to attack with Tunis as its objective. The break-in was to be on a narrow two-divisional front, 4th British Division right, 4th Indian Division left. As soon as the initial objectives were gained, the 6th and 7th Armoured Divisions would pass through and make for Tunis, some thirty miles away. "H"-Hour would be 3 a.m. on the 6th May.

The 5th Indian Brigade would lead the Indian Division's attack, and the Brigade plan allowed for the 1/9th Gurkhas to lead and secure the enemy outpost line. As soon as this was captured the 1/4th Essex was to pass through and go for the enemy main position. The Essex would have "under command" for the operation the 145th Regiment R.A.C. (Churchill tanks), the 432nd Anti-Tank Battery, a M.M.G. Company of the 6/6th Rajputana Rifles, a detachment of Sappers and Miners, and a troop of flail tanks.

Immediately after the plan had been explained, Lieutenant-Colonel Noble put his companies to practising a drill for attacking and destroying enemy in pill-boxes, which were said to abound in the enemy's defences. This was a form of defence not yet met with in mass by the 1/4th Essex in this war.

The move-up began on the 3rd May, and stage by stage the Battalion advanced into the new concentration area. On the 5th May the Commanding Officer issued his orders, for operations were to start at 3 a.m. the following morning. There had been no patrolling, since it was essential that there should be no risk of prisoners and possible identification of the arrival of the 4th Indian Division on the First Army front. The attack had to be planned and launched on information from units which had been actually holding the line. "This information was generally found to be scant," says a contemporary document rather scathingly. Perhaps the entry is an indication of the feeling that for a time existed between the two Armies, but which was soon to fade in recognition of each other's fighting ability.

At 12.30 a.m. the 6th May the 1/4th Essex moved out of its bivouac area, and after marching through the night was, at 4.45 a.m., in position on the Brigade start-line, with "A" and "C" Companies forward, "B" Company immediately behind with a mopping-up role, and "D" Company in reserve behind Battalion Headquarters. There had been some slight shelling and mortar fire as the companies closed up, but only 1 other rank had been wounded.

By 3.30 a.m. companies had linked up with the tank squadrons, but unfortunately the latter had had three tanks blown up in the approach march by running into some mines that had been lifted and laid at the side of a track. By 7 a.m. the Battalion was in an area immediately in rear of a feature known as Point 165 which had been captured by the 1/9th Gurkhas. In front of this was Point 166, the main objective. At 8 a.m. the 1/4th Essex, covered by artillery concentration of smoke and high explosive on the objective, crossed the start-line.

Two quotations will serve to describe the last battle of the 1/4th Essex in North Africa. The first is from the *History of the 4th Indian Division*, by Lieutenant-Colonel G. R. Stevens.

"As 1/4th Essex passed through the Gurkhas they veered to the right, across the front of 4 British Division. The tanks had closed up, and the Home County men moved on to their final objective with an escort of thirty Churchills. The confident spirit of this great Battalion was reflected by their transport, of which some seventy vehicles followed less than 800 yards behind the firing line."

So much for the broad picture: now for the detail as given in a contemporary report.

"By 8.20 a.m. both 'A' and 'C' Companies reported that they were in position on their objective, 'C' Company (Captain W. A. Matthews) having captured five nebelwerfers (a six-barrelled German mortar which had caused so many casualties amongst us in the Garci battle) with crews and a quantity of ammunition.

"During the course of the advance the tanks with 'A' Company (Captain H. C. Gregory) had a delightful battle with two 88-mm. enemy guns. These guns were situated on the top of a hill across a valley through which our troops had to advance. When the tanks appeared on the hill opposite, the guns opened up, and a pitched battle at almost point-blank range began, with the result that one of the 88-mm. was set on fire and the other abandoned.

"The Support Company, and the remaining supporting arms (except the sappers) who were following close behind 'D' Company then moved up to forward companies to support them against any possible counter-attack, and very soon news was received that our main armour had been released and was passing through on its way to Tunis.

"'C' Company (Captain W. A. Matthews) then went out in his carrier to the village of Bj Frendj, where he found a motor-car full of Germans, whom he captured and forced to drive him back to his Headquarters in their car. The total P.W. captured by 'C' Company is 37.

"At the same time 'A' Company had sent forward a patrol on to the ridge in front of them and a party of 4 Germans surrendered."

The picture is clear. The plan had been overwhelmingly successful, and a triumphant army, at the end of a long journey, was moving in to the kill.

At 9.30 a.m. the 7th Indian Brigade passed through to exploit success, and the Essex had little else but mopping up to do.

The battle for North Africa was almost over. Tunis fell on the 7th May, and on the 13th May Marshal Messe, the Italian Commander-in-Chief who had taken over command, ordered all remaining troops to lay down their arms. Over a quarter of a million prisoners were taken, including the remnants of the famous German Afrika Korps.

In the events leading up to this notable victory, the 1/4th Essex had played a conspicuous and honourable part.

On the 12th May, 1943, the following 4th Indian Division order was published:

"The Division today captured many thousands of prisoners, amongst them General Von Arnim, the Commander-in-Chief of the Axis Forces in Africa, and General Kramm, the Commander of the 5th Panzer Army, together with their H.Q.s and Staff.

"This is a very fitting conclusion to all the battles we have fought in Africa. It marks the final defeat of the Axis in this country. Please tell your men."

For the rest of May and the first part of June the Essex stayed by the sea at Misurata, whither they had been withdrawn after the battle for Tunis. Moved temporarily to Tripoli, the Battalion was visited by Lieutenant-General Brian Horrocks. It was his farewell visit, for the 4th Indian Division was now to leave the 10th Corps and return to the Nile Delta to refit.

On the 19th June the Battalion paraded on the Tripoli–Castel Benito road for inspection by His Majesty the King. On the 22nd June it left Misurata, and moved by easy stages to Alexandria, arriving on the evening of the 6th July, 1943. Camp was established approximately ten miles west of Alexandria, and the Battalion stayed there for ten days. Here they heard of further awards: the D.S.O. to Lieutenant-Colonel A. Noble and Captain J. Watt, M.C.; the M.C. to Major H. J. Young and Lieutenant C. Hailes; the M.M. to Corporal H. T. Brewer ("D" Company) and L/Corporal G. Hudson (Signal Platoon). From here, too, Major H. J. Young and 13 other ranks left the Battalion on posting to the home establishment, and were replaced by a draft from the 2nd Battalion.

There was also, by the accident of war, a meeting with the 5th Essex then in camp not far away, at Burg-el-Arab.

On the 16th July the 1/4th Essex moved across to the Burg-el-Arab area, and a football match 1/4th Essex *v.* 5th Essex was played, the 1/4th Battalion winning two goals to none. There also a Church Parade was held, conducted by Lieutenant-Colonel the Reverend B. K. Bond, then a Deputy Assistant Chaplain-General, but twenty-five years earlier the Chaplain to the 4th Essex with the 161st (East Anglian) Brigade, in the Palestine campaign.

More distinction came the way of the Battalion in a supplement to the *London Gazette* of the 2nd June, 1943, which was received on the 7th August, and which notified mentions in dispatches to Lieutenant-Colonel A. Noble, Captain D. J. Beech, M.C., Regimental Sergeant-Major C. J. Rose, Company Sergeant-Major S. J. Day, who had been killed on Ruweisat Ridge, and Corporal H. T. Taylor.

Those were care-free days. There was plenty of training, and lectures on mountain warfare preparatory to a move to a mountain-warfare training centre in Syria. There was also ceremonial and much recreation to balance the days: football with the 1/9th Gurkha Rifles, beating retreat by the 1/9th Gurkhas attended by all ranks of the 1/4th Essex, and a visit to the Battalion by the C.-in-C. M.E.F., General Sir Henry Maitland Wilson. Hockey matches, too, were played against 5th Brigade Headquarters, the 31st Field Regiment R.A., and other teams, and short leave into Cairo was granted. There was even cricket, a match against a Union Defence Force of South Africa eleven having almost a test-match character.

Before the Battalion moved on from Egypt, Captain B. P. Tully, M.C., R.A.M.C., left the Battalion. During the battles from Mareth to Tunis, Captain Tully, with the regimental stretcher-bearers, had given magnificent service. He was succeeded by Captain R. J. N. Pellow, R.A.M.C.

Some training—dry-shod—in combined operations was found possible in September and October, and then a move was made to Kabrit on the Suez Canal, where wet-shod training was carried out. From Kabrit the Battalion moved to Baalbek in Syria, preparatory to training in mountain warfare, but very soon moved back to Egypt. It was remobilised at El Tahag, and embarked in mid-November at Alexandria in the transports *Cuba* and *Staffordshire*.

The convoy left Alexandria on the 18th November to berth at Taranto, Italy, on the 22nd November. The Battalion disembarked straightway and marched to the 16th Indian Reinforcement Camp at Statte, where it joined the advanced party for the move of the 4th Indian Division to Italy.

Section VI

THE ITALIAN CAMPAIGN, 1943-44

The 1/4th Essex disembarked in heavy rain, an ominous portent of the unpleasant winter days that lay ahead.

The order of battle of the 4th Indian Division on landing was:

G.O.C. Major-General F. I. S. Tuker, C.B., D.S.O., O.B.E.

5th Indian Infantry Brigade (Brigadier D. R. Bateman, D.S.O., O.B.E.)	1/4th Essex Regiment 1/6th Rajputana Rifles 1/9th Gurkha Rifles
7th Indian Infantry Brigade	1st Royal Sussex 4/16th Punjab Regiment 1/2nd Gurkha Rifles
11th Indian Infantry Brigade	2nd Cameron Highlanders 4/6th Rajputana Rifles 2/7th Gurkha Rifles
Divisional Reconnaissance Regiment	Central India Horse
Machine-gun Battalion	6th Machine-gun Battalion Rajputana Rifles
Artillery	1st Field Regiment R.A. 11th Field Regiment R.A. 31st Field Regiment R.A. 149th Anti-Tank Regiment 57th Light A.A. Regiment

Engineers	4th, 12th, and 21st Field Companies (Sappers and Miners)
	11th Field Park Company
	5th Bridging Platoon
Medical Services	17th, 26th, and 32nd Field Ambulances
	15th Indian Field Hygiene Section

Sicily had been captured in August 1943, and the Eighth Army had landed in Italy on the 3rd September, followed on the 9th September by the American Fifth Army at Salerno. An Italian armistice had been signed, but the Germans in Italy fought on.

By the 1st January, 1944, the Eighth Army had fought its way northwards over the Rivers Trigno, Sangro, and Moro. Ortona had been captured. The Fifth Army, capturing Naples, had pushed on in the direction of Rome, and was near Cassino.

It was ideal defensive country and every mile was strongly contested. The Eighth Army offensive across and north of the River Sangro had bitten deeply into the German winter defensive positions, and the enemy was only giving ground under heavy pressure. There was no continuous front in the sense of a connected trench system, and with a wide "no man's land" between the two armies there was much scope for patrols. Casualties had been heavy and the "going" almost impossibly difficult, the forward areas being in the main supplied by mule transport. The rivers still to be crossed before the strategically important Pescara–Rome road could be reached were numerous and fast running. The coastal plain was a mass of mud and the mountains snow-bound.

A week before Christmas Lieutenant-Colonel Noble and his Intelligence Officer, Lieutenant J. S. Horsington, were able to visit the 5th Essex and spend a night with them just before they moved up for the Villa Grande battle.

Christmas 1943 was spent at Avigliano, where intense training was carried out in appalling weather conditions.

On the 10th January, 1944, there was a warning that the 5th Indian Infantry Brigade would probably move up behind the 2nd New Zealand Division on the 15th January. The 1/4th Essex, still at Avigliano, began to make ready. Patrol appointments were made, Captain D. J. V. Fisher becoming Battalion patrol master, and Major L. W. A. Chappell, M.C., the Brigade patrol master.

As the Battalion began to move forward into the battle area once more, the following special order by Major-General Tuker was made known to all ranks:

"Since September 1942 it has been the proud claim of the Division that an objective once captured is never given up. The 4th Indian Division is never counter-attacked off these positions.

"We have also claimed that no officer or man who wears the Red Eagle is ever taken prisoner unless so badly wounded that he can no longer use his weapons.

"The Division relies on each individual officer and man to live up to these claims.

"These are our claims, and these things win us our battles, for we are always stauncher than our enemy."

The Battalion moved up by stages, through Potenza, Gravina, and Canosa to reach Lanciano on the 15th January and to receive orders to relieve the 22nd N.Z. Motor Battalion in the area of Salarolo and the N.Z. Divisional Cavalry Regiment around Bianco.

These positions on the upper Sangro were taken over on the 17th and held until the night of the 21st/22nd, when the 1/4th Essex was in turn relieved by the Westminster Regiment of Canada and moved into reserve at Castel Frentano.

This short spell in the line served to show the nature of the operations on the Eighth Army front at that time. Widely separated platoon localities and company areas, deep patrolling and spasmodic shelling and mortaring both by day and night were the broad picture. To it there must be added the constant threat of enemy raids or incursions by his patrols. A party would go out at first light to an O.P. to find it had been slept in the night before by the enemy; civilians would report enemy whereabouts and clamour, too, for food, for A.M.G.O.T. (Allied Military Government of Occupied Territory) was not yet functioning in these forward areas.

But the 1/4th Essex was not in fact to be committed to this front. The Army Group Commander, appreciating that decisive results were not attainable on the Eighth Army front under winter conditions, had decided to switch a portion of that Army across to reinforce General Mark Clark's Fifth Army, and then to attack northwards in conjunction with a fresh landing shortly to take place at Anzio. The prize was Rome.

The Battles for Cassino, February–March, 1944

On the 2nd February, 1944, the 4th Indian Division was transferred across the Apennines to join the Fifth Army. This Army, after its gallant crossing of the River Garigliano, had reached the area round the small town of Cassino which blocked the southern entrance to the Via Cassilina. In the first week of February the efforts of the Fifth Army to capture it had been fought to a standstill.

To the 1/4th Essex, arriving in the area of Pietramelara on the 4th February, the climatic conditions seemed as unpleasant as those experienced east of the Apennines and quite unfavourable to an attack that would permit the mobility of a modern army to be fully utilised. The strategical and tactical situation, likewise, was unfavourable. The first efforts, prolonged and bitterly fought, to capture the Cassino area and push through to a junction at Anzio with the forces landed there on the 22nd January had failed. It was clear that there was to be no rapid advance west of the Apennines and that there was practically a stalemate on the Italian fronts.

On the 12th February the 1/4th Essex Regiment moved forward from Pietramelara to the Wadi Portella, where it lay, under shell fire, in reserve for the next few days while future operations were outlined. From a distance Monte Cassino appears bare, smooth, and offering little natural cover. It is in fact a mass of rough, broken ground indented with hollows and studded with knolls, the whole broken by innumerable ridges and ravines. Boulders, caves, scrub, all offer cover to a clever infantryman and his supporting weapons. With power tools to aid the natural cover, the whole had been converted into a fortress guarded by wire and minefields.

On the 18th February the 1/4th Essex was moved forward from the Wadi Portella to the Wadi Villa in preparation for an almost immediate attack. Cassino and the massive Monastery Hill had been attacked by heavy bombers on the 15th February, and bombed again on the 16th and 17th February. Despite this softening up, the infantry attack on the 18th February, which included the 7th Indian Infantry Brigade, fared so badly that the Army Group Commander, General Sir Harold Alexander, quickly intervened and stopped it. The 1/4th Essex, in reserve, was not therefore required.

Various reconnaissances were made, both in the hills towards the

Monastery and towards Cassino town, in the next few weeks, as various plans were explored and discarded.

The last half of February and the first weeks of March were unpleasant. It was a month of uninterrupted shelling, heavy at times, that caused casualties and restricted movement already extremely limited owing to the enemy's powers of observation from the high ground overlooking the Allied positions. It was a month, too, of extremely bad weather. "It rained as only it can in southern Italy, and down the mountains it came," says Captain J. Beazley, O.C. "B" Company. "It filled the river-bed and swept through our lines, taking with it blankets, equipment, and even a medium machine gun. Just as our morale was sadly needing a fillip, we had news that the attack on Cassino was to start."

The 4th Indian Division was now part of the New Zealand Corps. On the 23rd February Lieutenant-Colonel Noble was called to Headquarters 5th Indian Infantry Brigade, where Brigadier Bateman gave details of a fresh attack by the New Zealand Corps, which would be preceded by the saturation bombing of Cassino town, and in which the Brigade task would be exploitation on the eastern slopes of Monte Cassino. The Battalion outline plan was:

"A" Company to take over Point 193 and the Castle area, and "B" Company to take over the lower shoulder of Point 193 and the northern approaches to Cassino from units of the 6th N.Z. Infantry Brigade and to establish a firm base there. "D" Company would give depth on Point 175 north-east of the Castle area, while "C" Company would attack and capture Point 165 and the hairpin road bend nearby.

The reconnaissance and preparation of positions started the following day. The bad weather, however, delayed the saturation bombing of the town which was to precede the attack, and the 1/4th Essex, weary of the constant shell fire and bad weather, grew tired of the message "Bradman not batting tomorrow." "Bradman" was the code-word for the start of the new attack.

On the 3rd March there was another conference at Corps Headquarters, at which General Freyberg added to the formidable tasks already allotted the 1/4th Essex by saying that the Battalion would, with a squadron of New Zealand tanks, capture the Monastery (the Abbé d'Monte Cassino). This Lieutenant-Colonel Noble passed on to those immediately affected at a conference that evening: "B" Company would support the tanks (and vice versa), infiltrate to the south of the Monastery, and then give covering fire to the remainder of the

Battalion infiltrating to an assault line east of the Monastery. For the actual attack there were two alternatives: if "C" Company had not had to fight for Point 165, then "C" (right) and "A" (left) would lead the assault, with "D" in reserve; but if "C" had had to fight hard for Point 165, then "A" and "D" Companies would lead and "C" would be in reserve.

On the morning of the 15th March, 1944, the fresh assault on the Cassino defences was launched. At 8.30 a.m. a heavy and sustained air attack was made, in which 514 bombers dropped some 1,400 tons of bombs on a target area of less than one square mile—a heavy concentration even for World War II. Immediately the bombing ceased a heavy artillery bombardment began, and as the artillery concentrations lifted from the enemy forward area the 6th N.Z. Infantry Brigade went in to the attack.

The 4th Indian Division, now under command of Major-General A. Galloway, C.B.E., D.S.O., M.C., was in support to the New Zealanders' attack, the 5th Indian Infantry Brigade being charged with the task of continuing the initial advance of the 6th N.Z. Brigade.

Despite the massive air attack and subsequent artillery bombardment, the attacking New Zealanders encountered very fierce resistance from the German paratroops who formed the garrison of the Cassino area. An added hindrance in Cassino town itself was the completeness of its destruction, for the attackers had not only to fight a skilful enemy, but fight over a vast rubble heap, every corner of which could, and very often did, hold a determined paratrooper.

Despite fanatical resistance, the 25th N.Z. Infantry Battalion had by 5.30 p.m., the 15th March, two platoons well established in the Castle on Point 193, and the 1/4th Essex three-quarters of an hour later left the Wadi Villa and began the move up to take over from the New Zealanders and continue the battle so gallantly begun.

Castle Hill was the first foothill behind the town on the way up to the Monastery at the summit of the Cassino feature. Rain fell, and the men climbing the steep slopes of Castle Hill in the darkness made slow going. "A" Company, held up by a pocket of enemy, was already fighting among the rubble at the foot of the hill, and "C" Company, passing through them, encountered further parties of German parachute troops and became dispersed in the darkness.

As the Battalion toiled and fought in the darkness, orders for the next phase came in from the Headquarters of the 5th Indian Infantry Brigade. The plan was for the 1/6th Rajputana Rifles to pass through and capture the bend in the road at Point 236 at 10.30 p.m. that night. At 9.30 p.m., therefore, Major Beckett's "C" Company was ordered to press on and take over Castle Hill from the New Zealanders. It was also to capture Point 165 despite the hold-up of "A" Company.

So difficult, however, were the conditions of weather, terrain, and enemy resistance that for about an hour the only part of "C" Company under Major Beckett's effective command was his Company Sergeant-Major, two signallers, and a runner. The 1/6th Rajputana Rifles had similar troubles. It was 11.40 p.m. before "A" Company at the foot of Castle Hill could report the 1/6th Rajputanas as passing through and out on to the slopes leading up to the Castle.

By approximately midnight, the 15th/16th March, the leading elements of "C" Company were established in the Castle. "A" Company held the approach to the Castle from the outskirts of Cassino town, while "D" Company held Point 175 across a ravine behind the Castle. "B" Company was in a reserve position, while Battalion Headquarters with "S" Company were in the vicinity of Point 175.

The Brigade operation had gone much more slowly than expected. At 3 a.m. the 16th March, when "C" Company had reported Point 165 and a building known as "Yellow House" captured, Lieutenant-Colonel Noble, after discussion with the Brigade Commander, informed the officer commanding the 4/6th Rajputana Rifles (11th Indian Infantry Brigade) that a projected relief of the 1/4th Essex by the 4/6th Rajputana Rifles in order to free the former for an assault on the monastery could not yet proceed.

Daylight, the 16th March, found the 1/4th Essex in and around the Castle and on Point 165. The whole area was alive with snipers. Intermingled with the 1/4th Essex were elements of the 1/6th Rajputana Rifles. The latter, passing through the 1/4th Essex in the darkness, had run almost immediately into strong opposition, and had been halted before they reached the objective, the vital Point 236, the possession of which would open the way for a drive up to Hangman's Hill (Point 435). This was a rocky platform some 200 yards below the Monastery abutting from the side of the main massif. On the platform stood the pylon of an aerial ropeway, a gibbet-like structure that quickly gained the feature its name of Hangman's Hill.

With the 1/4th Essex and 1/6th Rajputana Rifles were elements of the 1/9th Gurkhas, who also had reached the forward positions above Cassino Town.

The situation on the morning of the 16th March was confused and difficult. By 10.30 a.m. the tanks allotted to "B" Company in the original plan of a drive up to Point 202, finding it impossible to get

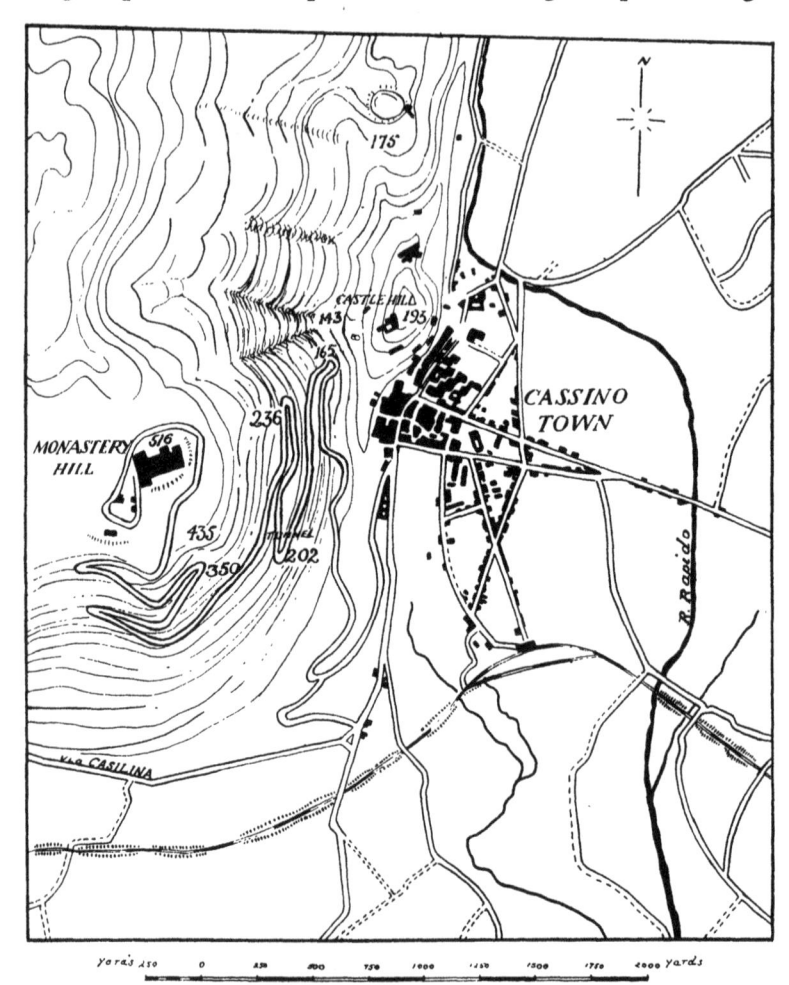

1/4TH ESSEX, THE BATTLE FOR CASSINO, MARCH 1944.

up the road, had withdrawn. Any movement brought fire from mortars and artillery as well as from snipers. By midday the decision was made to place the two forward companies 1/6th Rajputana Rifles under Essex command for a further attack, with artillery support on Point 236 at 7 p.m. that night.

This operation was launched as planned. Shortly after midnight, the 16th/17th March, an R.A. observation-post report gave Point 202 in our hands, but it was not until 5.50 a.m. that wireless contact was made with the 1/6th Rajputana Rifles, who reported they had in fact reached Points 202 and 236, only to be pushed off during subsequent severe fighting.

While this fighting was in progress, the 1/9th Gurkha Rifles had been committed from below the Castle. Slipping through the front of the 1/6th Rajputana Rifles and the New Zealanders on the lower slopes of the Monastery Hill, they began to infiltrate up on to Hangman's Hill.

Shortly after dawn, the 17th March, after taking more than eight hours to infiltrate through the confused fighting, the Gurkhas reached Hangman's Hill.

With the 1/9th Gurkhas established on Hangman's Hill (Point 435), it now appeared that further progress would be possible, and the 1/4th Essex was ordered to attack Point 236 from which the 1/6th Rajputanas had been dislodged.

The following orders were issued to "B" and "D" Companies:

"Intention: Hold Point 193, capture Point 236, and restore situation, link up with 1/9th Gurkhas on Point 435 and contact the New Zealanders on the lower slopes.
"Method: 'B' Company (Captain Beazley) capture Point 236 and reorganise. 'D' Company (Captain Kenrick) capture and re-establish Point 202, link up with the 1/9th Gurkhas, and contact the New Zealanders. 'C' Company (Major Beckett) consolidate Point 193 and Point 165. 'A' Company (Major Ketteley) as reserve in Castle."

The afternoon of the 18th March was difficult, as "B" and "D" Companies moved up to join with "A" and "C" preparatory to the advance on Point 236 and the Monastery itself.

Captain Beazley says: "Lieutenant Pat Coghlan had a platoon in a very precarious position forward of the Castle by about 200 yards. This platoon was tucked away in the remains of a house, and from here they had a close-up of German snipers who were doing their best to make the house untenable. In addition to his troubles, his No. 38 set had been doing overtime, and he needed a battery to regain wireless touch with his company commander (Major Beckett).

"As O.C. 'B' Company, I was asked to call on Lieutenant Coghlan and see the ground and its inhabitants, as it was likely that 'B' Company would be a leading company in any attack on the hill.

"It was late afternoon when my batman and a signaller from 'C' Company (who had been ordered to take up a spare wireless battery) followed me over the Castle wall bound for Coghlan's position. 'Bound one,' a cluster of large boulders, was reached without incident, but we had been spotted and came under rifle fire when we left our cover. The 'C' Company boy was shot in the leg. Communication back to Major Beckett was quickly made. Major Beckett and one of his stretcher-bearers brought in the wounded man. Major Beckett also arranged for 2-inch mortar smoke to be put down to cover our remaining 100 yards to the house."

The Castle area was very congested, and to make matters more difficult, a double-towered building south of the Castle was an enemy strong-point which had to be cleared before any progress could be made. This was to be shot up by New Zealand tanks and then cleared by "A" Company. This and other difficulties led Lieutenant-Colonel Noble to inform Brigadier Bateman at 4.46 p.m. that the advance against Point 236 would have to be a night attack.

Unfortunately, the tank shoot collapsed a wall of the Castle and caused casualties and lost weapons in companies. "A" Company had a number of men buried under the debris, while "B" Company lost men who fell to their death down a 150-foot cliff. Major Beazley speaks of the episode when he says: "From the house it could be seen that New Zealand tanks on the far side of the Castle Hill, using solid shot on the houses on the hill, were hitting the Castle itself with disastrous results. A wall of the Castle collapsed, burying some of our men and weapons."

Two hours later a further report to Brigade confirmed that it had been impossible to get the attack mounted before nightfall. By 7.30 p.m., after contact had been gained with the incoming 4/6th Rajputana Rifles, a message was relayed to the 1/9th Gurkhas on Hangman's Hill telling them to expect the attack on the Monastery to start at 6 a.m. the 19th March.

Between 8 p.m. and 10 p.m. Lieutenant-Colonel Noble visited the companies in the Castle area, and then made his way back to Brigade Headquarters, where at about 10.30 p.m. he explained the situation in the forward area to Brigadier Bateman.

Making his way forward once more, Lieutenant-Colonel Noble at 12.05 a.m. the 19th March confirmed previous orders—"B" Company was to capture Point 236 and "D" Company was to capture Point 202 —move at first light—relief of "A" and "C" Companies by the 4/6th Rajputana Rifles to proceed forthwith.

At 3.25 a.m. the Brigade Commander, accompanied by his G.S.O. III, arrived to set up his tactical (Tac) headquarters in Battalion Headquarters, since the 1/4th Essex was in contact with the whole Brigade by wireless, and communications otherwise were so poor as to be almost non-existent.

In the cold early morning of the 19th March, the 4/6th Rajputana Rifles began the relief of "A" and "C" Companies. By 5.30 a.m., when "B" and "D" Companies set off up the hill to their objectives, the relief of Point 165 had been accomplished, and the hand-over of posts within the Castle was under way.

"A" and "C" Companies were in fact beginning to organise themselves to go forward in the second wave behind the leading companies who had not advanced very far when information was received that Germans in strength were approaching from the Monastery area. Almost immediately heavy machine-gun fire swept the whole area, and it became evident a major counter-attack was being mounted. "A" and "C" Companies, in the process of relief by the 4/6th Rajputana Rifles, were the first to feel this attack, which was put in by about 200 to 300 determined men of the 1st German Parachute Division. It was decided that "A" and "C" should hold the Castle area, whilst the 4/6th Rajputanas should assist in ammunition duties and form a counter-attack reserve.

As communications were established from the area of Point 175, the move of Battalion Headquarters was delayed while the German attack was developing. Lieutenant-Colonel Noble ordered "B" and "D" Companies (by wireless), who were on the move-up in the first phase of the attack on Points 236 and 202, to engage the enemy from the flank by fire, but it was decided by the Brigade Commander that these two companies were to move up towards Hangman's Hill to reinforce the 1/9th Gurkhas. The German attack was anxiously watched from Battalion Headquarters, and maximum defensive fire was organised from "S" Company (Major H. C. Gregory, M.C.). The medium machine guns engaged with direct fire, and the 3-inch mortars gave sustained concentrations on the waves of the enemy moving on to the Castle. This fire caused many casualties to the enemy and blunted his attack.

Despite all this, the first charge almost carried the German Paratroops to victory, so great was the surprise, but they were driven back with heavy casualties. Fighting was bitter and close. The commander of the garrison, Major F. J. Ketteley, M.C., was killed early on, and by the end of the day all the officers of the Battalion in the Castle had been killed or wounded. Every available medium machine gun and mortar was in action almost continuously. Ammunition ran short, and many detachments would have fared badly but for the strenuous efforts of the ammunition parties organised by Regimental Sergeant-Major C. J. Rose, D.C.M., who was to gain a bar to his D.C.M. in these operations.

Major D. A. Beckett, O.C. "C" Company in the Castle, continues the narrative: "The enemy counter-attack opened with intense machine-gun fire sweeping the Castle. I have never known anything like it. It came from every angle. This lasted about ten minutes, then they were on us. We could not use our artillery D.F., because we did not know how the Rajputana Rifles or our own people were faring out in front. Our mortars had not even been registered. It had to be fought out with infantry weapons man to man.

"Frank (Major F. J. Ketteley, M.C.) went on the 'blower' to tell Battalion, whilst I did the best I could to organise the defences.

"The first attack very nearly succeeded. One or two tried to penetrate the courtyard and many were stopped only a few yards from the walls. We broke him up with Mills grenades, tommy-guns, and Brens."

This first counter-attack was smashed by the fighting spirit of men like Lieutenant P. M. F. Coghlan, O.C., No. 14 Platoon, Corporal E. Parker, and Private K. Smith, to name only three. Coghlan had just been relieved in the house which lay at the bend of Point 165. As soon as he saw what was afoot, he rallied his platoon, and to encourage them stood up directing operations in full view of the enemy. He was killed by a burst of automatic fire. Corporal Parker fought his section post coolly and efficiently until all his men were killed or wounded. The German dead, still unburied long after, bore grim testimony to his gallant work. Parker was in the end killed himself, but it is due to men like him that the only Germans to get inside the Castle were wounded, prisoners, and one emissary to request an armistice.

In the Castle a Bren gunner firing through an arrow slit, at that time vital to the defence, had been killed by a sniper. Another man moved up to take his place, and was similarly shot through the head. The German was now firing regularly at the arrow slit, the only one which covered a particular breach in the Castle walls, and so one that could not be left unmanned. Undeterred by the evident price of manning the post, Private K. Smith unhesitatingly took up the duty—and killed the sniper. He was subsequently awarded the Military Medal.

At 7.50 a.m. the Brigade Commander sent a personal message to "A" and "C" Companies, "You have done very well," but the danger was not passed, and Major Beckett continues the story:

"The lull did not last very long. The enemy had taken advantage of his first push to occupy very favourable ground and this time began with a shower of stick grenades. But we, too, were more prepared, and I had been on to Battalion Headquarters to arrange for our Vickers guns to bring enfilade fire on the western edge of the Castle. The 3-inch mortars too were used with telling effect, though the problem here was to find a place to observe from."

The time now was approximately 9.30 a.m. Little had been heard since about 7 a.m. of "B" and "D" Companies struggling towards Hangman's Hill until at 9 a.m. Sergeant Pitter (Commander No. 10 Platoon) and his Platoon Sergeant (L/Sergeant Gowlett) came into Battalion Headquarters. They reported that "B" Company had left the Castle at first light two platoons strong (reorganised into two platoons after casualties in the tank shoot of the evening before). The Company had met strong enemy forces just outside the Castle, and in the heavy fighting that ensued No. 10 Platoon was divorced from the remainder of the Company. They had tried to fight their way back into the Castle, but were surrounded by the enemy and under heavy M.G. fire from our own guns. So the platoon withdrew—seven strong—to Battalion Headquarters.

By 11.45 a.m. a message came from the 1/9th Gurkhas on Hangman's Hill to say "B" and "D" Companies had arrived in their area at an estimated strength of 40, plus 30 wounded.

A third counter-attack on the Castle was defeated during the morning. Of this attack Major Beckett says in a contemporary letter: "Battalion now warned us to expect a third counter-attack, and asked if we could state whether Point 165 was clear of our own troops. Captain Jenkins (Rajputana Rifles) said he had not been in touch with his men for two hours and would assume they had been overrun. Defensive fire was therefore laid on very close in, and as soon as the attack started a full 'blunderbuss' of artillery, mortars, medium machine guns, and small arms was brought to bear. This counter-attack was supported by a tank from the road bend above Point 165 and a systematic shoot aimed at the destruction of our west wall commenced. As a result the wall collapsed, burying about 10 of our party."

However, this attack was not pressed home, owing to the effectiveness of the defensive fire.

In the afternoon two enemy stretcher-bearers approached the Castle walls under a Red Cross flag, and "C" Company took advantage of the lull to dig in the ruins for the buried men, who included Captain D. J. Beech, M.C., and Lieutenant R. A. Ulph.

During all this action the Battalion was, as ever during the campaign, magnificently supported by the 1st Field Regiment Royal Artillery. In addition to the forward observation officer attached to "C" Company were Major O. R. W. Oswald, D.S.O., and an O.P. party waiting to go forward to join the 1/9th Gurkha Rifles. Not only did they maintain the highest traditions of the Royal Regiment in manning continuously in spite of casualties an exposed O.P. within a few yards of the enemy, but they set a splendid example in fighting as infantry as occasion demanded.

The operations for the capture of the Monastery now had to be abandoned. At 4.30 p.m., on the 19th March, after more than twelve hours of almost continuous close-quarter fighting, the Brigade Commander gave orders for the relief of the companies in the Castle, and for the return of "B" and "D" Companies from the position of the 1/9th Gurkhas on Point 435. The 1/4th Essex was relieved that night by the 6th Royal West Kent, a battalion of the 78th Division.

By 6 a.m., on the morning of the 20th, the remnants of the Battalion assembled in the old area in the Wadi Villa whence they had set out five days before. Casualties had been heavy, and exceeded 150 exclusive of those still forward with the 1/9th Gurkhas. "A" Company numbered 21 and "C" Company 13. Major D. A. Beckett was the only officer to return from "A" and "C" Companies, and Major C. J. Kenrick the only officer to return from "B" and "D." Both had been wounded and were evacuated. Lieutenant-Colonel A. Noble was severely wounded during the afternoon of the 19th March whilst taking the Divisional Commander to an observation post forward of Battalion Headquarters. Major L. W. A. Chappell, M.C., assumed command, Major H. C. Gregory, M.C., acting until Major Chappell could get to Battalion Headquarters. Lieutenant-Colonel Noble had commanded since November 1941, a distinguished period of command, in which the 1/4th Essex had gained renown. Apart from his personal qualities, it was probably his power to express his orders with complete clarity that enabled him to lead his battalion with such great success throughout a prolonged period of active warfare.

Back in the Wadi Villa the Battalion continued to suffer casualties from continuous shelling and mortaring, while they waited in reserve for the return of the remnants of "B" and "D" Companies from Hangman's Hill. Here they had been holding on with the Gurkhas, although completely cut off from the British lines.

The shortage of water was acute, and the job of water-finder fell on Sergeant Brewer, who every evening, despite the continuous shelling and mortaring put down by both sides, would take as many water-bottles as he could carry and return with them filled. Despite its peculiar taste no questions were asked: it was wet and everbody was glad to have it. On the fourth night, Brewer returned from his trip much later than usual but with water.

Questioned, "as we had suspected the water came from a shell hole and as he was about to start refilling operations a Very light had disclosed a former occupant 'in residence'—a dead mule which Brewer assessed as having been there for about three weeks."

On the 23rd March, the Brigade Commander asked Lieutenant-Colonel Chappell to find an officer who would make his way forward to Hangman's Hill and take the Gurkhas orders for their withdrawal.

Major Beckett continues:

"The story of Cassino would not be complete without reference to the exploits of the late Major M. S. Mallinson, who was awarded the M.C. for great gallantry on Hangman's Hill. He had been left out of battle (L.O.B.) earlier in the battle, but on March 23rd the decision was taken to evacuate the Gurkhas from Hangman's Hill, and accordingly three officers from the Brigade volunteered to find their way through to them with these orders. Each was given a pigeon with a small cylinder containing slips of paper. On these was written St. George, St. Andrew, and St. David, according to the nationality of the officer concerned. The pigeon was to be sent back with one slip if the officer succeeded, and two if he was wounded or otherwise unsuccessful.

"After what must have seemed an age to those waiting anxiously for news one pigeon flew in. It carried two slips of paper. For a time hopes fell, the difficulties were so great. Then two little specks appeared in the sky, and the remaining two pigeons arrived bringing news that Major Mallinson's efforts were successful and the Gurkhas, with some of our wounded under the care of L/Corporal Hazle, D.C.M., were led safely off Hangman's Hill."

It is proposed to interpose here a letter written after the war by L/Corporal A. J. Smith, a section commander under Lieutenant T. Stead, as illustrating the conditions for those on Hangman's Hill:

"Our task was to link up with gallant 'Johnny Gurkha' well up on Hangman's Hill. . . . We made our way through the ruins of Cassino up to the damaged Castle, and at 4 a.m. went through an archway and immediately grounded, and I found I had a 'sangar' of dead bodies, much to my disagreeable surprise.

"As light approached, we made our way up the notorious Hill, and as I glanced back I saw two Jerry parachutists just disappearing into the then slightly damaged Yellow House. I soon found out their purpose, as one of them just nicked my right thigh with a bullet.

"By this time the R.A. were plastering our surroundings with 25-pounder smoke shells, and we were well covered from view for most of the time.

"After taking up positions in a hole alongside the winding road which circled the hill up to the Monastery, I gave orders for the lads to keep their eyes open for any move by the rest of the platoon, as I was going to watch the extreme edge of our position for possible Jerry infiltration.

"There was no sign of the rest of the platoon, so I made my mind up to try and link with the Gurkhas, and started to advance cautiously uphill, and was rudely told to 'halt' by a pleasant-sounding voice. . . . I found I was on the position of 'C' Company 2nd N.Z. Battalion, and was taken to see Major Reynolds, the company commander.

"He told us to take up position with his lads. His H.Q. was in a well that was more like a cave, for one went in through a doorway, and about 10 feet inside was the water well, but he also had about four wounded chaps in there out of the way of the mortars Jerry so persistently poured down. After a while I went to see the Major, and was about to return when a mortar landed right in front of the Major, myself, and about eight New Zealanders. After the initial stunning, I found I had fourteen different holes in me, luckily none very large, and four other chaps were hit also. The injured medical orderly patched his pals up and then gave my many punctures treatment.

"During the next five days we were in that well we had little to eat, but I had many Oxos, as I was carrying them in my haversack, for I was canteen corporal for our section. The American Air Force tried dropping food and medical supplies to us, but it was only on the fifth night that we managed to obtain one of the canisters, and that had Gurkha rations—chappatties—in it, also a gallon of rum.

"With more chaps getting wounded and coming into the well, and the 'Black trackers'—Maoris—trying to link up with us and so release us from being surrounded by the Jerries, we were in a tight fix.

"On the fifth night Major Reynolds had orders to vacate the positions and retire to the destroyed town. He said he felt a cad, but had to leave us wounded behind. So we fixed up a Red Cross flag by using a white parachute and tearing strips off another red parachute for the cross, and put that on a long stick ready for the morning to show it was now an aid post, and we weren't mortared any more after that.

"The walking wounded went out at 9 a.m. the next morning, carrying another Red Cross flag improvised from the same parachutes, and we had been told that the New Zealand stretcher-parties would come for us that morning some time. Time went on, and we heard shouts from the stretcher-bearers, but couldn't make them hear us. About one o'clock in the afternoon I suggested to the New Zealanders that we try to hobble our way to the Castle in daylight, as I thought it was about 600 yards, and we ought to make it by darkness at 6 p.m. if we left at three o'clock.

"This we did after a tot of rum (horrible stuff for a T.T.), but we got held up by one of the chaps complaining of his ankle, which I heard later was fractured. As luck had it, the S.-B.s had decided at another go for us that afternoon, and I spotted them leaving the Castle and told the boys to relax, as all was now well. After a while the S.-B.s (nearly all officers and sergeants) reached us, and we were being carried towards the Castle when a Jerry parachutist medical orderly stopped our party and told us to go back from whence we had come, as the Jerries had supposed to have seen some of their wounded turned back by our people.

"Well, we just sat down in the open, and the officers started appealing to the orderly whilst we sat very dejected at this turn of events when our long ordeal seemed over. I don't think I ever felt so delighted and so dejected in so short a period.

"The Jerry suggested that two of our party should go to see their commander to negotiate, but the New Zealanders were a trifle wary about this, as two of them had been nearly 'snaffled' in a similar situation in the desert. But an officer and a sergeant volunteered to go with the orderly, and they disappeared over the crest of the hill with us left sitting very disheartened awaiting the 'Yea or Nay' which meant so much to us.

"About twenty minutes later they came back with a tough-looking Jerry sergeant, who was nearly blown up by a German mortar which, though aimed at the Castle, fell well short of the target near him.

"The news was music to our ears, as the commander had allowed us to advance on our journey. I was so delighted once more that I completely forgot the holes in my leg, and started to walk very fast towards the Castle, but it only opened my wounds again, causing me to be carried once more.

"On reaching the advanced R.A.P., we must have looked a sight with seven days' beard and our bandages filthy on our wounds. My arm wound was in an advanced state of gangrene, and a new and clean bandage was a very welcome sight. So, after being wounded on the 19th March, it was the 26th before I found myself in the very comfortable surroundings of the 14th Canadian Hospital."

Among those who had gone forward with "B" and "D" Companies had been L/Corporal E. B. Hazle, one of the Battalion stretcher-bearers. Hazle had already greatly distinguished himself at the battle of Alamein by rescuing British and Indian wounded under heavy fire, although he himself had been severely wounded, work for which he was awarded the D.C.M.

In the advance to Hangman's Hill and the subsequent holding of the position, there was no medical officer with the Essex and Gurkha personnel on the Hill. Hazle, however, was equal to the occasion, and took over the duties of R.M.O., and for six days treated more than 70 wounded, both British and Indian. For this L/Corporal Hazle, who had been ably assisted by L/Corporal Piper, received a Bar to his D.C.M.

The story of the 1/4th Essex at Cassino would be incomplete without mention of the regimental medical officer, Captain R. J. Pellow, R.A.M.C., who, while the battle for the Castle was being fought out above and around him, was tending an ever-growing company of wounded, which included British, New Zealanders, Gurkhas, Indians, both Hindu and Mohammedan, and a Sikh, as well as several Germans. The tiny aid post, very exposed in a tiny courtyard, became hopelessly overcrowded, but despite the difficulties, care for the wounded was never for one moment relaxed. He was to be awarded the Military Cross for his services with the Battalion in Italy.

On the 2nd April, 1944, the 1/4th Essex left the Fifth Army and the area of Cassino with few regrets.

With the Eighth Army, 1944

Back with the Eighth Army, the Battalion moved across to Termoli on the Adriatic coast near the mouth of the River Trigno, and from thence across to Lanciano, finally taking over a sector of the front line near Consalvi on the 9th April.

No rest period had been given to the Battalion after Cassino, nor yet had there been reinforcements to bring companies anywhere near war establishment. Even three rifle companies in the line, each some fifty strong, were hard to organise and harder to maintain. The front was a complete contrast to the close quarters of Cassino, a widely dispersed battalion layout with a no-man's-land some miles in extent. It was once more a war of patrols and raids, shelling and counter-shelling.

On the 14th April the 1/4th Essex was relieved by the 1/6th Rajputana Rifles and moved into brigade reserve.

Into the line again on the 20th April in the vicinity of Orsogna, the Battalion suffered two blows before it was again relieved. "C" Company Headquarters received a direct hit on the afternoon of the 22nd April, Major Mallinson and 7 other ranks being killed. This was the first misfortune. Then the following day a message was received at 6 a.m. at "C" Company Headquarters from No. 15 Platoon: "We are being attacked." It was the only message. The platoon had been suddenly raided and killed or taken prisoner to a man. Patrols on the ground and a reconnaissance by an air O.P. failed to disclose any trace. It must be appreciated that at this stage very large frontages were being held. There was no connected front line on either side and no-man's-land in some cases was several miles wide. Thus platoons and sections were isolated and far from immediate support in the event of sudden and surprise raid or attack.

Major D. A. Beckett, D.S.O., writing after the war says: "The attack on No. 15 Platoon and its successful outcome from the German point of view was explained after a walk over the ground when the Germans withdrew five weeks later.

"No. 15 Platoon position consisted of a cave, with two slit trenches just outside the mouth and two in the mouth itself. The remainder of the platoon usually sat in the cave. This could only be reached from the British lines after dark, as it was situated on a forward slope about 400 yards from the German position at Orsogna. It could not be supported directly by the other platoons of the company.

"I was told at a later date by two members of the platoon who were taken prisoner and subsequently escaped, that the Germans attacked shortly after first light, and having killed or wounded the men in the slit trenches at the outer edge of the cave position, brought the cave itself under direct fire. They then threw small tear-gas bombs, which effectively reduced the efficiency of the defenders, who had no gas masks with them.

"After an interval to allow the gas to take effect, the enemy charged the cave, and one of their number addressed the little garrison in English, threatening to seal up the mouth of the cave with an explosive charge unless the survivors came out and surrendered.

"Utterly isolated, demoralised by the tear-gas, and realising that their position was incapable of successful defence, the platoon surrendered. They were now to learn yet another bitter lesson, for their captors took them to another cave, almost identical with their platoon position, immediately below them. Here they remained all that day, learning that the raid had been planned weeks before. They were then removed to Orsogna after dark and eventually to Arezzo, from where two, L/Corporal Gaskell and Private Mahoney, subsequently escaped."

In studying this minor set-back it is clear that the position was ideally suited as an objective for a raid such as occurred. The position had been occupied by many battalions during the previous four months in which the front had been static in front of Orsogna. It was bad luck for the 1/4th Essex that the raid, assiduously practised for weeks, should have been put into effect during their tour of duty in that sector of the front.

Towards the end of the month the award of the D.S.O. to Major D. A. Beckett was announced. This was the fourth D.S.O. to be won by the 1/4th Essex.

The whole of May was spent in alternating spells in the front line and in reserve in the area of Orsogna.

It was a month of intense patrolling activity, with units holding very extended frontages, for once more General Alexander had transferred part of his forces west of the Apennines in order to attack on the front between Cassino and the sea. This attack was successful, the Gustav Line broken, and a junction at last made with the force at Anzio.

But the 4th Indian Division this time remained on the Adriatic sector of the front, holding, as has been said, a very wide frontage.

One night a 1/4th Essex fighting patrol of 9 men left the Battalion area at dusk with the task of forming an ambush on a suspected enemy patrol route. The patrol reached the ambush area and, forming three sides of a square, settled down to a long, cold, and silent wait. After a long time it was suddenly noted that the patrol was now 10 strong, a tenth member had slipped quietly into position next to Private Card,

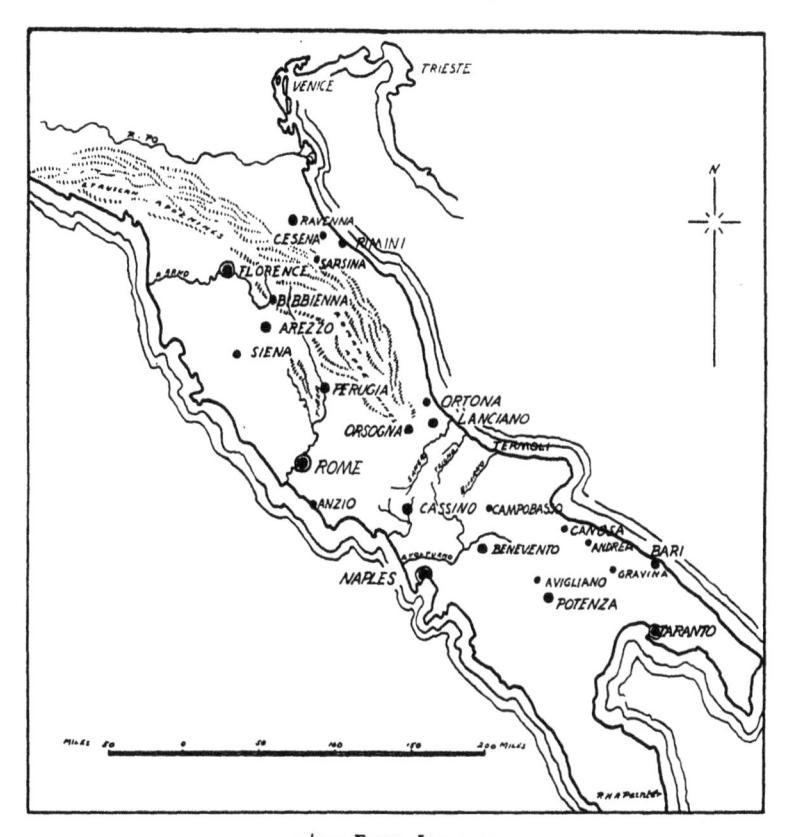

1/4TH ESSEX, ITALY, 1944.

the end man on one side of the square. Nobody moved or spoke, and the situation was tense. To deal with the intruder would be to give away the ambush, but shortly before the patrol leader decided to withdraw, the tenth member quietly stood up, yawned, and, noiselessly as he had come, moved off. It was a fox, and it had remained with the patrol for more than half an hour.

However, other patrols were not to escape so easily. There was the patrol from No. 8 Platoon, led by Lieutenant E. Rivers, which ran into an area of British anti-personnel mines well out in no-man's-land. Four casualties were caused by the first "S" mine, and then the patrol, bunched up as they were carrying the 4 casualties, stumbled across the trip wire of yet another mine. Lieutenant Rivers and 5 other ranks were killed and 11 were wounded. The Divisional Commander telephoned Lieutenant-Colonel Chappell and expressed his regrets at the mishap which had cost the Battalion dear.

In June 1944 the 1/4th Essex was switched to Campobasso for training in hill warfare, but on the 10th July arrived back in the Divisional concentration area at Andrea.

Since they had last been in the line, the Fifth Army, reinforced by a large proportion of the Eighth Army, had entered Rome on the 4th June. The retreating Germans had been pursued northwards, Perugia, in the central sector, being entered on the 20th June and Siena a little later. But forces withdrawn from the Fifth and Eighth Armies for the landings in France had so weakened General Alexander's hand that he was unable to prevent Marshal Kesselring falling back in comparatively good order to the Gothic Line running through Florence and Rimini.

It was to the central sector of the British front south of the formidable German defensive line that the 1/4th Essex moved from the concentration area at Andrea. In this central sector the German forces were still some distance from the main Gothic Line, and it was their purpose to delay the advance of the Allied army by every means within their powers for as long as possible.

After the fall of Siena at the end of June there were to be seven weeks of severe fighting before the thirty miles that lay between Siena and Florence could be covered. Similarly, seven weeks of stubborn fighting were ahead of the 1/4th Essex in their advance to Arezzo to the north-east of Siena. As Major Beckett says: "To give them their due, the Germans were good defensive fighters. Pounded by day and night from the air, their transport decimated by continual bombing, they hauled their guns and equipment back by oxen and mules. Driven from the main roads, they took to mountain trails and country byways overhung with trees. As they moved north, they laid waste villages, carried out extensive demolitions, and committed atrocities upon any civilian who attempted to impede them."

The line of advance took the 1/4th Essex from Andrea to Vincenco, to Gio Jello and to Pezzano, and on the 22nd July into Arezzo. They had been days of slow advance in thickly wooded and difficult country. Ammunition and supplies had to be brought up to forward companies by pack mules, many of which were lost from machine-gun fire as they moved along the narrow tracks. The companies, too, suffered constant casualties from machine guns and shell fire. Air support and artillery fire could not assist our advance to any great degree, owing to the nebulous nature of the defence, and the lack of any firm line. Mines were found everywhere, and at any moment the advance might be countered by enemy infiltration round the flanks.

Arezzo had just fallen to the New Zealanders. As the 4th Indian Division came up to the town the Divisional Commander was anxious to push on. The Battalion was warned as it moved into the town on 22nd July that the 5th Indian Infantry Brigade would move forward the following day, and be prepared to attack on the 25th the positions of the German 305th Division on Route 73 and at Piantolle. The Brigade would be required to capture Gello and Guaccano and be prepared for heavy counter-attacks and mortaring. There was little knowledge of the enemy, and therefore it was not possible to carry out any artillery registration on his positions.

The attack was carried out by the 1/9th Gurkhas and the 3/10th Baluch Regiment. The 1/4th Essex, in reserve at Antria and organised on a mule-pack transport basis, suffered considerably from shelling, losing 6 killed and 14 wounded before it moved forward to pass through the 3/10th Baluch. It reached Gello on the 27th July.

Before advancing farther, the 1/4th Essex was able to send 50 men under Major H. C. Gregory, M.C., back to Arezzo, where they paraded with other units of the 4th Indian Division on the evening of the 25th July, on the occasion of the visit of His Majesty the King to Arezzo. It was the second time His Majesty had seen the 1/4th Essex during the war, the first occasion being at Tripoli in June 1943.

"It was in Gello," to quote from the booklet *The Tiger Triumphs*, "that the ghost music was heard. The sentimental Boche, carolling his *lieder*, has guided his assailants on more than one dark night. But never before had thin instrumental strains come down the wind, to rise, to die, to pause and begin again, and ever to draw nearer. Along a steep mountain pathway the Essex stood to arms. A German corporal came ambling up the trail playing his mouth-organ. He was sure the English would not shoot him if they heard music. He was a soldier of eleven years' service who had fought in Norway, in France, and at El

Alamein. His company commander was an idiot. He preferred to desert rather than to serve under such a fool."

Throughout this district the Germans had made war in no uncertain fashion. Rape, murder, and cases of arson were frequent. Suspected partisans were hanged, their relatives deported or shot, and their villages destroyed. Reprisals were fierce. When a patrol from the 1/4th Essex shot up an enemy garrison in Guilano, the Germans quickly burnt the village. Every device was utilised to delay the Allied advance, but without success.

Pushing on from Gello, the 1/4th Essex, by limited company advances, had reached Scille by the 1st August. The forward movement was now going more quickly, for the enemy was nearing his Gothic Line and so falling back into his prepared defences, followed up both by the 4th Indian Division and by the 10th Indian Division on its flank.

With his forces now up to the Gothic Line, General Alexander planned to attack that major obstacle towards the end of August 1944. On the 3rd August the 1/4th Essex received the following message from Headquarters Eighth Army:

"PERSONAL MESSAGE
FROM THE
ARMY COMMANDER

"You have won great victories. To advance 220 miles from Cassino to Florence in three months is a notable achievement in the Eighth Army's history—to each one of you in the Eighth Army and in the Desert Air Force, my grateful thanks.

"Now we begin the last lap. Swiftly and secretly, once again, we have moved right across Italy an army of immense strength and fighting power—to break the Gothic Line.

"Victory in the coming battles means the beginning of the end for the German Armies in Italy.

"Let every man do his utmost, and again success will be ours.

"Good luck to you all.
"OLIVER LEESE,
"*Lieutenant-General.*

"TAC. H.Q.,
 "EIGHTH ARMY,
  "*August* 1944."

But the 1/4th Essex had suffered heavily at Cassino in March. It had been granted no rest after that gruelling test, and had been almost continuously in action ever since under very trying conditions. Now, at the beginning of August, after almost four and a half months of battle, not unnaturally the Battalion was tired. So when, with the prospect of yet another major attack ahead, the Brigade Commander visited Lieutenant-Colonel Chappell and questioned its ability to endure another severe test in its present state, the Commanding Officer, very rightly, agreed that he could not guarantee it.

The 1/4th Essex had fought its way back to El Alamein in June and July 1942. It had fought its way forward from El Alamein to Tunis in 1942 and 1943. With Cassino as a battle honour it had, perhaps, had more than its share of the Italian campaign in 1944. The Battalion had been bled white: reinforcements and an adequate period of training were vitally necessary, even if it meant leaving the 4th Indian Division.

The 1/4th Essex remained in the line until the 10th August, 1944, maintaining fighting patrols and receiving casualties from shell fire to the last moment before it was relieved by the 1st King's Own from the 10th Indian Division. The next day the unit was visited by the Divisional Commander. He explained his full appreciation that the Battalion needed a period of reorganisation, including changes in battle-worn personnel, and said that it was to leave the operational command of the 4th Indian Division for a time, but would continue its association by retaining the right to wear the divisional sign.

On the 12th August the Commander of the 10th Corps (Lieutenant-General Sir Richard L. McCreery, K.C.B., D.S.O., M.B.E., M.C.) visited the Commanding Officer and was told the history of the Battalion. He agreed that changes in personnel were necessary, as was, also, a period out of the line for reorganisation. He suggested that this period should be either two or three months in Italy or a period of approximately six weeks in the United Kingdom.

Before the 1/4th Essex was withdrawn from the 5th Indian Infantry Brigade, letters of appreciation were received by the Commanding Officer from the Commanding Officers of the 1/9th Gurkha Rifles and the 3/10th Baluch Regiments, battalions which had been companions with the 1/4th Essex in so many victories on the long road from El Alamein. In addition, a deputation of British and Gurkha officers from the 1/9th Gurkha Rifles visited the Battalion, and made a ceremonial presentation to the Commanding Officer of a kukri as a token of that Battalion's esteem of the 1/4th Essex. The kukri was issue pattern and had been used in battle.

And so, after a short period in the line with the 10th Indian Division, the 1/4th Essex, still wearing the "Eagle" flashes of the 4th Indian Division, was withdrawn on the 20th August 1944 to rest and retrain. The Corps Commander told Lieutenant-Colonel Chappell that he must start intensive training by the 2nd September, and be ready to join a division by the 7th October. In all problems of rehabilitation of the Battalion, the very greatest assistance was received from Lieutenant-General Sir Richard McCreery, the Commander 10th Corps, from Lieutenant-General Sir John Harding, Chief of Staff to the C.-in-C. Allied Armies, Italy, and from Brigadier C. M. Paton, the Deputy Adjutant-General at A.A.I. Headquarters.

On the 1st October, 1944, the Battalion was again ready for battle, and received orders to reorganise forthwith on a three-rifle company basis with an establishment of 30 officers and 700 other ranks. Those surplus to the new establishment left the next day, and the Battalion moved forward towards the front.

To quote Major Beckett:

"The landscape was changing when the Battalion returned to the line. Already the hand of autumn had touched the great hills of the Apennines. The leaves were thinning on the trees and rain was plentiful. It was a pleasant period as we joined forces with old friends of Desert days."

When it arrived in Savio Valley, the Battalion found itself once more under 10th Corps, and part of a small group of units known as Wheelerforce charged with the opening up of Route 71 to effect a junction with the main forces then engaged in heavy fighting before the Lombardy Plains.

The immediate obstacle to this was a strongly held German position dominating the road above Sarsina, a small town tucked into the side of a hill and rising steeply from the river. Forward of this, on the British side of the town, the Germans had blown two stretches of road. Further work by engineers on these two rather forbidding demolitions was impracticable without the capture of the high ground beyond. The key feature on the ridge was Tezzo, a collection of buildings on a "gaunt green whaleback," from which the enemy maintained observation on all British movements.

In the first week of October it was decided to assault these defences. The details were settled at a conference attended by the acting Corps

Commander 10th Corps, Lieutenant-Colonel Lindsay, commanding a small force "Lindforce," Lieutenant-Colonel L. W. A. Chappell, M.C., 1/4th Essex, and the Commanding Officer of the Nabhar Akal, a battalion of Indian State Troops.

On the night of 4th/5th October, "a dark night lashed with rain," says Major Beckett, "our men, led by Major C. J. Kenrick, M.C., with an Indian State Troops battalion (the Nabhar Akal), on their left, toiled up the steep slopes to put out the enemy's eyes and drive him from his observation posts. Going in with tommy-gun and bayonet, they gained the heights in a matter of minutes, killing, wounding, or taking prisoner most of the garrison.

"They gained some very useful information, and succeeded in capturing a complete overprint of the Gothic Line defences. Also a marked map showing their gun positions conveniently left behind by a German F.O.O. Both were eagerly snapped up, and our gunners gave the enemy batteries such effective attention that they did not trouble us again for some time."

The capture of Tezzo had a marked, if not decisive effect on the operation. A heavy artillery attack on a strong-point east of the river forced a further withdrawal.

The advance was continued from Sarsina to Monte Petra, and on to La Gondolfo. Many casualties were sustained, but the advance continued. Headquarters Eighth Army wrote to say they offered their congratulations on the capture of Tezzo, and that the prisoners taken brought the Army total in the present operations to 10,000.

Better still, on the 15th October, 1944, after another week's pressure on the enemy by the 1/4th Essex, Lieutenant-General Sir Richard L. McCreery, K.C.B., D.S.O., M.B.E., M.C., now the Commander of the Eighth Army, wrote:

> "Main Headquarters,
> "Eighth Army,
> C.M.F.
> "15th October, '44.

"Dear Chappell,

"I want to send you and all ranks of your Battalion my congratulations on the excellent record of your Battalion during your recent operations to the West of Route 71.

"The Battalion has shown a fine determination, skill, endurance, and initiative, often in very bad weather, which has enabled you to achieve excellent progress with a very limited force. Your operations on the axis of Route 71 have greatly contributed to the success of 5th Corps on your right, and I am certain that the pressure which you have been able to maintain will also greatly contribute to the operations of the Polish Corps.

"My best congratulations and thanks to you all, and good luck and success in the future.

"Yours sincerely,
R. L. McCreery.

LIEUTENANT-COLONEL L. W. A. CHAPPELL, M.C.,
Commanding 1/4th Essex.

On the 16th October Lieutenant-Colonel Chappell was wounded by shell fire at Schiazzano. Command was assumed temporarily by Major H. C. Gregory, M.C., until the arrival, on the 4th November, of Lieutenant-Colonel V. C. Magill-Cuerdon.

Meanwhile, the enemy commenced a further withdrawal, and our patrols, moving with considerable skill, gave him little peace.

"For his part," says Major Beckett, "the Germans sowed the area behind them thick with mines, and one night a party of men from 'A' Company, on a harassing mission, suffered casualties from anti-personnel mines within a few yards of a German position. Notwithstanding the risks involved, the medical officer, Captain R. Pellow, M.C., set out with a party of stretcher-bearers and recovered the wounded under the very noses of the enemy. At the same time he earned the distinction of being, as far as we knew, the first M.O. (other than as a P.W.) to give a plasma transfusion before an audience of German soldiers, who, to do them justice, permitted them to continue in their work unhindered."

On the 21st October, it was decided to send a fighting patrol from "A" Company under Captain G. Stuart to Giaggiola, after having first established a firm base at Pieve Ravoschio. This patrol was very successful. It took a prisoner at Cassa Curboroa, who proved to be a deserter from the 871st Regiment of the 336th Division, and who gave information of the enemy garrison in Giaggiola.

After a night march through mud and rain, Captain Stuart's patrol surprised the German garrison from the 2nd Battalion 870th Grenadier Regiment and took all 13 men prisoners. This penetration was quickly exploited. Important gains were made by the Battalion itself and by flanking units who, driving from the north-east, made valuable progress towards the hills dominating the approaches to Cesena.

On the 29th October the 18th Lorried Infantry Brigade, in which the 1/4th Essex was now serving, was transferred from under command of the 1st Armoured Division to command of the Polish Corps, and on the 31st October was withdrawn via Civitella–San Sofia–Bibbienna to Arezzo, where it was given three days' rest.

During this period, on the 2nd November, the 1/4th Essex received yet another complimentary letter. This time on the subject of the patrol which had carried out the rapid advance to Giaggiola under extremely adverse weather conditions. The message had come from the Headquarters of 1st Armoured Division and said: "A patrol from your 'A' Company recently carried out a rapid advance to Giaggiola under extremely adverse conditions and captured 14 P.W. When General Anders, G.O.C. Polish Corps, was informed of this incident, he at once rang up General Hull, G.O.C. 1st British Armoured Division, and asked that his personal congratulations should be conveyed to all concerned in this excellent piece of work. He remarked that he was proud to have such enterprising and vigorous troops under his command."

At the end of their short rest, the Battalion embussed on the 4th November, and moved from Arezzo to Rimini, the Adriatic port at the eastern flank of the Gothic Line which had been captured towards the end of September 1944. Here the 1/4th Essex joined "Porterforce," a small but interesting force named after its commander, Lieutenant-Colonel A. M. Horsbrugh-Porter, D.S.O., with which it was to serve until the 13th November.

The 1/4th Essex was now at last out of the close and mountainous country in which it had lived and fought for so long. Now on the bleak and windswept plains of Lombardy all ranks had the unfamiliar experience of fighting over flat country interspersed with farmsteads and cut by canals and deep ditches, which with the autumn rain had spread over fields and marshes.

The 1/4th Essex took up positions between Rence and the Fussate Canal. Its task, with the 27th Lancers, the 2nd Canadian Field Regiment, the 5th Medium Regiment R.C.A., and other units in, or in support of, "Porterforce," was to squeeze the Germans from a strongly defended position by every means short of actual direct assault. "This," as Major Beckett says, "called for very active patrolling to discover all we could about him, and then leave the guns and tanks and small fighting patrols to force him from his posts by sheer fire power." This task was accomplished. Pushing forward with comparatively light casualties, the 1/4th worked its way from Zaccaria to Gambellara. On the 14th the Battalion was relieved by the Westminster Regiment of Canada and concentrated at San Pietro in Vincon.

The long and arduous Italian campaign was, for the 1/4th Essex, now over. It moved first to Rimini on the 16th November and then by road and rail to Taranto. Here it rejoined the 5th Indian Brigade and 4th Indian Division, and sailed, on the 7th December, 1944, for further service in Greece.

Up to the time of sailing for Greece, the 1/4th Essex had been awarded the following honours: 4 D.S.O.s, 2 Bars to the M.C., 10 M.C.s, 2 Bars to the D.C.M., 5 D.C.M.s, and 22 M.M.s, a total of 45 awards for gallant and distinguished services in the field. A complete list of honours and awards given to the Battalion appears as an appendix to this chapter.

Section VII

GREECE, 1944-46

Greek guerrilla bands had been fighting the Germans since 1942. These were nominally under the command of the Supreme Allied Commander in the Middle East, and were formed into five separate organisations, of which the most important were E.L.A.S. (National Popular Liberation Army), E.D.E.S. (National Democratic Greek Army) and E.A.M. (National Liberation Party).

By the autumn of 1944 the southern areas of Greece had been almost cleared of Germans. On the 14th October Athens and the Piræus had been occupied by the British and efforts made to reconcile the now openly fighting National Bands in an effort to throw out the Germans and to unite the Greeks for the physical and economic recovery of the country under a democratic government. The party that had the largest support in the country was E.A.M., and its leader—Papandreou—sought to form a representative government. This, however, was impossible so long as the forces of E.L.A.S. and E.D.E.S. were in being and terrorising the districts in which they had a superiority.

The Greek Government, with the support of Lieutenant-General Sir Ronald Scobie, Commander-in-Chief of the new Greek Army, announced its determination to disband these resistance groups by the

10th December, 1944, and to re-form the Greek Army as the regular armed forces of the nation.

It was necessary to have additional British troops in the country if this policy was to succeed. Among the formations sent was the 4th Indian Division.

At the moment of the landing of the 5th Indian Infantry Brigade in the Piræus, the 2/5th Leicesters and 16th D.L.I. of the 139th Infantry Brigade were holding a tiny perimeter round naval installations at the Piræus. Their task had been clearing the harbour area and maintaining sea communication with Athens, but they were inadequate for the task. It was thus determined that the first task of the 5th Infantry Brigade would be to join up with the forces already there.

Except for the tiny area held by "Block" force as it was known, all the rest of the Piræus and Athens was held by the E.L.A.S. guerrilla forces, with an estimated strength of anything between 30,000 and 45,000. This larger force had to be defeated by the smaller British forces, which were handicapped by lack of local knowledge, whereas their opponents knew every street and alley in the city. Also, resistance groups can in emergency swiftly change from their semi-uniform to full civilian clothes and so mingle with crowds and effect a get-away.

This was the situation when the 1/4th Essex came ashore at Quay 8, Piræus, during the night 9th/10th December, 1944, to take up positions on the left flank of the 2/5th Leicesters.

Next morning the Essex passed through the left of the Leicesters and began to clear up the nearby built-up area. This was the first stage of an advance, supported by some tanks and the fire from a corvette, to seal off an area big enough to enable the rest of the 5th Brigade to land and undertake a sweeping operation to clear the whole of the eastern side of the harbour.

By the evening of the 11th December the cordon was completed, and the 3/10th Baluch and 1/9th Gurkhas, who had now landed, began to winkle out all E.L.A.S. pockets in the lower peninsula. This task was completed by the night of the 13th December, and all ground up to the Essex cordon cleared of the enemy.

This methodical clearance of the area street by street and block by block had been achieved in the face of fanatical resistance supported by machine-gun and mortar fire, and had cost the 1/4th Essex several casualties each day since the landing.

During the 14th and 15th the Battalion battled its way along the water-front in the face of stiff opposition. On the 16th it was swung

1/4TH ESSEX, GREECE, 1944-45.

from left to right of the line and came up on the right of the 16th D.L.I. In doing so it effected a partial break-out and finally cleared the enemy from the peninsula.

Thus the first intentions of the 5th Indian Infantry Brigade had been achieved—the clearance of the Kallipolis peninsula and the establishment of communication between the port of Piræus and Athens itself.

On the night of the 20th December, the 1/4th Essex was relieved by the 16th D.L.I. On the night of the 21st/22nd it was launched in a small amphibious operation across the harbour to land with other units of the Brigade on the north side of Megas Linin and clear the inner harbour of E.L.A.S. bands.

The 4th British Division was now landing. It was essential that all landing jetties should be free from small-arms fire, and so again the 1/4th Essex was committed to the same slow advance, block by block, harassed all the time by snipers.

At first tactical surprise had been achieved from the landing, but within forty-eight hours E.L.A.S. had reacted with vigour and strong counter-attacks, supported by mortar and M.G. fire, were experienced. Their failure was the turning-point of the campaign. A drive started that was to take the British forces through to the northern outskirts of the city.

In the advance, a boot and shoe store near Battalion H.Q. had been badly damaged. Strong orders had already been issued on looting, but in view of the temptation afforded by this damaged and derelict store, the Adjutant thought it advisable to issue a gentle reminder on the subject of looting. Although no proof had been offered, it was also thought advisable to parade three old warriors and personally warn them, not only against future looting, but that if they had been tempted they were to return the loot immediately. Dismissing them, one of whom was his batman, the Adjutant went to his quarters ahead of the batman, only to find an extremely smart pair of bedroom slippers peeping discreetly from beneath the camp bed. He was sadly in need of such things and they fitted perfectly.

On Christmas Day, 1944, "C" Company stormed Papastratos Cigarette Factory, a very large block of buildings forming a strongpoint at the north-east corner of the harbour. After half an hour's bombardment by tanks, mortars, and machine guns, "C" Company forced the surrender of the garrison and took 300 prisoners. To its amazement, when the company searched the cellars of the factory, 800 women and children were found seeking refuge there. An urgent message was sent back for food for them. By evening a soup kitchen had been set up and all had been fed, for many of them the first meal for four or five days.

This Christmas of fighting in Athens was, ironically, the first war-time Christmas spent in action: 1939, Kelvedon and Witham; 1940, Freetown; 1941, Cyprus; 1942, El Adem; 1943, South Italy; and now 1944, in action in Athens.

The fight was to continue until the 8th January, 1945, when the Battalion was able to enjoy a belated Christmas Dinner at Volos, whither it had moved. On the 15th January hostilities with E.L.A.S. officially ceased. The war for the 1/4th Essex was over.

The Battalion returned to the Piræus and on the 6th February moved to Kifisia. Here it was inspected by Major-General C. H. Boucher, C.B.E., D.S.O., now commanding the 4th Indian Division. From Kifisia it was moved to Portaria and Leehonia, and from there, on the 27th March, to Edhessa.

In mid-April, as the army in Italy moved to the final offensive, every unit in the Mediterranean area received a Special Order of the Day from General Alexander:

"ALLIED FORCE HEADQUARTERS,
"*April* 1945.
"SPECIAL ORDER OF THE DAY

"Soldiers, Sailors, and Airmen of the Allied Forces in the Mediterranean Theatre.

"Final Victory is near. The German Forces are now very groggy, and only need one mighty punch to knock them out for good. The moment has now come for us to take the field for the last battle which will end the war in Europe. You know what our comrades in the West and East are doing on the battlefields. It is now our turn to play our decisive part. It will not be a walk-over: a mortally wounded beast can still be very dangerous. You must be prepared for a hard and bitter fight; but the end is quite certain—there is not the slightest shadow of doubt about that. You, who have won every battle you have fought, are going to win the last one.

"Forward then into battle with confidence, faith, and determination to see it through to the end. Godspeed and good luck to you all.
"H. R. ALEXANDER,
"*Field-Marshal*,
"*Supreme Allied Commander*
"*Mediterranean Theatre.*"

His Majesty King George VI inspects the 1/4th Battalion The Essex Regiment and stops to greet Lieutenant-Colonel A. Noble, D.S.O. Tripoli-Castel Benito Road. 19th June, 1943.

(*Imperial War Museum*)

(Inter-Services Public Relations Directorate, G.H.Q., New Delhi)
1/4TH BATTALION THE ESSEX REGIMENT. THE AREA OF MONTE CASSINO AND THE ABBE D'MONTE CASSINO. MARCH 1943.

1/4TH BATTALION THE ESSEX REGIMENT. A GROUP OF SURVIVORS OF "B" AND "D" COMPANIES AFTER THE ASSAULT ON MONASTERY HILL, 18TH/19TH MARCH, 1943.

The group includes Major M. S. Mallinson, M.C., Captain A. Lee, Captain T. R. Stead, Lieutenant D. J. Patman, Sergeants Palmer and Clatworthy, Corporals Austrin, Wilson, L/Cpls. E. B. Hazle, D.C.M., Piper, and Brewster, Privates Whipps, Horsley, Pritchard, Hawes, Clements, Hencham, Bond, Saville, Horsman, Pryce, Card, Palmer, Crane, Pell, Minchella, Harding, Mawson, Burton, Freeman, Smith, Averil, and Hedles.

And so, on the 9th April, 1945, the Eighth Army, with whom the 1/4th Essex had served so long, entered upon its last offensive to enter Austria before the surrender of the Axis forces and so complete that long journey from El Alamein.

The 1/4th Essex, celebrating V.E.-Day by a Thanksgiving Service in Edhessa, gave thought to all who had fallen along the long road, and particularly to those comrades who, in life and in death, had added lustre to the name of their regiment.

There was little time for victory celebrations, as the Battalion was now responsible for some 2,000 square miles—an area larger than that of the County of Essex—of Western Macedonia, including the whole of the frontier between Greece and Jugoslavia and a portion of the Greek frontier with Albania.

It was one of the least-settled areas in Greece, having suffered much from the occupation of Germans, Bulgarians, and Italians. Roads, transportation, and municipal service were in a chaotic state, and the whole area was a happy hunting-ground for bandits.

Under the command of Lieutenant-Colonel A. Lovelace, M.B.E., M.C., who had now taken over from Lieutenant-Colonel V. C. Magill-Cuerdon, backed by the services of the 4th Indian Division and aided by the B.R.C.S. and U.N.R.R.A., the Battalion and troops under command, including Greek National Guard and Gendarmerie at one time amounting to nearly 3,000 men, gradually restored order out of chaos.

The bandits were always reluctant to engage the British forces, and the Battalion only lost 1 killed and 2 wounded, although the Greek supporting forces suffered many more casualties.

By September 1945, as control passed progressively from Battalion hands to the Greek authorities, the 1/4th Essex was concentrated in Edhessa, the capital city of the district, where a very close liaison with, and affection for, the Battalion had grown up in the months that the Headquarters had been in the town and the Battalion scattered across the district.

It was a token of this esteem for the 1/4th Essex when, on the 21st September, 1945, the Municipal Council of Edhessa unanimously elected the Battalion as "The Honorary Regiment" of the City, and conferred the freedom of the city on the Commanding Officer, Lieutenant-Colonel Lovelace, in the following terms:

KINGDOM OF GREECE
MUNICIPALITY OF EDHESSA

The Municipal Council of Edhessa unanimously passed a resolution on the 21st September, 1945,

whereby THE
1/4TH BATTALION THE ESSEX REGIMENT
becomes
HONORARY REGIMENT
and the

Commanding Officer,

Lieutenant-Colonel A. Lovelace, M.B.E., M.C.,

becomes a Freeman of the City of Edhessa, in recognition of the many services they have rendered to the town in establishing order and security in the PELLA NOME.

Edhessa, 21st September, 1945.
(Signed)   The Nomarch (Mayor) and
Members of the Municipal Council.

As a memento of the occasion, both the Battalion and the Commanding Officer were presented with silk National flags, suitably embroidered.

By reason of his Freedom, Lieutenant-Colonel Lovelace was entitled to vote in the Greek elections.

This ceremony took place one evening in the pouring rain when the streets were flooded. Lieutenant-Colonel Lovelace continues: "In an endeavour to clear the water in front of the Town Hall, someone had taken out the manhole cover from a drain. Flushed with congratulations and Greek wine, I left the Hall saluting obvious personages, went towards the staff car and disappeared down the drain." As the Adjutant put it: "The C.O. was so keen in his new-found civic responsibilities, that he started a tour of inspection of the city's sewers right away."

Very shortly afterwards Lieutenant-Colonel Lovelace handed over command to Major R. E. O. Bell, M.C. (Sherwood Foresters), but before he went he was assured that he could always come back and become Mayor of Edhessa if he failed to find employment in Britain.

Just before Christmas 1945 Lieutenant-Colonel L. W. W. Mariott took over command.

The run-down of units and formations was now in full swing,

and the training of the new drafts and the general maintenance of a high standard of efficiency in the Battalion presented a real problem under the conditions then prevailing in the north of Greece.

On the 1st March, 1946, the 1/4th Essex moved from Edhessa to Salonika, where it embarked for Piræus. The new station was Palfalipon (Athens). The move severed the last link between the 1/4th Essex and the 4th Indian Division, now a skeleton of its former self. In Athens the Battalion came under the orders of the 13th British Division (Major-General A. H. S. Adair), and was accommodated in numerous and widely dispersed requisitioned buildings. There was a very rapid turn-over of personnel due for release. Those available were almost exclusively employed on heavy guard and security duties, for thieving by the local populace was widespread. But nevertheless determined efforts to achieve efficiency were made during the last few months of the Battalion's active life, efforts to maintain to the end the excellent record of the 1/4th Essex throughout the war.

Mention must be made of the excellent sporting name the Battalion made in 1946 by winning first the "Northern Greece" Football Tournament, and then the "All Greece" or "Plastiras" Cup. This latter victory over the 1/6th East Surreys qualified the 1/4th Essex to represent the Army in Greece against the Army in Italy.

Unfortunately, the match in Italy—1/4th Essex versus the Polish Army—was lost by the odd goal, but, then, it is rare that a battalion side has as its opponents the best of a small national army.

At the beginning of May 1946 the 1/4th Essex was put into suspended animation. So was ended a period of service by a Territorial infantry battalion that has few peers, a period in which the 1/4th Essex added distinction to their Regiment's history and brought added renown to the Territorial Army.

The 4th Battalion was resuscitated in May 1947 with the start of the post-war Territorial Army, and a short account of its activities between 1947 and 1950 is given in the last chapter of this book.

APPENDIX A

Honours and Awards, 1/4th Battalion the Essex Regiment

Distinguished Service Order

Major D. A. Beckett.
Lieutenant-Colonel A. Noble.
Major D. J. M. Smith.
Captain J. Watt.

Bar to Military Cross

Captain D. J. Beech.
Major H. C. Gregory.

Military Cross

Lieutenant D. J. Beech.
Major L. W. A. Chappell.
Captain H. C. Gregory.
Lieutenant C. Hailes.
Major C. J. Kenrick (R. Warwicks).
Captain F. J. Ketteley.
Captain M. S. Mallinson.
Captain R. J. N. Pellow (R.A.M.C.).
Captain B. P. Tully (R.A.M.C.).
Captain J. Watt.
Major H. J. Young.

Bar to Distinguished Conduct Medal

L/Corporal E. B. Hazle.
Regimental Sergeant-Major C. J. Rose.

Distinguished Conduct Medal

Sergeant E. K. Chapman.
Company Sergeant-Major W. H. Cook.
Private E. B. Hazle.
Private G. Jackson.
Regimental Sergeant-Major C. J. Rose.

Military Medal

L/Corporal C. Bartlett.
L/Sergeant H. T. Brewer.
L/Corporal G. Z. F. M. Carter.
Corporal H. Chinick.
Sergeant N. Cronk.
Sergeant J. R. Cross.
Private E. D. Davies.
L/Corporal J. Glibbery.
Private E. Gooderidge.
Private W. Hazell.
Company Sergeant-Major T. Horne.

L/Corporal G. Hudson.
Company Sergeant-Major T. S. Jones.
Sergeant J. La Plain.
Private P. G. Lewis.
L/Sergeant A. Marjoram.
L/Corporal J. E. O'Donoghue.
Corporal J. S. A. Reeder.
Private K. Smith.
Private J. Stringer.
Corporal H. T. Taylor.
Corporal H. Thompson.
Colour Sergeant (C.Q.M.S.) R. G. Wheeler.

Mention in Despatches

Corporal D. Aulem.
Corporal S. C. Bacon.
Corporal W. Bristow.
Major L. W. A. Chappell, M.C.
L/Sergeant V. Clatworthy.
Company Sergeant-Major R. Cox.
Regimental Quartermaster Sergeant N. T. H. Croucher.
Company Sergeant-Major S. Day.
Captain K. D. Edrupt.
Lieutenant-Colonel G. M. Gibson, T.D. (2)
Sergeant A. Lungley.
Lieutenant (Q.M.) S. G. Mason.
Corporal J. McQueen.
Private T. C. Nethercoat.
Lieutenant-Colonel A. Noble, D.S.O., T.D. (2)
L/Corporal L. Piper.
Private R. Richardson.
Regimental Sergeant-Major C. J. Rose, D.C.M.
Sergeant F. J. Roy.
L/Corporal A. Seagram.
Corporal H. T. Taylor
Private A. White.
Private L. Wiley.
Private R. Woodwards.

Ranks shown are those held at the time of the award.

APPENDIX B

Battle Casualties, 1/4th Battalion the Essex Regiment

Date and Action	Killed or Died of Wounds	Prisoner of War	Wounded	Missing
1942. Matruh	9 14 (whilst P.W.)	106	25	—
Alamein	26	—	83	—
1943. Benghazi (air action)	6	—	10	—
Mareth	6	—	17	—
Akarit	10	—	25	—
Enfidaville	12	—	76	3
Tunis	4	—	16	—
1944. Prior to Cassino	15	—	27	—
Cassino	49	13	108	15
After	51	16	73	—
1945–46. Greece	4	—	41	—

APPENDIX C

Battle of Djebel Garci

Report by Corporal-Thompson, 1/4th Essex, on a long-range patrol carried out under the command of Lieutenant Hailes.

Start-point: Pt. 100 (204821) before the Dj Garci.
Strength: 1 Officer, 15 O.R.s, including 1 Medical Cpl.

Leaving "B" Coy. area (Pt. 100) on the evening of the 19th April, and accompanied by a 4th Rajputana Rifles patrol, we advanced towards the enemy lines.

After moving about 800 yards, we left the Indian patrol behind us, and made our way over open ground until we reached the foothills. We had advanced through the hills for about two or three hundred yards, when suddenly we were fired on by a machine gun slightly to our right front and a mortar on our left. Hearing the enemy giving orders, we moved into a suitable position and returned their fire. On a hill to our right flank and slightly to our rear another M.G. started firing, and finding we were nearly surrounded, Lt. Hailes decided we should have to move on to the left down into a narrow wadi. We advanced along the wadi on the enemy's right flank, passing a pile of Lee Enfield rifles stacked beside a track. We continued through the hills, and suddenly our barrage opened up, the shells dropping directly to our front 150 yards distant. We immediately sought cover and remained there until the barrage lifted.

Lt. Hailes issued orders for the patrol to advance under cover of the smoke caused by the barrage, and this we did for 150 yards until the air cleared. We were making our way round the base of a small hill when we observed forward of us about 100 yards three square objects which appeared to be camouflaged vehicles or guns. Lt. Hailes ordered the patrol to surround and attack these, but on doing so we discovered that the objects were haystacks, and no enemy were seen.

We continued our advance round the base of some small hills, when suddenly voices were heard coming from the top of one of the hills. Figures were seen moving about, and we all dropped down in a long narrow trench, when one of the figures was seen coming down the hill towards our position. Directly he was level with us, Lt. Hailes jumped up and levelled his revolver, ordering the enemy into our trench. He was a German officer, and was disarmed and placed under the guard of Pte. Marsh. The patrol moved off, and observing this the German attempted to disarm Pte. Marsh; however, L/Cpl. Patrick spotted this, and opened fire with his tommy-gun, whereupon the German collapsed screaming and the patrol continued without delay.

The enemy again opened fire on us, but we kept going, bypassing enemy positions in our way. Suddenly we encountered enemy directly to our front, and on carrying out Lt. Hailes' orders for a frontal attack, we killed three of them.

We continued until we came upon more enemy positions. Lt. Hailes again ordered a frontal attack, and while shots were being exchanged two enemy were killed.

We moved on, and another M.G. opened fire on us. This we avoided, but looking to our rear we observed figures advancing towards us. The enemy were surrounding us and holding their fire, but we still advanced, making wide sweeps to avoid them.

Our route was now not a chosen one, but we kept going, crossing over a secondary road (178854) which had been blown, possibly by bombs, and then into a cornfield. The enemy were close behind, when suddenly voices to the right called on us to halt. Voices could also be heard on our left, but there was no shooting, so we kept moving at a fast rate.

We next approached a cactus hedge, and passing through saw a small building and the dugouts of a previously inhabited position. The building was deserted, and we rested here while Lt. Hailes and Sgt. Lawton made a recce. On their return, after ten minutes mortar bombs began to fall, and these made us move on. After marching for 150 yards we came to an A.-Tk. ditch (173863) which we crossed, carrying on in almost a half-circle. We found excellent cover in the dry gully of a river-bed. As mortar bombs were dropping close now, Lt. Hailes decided to halt for protection. Twenty minutes later Lt. Hailes decided to push on, but as we got out into the open the mortaring started again, and Sgt. Lawton was seriously wounded in both legs. We retired to the wadi, and Cpl. Taylor gave medical attention to the Sgt., who was bleeding profusely.

It was now 0115 hours on the 20th, and Lt. Hailes decided that we should have to remain in the wadi until it was dawn, as it was impossible to move Sgt. Lawton. Sentries were posted.

At 0530 hours Lt. Hailes made a recce with L/Cpl. Patrick, leaving with me his map and instructions in case he failed to return. The position we were in was facing British lines, with the tank trap in our rear and the main road on our left.

Lt. Hailes returned with L/Cpl. Patrick after 30 minutes, and told us we could move and that our chances were good. Sgt. Lawton would have to be left, and Cpl. Taylor said that it was imperative that he should stop and attend to him. Pte. Stringer volunteered to stay and give protection. Rations and water were left with the three men, and Lt. Hailes gave orders that if we could not get help to them by 1400 hours, they were to use their own initiative and try to get Sgt. Lawton back.

At 0845 hours the patrol moved out of the gully into the open in two sections, Lt. Hailes leading. We gained concealment in some scrub and bushes on our right and moved in the direction of our own lines. No shots were fired at us for 150 yards, when we reached ground that afforded us no cover whatsoever. Directly to our front were two farmhouses, and Lt. Hailes decided to make for these. We were about 80 yards from the buildings, when intensive M.G. fire was brought to bear on us, whereupon the patrol dropped down and moved into a fire position in the belief that the fire was coming from the buildings. Lt. Hailes ordered a frontal attack, and then, realising that we were being fired on from the rear, we passed behind the buildings and took up a position under cover. Pte. Burns received a bullet in the arm and was bleeding profusely, while Lt. Hailes received a slight graze on the leg. I dressed Pte. Burns' arm while Lt. Hailes placed the Bren gunners round the house, his intention being to silence the enemy M.G.

After five to ten minutes mortar bombs began to drop very close to the buildings and the enemy machine gunners kept up a steady fire. We were apparently a very good target, for every movement we made was seen, and yet we could not locate the enemy position. We were forced to move through a cactus hedge and away from the building. Pte. Burns, being in a weak condition, we had to relieve him of his equipment and leave it.

We carried on in short rushes, and taking advantage of some trees which afforded good cover, we pushed forward, on our left being a cactus hedge which ran near the main road. Lt. Hailes decided we should cross the road and take cover behind some ridges. We went through the cactus hedge into the open, and by running and weaving managed to reach cover without a casualty.

M.G. fire was intense, and the whole of the road was being sprayed, so we could not possibly move in that direction.

After resting in this position for five or ten minutes, Lt. Hailes decided that our only way was to surmount the small ridge forward of us in pairs. This we did, and found we were in a narrow wadi winding to the left. We moved down this in single file for about 200 yards, until we reached a spot where we had to step up on to higher ground. Lt. Hailes was leading, and we had moved no more than 6 yards when I heard a shot, and saw Lt. Hailes place his hand on his back, moan, and fall down. I looked forward, and about 30 yards away I saw what appeared to be a puff of smoke. This I think was the sniper's position.

We dropped to the ground and crawled back out of view, as a M.G. was now firing at us from higher ground. I placed the Bren Gunners in position, and spread out the remainder of the patrol for all-round defence, the enemy fire being very intense. I waited five minutes, hoping Lt. Hailes would crawl back, as I did not at that time know the full extent of his wounds. As he did not appear, I called for two men to go out to him. Pte. Jackson immediately volunteered, and on my giving him instructions he moved off. The enemy opened fire immediately, but after a few minutes Pte. Jackson returned and informed me that Lt. Hailes was badly wounded and needed dressing. I obtained a shell dressing and gave it to Pte. Jackson. Pte. Marsh then asked if he could go as well, as he was Lt. Hailes' batman, so I gave them both instructions which were for them to try to get Lt. Hailes back. Lt. Hailes could not and did not want to be moved, but while dressing him Pte. Marsh was shot and killed.

Pte. Jackson reported the situation to me, and I told him to ask Lt. Hailes for orders. Lt. Hailes said that nothing could be done for him; he wished to surrender, because he needed medical attention, and he stated that he would be all right that way. So he handed over his binoculars and compass and also his wrist-watch, but he would not part with his revolver. He requested a white handkerchief, saying that before waving it he would allow me time to get the patrol away. Then he told me what route to take, thinking it best that we should keep by the road.

Explaining the whole situation to the patrol, I told them that our whereabouts were known to at least three enemy positions. I then issued orders for all surplus kit to be left, as we needed to move quick and light. This was done. I then decided to move back through the wadi the way we had come, and this was done singly by crawling and quick rushes.

I moved the patrol to a hidden position about 200 yards from Lt.

Hailes, and on the way heard two revolver shots from his direction. On reaching the chosen spot in the wadi, I placed my men out in such a way that should we be surprised only part of the patrol would be seen.

It was now about 1100 hours, and making a recce I found that I could not get the patrol out this way, as the enemy were covering the rear and our right flank from whence we had withdrawn. I informed the patrol that our only chance was to move by night, and so I ordered a complete silence and immobility. This was obeyed.

Eight hours later darkness came, and I decided to move before the moon rose (during the day I observed that the enemy had heavy guns to our rear and slightly to the left a large number of M.G.s and a mortar position).

I noticed that the compass Lt. Hailes had left me was set at 300 degrees, but on taking the back bearings I found it led right across the enemy's strongest position, so I decided on a back bearing of 210 degrees, which would give the patrol a good chance of bypassing the enemy posts.

We crossed the main road and moved up into the hills, twice bypassing enemy localities. No fire was brought to bear on us.

After six hours' marching we arrived at a 4th Ind. Div. R.A. command post, where I had Pte. Burns evacuated. The O.C. informed me of the Bn.'s position, the time now being 0230 hours on the 21st. At 0800 hours I made my way back to the Bn. arriving at "C" Coy H.Q. at 1200 hours on Wednesday.

In a subsequent report Corporal Taylor says that Sergeant Lawton, Private Stringer and himself started back after dark on the night 20th/21st April, but after moving about a thousand yards they halted for three days to enable Sergeant Lawton to regain strength.

During this time Corporal Taylor observed the location of many enemy weapons, and noted spots where our own shells were falling.

On the 23rd April the journey was resumed, Private Stringer leading and Corporal Taylor supporting Sergeant Lawton.

At 2200 hours the party contacted an anti-tank regiment attached to the Free French, who directed them to a U.S. A.D.S., from where they were able to return to their unit.

Chapter Five

THE 2/4TH BATTALION THE ESSEX REGIMENT, 1939-45

THE fortunes of war can seldom be shared equally either by individuals or by units. Some will have greater opportunities and a greater share of the centre of the stage than others. Some must have less conspicuous but none the less arduous and vital roles to perform. For among units there must be, for every one in the forefront of the battle, one, and more than one, in the lines of communication, at the the base, and in the Home Country. Men must be trained, held, and dispatched overseas; returned casualties must be refitted; the safety of the home base must be assured. Few could know as war came, or indeed during war itself, whether their role would be to fight in the limelight of world opinion and acclaim, or whether they would be required to stand and serve in some less conspicuous way.

It was the fate of the 2/4th Battalion to be denied an overseas role. It was to be one of the many units whose role was not to be spectacular, but nevertheless essential in the preparation for and attainment of final victory.

Raised side by side with the sister battalion, the 1/4th Essex, the approach of war found the 2/4th with headquarters at Ilford under the command of Lieutenant-Colonel Lord Edward Hay.

Plans down to the smallest detail had been carefully prepared in the last years of peace to meet the emergency of war, and one of the very first duties to fall on Regular and Territorial units alike was, as war became imminent, to guard places vital to the safety and well-being of the country, such as oil depots, important bridges, viaducts and railway junctions, canals, docks, and airfields.

It was the 27th August, 1939, when the code message ordering the guarding of these vulnerable points, as laid down in the mobilisation scheme, was received at Battalion Headquarters.

It was not an easy task. It required common sense, loyalty, and an innate sense of discipline to go out, with little authority and experience, far from Battalion or Company Headquarters, and assume the duty of safeguarding some vital area. The while the rest of the country went on holiday or about their daily business with what seemed to be singularly little appreciation of the crisis so rapidly approaching.

But the men of the 2/4th Essex, and indeed the men of all units, overcame their difficulties, whether the lack of proper guard orders, non-co-operation on the part of those whose property was to be guarded, the lack of billets, or the complete impossibility of getting food either by subsistence allowance or from rations.

The duties assigned to the Battalion were quickly assumed at Clacton, Dagenham, Shoeburyness, and Romford.

Events moved quickly. On the 1st September all Territorials were ordered over the wireless to join their units. Later that day the mobilisation order itself was issued by H.Q. 54th (East Anglian) Division. On the 3rd September, 1939, came the declaration of war, so quickly followed by the air-raid sirens over Essex and London. It was a false alarm, but a foretaste of things to come.

The 2/4th Essex started the war as a unit of 161st (Duplicate) Infantry Brigade, rechristened during September 1939 as 163rd Infantry Brigade, a part of the 54th (East Anglian) Division.

There were to be few thrills and no easy road to glory. The Battalion remained in its unspectacular role of V.P. protection till the end of October 1939, seeing other and more fortunate units move overseas.

And then came a change of duty and of scene. Ordered to move on the 2nd November, 1939, to Suffolk, the 2/4th was given a sector of the east coast to defend. Battalion Headquarters were at Saxmundham and forward companies at Leiston and Aldeburgh. It was that curious period of lull and unreality which occurred after the outbreak of war, with little to enliven the long hours of guard duty and training. There were the occasional mine on the shore, flares and gun-fire well out to sea as some east-coast convoy was attacked, and the sound of aircraft engines by night as enemy aeroplanes flew in to drop magnetic mines in harbours or on the coastal sea routes. There was also an occasional spy scare to break monotony and keep sentries on their toes.

Then came another move. This time the 54th Division was to go northwards into Northumberland, and on the 18th April the 2/4th Essex moved to Hexham. Here the Battalion found volunteers for No. 3 Independent Company formed with the East Anglian Division for immediate service in Norway, and as with the other Essex Territorial battalions, the supply of volunteers greatly exceeded the vacancies to be filled.

Next followed a move to Lambton Castle on the 31st May, at the very height of the crisis of Dunkirk, when anything seemed likely to happen.

An officer writes: "The Dunkirk days in 1940 will remain a live memory for those in the Battalion at the time. We were at a few hours' notice to move, and for days kitbags remained packed. There was 'stand-to' at first light and at dusk, and during the day companies went trench digging, in solid rock in places, at Fallowfield, in the Roman Wall country.

"The order to move came one night about 11 p.m., and the people of Hexham awoke the next morning to find the Battalion gone. In requisitioned transport and buses, the 2/4th Essex travelled to Lambton Park, Co. Durham, which was nearer the coast, where with practically no tentage we bivouacked in glorious weather until ordered to Sunderland to spend months amid an area of concrete road blocks and strongpoints."

There were no doubts as to the efficiency of the road blocks and defence posts occupied by the Battalion at any time, but certainly the post-Dunkirk days till the autumn of 1940 were the climax of defensive effort and enthusiasm. Thereafter the pendulum swung to preparation for offence and to offensive action itself.

But that era lay ahead, and in June 1940 defence was the only thought at battalion level. It was a time of air raids, parachute scares, and potential landings. Every night and every day could, and many times did, bring bombing raids, every quiet and windless night was a possible occasion for parachute landings, and every spring tide a time for possible seaborne landings.

One night the N.C.O. in charge of a post on the sea front saw the shapes of warships steaming in towards him. Before he could do anything they were ashore, well ashore on the rocks. They turned out to be two British destroyers—*Ashanti* and *Fame*—which, losing direction, had just collided and then run ashore.

Both were badly damaged and helpless, a good target for enemy aircraft, and the task was to get them afloat and into dock as quickly as possible. Working in relays, men of the 2/4th Essex formed a human chain, only possible at low tide, and for several days laboured to lighten ship, ammunition and stores of every description being passed from hand to hand until the destroyers could be refloated. During these operations an officer of one of the ships remarked to Major E. R. Meggy that possibly *Ashanti* and *Fame* would be merged into one during reconstruction, and that the new destroyer might well be named H.M.S. *Ashame*. But both lived to fight with honour another day.

It was at Seaburn on the 3rd August, 1940, almost a year since the first preparatory code word galvanised the Battalion orderly room into action, a year of varied experience and greatly increased efficiency, that the 2/4th Essex had their first post-war change of command, Lieutenant-Colonel J. W. Hurrell, M.C., taking over from Lieutenant-Colonel Lord Edward Hay.

The summer of 1940 was an increasing crescendo of air raids and mounting tension, until, on the evening of the 7th September the code word "Cromwell"—Invasion imminent—was received by Battalion Headquarters. It was the climax. Posts were manned and every possible precaution taken. But invasion was not to follow. Then tension slowly relaxed as the autumnal weather made seaborne invasion less and less feasible. As did, too, the mounting strength of Britain.

On the 11th October the 2/4th Essex moved to Chester-le-Street, County Durham, where the New Year of 1941 was to find them. Despite the severe weather of that winter, training was resumed, the emphasis already swinging towards the offensive. But life was not all training and there were battalion concerts and other entertainments. Here "Out of the Rag Bag," the first of a very successful series of revues, was produced by Major J. G. Gibson.

The Battalion was to remain at Chester-le-Street until the 28th March, 1941, on which day a road and rail move to Fairford, Gloucestershire, was carried out. Here the 54th Division became part of the 8th Corps.

The months at Fairford were a period of hard and large-scale training, the exercises extending as far south as Devon and as far north as Wales. At Fairford the Battalion found a Guard of Honour for Field-Marshal Lord Birdwood. The guard, whose drill and bearing were excellent, genuinely impressed the Field-Marshal as he inspected the men paraded in shirt-sleeves order, bronzed and fit through many weeks of strenuous training.

The Battalion had nearly four months of valuable training experience under 8th Corps before it was ordered to Henley-on-Thames on the 22nd July, 1941. Here it came under 11th Corps, and it was from Henley that the 2/4th moved in September on Exercise "Bumper," the largest and most spectacular exercise so far mounted in England. It was fourteen days' hard work for the 2/4th Essex, and the whole of the 54th Division, in their role of enemy, for they took the part of the Sixth German Army.

Shortly after this experience the Battalion moved once more. The 21st November, 1941, found it at Aldeburgh for another turn of beach defence duty, still under command of 11th Corps. It was not at all dull routine. There was still a possibility of invasion or at least of seaborne raids upon the English coast, and alarms kept the Battalion on its toes, as a contemporary document goes to show:

"10.25 hours: 50 ships reported off Dunwich by 163 Brigade. Coys. ordered to man fwd. posn. Supporting arty. (462.328.353 Btys. of 547 Coastal Defence Regt.) informed. Also R.N.O.

"10.45 hours: All Coys. man fwd. posns.

"11.15 hours: 5 Trawlers passed Aldeburgh steaming South. One flying barrage balloon.

"11.35 hours: Bn. reverts to normal state of readiness."

On the 15th March, 1942, Battalion Headquarters moved to Leiston, and there it was to stay for the remainder of the year.

On 15th May, 1942, Lieutenant-Colonel C. S. Mills took over command from Lieutenant-Colonel J. W. Hurrell, who was posted to another appointment.

The period in Leiston saw the disintegration of the original T.A. battalion, which had remained almost intact for over two years.

Although the invasion scare had died down, coast defence remained the priority role of the Battalion. By frequently relieving the forward companies astride the Sizewell Gap, Lieutenant-Colonel Mills was able to continue vigorous training and recreation throughout the summer. The interest in cricket was inspired by Lieutenant Peter Smith, the well-known Essex county player, and the reappearance of "Rag-Bag" fully occupied the spare time of more than forty members of the Battalion.

The autumn, however, brought drastic changes in the composition of the Battalion. Officers were urgently needed for the Indian Army, officers and other ranks were wanted for the new divisions being formed in East and West Africa, and the fluctuating fortunes of war in the Western Desert in the months before El Alamein called for large drafts of reinforcements.

At the same time, together with all units in the Division, the Battalion was allotted an additional role of lifting sugar beet.

DRUMS OF THE 5TH BATTALION THE ESSEX REGIMENT. LATAKIA, SYRIA. MAY 1943.

(Imperial War Museum)
5TH BATTALION THE ESSEX REGIMENT NEAR LANCIANO (SOUTH ITALY). 9TH DECEMBER, 1943.
The road working party includes Privates S. Puzey (Isleworth), F. Brown (Ilford), K. Livermore (Chelmsford), and P. Bradley (Chelmsford).

(Imperial War Museum)
5TH BATTALION THE ESSEX REGIMENT. ROAD DRAINAGE AND REPAIR NEAR LANCIANO. 9TH DECEMBER, 1943.

(Imperial War Museum)
5TH BATTALION THE ESSEX REGIMENT. A SECTION (CORPORAL COX) RELIEF ON THE RIVER ARIELLI SECTOR, NEAR VILLA GRANDE. 15TH JANUARY, 1944.

Recruits with only a few weeks of primary and corps training were in the meantime being fed in from the Training Centre at Warley. At first they were given a fair measure of training, but later, as the commitments grew, their seasoning was little more than that they acquired in the root fields.

By mid-winter the Battalion had been reduced to a cadre of 15 officers and 190 other ranks, for by now more than 60 officers and nearly 1,000 men had passed through its ranks.

By the New Year, 1943, the Battalion was again brought up to establishment in part by a large draft from the 9th (Home Counties) Parachute Battalion, until recently the 10th Essex. For a while drafting commitments were eased, until after Exercise "Spartan," in which the Battalion defended the line of the Thames between Henley and Sonning against the Canadian First Army. For this exercise the Battalion was afforded an uninterrupted period of three weeks in which to reach a marching standard of 90 miles in 3 days.

After "Spartan," a change of station was ordered, and on the 12th April, 1943, the Battalion found itself in Old Park Barracks, Dover. Here, on the 1st May, the 2/4th Essex was very pleased to be honoured by the visit of the Colonel of the Regiment, Lieutenant-General Sir Geoffrey W. Howard, K.C.B., C.M.G., D.S.O., D.L. Luckily, the Colonel's visit did not coincide with one of the bouts of cross-Channel shelling which were a feature of the Dover area in 1943. During their six weeks' stay in Dover, the Battalion witnessed several of these heavy duels between British heavy batteries and the German guns mounted on the French coast. No casualties were sustained by the Battalion, although they were numerous among the civilian population.

The stay was short, and by the 18th May the 2/4th Essex found themselves in Bradford Down Camp, Dorchester. It was here that Brigadier-General J. T. Wigan, C.B., C.M.G., D.S.O., T.D., Honorary Colonel of the 4th Battalion The Essex Regiment, visited his unit, a visit welcomed by all ranks and marked by a battalion inspection and march past.

The stay at Dorchester was again comparatively short, for July saw the Battalion on Southampton Common, and at Botley busily digging hundreds of trenches. The whole operation was shrouded in mystery and secrecy, for it could not then be known that this humdrum duty was an essential part of the detailed scheme of preparation for the immense concentration of troops that was to be built up round that area in 1944, the forming-up area for the invasion of Europe.

From Southampton the Battalion crossed to the Isle of Wight, there to become part of the 47th (London) Division, at the time commanded by Major-General A. E. Robertson, D.S.O. Here the 2/4th joined the 140th Infantry Brigade.

Not much time was allowed in the Isle of Wight, for in January 1944 a complete change of scene was experienced, when the whole of the 47th Division was transferred to the North Riding of Yorkshire, to form part of the 8th Corps.

Battalion Headquarters was first at Hutton Rudby and then at Stokesley, and it was from here that the Battalion took part in Exercise "Eagle," which was to practise 8th Corps in an attack against a typical "Hedgehog" position. The 2nd Essex on the right and the 2/4th Essex on the left had to dig in and live underground, and under several inches of snow too for much of the time, until overrun by the attackers ten days later. The fitness and morale of the troops were borne out by the extremely small sick rate.

On the 25th March, 1944, the Battalion, now with the 25th Infantry Brigade (Brigadier A. H. Blest), left for "Special Static" duties in connection with D-Day in the Gosport area. The marshalling of invasion troops preparatory to embarkation was their role, which included feeding, equipping, and general welfare, and also disembarkation and reception of survivors and prisoners. There was much to do and much to see.

With the invasion safely launched, the Battalion was relieved of its embarkation duties and moved to Greatham. Here all available fit men were posted as reinforcements, many to a battalion of the Dorsetshire Regiment, with which an Essex company was soon fighting in France. They were sad to go, for many had served full five years with the 2/4th Essex all over England and yet showed a willing response. It was the luck of the draw.

The lot, too, of those left behind was hard. Barely 200 remained on the Battalion strength after drafting. Lieutenant-Colonel C. S. Mills had himself gone to command the 7th North Staffords on the 16th July, 1944, and the Commanding Officer was now Lieutenant-Colonel J. L. L. Lotinga, M.C., Royal Fusiliers. This link with the Royal Fusiliers was soon to be greater, for the 2/4th Essex, being now less than 200 strong, was amalgamated with the 12th Royal Fusiliers, and on the 30th August, 1944, moved to Southwold to act as a training battalion, principally for young soldiers.

By 1st November the new 2/4th Essex had been moved to Shorncliffe, where it was still serving on V.E.-Day.

There is little more to tell. Lieutenant-Colonel Lotinga handed over command in October 1945 to Lieutenant-Colonel C. L. Archdale, who took the Battalion to Aylsham, in Norfolk, and thence to Ketteringham, near Norwich. Demobilisation was now in progress, and "Age and Service Groups" the topic of the day. With the turn of the year, the 2/4th Battalion had ceased to exist as an active unit, and had been placed in suspended animation.

The role of the Battalion had been unspectacular but important. It had, for the six and a half years of its active life, at all times done its duty in the best tradition of the Essex Regiment. Many people to this day all over England, whether at Chester-le-Street in Durham, Fairford in Gloucester, or at Dorchester, think kindly of the Essex Regiment and of the men who served in its ranks. That they do so is because of the happy impression left behind them in their travels by the 2/4th Battalion The Essex Regiment.

Chapter Six

THE 5TH (1/5TH) BATTALION THE ESSEX REGIMENT, 1939-50

FOREWORD

by Lieutenant-General Sir Dudley Russell, K.B.E., C.B., D.S.O., M.C., Commander 8th (Indian) Division, 1943-44.

As Divisional Commander of the 5th (1/5th) Battalion The Essex Regiment from January 1943 to March 1944, I was in a position, possibly more than anyone else, to assess the value of their courage, endurance, and loss from the wider point of view. Their contribution to overall success in battle was a magnificent one and their heavy casualties not in vain.

It was impossible to ease the Battalion gradually into battle, as is so desirable, and they therefore found themselves launched into the tough Trigno fight without preliminary initiation. Mist, lack of information, and German paratroopers made it an extremely difficult operation. Success was achieved elsewhere largely as a result of this Battalion's fine fight.

It says much for the spirit of the Battalion and its early training that it was ready to fight hard again in such a short time at the Sangro. The story of how almost insurmountable difficulties were overcome is well told, but I think all would like to know that General Montgomery told me personally that without success at Il Calvario the Sangro crossing would have been a much more difficult operation, and that casualties in seizing this feature were very worth-while.

With the loss of many leaders and a further influx of miscellaneous reinforcements, the Battalion still went on fighting and produced a punch at Villa Grande which was, perhaps, their most wonderful effort, remembering the circumstances. They had now done more than could be expected of any unit and I reluctantly said good-bye to them. I am glad their final battle in Europe was such a well-deserved success.

It was a great honour to be asked to write this Foreword to a story so well told, and thus to be associated with such exemplary gallantry.

Lieutenant-General, Chief British Adviser to the Indian Army.

THE 5TH (1/5TH) BATTALION THE ESSEX REGIMENT

Section I

HOME DEFENCE, 1939-41

THE old Essex Volunteers became part of the Essex Regiment in 1883, the 2nd Volunteer Battalion having its headquarters at Braintree. In 1908, with the inauguration of the Territorial Force, this 2nd Volunteer Battalion of the Essex Regiment became the 5th Battalion The Essex Regiment (T.F.). Its headquarters were established at Colchester, and moved to Chelmsford in 1911.

The Territorial Army was reconstituted on the 16th February, 1920, the 5th Battalion The Essex Regiment T.A. having its headquarters at Market Road, Chelmsford.

In the spring of 1939 a decision was taken to duplicate the Territorial Army. It was finally agreed not to raise the second line battalion side by side with the existing battalion, but to divide the recruiting area geographically into an east zone and a west zone.

On the 1st June, 1939, the 5th Battalion was thus divided into the 1/5th (West) Battalion and the 2/5th (East) Battalion of the Essex Regiment. The 1/5th Battalion had its headquarters at Market Road, Chelmsford, and was, in August 1939, commanded by Lieutenant-Colonel H. C. N. Trollope, D.S.O., M.C.; it was part of the 161st Infantry Brigade, and of the 54th (East Anglian) Division.

With the imminence of war, personnel of the Territorial Army were called out, on the 25th August, 1939, to undertake the guarding of certain vulnerable points, and this order was quickly followed, on the 1st September, 1939, by orders to mobilise. On the 3rd September the embodied strength of the Battalion was 23 officers and 635 other ranks.

Embodiment had been carried out at company stations: "W" Company, Chelmsford (Major P. V. Upton); "X" Company, Saffron Walden (Captain F. Barrett); "Y" Company, Dunmow and Stanstead (Lieutenant N. Davey); "Z" Company, Maldon (Captain D. C. Capel Dunn); and Headquarter Company, Chelmsford (Captain J. F. Cramphorn). Major J. P. Nott was Second-in-Command, and Captain G. H. Walker was Adjutant. Lieutenant A. L. Ostler was Quartermaster.

The Battalion concentrated in Chelmsford in October, being accommodated in billets and requisitioned buildings.

There was much to do in those early months. Army intake drafts had to be received and trained, immatures sorted out and regretfully sent elsewhere, while the training of the Battalion had to receive the highest priority, for many were soldiers of comparatively little service, and all stood in need of training in modern weapons and methods. And so junior-officer courses and training-cadre courses for non-commissioned officers were instituted, with great benefit to the Battalion.

On top of everything, there had to be constant work in connection with the scheme for the defence of the east coast, as the 1/5th had, in common with the other Essex territorial infantry battalions, much the same role as the Battalion had had in 1914 and 1915.

Days were not exciting, enlivened even as they were by the occasional air-raid warning, but it was an important period, for on the foundation laid in Essex in the months following September 1939 was built the success the Battalion was to attain later in the war.

It is not good for a unit to stay too long in its home area. The spirit of adventure calls for new fields to explore, and all were glad when the Battalion advance party left on the 3rd April 1940, for Beal in Northumberland.

Perhaps the move could have been better timed from the Battalion's point of view, for the same day as the move order was received, a draft of 287 army-class intake joined. This is a very large number for any battalion to absorb and train at any one time, and to receive them on the eve of the first major move since the outbreak of war did not make matters easier.

However, dividing the draft into thirty squads, each named after a battle honour of the Essex Regiment, the 1/5th cheerfully set about its task. By the 15th April, 1940, the recruits had been clothed, equipped, and at least partially trained. On that day the Battalion entrained at Chelmsford station in excellent order, and arrived at Beal the following morning.

The prospect of active warfare was now much nearer than it had been in those early days in and around Chelmsford, and there was a large and immediate answer to the call made, on the 26th April, 1940, for volunteers to serve in an independent company to be formed within the 54th Division for service in Norway.

This was No. 3 Independent Company, commanded by Major A. C. Newman, of the 1/4th Essex.

Lieutenant H. G. Hopwood took the section from the 1/5th Essex to join the platoon commanded by Lieutenant M. J. Wootton (1/5th

THE 5TH (1/5TH) BATTALION THE ESSEX REGIMENT 359

Essex). The section was 13 strong. Shortly afterwards, they were to land at Bodo, in the Arctic Circle, and to march south for about one hundred and fifty miles to link up with the 2nd Scots Guards. Then, reinforced by Nos. 2, 4, and 5 Independent Companies, the 1st Irish Guards and the 2nd South Wales Borderers, they fought a three weeks' rear-guard action back to Bodo, the task of this composite force under Brigadier C. McV. Gubbins being to delay the northward advance of the enemy towards Narvik.

No. 3 Independent Company with No. 4 (42nd East Lancashire Division) and No. 5 (London Division) were then formed into No. 2 Commando under Major Newman. Lieutenant Hopwood, with Sergeant Oxley, Corporals Macklin and Wakelin, and Private Tedder of the 1/5th Essex all joined this Commando. Hopwood (now Captain) was, however, the only 1/5th Essex representative in No. 2 Commando's famous raid of St. Nazaire on the 28th March, 1942. He was taken prisoner in the raid, being subsequently awarded the Croix de Guerre (*avec* Palme) and mentioned in dispatches.

The German attack on Holland, France, and Belgium soon followed, and on the 10th May, 1940, we read, "Invasion by Germany of Low Countries caused considerable alteration in the routine of the Battalion."

With the writing on the wall in Holland, it was clear that a possibility of invasion, or at least of large-scale raids, now existed. The 161st Infantry Brigade, part of G.H.Q. strategic reserve in the United Kingdom, was put at six hours' notice to move, and all ranks confined to their battalion areas. Work on defences was accelerated to the greatest possible degree, and the Battalion daily "stood to" at the half-hour before and after dawn and dusk.

It was a time of high endeavour, and every task given to the 1/5th Essex was willingly accepted and efficiently performed.

From Beal the Battalion moved on the 18th June to the area of Newcastle-on-Tyne, and shortly afterwards to Hexham and Prudhoe, where, on the 21st August, 1940, the 1/5th Essex first received the order to mobilise for service overseas.

Very great efforts were made to complete mobilisation in the time allowed, but in the end the orders were cancelled and the 1/5th reverted to brigade control. Had the original orders been carried through, the Battalion would have gone to "salubrious" Freetown in Sierra Leone, so perhaps more was gained than lost by this last-minute cancellation of orders.

Tropical kit issued during mobilisation was not withdrawn. It was a warning to the men that they were not to remain indefinitely at home, but its retention was to be a headache to the Quartermaster.

At Prudhoe, too, the 1/5th was to experience the alarms and excitements engendered by the receipt on the evening of the 7th September, 1940, of the code-word "Cromwell"—Invasion imminent. Put at one hour's notice, the Battalion remained poised for action until the crisis passed and a more relaxed degree of readiness was permitted.

On the 19th December the 1/5th Essex left Hexham—and the 54th Division—to move to Kent. Here the Battalion came under the command of the 43rd (Wessex) Division, relieving the 11th Royal Marine Battalion in the defended area of Deal and Sandwich.

The district held by the 43rd Division was probably vital to the safety of England, and it was an immediate German objective under their invasion plans as was disclosed after the war. It was under periodical shell fire from enemy coastal batteries and was heavily fortified. Beaches and their approaches were mined, and became a constant danger to the most circumspect patrol, as the 1/5th Essex found a very few days after arrival, when a patrol was blown up and 3 men killed.

At Sandwich, the 1/5th Essex was visited by Lieutenant-General Sir Geoffrey W. Howard, K.C.B., C.M.G., D.S.O., Colonel of the Regiment, the corps of drums parading with the Guard of Honour in the Market Square. Special mention is made of the corps of drums, for it is clear that they played a prominent part in the corporate life of the Battalion, and that much of the state of high morale maintained throughout the war years was due to pride in them. They outwardly displayed the pride the Battalion felt in itself.

After a short stay in Dover in February 1941, during which time the Battalion experienced bombardment of the area from batteries on the French coast, on the 1st March the 1/5th moved across Kent into Milton Barracks, Gravesend. Here they were to stay until June. The Battalion was concentrated for the first time and there was a chance to train. Captain A. L. Ostler says: "It was the first opportunity really to get the Battalion together, and many will remember the new Adjutant, Captain Elliott, a former Coldstream Guardsman, who put the Battalion—including the officers—through their paces." An A.T.S. company in Milton Barracks meant that men were relieved of duties in cookhouses, messes, and telephone exchanges, and so made available for training parades they would have otherwise missed.

By April and May such entries in Battalion records as "24 hours' exercise: Battalion marched 30 miles in eleven hours," are common, and denote the high standard of training that had been reached.

Towards the end of May 1941, orders to mobilise for service overseas were again received, and the Battalion was in the throes of that involved process when, on the 4th June, it received a farewell visit from the commander of the South-eastern Army, Lieutenant-General B. C. T. Paget, C.B., D.S.O., M.C.

On the 25th June, 1941, the 1/5th Essex moved to Gourock, Scotland, there to embark in H.M.T. *Oronsay*, which sailed the following day for an unknown destination.

Section II

THE MIDDLE EAST, 1941–43

Heading south from Freetown, for the past six months the station of the 1/4th and 2/5th Essex, the *Oronsay* was routed to Durban. The 1/5th had expected to meet the 1/4th and 2/5th at Freetown, but Headquarters 161st Infantry Brigade, with the two battalions under command, had already sailed for the Middle East.

At Durban, where the troops were put ashore for exercise and recreation, a ceremonial parade was held, in which the 1/5th Essex, headed by the drums, marched past the Mayor of Durban, an event that received wide publicity in South African newspapers.

As they headed north-west from Aden, any lingering doubts that the Battalion might be sent to India were dispelled, and on the 22nd August, 1941, the 1/5th Essex disembarked at Port Tewfik, and passed, as was the lot of nearly every new arrival in the Middle East, to Qassassin and the El Tahag Camps.

In El Tahag the Battalion linked up with its advanced party, which had left Gravesend four weeks ahead of the main body, and on the 13th September moved out into the Western Desert, there to rejoin the 161st (Essex) Infantry Brigade and take over a share of the responsibility for the ground and air defence of Western Desert landing-grounds.

Officers on the strength as the 1/5th Essex joined the Middle East Forces were: Lieutenant-Colonel H. C. N. Trollope, D.S.O., M.C.; Majors G. H. Walker, J. P. Nott, and P. V. Upton; Captains M. T. Nash, C. O. P. Trimble, E. I. Elliott, L. C. Kaye, I. P. Foster, M. J.

Wootton; Lieutenants J. N. Lyster, F. J. Symington, J. F. Halbert, V. A. L. May; 2/Lieutenants C. E. A. Whyte, J. P. Kaye, M. Tye, W. W. Buzza, C. F. M. Beard, T. C. Loder, A. R. Lee, J. Mann, H. E. Chandler-Honnor, D. M. Gibbs, R. T. Butcher, F. L. Pagniez, M. I. Law, G. A. Whyte, and H. R. Horobin. Lieutenant A. L. Ostler was Quartermaster.

Captain M. T. Nash was soon to leave the Battalion—to take up the appointment of Staff Captain at H.Q. 88 Area in Tobruk, and incidentally to become the second prisoner of war from the Battalion, being captured in the fall of Tobruk in June 1942. Captain Hopwood, captured at St. Nazaire in March 1942, was the first.

From El Daba in the Western Desert the 1/5th Essex sent a platoon under 2/Lieutenant J. Mann to act as defence platoon to the headquarters of Western Desert Force, receiving later a most appreciative letter from Lieutenant-General A. R. Godwin-Austen, the Commander of the 13th Corps.

Relieved of duties on landing-grounds, the Battalion moved into the Bagush Box on the 27th September, there to hear the unwelcome news that the 161st Brigade was to change its composition and the three Essex Territorial battalions were to be scattered. It was a blow to morale and regimental sentiment, for all ranks knew of and wished to emulate the fine work of the Essex Territorial Brigade at Gallipoli and in the Palestine campaign in the First World War.

Three British infantry battalions were required to complete the infantry component of the 8th Indian Division now in the Middle East, and the 1st Royal Fusiliers, 1/5th Essex, and 2/5th Essex were selected. The 1/4th Essex was chosen to join the 5th and later the 4th Indian Division. Relieved in the Bagush Box by the Kaffararian Rifles of the South African Defence Forces, the 1/5th Essex moved, on the 13th October, to Port Said in relief of the 4/7th Rajputs.

At Port Said Lieutenant-Colonel Trollope left the Battalion on appointment as a Sub-area Commander. His place as commanding officer was taken temporarily by Major P. V. Upton, for Major J. P. Nott had already gone ahead with an advanced party on the next move—to Iraq.

Major Upton had little time to get accustomed to his command before a few days later, on the 3rd December, 1941, the Battalion was moved eastwards across the Suez Canal on the first stage of the long journey to join up with the 8th Indian Division in Iraq.

Iraq and Persia had become of added strategical importance within the past six months. There was the need to retain a garrison in Iraq after the rebellion earlier in the year, in the suppression of which the 1st Essex had taken a leading and notable part; then there was the necessity to hold troops in Syria and Mosul as a barrier to any German advance through Turkey and down the valleys of the Tigris and the Euphrates to the Persian Gulf. Finally, with the Russian withdrawals to the Caucasus then in progress, it was necessary to organise a potential barrier in Persia against any German penetration south of the Caucasus.

Entraining at Kantara (East), each man with a more than adequate ration supplied by some care-free Australians working under the orders of Movement Control, they reached Haifa on the 4th December.

The move did not go too smoothly, for the official movement order had not arrived before the Battalion left Kantara, and so their arrival at Haifa may be termed "demi-official." Major Upton went to H.Q. Movements, where "disorganisation reigned supreme. We were only half expected (the missing movement order)."

However, tentage and rations were eventually provided, and the 1/5th Essex encamped for the night in an olive grove eight miles out of Haifa. There the next morning a most astounding collection of ramshackle buses arrived, and the Battalion was invited to step in and start on the long trans-desert journey to Baghdad.

Many seriously doubted they would ever reach their journey's end, for by no stretch of imagination could the buses, driven by Jews and Arabs, be called desert-worthy. A sound tyre was a matter of congratulation, a spare tyre unheard of. But Allah and Jehovah willed, and after a long, monotonous, and hot journey by Mafraq, H.5, H.3, and Rutbah Wells, the column reached Habbaniya.

Crossing the River Jordan, the chaplain and others went down to the river, "And I have an idea," says Major Upton, "that the Padre's water-bottle came back full of holy water for future reference."

At H.5, the commander of the post "had a delightful bull terrier, and the next time I saw it was in Baghdad." One simply cannot stop some dogs from camp following.

It did not prove easy to obtain baths and other amenities in Habbaniya Cantonment. The majority of the Battalion had had no opportunity to bathe or wash their drill clothing and underclothes for nine days, but luckily, after a period of frustration, Major Upton found Major Cariappa, the D.A.A. and Q.M.G. of the 10th Indian Division, who proved most helpful. Major Cariappa is better known as the first Indian Commander-in-Chief of the Army of India.

A heavy dust storm raged for some days at Habbaniya, and altogether the Battalion was glad to pass on through Baghdad to Buqaq, some thirty miles north of Mosul. There the 1/5th Essex joined the 19th Indian Infantry Brigade of the 8th Indian Division. There also was found the advance party under Major J. P. Nott which had been on ahead for six weeks. "We opened our eyes a bit at the advance party," reports Major Upton, "as they were nearly all arrayed in a weird and wonderful mixture of Indian Army issue and local purchase 'wog' clothing."

Conditions in Mosul were found to be far from easy. The Battalion was straightway set to digging its portion of a defensive system northwest of Buqaq, in case of any German break-through from Trans-Caucasia.

Christmas Day, 1941, was spent in heavy rain and such entertainment as could be improvised, while Boxing Day was occupied in repitching camp and digging vehicles out of the quagmire caused by the rains of the day before.

Living conditions were bad. Tentage was extremely short and the weather very cold. Temperature was down to zero on many occasions, and during January 1942 there were fourteen consecutive days of snow. There were no camp roads to speak of, and owing to the lack of a metalled road between Buqaq and Mosul, the Brigade was almost cut off for a fortnight. The only heating was by charcoal braziers, and needless to say, there was a fuel crisis with charcoal in short supply. This came from the wooded hills near the Turkish border, north of Mosul, and with the Army competing with civilian demands, the price rocketed and supply became very difficult.

So, regrettably, was the supply of boots and winter underclothes, and altogether the Battalion was not sorry to get through to the warmer days of spring.

On the 19th January, 1942, Lieutenant-Colonel B. G. Allen, the Sherwood Foresters, assumed command.

In February, as the weather improved and as the local defences were completed, training became possible. A camp was set up between Mosul and Kirkuk, and intensive company training started, but even late in the month heavy rains and high winds were liable to reduce the camp to a shambles.

In March a move was made to Altun Köpri, some twenty-five miles north-west of Kirkuk, where work was started on an elaborate brigade defensive position covering the river and including the village of Altun Köpri itself, which was to be made into a fortress.

These defences were completed in every detail except for wiring and the laying of mines. With its concrete-filled houses all carefully camouflaged, the village became a show-piece, and was used for demonstration purposes, being visited by parties from all over the Middle East. The communication trenches in the battalion area alone totalled over twelve miles in length.

In May came a move back to Mosul. It was now very hot, but collective training went on. Few will forget the exercise when they had to march eighteen miles and fight three actions, one after another, with the shade temperature never below 112 degrees.

While the Battalion was at Mosul, it was called upon to find the Guard of Honour when H.R.H. the Duke of Gloucester visited the area. His Royal Highness, who later inspected the whole Battalion on a brigade parade, was pleased to say it was "a very good guard."

As the summer advanced, the Essex found conditions as trying as they had been in the cold weather. Tentage was still short, and the shade temperature often reached 125 degrees. It was not until November that Lieutenant-Colonel Allen was able to write to Colonel Sir Carne Rasch, Bart., Honorary Colonel of the 5th Essex, and say, "We did last month get some shelters for the men's dining halls, but until then they were in the sun all day, except when in their own 180-pound living tents, where they are 12-14 in number. This last week we got tables and forms, and for the first time in a year they have such things to feed off."

In July 1942 the Battalion had a spell in the so-called holiday camp at Shaqlawa, among the foothills, 150 miles north-east of Mosul.

At this time the Commanding Officer led a strong battalion and company reconnaissance party into Persia, where they took part in the detailed planning of a brigade defensive position at Buru Jird in the mountains near Hamadan. The party were some six weeks at an altitude of 6,000 feet, and the defences went up to 10,000 feet. Later on these defences were dug by civilian labour and left to be manned in case of a Russian collapse in the Caucasus. Major J. P. Nott was appointed fortress commander, and spent about six months away from the Battalion on this duty.

At Shaqlawa, although it was still very hot, there were trees and shade, a great improvement on the bare rock and dust of Mosul. Unfortunately fear of civil disturbance cut short the rest period, and the Battalion had to return hurriedly to Mosul, where it was to remain until November.

With the cooler weather in October and November, field training started once more, and the Battalion resigned itself to another winter in Iraq.

It was a time of reorganisation. The 8th Indian Division had been reduced to a skeleton during the summer, when the 17th and 18th Brigade groups with all the divisional artillery had been rushed westwards during the crisis that ended with the stabilisation of the British front near El Alamein.

Included in the 18th Infantry Brigade group had been the 2/5th Essex, and as that battalion passed through Mosul in June 1942, many old friendships were renewed for the last time until after the war.

With these departures, the 1/5th Essex had become the only British infantry battalion left in Iraq and Persia, and had, therefore, been called upon to find many officers and men for employments within the Command. Up to November 1942, it had lost some 80 non-commissioned officers or potential non-commissioned officers for various employments, and in October alone had had to find 4 officers for third-grade staff appointments. This was a serious drain on a battalion which for some six months had not had a single infantry platoon commanded by an officer.

However, in December 1942 the 56th (London) Division arrived in the Command, and it and the 8th Indian Division were grouped into the 21st Indian Corps, under Lieutenant-General A. G. O. M. Mayne. In the following month Major-General D. Russell took command of the 8th Indian Division: he had been for the past six months the Brigade Commander of the 1/4th Essex in the 5th and 4th Indian Divisions.

In November the Battalion moved to Kifri, and Lieutenant-Colonel Allen wrote to Lieutenant-General Sir Geoffrey Howard:

"We are more favoured as regards amenities and welfare in this camp; we are certainly much better off than we have ever been as regards tentage, etc., but I must confess that the amenities provided for troops in this country fall far short of those anywhere else as far as I know. There are no officers' clubs in the country; there are very few and inadequate Y.M.C.A. Hostels for the men, and except in Baghdad and one or two large towns like that, the standing camps have no properly constructed cinemas. We have to rely almost entirely upon ourselves to keep the men happy and occupied when not training.

We have managed to start in the evening, during non-training hours, quite a useful education programme, and officers and N.C.O.s voluntarily run classes in German, French, Spanish, shorthand, bookkeeping, and Urdu. The latter is also a compulsory subject now for officers and senior N.C.O.s. Unfortunately, there are no education officers, or at any rate we have not seen one, and education is carried out under considerable difficulties as regards provision of stationery, text-books, and even lighting is a problem, but we are really doing something in this way.

"The men had a very good Christmas. We managed to give them an excellent dinner, and the weather has been kind to us. Everybody enjoyed themselves. There was even no grousing on account of the non-arrival of Christmas mail. This, however, has reached us since, or at any rate the bulk of it; 69 bags of mail arrived on 31st January.

"The health of the troops is really excellent, particularly when one considers the conditions under which they were living during the extreme heat of the summer out here. It is, at times, particularly on night training, uncomfortably cold, and there have been several occasions when the men have got very wet, but taking it all round we have been lucky, and I feel that the Battalion is fighting fit and ready for active operations from a physical as well as an efficiency point of view. Though I confess again that my one worry is the junior officer shortage."

In April 1943, the 1/5th Essex left Kifri, and moved, by Lancer Camp, Baghdad, across the desert to Rutbah and to Staging Camp H4.

On the 29th April they crossed into Transjordania. The 1/5th Essex had been in Iraq since December 1941, and in the opinion of all ranks it had been far too long.

There were few regrets. Perhaps Private Tanti had some lingering feeling of loss for his incinerator—Tanti's Inferno as it was universally known—that he had tended with such care. Perhaps too some thoughts for the cigarettes at ten for 5*d*., and a few for the shooting and fishing they had occasionally enjoyed in their leisure hours.

"A party got a 55-pound fish out of a local river," Lieutenant-Colonel Allen once wrote; "I think it was a Tigris salmon. I won't confess how they got it. But it pretty well fed a company."

As they passed out of the land of bondage, Lieutenant-Colonel B. G. Allen was still in command, but Major E. E. Owen was now Second-in-Command, for Major J. P. Nott had been posted to the Iraq Levies and Major P. V. Upton to a first-grade staff appointment. Captain

C. E. A. Whyte was Adjutant, and Captain A. L. Ostler, needless to say, was still Quartermaster.

Of the officers who had embarked with the Battalion on the 25th June, 1941, the following were still on the strength on the 29th April, 1943, as the 5th Essex moved into Transjordania: Captains C. O. P. Trimble, L. C. Kaye, M. J. Wootton, F. J. Symington, J. N. Lyster, J. P. Kaye, W. W. Buzza, C. E. A. Whyte, M. Tye, C. F. M. Beard, H. E. Chandler-Honnor; Lieutenants D. M. H. Gibbs, F. L. Pagniez, M. I. Law, G. A. Whyte, H. R. Horobin, and Captain (Q.M.) A. L. Ostler.

Lieutenant Horobin was unfortunately killed in an accident a very few days later.

The Battalion crossed, on the 1st May, 1943, into Syria and moved into camp at Latakia (Lattaquie). It was now part of the Ninth Army.

On the 8th May, 1943, notification was received from the War Office that the Battalion had been redesignated the 5th Battalion The Essex Regiment.

The War Office had written in November 1942 to Colonel Sir Carne Rasch to say that, owing to the heavy losses sustained by the 2/5th Essex, that battalion had been placed into suspended animation, and that it was therefore proposed to change the designation of the 1/5th Battalion to "5 Battalion The Essex Regiment, T.A." By May 1943 the relevant Army Council instruction had reached the Battalion.

At Latakia, on the Syrian coast near the Turkish frontier, and later at the mountain warfare school in the Lebanon near Tripoli, the Battalion was put to training in hill warfare. Here it was they got the experience in the handling of mule transport which was to be so useful to them in Italy.

Of Latakia, Lieutenant-Colonel Allen writes:

"This was an attractive little town; very French; and we were the first British troops to be there in any numbers. The country around was also delightful. I made a point of calling on the local French Army who were a colonial battalion from West Africa, who had always been Free French. They were a good crowd, and their reaction was almost embarrassing. When they entertained the Regiment they turned out the guard for me, and presented me with one of their Free French badges. Our drums played for them in a local Red Cross fête, and generally speaking the relations between ourselves and the French there were excellent."

The Battalion was not to remain there long, for on the 27th May it was sent hurriedly on a new task. This was to go to Sofaga, on the Red Sea, and to prepare a defensive position for an attack by the 231st Infantry Brigade in a combined operation exercise. This brigade had garrisoned Malta, during the siege, 1941-43, and now formed part of the 30th Corps. It was, in poetic justice, about to take part in the invasion of Sicily.

Of this move from Syria to Sofaga Lieutenant-Colonel Allen, in a contemporary letter, says:

"The Battalion moved from Lattaquie towards the end of May and travelled by road right through Syria and Palestine, to Cairo, and then down the Nile Valley to Sofaga, on the Red Sea, cutting across from Qena, forty miles north of Luxor, by a new road. At Sofaga we were to do 'enemy' for certain units being trained in combined operations, and we spent ten days hard at work preparing the position which was to be attacked. However, when it came to the day itself, in spite of all the preparations which had been made, and with many staff officers present, it was discovered that the sea was, unfortunately, too rough for landing craft to operate; and not only that—it was almost certain to continue being so rough that it was no good carrying on with the original scheme. They did, however, move us eighty miles farther north, up the Red Sea, to another spot, where they hoped landing operations would be possible. There we had to re-dig, and to some extent wire, a new position, which we did in twelve hours. I regret to say that again the anchorage for the troopships was found to be unsuitable for the use of landing craft at that time of the year, so our long journey down to the Red Sea was really a waste of time. The Corps Commander concerned, General Leese, who came down to see the operation, had quite a lot to say about it, as you may imagine, but I am glad to say that he gave us a very good chit in public for our work down there, and also wrote a very nice letter to our Divisional Commander about what we had done."

The whole exercise was called off on the 14th June, for time was too short for further delay. The invasion of Sicily was planned for the 10th July.

After this thousand-mile jaunt down from Syria, Lieutenant-Colonel Allen says:

"We moved from Sofaga on the 18th June to carry out dry-shod combined operations training at Burg-el-Arab, just thirty miles west of Alexandria. On the way we spent four days at a camp at Mena, just outside Cairo. We found in this camp at Mena various mock-up landing towers, etc., so we did not waste any time, and started our dry-shod training straightway, thus making three days on the rest of the Brigade."

On arriving at Burg-el-Arab, the rest of the Brigade joined up with the 5th Essex, and Lieutenant-Colonel Allen continues his story by saying:

"We were a little unfortunate over the dry-shod training, as we were the first people to come to this camp for that purpose, and the mock-ups, etc., were not completed, or as good as they were at Mena. In addition, the combined operations training team had only just arrived at the camp, and had not all their complete stores, so that training was, to some degree, rather spasmodic and not laid on as it should have been.

"We have, however, learnt quite a lot about the operation, and in the end carried out a night scheme set by Brigade, which included landing from mock-up craft on the imaginary beach, and the occupation of a beach-head position. This involved the blowing up of wire with Bangalore torpedoes, etc.

"Whilst at Burg-el-Arab, our Divisional Commander, General Russell, visited us, and one day took a large number of officers from the Brigade out to the Alamein battlefield. He commanded the Brigade in the 4th Indian Division in which the 1/4th served, so that all he showed us there was not only of general interest, but of particular interest to us from a Regimental point of view. In addition, a fact which I do not think any of us were aware of, he showed us how the 2/5th position actually covered his Brigade while it was preparing to occupy the position held by it for some months. I personally did not realise that the 2/5th position was so close to the Alamein battlefield; in actual fact, it became really a reserve battalion area for the Germans. We made, at that time, a very quick search of the locality said to be occupied by the 2/5th, and at once found definite identification that they were there. Later, I went out again with another party, and also sent out my I.O. and section to search the area, and to make a sketch-map; I have not seen the map yet, as it is not completed, but we understand that he identified all the positions occupied by the companies in the Battalion, and I myself found the H.Q. and 'B' Echelon area. I have, in my possession, shoulder-titles and a cap-badge which I found, and lying about were kit-bags used by the Italians or Germans as sand-bags, etc., etc. Even a few hockey sticks were still there, showing how very quickly the Battalion was thrown into the battle."

To obtain officers of the Regiment to serve in the various battalions was always a pressing concern of all commanding officers, and Lieutenant-Colonel Allen goes on:

"When in Cairo, I took the opportunity to go and see A.G.3 at Middle East G.H.Q., where a lady staff officer gave me four new officers, three of whom have just passed through the O.C.T.U. here, and another who had been with the 2/4th Battalion at home. They were all Essex Regiment, and should prove a useful addition to our officer strength, which is now only one under war establishment."

On the 18th July, 1943, the 5th Essex moved back to Syria, this time to Tripoli, where training in hill and mountain warfare was resumed.

Sicily had, by now, been attacked and it was clear the invasion of Italy would not be long delayed. The 8th Indian Division, so long away from an active theatre of warfare, hoped it would be called to join the Eighth Army.

In August the Battalion went to Qatana, about twelve miles from Damascus, and there, on the 6th September, 1943, was received the first of the long sequence of move orders that was to take the 5th Essex from Qatana to Haifa, from Haifa to El Kantara, and to the Ikingi staging camp near Alexandria, whence the Battalion sailed for Italy.

The 5th Essex had served in the Middle East for twenty-five months, practically all of which time had been spent east of the Suez Canal. It had had more than its share of training and of the construction of defences, and all eagerly awaited the active role for which the 8th Indian Division had at long last been selected.

Section III

THE ITALIAN CAMPAIGN, 1943-44

The order of battle of the three infantry brigades of the 8th Indian Division as they landed at Taranto in September 1943 was:

G.O.C.: Major-General D. Russell, C.B.E., D.S.O., M.C.

17th Infantry Brigade: 1st Royal Fusiliers.
    1/12th Frontier Force Rifles.
    1/5th Royal Gurkha Rifles.
19th Infantry Brigade: Brigadier T. S. Dobree, D.S.O., M.C.
    5th Essex.
    3/8th Punjab Regiment.
    6/13th Royal Frontier Force Rifles.

21st Infantry Brigade: 5th Royal West Kent.
1/5th Mahratta Light Infantry.
3/15th Punjab Regiment.
M.G. battalion: 5/5th Mahratta Light Infantry.

The 5th Essex landed at Taranto on the 24th September, 1943, and was straightway moved some six miles outside the dock area to some olive groves, where the Battalion bivouacked.

Officers who landed in Italy with the Battalion included: Lieutenant-Colonel B. G. Allen; Majors E. E. Owen, E. I. Elliott, C. O. P. Trimble; Captains L. C. Kaye, J. P. Kaye, C. E. A. Whyte (Adjutant), M. J. Wootton, W. W. Buzza, J. N. Lyster, M. Tye, C. F. M. Beard; Lieutenants M. I. Law, J. G. S. Trelawney, W. F. Griffen, D. M. H. Gibbs, H. E. Chandler-Honner, R. C. G. Hill, C. Baldwin, G. F. Harding, E. G. Ainsworth, G. A. Whyte, A. H. Manning, R. C. Purdie, F. J. Thornton, D. L. Maxwell, N. L. Starkey, B. A. Porte, W. Howes, R. P. Dann; 2/Lieutenants R. H. Ettershank, G. C. May, W. G. Lampard; Captain (Q.M.) A. L. Ostler, Captain C. C. Wright, R.A.M.C., and the Reverend R. J. Holmes, R.A.Ch.D.

In his first letter from Italy, Lieutenant-Colonel Allen says:

"We are quite comfortable, bivouacked in the olive groves: at the moment, though, rations are very much on the hard-scale, and we are not allowed to buy foodstuff locally owing to the civilian shortage in the country. Actually there does not appear to be much to buy. We can, however, get plenty of grapes, and there is some local wine of a rather doubtful quality.

"The local Italians are apparently very friendly, but it has been rather difficult to know exactly how to treat them—whether as allies or defeated enemies. However, to treat them firmly, but courteously, seems to meet the case. It is indeed strange to walk about a large town near here, amongst many of their armed forces, still carrying their weapons. The town, incidentally, is pretty well intact, except for the railway station, which was bombed rather badly, but most of the shops are closed, and it really offers, at the moment, very few attractions for the troops.

"We have no N.A.A.F.I.s open yet here, but have not yet exhausted our own stocks which we brought with us.

"We have managed to smuggle our drums with us here, because I do not see why Scottish regiments should be the only ones who are allowed any music on active service, and whilst they are run on a voluntary basis, they have already been playing for us here, and I hope we shall manage to keep them going during quiet periods for some time to come. Naturally, there is some risk of losing them, or having them damaged, but I feel that their value is so great during times like this, in keeping the Regimental spirit going, that the financial risk was well worth while, and I hope you agree. In actual fact, we are the only Battalion in the Division who have drums, and I hope in days to come we shall be able to head the march into various enemy towns."

The 8th Indian Division was the first Indian formation to be employed in Italy, joining on landing the Eighth Army, under General Sir Bernard L. Montgomery. It formed part of the 5th Corps under Lieutenant-General C. W. Allfrey and as the 5th Essex moved northwards from Taranto, first to Addario and then at the beginning of October towards Foggia, it is perhaps opportune to review the situation in Italy at that time.

Italy had been invaded on the 3rd September by a landing of the Eighth Army from Sicily across the Straits of Messina. The Fifth American Army, containing British formations, landed at Salerno six days later.

The Italians surrendered, but the powerful German Army in Italy fought on.

The Eighth Army had pushed back a screen of rear-guards, and had advanced through Calabria, Basilicata, and Apulia to link with the Fifth Army, so that by the 1st October these two armies, operating under H.Q. Fifteenth Army Group, had reached the general line Foggia–Naples.

The Eighth Army had thus left the plains of the southern toe of Italy, and by now was into broken country. On the Adriatic side of the peninsula there were many miles of rolling ridges and steep valleys, with rivers running swift and deep from west to east, each constituting an obstacle to any force advancing northwards. Where spurs from the central mountain spine approached the coast, these ridges became sharp and the valleys deeper.

Every available inch of this countryside is intensively cultivated, and garden patches, vines, and trees abound. Olive trees, willows, and larches grow everywhere where ground is cultivated, while scrub covers all ground unfit to till. The husbandmen's houses and the jumble of villages stand on the higher ridges, and are ideal for observation posts and for defence.

It was in this country that the Germans made their first main

5TH ESSEX, ITALY, 1943-44.

stand—the Gustav line running from near the mouth of the River Sangro on the Adriatic coast up the Sangro valley to Montegreco and then along the Volturno valley through to the Mediterranean coast.

The capture of Foggia on the 27th September was followed, on the 2nd/3rd October, by the capture of Termoli. This success by the 78th Division caused the enemy to reinforce the Adriatic sector with the 16th Panzer Division from the area of Naples, and some very bitter fighting followed. But the 78th Division held firm, and on the 7th October, 1943, the Germans fell back from the line of the River Biferno to that of the River Trigno.

This then was the situation as the 5th Essex came into the forward area in Foggia. The Battalion had been ordered forward ahead of the 8th Indian Division to restore order in the town and stop looting. The few military government officers already in the town had no staff, and were unable to cope with the civilian situation. Lieutenant-Colonel Allen was made Military Governor of the town, which had been very badly bombed, was without electric light, water, or medical services, and had only a depleted and disorganised police force. Lieutenant-Colonel Allen says: "The Battalion was equal to the task. The Second-in-Command was made acting Town Major to deal with accommodation problems, the intelligence section with Private Tanti as official interpreter, our only one, took over control of the police and security. We ran three improvised prisons for civilians guilty of looting, breaking curfew, and so on. We found an American army engineer who was used in civilian life to dealing with 'public utilities' and who got the water supply and electric power partly restored. It was the Battalion's first real active service job and they did it well."

The Approach to and the Battle of the River Trigno

The Eighth Army plan for the crossing of the River Trigno was that the 5th Corps (78th British and 8th Indian Divisions) would assault the river line, the attack being preceded by a drive of the 13th Corps (5th British and 1st Canadian Division) on Isernia.

Thus, on the 20th October, the 5th Essex left Foggia and began a move up to the forward areas, first to Ururi and then on the 23rd to Larino, where "X" Company was detached and sent forward to guard the bridge over the River Biferno.

The 5th Battalion was now commanded by Lieutenant-Colonel W. L. R. Benyon, Royal Welch Fusiliers, for Lieutenant-Colonel

Allen had been left at Foggia. Much to his regret and to that of the Battalion, he had been considered by the Army Commander too old to take the unit into battle, and had been superseded.

At Larino, Lieutenant-Colonel Benyon had to go sick, and was admitted to No. 9 Casualty Clearing Station. Command of the Battalion was taken by Major E. E. Owen. Major E. I. Elliott became Second-in-Command, and remained in command of H.Q. Company. These rapid changes in command on the eve of battle were unfortunate and disturbing, as were climatic conditions. The weather had broken, and heavy autumnal rains were now descending in sheets, turning streams into torrents, and fields and hillsides into quagmires. Small country roads, built for light-wheeled traffic at most, crumbled under the heavy army traffic, and became almost impassable even without the additional hazards of mines and destroyed culverts and bridges.

On the 24th October another step forward took the Battalion to a concentration area west of the River Biferno. From there the following day it was stepped up to occupy a defensive position west of Acquaviva.

The 3/8th Punjab Regiment and 6/13th R.F.F.R. were the forward battalions at this stage, with the 5th Essex in brigade reserve.

The 19th Indian Infantry Brigade group was now the leading echelon of the Division, and the advance on the 26th took the 5th Essex as far as San Felice.

Although to the forward troops demolitions and destruction were constant reminders of the enemy, there was no physical contact, and it was difficult to convince the man in the ranks that there was in fact nothing between him and the enemy. As a contemporary letter put it: "The Brigade had been pushing on almost unopposed, the enemy only attempting to delay us on natural lines of defence such as rivers. It was altogether different to anything any of us had imagined." Suppressed excitement was evident and a terrific keenness, but the absence of any enemy was an anti-climax.

An ominous portent for the future, however, was the identification on the divisional front of the German 1st Parachute Division, one of the most skilful and belligerent of German formations, but of this the rank and file of the 5th Essex were still happily ignorant.

On the night of the 26th/27th October the 3/8th Punjab Regiment attacked and occupied Monte Falcone, and the following morning the 5th Essex was ordered forward to capture and consolidate Monte

Mitro and from there to patrol forward to the line of the River Trigno. The advance was without incident except for a bad demolition on the main track up which the Battalion was moving. This held up most of the transport except for the carriers.

The occupation of Monte Mitro and Monte Falcone gave the 19th

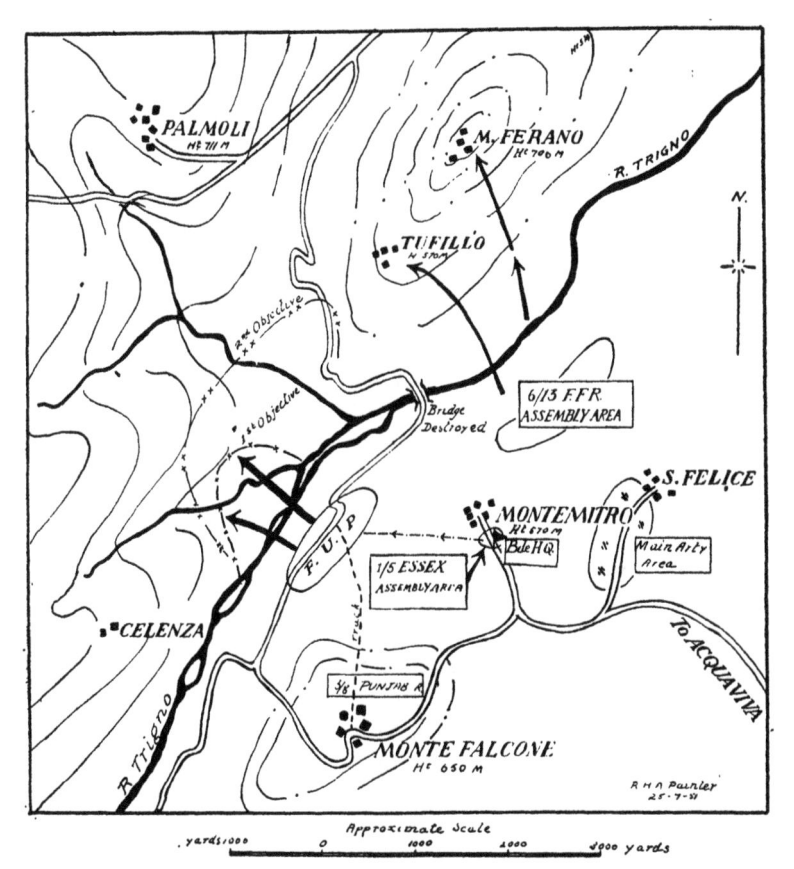

5TH ESSEX, THE CROSSING OF THE RIVER TRIGNO, NOVEMBER 1943.

Indian Infantry Brigade a firm grip on the south bank of the Trigno, and during the night the 27th/28th October the first patrols from the 5th Essex made their way down to the river line.

In this area the Trigno runs between steep escarpments, with crests nearly 1,500 feet above the bottom of the valley. In places the banks were sheer. The river was wide—from 60 to 100 yards—with a stony bottom split up into a number of channels, quite shallow, and easily fordable. The whole river-bed with water channels and shingle banks was some 400 yards wide and in full view of an enemy on the north bank.

Monte Mitro itself is a typical south Italian village perched on the top of the hill, looking down on to the river 1,500 feet below, the bank of which could be reached by a steep and tortuous footpath. This debouched into a field, fringed with trees, adjoining another field which sloped to the river. To the left a road came down the valley running parallel to the river and crossed the stream below Monte Mitro by a bridge which, however, had been destroyed.

The 5th Essex, now on the eve of battle, had been described a few days earlier, in Foggia, by Brigadier T. S. Dobree as an efficient, well-disciplined, and well-administered unit. Writing to Lieutenant-Colonel B. G. Allen on the 19th October, the Brigadier had said: "I think you know what a very high opinion I have of your Battalion, their discipline, and their training, and the state to which you have brought them." They had, too, since moving up to the forward areas, sent officers and other ranks for battle inoculation to the 78th British Infantry Division—the "Battleaxe" Division—a formation with an unsurpassed reputation.

From the night the 27th/28th October patrols were pushed, by day and night, down the river without meeting enemy resistance or drawing fire. However, intermittent shell fire over the battalion area, on the 29th October, caused the first 5th Essex casualties of the campaign, 1 man being killed and 6 wounded.

The weather continued to be bad, and the state of the roads became worse. "B" Echelon, lying back to the west of Acquaviva, became stuck in the mud and unable to bring supplies to the forward echelon. Rations came up by mule, for in view of the mountain warfare conditions anticipated in the drive up the mountainous backbone of Italy, each battalion had been issued with about sixty mules from two Indian mule companies which were now part of the Division. It is certain that the 5th Essex were supplied on many critical days only by the use of these mules and the devotion of those who led them.

On the 31st October, with the weather still extremely bad, came orders for the 5th Essex to cross the Trigno the following day. A subsequent order put back timings by twenty-four hours, and the attack was therefore laid on for the early morning of the 2nd November, 1943.

Information about the enemy was extremely scanty and intelligence reports from higher formations uninformative. Patrols down the river had failed to make the enemy disclose his positions, and Captain C. E. A. Whyte, the Adjutant, had to frame his information paragraph:

"*Enemy*. Information uncertain and confused. Some posts are sometimes held and he probably uses mortars in a mobile role; no entrenchments are visible; there is little artillery; there are rumours of tanks, but it is more than likely these are self-propelled guns."

That is all the 5th Essex could be told in the operation orders for a difficult night approach march, a river crossing, and an attack.

Captain C. E. A. Whyte perhaps understates things when he writes: "I think 'I' staff must have underestimated the strength of the enemy." Captain J. N. Lyster says: "Repeated assurances from the Brigadier and the Commanding Officer that the Germans were ready to go and that it was only necessary for us to show a bold front to shift them helped to allay some of my fears. How we grew to mistrust the cry—'they are pulling out.'"

On the enemy side Tufillo dominated the front, and the rising ground on each side of the spur, with numerous undulations and small copses, farm-houses and the like, made it a very strong defensive position when held by a skilful and determined enemy.

The capture of Tufillo was essential to the success of the crossing, and in consequence the Brigade plan was for the 6/13th R.F.F.R. to cross on the right and attack and seize the Tufillo spur during the night. On the left the 5th Essex was to attack at dawn across the wide river-bed, establish a bridge-head, and pursue up the road. The attack would be supported by "B" Squadron 50th Royal Tank Regiment, the 8th Indian Divisional Artillery, one army field regiment, and two troops from the 15th Anti-Tank Battery. Meanwhile, after dawn the 6/13th R.F.F.R. would continue the advance on the right and take Monte Ferano. The 3/8th Punjab Regiment was to remain in reserve in the area of Monte Falcone and cover the left flank towards Celenza. After the 5th Essex bridge-head was established, the trackway was to be continued forward to the river and linked up with the road. Nearly all the artillery would support each attack in turn.

The attack plan of the 5th Essex was worked out in two phases:

In Phase I, "Y" Company would take up positions to cover the Battalion assembly area. Then "W" and "Z" Companies would pass through, cross the River Trigno, and establish themselves on two features on the north bank known as Lone Tree Ridge and "K" Farm Ridge. "X" and "Y" Companies would follow in reserve as ordered. On the introduction of Phase II, "X" Company was to pass through the forward companies and establish itself on a further feature known as White Farm Ridge and then exploit right-handed to further high ground. "Y" Company was the reserve under the commanding officer's hand. The Company was to establish itself covering the assembly area by 2 a.m., the 2nd November, and zero for "W" and "Z" to pass through was fixed for 5.30 a.m.

Few slept that night. It was the first battle, and there was natural anxiety, coupled with physical discomfort. The fleas and the weather were against sleep, and many were anxious about the coming battle. "... Part of my anxiety was due to the fact that I had been unable to have a decent look at the assembly area," says Captain J. N. Lyster, then Second-in-Command of "Y" Company. Others were more than anxious about the lack of information as to the enemy's strength and dispositions.

To make matters worse, there was that night an extremely thick mist, which reduced visibility to from five to twenty yards as "Y," the leading company, made its way in the darkness down the steep footpath leading to the river line. The path and assembly area was taped out, but even so it was not an easy operation. "W" and "Z" Companies followed down to time, but main Battalion Headquarters was late in starting owing to trouble with the mules carrying the rear link set and its batteries.

The guns started their slow concentrations, gradually stepping up to normal as "Y" Company (Major C. O. P. Trimble) was slowly wending its way down to the assembly area.

At 3.45 a.m. the 6/13th R.F.F.R. on the right began to cross the river under cover of a barrage and started to move up the spurs ahead of them.

Brigadier Dobree says of this phase: "The 6/13th went off successfully, and though they were, in the middle stage, behind the artillery, they reached the Tufillo spur on time, and their cheers and shouts, as they moved on to the village, could be heard floating across the valley at Advanced Brigade Headquarters. But they could not get into the village.

Before 5.30 a.m., despite the mud, darkness, and the mist, all the 5th Essex companies were in position in the assembly area, but in some cases forward observation officers, Royal Artillery, had not succeeded in joining up with the companies.

The morning of the 2nd November was very misty, and smoke made visibility very poor. Nevertheless, the attack began on time, and "W" Company (Captain M. J. Wootton), left forward company and "Z" (Major L. C. Kaye), right forward company, began to cross in the wake of the barrage. Behind in support was "X" Company (Captain J. P. Kaye), while "Y" (Major C. O. P. Trimble) lay in reserve.

As they came to the river, it was found to be shallow and fast running but with much loose sand in its bed, which made a quick crossing difficult if not impossible. As soon as the leading elements came into the river, they met heavy and accurate artillery fire and fire from machine guns on fixed lines. There was also mortar fire, and "W" and "Z" began to suffer casualties.

Coming out of the river-bed, "W" lost direction in the mist, and began to veer to the left of the correct axis of advance, but "Z" kept straight for its objective. As it advanced, "Z" Company was held up by a machine-gun post hidden in a house not far from the river-bank. This post Major L. C. Kaye rushed and knocked out, thus enabling his company to continue its advance. For this action and for his leadership during the battle of the River Trigno Major Kaye was to be awarded the Military Cross, but unfortunately did not live to hear of the distinction he had gained.

By about 8 a.m., "Z" Company, now reduced to a strength of about 20, succeeded in reaching its objective.

"X" Company (Captain J. P. Kaye) had by now crossed the river. Passing through the leading troops, it had after severe fighting reached its objective on the White Farm Ridge feature, but after suffering heavy casualties was forced off and joined up with "Z" Company.

At an early stage communications within the Battalion failed. Battalion Headquarters had been established in the first field at the foot of the escarpment, farther back by about 150 yards than had originally been intended. Faulty information in the dark, smoke, and mist led to this change of location, which in the event was to prove of importance, because of the failure of the wireless link between companies and Battalion Headquarters and lack of knowledge as to the exact location of Battalion Headquarters.

"Communications were dreadful and I could get no information," states Captain Whyte, the Adjutant. "'Z' Company's set seemed to be the only one working, and though they appeared to be making steady progress on the right, they couldn't tell me anything of the other companies." (Of "W" Company's operators, one was killed and the other badly wounded: the bullet which killed the former went right through the No. 18 set.)

Meanwhile, in the assembly area Major Trimble had realised that "W" Company was off its line and thus had failed to get its objective. He therefore decided to commit "Y" Company to take "W" Company's objective.

"Y" Company had unfortunately got scattered in the dense mist and smoke, and Captain J. N. Lyster could only collect up No. 14 Platoon (2/Lieutenant R. H. Ettershank) and No. 15 Platoon (Lieutenant D. L. Maxwell). "I took 14 and 15 down to the company commander," says Captain Lyster, "and he said we could wait no longer, and even though we were short of one platoon and—most important of all—our wireless set, and supporting arms commanders, we must take 'W's' objective. So we set off across the 500 yards of stony riverbed with its 60–70 yards of two-foot-deep river. For some time we could see little through the mist and smoke, but the enemy were firing, presumably on fixed lines, down the river-bed and one or two men were hit. Corporal Cornell fell near me, and we dragged him under a small bank and told him to wait till the stretcher-bearers could get him.

"It was quite a relief to reach the far bank, but this was momentary, as a grenade was flung from the bushes above us. 14 Platoon cleared these bushes with great dash, while 15 Platoon went on towards the objective. They came under fire from a machine gun, and I appeared with 14 Platoon just in time to see a section put in a first-rate bayonet charge with covering fire from another section and knock out the machine gun."

Following up with 14 Platoon, Captain Lyster reached the top of the small hill that was "Y" Company's objective, and had a look round. "Not a very enthralling sight, as not a sign could we see of the other companies, and there was plenty of fire coming at us from their objectives. We shot back with vigour, but it was very worrying that we had absolutely no contact with the other companies, with Battalion Headquarters, or our supporting arms."

This isolated company now became the target for the German fire, and under cover of his fire the enemy began encircling, so Major Trimble sent Captain Lyster back to find the Commanding Officer's Headquarters and get information, orders, and supporting fire.

He took Private Watts with him, and they worked their way back to the river's edge which the enemy was mortaring hard. "We had gone some 200 yards in close cover when a movement caught my eye, and I saw a section of Germans creeping to the top of a bank some 200 yards away on our right. I saw the light machine gunner of the section get into a firing position and take aim; and looking in the direction in which he was aiming, I could see several men of 'Y' Company who had obviously not spotted this enemy party on their left rear. Fortunately, the spandau must have had a stoppage, because before they could fire Watts and I let them have a couple of rounds apiece and they scrambled into cover and disappeared.

"The prospect of the wide river-bed from which the mist had now disappeared was extremely bleak," continues Captain Lyster, "but we had to get across somehow, and anyhow, our present position in the centre of their mortar concentrations was far from attractive. So telling Watts to give me twenty yards start, we jumped up and ran for our lives.

"The bushes on the far bank seemed to be in another unattainable world and the water seemed to have changed into treacle. As, I suppose, we were the only living persons visible in the river-bed, we provided great sport for the enemy. Watts, unfortunately, was killed, but by great good luck I eventually found myself very frightened and out of breath among the bushes."

At this time, owing to communications difficulty and his inability to find "Y" Company on the near side of the river, Lieutenant-Colonel Owen decided to cross the river with a small tactical headquarters. This he did without difficulty, to find "Y" Company Headquarters on the other side, but no sign of Major Trimble.

Lieutenant-Colonel Owen, in attempting to make a reconnaissance forward, was wounded. He gained touch with Captain J. P. Kaye ("X" Company) who was also wounded at this time, and in view of the general situation decided to recross the river and gain touch with Brigade H.Q. This he managed to do without trouble from the enemy, and making his way through Headquarter Company area contacted Brigade. He then unfortunately had to be evacuated.

"Y" Company, shortly after Lieutenant-Colonel Owen and Captain Lyster had left, had been heavily counter-attacked and driven off its objective. Major Trimble decided to withdraw the remnants of his company back across the river. They had had heavy casualties, and the Commanders of No. 14 and No. 15 Platoons, Lieutenant Maxwell and 2/Lieutenant Ettershank, had both been wounded and taken prisoner.

The withdrawal of "Y" Company again isolated the remnants of "W," "X," and "Z" Companies, and the position about 9.30 a.m. can be summarised as follows:

"W" Company, having gone too far left-handed in the initial advance in the mist from the river-bed, had lost contact with the rest of the Battalion. No. 7 Platoon (Captain J. G. S. Trelawney) had gone too far forward and had by now disappeared. The Company Commander, Captain M. J. Wootton, had been seriously wounded (he was to die from his wounds), and the lost and now somewhat leaderless company was in great trouble, out of touch, and without supporting fire of any nature.

"X" Company, having crossed after "W" and "Z" Companies, did take its objective assisted by "Z," now firmly on its own objective and by the missing No. 13 platoon of "Y" Company which had joined in with the "X" Company advance. Lieutenant A. H. Manning and Lieutenant W. G. Lampard had been killed, and all platoons had had heavy casualties. 2/Lieutenant G. C. May, O.C. 13 Platoon, had been badly wounded, and was to be picked up, still alive, two days later. The remnants of the company now fell back on the firm base provided by "Z" Company.

The remnants of "W" and "X" were taken under command by Major L. C. Kaye, O.C. "Z" Company. Largely owing to Major Kaye's leadership, "Z" Company, with the remnants of the other companies, stubbornly held their ground in face of repeated counter-attacks for about six hours until, about 1.30 p.m., a withdrawal was ordered by Brigade Headquarters. This most difficult withdrawal was skilfully conducted with few casualties. Major Kaye got the bulk of the Battalion back across the river by about 4 p.m., the remnants of No. 18 Platoon—Sergeant W. J. Swan—the last back over the river, coming in under cover of darkness about 6 p.m. Shortly before this platoon got back, "Y" Company Headquarters also completed their withdrawal. They had come under extremely heavy fire when crossing the river, and had been forced to take cover behind a small shingle bank, and there they had spent the whole afternoon lying in the water.

And so shortly after nightfall the 5th Essex were back over the Trigno, having suffered during the day 139 casualties, including 10 officers and 41 non-commissioned officers. The loss of 51 leaders was a severe blow.

Lieutenants G. A. Whyte, W. G. Lampard, and A. H. Manning had been killed; Lieutenant-Colonel E. E. Owen, Captain J. P. Kaye, 2/Lieutenant G. C. May, and Captain M. J. Wootton had been wounded, and Captain J. G. S. Trelawney, 2/Lieutenant R. H. Ettershank, and Lieutenant D. L. Maxwell were missing.

Of Captain Trelawney it is said that when his Company Commander became a casualty, Headquarters made an effort on the wireless to get him back to his own Company Headquarters to take over command. But the reason was not given over the wireless, and back came Captain Trelawney's answer, "To hell with that, I'm not coming; I'm having too good a time here." Shortly afterwards he and the platoon he was then with were overwhelmed by the enemy.

Very great gallantry had been displayed. There is, for example, the story of Corporal E. J. P. Dale who took charge of his platoon after both his platoon officer and platoon sergeant had been killed, and at a time when it was held up by three machine guns and an anti-tank gun. The latter was firing at the platoon at a range of only thirty yards, but Corporal Dale got to his feet, and with his tommy-gun shot the two Germans manning the anti-tank gun. He continued to fire, and killed the remainder of the gun crew as they rushed to man the gun. Having done this, Corporal Dale turned to his platoon and said quietly, "Christ, I was frightened," and then without more ado led his platoon on against further opposition. For this action Corporal Dale was given an immediate award of the Military Medal.

The night 2nd/3rd November was spent patrolling along the river looking for any stragglers and wounded who might be trying to rejoin. Quite a number managed to get back. Private Bryce of "Y" Company was one. Wounded in both legs, he had lain up under cover during daylight and at night had dragged himself back across the river, an astonishing feat of endurance.

By the morning of the 3rd November, everyone had had a hot meal, and the Battalion had shaken itself into a rough defensive position. It was temporarily commanded by Major C. O. P. Trimble.

During the morning, Major K. Wilkinson (The East Yorkshire Regiment, attached 1st Royal Fusiliers) took over command, and infused new life into a somewhat shaken battalion. They had been hard hit in their first battle, an action in which they had been told to expect little opposition, but in which in fact they met with the most stubborn resistance from a determined enemy in a highly organised defensive position.

Owing to the heavy casualties, Major Wilkinson temporarily reorganised the Battalion into two companies, "W" and "X" forming one company, "Y" and "Z" the other.

Of the Trigno action Brigadier Dobree, writing in 1951, says: "For their first serious battle, this Trigno crossing was a very severe and bitter trial. They came up against the best trained and toughest German troops in Italy in a very carefully prepared position. The 5th Essex made a most gallant and desperate attempt to overcome odds which proved too strong for them, but gave the enemy such a hard knock that he had to go after two more days' constant harassing. Casualties were unfortunately heavy. The C.O., among many, was wounded near the farthest point reached, and many officers and men lost their lives. The Battalion was put in Brigade reserve, and had the opportunity, at once, of searching for and burying their comrades."

Lieutenant-General Sir Dudley Russell wrote to say: "I visited Battalion H.Q. during the morning of the battle, and found them a little breathless, sad over lost friends, but efficiently active in reorganising to get on with the fight. I spoke to many of their wounded who were in great heart and the remarks of one: 'What a party, sir. I bet those paratroopers didn't like it either,' was indicative of their spirit. Had it not been for the fine soldierly bearing, the battalion spirit and devotion to duty of all ranks, the unit would never have recovered as quickly as it did. Success was achieved elsewhere largely as a result of the 5th Battalion's fine fight."

On the 5th November the composite company commanded by Major L. C. Kaye was ordered to send a patrol across the river, which would be followed by the remainder of the company if little or no opposition was encountered. The patrol was fired on and held up, but Major Kaye, convinced that the enemy was withdrawing, went ahead of the patrol and made his way to the objective of two days before. The patrol followed, and later the rest of the company followed up. Then the Battalion crossed.

So ended the battle of the River Trigno. It had been a hard introduction to battle.

Certainly faulty intelligence and the dense mist mitigated the chances of success. Bad communication within the Battalion was an added handicap, as was the ground over which the attack had to go, offering as it did little or no scope for manœuvre.

But whatever the causes of this set-back, it was certainly not for lack of fighting spirit. An extract from a contemporary letter written by Major E. I. Elliott reads:

"There can be many reasons why it [the attack] failed, but most certainly not through lack of gallantry. I walked the battlefield shortly after, and our fellows had fought like fiends: evidence of that was plentiful—young Gerry Whyte, Arthur Manning, Lampard, others, and many N.C.O.s lying face on to machine guns which they had crippled in their last moments."

Where so great gallantry had been shown by so many, it is not possible to name all those who distinguished themselves, but the River Trigno cannot be left behind without naming Major L. C. Kaye, Sergeants D. D. Smith and C. T. Snowdon, Corporals P. J. Leppard and E. J. Dale, and Privates G. N. Elsmore, C. H. King, Keeley-Callan, and E. Wiffin.

On the evening of the 5th November the 5th Essex, now assembled in the original objective area, was ordered to occupy Palmoli on the following morning.

The Approach to the River Sangro

Captain R. C. G. Hill says of the advance northwards from the Trigno:

"Brigadier Dobree ordered an advance on Palmoli. This was a typical compact Italian hill-top town about five miles from the river and overlooking the road up from the river. Majors Kaye and Lyster, Company Commanders of 'Z' and 'Y' Companies, were on reconnaissance at the time, and as Second-in-Command 'Z' Company I was the senior officer available and was ordered to take 'Y' Company, the carrier and mortar platoons, and leave in half an hour.

"The strength of 'Y' Company was approximately 40, and we started off riding in the carriers, but owing to mines in the road progress was slow, and after $1\frac{1}{2}$ miles I dismounted 'Y' Company under a hill, where there was cover from observation in Palmoli.

"We advanced over the hill while the carriers under Captain Griffen advanced along the road. We were in wireless communication with the carriers and mortars, but not with Battalion H.Q. But I had a previously arranged success signal of three white Very lights to be fired when in Palmoli.

"After advancing through olive groves and tomato fields (the tomatoes quenched our thirst) for about twenty minutes, we saw an

Italian running across the fields. I decided to take him and question him: he said there were many Tedeschi in Palmoli, finally giving the figure at 25. This heartened everyone, and we pressed on, taking the Italian with us; he was one of the many who had been to America and proud of his English.

"The remaining distance was crossed without incident, and we reached a small copse 300 yards from the village. From there we could see a mile of road, but there was no sound or sign of the carriers with whom we were now out of wireless touch. I didn't like to take the village without their support.

"There was no sign of life in Palmoli. I was beginning a reconnaissance when there was a loud explosion from the centre of the village, followed by a cloud of smoke.

"A few seconds later half a dozen Italians came running out of the village. The Italian with us shouted before we could prevent him, but no damage was done. They had come to find us and tell us the Germans were leaving from the other end of the village and the explosion was their ammunition dump blowing up under the town hall."

Palmoli was occupied on the 6th November and the 5th Essex remained there until the 12th.

There, four rifle companies were re-formed and commanded respectively by Captain M. Tye ("W"), Captain D. M. Gibbs ("X"), Major J. N. Lyster ("Y"), and Major L. C. Kaye ("Z"). Captain W. W. Buzza took H.Q. Company, Captain W. F. Griffen the Carrier Platoon (No. 4), while Lieutenant C. F. M. Beard took No. 5 Platoon (Anti-tank), Lieutenant E. G. Ainsworth (formerly the regimental sergeant-major) was transferred from the mortar platoon to be second-in-command of "Y" company. Administration was overhauled and reorganised in the light of the lessons of battle.

From Palmoli the Battalion moved first to San Buono, then to Casalanguida, and on the 17th November further company reorganisation sent Captain R. C. G. Hill to "W" Company as Second-in-Command, and Captain W. W. Buzza as Second-in-Command of "Z."

Captain C. Wright was still the medical officer. He had performed heroic work under extremely difficult circumstances during the Trigno battle, as had too the Chaplain, the Reverend R. J. Holmes, C.F. Both had done far more than was their share in the first battle of the 5th Essex.

In the subsequent advance after the capture of the heights round

Palmoli, the 19th Indian Infantry Brigade was in reserve. It was an advance across difficult mountainous country, with deep river-beds, and as every bridge was blown, progress was slow. Sergeant L. G. Ketley and the pioneer platoon did outstanding work in clearing the numerous mines that were found in every direction. This slow advance gave time to the Essex to complete their reorganisation after the heavy casualties on the Trigno.

After the 1/5th Royal Gurkhas of 17th Infantry Brigade had captured Atessa, the 19th Indian Infantry Brigade took the lead with the object of clearing the enemy from the south side of the River Sangro, from Piazzano to the heights above Archi, and also covering the deployment of the New Zealand Division in its preparation for an attack across the river.

Meanwhile the rest of the 8th Indian Division had moved north-east to the area of Paglietta in readiness for the battle of the Sangro. The 19th Indian Infantry Brigade thus came temporarily under command of General Freyberg's New Zealand Division.

Contact was soon gained with the enemy and shelling started. There were no casualties except for Captain D. M. Gibbs, who was in a slit trench in rear of a haystack when a dud shell, coming through the haystack, made a direct hit. It was indeed the thousandth chance. Captain R. C. G. Hill took over "X" Company.

"We were at this time," says a contemporary letter, "fighting a most peculiar type of action, advancing along high ground, a valley on our left, with more high ground farther across, on which the Boche was sitting. We were pushing north along our high ground and he, sitting on our left flank (the west) could hit us with everything except the kitchen sink, and frequently did so, including harassing patrols by night, which on occasion got into our gun lines, and one night Brigade Headquarters fought."

After a short engagement at dusk, the 6/13th R.F.F.R. took San Marco, but the very dominating village heights of Perano and Archi strongly held by rear-guards had to be seized before the river line could be reached. The 3/8th Punjab Regiment, in a fierce and violent afternoon battle, with the help of tanks took Perano, and the next night the 6/13th R.F.F.R., after encountering some opposition, drove the enemy from Archi, a magnificent old walled town with a most commanding view. Mules were used to supply both battalions direct across-country.

Meanwhile, the 5th Essex was in reserve at Atessa, and on the 19th

November moved another step forward to a position midway between Archi and Perano. Here 115 reinforcements joined. From view-points nearby, the whole Sangro valley could be seen stretching away to the east, while to the west broken mountainous country, virtually unoccupied by either side, faded into the distance.

The Crossing of the River Sangro

Now the New Zealand Division began to come up and make preparations for the battle of the Sangro, "and it soon became evident," says Brigadier Dobree, "that in order to ensure that the N.Z. attacks would not be severely jeopardised, it was essential to drive the enemy from the spur of San Angelo which was formed between the junction of the Sangro and Aventino on the left flank."

The 19th Indian Infantry Brigade was therefore ordered to capture and hold this on a date previous to the main attack. The bridge to San Angelo had been destroyed except for the piers, and movement along the forward lateral road was not possible in daylight except by single vehicles at speed and hazard. The river was fordable provided heavy rain did not fall.

The hill-top of Il Calvario was the key-point to be captured, as it gave observation, not only right along the Sangro, but on to the village of San Angelo. The village was expected to be strongly held, standing as it did almost sheer out of the river. Il Calvario was high and crowned with scrub and trees. Both were most difficult objectives even had they not been across the river.

On the 20th November the 5th Essex was ordered to cross the Sangro and occupy San Angelo at dawn the following morning. The first order for an almost immediate crossing was postponed because of Lieutenant-Colonel Benyon's representations that nobody had seen the ground, and there was not the time to make the necessary preparations for a river crossing.

Lieutenant-Colonel Benyon, writing in 1951, says:

"The original order to cross the Sangro at dawn on the 21st November, without reconnaissance, remains one of my most vivid memories of this period. I regarded it as impossible." A subsequent postponement was made necessary because of the weather turning unfavourable, the river rising in flood, transport getting bogged down, and the administrative situation becoming threatening.

Major E. I. Elliott writes of this phase:

"Here began the most desperate hard work that I have ever undertaken. On the 19th November we advanced to occupy the Archi-Perano ridge... and the problem was to get supplies and ammunition into the Battalion. The road could not be used, anything that showed on it was slaughtered. We built a track winding through four miles of most difficult country, and despite rain, took all our light transport across it. I nearly killed by hard work a hundred men in two nights, and remember waking up under a hedge about seven o'clock the second morning: the men were strewn along the track asleep with exhaustion, but the job was finished. It later proved our salvation."

The plan which—after postponement—was put into effect on the 23rd November was: the 3/8th Punjab Regiment, by a silent attack at night, would capture Il Calvario. This would be the first phase, and if successful would, it was hoped, cut off San Angelo. The 5th Essex would cross silently during the night and assemble on the far bank, launching an attack on the village of San Angelo just before dawn, after a short and intense bombardment of the village by all available artillery.

Major J. N. Lyster takes up the story: "On the 20th November 'Y' Company, of which I was the commander, were working hard to clear the mass of rubble blocking the main street of Archi and allow through the Battalion's transport. I was walking from one road block to another when a particularly filthy-looking peasant hobbled up to me holding out his hand and saying, 'My God, Major, I'm glad to see you.' He was a captain in the South African Air Force, who had escaped from a prison camp in September and been hiding up ever since.

"Thinking he might have valuable information, I took him down to Battalion Headquarters, and on the way passed the Brigadier talking to the Commanding Officer, and from the look on Colonel Benyon's face I gathered that something exceedingly unpleasant was to happen to the 5th Essex in the immediate future."

On the following day, the 21st November, Major Lyster was ordered to send a daylight patrol to accompany a sapper officer of the N.Z. Division to find the best place to cross the River Sangro on the Battalion front. Major Lyster goes on: "Lieutenant G. F. Harding took this patrol, and in spite of getting exceedingly wet, during which process I suspect that everyone who watched it, both friend and foe, laughed a great deal, he could find no place that was fordable." It was followed by further patrols during the 22nd.

By midnight the 22nd/23rd November, only one possible crossing place had been found, a ford about 800 yards to the left of the demolished bridge. This had been discovered by a patrol under Sergeant W. J. Swan. He had been with earlier patrols, and now reported a difference of three feet in the river level to that noted earlier. The effect on the Sangro of flood-water had not then been appreciated, but events during the battle were to confirm the correctness of his observations.

With a possible crossing place now found, the Brigade plan already outlined can be taken a step farther by dealing with the problem as it faced the 5th Essex. The task was formidable. The village of San Angelo was across a deep and unpredictable river, and lay between two arms of that river. The river itself was about thirty yards wide at its narrowest point, bitterly cold with snow water from the mountains, and running at high speed. Its depth was variable, but the mean was perhaps about three and a half feet. The approach was down the face of a bleak hill about 2,000 feet above sea-level, on the forward slopes of which the 5th Essex were established. The bridge to San Angelo was blown, and the road coming in along the line of the river on the right front of the 5th Essex sector was cratered in a most business-like manner and under full observation from the Sangro ridge across the river. Nevertheless, the Battalion was obliged to use this road on occasions, and Lieutenant C. Baldwin, the Battalion Transport Officer, had an uncomfortable adventure there one night.

The quartermaster of the 3/8th Punjab Regiment preceding Lieutenant Baldwin across the diversion was hit by a shell and killed outright. Baldwin, "concerned with getting over, led his convoy of four vehicles at speed, and missing his right road went straight down to the bridge instead of turning left, and did not discover his mistake until he came under the direct fire of an 88-mm. gun and some mortars." However, except for 2 minor casualties and damage to two vehicles, the convoy was able to extricate itself.

Across the river was the vital ground now held by the enemy, from which they had commanding views down the river on the front and to the right of the 19th Indian Infantry Brigade sector, where the N.Z. Division was to cross. It was a long spur about 2,000 feet high on the left and about 700 feet on the right. It was some 3,000 yards long and jutted out towards the river on the right.

The frontage allotted to the 5th Essex was about 2,000 yards, and included the village of San Angelo. From the village the ground rose in a series of ridges to a high feature about two miles from San Angelo, on which was the village of Casoli. The right of the 5th Essex sector was bounded by a tributary of the Sangro which ran away to the north: the left was marked by a distinctive knoll and a line of trees. Between the 5th Essex left and the sector of the 3/8th Punjab was a gap of about 1,000 yards.

As has already been said, by midnight, the 22nd/23rd November, only one crossing place had been found, and the plan, which had been to go over on a two-company front using two crossing places, had to be amended. The new plan was to put the Battalion across much farther to the left than had been hoped, as the only ford was some 800 yards upstream from the broken bridge. The amended plan for the crossing was for the two forward companies to send platoons across with some New Zealand sappers who, with the help of the Battalion pioneers, would fix ropes to assist the remainder of the Battalion to cross.

"X" Company (Captain R. C. G. Hill) would take the right side of the San Angelo feature, "Z" Company (Major L. C. Kaye) the left and the village of San Angelo. "W" Company (Captain M. Tye) and "Y" Company (Major J. N. Lyster) were in reserve.

At 1.30 a.m., the 23rd November, the 5th Essex began the long march, in pouring rain, down to the forming-up places in the scrub and low bushes on the south bank of the river. There was much anxious speculation as to how deep would be the river as the companies moved slowly down the steep escarpment.

"When we reached our forming-up place," remarks Major Lyster, "it looked as if the Germans were expecting us, as they suddenly shelled the area pretty heavily, but there were few, if any, casualties, and the forward companies set off to the river on time."

"It was a horrible sensation entering the water, which was up to the waist of the average man," said Lieutenant-Colonel Benyon; "it was raining really hard by now, and a chill wind froze the sweat of two hours' marching. Curiously the water was warmer, if such a term is applicable, than had been anticipated. The farther shore was very muddy and slippery. It was very dark.

"Nevertheless, 'X' and 'Z' Companies crossed without much difficulty and disappeared up the re-entrant without a shot being fired, but the river was again rising at tremendous speed, and the following companies would not have got across without the help of the two large and stalwart N.Z. engineers who stood in the river during almost the whole crossing, supporting a rope which gave hold to those crossing over, and saved many from being carried away and drowned."

Captain H. E. Chandler-Honnor and the intelligence section also

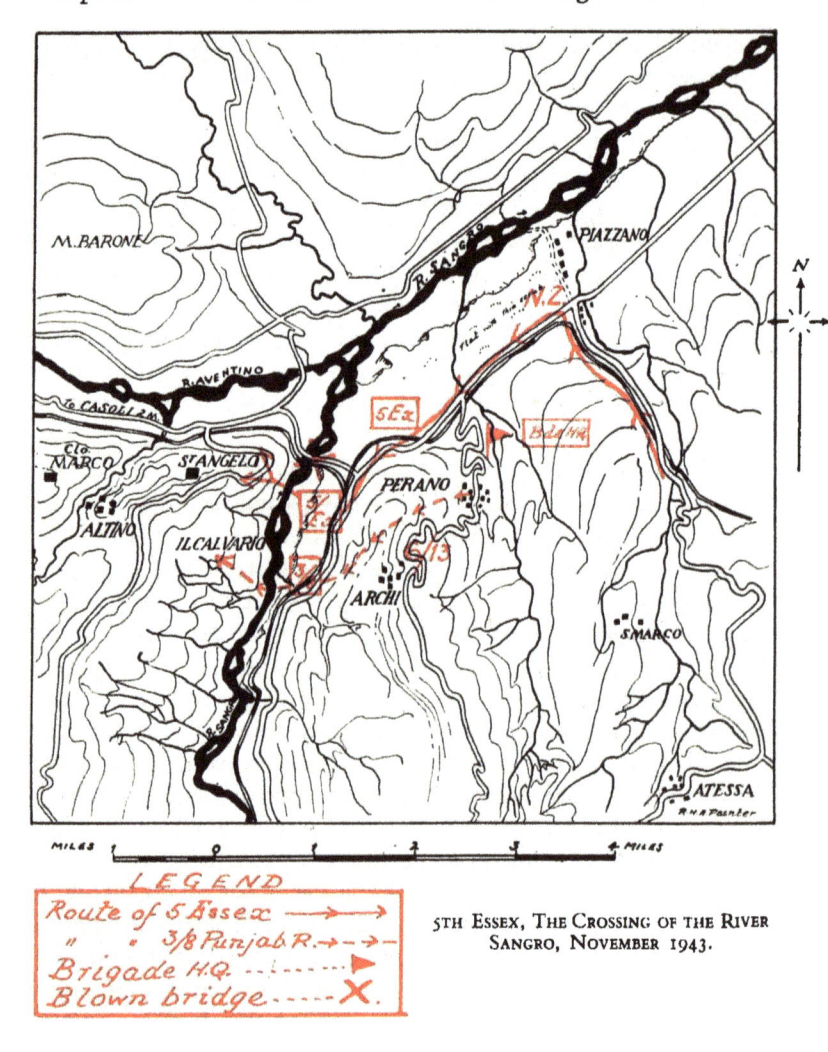

5TH ESSEX, THE CROSSING OF THE RIVER SANGRO, NOVEMBER 1943.

played a notable part, not only in the physical crossing, but in all the reconnaissances that were carried out to find a crossing place.

The rain and the roar of the river drowned any noises, and there was no interference until the leading companies reached the outskirts of

San Angelo after climbing the steep slopes up from the river. It appeared that the enemy was taken completely by surprise, "and we afterwards found out," remarks Major Lyster, "that at midnight the battalion of Panzer Grenadiers, whom we had expected to meet, had been relieved by our old adversaries of the Trigno, the 3rd Parachute Battalion. This for us was extremely fortunate, as the 3rd Paratroops didn't really know their new position and, in my opinion, most of them were asleep when 'X' and 'Z' attacked them. However, they were not the troops to refuse a fight, and they came rapidly to life when the forward companies were just short of their objective."

The inevitable dog-fight began. "X" Company on the right soon had casualties and eventually got stuck just short of the top of its ridge. "Z" Company reached its objective with almost no resistance, but as the two leading platoons were passing through San Angelo and Major L. C. Kaye was just speaking to his company sergeant-major (C.S.M. Pratt) about a bloodless battle, a German sentry stepped from a doorway some ten yards distant and fired a burst. Major L. C. Kaye was killed instantly, a grievous loss to the Battalion.

Captain R. C. G. Hill, with his "X" Company, holding an olive grove 100 yards from the top of the ridge of the San Angelo feature, had early in the morning detailed one platoon to protect his right flank. This, according to the original plan, was to have been the responsibility of Captain Griffen's carrier platoon. Captain Griffen says: "Our task was to afford right-flank protection to the main crossing by getting over at the demolished bridge. When we arrived at the bridge, it was found that the river had risen considerably and the bridge covered by M.G. fire. This effectively kept us pinned down up to our thighs in water, under shell fire, for the rest of the day. We did, however, manage to cross over when dusk fell and join 'Z' Company."

"X" Company's flank-protection platoon was that commanded by Lieutenant Thornton, who was killed early in the action. His platoon later became pinned down. No messages were received from this platoon reporting its progress. Captain Hill was therefore handicapped by the apparent loss of his right-flank platoon and also by the absence of the carrier platoon. However, despite difficulties, "X" Company held its ground throughout the day.

The forward platoons of "Z" Company also had severe fighting as they passed through San Angelo. Lieutenant Starkey's platoon overshot its objective and was rounded up by the enemy later in the day.

By the time "X" and "Z" Companies were being brought to a

standstill, it was beginning to get light, and Battalion H.Q. and "Y" were crossing the river.

"It was an extremely nasty period," to quote Major Lyster. "The river had risen enormously, and it would have been quite impossible for anyone to cross without the aid of the rope. As it was, one or two men were swept away and drowned, and a man of small stature could only just manage to keep his head out of the tremendous current."

Captain C. E. A. Whyte, the Adjutant, and the Medical Officer, Captain C. Wright, crossing with Battalion H.Q., found a kind of cave hollowed under a bank, about seventy yards from the river. "Here," says Captain Whyte, "we set up our wireless sets and an R.A.P. Owing to screening, we were out of touch with the companies, but we could hear the set with the C.O.'s Tactical Headquarters. I then heard the Signal Officer (Captain M. I. Law) on the C.O.'s set telling me to report to 'Tac H.Q.,' and 'mind the snipers.' I found them in the buildings east of 'Z' Company's objective."

"W" Company was by now committed to the support of "X" and "Z," and Lieutenant-Colonel Benyon now ordered "Y" Company to clear San Angelo, on the edge of which were the remains of "Z" Company, and then to push on to the top of the ridge above and beyond it.

"We cleared three-quarters of the village," says the Company Commander, "without much difficulty, but then ran into some stubborn L.M.G. posts which were placed on the edge of an olive grove some hundred yards beyond the village, and these had a clear field of fire at anyone appearing from the village. Also a few of the enemy were sniping from the last houses of the village. We cleared these out and tried to work round the right flank of the M.G.s, behind a smoke screen, but the ground was very open and No. 14 Platoon had heavy losses.

"These were lying dead or dying out in the open, and my stretcher-bearers behaved with foolhardy gallantry trying to get in the wounded. But the Germans cared little, and two stretcher-bearers were killed. Private King especially behaved with great gallantry, and I was very sorry he was not given the decoration for which I recommended him."

And so the day wore on, the forward companies being particularly worried by an isolated and very strong building on a small rise which overlooked the western edge of the village. This, after close and accurate artillery bombardment, was cleared on the following morning.

Meanwhile, above the 5th Essex to the west the 3/8th Punjab Regiment was having a desperate battle on Il Calvario, in which very heavy casualties were suffered. Last light on the 23rd November found both battalions clinging rather precariously to their objectives. The 5th Essex had during the day lost about 100 killed, wounded, or missing.

Brigadier Dobree now takes up the story. "It was on this first day and night that the river continued to rise in alarming fashion and became quite unfordable by the second day. Both battalions were practically cut off. Men were drowned in attempting the crossing, particularly in the 3/8th Punjab Regiment area, whose crossing place was subject to constant fierce bombardment. Desperate expedients were proposed and about to be put in operation, including a suggestion of General Freyberg's to get the Navy to send up rocket apparatus. Fortunately, the enemy, after their first efforts, made no serious counter-attack, and just as the river seemed to be getting worse, the skies cleared, the water went down with great speed, the sun shone, and everything dried up. Both battalions were firmly established.

However, to the 5th Essex companies this period was one of much anxiety. Major Lyster gives the Battalion picture for the remaining days on San Angelo:

"The fly in the ointment, and a large one at that, was that the river was hopelessly swollen, and that we had not a hope of getting across to us any tanks, anti-tank guns, or other supporting arms. In fact, the situation was most unenviable, and if, as seemed likely, the enemy counter-attacked in the morning, and especially if he had any tanks, we should have very little hope.

"And so we spent a particularly uncomfortable and uneasy night. In the early part of it the enemy did succeed in getting into the edge of the village, but we managed to hold them there. I think they must have thought that we had crossed in much greater strength than we actually had, because in the latter part of the night they hauled off altogether and at dawn we discovered that they had disappeared.

"We thereupon immediately occupied our objective completely, and reorganised into a good defensive position. We all felt very much happier about the situation now, though it was still not exactly a comfortable one: it appeared that the 3/8th Punjab on our left had been severely counter-attacked, and it was thought that their objective, which completely overlooked our position, was still in enemy hands, though later it became known that the enemy had abandoned this too.

"Also the river was still in full flood, and consequently the main Eighth Army attack had had to be postponed yet again, and we could still not get our supporting arms across.

"And so the situation remained for four uneasy days, until to our great joy and relief we watched the main Eighth Army crossing take place.

"It will always remain a mystery to me why the enemy didn't counter-attack us in force; the San Angelo feature was the key to the main crossing—whoever held it completely dominated that area of the river, and if the enemy had counter-attacked in strength with tanks, we should have had little hope of stopping him."

"The capture of the San Angelo spur received a special message of congratulation from the Army Commander," says Brigadier Dobree. He goes on: "The Essex again had had a very difficult task which they had carried out with verve and determination and shown themselves to be a fine fighting battalion after the hammering they had received such a short time before on the River Trigno."

Again the price paid had been high. One hundred and nine casualties, including 5 officers and a high proportion of non-commissioned officers.

Coys.	Killed Offrs.	Killed O.R.s	Wounded Offrs.	Wounded O.R.s	Missing Offrs.	Missing O.R.s	Total Offrs.	Total O.R.s
H.Q.	—	4	1	15	—	—	1	19
"W"	—	6	—	15	—	—	—	21
"X"	2	6	—	15	—	12	2	33
"Y"	—	4	—	7	—	2	—	13
"Z"	1	4	—	7	1	7	2	18
Total	3	24	1	59	1	21	5	104

Forward on the final objectives, administration became difficult, for Lower Archi, the site of the rear echelon, was under constant shell fire, as was the route up to the crossing place. That the forward echelon was replenished was largely due to the work of the company quartermaster-sergeants and Sergeant L. G. Ketley. Company Quartermaster-Sergeant H. W. Penson, for example, was in charge of the mule teams bringing supplies to the crossing places. The column was repeatedly and heavily shelled, those mules not killed stampeding on one occasion into a heavily mined area. But the supplies were got up and across the river into the forward echelon. Major E. I. Elliott wrote in early 1944: "We were shelled to blazes in the mule area, losing fifty-odd mules, and through that and the mines we had the hell of a job to get anything over. However, it was vital, and we did it: clerks, batmen, mess staff, drivers, cooks, all carried daily for nearly a week under shell fire, mortars, and what have you. I was very proud of them."

Sergeant Ketley, too, when the crossing place had been neutralised by heavy fire, and the first cable swept away, had under indescribable conditions of weather and enemy action reconnoitred and found a subsidiary crossing place near the ruined bridge which he proceeded to organise. Had Sergeant Ketley failed, the whole Battalion would have been in jeopardy. It is satisfying to know that both Company Quartermaster-Sergeant H. W. Penson and Sergeant L. G. Ketley received the Military Medal.

With the loss of 5 more officers in the Sangro battle, a shuffle of company commanders was again necessary. Captain C. F. M. Beard was given "W" Company, Captain R. C. G. Hill "X," and Captain W. W. Buzza was appointed to "Z." Major J. N. Lyster remained in command of "Y" Company.

On the 27th November the main 5th Corps attack went in and was supported, as had been planned, by the 5th Essex and other units of the 19th Indian Infantry Brigade now firmly in possession of their objectives.

Then, on the afternoon of the 29th November, the 5th New Zealand Infantry Brigade attacked Monte Barone across the Sangro and to the left of San Angelo. This proved to be the final straw, and caused the enemy resistance in front of the 19th Indian Infantry Brigade to crumble. First the 3/8th Punjab was withdrawn, and then on the 30th November the 5th Essex came back, the San Angelo position being abandoned without relief.

As the 5th Essex marched back through San Marco to Atessa, the whole of the Sangro Ridge was falling into the hands of the 5th Corps.

Since first being committed to battle a short five weeks earlier, the battle casualties of the 5th Essex had been 15 officers and approximately 250 other ranks. The Battalion had suffered a serious blow, for non-commissioned ranks had suffered the same high proportion of losses as had commissioned ranks.

Lieutenant-General Sir Dudley Russell wrote of this battle in 1951 and said: "The Battalion was ready for a fight again in a remarkably short time, and this came at the Sangro River which was hard going with inclement weather. The following is, I think, worthy of record. Shortly after the capture of the Il Calvario feature by the 19th Brigade, General Montgomery asked General Freyberg and me to meet him at a good view-point near Paglietta. He called our attention to Il Calvario and, as far as I can remember, said, 'Just look at that hill. Without it this Sangro crossing would have been a much more difficult operation. I understand, Freyberg, that this was captured by a brigade of the 8th Indian Division under your command. I am told they suffered heavy casualties, Russell. Tell them every one was worth it.' "

It appears unfortunate, however, that a battalion, fresh to a theatre of active operations, should have had so severe a baptism of fire as did the 5th Essex at the crossings of the Trigno and Sangro, soon to be followed up by even more bloody fighting. The Battalion had been given no preliminary period in a quiet sector, where the many lessons of active service, unteachable on training, might be absorbed in a defensive role punctuated by active patrolling.

The Advance towards Villa Grande, December 1943

There was to be no rest in Atessa. The Battalion had barely arrived on the 30th November when orders were received saying it was to move early the following morning in relief of a battalion of the 21st Infantry Brigade. Captain Whyte must have sighed as he sat down to prepare yet another operation order.

Leaving Atessa, they went to Paglietta, and after a halt for twenty-four hours moved on the 3rd December to relieve the 1/5th Mahrattas at Andreoli.

At Andreoli, the day after arrival, the 5th Essex received a draft of 6 officers and 200 other ranks, bringing the reinforcement total since the 20th November to 334 other ranks. It is not easy for a battalion under the best of circumstances to absorb and digest so large a draft, and it is extremely difficult to do so when almost continuously on the move in the forward areas.

Over thirty regiments were now represented in the Battalion. It was only too clear that there was to be no break in operations and no rest period, and that before very long the 5th Essex, now numerically at battle strength, but in truth diluted by officers, non-commissioned officers and men almost unknown to their comrades, would again be committed to battle. It is a very great tribute to the spirit of the 5th Essex that it was to fight so magnificently in its next battle, a proof that the Battalion absorbed the drafts and not the drafts the Battalion. Indeed, many were the requests to be sent back to the 5th Essex from these new arrivals when, a few weeks later, they lay wounded in hospital.

We have Lieutenant-Colonel W. L. R. Benyon's letter of the 11th December to explain the problem and give his solution. He was writing to the Colonel of the Regiment:

"With the considerable reinforcements required, it was inevitable that we should be joined by men of other units, but I did not anticipate quite such a mixture as we have at present. The main drafts we have received consisted of 130 Oxford and Bucks and 200 Cameronians. The former draft arrived immediately prior to our last action, and had, of necessity, to be posted to companies where most required. The latter draft arrived in a period of comparative quiet, and I discovered that they, with their officers (6 in number), formed part of a Cameronian battalion recently converted to draft finding. I have, therefore, taken the unusual step of forming two Essex companies ('Y' and 'Z') and two Cameronian companies ('W' and 'X'). This, I know, must seem to you unfortunate, but I did it largely so that I could keep together officers and men who had trained together and knew each other, as I think by so doing, better results will be obtained in action; and I took counsel before implementing my decision, not only of my Company Commanders, but of such old soldiers as the Quartermaster (Captain A. L. Ostler) and the Regimental Sergeant-Major (R.S.M. R. A. Lambert)."

Major D. O. Liddell, M.C., who was the senior officer with the Cameronian companies, says: "Our Battalion had come direct from the Faroe Islands. On hearing we would be kept together I passed on the news to the men. It was a great tonic, and all Cameronians felt a great debt of gratitude to Colonel Benyon, a debt that increased as the campaign went on, due to the co-operation and kindness of everyone on the staff of the 5th Essex. I am sure it made us give that little bit extra."

The draft from the Oxford and Buckinghamshire Light Infantry was used to make Headquarter Company up to strength.

To complete the picture of the 5th Essex at this time, the roll of officers on the strength on the 11th December, 1943, was as follows:

Lieut.-Colonel W. L. R. Benyon, R.W.F.
Major E. I. Elliott, Essex.
Major G. N. Ross, Gordons.
Major J. N. Lyster, Essex.
Major D. O. Liddell, Cameronians.
Capt. W. W. Buzza, Essex.
Capt. D. McF. Hathorn, Cameronians.
Capt. C. E. A. Whyte, Essex.
Capt. R. C. G. Hill, Wiltshire.
Capt. C. F. M. Beard, Essex.
Capt. W. F. Griffen, Wiltshire.
Capt. M. I. Law, Essex.
Capt. C. Baldwin, Essex.
Lieut. B. A. Porte, Essex.
Lieut. A. B. W. Clarke, D.C.L.I.
Lieut. L. L. M. Clark, Essex.
Lieut. A. S. Steedman, Cameronians.
Lieut. W. H. W. Howes, Essex.
Lieut. J. M. Davidson, Cameronians.
Lieut. G. F. Harding, Essex.
Lieut. W. P. Howard, K.R.R.C.
Lieut. J. W. Harvey, K.R.R.C.
2/Lt. R. Purdie, Essex.
2/Lt. R. P. Dann, Essex.
Capt. (Q.M.) A. L. Ostler, Essex.

On the 3rd December elements of the 5th Corps had, after stiff fighting, reached the general line San Vito–Lanciano, and two days later the 5th Essex was moved up into Lanciano. The enemy, forced off the line of the Sangro, was now giving ground only under pressure, and not going back from one main natural feature to another as he had done between the Rivers Biferno and Sangro.

Despite the difficult country and the appalling weather, the Eighth Army Commander continued his offensive, regrouping his formations after the battle of the Sangro with that object in view. The 1st Canadian and the 8th Indian Divisions formed the 5th Corps on the right of the Army front, and to the left was the 13th Corps of the 5th British and New Zealand Divisions. The 78th Division, which had fought continuously since the Sicily landings, was temporarily withdrawn to rest.

On the 7th December Brigadier Dobree visited the Battalion, giving the Commanding Officer little or no hope of an early opportunity to retrain and absorb the new material into the team. There was, of course, no chance to do this in Lanciano, which was virtually in the front line, and under frequent shell fire. Nine other ranks were killed or wounded there.

Captain W. F. Griffen says: "At Lanciano we had several very uncomfortable nights, owing to the uncannily accurate enemy artillery fire. This was later put down to there being an enemy O.P. still in the town."

On the 10th December the 1st Canadian Division forced a crossing of the River Moro and the long fight that was to lead to Ortona had started.

That evening the 5th Essex was ordered to move forward on the 11th December to Casone as part of a general advance by the 8th Indian Division, but the 21st Infantry Brigade, which was acting as leading brigade, was counter-attacked and the advance was halted. The 5th Essex returned to Lanciano, where they sat for another three days.

Then a new attack, this time by the 17th Indian Infantry Brigade, was put in with success, and the 5th Essex cheerfully set off once more for Casone. Half-way it was told there was no room, so the Battalion was turned about and once more arrived in Lanciano, whose inhabitants must have been getting quite dizzy with all these changes of mind on the part of the 5th Essex. But possibly the only person seriously upset was the Town-Major with all these alterations to his housing schemes.

On the 15th December the 5th Essex succeeded in getting to Casone, only to receive orders to proceed forthwith to Ruatti, there to relieve the 5th R.W.K. The sector was taken over by 6 p.m. and active patrolling started from the moment they were in position. At Ruatti the 5th Battalion was very pleased to have a short visit from Lieutenant-Colonel A. Noble, D.S.O., the Commanding Officer of the 1/4th Essex who had just arrived in Italy with the 4th Indian Division.

Brigadier Dobree says: "The 19th Indian Infantry Brigade remained in reserve until the 15th December, having moved forward to various reserve positions while the Division fought its way to the Ortona–Orsogna road. The 6/13th R.F.F.R. crossed the road beyond Caldari and pressed on to the north-west against much opposition. On the coast the Canadians were meeting with very fierce resistance in their efforts to take Ortona."

In between lay the village of Villa Grande, strongly defended by the 1st Parachute Division and barring the way forward.

The Ruatti sector was held during the 16th and 17th December, and on the 18th an advance was made to the area of Caldari station.

Since crossing the Sangro the carrier platoon had been in reserve "carrying out fatigues, such as road repairs, bridging, and guards," says Captain Griffen. "It was when proceeding on one such a task, a few miles north of Lanciano, that we had the unpleasant task of riding in an anti-tank portee along an enemy-observed road on top of a high ridge. Shelling immediately commenced, and a German fighter machine gunned us as it flew past *below* our level, being in the valley on our right. Needless to say, we were glad to get off that ridge."

Captain R. C. G. Hill and Major J. N. Lyster were both wounded and evacuated from Ruatti, as was Major E. I. Elliott who was sick, Major G. N. Ross taking over the duties of Second-in-Command. Major J. W. G. Lee joined the Battalion whilst it was at Ruatti, and was posted in the first instance to Headquarter Company.

The Battle for Villa Grande

On the 19th December a further advance in the face of slight opposition took the 5th Essex to a small hamlet, to be known as Villa Rosa, about three-quarters of a mile south of the village of Villa Grande. Here Captain W. W. Buzza was wounded, and on the 21st December Major J. W. G. Lee came forward to command "Z" Company.

This same day the Battalion received orders to attack Villa Grande on the 22nd December.

The officer casualties of the past three days had not eased the problems of command and administration within the Battalion, and an added worry was that during the day a sudden sharp attack had rounded up half a platoon from "Y" Company. Thus the enemy had identifications, whereas the 5th Essex did not know the nature of the garrison holding Villa Grande.

The Battalion operation order for the attack gives the information about the enemy as: "There are indications that the enemy has pulled out to some extent, but may resist stubbornly." There is nothing else, and once more one is led to the conclusion that 5th Essex was committed to an attack on inadequate intelligence.

"Verbal orders that evening from the C.O. sounded quite cheering," says Major Lee, "as it was not known that the objective was held by troops of the 1st German Parachute Division, and we were getting what looked like a good ration of supporting arms."

The plan as confirmed by written orders was for the 5th Essex to attack early on the 22nd December.

To assist the Essex attack the 6/13th R.F.F.R. on the 5th Essex left would send out strong patrols just before first light, whilst the troops of the 1st Canadian Division, now believed to be in Ortona, would send out a fighting patrol. The 3/8th Punjab Regiment would relieve the Essex in Villa Rosa by 3 a.m., the 22nd December, and would, at 6.30 a.m., stage a diversion to the north-west.

The troops in support of the 5th Essex attack which so cheered

Major Lee and others when they heard of them were to be "C" Squadron 50th Royal Tank Regiment, the 5th Corps Artillery, one platoon from 69th Field Company, and one platoon (M.G.) from "C" Company 5th Mahrattas.

The 5th Essex attack was to be in two phases. In the first phase "W" Company would attack the Outhouses, a small group of buildings some 100 yards from Villa Grande, and would be covered by concentrations of two field regiments on the Outhouses and two on the village of Villa Grande itself. The rate of advance was to be 100 yards every five minutes. On gaining its objective "W" Company was to be relieved and go into battalion reserve.

Then the second phase would operate. "X" Company, with two troops of tanks in support, was to move forward, and passing to the left of the Outhouses area and along a spur to the left of Villa Grande, was to take up a position from where it could guard the left flank and overlook, and if necessary block, the far exits from the village. With "X" Company in position, the main assault companies—"Y" and "Z"—would advance with the task of capturing Villa Grande itself. "Z" Company on the right was to form up behind "W" Company and "Y" on the left behind "X" Company.

The timings were planned so that these companies would pass through "W" Company and the Outhouses after capture, and go on to cross a start-line at the near end of the village at 6.45 a.m.

At 6 a.m., the 22nd December, after a night of bitter frost, "W" Company (Major D. O. Liddell) began to move forward in the half-light at the same time as the artillery concentrations came down on Outhouses.

Major Lee carries on the narrative. "At first not much happened, and 'W' Company, with two platoons up, were well on their way and the leading platoon of 'Z' Company and 'Z' Company 'Tac H.Q.' were following up and just clear of Villa Rosa when down came the German D.F. (defensive fire) right on these troops. German machine guns also opened up on fixed lines, using quite a lot of tracer.

"This D.F. was terrific, and when I looked at the ground afterwards, the space from Villa Rosa to Outhouses was a network of craters stretching for quite a distance on both sides of the road."

The attack had, as Brigadier Dobree says, "gone in with fine determination, but the artillery had had little effect on the stone houses and defences, and even in some places made the defences more difficult to find and get at." There were many casualties.

"W" Company had now two platoons under heavy fire in front of the Outhouses, and the right forward platoon, about 100 yards away and in exposed ground, under heavy machine-gun fire. Major Liddell himself went over to this platoon which was temporarily pinned down and personally rushed a machine-gun post and put it out of action, at the same time being wounded in the eye.

In the meantime, the other two platoons of "W" Company had moved in and captured the Outhouses, but did not recognise them as their objective. Nor did the right forward platoon, which, under its wounded company commander, charged in to establish a footing in the first house of Villa Grande, thinking it was entering the Outhouses. At dusk that day Major Liddell at last allowed himself to be evacuated, having been wounded some ten hours previously.

At about 10 a.m. the two platoons of "W" Company in the Outhouses, still thinking they had not captured their objective, went forward under smoke and joined their other platoon in the outskirts of Villa Grande.

Thus the position at this hour was that "W" Company (now reduced to the strength of a platoon) was in Villa Grande and "Z" Company was in the Outhouses. The ground between Outhouses and Villa Grande was by now so swept by fire that all attempts by No. 18 Platoon (Sergeant W. J. Swan) to move forward were foiled.

In the meantime, on the left flank "X" Company had set off to gain its preselected position, but early in its advance had come under heavy and accurate fire. Within half an hour the Company Commander, Captain D. Mc. F. Hathorn, and Lieutenant A. S. Steedman, the Company Second-in-Command, had been killed, and the company sergeant-major wounded.

That the company could be brought forward into a suitable position where it could dig in and harass the enemy was due to Captain Hudson, the F.O.O. accompanying "X" Company and to L/Corporal J. W. Lofthouse, who quite early in the action was the only N.C.O. left actively in command. Lofthouse was later joined by the L.O.B. (left out of battle) party under a sergeant, but the latter was soon to be killed, and Lofthouse was again the senior surviving non-commissioned officer. He led most gallantly through most of the day, only to be himself killed late in the afternoon. He was given a posthumous award of the Military Medal.

"W" Company from the southern outskirts of Villa Grande could see three tanks of the 50th Royal Tank Regiment receive direct hits as they came over the high ridge of the spur on the left flank, in support of "X" Company. It was then that Private J. Hastie of "W" Company, entirely on his own initiative, went forward into Villa Grande to try to locate the anti-tank gun which was doing all the damage. Hastie destroyed the crew of the gun, and for his outstanding courage was awarded the Military Medal.

Lieutenant G. F. Harding, from "Y" Company, was sent out to take over command during the night of the 22nd/23rd December.

To return to Villa Grande—No. 18 Platoon "Z" Company moved in after dark and reached the village but, missing "W" Company completely, occupied four more houses.

Any movement in the village drew fire, and in the darkness nothing could be done. In the dark interiors of houses which had not been even seen, let alone entered in daylight, and in which the Germans had lived for days, the mental strain of that night can hardly be imagined. "We—25 men and myself—all that was left of 'W' Company," said Major Liddell, "occupied three rooms of the first building on the evening of the 22nd. The Germans could clearly be heard next door through the walls."

At first light on the 23rd December No. 16 Platoon, "Z" Company (Lieutenant J. W. Harvey) was sent in to join up with the remnants of "W" Company and No. 18 Platoon. It was not heard of again, and must have missed the houses occupied by "W" and "Z" platoons in the morning mist and walked straight into the hands of the enemy.

By daylight the few men in Villa Grande were having a most unpleasant time, and No. 18 Platoon, which was busy capturing more houses, was heavily counter-attacked and reduced to Sergeant Swan and 5 men.

As luck would have it at this time, the remaining platoon of "Z" Company (No. 17 Platoon, Lieutenant W. P. Howard) and "Z" Company Headquarters went in under smoke and met this counter-attack head on. Lieutenant Howard fell wounded as he reached the village, but the Germans withdrew and left the 5th Essex established in Villa Grande. The success had been costly, as by nightfall on the 23rd December "X" Company was holding its ridge with about 20 men, and Villa Grande had only been nibbled at, the first few houses being held by "Z" Company Headquarters with under command the survivors of "W" Company formed into one platoon and the survivors of "Z" Company into another.

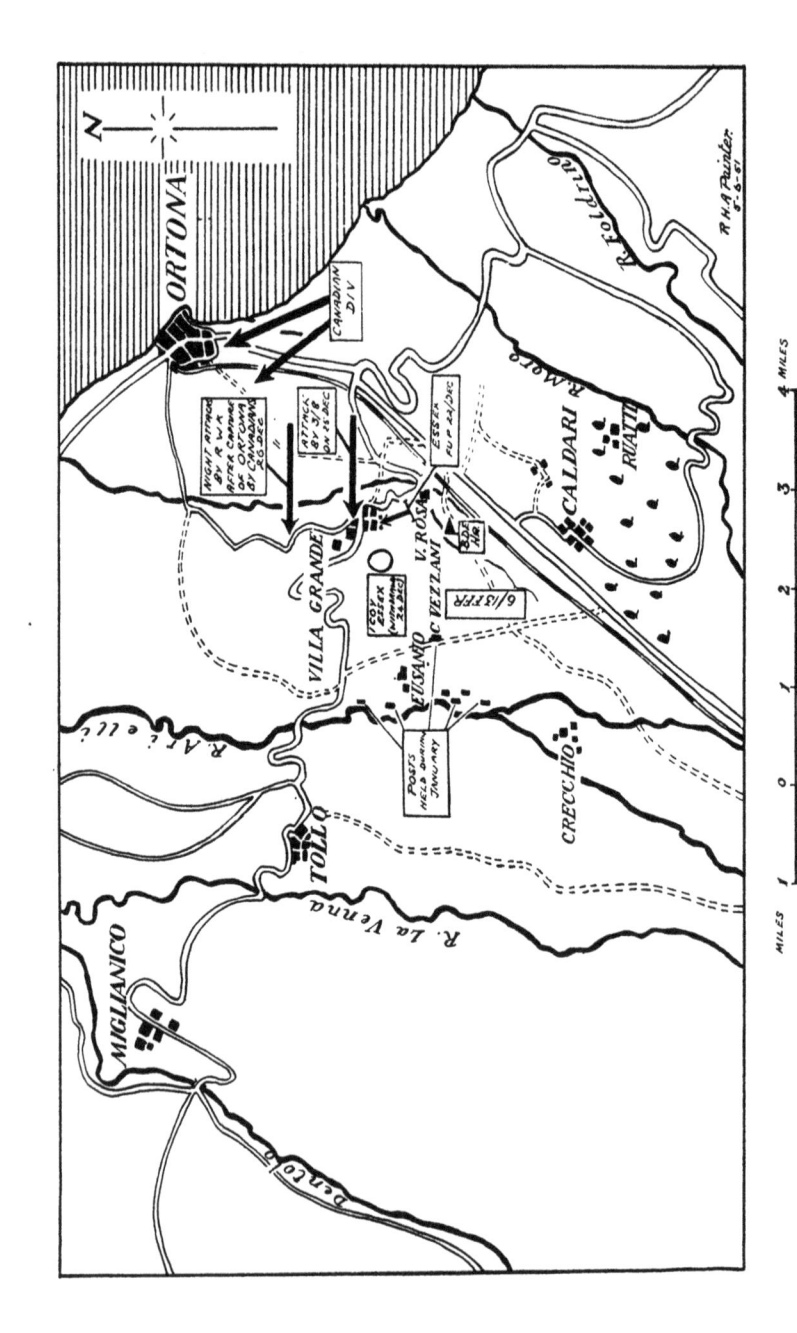

5TH ESSEX, THE BATTLE FOR VILLA GRANDE AND SUBSEQUENT OPERATIONS, RIVER ARIELLI, DECEMBER 1943–MARCH 1944.

After this it was pure street fighting and a battle for junior leaders under continuous shell and mortar fire.

Sections moved from house to house, from cellar to loft, and from one rubble pile to another, and every yard was contested. Generally a section would push forward with another covering, but often there was not room for even section manœuvre, and individuals had to do their gallant best. It was a deadly and nerve-racking type of warfare, and Essex casualties were heavy. Night and day this bitter battle was fought, and bit by bit, room by room, and house by house, the southern tip of Villa Grande was wrenched from enemy hands.

During the morning of the 24th December, Lieutenant-Colonel Benyon sent No. 4 Platoon (Carriers) to operate from the right flank as a diversion to the main attack.

Captain W. F. Griffen, who led this platoon, says: "The plan was for the rifle companies to advance on the axis of the road with the carrier platoon acting as right flank guard and in liaison with the Canadians on the east coast.

"We were to approach the village from the east in the carriers. This, however, proved quite impracticable, as the only bridge was heavily mined and booby-trapped, and the gully it spanned a natural anti-tank obstacle. We therefore left the carriers and drivers on the lateral road. The latter were to carry out splendid work later in the battle, keeping open a line of communication and evacuating casualties.

"The whole of this area had been devastated by artillery fire from both sides, and there was never a dull moment, a moment free from shell and multiple-barrel mortar fire. There was a French-Canadian battalion on the right. It had suffered very heavy casualties and was commanded by a captain. They were most co-operative, giving me supporting fire, and even some precious N.A.A.F.I. supplies for the platoon.

"I found we were up against at least a company in strength, well dug in and ready for anything.

"We advanced along the axis of the road from the east, and succeeded in reaching a group of houses half-way to Villa Grande, only to find we were surrounded.

"However, at dusk we managed to fight our way out, with few casualties, to consolidate short of these houses and wait for dawn. Sergeant Bush was fortunate in escaping unharmed when the tripod of his L.M.G. was shot away, and Sergeant Smith and I were not amused when a typical Italian village lavatory in which we were sheltering collapsed about our ears.

"At dawn on the 25th—Christmas Day—we again advanced, this time with a troop of tanks giving us fire support, but this petered out when two of the tanks were disabled by mines." It must be remembered the strength of the dismounted carrier platoon was never more than 16, so they could not hold much ground.

Meanwhile, with the carrier platoon now out on the right flank and with the devoted efforts of "Z" Company's composite platoons in the village, the Commanding Officer, on the 24th December, had got "Y" Company through "X" on the left flank and established forward on the spur to the north-west of Villa Grande.

By the morning of the 25th December "Z" Company had gained sufficient elbow room in Villa Grande to allow of it being reinforced, and the remnants of "X" Company, about 20 strong, were brought up. Together these companies advanced to the centre of the village. The area was still infested with paratroopers who clung to their broken burrows and fought fanatically to the last, the area round the village church being particularly difficult to clear.

At midday on Christmas Day the Germans put out Red Cross flags, and both Essex and Germans brought in their wounded.

During Christmas afternoon Battalion "Tac H.Q." moved up to the southern edge of the village with supporting weapons, and "C" Company 3/8th Punjab Regiment, now under command, was put in to attack.

On the outskirts of the village the Punjabis were met with machine-gun and rifle fire from positions previously cleared by the Essex, and again reoccupied under cover of darkness by fresh fanatical fighters. But the momentum of the attacks was continued, and the Punjabis entered the village and joined up with the Essex companies.

Brigadier Dobree of this phase says: "On Christmas morning, after a reconnaissance from the east of the village, a plan was made for a company of the 3/8th Punjab Regiment, with a troop of 50th Royal Tank Regiment (who throughout had given the Essex every possible assistance), to attack from the east and get behind the defenders. It appeared at first as if this attack would bring success and relief to the Essex, but again, after they got a firm hold on the edge of the village, progress was almost halted by the defenders."

But even now the stubborn enemy resistance held. All through Boxing Day repeated efforts were made to clear the remainder of the village. The Essex companies attacked from the south end, the 5th Royal West Kent, from 21st Indian Infantry Brigade, pressed in from the south-east, and the Essex carrier platoon from the east, but despite all these efforts the advance was still held.

On the 27th December, despite intensive defensive fire and mounting casualties, the remnants of Captain Griffen's carrier platoon succeeded in reaching a group of houses on the eastern edge of Villa Grande, inflicting considerable casualties on the enemy and taking 18 prisoners. Another attack from the south failed. In the attack Captain H. E. Chandler-Honnor was killed, as was Lieutenant A. B. W. Clarke when the house he was in received a direct hit or was blown up by a mine.

These losses were serious, for many other officers—Captain B. A. Porte, Major D. O. Liddell, Lieutenant J. M. Davidson, Lieutenant W. P. Howard, Lieutenant J. W. Harvey, Captain D. McF. Hathorn, Lieutenant A. S. Steedman to name only some—had been killed or evacuated as casualties. In fact, when Lieutenant A. B. W. Clarke was killed during the 27th December, he was the thirteenth officer casualty in the 5th Essex since the 20th December, a rate almost crippling to any unit, but particularly so when added to the very heavy losses already sustained in the campaign since the crossing of the Trigno less than two months before. Non-commissioned officer casualties had been proportionately as heavy, and included Sergeant Swan, who by now had been severely wounded.

But the relentless pressure and fighting spirit of the 5th Essex in the end prevailed and the enemy resistance began to weaken.

During the night of the 27th/28th December the enemy withdrew to the north of the village of Villa Grande. An attack by a company of the 1/5th Mahrattas was put in on the morning of the 28th December and was successful. The rest of the village was taken. "The Indians entered the village to find it a shambles, with dead Germans sprawled on the rubbish heaps, in the entrances to dug-outs, or floating in water-filled slit trenches."

Villa Grande, as one correspondent put it, "looked as though a giant had trodden on a child's box of bricks."

But Villa Grande belonged to the 5th Essex, and "Z" Company moved up to the north end of the village, and at 8 a.m. on the 28th December relieved the Mahratta Company after its attack. Almost simultaneously the 5th R.W.K. attack came in to capture the remnants of the enemy in their fresh positions north of the village.

The Battle of Villa Grande was over, and there is little more to tell. The operation had been a costly and harrowing experience in the most difficult type of fighting under the worst conditions. That the Battalion "stuck to it so gallantly and persevered after their first check was a lasting credit to them." So writes their Brigadier.

On the 29th December the 5th Essex, or what was left of them, relieved by the 1/12th F.F.R., made their way back to Ruatti. In the seven-day struggle for Villa Grande, the Battalion had had 13 officers and 266 other ranks battle casualties.

CASUALTIES—VILLA GRANDE
20th–27th December, 1943

Coys.	Killed Offrs.	Killed O.R.s	Wounded Offrs.	Wounded O.R.s	Missing Offrs.	Missing O.R.s	Total Offrs.	Total O.R.s
H.Q.	1	9	1	19	—	3	2	31
"W"	—	22	1	42	—	1	1	65
"X"	3	15	2	45	—	7	5	67
"Y"	—	12	2	21	—	10	2	43
"Z"	—	5	2	45	1	10	3	60
Total	4	63	8	172	1	31	13	266

When such great gallantry was displayed by so many, it is invidious to attempt to single out individuals by name, but nevertheless mention must be made of Major J. W. G. Lee, who was awarded the D.S.O., and his company sergeant-major, A. H. Mummery, who was to be given the D.C.M., as was Sergeant W. J. Swan ("Z" Company). Then there were Major D. O. Liddell ("W" Company) and Captain W. F. Griffen (Carrier Platoon), both of whom gained the M.C.; while Sergeant G. D. Syme, L/Corporal J. W. Lofthouse and Private J. Hastie gained the M.M. Major Liddell, Sergeant Syme, L/Corporal Lofthouse, and Rifleman (Private) Hastie were Cameronians. Others brought to notice included Corporal I. E. Hill, Private L. A. Flatman, Corporal G. S. Leggett, L/Corporal S. W. Messias, and Private E. J. White. Those are only some of the many who fought with distinction and gallantry in a most bitter battle, perhaps one of the most bitter of the whole campaign.

Their losses had been a cruel blow to the 5th Essex. Added to those incurred since the initial action on the Trigno, it meant that the Battalion, between the 1st November and the 31st December, 1943, had incurred 536 battle casualties.

A high price had been paid for relatively unimportant gains, and the need to sacrifice so much for so little of real strategic importance can be fairly questioned. It is perhaps not inappropriate to quote from the book *Operation Victory*, by Major-General Sir Francis De Guingand, K.B.E., C.B.E., D.S.O., Chief of Staff Eighth Army: "The fighting during the period had been fairly costly, and one rather wonders what we achieved. Enemy formations were certainly pulled over from opposite the Fifth U.S. Army and heavy casualties were inflicted on the Germans. With snow in the mountains and mud everywhere, we began to think about Passchendaele. Had we gone on too long? Were troops being driven too hard? I feel very definitely that a mistake was made in pressing the Sangro offensive as far as it was. When once the weather had broken, it was extremely unlikely that we could have advanced across the mountains, even if we had reached the Pescara–Rome road." [1]

The losses could not but leave a mark upon the Battalion, and detract something from its spirit and fighting efficiency. That the 5th Essex fought so well at Villa Grande is a tribute both to the fighting spirit of the Cameronian and Light Infantry reinforcements who supplied half of the battle strength, and to the indefinable morale and esprit of the Battalion which could absorb those reinforcements in so very short a time before battle and cause them to fight as the 5th Essex always fought.

Back in Ruatti, the Battalion rested and reorganised. They were visited on the 30th December by their Brigade Commander, and on the 31st, New Year's Eve, the Battalion celebrated Christmas Day a little late that year. No doubt the Cameronian personnel thought this rather a good idea, this celebration of the Sassenach's Christmas at midday and then straight on into the Hogmanay celebrations.

Reinforcements started to arrive early in the New Year, 114 arriving on the 2nd January, 1944, and then 83 Black Watch personnel the 3rd January. These were posted *en masse*, and became "X" Company, under command of Captain Griffen, who was transferred from the carrier platoon.

These two drafts of 197 other ranks less than replaced the wastage

[1] *Operation Victory*, pp. 333-34.

from the battle of Villa Grande, but raised the strength from the low figure of 479 to which the Battalion had been reduced on the 1st January, 1944.

The officer situation was even worse. It had fallen to a strength of 9, but on the 5th January 13 officers were posted, 8 from the Rifle Brigade and 5 from the Union Defence Forces of South Africa. The 5th Essex was now extremely cosmopolitan, and the number of units represented in its ranks had risen to thirty-six. The situation would have been almost ludicrous had it not been so serious, but despite the heavy losses and the overwhelming need for a period of rest and reorganisation, it was apparently found impossible to grant it to this overtried Battalion. "I had a feeling of utter despair," says Lieutenant-Colonel Benyon, "when we were ordered into the line again just four days after Villa Grande."

The Arielli, January/February 1944

Withdrawn from Villa Grande to Ruatti on the 29th December, by the 2nd January, 1944, first one company was called forward to relieve a company of the 1st Royal Fusiliers at Villa Marcone, and then on the 4th January the whole Battalion went in relief of the Fusiliers. They were at Marcone only two days, during which time another large draft, this time from the Duke of Wellingtons, joined the Battalion. The 5th Essex then moved to Vezzani, where it was once more in the front line towards the banks of the River Arielli.

By now there had been the first snow-fall, and the weather was bitterly cold. The Battalion was more than grateful for the mufflers, socks, and other comforts reaching them, thanks to the devoted efforts of Lady Howard and the ladies of the Essex Regiment Comforts Fund (44th and 56th), whose honorary Secretary was Mrs. Lister, wife of the Reverend G. M. Lister, M.C., C.F., Chaplain at the Regimental Centre at Warley. In all, some 40,000 comforts were collected and distributed to battalions of the Regiment during the war.

The enemy, battalions of the 3rd and 4th German Parachute Regiments and the 200th Panzer Grenadiers, supported by some thirty Mark IV tanks, was now building a defensive line between the rivers La Venna and Dentolo, with positions along the western bank of the River Arielli.

The 8th Indian Division was now disposed with the 17th and 19th Brigades forward and with the 21st Brigade in reserve. On the right of the 19th Brigade lay the 17th Indian Infantry Brigade; on the left the 2nd Independent Parachute Brigade under command of the 2nd N.Z. Division. The 19th Indian Infantry Brigade had the 5th Essex and the 3/8th Punjab Regiment forward, with the 6/13th R.F.F.R. in reserve. The task was to secure all ground within the brigade boundary up to the River Arielli.

No further major advance was contemplated for the winter, but the intention was to harass the enemy and keep him occupied with raids.

The Brigade position was up to and along the east bank of the River Arielli south of the Tollo road. Many battered houses and strongpoints were held in depth. These covered one another, but gaps in the line made it possible for patrols on either side to pass through the forward defences to a limited degree. The enemy was known to be enterprising and his patrols were very active, mining tracks within the British area by night, cutting telephone wires, and attaching "S" mines to the cut ends. Most of the troops lived in the farmhouses and outbuildings scattered over the hill-sides, sallying forth after dark to prowl into no-man's-land. Many and bitter were the sudden encounters.

The 5th Essex had relieved the 3/15th Punjab Regiment of the 21st Indian Infantry Brigade in the area of Vezzani-Eusanio, and there the Battalion was to remain until relieved by the 1/12th F.F.R. on the 16th January.

It was a difficult period for the 5th Essex. With 600 battle casualties in less than three months, men did not know their section commanders, nor section leaders their platoon officers. Had all reinforcements been of the Essex Regiment, the problem would have been difficult enough, but there would at least have been a common upbringing and background, a bond to hold them together in times of strain. But they were from every regiment, and the difficulties in trying to weld together such a variety of men cannot be exaggerated, particularly as among the casualties had been so high a proportion of officers and senior N.C.O.s.

In the difficult winter conditions and in the type of defence where it was essential to have a series of small defensive positions mutually supporting against an active enemy, the feeling of confidence in "knowing the next man" was a necessity. This could not be achieved without considerable training in easy conditions which the 5th Essex had been denied. "It is difficult," wrote Lieutenant-Colonel Benyon in 1951, "to bring home the peculiar horror of the two months—January and February 1944—spent in defensive positions, with night movement only as a rule, and a half-trained battalion." So casualties and incidents that would not have occurred with a more compact battalion were to be expected.

There was one such incident within two days of taking over positions on the Arielli. "X" Company, now commanded by Major J. N. Saunders (Union of South Africa Forces), with Captain W. F. Griffen (Wiltshire Regiment) as second-in-command, had one platoon forward, one on the right flank, and the third in reserve round company headquarters. About 2 a.m. on the second morning on the Arielli, Sergeant McIntosh, the platoon sergeant of the forward platoon, staggered into Company Headquarters badly wounded, with a message to say his platoon had been overrun by a strong enemy patrol and, except for those badly wounded, had been captured.

Major Saunders immediately went forward with a strong patrol to find only half a dozen wounded in the platoon position. These were taken back to Company Headquarters, but not finally evacuated for several days because of the difficulties imposed by the excessively heavy shelling by day and the vigorous patrolling by night.

The Germans foolishly returned to the overrun platoon position the following night and suffered heavy casualties from machine guns arranged to fire on fixed lines. On another night a large-scale enemy raid reoccupied Eusanio, but "W" Company recaptured the position the same night.

It had now temporarily thawed and the whole battalion area was a morass. Trench digging was impossible, as the water level was only a few inches below ground. Casualties from shell fire and in raids and patrols were continuous. By the time they were relieved the 5th Essex had had another 149 battle casualties.

Major D. O. Liddell had been wounded once more, as had Captain C. F. Adams and Lieutenants R. G. Clark and M. G. Power. All except Lieutenant Clark, who remained at duty, had to be evacuated.

On relief, the Battalion moved back to Ruatti, where it was converted to a new war establishment and reorganised on the six-company basis with Headquarter Company, support company, and four rifle companies. These were to be "W," "X," "Y," and "Z" as before. Nevertheless, the reorganisation did not immediately increase efficiency, being yet another shuffle of personnel already insufficiently acquainted with each other.

From Ruatti the 5th Essex moved, on the 26th January, back to Lanciano in the reserve brigade area, the farthest from the war they had

THE RIVER ARIELLI
4th–17th January, 1944

Coys.	Killed Offrs.	Killed O.R.s	Wounded Offrs.	Wounded O.R.s	Missing Offrs.	Missing O.R.s	Totals Offrs.	Totals O.R.s
H.Q.	—	1	—	7	—	2	—	10
S.P.	—	2	—	8	—	7	—	17
"W"	—	4	3	21	—	6	3	31
"X"	—	1	—	17	—	22	—	40
"Y"	—	11	1	20	—	3	1	34
"Z"	—	7	—	6	—	—	—	13
Total	—	26	4	79	—	40	4	145

been for many weeks. The most was made of this short period of rest and reorganisation, which was to last until the 5th February. Towards the end a Battalion church parade service was held with the band of the Irish Guards on parade. The service was taken by the Reverend V. J. Pike, the D.A.C.G. of the 5th Corps, and the salute by the Divisional Commander, Major-General D. Russell, C.B.E., D.S.O., M.C.

At the end of the rest period the 5th Essex moved once more into the front line. The 19th Indian Infantry Brigade was at the time relieving the 11th Canadian Infantry Brigade, and the three moves of the 5th Essex to the forward area meant relieving first the 3/15th Punjab Regiment at Mancelli, then the Royal 22nd Regiment of Canada at Caldari, and finally the Irish Regiment of Canada at Casa Salvini, near Orsogna.

The weather was bitterly cold and there was much snow, for the 8th Indian Division had in these reliefs side-stepped farther into the hills and was spread over a front of some twenty miles between Orsogna and the Maiella Mountains. Patrolling was carried out in white camouflage suits which proved most effective—in fact, almost too much so, for on occasion a patrol would lose contact within its own organisation.

At Casa Salvini the "old hands" were glad to welcome Major J. N. Lyster, who returned to the Battalion from No. 11 Convalescent Depot.

The 5th Essex remained in the line between the 5th and 26th February, when it was relieved by the 1/5th Mahrattas and returned to Lanciano. In this last three weeks of winter warfare, another 57 battle casualties had been incurred, for there were many raids and much mortar fire on the widely dispersed battalion.

ORSOGNA
5th–26th February, 1944

Coys.	Killed Offrs.	Killed O.R.s	Wounded Offrs.	Wounded O.R.s	Missing Offrs.	Missing O.R.s	Totals Offrs.	Totals O.R.s
H.Q.	—	—	—	—	—	—	—	—
S.P.	—	1	—	3	—	—	—	4
"W"	—	—	—	3	—	—	—	3
"X"	—	—	—	2	—	3	—	5
"Y"	—	3	—	15	—	2	—	20
"Z"	—	4	1	11	—	9	1	24
Total	—	8	1	34	—	14	1	56

Brigadier Dobree says: "They held the line and patrolled actively, but it was evident that the first opportunity must be given them to have adequate rest and proper training. In mid-February the 2nd Argyll and Sutherland Highlanders was nominated to take the 5th Essex place in the brigade, and before the end of the month the Essex moved to a back area."

The 5th Essex left Lanciano and the 8th Indian Division on the 2nd March, 1944, having been a part of that formation since December 1941. It passed into 5th Corps reserve, and moved back into the village of Monte Odorisio, near Vasto, where the next ten weeks were to be spent.

Before leaving this phase of winter operations, mention must be made of the excellent work of the company quartermaster-sergeants, without whose activities the forward companies on the Arielli and towards the Maiella mountains would have fared ill. Captain R. C. G. Hill says: "In this last phase I was O.C. H.Q. Company, and had advanced 'A' Echelon with me. Each evening the rations, ammunition, mail, and stores were loaded on to mules with Indian muleteers (very cheerful but not speaking English: our Urdu was just sufficient to make them understand). In all weathers—snow, rain, bitter frost, and thick mud—the C.Q.M.S.s got their supplies up without fail, despite shelling and machine guns on fixed lines.

"The round trip took them four hours; then, after a short rest, they left at dawn for Lanciano with jeeps and trailers for the following night's supplies, arriving back in time to split into mule loads before leaving again for the line. I personally did each trip once, and am sure that doing it night after night for three weeks must have been extremely exhausting."

Many had distinguished themselves in those hard winter months, among them Captain M. I. Law, Private G. McDougall, Captain J. Lipscombe, Private A. P. Stephenson, Lieutenant R. C. Purdie, Private M. Stonehouse, Company Quartermaster - Sergeant C. Burgess and Company Quartermaster-Sergeant G. Thompson. Then there was Private A. Whittaker, Private R. Clyde, Corporal H. Spearman, and Sergeant L. Taylor. There were many others.

Back in Monte Odorisio, the Battalion underwent military re-education, starting with individual training, and culminating in practice in combined operations. There was a possibility that they might be called upon to carry out a "Sea-hook" on the Adriatic coast near Pescara.

During all this training Lieutenant-Colonel Benyon had the greatest aid from Lieutenant-General C. W. Allfrey, C.B., D.S.O., M.C., who was still commanding the 5th Corps. He personally interested himself in the Battalion, and on the 15th April came to present decorations for the following officers and other ranks: Major J. W. G. Lee, D.S.O.; Captain W. F. Griffen, M.C.; Sergeant W. J. Swan, D.C.M.; Company Quartermaster-Sergeant H. W. Penson, M.M.; Sergeant L. G. Ketley, M.M.; Sergeant D. D. Smith, M.M.; L/Sergeant E. J. P. Dale, M.M.; Corporal A. F. Armsby, M.M.; Private G. N. Elsmore, M.M.; and Private J. Hastie, M.M.

Concentrating once more at Monte Odorisio after withdrawing detachments from Termoli, where they had been running a combined training centre, the 5th Essex was again warned to be ready for active operations.

"I must mention the extraordinary 'feel' of the Battalion," writes Lieutenant-Colonel Benyon, "when we returned to the line in May after those two months' training. I am confident we were a first-class unit at that time, and I was sorry we were never really tested."

With the 10th Corps, May–June 1944

On the 21st May, 1944, the Battalion moved to Colle Croce, just north of Isernia, and passed under command of the 2nd N.Z. Division.

In its new formation the 5th Essex was, on the 23rd May, made part of a mobile force known as "Pleasant Force," commanded by the second-in-command of the N.Z. Armoured Brigade, and consisting of the motor battalion of the N.Z. Armoured Brigade and the 2nd N.Z. Divisional Cavalry Regiment. The task was the "follow up" of the enemy withdrawing after the battle of Cassino, and the 5th Essex role was principally that of occupying ground that had been passed over by the advancing motorised units.

A week was spent with "Pleasant Force," during which time they moved from Colle Croce to Acquafondata and on to Monte Faiillo. Battalion Headquarters was finally established at Casa Luciense, northwest of San Elia, where they took over from the 24th N.Z. Battalion. The position was overlooked by the enemy, and movement by day was almost impossible, quickly drawing mortar and artillery fire. There was, however, no other contact with the withdrawing enemy, and after three or four days the Battalion was once more left behind by the war, and companies were pulled in to the area of Battalion Headquarters at Casa Luciense. This was on the 28th May, and it is evident that the week of contact with the enemy had merely been an interruption in the 'real war,' for the very next entry in contemporary records is "30th May. Salvage drive continues."

On the 30th May the 5th Essex passed to the command of the 10th Corps on ceasing to be employed with "Pleasant Force." It was promptly set to advance over some very mountainous country up towards Pescasseroli, a town to the west of Castel di Sangro. Once again the Battalion was attached to the N.Z. Division.

There is little to be said of this phase, for it was the follow-up of an enemy with whom contact had been lost. The whole area was, however, heavily mined, and in the first daylight patrol on the front, Lieutenant St. J. C. Bally was killed, together with several other ranks.

This was the last operation of the 5th Essex in the campaign in Italy.

On the 19th June, 1944, the Battalion was ordered back to Afragola near Naples, where it was disclosed that the 5th Essex was going to the Middle East, and would be under command of the 5th British Division for the move.

At Afragola stores and transport were handed in and preparations made for embarkation.

This plan had come as a surprise to Lieutenant-Colonel Benyon, for he had been told, on completion of the Pescasseroli operation, the Battalion would revert to the 5th Corps. But apparently the 5th Division, which after a gruelling time in the Anzio beach-head was being withdrawn to the Middle East for retraining, was leaving a battalion in Italy, and the 5th Essex, at the time unbrigaded, was to take its place.

Section IV

THE MIDDLE EAST, 1944-45

And so, under command of, but not yet part of, the 5th Division, the 5th Essex embarked at Taranto on the 3rd July, 1944, in S.S. *Batory*, and three days later landed at Alexandria.

Here the Battalion became part of the 5th Division, and after a week spent at Qassassin (very near the Battalion's first camp in Egypt three years earlier) where it was re-equipped, the 5th Essex moved up to Palestine with the remainder of the Division.

There is little doubt that as the 5th Essex settled into its new formation, there was a great feeling of relief and encouragement. A long-established formation, the 5th Division had a high standard of administration and staff work, and there was in it, as one officer puts it, "a great feeling of family life and *esprit de division*."

Under these conditions the 5th Essex entered upon a new lease of life, and the last joined of the numerous reinforcements from thirty-eight regiments settled down to render loyal service to their new Battalion.

The first station was Beit Lid near Tulkarm, where the 5th Essex, on the 16th July, 1944, took its place alongside the 2nd Cameronians and 2nd Wilts in the 13th Infantry Brigade under Brigadier L. M. Campbell, V.C., D.S.O., T.D.

The official forecast was that they would do one month's training at Tulkarm and then go with the rest of the brigade for approximately two months' battalion and brigade training in Syria, after which the 5th Division would return to the European theatre of operations, probably to Italy.

Drafts now brought the 5th Essex up to strength, and it is notable that the percentage of Essex officers serving with the Battalion had now increased. The nominal roll of those on the posted strength on the 11th August, 1944, is given as follows:

Lieutenant-Colonel W. L. R. Benyon (R.W.F.)
Major G. N. Ross (Gordons)
Major T. N. Saunders (U.D.F.)
Major J. W. G. Lee, D.S.O. (Essex)
Major J. N. Lyster (Essex)
Major C. F. M. Beard (Essex)
Captain R. W. de Jager (U.D.F.)
Captain W. J. Whiteley, M.C. (U.D.F.)
Captain C. E. A. Whyte (Essex)
Captain M. Tye (Essex)
Captain E. A. Towndrow (Buffs)
Captain R. C. G. Hill (Wilts)
Captain M. I. Law (Essex)
Captain W. F. Griffen, M.C. (Wilts)
Captain G. N. R. Stayton (Suffolk)
Captain C. Baldwin (Essex)
Captain J. Lipscombe (K.R.R.C.)
Lieutenant J. F. Halbert (Essex)
Lieutenant C. A. Emanuel (Hamps)
Lieutenant L. M. L. Clark (Cameronians)
Lieutenant D. W. Lardner-Burke (U.D.F.)
Lieutenant J.R. McComish (Essex)
Lieutenant J. M. Davidson (Cameronians)
Lieutenant G. F. Harding (Essex)
Lieutenant R. C. Purdie (Essex)
Lieutenant R. P. Dann (Essex)
Lieutenant J. E. A. Tansey (Buffs)
Lieutenant K. R. Barge (Essex)
Lieutenant P. P. S. Thorn (Essex)
Lieutenant G. M. Davis (Northamptons)
Lieutenant G. J. D. Baird (Norfolks)
Lieutenant R. G. Clark (Essex)
Lieutenant M. B. Thomson (Essex)
Lieutenant G. F. Chinnery (Essex)
Lieutenant H. F. Ebbs (Norfolk)
2nd Lieutenant H. D. Kitchener (Buffs)
2/Lieutenant D. J. Hooton (Essex)
Captain K. D. Wood (R.A.M.C.)
The Reverend J. Hayes (R.A. Ch.D.)

Captain C. E. A. Whyte, who had been adjutant for over two years and whose work in and out of battle had been done so efficiently and unobtrusively that it was perhaps taken for granted, had just handed over to Captain J. Lipscombe. Captain A. L. Ostler was still Quartermaster, but this is possibly a redundant statement, for Lieutenant Ostler was Quartermaster when the Battalion was embodied in August 1939 and Captain A. L. Ostler, M.B.E., was still Quartermaster on V.E. Day 1945. In fact, he was still Q.M. when the Battalion disbanded in

June 1946, and maybe he is still Quartermaster of some disembodied 5th Essex for old soldiers. . . .

It was fortunate that about this time the 19th Essex, a battalion formed in the Middle East from surplus Home County personnel in the infantry depots, was disbanded, and thus Essex personnel became available for drafting to the 5th Battalion. One hundred and twenty of these men joined during August.

On the 2nd September the 5th Essex moved by road to Jebel Mazaar, Syria, where it stayed until, on the 15th October, the Battalion moved back to Khassa, in the Gaza area of Palestine.

Up in the Lebanon, "Z" Company was party to a strange bargain. Lieutenant R. Powell's platoon, during a divisional mountain warfare exercise, was in a village high up a mountain-side. It was occupying a small stone house, and in the bustle of moving in, the platoon tea ration disappeared. No doubt the Arab owner of the house could say where, but he didn't. When he had the chance, Lieutenant Powell got to the R.A.P. and asked the medical officer if there were any "comforts" to spare. After many negatives the doctor said if the platoon could give him something to help his first-aid classes he would consider a deal. Back despondently to the platoon who were told "no tea." "But," said one L/Corporal Short, "there is a death pit in one of the section areas, and it is full of skeletons." "I went down the slope," says Lieutenant Powell, "and was shown a round hole about 1½ yards in diameter, widening out into a circular stone pit, and about six feet down there were many, many skeletons—quite old, I should think." Needless to say, the platoon got their tea.

It was a time of hard training, and the successes of the 5th Essex in training and recreation should be recorded. In the Divisional interplatoon "Skill at Arms" competition, No. 7 Platoon and No. 4 Platoon of the 5th Essex took second and third places, an excellent result when one considers the very high standard of shooting and physical fitness required, and the keenness to win shown by all battalions in the Division.

"The Divisional Commander wishes to congratulate 5th Essex in their high standard of shooting which both their teams displayed during the Skill at Arms Competition."—*5th November, 1944.*

The 5th Essex won, too, the 5th Division inter-unit football competition. The final was played on the Jerusalem Stadium, where a crowd of over ten thousand saw the 5th Essex beat the 2nd Royal Scots Fusiliers by one goal to nothing.

Then there was the anti-terrorist operation against the town of Natanya to add realism to training. This operation was most successful, some 35 suspects and 12 wanted terrorists being apprehended. The great success of the operation was due primarily to the speed at which the "cordoning off" was done by the Essex and the very high security measures that were adopted—nobody in companies knowing the name of the actual town to be raided until ninety minutes before the start of the raid.

By September the 5th Essex had reached a strength of 1,004, the highest in its history, and it was while at this high parade strength that Brigadier F. R. G. Matthews, the new 13th Infantry Brigade Commander, first saw the Battalion.

In November, Lieutenant-Colonel W. L. R. Benyon was appointed to the staff, and Lieutenant-Colonel W. A. Heal, The Suffolk Regiment, came to the Battalion, assuming command on the 23rd November, 1944. He was quick to note that, despite the dilution of the Battalion by men of different regiments (forty-one regiments were by now represented in the 5th Essex), "the very close relationship of the old pre-war Territorial was most marked, and they tended to gather by districts: the men from Saffron Walden in one corner, those of Chelmsford in another, and so on."

The stay in Palestine and Syria proved longer than had been originally anticipated. But in December the Battalion was put under orders to stand by for embarkation to Italy. The advance party had actually taken over the heavy equipment and transport from a battalion in the 4th Division, when the move was cancelled, and the New Year saw the 5th Essex still in Khassa. "Christmas Day—very heavy rain all day, but all ranks enjoyed the day immensely," says one report, and many must have thought of the Christmas Day of a year ago spent in the noise and stench of Villa Grande.

Section V

North-west Europe, April–May 1945

On the 10th January, 1945, a warning order was again received, saying the 5th Division was to return to the Central Mediterranean Force. Towards the end of the month the Battalion advance party left for Italy, to take over from the Lancashire Fusiliers of the 4th

Division. On the 12th February the main body sailed from Haifa in S.S. *Banfora*.

The voyage was without incident, and on the 16th February the 5th Battalion found itself once more in Taranto. Plans had, however, changed, and the unit entrained the day after disembarkation for Salerno, where it stayed between the 19th and 28th February in an atmosphere fraught with security. On the 28th the 5th Essex proceeded to Naples, and embarking in H.M.T. *Esperance Bay*, sailed the following day, after one of the shortest Italian tours on record. Not that the Battalion quarrelled with these new plans, for many in its ranks had had a taste of Italy in winter a year before.

Disembarking at Marseilles on the 2nd March, 1945, the 5th Essex entrained the next day for Wetteren, in Belgium, where it arrived on the 6th. Palestine, Italy, France, and Belgium, all between the 12th February and the 6th March. It had been quite a Cook's tour.

But things were to be better still. Moving from Wetteren to Mont St. Amand, on the outskirts of Ghent, the Battalion was billeted in civilian houses. This was good after the canvas and ruined houses of the Middle East and Italy, but best of all was the news that all ranks were to be granted seven days' U.K. leave before further operations. The first party left the next day.

Those not on leave, and leave parties as they returned, were straightway initiated into the new weapons of war that had come into general use since the 5th Essex was last in action—Wasp flame-throwing equipment, and Windsor-type carriers to tow the six-pounder anti-tank guns for example. The 5th Essex and the 5th Division, too, had to be inculcated with the spirit and habits of the 21st Army Group, and Field-Marshal Sir B. L. Montgomery came in person to do it. He inspected a detachment of the 5th Essex in Ghent, and afterwards lectured to all officers, warrant officers, and colour-sergeants of the 5th Infantry Division in the Café Quebec, Ghent. Those who have had the privilege of hearing the Field-Marshal on one of those occasions will realise that the senior ranks of the Division dispersed to their units with no doubts of what was expected of them in the future.

The 5th Essex was not committed to battle until the 20th April, 1945, and until shortly before this date remained in Ghent. That time was not wasted, and that all ranks of the 5th Essex were filled with the best traditions of the Essex Regiment is perhaps shown by the following letter registered "in" in the orderly room post-book on the 9th June, 1945:

"G%%HENT%%, 2nd June, 1945.
"S%%IR%%,
"Respectfully we take the liberty of requesting a favour. The people of Mt. St. Amand-Ghent admire so much the soldiers of the Essex Regiment of England who stayed with us to our pleasure during the months of March/April, that we again request their pleasure with us.

"We appreciate the splendid qualities of the officers and men as gentlemen and soldiers, and thus dare to ask you to kindly grant them a stay in Ghent–Mt. St. Amand.

"It would create happiness for the people of our district to extend our hospitality and friendship to the soldiers of your regiment and perhaps offer a little joy to them.

"In anticipation, we thank you and ask God to bless you and your armies.

"We beg your consideration in our request.
"Sincerely.
"T%%HE%% C%%OMMANDING%% O%%FFICER%%,
"T%%HE%% E%%SSEX%% R%%EGIMENT%% (5%%TH%% B%%N%%.)
"21%%ST%% A%%RMY%% G%%ROUP%%,
"A.E.F."

This letter is signed by nearly one hundred citizens of Ghent, who give their full names and addresses. But this is anticipating, for it is only April and the war has yet to be won.

Leaving Ghent on the 14th April, very shortly after the corps of drums had paraded amid great appreciation at the Town Hall, the 5th Essex began to stage up to the forward areas, where advanced elements were now rapidly approaching the River Elbe.

The route was through Goch and Issum to a divisional concentration east of Hessbeck, where the 5th Division came under command of the 8th Corps. As the 5th Essex moved out of this concentration area near Uelzen on the morning of the 20th April, the Battalion was once more forward troops, and its task was to advance to the Elbe.

Opposition was expected to be stiff, but was in fact light. "W" Company crossed the start-line at 6 a.m. the 21st April, and through the day companies were leap-frogged through by M.T. "It was," says Lieutenant-Colonel W. A. Heal, "an almost copy-book advanced-guard move, the leading companies with their scouts ahead, point section and so on, and the rear companies ferrying up in the Battalion transport." During the morning a reconnaissance patrol found from the carrier platoon and sent to contact the 6th Seaforths on the right flank ran into a locality occupied by a self-propelled gun. The leading carriers received a direct hit. Lieutenant D. W. Lardner-Burke and 4 other ranks were killed and 1 other rank wounded. It was evening before any further contact was gained with the enemy. This was when the 5th Reconnaissance Regiment reported the enemy to be offering stubborn resistance in Barskamp.

"H-Hour" was fixed for 8 p.m. "Z" (right) Company and "W" (left) Company were to go forward covered by "Y" Company, while "X" Company would be in reserve. The attack was to be supported by "Q" Battery of the 91st Field Regiment and a troop from the 52nd Anti-Tank Regiment. The plan was quickly made, and at 8.6 p.m. the barrage came down. "The field battery," says Major Lee, "for some reason was unable to fire and the barrage consisted of the 17-pounder anti-tank guns and the Battalion 3-inch mortars. This was most effective, and the German civilians in the village were terrified when they found solid shot sometimes going through their houses in a row. One house must have had a key joist hit, as it collapsed like a pack of cards." The attack was entirely successful, and the enemy withdrew after offering only token resistance. By 8.15 p.m. Barskamp village had been captured at the cost of 2 other ranks only slightly wounded. Fifteen prisoners were taken during the day.

On the 22nd April "X" Company, with a section of 3-inch mortars and a section of carriers under command, left its bivouac area near Barskamp to find the enemy. They left at 7 a.m., and by 7.20 had run into a small party of the enemy and had suffered casualties, 2 being killed, and 1 wounded. But the enemy did not stand, and by evening patrols had reached the south bank of the River Elbe.

On the next day the whole of the 13th Infantry Brigade moved up to the line of the river with the object of preventing any attempt by the enemy to cross back over the river and patrol. The 5th Essex was on the right of the Brigade sector, with the 2nd Wilts in the centre and 2nd Cameronians on the left. While Battalion Headquarters remained at Barskamp, forward companies patrolled the south bank of the Elbe, paying particular attention to ferry sites and similar likely crossing places.

The situation remained quiet during the 23rd and 24th April and there was no contact. Listening posts remained established on the river line, while companies patrolled and searched the woods in their area to round up stray prisoners, but none was found.

It was so quiet that officers had some difficulty in making the troops take reasonable front-line precautions. No shell had landed in the battalion area since the 21st April, but nevertheless the south bank of the River Elbe had to be continuously dominated by patrolling, so as to prevent the enemy recrossing the river, particularly at the more likely crossing places. Only one boat came towards the 5th Essex bank —during one night—but a burst of Bren fire turned it back and it was neither seen nor heard again.

All civilians had been evacuated from the brigade area, leaving their live-stock behind, and it did not take the 5th Essex long to organise a butcher's shop and dairy. The Battalion lived very well.

On the 24th April it became clear that the present areas would be occupied for some days, and so it was arranged that companies should be given forty-eight hours' rest periods in Barskamp.

It was rest more in name than in fact, for Lieutenant Powell says: "We were kept busier than ever doing odd jobs, from clearing woods that were all clear to milking cows that were not sent back with their German owners. Another spell on the river was a welcome break, although keeping under cover was very tedious when there was no obvious incentive."

However, on the 28th April orders for the relief of the 13th Infantry Brigade by the 505 U.S. Infantry Regiment were issued, the Brigade to move to a concentration area south of Melbeck on relief.

The first intimation that "Z" Company had of this up on the river line was when it had a surprise visit from a party of about eleven Americans all piled into two jeeps. They said their division was going to take over from the 5th Essex (and the rest of the "Limeys") on the 29th, and they were to do a reconnaissance patrol into the village of Stiepelse, on the north side of the Elbe.

Their officer said his orders were to land on the jetty steps, and as "Z" Company knew there was a German sentry there, they did their unavailing best to deter the 505 U.S. Infantry Regiment. As the Americans drove their reconnaissance boat down to the river, the 5th Essex took protective action. Covering fire parties were posted, as the American expedition set out. The Elbe was 400 to 500 yards wide and running fast and cold.

After a while sharp small-arms fire broke out from the opposite bank, but the patrol was by then too near the north bank for the Essex to help. About three hours later one stark-naked American staggered into "Z" Company H.Q. He said the boat received heavy fire when about fifteen yards from the enemy bank. His gun jammed and he jumped overboard—those were his orders. "He undressed in the water and swam back, being carried perhaps 1½ miles before he reached our bank. He was wrapped in a blanket, given a cigarette and whisky, and then the American pressman who had awaited the patrol's return brought out his camera and said, 'Smile, please—gee, this'll make a swell picture for the folks back home.' That shook 'Z' Company."

However, despite this unsatisfactory beginning, the relief was accomplished during the afternoon of the 29th April, and the 5th Essex moved by M.T. to the brigade concentration area.

Here, on the 30th April, they heard the plan for the next day. 13th Infantry Brigade was to move into the bridge-head already established across the Elbe by the 15th (Scottish) Division; the Brigade would then break out of the bridge-head as early as possible with its objective as Lubeck.

The war was visibly coming to an end, and British strategy dictated that troops of the 21st Army Group should be across the south of the Schleswig-Holstein Peninsula and through to the Baltic coast before the "Cease-fire," if humanly possible.

The approach march was by M.T.—slow, tedious, and cold. A few German jet fighters, the first seen, flew over, but there was no interference. The pontoon bridge across the Elbe looked longer and more precarious than ever, but soon the Battalion was debussing in a little lane. "There were dead Germans, and it was clear that the ground had not long been ours."

"One of my most vivid memories," continues Lieutenant Powell, "was going round 'Z' Company sentries at about 9 p.m. I passed a Company H.Q. group and they were listening to the B.B.C. News. 'Hitler's dead,' the operator said. But what difference could that make, for we 'go in' tomorrow. Little did we guess that this was the end, and the only live Germans we were to see thereafter were surrendering."

On the 2nd May there was a break-out from the bridge-head. The 5th Division was directed on Lubeck, the 13th Infantry Brigade on the right on the road leading to Brettenfelde, with the 17th Infantry Brigade group on the left. Behind the 13th Brigade group followed the 15th Infantry Brigade ready to pass through and continue the advance should the leading brigade be seriously committed at Molln. The 13th Infantry Brigade's intention was that it would advance "at best speed" with the 2nd Wilts in the lead followed by the 5th Essex, 2nd Cameronians, and the 91st Field Regiment.

The 5th Essex moved first to Dalldorf. Progress was very fast, at times thirty miles in the hour for the Brigade column. Resistance, which at the Elbe crossing and at Potrau on the 1st May had still been stiff, was now ceasing, and no contact was made that morning except with those who wished to surrender.

By the afternoon the 5th Essex approached Molln. Prisoners were pouring in, giving themselves up everywhere. At 2 p.m., as they moved into Molln itself, a general staff officer of the 245th Infantry Division arrived at Battalion Headquarters and offered to surrender the entire division to the 5th Essex. The offer was accepted. As this division had been dug in on the line of the 5th Essex approach, the Battalion was grateful for the timely surrender, for nobody wanted a major battle at this late stage of the campaign.

The Commander of the 245th Infantry Division, Lieutenant-General Sander, did not at first appear—the tiresome business of arranging the surrender of his division was left to a second-grade staff officer—but he was taken prisoner later. By 5 p.m. it was estimated that some 1,500 prisoners had passed through the Battalion's prisoner-of-war cage.

But the 5th Essex was not given time to complete this task, for Lubeck was still the prize. At 6.15 p.m. it made the next bound forward to Ratzeburg. Here chaos was evident. Germans were wanting to surrender faster than the 5th Essex could cope with them. The pile of arms at "Z" Company check post rapidly grew to a mound. "All night they came, and I well remember one German Major being asked if his company had brought their rations. 'Nein,' he said. 'Well, go back and fetch them,' we said. 'You ought to know better than to surrender without food.' It was quite fantastic. Many Germans genuinely thought they were handing in their arms so that they could be issued with allied weapons to help us fight the Russians."

That evening the sword of honour of Marshal von Rondstedt, the sword presented to him on first being commissioned into the German army, was found. It has since been placed in the Museum of the Essex Regiment at Warley.

On the morning of the 3rd May the 5th Essex was relieved by the 1st K.O.Y.L.I., from the 15th Infantry Brigade, and moved to Grosse Gronau, where the task was to sweep an area and bring in any enemy who were not giving themselves up. That afternoon the other two battalions of the 13th Infantry Brigade reached Lubeck itself.

The enemy did not require much sweeping of areas to force them to surrender. The problem was to know what to do with those already in British hands. By the evening of the 3rd May there were some 6,000 in the Battalion's prisoner-of-war cage, and four generals had been passed through to Division.

On the 4th, 5,000 were marched off to Molln with an escort of two carriers to every thousand prisoners. The prisoners had no food or water, for it was quite impossible for the 5th Essex to do anything effective in the face of a problem of such magnitude. Another 2,000 prisoners were sent back in M.T.

At 8.30 a.m., on the 5th May, 1945, the 5th Essex received a message saying that the "cease fire" had sounded at 8 a.m. that morning on the Second British Army front.

But although fighting was over, work was not, for "Operation Eclipse" was now launched. Under this scheme tasks were many—prisoners had to be rounded up and disarmed, dangerous prisoners, such as S.S. men, had to be segregated and normal prisoners caged or at least corralled under local guard. Then small arms had to be collected in dumps and prepared for destruction, while guns and armoured fighting vehicles had to be organised into gun and vehicle parks. Burgomasters had to be contacted, and all information got from them on such things as resistance movements, whereabouts of Nazi and S.S. Leaders, and dumps.

In addition, the 5th Essex had the task of preventing civilians withdrawing ahead of the Russian army from crossing the Brigade boundary from the east.

On the 5th May, Battalion Headquarters moved to Krumesse, where they were still quartered on V.E.-Day.

The day was marked by a ceremonial parade in Lubeck, to which every unit in the 5th Division sent a detachment. Three officers and 60 men of the 5th Essex were on parade when the Union Jack was hoisted in Lubeck and the representative detachments marched past their Divisional Commander.

The 5th Battalion the Essex Regiment had gone far and done well during the years of war and had worthily upheld the high traditions of the Essex Regiment. It had served at home and in Egypt, Palestine, Syria, Iraq, Italy, Belgium, and Germany. In Italy it had taken part in some of the most bitter fighting of the whole war.

In conclusion, it is proposed to quote from the farewell message from Brigadier T. S. Dobree, D.S.O., to the 19th Indian Infantry Brigade on his relinquishing command in June 1945:

"In giving up command of the 19th Indian Infantry Brigade after more than two years, I want to thank all ranks for their splendid performance, loyal help, and untiring efforts. Together we had a continual series of successes in battle through the length of Italy. The foundation for these was laid in our training in Iraq and Syria in 1943, where we first got to know so well the other arms in the Division who have always given us such unswerving support. . . .

"We will remember the 5th Essex, who came with us to Italy, and how bravely they battled at Villa Grande. . . ."

Section VI

MAY 1945–JUNE 1946

It was not long before the immediate task of rounding up the surrendered enemy personnel and displaced persons was accomplished, and the 5th Essex was pleased to be moved into Wismar, a pleasant sea-port on the Baltic, with wide tree-lined streets and pretty parks. It was the most easterly town reached by the Allies.

Here the 5th Essex took over from the 9th Parachute Battalion, for the 6th Airborne Division was packing up preparatory to a move back to England, there to retrain in case it was needed for the war against Japan. It was almost a relief between two Essex battalions, for the 9th Parachute Battalion had been formed in November 1942 from the 10th Essex.

The last few hours of the war had seen a race between the Airborne Division and Russian tanks for possession of Wismar. The airborne troops had won, but only just, the inter-zonal boundary being almost immediately east of the town.

The Corps of Drums of the 5th Essex very much came into their own at Wismar, beating Retreat on the main square, leading the Battalion to church, and attending ceremonial guard-mounting parades. There is little doubt that their smart turn-out and efficiency did much to impress the Germans with their so great love of ceremony.

Early in June a move was ordered to Bad Kleinan, on the Schweriner See about twelve miles from Wismar. Here the Battalion was to enjoy excellent sailing and boating in beautiful weather.

Bad Kleinan was right on the inter-zonal boundary, and the Battalion had a good opportunity of summing up the Russians and their army. Liaison visits were paid across the boundary, and on the 7th June one reads:

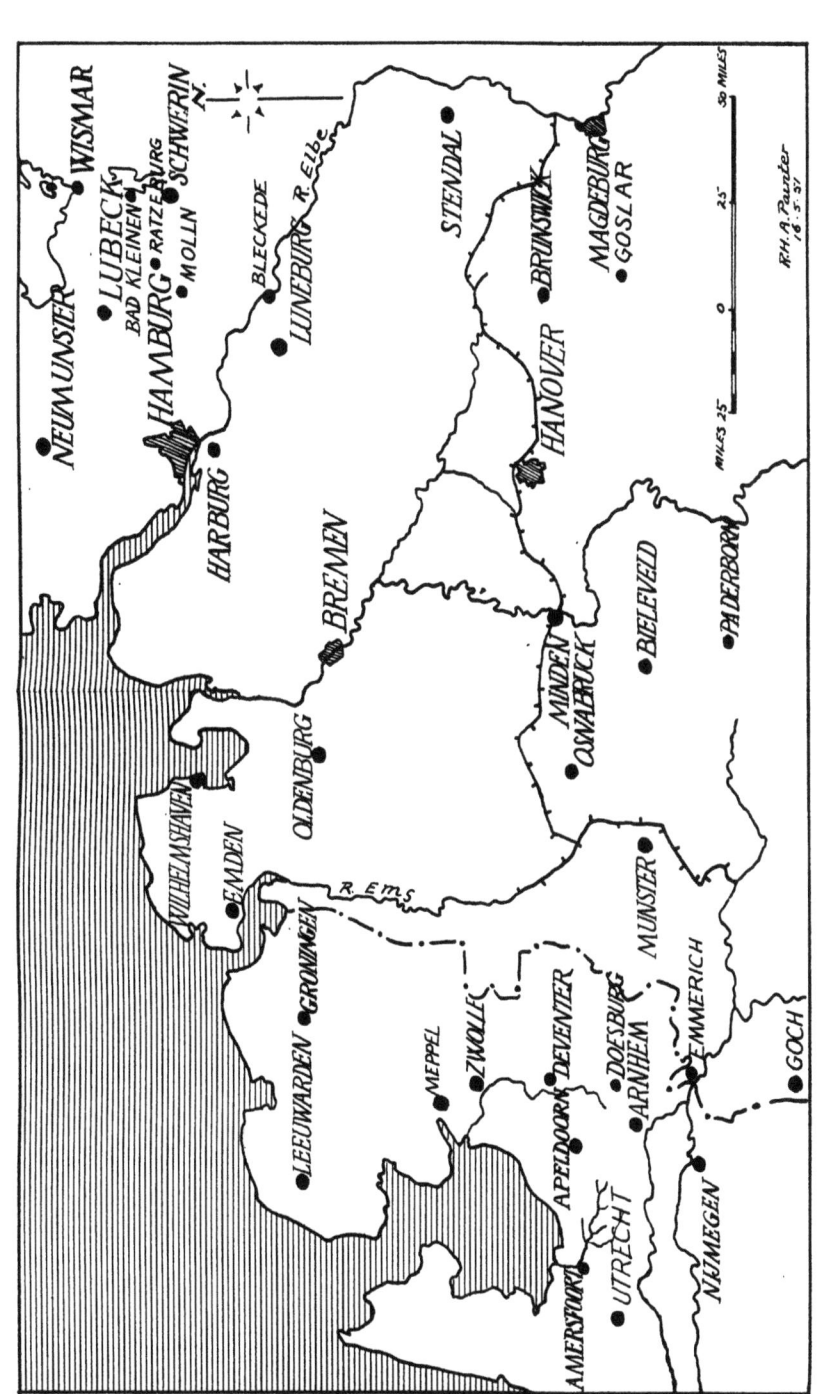

5TH ESSEX. NORTH-EAST GERMANY. APRIL-MAY, 1945.

"10.30. C.O. and O.C. X Coy pay a liaison visit to the Russian unit facing the Bn."

"11.30. C.O. returns."

What was the fate of O.C. "X" Company, one wonders? The record is silent, and as the next entry is three days later and deals with the move of the Battalion to Osterburg, one can only fear the worst.

Osterburg is west of the Elbe, not far from Stendal, and the stay there was short. It was a time of inter-zonal boundary adjustments, and on the 1st July the area was given over to the Russians. "W" Company stayed behind for twenty-four hours to maintain order, while the change over in zonal authorities took place, and thus had an excellent opportunity of seeing the Red Army at really close quarters. The virtual absence of mechanical transport and the army's almost complete reliance on requisitioned farm wagons and carts seems to have been the most striking impression.

The new move took the 5th Essex to Goslar, on the edge of the Harz mountains. Battalion Headquarters was set up in the village of Oker, some five miles outside the town. For a time the Battalion had a quiet and peaceful life, the first rest period since the end of the war, and it was the more appreciated because of the excellent billets and amenities found in Goslar. "We are," wrote Lieutenant-Colonel Heal, "chiefly engaged in guarding important installations, looking after the area, and getting as many amusements for the troops going as we can. The drums are in great form and impress the Germans tremendously."

Here in mid-July the release scheme began to operate, the first man of the Battalion to go being Private Tanti. One hopes that a suitable relief to maintain "Tanti's inferno" had been found before he went.

This release was the forerunner of a period of great change, as repatriation to the U.K. under the "Python" Scheme and leave in lieu of Python (Lilop) began to operate as well as the release scheme. Within the next ten days nearly 400 officers and men were sent home.

But movement was not all homewards, for on the 28th July, 1945, the Colours were brought out from England.

At the beginning of August a 5th Divisional routine order gave the news that the following additional personnel had been "mentioned in despatches": Captain C. E. A. Whyte, Company Quartermaster-Sergeant I. Shortland, and Privates M. A. Stebbing and G. Stevenson.

E.R.—28

Now in October came another move and a change in command, the 5th Essex moving to Bleckede, on the River Elbe, and coming under the 43rd Wessex Division. All ranks were extremely sorry to sever their connection with the 5th Division.

At Bleckede, which was near the scene of active operations by the Battalion in 1945, the 5th Essex was again on the borders of the Russian Zone, though this time there was the River Elbe between the two armies.

The task was now that of internal security in the Kreis Luneburg. Duties ranged from guarding prisoners awaiting the Belsen Camp trials, searching villages for contraband, to mounting guard at Divisional Headquarters. The duties to be performed were many, and began to bear heavily on the Battalion, as the establishment was reduced by the disbandment of the support company, and numbers fell by the operation of the age and service group release scheme. A compensation was that the countryside teemed with game of all descriptions from deer to partridges. Many had shot-guns, and no mess or cookhouse was ever short of some addition to the diet.

In the New Year, the run-down became even more rapid, age and service Groups 25 and 26 taking 300 men into civil life. These men were largely the original members of the 5th Essex, and in many ways their departure meant the removal of the old backbone of the Battalion.

At the end of February 1946, the 5th Essex moved for a five weeks' stay at Munster Lager, five weeks too long in the opinion of many. It was a case of bad billets, bad weather—snow and mud everywhere—and guard duty every other night, the task being the almost impossible one of guarding about 20,000 German prisoners in a camp area some four miles across. There was, too, no record of those who were supposed to be in the camp.

Lieutenant-Colonel W. A. Heal, O.B.E., who had commanded since the 23rd November, 1944, now left the Battalion, his place being taken by Major B. H. Craig, The Buffs, who unfortunately was not to command for long, for on the 24th April, 1946, the Battalion was placed in suspended animation.

It had only just been transferred in early April to Luchow, an attractive little town on the border of the Russian Zone, and all ranks were busily settling themselves in when this unpleasant news was received. Luchow was in the Kreis Dannenberg, of which Colonel B. G. Allen was the Military Government Officer, a curious coincidence, for from Foggia to Dannenberg is a long, long way.

The official date of disbandment was 20th May, 1946, but despite all posting orders being filled immediately, there were still 9 officers and 112 other ranks on the strength on this day. The residue was posted to Luneberg for final dispersal, which was completed on the 13th June, 1946.

The last posting was that of Captain A. L. Ostler, M.B.E., the Quartermaster, who had the remarkable record of being embodied with the Battalion on 3rd September, 1939, and having remained on the strength, without a break, being the last to be posted from the Battalion on the 13th June, 1946.

Almost the last act of Captain Ostler had been to pack and dispatch to Chelmsford the drums of the Battalion, the drums that had been so great a feature in the life of the Battalion throughout the war, and which had been beaten, to the pride of the Battalion and admiration of the onlookers, in England, South Africa, Egypt, Iraq, Syria, Palestine, Italy, Belgium, and Germany.

Section VII

THE POST-WAR STORY

On the 1st May, 1947, the 5th Battalion The Essex Regiment was reconstituted in the new Order of Battle as 646 H.A.A. Regiment R.A. (5th Battalion The Essex Regiment), under the command of Lieutenant-Colonel J. F. Cramphorn, T.D. Batteries were originally formed in Chelmsford, with detachments at Witham and Maldon (Major J. C. Sheldrake); in Braintree, with detachments at Dunmow and Halstead (Major A. L. Cullen, M.C.): and in Colchester (Major R. A. Hill). A striking ceremony was held on the 13th September, 1947, when the Battalion Colours were handed back to the Regiment by a detachment from Warley, in the presence of the Lord-Lieutenant, Colonel Sir Francis H. D. C. Whitmore, K.C.B., C.B., C.M.G., D.S.O., T.D., J.P., and many Deputy-Lieutenants. After the ceremony, a Service was held in Chelmsford Cathedral, followed by a reunion of hundreds of members and ex-members of the Battalion, many of whom came from literally all over England.

The Regiment went to its first camp at Bude in June 1948 with 16 officers and 38 other ranks. At the end of 1948, the Regiment underwent a second conversion, this time to Light Anti-Aircraft. The Colchester battery was expanded to form a new regiment (530 L.A.A.), leaving 646 with batteries at Chelmsford, Braintree, and Saffron Walden. The Regiment went to camp at Bude again in June 1949, 21 officers and 79 other ranks strong, this time with Bofors guns. The War Office recruiting campaign during 1949 was carried out energetically, but at the close of the year, the strength was 20 officers and 96 other ranks.

In 1950, camp was again at Bude and again highly successful. Nineteen-fifty saw the biggest change of all, in the reception of national service men doing their obligatory training.

In September 1950, Colonel Sir F. Carne Rasch, Bart., T.D., D.L., J.P., retired from his appointment as Honorary Colonel, his place being taken by Colonel C. Portway, M.C., T.D., D.L., J.P., who had commanded the 5th Battalion from 1928 to 1935.

APPENDIX A

BATTLE CASUALTIES 5TH (1/5TH) BATTALION THE ESSEX REGIMENT

The total battle casualties of the 5th Essex were approximately 797 killed, wounded, and missing. The bulk of these were incurred in five operations.

Date	Operation	Officer Casualties	O.R. Casualties	Total Casualties
2nd–5th Nov., 1943	River Trigno	10	129	139
22nd–25th Nov., 1943	River Sangro	5	104	109
22nd–27th Dec., 1943	Villa Grande	13	266	279
4th–17th Jan., 1944	River Arielli	4	145	149
5th–26th Feb., 1944	Orsogna	1	56	57
	Total . .	33	700	733

APPENDIX B

Location by Date, 5th (1/5th) Battalion The Essex Regiment

Date	Brigade	Division	Location
Sept. 1939–Apr. 1940	161 Inf. Bde.	54 East Anglian Div.	Chelmsford Area
Apr.–June 1940	161 Inf. Bde.	54 East Anglian Div.	Beal, Northumberland
June–Dec. 1940	161 Inf. Bde.	54 East Anglian Div.	Prudhoe. Hexham
Dec. 1940–Jan. 1941	Deal Area	43 Wessex Div.	Sandwich, Deal
Feb. 1941	—	43 Wessex Div.	Dover
March–June 1941	—	43 Wessex Div.	Gravesend
26th June–22nd Aug., 1941	*Embarked H.M.T. *Oronsay* in transit to Middle East Disembarked H.M.T. *Oronsay*		(Gourock) (Suez)
Sept. 1941	161 Inf. Bde.	—	Western Desert
Nov. 1941	—	—	Port Said
Dec. 1941	Moved to Iraq	—	—
Dec. 1941–Dec. 1942	19 Indian Inf. Bde.	8 Indian Div.	British Troops Iraq. Paiforce

5th Battalion the Essex Regiment. (1/5th redesignated Jan. 1943)

Date	Brigade	Division	Location
Jan.–Apr. 1943	19 Indian Inf. Bde.	8 Indian Div.	Mosul, Iraq
May–Sept. 1943	19 Indian Inf. Bde.	8 Indian Div.	Syria, Egypt, and Palestine
Sept. 1943–March 1944	19 Indian Inf. Bde.	8 Indian Div. & Eighth Army	C.M.F., Italy
March–July 1944	—	5 Corps, & 10 Corps	C.M.F., Italy
July 1944–Feb. 1945	13 Inf. Bde.	5 British Div.	Palestine and Syria
March 1945	13 Inf. Bde.	5 British Div.	C.M.F., Italy
March–Sept. 1945	13 Ind. Bde.	5 British Div.	21 Army Group, Germany
Oct. 1945–May 1946	214 Inf. Bde.	43 Wessex Div.	B.A.O.R., Germany

* Spent four days in Durban, 1st–5th August.

Chapter Seven

THE 2/5TH BATTALION THE ESSEX REGIMENT, 1939-42

FOREWORD

by *Lieutenant-General Sir Willoughby Norrie, K.C.M.G., C.B., D.S.O., M.C., General Officer Commanding 30th Corps, 1941-42, and Governor of South Australia since 1945*

Exactly nine years ago today, the 2/5th Battalion The Essex Regiment was fighting its first and last battle in the Libyan Desert.

The story of the stand of the 18th Indian Infantry Brigade and the part the Battalion played at Deir-el-Shein is told in the following pages.

As Commander of 30th Corps at the time this action took place, I am very pleased to have this opportunity of recording my high appreciation of the gallant part played by the 2/5th Battalion The Essex Regiment, who bore the brunt of the enemy attack.

On the 27th June the Battalion arrived at El Alamein, and in forty-eight hours despite extreme handicaps—such as lack of transport, shortage of all R.E. stores, mines, and wire, the Essex Regiment, under Lieutenant-Colonel K. F. May, converted by indomitable work a piece of bare desert into a reasonable defended locality. The position was in the shape of a saucer, with good observation points on the edges, but digging on the ridge itself was very difficult owing to its rocky nature, though there were some patches of sand.

The 1st July was a hot and very unpleasant day, with a heavy sandstorm blowing. In fact, the "fog of war" became so intense that troops ordered to support the Brigade lost themselves in the maelstrom.

First news of the attack by the 15th Panzer Division was sent back in high-grade cypher on the wireless, which unfortunately wasted valuable time, when every minute was of vital importance. The Battalion put up a very stout fight all day against overwhelming odds, but the 18th Indian Infantry Brigade was eventually overrun after stalwart resistance, yet the fighting spirit of the 2/5th Essex was outstanding to the end.

When the Official History of the War is completed the delay imposed upon the enemy at Deir-el-Shein will be found an important factor in the successful defence of El Alamein at a critical period of the Libyan Campaign.

The evidence of captured German documents confirms that the resistance of this Brigade in general and of the 2/5th Essex in particular, dealt a severe blow to the German armour, and effectively limited their offensive power in the succeeding days.

I am proud to have had troops of the calibre of the 2/5th Battalion The Essex Regiment under my command.

I congratulate Colonel May, his officers and men. They did their duty and did it right well.

ADELAIDE.
1st July, 1951.

Willoughby Norrie

Lieutenant-General.

Section I

HOME DEFENCE, 1939-40

OFFICIALLY formed on the 1st June, 1939, the 2/5th Essex had little time to find its feet as a unit before, on the 1st September, it was embodied as part of the 161st (Essex) Infantry Brigade in the 54th (East Anglian) Division.

The official designation was the 2/5th (East) Battalion The Essex Regiment, for on the duplication of the Territorial Army, the old 5th Battalion had been split geographically into two parts, an East Battalion and a West.

The peace-time distribution of the 2/5th Battalion was Headquarters at Colchester, with Headquarters Company at Colchester, Manningtree, and West Mersea; "A" Company was split between Thorpe-le-Soken and Brightlingsea; "B" Company at Halstead and Earls Colne; "C" Company at Braintree, and "D" Company at Witham and Kelvedon.

On embodiment, Lieutenant-Colonel C. Portway, M.C., T.D., had his headquarters at St. George's Hall, Colchester. Major C. A. Brooks was his Second-in-Command and Captain A. Balden his Adjutant.

The Regimental Sergeant-Major was Mr. G. W. Amey, who had spent most of his service with the "Pompadours." The duty of the Battalion was to guard vulnerable points and to be responsible for the defence of a sector of the east coast, principally the landward defences of Harwich. This duty was, by coincidence, the same as the first task given to the 5th Essex in 1914, and fell in 1939 to "C" Company, commanded by Captain A. J. Hills.

"D" Company also went to Harwich with orders to convert Warner's holiday camp into an internment camp, while the remainder of the Battalion was deployed to guard vulnerable points.

Very shortly after embodiment the Divisional Commander, Major-General J. H. T. Priestman, C.B.E., D.S.O., M.C., and Brigadier H. Pawle (soon to be followed in command of the 161st (Essex) Infantry Brigade by Brigadier J. W. L. S. Hobart, D.S.O., M.C.) came to check and approve the battalion layout.

That first September of war was an extremely busy month for all units, but doubly so for a battalion so recently established as the 2/5th Essex. Men in essential occupations had to be "combed out" and discharged, the immature "under nineteens" had to be posted to home defence units, instructors had to be found for the newly formed Infantry Training Centre at Warley, and drafts of Army class intake had to be received and absorbed. In addition, the whole Battalion, as well as the Army class recruits, had to be trained. There was no spare time, even on Sundays, and yet on the 24th September, 1939, one can read a complaint that church parade could not be held: "Still no church parades owing to the order from Brigade that members of H.M. Forces and civilians should not be in church together in case air-raid warning should be sounded." A reminder of the curious mentality of those days.

Gradually, defence duties were handed over to home defence and other units, and early in 1940 Lieutenant-Colonel Portway was able to concentrate most of his battalion in Colchester. A great acceleration in training and general efficiency was soon apparent, for not only was administration much easier now the Battalion was concentrated, but tactical training could be carried out in Wivenhoe Park, while field firing could be practised on the new range at Fingringhoe, which was opened by the 2/5th Essex.

By the 22nd March, 1940, the 7th (H.D.) Essex had taken over the last V.P., and the whole of the 2/5th was concentrated in Colchester. But nor for long, for on the 16th April the Battalion moved to

Northumberland. The move was complicated by the fact that a very large army intake draft joined just after the warning order to move had been received, and no fewer than 255 men had to be clothed, equipped, and squadded while the Battalion was packing up. This, of course, did not make the first major move of the war any easier.

The duties of Adjutant had been handed over by Captain Balden to Captain J. F. Finn, M.C., who had held that post with the 5th Essex in 1918. On the 14th January, Captain V. C. Magill-Cuerdon took over the duties, and his experience as a regular soldier was to prove useful in organising the move to Northumberland, which went smoothly.

Lieutenant-Colonel Portway did not go with the Battalion, which was commanded during the move, and while they were settling themselves down in Northumberland, by Major C. A. Brooks. Lieutenant-Colonel C. M. Paton, who had come from a staff appointment in the War Office, assumed command on the 19th April, 1940.

Battalion Headquarters was at Mansfield House, Lowick, and the companies were scattered round in Lowick, Heatherslaw, Nesbitt, Ford, and Doddington.

An intense period of administration and training followed, and the 2/5th Essex, now in competition with the 1/4th and 1/5th Essex—for the whole of the 54th Division had moved into Northumberland—began to progress towards the goal of fitness for battle. Training was made the easier because the local inhabitants were friendly, and viewed with favour these men of Essex who did not break down hedges nor leave gates open like their predecessors from industrial towns in another northern county, and who were always ready—in their scant spare moments—to lend a hand with any agricultural work.

From the 10th May, 1940, the Battalion was put at six hours' notice to move to counter any enemy seaborne or airborne landings, for if invasion was not yet probable, there was at least a chance of raids to increase the disorders and chaos that the enemy hoped to achieve from a successful offensive in Western Europe.

The Battalion had been made mobile by the provision of a heterogeneous mass of coaches, lorries, and trucks, and on the night of the 31st May, 1940, as the crisis of Dunkirk moved steadily to a head, intensive digging and wiring of the beaches started.

A proof of the steady progress made by the Battalion in the past six weeks lay in the fact that, though only a limited reconnaissance by a few officers had taken place, the 2/5th was able to move to the beaches

THE 2/5TH BATTALION THE ESSEX REGIMENT 443

by M.T., an average distance of fourteen miles, after nightfall on the night 31st May/1st June, and to start digging tasks by moonlight. When daylight came, only one small section of trench was found to require resiting.

As with most other units, memories of the Battalion of that summer of 1940 must be chiefly the digging of coast defences, putting up road blocks, practice mannings, sudden moves, and experiments with strange and makeshift weapons of defence. "Major Brooks demonstrated the use of Molotoff bombs," says one account, and such was the spirit of those days that every man was prepared to take on single-handed any enemy tank that might appear, and so pass on the knowledge gained from Major Brooks' demonstration.

With the fall of Dunkirk began that shuffle of units that was to be such a feature of life in the United Kingdom in those years of home defence. Unit moves and moves within the unit itself were of frequent occurrence, for it seemed that no sooner had a unit put its billets in order than it was at once moved elsewhere. Other antidotes to monotony or loss of security, or whatever it was, were the "road-block routine," under which the nature and site of blocks were changed twice weekly, and the "special-role" procedure, which assigned to battalions an ever-changing series of tasks of the most remarkable type.

On the 16th June the Battalion moved to the Corbridge area, with companies at Corbridge, Stocksfield, Aydon, and Newton, but Battalion Headquarters had hardly settled before it was moved to Belford and again shortly afterwards to Ellingham Hall, Chathill.

It was a time of alarms and rumours—air-raid alarms and rumours of parachutists and enemy coast landings. Even fishing vessels were reported to have left Germany carrying fifth columnists who were to land during the night of the 19th/20th July. Special vigilance was ordered, but needless to say, the 2/5th saw nothing, nor yet did any other unit.

By this time the Battalion had knitted into a live unit, with capacity to move quickly and to operate effectively. There is the story of the officer's wife who, stranded in some remote village with no means of transport, was included as an emergency measure in a closed van with the company stores on the basis that the Battalion move from X to Y would only take a couple of hours. Unfortunately, Division took control of the move at the last minute, and produced a route modelled on an Alpine motor endurance test, with the result that the unhappy woman underwent some ten hours' solitary and uncomfortable confinement.

Every opportunity was taken to train, and even though the construction of defences had overriding priority, the organisation of tank-hunting platoons and the issue of surprise alarm orders kept the principles of offensive action and mobility in the forefront of everyone's mind.

In early September Battalion Headquarters moved to Throckley, Newcastle-on-Tyne, and received there, on the evening of the 7th September, 1940, the warning of imminent invasion.

But the crisis passed, and as autumn replaced summer so the risks of invasion lessened, until the finer weather and calmer seas of spring would again make it a feasible operation of war.

So as the tension on the coast slowly relaxed, the Battalion gradually moved inland and, intermixed with the eternal moving of billets, a period of brigade, divisional, and even corps training began.

By the 15th October the 2/5th Essex had taken part in the first 54th Divisional training exercise, held in the Long Framlington area.

Immediately afterwards they moved to the Haltwhistle area, and were still there when, on the 30th November, 1940, a message was received from Headquarters 10th Corps to say that the 2/5th Essex was forthwith under War Office operational control, and was to be ready to move overseas on or after the 8th December.

The ensuing fortnight was one of desperate endeavour, but finally the Battalion stood mobilised and ready for service overseas. The destination was secret, but the fact that the 1/4th Essex was in Sierra Leone, coupled with the issue in the tropical outfit of such articles as mosquito boots and mosquito nets, pointed to West Africa. On the other hand, the issue of gumboots and thick pyjamas and "underclothes, thick woollen," pointed to Iceland or the Falkland Islands.

On the 17th December, 1940, the 2/5th Essex embarked at Glasgow in H.M.T. *Neuralia*. She sailed next day for an unknown destination.

Section II

WEST AFRICA, 1941

The *Neuralia* was an elderly trooper well known to regular members of the Regiment, for her sedate voyaging to and from the East in the years between the wars.

On board, the 2/5th Essex shared the very limited accommodation with the Headquarters of the 161st Infantry Brigade, a General Hospital, and some details. The *Neuralia* had been substituted at short notice for another and larger ship which had unfortunately been bombed, and fitting in all the troops that had to be carried was no easy task. Things were not facilitated by the fact that there was a dock strike, but owing to the efforts of the ship's officers and men and of Brigadier Hobart and his Brigade Staff, the *Neuralia* sailed on time, although short of a proportion of fuel and stores.

For the majority of the Battalion it was the first long sea voyage. Indeed, it is worth recording that Major J. F. Finn, M.C., and Regimental Quartermaster-Sergeant S. C. Proom were the only two members of the old 161st Essex Infantry Brigade who sailed to Gallipoli in 1915 to proceed overseas with the new 161st Essex Infantry Brigade in 1940.

The convoy was large and had a powerful escort, which at times included two aircraft carriers and three cruisers, together with destroyers, sloops, and corvettes.

The voyage was quiet for a time, except when one night the ship next ahead of the *Neuralia*, the *Empire Trooper*, had a break-down in her engine-room and was nearly rammed. Falling out of the convoy for a time, she eventually rejoined, and became the next astern of the *Neuralia*, a fortunate change of position for the *Neuralia*, as will be seen.

Early on Christmas morning, heavy gunfire was heard, and almost immediately the next astern was hit and the *Neuralia* straddled. The German eight-inch cruiser *Hipper* had located Convoy W.S.8A.

It was rough and visibility was poor, and the *Hipper* rapidly closed on the convoy to attack by gunfire, apparently quite unaware of the strength of the escort, which that Christmas morning included the cruisers *Berwick*, *Bonaventure*, and *Dunedin*.

It was exciting for those on deck. Guns were firing, shells were dropping, and the already poor visibility was quickly being lessened as every ship in the convoy made smoke as rapidly as she could. The *Hipper* was immediately engaged by *Berwick* and *Bonaventure*, and there was a brief sharp engagement, in which both *Berwick* and the *Hipper* received damage. The *Hipper* made off at high speed in the low visibility, and eventually made harbour at Brest. A German supply ship—the *Baden*—accompanying the *Hipper* was sunk. The *Empire Trooper* next astern of the *Neuralia* fell out of the convoy, but reached Gibraltar in safety.

It was an exciting start to Christmas Day, but the action was apparently considered by the 2/5th Essex to be a private war on the part of the Royal Navy, for it receives no mention whatsoever in the Battalion's records.

Nevertheless, as the convoy lay in the steamy heat of Freetown Harbour on the 5th January, 1941, and the Essex prepared to disembark, it was with a prayer of heartfelt gratitude to the Royal Navy for its safe conduct.

The Battalion thought itself a bit odd in tropical kit for the first time. "Everyone looked very quaint to start with, as very few of us had worn tropical kit before. The 'shorts-long,' with their frightful turn-ups above the knee, did not make it any easier to produce an appearance of smartness." However, conquering their diffidence, the 2/5th Essex disembarked and moved into Benguema Camp, near Waterloo, Sierra Leone, where everything possible had been done by Lieutenant-Colonel G. M. Gibson, T.D., and all ranks of the 1/4th Essex to prepare for the arrival of the sister battalion. The 1/4th had already had nearly five months in the Colony, and both battalions were to remain for a further six.

It was a difficult period for troops fresh from the United Kingdom. The climatic conditions are too well known to require much enlarging upon. The hot-house atmosphere for many months in the year, the malaria risk, the then current fear of blackwater fever, the tendency for cuts and wounds to refuse to heal, and the insidious attack made by the climate on any old injuries or weaknesses—all these exercised a cumulative effect.

Camp sites in Sierra Leone were limited, and it was unfortunate that both those occupied during the Battalion's stay had already been condemned by the medical authorities as unfit for habitation by white troops. There was perhaps a tendency to lay down that British troops must be accustomed to work and train under exactly the same conditions as Africans. These included training all night in malarial areas, despite the lessons that should have been learnt from the malarial incidence caused in the 1/4th Essex by its occupation of similar positions a few months earlier. It was, perhaps, a failure to appreciate the risks that must be run in actual operations and the risks that may be run in training. Reason was, however, restored through the representation of Brigadier Hobart, assisted by medical advice from the two magnificent Territorial general hospitals, which, fortunately, were now stationed in Sierra Leone.

Nevertheless, Benguema Camp was low lying, as was Lumley, and the malarial risk was always present. Lumley, right by the sea, had, however, the compensation of the splendid bathing on nearby Lumley Beach, an amenity enjoyed by the greater part of the Battalion almost every day of its stay.

Much useful training was possible, despite climatic limitations; range work, bush warfare, and some experience in elementary combined training with the Royal Navy, elementary because of lack of landing craft and because the full technique had yet to be evolved. There were three assault landing craft and one motor landing craft only at Freetown at the time.

The Royal Navy paid return visits to the Essex camps, especially destroyer crews in port for forty-eight hours' boiler cleaning after long spells of anti-submarine or convoy work. "The matelots enjoyed themselves hugely, and wondered why they had chosen the sea until taken for a ride on an armoured carrier through rough bush country in full sun and heat."

Much of this training was watched by Major-General C. G. Woolner, M.C., who commanded the Sierra Leone area, by Brigadier Hobart, and by Brigadier M. A. Green, the commander of the West African Infantry Brigade quartered in the Colony.

One of the first visits by General Woolner to the Battalion took place when a company was engaged in training in the bush. Few of the Essex Territorials had ever before seen a general in tropical kit. The officer commanding the company at exercise, Captain A. E. C. Alston, was suddenly interrupted at a ticklish moment by an officer in tropical kit wearing no red hat or red tabs, and whose insignia Alston took to be those of a second lieutenant in the Army Physical Training Corps. Captain Alston replied to his questions with the shortness and abruptness that one of that rank deserved. When later he learned the truth, he was very horrified, but in actual fact the General was highly delighted.

Towards the end of April 1941 the 2/5th Essex, together with the 1/4th Essex, were put under preparatory orders for "Operation Shrapnel." At the time "top secret" and the reason of much unexplained and mysterious activity such as the filling of four thousand 2-gallon cans with drinking water and loading them into a ship, its purpose was made public by Mr. Winston Churchill in his work, *The Second World War*, vol. II, where he says: "We held ready a strong brigade with four suitable fast transports to seize or occupy some of the Atlantic islands. Alternatively, if the Portuguese Government agreed that we might for this purpose invoke the Anglo-Portuguese Alliance of

1373 'Friends to friends, and foes to foes,' we might set up with all speed a base in the Cape Verde Islands. This operation called 'Shrapnel' would secure us the necessary air and refuelling bases to maintain naval control of the critical stretch of the route round the Coast."[1]

About this time Captain V. C. Magill-Cuerdon moved to Brigade Headquarters, and the duties of Adjutant were taken over by Captain P. B. Lake. Recreation went with training. The Reverend D. W. Thompson, the padre to the Battalion, was particularly active in arranging outings for the other ranks to whom living in a West African Colony was a great novelty.

On one of these, Majors Brooks and Hills, with a party of about 40 other ranks, set off in a chartered native motor-boat in an attempt to reach the Banana Islands some way down the coast to the south. It soon became obvious that time would not permit reaching the Banana Islands and returning before dark. So instead, the party was put ashore at a small village named York, on the mainland. It was arranged to depart some two hours later, but when the party mustered, nothing could be found of the native crew. They were eventually located returning from the village accompanied by most of the inhabitants and a large stone jar of palm wine. They all appeared to have partaken freely of wine before leaving the village. The boat was eventually got under way and safely out of the very narrow, rocky inlet and turned its nose for home.

Major Brooks immediately placed the palm wine under guard, and urged the native captain to keep up his best speed in an endeavour to make up the hour and a half which had been lost. It was useless, and before the party could approach the boom defences, darkness had fallen. The natives, however, put their motor-boat hard at the boom close by the boom-defence vessel. The boat hit the first wire and lurched drunkenly over it, coming to a stop against the second wire amidst a burst of profanity from the boom vessel. The natives immediately dropped down into the bilge of the boat. The captain was gripped by the scruff of the neck and made by Major Brooks to stand on the bow and give an explanation to the boom-vessel crew. This was supplemented by Major Brooks. The wires were slacked off, and the boat made its way without lights up Freetown Harbour, where it was several times in immediate danger of being run down by picket boats. It was with a sigh of relief that the party got ashore and found the M.T. that had been waiting two hours to take them to camp.

[1] W. S. Churchill, *Their Finest Hour*, p. 552.

Another antidote to monotony was the visit, two or three times a week, of a Vichy French reconnaissance aeroplane from Dakar, which came to photograph the harbour and defence works. These machines were Glenn Martins of recent American design, and at the time there was no aircraft in British West Africa suitable to attack and drive them off. However, one week one was brought down by the anti-aircraft defences, much to everyone's satisfaction.

Much of French Equatorial Africa had adhered to Marshal Petain and the Vichy Government, and the garrisons of the French colonies greatly outnumbered the forces in British West Africa, particularly in Gambia and Sierra Leone.

So when in June 1941 it was thought that the British occupation of Syria might well provoke Vichy France to retaliatory action, Sierra Leone was particularly threatened, and on the 7th June, 1941, the 2/5th Essex was warned of the immediate danger of war with France.

But the crisis passed, and the already ordered relief of the 161st (Essex) Infantry Brigade by a West African brigade from Nigeria proceeded without interruption.

The 19th June, 1941, saw the 2/5th Essex embarking in H.M.T. *Bergensfjord* with a strength of 32 officers and 725 other ranks.

Brigade H.Q. and the 1/4th Essex had already embarked, and as the 2/5th went aboard, they were greeted with cries of "Come aboard the *Altmark*." [1] The 1/4th had travelled to Sierra Leone in the then unconverted luxury liner *Monarch of Bermuda*, and the men of the 2/5th soon gave these "tourists" other ideas, as the accommodation in the *Bergensfjord* was found to be a distinct improvement on that in the *Neuralia*.

As the ship sailed on the afternoon of the 20th June, Lieutenant-Colonel Paton received the following congratulatory letter from Brigadier Hobart:

"HEADQUARTERS, 161ST INFANTRY BRIGADE,
"c/o A.P.O. 1000.
"20th June, 1941.

"DEAR PATON,

"On the eve of our departure from Sierra Leone, I wish to congratulate you on the way your unit has carried out its duties and the way your troops have behaved during their stay here.

---

[1] The *Altmark*, an auxiliary of the German battleship *Von Spee* when commerce raiding in 1939–40, was used as a prison ship for the crews of our sunk merchant ships. Her name became synonymous for a transport with poor accommodation.

"They have earned the admiration and respect of all those with whom they have come in contact.

"In spite of the trying climate, they have displayed remarkable energy, discipline, and keenness in all their work and play.

"Our stay in Sierra Leone has been a valuable experience, and we have made full and very good use of our opportunities to train in all phases of warfare.

"We are now on our way to the Middle East, and I hope will shortly have the opportunity for which we have been working and waiting, to fight the enemy.

"I have the greatest confidence in you and your unit, and am convinced they will give a good account of themselves.

"I would be glad if you would bring this to the notice of your troops.

"May fortune favour us.
"Yours sincerely,
"(*Sgd.*) J. S. HOBART.

"LIEUTENANT-COLONEL C. M. PATON,
"*Commanding 2/5th Battalion the Essex Regiment.*"

Section III

THE MIDDLE EAST, 1941–42

The voyage southwards was without alarm, the Line being crossed with traditional ceremony on the 23rd June, when the many novices duly attended at the Court. On the 4th July the *Bergensfjord* docked at Durban.

Five days followed, in which the hospitality shown to all ranks was almost embarrassing, but the 2/5th Essex maintained their steady record for good behaviour, the local authorities saying that they had never had better-conducted guests.

On the 9th July the Battalion re-embarked on the *Ile de France*, a large and fast liner, which sailed on the 11th July in a 20-knot convoy. Brigade Headquarters and the 1/4th Essex were also on board, and the two Essex battalions mounted over one hundred Brens for the anti-aircraft defence of the ship, as well as some Vickers medium machine guns.

Ashrafi Roads at the southern end of the Gulf of Suez were

reached on the 21st July. Here the *Ile de France* waited for several days, during which time a little light relief was provided by an elderly senior medical officer who boarded the ship in a condition of incipient frenzy, having been told that there was on board a battalion direct from the United Kingdom with 200 malaria cases in the ship's hospital.

Interest, too, was afforded by the *Queen Elizabeth* and *Aquitania*, full of Australian and New Zealand troops, which were also lying in the Ashrafi Roads. The 43,000-ton *Ile de France* appeared quite small against the giant *Queen Elizabeth*.

On the 27th July the Battalion disembarked at Port Tewfik, Egypt, and proceeded to Camp 20, El Tahag, where they expected to be given a special rest period to mitigate the effects of the West African climate. But this amenity failed to materialise, and Lieutenant-Colonel Paton was warned that his battalion would move almost immediately to an area east of Mersa Matruh on lines of communication duty.

On the 5th August, the 2/5th Essex entrained at El Qassassin and arrived the following day at Sidi Haneish, where it was made responsible for a sector of the Bagush Box. This was a defended locality of remarkable size and construction, situated about 160 miles behind the front line of July 1941, which was at the time in the region of the Egyptian frontier. Headquarters 161st Infantry Brigade and the 1/4th Essex were also in the Box, but owing to operational requirements the 2/5th was temporarily removed from Brigadier Hobart's command and placed under the 11th Indian Infantry Brigade of the famous 4th Indian Division.

Major-General F. W. Messervy, the divisional commander, visited the Battalion on the 11th August, as, on the 19th August, did Lieutenant-General Sir N. M. Beresford-Peirse, K.B.E., D.S.O., Commander of the Western Desert Force. Between these visits the Battalion was very pleased to welcome the Deputy Assistant Chaplain-General of the Desert Force, the Reverend B. K. Bond, who had been chaplain attached to the 5th Essex in the Mediterranean Expeditionary Force between 1915 and 1917.

Training in desert warfare under the guidance of the 4/16th Punjab Regiment and work on the sector defences in the Bagush Box filled the days, the 2/5th Essex rapidly becoming used to desert conditions. On the 21st August the Battalion reverted to the control of the 161st Infantry Brigade, and three days later "B" Company, under Captain D. A. C. Wilkinson, moved to Sidi Barrani, there to carry out work on the defences. Sidi Barrani is well known to many members of the

Regiment, the first defences there being constructed by the "Pompadours" in 1935-36. It is a tribute to their work that the trenches and shelters then constructed were still usable in 1941.

Enemy action was slight in the rear areas, and the work and training of the 2/5th received little interference. Next, on the 29th August, came orders to say the Battalion had temporarily no operational role, but would be for the time responsible for care and maintenance of four sub-sectors of the Bagush Box. This continued till the 13th September, when the task was thankfully handed over to the 18th and 19th N.Z. Battalions.

Next came a period of responsibility for the ground and A.A. defence of numerous air landing grounds which necessitated the widespread dispersion of companies. It was whilst on this duty that, says Captain A. E. C. Alston, "the first shots at the enemy were fired. The Battalion had been bombed in Northumberland and shelled at sea, but the first time any part of it fired shots back at the enemy was when 'C' Company and some of the carrier platoon were sitting at Fuka. He usually 'had a go' at the time of the full moon, and sure enough he came in nice and low. Alas, we didn't bring one down, but a tail-gunner exchanged shots with a couple of our posts, and we felt we really had been near. He got an ammunition train in the station near the landing ground, which went up in a series of marvellous explosions...."

Meanwhile, the 1/5th Essex had now arrived in the Middle East and joined up with 161st Infantry Brigade. But circumstances were not to allow the Essex Territorial Brigade long life.

It was a time of reorganisation in the Western Desert, and the 161st (Essex) Infantry Brigade was to suffer in that reorganisation. It was not to fight as an Essex brigade, and the three battalions were to be dispersed. It was a bitter disappointment, for all remembered and wished to emulate the gallant exploits of the old 161st Infantry Brigade at Gallipoli and at Gaza, and indeed throughout the years of the First World War.

But regimental sentiment had to take second place to the material needs of the moment. The 8th and 10th Indian Divisions, now in Iraq, were without their proper complement of British infantry battalions, and changes were being made in the establishment of the older 5th Indian Division.

And so, one by one, the three Essex battalions left their old brigade to join new formations.

But before the 2/5th Essex left the Brigade, they saw Lieutenant-Colonel Paton go on appointment as A.A.G. Headquarters Western Army, the Eighth Army. He left on the 20th September, 1941, and command was temporarily taken over by Major C. A. Brooks, until Lieutenant-Colonel K. F. May could join from the 1st Essex, then in Syria.

It is perhaps a suitable opportunity to record the names of the officers serving with the Battalion at this date:

Majors C. A. Brooks, A. J. Hills, J. F. Finn, M.C.; Captains D. A. C. Wilkinson, S. K. Clover, A. L. Cullen, F. Stanger, E. B. Cooper, H. J. L. Wright, A. E. C. Alston, P. B. Lake; Lieutenants M. H. Murray, P. W. Daniell, E. E. Sanderson, H. S. Lashbrook, D. P. Oexle, J. A. Porter, P. R. Perfect, J. P. Potts, T. Thaw, R. D. Barnsdale, F. G. Coe, D. W. March, G. E. M. Carter, and Lieutenant (Q.M.) P. H. Brooks.

It was to be some weeks before the Battalion was to be finally transferred. In the meantime it moved to El Daba, where the 2/5th lived among the sandhills on the sea coast, and shared accommodation with the myriads of sand fleas which inhabited that area and which encouraged the battalion poet into verse. Here Lieutenant-Colonel K. F. May joined the Battalion and assumed command.

On the 20th October the 2/5th Essex left the Western Desert and moved into Ranpur Camp, Suez, where the Battalion learnt that it was shortly to go to Iraq and there join the 18th Infantry Brigade of the 8th Indian Division. It wasn't a very entrancing prospect, particularly for Lieutenant-Colonel May, who had already been to Iraq earlier in the year with the 1st Essex and knew the nature of the country only too well.

The 2/5th Essex was to stay in Ranpur Camp until the 13th December, and these two months on the Canal have little interest. Companies were employed on guard duties at vulnerable points in the Suez Canal area and in port protection duties. The employments were varied and, especially in the dock areas, not without danger. Casualties were caused by enemy bombing. Thanks were received on one occasion from the Naval authorities for prompt action which prevented a mined vessel from slewing across and blocking the Suez Canal.

Before leaving Suez, Regimental Sergeant-Major C. W. Small joined the Battalion on posting from the 1st Essex in Tobruk. He reported with two black eyes, part of the skin off his face, and unshaven. The 2/5th Essex had a good laugh when they saw him arrive. Many varied and ribald suggestions were made as to how he had come by his injuries, until it became known that he had been torpedoed between Tobruk and Alexandria, flung into the sea by the explosion, and had hit a raft with his face.

The Battalion left Suez without many regrets on the 13th December, moving the next day to Haifa on the first stage of the long journey to Mosul. Two days later the Battalion was lifted by No. 40 M.T. Company R.A.S.C. (aided by a collection of ramshackle civilian buses from Tel-Aviv and Jerusalem) and taken in the wheel tracks of the 1st Essex to Rutbah and Habbaniya.

The advance party under Major A. J. Hills had gone ahead over two months before. Major Hills says: "My orders on leaving the Battalion in the Western Desert were to take the advance party to Palestine. I can well remember my astonishment when I was told by a staff officer at the Tulkarm station to take my party in four buses driven by Arabs. I was told I could not be informed of our destination, but the journey would take about four days and the drivers knew the way. It was an extraordinary sort of movement order to receive, and I have often thought since that I was a bit silly to act on a movement order of that sort. However I did, and in due course we arrived in Baghdad and were put on the train up to Mosul, where we joined the 18th Indian Infantry Brigade."

And now, at last, the main body was on the way to join them. Lieutenant-Colonel May says: "I led and set the pace and went my own route. Each company had its own flag front and rear, so we could tell who was which. The drill was, after the long midday halt the R.S.M. went ahead with two lorries with the cooks and guides from each company. They cracked ahead so that when the Battalion arrived in convoy each company on passing the dispersal flag drove to its company area which was flagged and bedded down. By which time a hot meal was ready. Bedding down consisted of hammering desert 'bivvies' (two-men type) into the sand and getting down to it. It's a simple drill, and always at the end of a day's run one would hear violent hammering for a quarter of an hour and then silence."

It took six days to cross the desert from Haifa to Baghdad, and as Lieutenant-Colonel May crossed the desert both with the 1st Battalion and again with the 2/5th, it is fitting that he should tell a brief story of this desert journey: "We left Haifa, skirting the Mount Carmel range, and then the road runs along the south side of the Plain of Esdraelon. From there it goes more or less due east via Jenin, via Jisr el Majami bridge over the Jordan. Here the road is running below sea-level.

Most of the country traversed so far has been agricultural with neat Jewish settlements off the main road, and the general impression is nice green farming country. Dropping down into the Jordan Valley, the ground is more barren and stony, but the views are magnificent. It is a very narrow bridge, and the road on the Transjordan side climbs over 2,500 feet in about eleven miles. The road then goes up and up and over the Transjordan plateau, running fairly near the Syrian frontier. At H.3, a pumping station belonging to the Iraq Petroleum Company and nearly in the middle of the desert, the road is then 3,000 feet above sea-level. Before arriving at H.3, the road crosses a lava belt about sixty miles in width, most of the rocks being about the size of your head. . . ."

As the column passed Rutbah Wells, a small walled fort with good water supplies, and surrounded by hills and valleys, Lieutenant-Colonel May goes on: "It is a most peculiar configuration to find in the middle of a desert, but, then, the Syrian Desert is quite different to the Western Desert. It fascinates me. One is always stumbling on something new. Maybe a salt-pan, or another as white as snow and as flat as a billiard table. There is plenty of water in the Syrian Desert if you know where to look, and the Arabs know. The track is just innumerable tyre tracks, made by the original column that went through to scotch the rebellion. Here and there you will see a new track which some driver has made, thinking that his route is better and quicker than the main one. Every five kilometres there is a notice board giving the distance to Ramadi on the Euphrates. The colour of the desert is generally brown, but it varies, and the colourings made by the sun setting have to be seen to be believed."

Two nights were spent on the plateau above the R.A.F. cantonment at Habbaniya, and then on from Habbaniya via Baghdad, Tekrit, and Qaiyara to Mosul.

There the advance party under Major A. J. Hills had been waiting for two and a half months. They had started work on laying out the defensive perimeter round Mosul and preparing the camp site, which lay outside the town itself but inside the defence perimeter. They could not complete the camp as the majority of the necessary tentage was coming with the main body.

The arrival of the Battalion kept being put off, and Major Hills says, "In our most depressed moments we used to say to each other, 'Well, the Battalion will arrive on Christmas Day and in the rain.'"

This is exactly what happened. It poured with rain, the mud road into the camp became a quagmire, and as the Battalion column rolled up on Christmas Day the great majority of the buses and trucks became bogged down.

However, Christmas is Christmas even in the midst of a Mosul bog, and everyone crowded in somewhere, including the civilian buses. Soon sing-songs to celebrate Christmas night were in full swing.

Boxing Day was spent digging in and pitching tentage, and by the 27th the Battalion had at least a canvas roof if not dry floors.

After a few days in which to settle in and clean up, on the 30th December, Major-General C. O. Harvey, C.B., C.V.O., C.B.E., M.C., the Commander of the 8th Indian Division, and the 18th Indian Infantry Brigade Commander, Brigadier R. G. Lochner, M.C., visited them and told the Battalion what was expected of it.

The other two battalions then in the Brigade were the 1/2nd Gurkhas and the 2/3rd Gurkhas, but the 1/2nd Gurkhas were shortly to be transferred to the 4th Indian Division, their place in the 18th Brigade being taken by the 4/11th Sikhs.

At first the 2/5th Essex was to find conditions somewhat strange, for until a short time before its arrival, the 8th Indian Division had been composed entirely of Indian Army units. The arrival of British infantry battalions meant that the Division was now in conformity with the established Indian divisional pattern, but much shaking down was necessary. For one cannot take a Territorial battalion from a British brigade, transport it to a far country, put it into an Indian division administered by India, and expect all mental reactions to be adjusted immediately.

Fortunately, the Battalion had a very good friend in the person of Major J. K. Shepheard, R.E., Brigade Major to the 18th Indian Infantry Brigade, who had been Brigade Major to Brigadier Hobart in the 161st Infantry Brigade. Major Shepheard was invaluable in smoothing out the many difficulties that arose.

Indeed, the adjustment of mental reactions was not needed only on the Essex side. "We found the staff and services all looking to Karachi and India, where we had been used all the time previously to looking to Accra (G.H.Q. West Africa Force) or Cairo and England for everything. I believe for a time our mail was routed via Karachi."

Soon the snow came down, and, by mid-January 1942, eight or more degrees of frost were being registered in the living-tents. The Battalion was still in tropical clothing in the daytime and found the days very cold, although quite pleasant in the sunshine. But spirits remained high, particularly on the day in mid-January when they sat down to an excellent if belated Christmas dinner of local turkey and N.A.A.F.I. plum pudding. Comforts, too, generously provided by ladies of India, were supplied through Division.

In the winter of 1941/42 there was a possibility that the Germans might well break through the Caucasus into Persia and Iraq, and the task of the 8th Indian Division was to prepare defences covering Mosul. And so the 2/5th soon found themselves at work on a battalion defensive position and at the same time assisted in the supervision of a mass of native labour engaged in the construction of an immense and circular anti-tank ditch. Everyone had grave doubts as to its usefulness, but "theirs not to reason why" and the work went on.

After some six weeks of this work, the Battalion was moved, on the 15th February, about forty miles farther east to a camp site about four miles from the quaint and very ancient walled city of Irbil, which "stuck up on the horizon like a large black tiered cake." Irbil, the ancient Arbela, is the oldest inhabited city extant.

Here the country was ideal for training, miles and miles of rolling country, passable by mechanical transport except after heavy rain and only dotted with an occasional Kurdish village. A unit could go anywhere and do anything without let or hindrance and a considerable amount of useful training was accomplished. Not before time, thought the men, for up to date the Battalion had spent its war digging or manning defences in England, West Africa, Egypt, and Iraq, and all were anxious to get down to the real thing.

At Irbil one night Brigadier Lochner was dining in the mess when a great gale of wind and rain hit the camp. Most of the canvas was flattened, but the Brigadier hung on for dear life to the tent pole of the mess tent, which went to an acute angle but did not finally collapse. At the height of the storm a dripping figure forced its way through the flapping canvas, and a plaintive voice said, "I'm lost. Can someone tell me where I am?" It was Regimental Sergeant-Major Small.

Such storms made life pretty uncomfortable, for, of course, there was nowhere to go when tents blew down, except into the transport vehicles, but spring was coming, and in spring life, even in Iraq, had its compensations.

"March in Iraq was a lovely month, masses of yellow Jericho daisies, and the country, which was largely desert and little else, looked quite lovely in places where you get miles of yellow consisting of these beautiful Jericho daisies."

For recreation it was possible to play football against the 1/5th Essex, now in the 19th Indian Infantry Brigade and not far away, with the 2/3rd Gurkhas and with the 121st Field Regiment, R.A. A very close liaison developed with the Battalion's link battery—275th Battery under Major W. K. Paul—a liaison that was to stand the strain of battle under most adverse conditions.

There was shooting, too, perhaps the best duck shooting in the world in winter, and with the spring, shooting at greater bustards and gazelle, with a few expeditions against wild boar.

On the 1st February, 1942, the Persia and Iraq Forces (Paiforce) were regrouped as the Tenth Army, under Lieutenant-General E. P. Quinan.

This reorganisation, as well as bringing the Tenth Army into being, transferred it from Indian command and administration to that of the Middle East with much benefit to the long-suffering British battalions as regards mail services, N.A.A.F.I., and the like. There is little doubt that troops in Persia and Iraq were much less well served than those in Egypt, Syria, and Palestine.

The reorganisation brought three separate armies under H.Q. Middle East, the Eighth Army in the Western Desert, the Ninth Army in Palestine and Syria, and the Tenth in Persia and Iraq.

The G.O.C.-in-C. Middle East Forces, General Sir Claude Auchinleck, accompanied by the Army Commander, Lieutenant-General Quinan, visited the 2/5th Essex whilst it was at Erbil.

The valuable training period at Irbil was broken by a move south to Baquba, on the River Diyala, about twenty-eight miles north-north-east of Baghdad, where the 2/5th Essex once more found itself constructing defences, but opportunity was taken of the proximity of Baghdad to send parties on leave to the city. At Baquba Captain H. J. L. Wright took over the duties of adjutant from Captain P. B. Lake. Then, as the defences neared completion, the Battalion was ordered back to Irbil.

Defences, carefully dug and lined with precious wood and even more precious corrugated iron, were left under village guard. The last trucks of the departing Essex saw the first marauding Arab bands swooping down to strip those so laboriously constructed defences. The Arab, who had always considered the English as "afflicted by Allah," must have thought them even more mad than usual to leave such treasures behind.

Not perhaps that the 2/5th Essex can afford to be too sanctimonious in such matters, for there were those vehicles left so trustingly in the Battalion lines when that Indian unit went to Cyprus at short notice. Curious how the 2/5th was never short of spare parts and never had a cracked cylinder head, however severe the frost.

Back at Irbil, on the 20th April, 1942, the Battalion underwent further intensive training and some last shooting in their spare time, for time in Iraq was drawing to a close. In the Western Desert the situation soon began to alter rapidly and for the worse.

Section IV

THE BATTLE OF DEIR-EL-SHEIN

At the end of May 1942 an offensive by the Axis forces under Rommel met with considerable success and, attacking all along the line, he had by the 10th June forced a general withdrawal of the Eighth Army. Reinforcements were an urgent necessity. These came from the Ninth Army in the first instance, and to replace them units and formations of the Tenth Army were moved westwards. Brigadier Lochner's 18th Indian Infantry Brigade Group, detached from the 8th Indian Division, was one of the formations so moved.

The Brigade Group consisted of Brigade Headquarters and Signal Section, the 121st Field Regiment R.A., the 2/5th Essex, 2/3rd Gurkha Rifles, and the 4/11th Sikhs, together with a field ambulance and the Brigade workshop section.

The group left Irbil on the 9th June, 1942, and travelling westwards through Mosul, Deir-ez-Zor, and Damascus, reached the area of Hadera and Acre in northern Palestine by the middle of the month.

The 2/5th Essex and indeed the whole 18th Indian Brigade Group were not equipped to war scale. The Essex had no carriers, for the Indian-pattern wheeled carriers had been withdrawn, and tracked carriers had not been issued. The one 2-pounder anti-tank gun issued to the Battalion for training had also been withdrawn. It seemed clear to all that the Brigade move had been to reinforce the Ninth Army, and no move even farther westward was thought of. Indeed, the general idea seemed to be that they would embark for Cyprus. But after only one week of comparative luxury in the Sidney Smith Barracks at Acre, the Battalion, with the rest of the Brigade Group, was suddenly ordered westwards into Egypt.

Brigade Headquarters, with the Brigade M.T. column, the 121st

Field Regiment, and the field ambulance, moved on the 23rd June by the Sinai Desert road with destination given as Mersa Matruh.

The three infantry battalions moved by rail on the 25th June, the 2/5th Essex entraining at Haifa. Their destination, too, was given as "Mersa Matruh if still in our hands." It sounded ominous.

A clear run was made from Haifa to Kantara, then across the Canal, and another straight run across Egypt, through Tanta, and skirting Alexandria, to Amriya. "Here, I suppose," said Lieutenant-Colonel May, "if the need had not been urgent, we should have unloaded all our light baggage, dropped a rear party (left out of battle party) and proceeded into the Western Desert in battle order only." After a brief halt the train moved on and reached the small station of Galal, the first station beyond and to the west of El Daba, about 9 p.m. on the evening of the 26th June. The Battalion was now well up into the forward areas, but, as has been explained, was not in operational order, nor had any opportunity for preparing for operations been given. Even their train was normal peace-time rolling stock of first-, second-, and third-class carriages painted white. Joining in Galal station a goods train facing east and a long line of wagons already halted in the area, it made "a long thick black streak on a yellowish background, a perfect air target."

It was quickly bombed, and the Essex were as promptly dispersed well off the railway track, but nevertheless had 2 killed and 4 or 5 injured. An Indian unit in the goods wagon train, not so quick to disperse, had more casualties. Bombs set alight some empty oil drums, and the blaze brought the enemy back to drop still further bombs.

Captain J. K. Drucquer, the Regimental Medical Officer, did excellent work that night.

Early next morning, the 27th June, all trains were headed eastwards and returned to El Alamein. Lying behind the Essex train and so ahead in this retrograde movement was the train containing the 4/11th Sikhs, which had come up during the night, and which had also suffered in the night's bombing.

Arriving at El Alamein station about 8 a.m. on the 27th, Lieutenant-Colonel May at once dispersed the 2/5th and the 4/11th Sikhs well astride of the railway. He found neither Brigade Headquarters nor M.T., but the 2/3rd Gurkhas were there and had already detrained.

The situation thus was as follows: the three infantry battalions were at El Alamein, but divorced from their M.T. and deficient of carriers and anti-tank guns. Brigade Headquarters, under Lieutenant-Colonel

C. E. Gray, 2/3rd Gurkhas (for Brigadier Lochner had remained sick in Palestine), the Brigade M.T., and the field regiment were somewhere between Sinai and Mersa Matruh. It was not exactly a promising situation, as Lieutenant-Colonel May, the senior lieutenant-colonel of the Brigade present at El Alamein, took command of the three battalions. He saw that some degree of chaos was already impending—"Hundreds of odd troops were milling round the water-point, hundreds of vehicles were jostling down the coast roads heading east. Scores more were following a track parallel to the railway."

Borrowing a vehicle, he went to the Headquarters of the 1st South African Division in the Alamein Box to get information and, if possible, orders. There Lieutenant-Colonel May found Lieutenant-General Sir Willoughby Norrie, the commander of 30th Corps, who was busily organising the rear position El Alamein–Qattara Depression.

General Norrie knew about the arrival of the 18th Indian Brigade Group, and hearing the location of the three battalions said, "Good, stay there, but send me a liaison officer." He gave it as his opinion that the Brigade was not likely to be needed, and that until it had got its transport, carriers, anti-tank guns, and ammunition, it would not be in a position to do anything.

However, the situation was now altering very rapidly and for the worse. The general situation on the 27th June was as follows: Tobruk had fallen on the 21st June, and following up his success Rommel had crossed the Egyptian frontier on the 23rd. Covered by rear-guards, the Eighth Army was in retreat eastwards from Sollum. Transport, nose to nose, in columns four abreast, crawled back to Mersa Matruh, and on to El Alamein.

It was at this moment of full withdrawal that the 18th Indian Infantry Brigade—in Iraq a short three weeks before—had detrained almost fortuitously at El Alamein. Separated from commander and staff and divorced from their transport and supporting arms, they had received on their westward journey no information that indicated they would be virtually in the front line the moment they detrained. So battalions were not organised for battle, no "left out of battle" parties had been formed, nor had they been given opportunity to shed their light baggage. Such things that had not been dumped beside the railway at El Alamein went forward with companies, and unit transport still carried kitbags, hockey sticks, and other sports gear as the debris of battle was all too soon to show.

At about 7 a.m., the 28th June, a staff officer from Headquarters

30th Corps arrived with operation orders. The 18th Indian Infantry Brigade Group was to take up a defensive position at Deir-el-Shein, a position about midway between El Alamein station and Kut Butara,

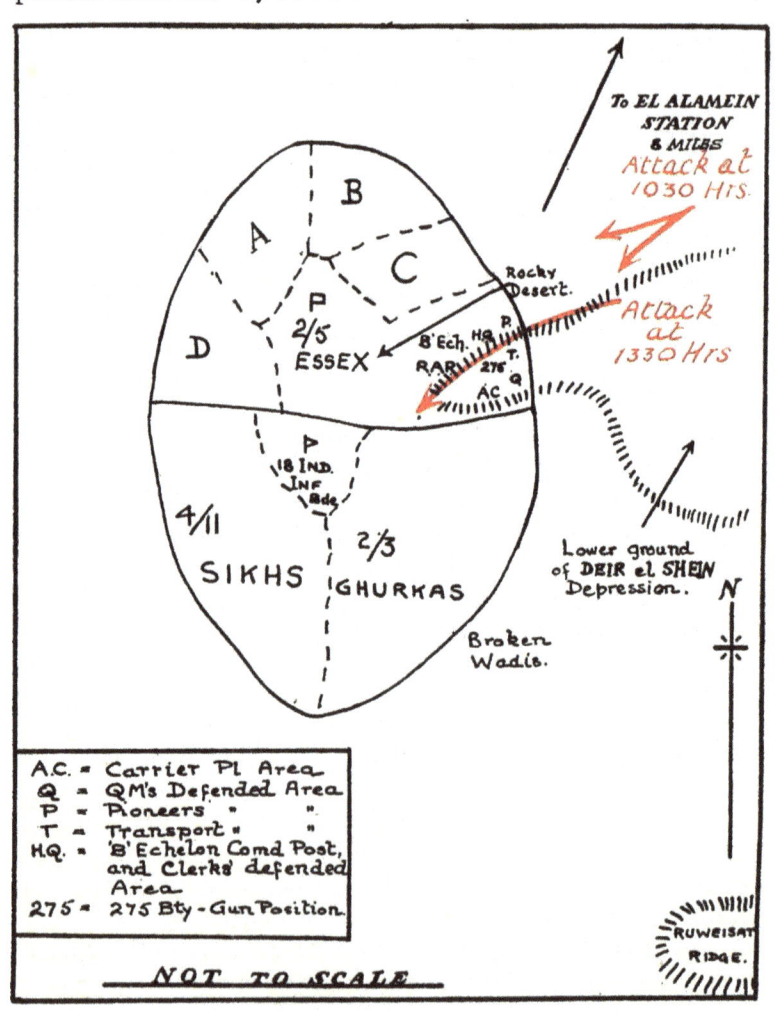

2/5TH ESSEX, DEIR-EL-SHEIN, 1ST JULY, 1942.

about eight miles to the south-south-west of Alamein station and some four miles to the north-west of the western tip of Ruweisat Ridge. Check points were also to be established to collect and direct units withdrawing eastwards across the desert.

Deir-el-Shein, a name on the map and little else, is a saucer-shaped depression in the desert, a series of ridges and nullahs, some wide and deep enough completely to conceal a tank. The whole configuration could easily contain a division, but one division would be insufficient to hold the whole position securely.

Two hours later battalion transport—that of the 2/5th Essex and 4/11th Sikhs—began to arrive at El Alamein, and it became possible to start a shuttle service out to Deir-el-Shein. By midnight, the 28th/29th June, the whole of the 18th Indian Infantry Brigade Group, except for the 121st Field Regiment, had been ferried out to the position. The 121st Field Regiment had been detached from the remainder of the Brigade road party and committed to action west of Deir-el-Shein (in the area of Mersa Matruh in support of the 1/4th Essex).

Early on the 28th June, Lieutenant-Colonel May went forward with the commanding officers of the 4/11th Sikhs and 2/3rd Gurkhas. A brigade position was selected and battalion defensive areas allotted, so that work could start as soon as the first troops reached the area.

In making his plan of defence, Lieutenant-Colonel May included a position for a second brigade, for the 30th Corps order had said that a brigade from the 50th Division would arrive in time to share the defence of Deir-el-Shein. In fact, no elements of this brigade ever arrived in the position.

In the evening of the 28th June Lieutenant-Colonel C. E. Gray, the acting brigade commander, arrived, and the layout having been approved, Lieutenant-Colonel May reassumed command of the 2/5th Essex.

Deir-el-Shein had at no time been regarded as a brigade or divisional box, and at the time of arrival of the leading troops of the 18th Indian Infantry Brigade on the morning of the 28th June, there were no defences whatsoever even in outline. Every available vehicle had to be used to bring up tools, wire, and mines, to fetch the troops and baggage from El Alamein, and to draw water from El Hamman, some fifty miles away. These duties continued to the moment of contact with the enemy, with the inevitable result that "B" Echelon could not be withdrawn and had to be incorporated in the defence.

There was very little time to prepare a defensive position capable of resisting a tank attack, for the Brigade had been warned that the enemy could be expected within forty-eight hours of the initial deployment at Deir-el-Shein. The ground was mainly stony, with sand only in patches, and much of the area had live rock within two feet of the surface. There were no power tools and only four bulldozers for the whole Brigade. Effective digging was impossible in a greater part of the area.

Private A. Gambier says: "The sand was only eighteen inches deep, beneath which was solid rock. South African engineers had started blasting operations to make holes in the rock, but on the day the enemy arrived, they had not reached 'B' Company and so the company had no deep weapon pits."

Despite this almost insurmountable difficulty, the Essex, working twenty hours in each twenty-four, had dug vehicles in as far as was possible, and had made what weapon pits they could. A triple dannert-wire obstacle had been run round the brigade area, though not, because of time and the shortage of wire, between the battalion areas. Mines were in very short supply, but sufficient had been obtained to lay a field fifty yards deep in front of the wire on all rifle company sectors. A 1,000 yards of front was, however, unmined. This was in part the sector occupied by "B" Echelon at the time of attack.

During the evening of the 30th June four 2-pounder anti-tank guns were collected from El Alamein. Two lacked sights, and the accompanying ammunition was extremely limited. There was not a single Bren carrier with the Battalion. However, six 6-pounder anti-tank guns manned by a company of the Buffs pulled in during the night and occupied positions that fortunately had been already prepared. This company of the Buffs was to perform yeoman service during the battle.

Eighteen 25-pounders from the 121st, 124th, and Kent Yeomanry Field Regiments also entered the box during the night the 30th June/1st July, and the six guns of the 275th Battery under Major W. K. Paul were placed in support of the 2/5th Essex. Thus was the liaison with the link battery resumed on the very eve of battle. Unfortunately, the battery had already been in action during the 30th June and was short of ammunition. Unfortunately, too, the guns had to be put down in the open, for there was no time to prepare gun positions. Finally, to complete the defensive picture, it remains to say the sole supply of small-arms ammunition available to the Brigade was the A.F.G. 1098 store brought in unit transport from Iraq. There was no reserve whatsoever.

The 1st July showed itself to be a day of poor visibility, and the dust haze was increased as elements of withdrawing formations, including a large portion of the 1st Armoured Division, continued to pull back through and to the flanks of the Deir-el-Shein Box.

2/5TH BATTALION THE ESSEX REGIMENT. A BELATED CHRISTMAS DINNER. MOSUL. JANUARY 1942.

Among those recognisable in the photograph are (left to right) Sgt. Pentney, C/Sgt. Middleton, Sgt. Eldridge, C.S.M. Lockmiller, Sgt. Harris, Sgt. Carter, P.S.M. King, Sgt. Surridge, Pte. Wilson, Sgt. Clary, Sgt. Thompson, L/Cpl. Joy, Sgt. Pennock, Sgt. Squirrell. Sgt. Foakes, Sgt. Holden, Capt. A. E. C. Alston, Sgt. Patmore, Sgt. Stubbs, Sgt. Clarke (holding a turkey), Sgt. Creswell, Sgt. Desborough, C/Sgt. Ransome, Sgt. A. B. Smith, Sgt. Toswell, Capt. Sanderson, Lt. P. Perfect, Major A. J. Hills, Lt. P. W. Daniel, Lt. (Q.M.) P. H. Brooks, Pte. Farrant, Pte. Johnson, Lt. F. G. Coe.

THE ESSEX REGIMENT CHAPEL, WARLEY.

There had been a continuous flow of units for the past thirty hours, and it was a strange coincidence of war that on the 30th June one shot-up station wagon withdrawing through the area of the 2/5th should be found to hold Lieutenant-Colonel A. Noble, the Commanding Officer of the 1/4th Essex. He told Lieutenant-Colonel May that he had pulled out of Fuka with part of his battalion, had had to fight his way out of a German trap at night, and that the 1/4th were re-forming on Ruweisıt Ridge, a few miles to the rear of Deir-el-Shein. Several more officers and many other ranks of the 1/4th were seen and spoken to during the day.

Towards 7 a.m., the 1st July, a fresh cloud of dust was reported moving up from the south-west. The screen of armoured cars of the Guides Cavalry reported that a large enemy column was advancing, and that the protective screen was being withdrawn east of Deir-el-Shein. This column was in fact elements of Rommel's Afrika Korps, chiefly the 15th Panzer Division.

It was preceded by reconnaissance elements, many in captured British vehicles, which made identification in the low visibility difficult. Captain A. E. C. Alston, O.C. "A" Company, says: "Shortly after stand-to on the 1st July another large column came in sight. Difficult to identify though some of it looked British. We reported it back to Battalion Headquarters. Yes, too true, a lot of the vehicles were British, but any lingering doubts about the column were rapidly dispelled by the arrival of some shells. One of them slap in the midst of No. 8 Platoon...."

This was followed by ranging on Deir-el-Shein by black airbursts from artillery in the main column still lying off to the south-east. The time was now about 8 a.m. This general registration was followed by ranging on "B" Echelon, and as the story of "B" Echelon's gallant action plays a prominent part in the account of the battle, it is proposed to go back a little and give the story from the start.

"B" Echelon had been allotted an area in the eastern portion of the Battalion's position. There was a small wadi running down from east to west, and the high ground (relatively) to the south of the wadi marked the point of junction of the 2/5th Essex with the 2/3rd Gurkhas. The high ground continued out eastwards beyond the battalion area and prevented a view down into the main portion of the Deir-el-Shein depression.

The wadi widened out into almost flat ground, with a little ridge bearing away to the north, where "B" Echelon joined on to "C"

Company's area. The ground between the main "C" Company localities and "B" Echelon's main position was rocky desert some 600 to 800 yards across.

"B" Echelon vehicles, cookhouse, Regimental aid post, baggage dump (for kitbags and other encumbrances were still with the Battalion), and stores were sited in the lower ground in this wadi, but the difference between the highest and lowest point was not more than about four to five feet.

Major C. A. Brooks, the Battalion Second-in-Command, was in command of "B" Echelon. He says: "After a number of vehicle pits had been dug in this softer ground in the wadi, accommodation had to be found for the 25-pounders of the 121st Field Regiment. 'B' Echelon was given under command some six Bren guns, manned by the carrier crews who had left their vehicles behind in Iraq. In order to ease the ammunition supply problem for these guns, three of them were allocated to the pioneer platoon, cooks and quartermaster staff. Carrier crews were thus six men to a gun instead of three.

"Dawn on the 1st July broke as the guns of the field regiments drew into position. Reconnaissance parties had arrived the night before, but no digging had been possible for the guns. Five of them were sited in the lower ground of the wadi, but it was not posssible to get them dug in in the short time before the enemy made his presence known.

"One gun, which was unserviceable but which was of quite good appearance, was towed out to a spot near the perimeter wire half-way between 'B' Echelon and 'C' Company in the hopes of drawing fire to a spot where it would be harmless."

As has already been said, this portion of the front had no minefield in front of the triple dannert fence, and the only protection, other than the perimeter wire, was a small section of wire fence, about 150 yards in length, running back along the line of junction with the Gurkhas. Weapon pits were not sited tactically, but in places where the ground allowed some digging-in to be done. There were no anti-tank guns with "B" Echelon and no mortars, although one detachment with "C" Company was able to fire on the ground in front of "B" Echelon.

First contact was "about 7.45 a.m., when he (the enemy) fired a few ranging shells in and around 'B' Echelon area. One of these first shells," says Major Brooks, "unluckily scored a direct hit on one of the two water-carts, killing the driver and mortally wounding his mate, and turning the water-cart into an inverted pepper-pot. The 25-pounders opened up in reply, but after a few shells nothing much more happened."

There was now a lull, except for desultory shelling as the enemy stood off. At about 10 a.m., Captain E. B. Cooper, O.C. "C" Company, reported back to Lieutenant-Colonel May that a Bren carrier was moving in towards the Essex lines flying a white flag.

In due course two blindfolded men were brought in to the Essex command post, where Lieutenant-Colonel Gray, the acting brigade commander, had just arrived. They wore no rank badges but stated they were two officers of the 50th Division who had been captured by the 15th Panzer Division and had been sent in by the divisional commander to order the British to surrender within half an hour to save unnecessary bloodshed. The 15th Panzer Division was said to have about sixty tanks, a lot of 25-pounders and anti-tank guns, together with much captured M.T., and plenty of petrol and water.

At that moment Brigadier J. S. Nichols, D.S.O., M.C., temporarily in command of the 10th Indian Division, rang up from Brigade Headquarters. He was told the situation and ordered the two officers to be sent down to him. As Brigadier Nichols had until very recently commanded the 151st Infantry Brigade in 50th Division, there is little doubt he received the delegation in a fitting manner.

About 10.30 a.m., under cover of light shelling, some of the enemy forward elements nosed up towards the wire on "A" Company front. About half a dozen vehicles were mined as the party made their way along the front until they got into a depression about 500 yards from "B" Echelon.

Major Brooks speaks of this when he says: "About 10.30 a.m. enemy shelling opened up quite heavily, and they obviously located the field guns when they replied. At the same time enemy tanks and troop-carrying half-track vehicles in large numbers were seen on the high ground to the east of 'B' Echelon. They appeared to be advancing for an attack, but Major W. K. Paul (O.C. 275th Battery), who was with O.C. 'B' Echelon, as there was not sufficient signal wire to enable him to be at Battalion Headquarters, was able to turn his guns on to this target with open sights, and they, with 'B' Echelon small-arms fire, undoubtedly caused the enemy considerable casualties as he quickly withdrew into dead ground in the Deir-el-Shein depression to the east."

The enemy shelling on the whole Battalion front now increased, and was stiffened up with what Captain Alston calls "pestilential mortars." The 4/11th Sikhs could now be heard in action by "A" Company.

Under cover of the fire, the enemy infantry approached "B" Echelon over the ridge that screened the depression and attempted an attack. This was repulsed by small-arms fire before the enemy could get to the perimeter wire.

By now the 275th Battery, heavily engaged by the enemy artillery, were suffering from lack of cover. Two guns were out of action and the personnel had suffered considerable casualties.

"'B' Echelon," continues Major Brooks, "had not suffered such heavy casualties owing to better protection, but there had been many near misses and a number of vehicles had been hit." Some were on fire and others were unserviceable. Some of the baggage was set alight and began to burn.

The enemy now established himself on the ridge, and the whole of "B" Echelon was swept with small-arms fire, which became intense when anybody tried to move. The area was also under continuous shell fire.

About midday, the wire to Battalion Headquarters was cut somewhere on that 800 yards of flat rocky desert which separated the main position from that held by "B" Echelon. A line party (L/Sergeant R. Smith and Private R. Fisher) made repeated efforts to repair the break, but eventually Fisher was killed and Smith forced into cover.

Major Brooks goes on to say: "Just before the line was cut, a remarkable incident took place. The enemy succeeded in bringing up an anti-tank gun to cover 'B' Echelon's area, and this was causing a great deal of damage to the vehicles, the field guns, etc. The field guns were unable to bear on this target, so help was asked from the mortars in 'C' Company's area. O.C. 'B' Echelon, in direct conversation over the line via Battalion Headquarters to the mortar detachment commander, was able to direct fire of the mortars on to the target which they could not see, and by a stroke of luck after a comparatively few rounds, a direct hit on the anti-tank gun was scored.

"The odds were too great for the end to be long delayed, and soon after 1 p.m. an enemy party, supported by fire from tanks as well as from the infantry on the ridge, advanced to the wire with a Bangalore torpedo.

"'B' Echelon—every available man—cooks, mess staff, clerks, M.T. personnel, and the quartermaster and his staff—were firing steadily, taking heavy toll of the enemy, but at the same time exhausting their slender stocks of ammunition.

"About 1.15 p.m. the enemy succeeded in blowing a breach in the wire opposite Sergeant Toswell's position. Immediately tanks and eight-wheeled armoured cars advanced through this with infantry support behind. Sergeant Toswell was killed and the post overrun."

There were no anti-tank weapons, the 25-pounders were nearly all out of action, and the meagre G 1098 supplies of small-arms ammunition exhausted.

Post by post, "B" Echelon was overrun. Owing to the great volume of fire produced by the enemy and the absolute lack of anti-tank defences, it was impossible to organise any form of counter-attack. At 1.30 p.m. "B" Echelon command post was overrun, and O.C. "B" Echelon and O.C. 275th Field Battery were captured.

The last serviceable 25-pounder gun and its crew, together with some survivors from the other gun crews, were able to pull out just before the final attack, and withdrew to join up with another battery elsewhere in the brigade box.

Tanks and infantry now passed on up the wadi, successfully overrunning the cookhouse position and the R.A.P. They then, according to Major Brooks' observations, seemed to come under fire from some anti-tank guns, and were not able to press on across the open ground towards Battalion Headquarters till later in the day.

The prisoners from "B" Echelon were taken some 800 to 1,000 yards away into a slight depression not very far from a concentration of German vehicles. These were shelled by the 25-pounders later in the afternoon and unfortunately a stray splinter killed the Quartermaster, Lieutenant P. H. Brooks. The Battalion chaplain, Captain the Reverend D. W. Thompson, and the Medical Officer, Captain J. K. Drucquer, R.A.M.C., had both been wounded earlier in the action.

Lieutenant-Colonel K. F. May says of the battle: "I cannot speak too highly of the action 'B' Echelon put up. They fought until practically all their ammunition was expended, and certainly extracted a high price from the enemy infantry, but against tanks it was impossible, and our 25-pounders and anti-tank guns were very thin on the ground."

The effect of this break-in meant that "C" Company, the right-hand Essex company, now had an open flank, and a large gap between it and the left-hand company of the 2/3rd Gurkhas.

After a pause to reorganise, the enemy began pushing along the flank of "C" Company towards Brigade Headquarters, and attempted to infiltrate into "C" Company area, but was prevented. A lively battle was seen to develop round the Brigade Headquarters area, probably between the German tanks and seven "Matildas" which had come into the box the evening before the battle. It was now about 2 p.m. Gun and mortar fire in the battalion area was heavy, but no major action had developed since "B" Echelon had been overrun half an hour before. "C" Company, however, reported tanks to be moving about in the distance.

The attack was not pressed, however, and the 6-pounder anti-tank guns, manned by the Buffs, did excellent service in delaying the enemy advance. It is probable, too, that he suspected minefields which undoubtedly would have been laid for the all-round defence of company areas had mines and time been available.

It was not till nearly 5 p.m. when, quoting Captain E. B. Cooper, O.C. "C" Company, "the enemy with about ten tanks and two mounted (self-propelled) guns supported by infantry attacked 'C' Company from the direction of 'B' Echelon. A severe dust-storm was blowing at the time, and visibility no more than fifty yards. By this time nearly all the British artillery had been knocked out, and the enemy tanks were able to drive right into the middle of 'C' Company position."

As "C" Company was overrun, "B" Company began to suffer.

Reference to the sketch map will show that by now the enemy had bitten deeply into the Essex defences, but soon after 5 p.m. Lieutenant-Colonel Gray rang up to say the 1st Armoured Division would be counter-attacking shortly, and the message, passed out to companies still in touch with Battalion Headquarters, put additional heart into the now hard-pressed Essex.

At about 5.30 p.m. the fight round Brigade Headquarters seemed to be getting fiercer, and there was intense shelling everywhere. The line to Brigade went "out" at this stage.

"B" Company was by now rounded up, and only "A" and "D" remained in action. About this time the enemy made progress as rapid as it was unexpected through the area of the 4/11th Sikhs to expose "D" Company's flank to heavy attack.

At 6 p.m. "A" Company was attacked. Captain A. E. C. Alston says: "Jerry attacked 'A' Company about 6 p.m. with a Mark IV, two Mark IIIs, and an armoured car, plus infantry. The one 2-pounder gun in our area was put out of action, and then we had nothing except

Brens and rifles. Company Headquarters was first overrun. Then No. 9 Platoon. We hung on, so Headquarters went shortly after 7 p.m., and afterwards I learnt that Nos. 7 and 8 Platoons were finally swept up just before dusk. In Company Headquarters the company sergeant-major was killed and the company clerk wounded."

Nevertheless, the enemy still had to fight hard for "D" Company's area, but by 7.30 p.m. the last post had been overrun and fighting ceased.

Shortly afterwards, H.Q. 18th Indian Infantry Brigade was captured, and one company of the 2/3rd Gurkha Rifles overrun. It was now nightfall, and under cover of darkness the remainder of the Gurkha battalion was able to disengage and join up during the night with the main British forces at El Alamein.

The events of the 1st July, 1942, are summarised in the dispatch by General Sir Claude J. E. Auchinleck, G.C.I., C.B., C.S.I., O.B.E., A.D.C., Commander-in-Chief the Middle East Forces, submitted on the 27th January, 1943, and published as a supplement to the *London Gazette* of the 13th January, 1948.

"On the morning of the 1st July, the enemy unsuccessfully attacked the 1st South African Division which was holding the fortifications round El Alamein itself. At the same time he launched an infantry attack with strong artillery support against the 18th Indian Infantry Brigade Group, holding the Deir-el-Shein defensive locality. This attack was beaten off. But the Brigade had just arrived from Iraq and suffered from inexperience and from the difficulties of having to take up a defensive position at very short notice.

"When a further attack, strongly supported by tanks, developed late in the afternoon under cover of a dust-storm, which undoubtedly favoured the attackers, the Brigade was eventually overrun, after five hours' stalwart resistance. Only one infantry battalion survived the attack, but the stand made by the Brigade certainly gained valuable time for the organisation of the El Alamein line generally."

Lieutenant-Colonel May and others made a dash for liberty, but without success. Private A. Gambier says:

"At El Daba I saw the Commanding Officer, Lieutenant-Colonel May, who asked me for a stretcher to carry a wounded soldier. A few minutes later he disappeared, and a figure was seen sitting in the back of a German truck going in the direction of Alamein. It was Colonel May. However, the C.O. joined the prisoners again at El Daba, but rumour has it that he tried at least twice to escape."

The action at Deir-el-Shein marked the finish of the 2/5th Essex, to whom the fortunes of war had not been kind. There were no reinforcements available with which to rebuild the Battalion, and the War Office eventually came to the decision that its reconstitution was not possible.

General Sir Willoughby Norrie, writing in 1944 to Colonel Sir Carne Rasch, Bart., the Honorary Colonel of the 5th Essex, said:

"The 2/5th Essex put up a very stout fight against what proved to be overwhelming odds on the 1st July, 1942. Although they were eventually scuppered, their resistance helped the general situation, and they were instrumental in knocking out, I should say, at least a dozen tanks, which at that time was a lot in the very diminished forces Rommel still had.

"The 18th Indian Infantry Brigade were brought up in a hurry from behind, had to dig themselves in, and were attacked within forty-eight hours of arrival.

"The full story has never been known."

For this action against overwhelming odds the 2/5th Essex were subsequently awarded two Military Crosses and two Military Medals.

These were awarded to Captain E. B. Cooper (O.C. "C" Company) and Captain A. L. Cullen (O.C. "B" Company), to L/Sergeant R. Smith for his gallantry in attempting the repair of the signal line between "B" Echelon and the main position, and to L/Corporal H. T. J. Dyer for gallantry with the M.T. Section in the defence of "B" Echelon. In addition, the Military Cross was awarded to Lieutenant R. V. Knight of 275th Battery R.A. in support.

Major C. A. Brooks, O.C. "B" Echelon, Private R. Fisher (killed in the attempt to repair "B" Echelon line), Sergeant R. G. Toswell (Pioneer sergeant), and Private C. Wiseman (a Boyes anti-tank rifleman with "B" Company) were all mentioned in dispatches.

To conclude the story of a gallant but unfortunate Battalion, it is not inappropriate to add that many officers and other ranks made strenuous and repeated efforts to escape while prisoners-of-war. A large number were successful following the surrender of Italy in 1943.

Altogether, for such attempts, successful and unsuccessful in Italy and Germany, Lieutenant-Colonel K. F. May was awarded the O.B.E. and other officers and other ranks were mentioned in dispatches. Amongst these were Lieutenant F. G. Coe, Lieutenant M. H. Murray,

L/Corporal J. W. South, and Private L. E. Francis, who was killed in Germany whilst a prisoner-of-war.

The Reverend D. W. Thompson, C.F., was also mentioned in dispatches for his good services whilst a prisoner-of-war in Germany.

It is thus clear that even in adversity the fighting spirit of the 2/5th Essex lived on.

Chapter Eight

OLD BATTALIONS IN A NEW ROLE, 1939-50

INTRODUCTION

THE year 1935 saw the 7th Battalion The Essex Regiment leave the Essex Territorial Infantry Brigade to turn over to an anti-aircraft role and become the 59th Anti-Aircraft Brigade R.A. Then in 1938 the 6th Battalion had to follow into anti-aircraft work, split into two halves, and become the 1/6th Battalion The Essex Regiment (64th Searchlight Regiment) and the 2/6th Battalion The Essex Regiment (65th Searchlight Regiment).

The past ten years has seen many changes in role and name for these old-established units, so long part of the Essex Regiment, first as Volunteer battalions, next as units in the Territorial Force, and then as part of the Territorial Army, but the passing years have seen little weakening of the bonds of sentiment and association that tie these units of Royal Artillery so closely to their parent regiment. The following accounts of the war-time activities of these old battalions of the Essex Regiment may, it is hoped, strengthen still further the ties between the two Regiments.

Section I

59TH (THE ESSEX REGIMENT) HEAVY ANTI-AIRCRAFT REGIMENT R.A., T.A. (LATE 7TH BATTALION THE ESSEX REGIMENT)

In 1935 the 7th Battalion The Essex Regiment T.A. was converted into a heavy anti-aircraft unit, under the designation 59th (The Essex Regiment) Heavy Anti-Aircraft Brigade R.A., T.A.

It was agreed with the War Office that the unit should retain the name of The Essex Regiment in its title, and personnel obtained permission to wear the Essex cap badge and buttons. The title was subsequently changed to 59th (The Essex Regiment) Heavy Anti-Aircraft

Regiment R.A., T.A., and it is under this name that the unit operated throughout the Second World War.

On the 22nd August, 1939, a preliminary warning of mobilisation was received, and on the 24th August the final stages were ordered, resulting in the immediate deployment of the Regiment under the command of Lieutenant-Colonel C. Needell, M.C., T.D., R.A., on the north side of the Thames Estuary.

The Regiment was completely ready for action at 9 a.m. the 25th August, 1939, and by then only 1 per cent. of the unit had failed to report for duty. The deployment was no mean feat, considering that the unit was deficient in transport and had to rely mainly on borrowed civilian vehicles.

On the declaration of war, an increased state of readiness was ordered, but fortunately no attack materialised, and, apart from occasional small raids, it was not until the second half of 1940 that real action began.

The Regiment's part in the "Battle of Britain" is difficult to assess, although, as is now known, a large number of enemy aircraft were destroyed. The 59th Regiment can at least claim to have been in the front row in many actions. It will be recalled that the German official figures show that during the period July/October 1940, 1,733 enemy aircraft were destroyed by fighter aircraft and anti-aircraft guns, and all regiments participating in the vulnerable areas can justifiably claim a share in this now-proved victory.

The first regimental casualties were sustained during this period, when bombs were dropped on a gun position at Stanford-le-Hope, and when another position at Hadleigh was machine-gunned by a crashing enemy aircraft.

In May 1941 it became clear that the Regiment was destined for a less static role, and a period of mobile training under regimental arrangements ensued. This was closely followed by a move to the Clyde and Newcastle, both of which had sustained heavy air raids.

In September 1941 the Regiment became part of the Anti-Aircraft Command mobile reserve, moving to Sittingbourne, Kent, and from there to Bristol, Plymouth, and back once more to Bristol in January 1942.

The unit was now warned for service overseas, and a period of intensive mobile training followed. During this period command was assumed by Lieutenant-Colonel A. D. G. Courage, M.C., R.A., with Major R. F. Kemball, T.D., R.A., as Second-in-Command. On completion of this training period, the Regiment was again deployed operationally in Bristol, Weston-super-Mare, Yeovil, and later Exeter, and in addition to continuing these operational duties, mobilisation and re-equipping were continued.

The final stages of mobilisation were concluded at Penkridge in Staffordshire. Lieutenant-Colonel G. W. F. Stewart was now in command, and Major G. F. Cumming, one of the original R.A. regimental officers, was reposted as Second-in-Command.

The 59th Regiment sailed for North Africa on the 11th December, 1942. In the course of the first night in the Mediterranean, the convoy was attacked by "U" boats, and the S.S. *Strathallen*, which was in direct line astern of the *Empire Pride* carrying the 59th Regiment, was torpedoed, with eventual heavy loss of life.

After many troubles the Regiment deployed at Bone, the First Army forward supply base. The results in Bone bear mention. It is estimated that during the period December 1942 to September 1943, nearly nine hundred enemy aircraft attacked the vulnerable area, of which it is estimated that 15 per cent. were brought down, or so badly damaged that they ceased to be operational.

The port of Bone was credited, up to May 1943, with providing the following build-up for the First Army:

Number of ships turned round—341.
Average daily tonnage discharged—3,129 tons.
Average daily tonnage sent forward to troops—2,396 tons.
Number of troops through port—78,000.

In July 1943 Lieutenant-Colonel Stewart was posted on promotion to A.A. Command, and returned to the United Kingdom. Lieutenant-Colonel T. W. Miller-Jones, R.A., assumed command of the Regiment.

In August 1943 orders for a move to re-equip were issued, and a transfer to Bizerta took place. The orders included a change of command, the 59th Regiment passing to the command of the American Fifth Army, perhaps the first time that an Essex unit came under American command.

On the 12th November, 1943, the 59th Regiment sailed in landing ships (tank) for Italy, there to be deployed in the anti-aircraft defence of Naples. It was during the stay there that the Regiment took over command of three Italian anti-aircraft batteries the personnel of which showed a tendency to mutiny on one or two occasions. At Naples, too, the Regiment was "diluted" by drafts of Basutos. These African troops proved first class in every respect, and an added point of interest is that they applied for, and obtained under special authority, permission to wear the Essex cap badge whilst with the unit.

The port of Naples, during the period the 59th Regiment was deployed, was an assembly port for the Anzio operations, and later for the invasion of the South of France. Remarkably few ships were damaged by enemy air activity whilst in harbour, and this can be attributed, to a large extent, to the anti-aircraft defences then operating.

On Boxing Day, 1944, the Regiment was ordered to Leghorn, then the forward port for the Fifth Army, and by the 1st January, 1945, all batteries were operationally deployed. There were occasional air attacks on Leghorn, and in addition to anti-aircraft duties, two troops of the Regiment were in a secondary role of coast defence, which provided additional activity. At the same time the Regiment was undergoing, by detachments, intensive training in "field shooting," and later had a gun attached to 76th H.A.A. Regiment at Via Reggio in a field role.

Orders were received for the Regiment to proceed "somewhere south of Genoa" in a field role, but just as the move was due to commence, hostilities in Italy were terminated.

It may be of interest to quote a report received from the coast defences commander on an action that took place on the night before the German capitulation. It was a last desperate attempt by a few Hitler fanatics, in fast motor-boats, on the harbour at Leghorn. The two 4-gun troops whose duties included coast defence took part, and the following letter was received by the Brigade Commander:

"Would you please convey my very best thanks to your chaps for the simply splendid show they put up for us during the scrap in the early morning of the 24th. Our combined efforts have been credited with two 'kills,' and the whole attack was wiped out. What could be better!"

There is little more to tell. Operational commitments ceased on the 4th May, 1945. The Basuto troops were detached, and returned via the Middle East to South Africa. 59th personnel remained to pack up guns and equipment, and eventually one battery was formed into a transport company, and two became, with some distinction, military police units in Trieste. These duties continued until total release had been completed.

The 59th Regiment had played its part in the achievement of

victory in the Italian campaign, on which His Majesty the King sent the following message to Field-Marshal Alexander:

"To you and all those under your Command I send my heartfelt congratulations on the overwhelming victory by which you are bringing to so triumphant an end your long and arduous campaign in Italy."

Placed into suspended animation and finally disbanded, the 59th Regiment was resuscitated on the rebirth of the Territorial Army in 1947, and re-formed on the 1st May, 1947, as the 459th (The Essex Regiment) (M.) Heavy Anti-Aircraft Regiment R.A., T.A.

The first commanding officer of the new Regiment was Lieutenant-Colonel R. F. Kemball, T.D., R.A., the Honorary Colonel of the Regiment being Colonel H. F. Kemball, T.D., D.L., an old Commanding Officer of the 7th Battalion The Essex Regiment.

Section II

64TH SEARCHLIGHT REGIMENT (LATE 1/6TH BATTALION THE ESSEX REGIMENT) 1938-45

Lieutenant-Colonel R. W. Wren, T.D., the Officer Commanding the 6th Battalion The Essex Regiment at the time of the change over to a searchlight role, took command of the new 1/6th Battalion The Essex Regiment (64th Searchlight Regiment) on its establishment on the 1st November, 1938.

Three companies were formed: 441 and 442 at the old 6th Battalion H.Q., The Cedars, West Ham, from the old infantry Headquarter Wing, and "A," "B," and "C" Companies and a new company, 443, at Chingford, where it was accommodated in huts until the completion of the new drill hall.

Major M. A. H. Ditton, M.B.E., was Second-in-Command of the new unit.

There was no time to spare, for the strength of the converted Battalion had to be built up from a few hundreds to an establishment of 1,300. This figure was achieved, and by the spring of 1939 all three companies had been recruited to full strength.

Early in 1939 collective training started, and nearly every evening detachments of Essex Territorials could be seen out on Wanstead Flats and at Epping Forest with their new equipment and engaged in air co-operation.

During the summer, the training period of fifteen days in camp was extended to one month, but only 442 Company had completed its training in an operational area before the embodiment of Anti-Aircraft Command and a general mobilisation of all air defences was ordered on the 24th August, 1939.

On mobilisation, the 1/6th Essex (64th Searchlight Regiment) assembled at Weybourne in Norfolk, and within a few days was deployed to war stations, mainly in the Fen country.

441 Company, with Regimental Headquarters, was near Wisbech, 442 Company at Narborough, and 443 at Walpole Highway, all companies being fortunate in drawing from the outset full equipment and so becoming operational.

As the searchlight sites were very isolated and established in fields, a considerable amount of work had to be done in making roads, hard standings, and revetments for the equipment, erecting the hutting, and generally preparing the sites for occupation throughout the winter. Night training was carried out at every opportunity, and the equipment was continually being brought up to date.

Considerable numbers of N.C.O.s and men were being sent to O.C.T.U.s at this period, and batches of army class intakes were received early in 1940.

Activity from enemy sources was non-existent until about June, when the local R.A.F. stations became targets for day and night raids.

During the summer of 1940, the Battalion became a unit of the Royal Artillery, the 1/6th Essex becoming the 64th Searchlight Regiment R.A., but permission was granted to continue to wear the badges and buttons of the Essex Regiment. The old title was bracketed with the new for domestic purposes.

From the autumn of 1940 hostile activity was more or less continuous, and new tactics and equipment for air defence were being tried out. New layouts of sites were ordered, and the Regiment was deployed over even larger areas. R.H.Q. moved to Billing near Northampton, 441 Battery to Towcester, 442 to Ramsey, Hunts, and 443 to Thrapston, Northants. The Regiment remained in these areas until 1943.

Then when enemy activity became concentrated on various cathedral towns, a move was made to Yorkshire with R.H.Q. and 443 Battery near Selby, 442 Battery at York, and 441 Battery at Easingwold. This activity died down, and early in 1944 the 64th (Essex) Searchlight Regiment R.A. moved back to Norfolk.

In mid-1944, when first V.1 activity and then V.2s began, the Regiment was moved to the London area. It was to remain there until, with the elimination of the flying-bomb menace there was a temporary surplus of searchlight regiments. Orders then came for conversion into a garrison regiment, Royal Artillery, to serve on the Continent.

Spring of 1945 thus found the 64th (Essex) Searchlight Regiment now redesignated the 639 Garrison Regiment R.A., at Osnabruck in Germany.

Here, in August 1945, Lieutenant-Colonel L. W. W. Marriott, a pre-war adjutant to the 6th Essex (1930–34), took over command from Lieutenant-Colonel D. J. Hedley. Despite the fact that for several months the duties had been largely looking after German ammunition dumps, arms factories, camps for displaced persons and similar routine duties, Lieutenant-Colonel Marriott found the Regiment very keen, well administered, and full of esprit-de-corps. The discipline and turn-out were exceptionally good. The Regiment was very proud of its connection with the Essex Regiment. There was real sorrow when it was placed in suspended animation early in 1946.

The Regiment had done its war-time tasks well. Much of the time had been spent in discomfort and monotony, but despite every drawback, it had at all times been a great credit to the County and the Regimental connection.

Reanimated on the 1st May, 1947, with the rebirth of the Territorial Army, the 599th (Essex) H.A.A. Regiment, R.A., T.A., became the linear descendant of the old 1/6th Essex. Now a mobile anti-aircraft unit armed with 3·7-inch guns, the Regiment has its headquarters and two batteries at the new drill hall in Chingford and one battery at the old drill hall in West Ham.

Section III

65TH SEARCHLIGHT REGIMENT (LATE 2/6TH BATTALION THE ESSEX REGIMENT), 1938–45

On the 1st November, 1938, the 6th Battalion The Essex Regiment, having been converted to a searchlight role, was divided into two.

The 2/6th Essex, under command of Lieutenant-Colonel P. L. Grimwood, M.C., T.D., a former commanding officer of the 6th Essex, was put on to a new establishment of a headquarters and three searchlight companies, with its new title as the 2/6th Battalion The Essex Regiment (65th Searchlight Regiment).

Battalion Headquarters and 444 Company were at Prittlewell, while 445 Company was formed with a nucleus taken over from the 28th Essex Searchlight Battalion at East Ham. 446 Company established itself with a small nucleus of Royal Signals personnel at Prittlewell, and had another drill hall at Grays, with a troop taken over from the Essex Fortress Engineers.

The task ahead of the new battalion was formidable. Not only had numbers to be increased from between 200 and 300 to 1,300, but all had to be trained and the unit made fully operational. Training was not confined to technical instruction on the newly issued equipment, for it can well be understood that with three companies, each of twenty-four searchlights, the administrative training required by officers and non-commissioned officers was as urgent a need as the operational training. With each detachment self-contained, messing presented a special problem, and this was met by drill hall classes, at each of which some thirty cooks performed on joints of meat on a petrol cooker.

In order to speed up training and try out the various equipment, anti-aircraft units had their camps extended to a one month's period in 1939. The searchlight units particularly found this most useful, as they were deployed in operational areas. Only one company of the 2/6th was able to do this, however, as general embodiment of the anti-aircraft defences began during August 1939.

Using Weybourne, Norfolk, as a base, the unit was soon establishing itself in North Norfolk, each company having an area of twenty-five miles by twelve miles in which its twenty-four lights were spaced. Only two companies, 445 at Guist and 446 at Raynham, were fortunate in drawing equipment early, but there was ample work for all to do in the preparation of permanent camps. This involved much making of roads and hard standings, together with revetments to protect the operational numbers manning the equipment. Sites were isolated in many cases, but the local people were extremely kind to the men, and their efforts, added to unit welfare measures, produced a good standard of comfort.

Training was naturally of an intensive kind, with "night manning practice" at every opportunity. Equipment was being continually modified and adapted, while the personnel also were subjected to considerable changes. Shortly before Christmas 1939, each company received some fifty "immatures" from infantry battalions, and no sooner were these absorbed than Army Class intakes in batches of eighty were received for training at Company H.Q. It may be said with some satisfaction that the unit was able to supply about 120 officer cadets within the first year of war.

Activity from enemy sources was almost non-existent until about May 1940. Until that time, air traffic had been mainly our own Coastal Command aircraft from Bircham Newton R.A.F. Station, or Bomber Command aircraft from West Raynham. In the space of a few nights the whole scene changed, and the area became a general crossing point for the Midlands raids, while the R.A.F. Stations themselves became targets for day and night raids.

Until this time there had been three types of searchlight units—Infantry, Royal Artillery, and Royal Engineers—all working on the same ideas, but administered differently. Redesignation as Royal Artillery became the order of the day, and the 2/6th Essex became the 65th Searchlight Regiment R.A. for official purposes, but with the old title bracketed for domestic purposes. Nevertheless, the Regiment was still allowed to wear the badges and buttons of the Essex Regiment, and this continues.

The technique of searchlights was ever changing, and modern equipment, with the beginnings of Radar control, was being deployed. This brought a decision in the autumn of 1940 to "cluster" the lights in groups of three, one of each group being a "master" light of 150 cm., as against the older 90s. There was an upheaval of everything—hutting, cookhouses, and even road material, to say nothing of the friendships and acquaintanceships that had developed.

Putting this into effect kept everybody fully employed, as hostile air activity by night and day was more or less continuous, and no sooner was completion in sight than the Regiment moved across to the Lincolnshire area. Operations were of a similar nature, though technique varied from time to time. A further move into the Humber G.D.A. (gun defended area) was much more interesting, as for the first time the Regiment came into a "hitting-back" atmosphere, where co-operation with the guns was in marked contrast to the earlier co-operation with night fighters.

Whilst still in Lincolnshire, Major A. C. Faulkner left to command a searchlight regiment, and was followed as Second-in-Command by Major R. G. Boulton, who shortly after also left on transfer to light anti-aircraft, and Major S. J. Smith became Second-in-Command.

Lieutenant-Colonel P. L. Grimwood also left, his place being taken by Lieutenant-Colonel D. J. Hedley.

In the Humber G.D.A., good results were achieved, and no raid actually penetrated either to Hull or Grimsby whilst the Regiment was stationed in the area. It is difficult to record practical successes against hostile aircraft when a unit is armed only with searchlights and light-calibre weapons, but several Category I.s were awarded as the direct result of the Regiment's searchlight offensive.

Towards the end of 1944 enemy activity was much reduced, and the Regiment ultimately joined a number of others for conversion into Royal Artillery garrison regiments for service on the Continent.

In November 1944, 607 Garrison Regiment R.A. moved to Brascheat, and to Kappellan in December 1944, both in the Antwerp area of Belgium.

Batteries were deployed: "B" to Bogi, "C" to Deurne, "D" to Malines, and "E" to Boechont. The duties were guarding petrol and other stores. This was a very nerve-racking period, due to the endless dropping of "V" missiles. Fortunately, there were no fatal and few minor casualties.

These caretaker duties required a much lower establishment than the thirteen-hundred-odd of a searchlight regiment, and 607 Garrison Regiment was much depleted in numbers, but still with some original T.A. volunteer element of pre-war days, including a number dating back to 1922.

In May 1945, R.H.Q. moved to Haelen, "B" Battery to Averbode, "C" to Kermpt, "D" to Lumen, and "E" to Kirkoven. The Regiment was now engaged in protecting large stocks of petrol which, at that time, had a very high black-market value. Many arrests were made, and by ceaseless patrolling the losses were reduced from thousands of gallons per month to a mere trickle. Two Belgians were wounded while trying to avoid arrest, and many were taken red-handed at all hours of the night.

In June 1945 the Regiment concentrated in Burg Leopold for training and moved to Minden in August 1945.

Lieutenant-Colonel E. C. Vander Kiste took over command in October 1945, thus being the first officer of the Essex Regiment to command since Lieutenant-Colonel Grimwood left in 1942.

In 1946 the Regiment was put in "suspended animation" and finally disbanded.

It had had a varied career and had suffered many changes in designation, but as was fitting for a unit with long and honourable Volunteer and Territorial service, it did not remain disbanded for long.

On the 1st May, 1947, 600 H.A.A. Regiment R.A. (Essex) T.A. came to life as the successor to 607 Garrison Regiment R.A., the mobile role with 3·7-inch guns being entirely new to the few old hands who responded. R.H.Q. was established at East Ham in the drill hall, which had been completed in 1939 and which was now to be called the T.A. Centre. "Q" and "R" Batteries were also to be housed there, while "P" Battery went to Prittlewell.

Lieutenant-Colonel J. E. Lloyd, T.D., R.A., who was appointed to command, has a long association with the Essex Regiment, having joined the 6th Battalion in 1921 and served as Adjutant, Battery Commander, and Second-in-Command during the war. Colonel C. E. Edwards, D.S.O., M.C., who had been associated with the Regiment in the Southend District before the war and with the National Defence Companies of the 6th Essex, was appointed Honorary Colonel.

Despite all changes, the link with the Essex Regiment lives on, and the castle badge and eagle buttons are worn with pride, while at the close of 1950 the designation of the Regiment has now become 600 H.A.A. Regiment R.A. (The Essex Regiment) T.A.

It is with pleasure that one reads in the short history of this Regiment issued to all volunteers and national service men joining, "The Regiment has retained its association with the Essex Regiment, and is still permitted to wear the Essex Regiment's badge and buttons and the right to carry colours on appropriate occasions."

Chapter Nine

THE NEW BATTALIONS, 1940-45

DURING the first nine months of the Second World War there was little or no expansion of infantry. The duplication of the Territorial Army in 1939 had provided sufficient infantry battalions to meet the needs of the army so visualised on the outbreak of war. Unless some form of static warfare became general, it seemed unlikely that there would be any great expansion of infantry.

The evacuation from Dunkirk and the very real threat of invasion that existed in the summer of 1940 were, if only temporarily, to alter this conception. One of the most urgent requirements of the Chiefs of Staff then was men on the ground—men who would guard our coasts and form a screen behind which the field-force formations could be refitted and trained, first in a counter-attack role should invasion occur, and then for the final counter-offensive without which the war could not be won.

There was thus a decision in June 1940 to raise an additional sixty infantry battalions with the primary task of coast defence. The 8th, 9th, and 10th Battalions of the Essex Regiment were three of these battalions.

As the invasion risk lessened and those responsible for the higher direction of war looked more and more towards the counter-offensive, and as the size of this country's contribution to overseas expeditions was determined, so the need for infantry battalions tended to lessen while the need for supporting arms grew greater.

Thus in 1942 we see the new Essex Battalions suffer a metamorphosis, the 8th Essex to become the 153rd Regiment R.A.C., the 9th Battalion the 11th (Essex) Medium Regiment R.A., and the 10th Essex the 9th Parachute Battalion.

One more battalion of the Essex Regiment was formed during the Second World War, the 19th Essex formed in Egypt in 1943, and the brief history of this battalion, too, is recorded in this chapter.[1]

[1] For this chapter see map facing page 428.

Section I

THE 8TH BATTALION THE ESSEX REGIMENT (THE 153RD REGIMENT R.A.C., AND "C" (ESSEX) SQUADRON 107TH REGIMENT R.A.C.)

Originally raised in 1908 as a unit of the Territorial Force, the 8th Essex served as a cyclist battalion throughout the First World War, and although it did not proceed overseas as a unit, its personnel served in practically every battalion of the Regiment. Disembodied in 1920, the 8th Essex was not re-formed as infantry in the post-war Territorial Army. Twenty years later, at a crisis in England's history, orders were received at the Infantry Training Centre, Warley, to form an Eighth Battalion of the Regiment.

It was on the 4th July, 1940, that the 8th Battalion came into being at Warley. Lieutenant-Colonel C. L. Wilson, M.C., was in command. He was given a cadre of 17 officers and 156 other ranks from the Infantry Training Centres at Warley and Blandford. Major D. R. Gahagan was his Second-in-Command, and a former orderly-room sergeant of the 1st Battalion, now Captain C. A. Webb, his adjutant.

By the 6th July the cadre 8th Battalion was at Park Attwood, near Kidderminster. By the 9th July it was established at Bentley Manor near Redditch, where there was hardly time to reconnoitre and prepare a camp site before the army intake drafts started to arrive. At the end of July, barely four weeks after birth, the Battalion had a strength of 27 officers and 967 other ranks.

The small leavening of regulars, amongst whom were the Commanding Officer, Second-in-Command, Captain M. H. Crocker, Captain R. H. A. Painter, 2/Lieutenant B. J. Palmer, Regimental Sergeant-Major L. Perry, D.C.M., and Company Sergeant-Major T. Wollin, M.M., soon instilled the customs and traditions of the Regiment into the newcomers.

There was no time to spare in that summer of 1940, but even by the standard of those days the creation of a battalion approximately one thousand strong within a matter of weeks was no mean achievement. From the outset, the 8th Essex had its share in the defence scheme for the Birmingham area.

It was hard work for the cadre to form and train at top speed a new battalion. The cadre themselves were a mixed lot—some just back from Dunkirk, some even more recently out of France through Cherbourg, while others were I.T.C. instructors, and most of the officers were very recently commissioned. Ten out of the first eighteen officers who joined at Warley were second lieutenants.

On the 10th October, 1940, the Battalion moved to Sherborne, where it came under the operational command of the 50th (Northumbrian) Division. A few days for reconnaissance, and then forward to the coast to take over beach defences from the 9th D.L.I.

Whilst at Sherborne, the 8th Essex was visited by the Commander 5th Corps, Lieutenant-General B. L. Montgomery, C.B., D.S.O.

Headquarters was at Litton Cheney, on the Dorset coast, and the battalion sector included Langton Herring, Fleet, Chickerell, Portisham, and Abbotsbury. On the Battalion's right was the 9th Essex; on the left the 8th Dorsets.

From now onwards the 8th Essex was principally engaged in the construction of beach defences—minefields were laid, beach scaffolding erected, and platoon localities, company areas, and gun positions all constructed.

So far as was possible inter-company reliefs were organised to allow one company "out" for training at a time, but in general it was a life of digging and wiring, more digging and more wiring, and then still more digging and wiring. All sorts of strange weapons of war were handed to the Battalion to deal with—"Blacker Bombards," "McNaughton Tubes," "Fougasses," and many others, some, if truth be told, more likely to strike fear in the hearts of their users than in those of the enemy.

The 8th Essex and other war-formed battalions were organised into beach, coastal, or county divisions, and although there was no doubt as to their primary role, all ranks hoped in due course to be allotted a field-force role. There was great keenness. No shortage of equipment was allowed to hinder training, and it was no uncommon sight in those autumn days of 1940 to see the mortar platoon in action, the mortar officer carrying out training by means of an old drain-pipe and some empty sherry bottles.

Eventually the Battalion began to get its equipment, and by the spring of 1941 was anxious to be relieved of beach defence for a period of camp and training in the offensive.

The 8th Essex, being static in its role of beach defence, suffered many changes of operational command as divisions and even corps in reserve behind the beaches moved on their lawful occasions. In December the Battalion was under 3rd Division, although still forming part of 210th Infantry Brigade, and at the end of February 1941 it was put under command of 226th Infantry Brigade (Brigadier G. W. R. Templer, C.B.E., D.S.O.).

In March 1941 H.R.H. the Duke of Gloucester visited the Abbotsbury Castle sector of the beach defences and inspected a representative party of the Battalion. Later that month they were inspected by the 5th Corps Commander and by Major-General G. I. Gartlan, C.B.E., D.S.O., M.C., who was then commanding the Dorset Coastal Division.

Although the threat of large-scale invasion had passed, the possibility of raids still remained, and special vigilance was ordered from time to time as intelligence reports denoted unusual activity, or, as was often the case, when conditions were suitable for landing—spring tides, calm seas, thick fog—those were the conditions that called for special patrolling of the beaches behind the now formidable defences.

In April the Abbotsbury sector was visited by the Commander-in-Chief Home Forces, General Sir Bernard Paget, and General the Hon. H. R. L. G. Alexander, commanding Southern Command. It was the last important happening to the 8th Essex on its first spell of beach defence.

On the 5th April, 1941, the Battalion was relieved by the 2nd East Yorks, and concentrated at Warden Hill, Evershott, for battalion and brigade training. Here it stayed for six weeks, and was again inspected by General Montgomery. He was obviously impressed, and permitted the Battalion to take part in the strenuous exercises of the 3rd Division before again relieving the 2nd East Yorks. During these exercises the marching abilities of the 8th Battalion surpassed even those of the "Iron Division," and, with other comparable battalions, was held out as an example at the next of General Montgomery's famous conferences.

The rest of the summer of 1941 was spent on the beaches, a move to winter quarters in Weymouth taking place at the end of October. This, however, proved to be of short duration, and on the 19th November the 8th Essex moved to Swindon. At Weymouth preliminary work in accordance with orders to reorganise as an armoured regiment had been carried out and at Swindon the conversion took place.

The 8th Battalion The Essex Regiment now ceased to exist, and the 153rd Regiment Royal Armoured Corps rose in its stead. It was to be an army tank battalion. The establishment of an armoured regiment is smaller than that of an infantry battalion: also the qualifications for a good infantryman are not necessarily the same as those required for a good tank-crew man, and so the 8th Battalion had to suffe rthe ordeal of an intelligence test, the psychiatrists and the scientific soldiers having their say. Those who survived the ordeal had regretfully to say good-bye to some 250 of the original members of the Battalion. Many went to form the defence company for Headquarters 5th Corps, the remainder being drafted to battalions of the Essex Regiment.

The 153rd Regiment R.A.C. was to remain in Wiltshire as part of 34th Army Tank Brigade through the winter of 1941/42, but practically every officer and other rank was away on conversion courses of one nature or another.

In February 1942 they received their first Churchill tanks, which were named with battle honours of the Essex Regiment, and training started on the Ogbourne Downs. The summer of 1942 saw the introduction of mixed divisions in place of purely infantry divisions. So in June the 34th Army Tank Brigade became the third formation of the 1st Division. The 153rd Regiment moved to Norfolk, and was soon visited by Lieutenant-General K. A. Anderson. Although the Regiment had barely passed the "troop training" stage, it here took part in its first large-scale exercise.

In July squadrons were sent in turn to Scotland for training in combined operations. First infantry, then tanks, and now in the hands of the Royal Navy! Indeed, a varied training. The Royal Navy taught them many things, from slinging a hammock and fitting a Mae West to much lower-deck slang. Apart from one officer who apparently mistook his tank for a submarine, there were no mishaps. Much was learnt, and all ranks enjoyed the training and change of scene.

The 1st Division was earmarked for "forthcoming operations" (in North Africa as events turned out), and the 34th Army Tank Brigade, not having completed its gunnery and tactical training, was replaced by an older formation that had. So in the autumn of 1942 yet another move took place, to Worthing, in Sussex, and later to Broome Park, near Canterbury, once the home of Lord Kitchener. The 34th Armoured Brigade now formed part of the 43rd (Wessex) Division.

Broome Park remained the home of 153rd Regiment for over a year, from where it carried out intensive tactical training, and gunnery practices on the few tank ranges established in various parts of the country. A squadron also did duty at the Battle School at Catterick, and thus learned to endure the missiles of friend and foe in demonstrations under battle and almost arctic conditions during December 1942 and the first months of 1943.

At Broome Park, too, changes in command took place, Major R. Wood, The Royal Tank Regiment, taking over from Major D. R. Gahagan as Second-in-Command and then assuming command in April 1943.

All 1943 was spent in training. Exercise followed exercise, those mighty bloodless battles in the United Kingdom, the memory of which will live on in hearts behind the ribbon of the Defence Medal when recollections of many smaller and bloody battles in France, Belgium, Holland, and Germany have slipped away.

In mid-1943 all four squadron commanders and the Adjutant of the 153rd Regiment, Royal Armoured Corps (Major D. M. Bishop, Major J. L. Paul, Major E. C. Garner, Major C. A. Webb and Captain G. R. Hamber), had been with the Regiment since its foundation as the 8th Essex in July 1940. This state of affairs could not last, for early in 1944 General Montgomery laid down that there was to be an exchange of officers between regiments which had battle experience in the Middle East and Italy, and those regiments who had long been training in the United Kingdom, and so a dilution of the Essex officer element was inevitable.

In March 1944 the 153rd Regiment R.A.C. took part in Exercise "Shudder," which was to practise procedure in landing on the continent of Europe. It was the last exercise in which the Regiment was to take part. It was now fully trained and ready for the invasion.

The Regiment landed at Arromanches on D 28, and was first committed to action on the 16th July, 1944, with the 8th Royal Scots in the attack to enlarge the bridge-head over the River Odon. This proved to be a stiff initial battle. Twelve tanks were knocked out and 16 officers and 80 other ranks became casualties.

The Regiment was rested after this action, and re-formed in a sodden cornfield close to Marcelet but was in action again within nine days.

Major E. C. Garner was now the sole remaining original Essex Regiment officer in command of a squadron.

While the Regiment was re-forming, it was visited by Lieutenant-General N. Ritchie, Commander 12th Corps, who personally congratulated all ranks on their fine performance during operation "Greenline," the enlargement of the Odon bridge-head.

After re-forming, the 153rd Regiment R.A.C. fought on in the battles of the break-out from the Normandy bridge-head, operating principally with the 59th Division, until, on the 17th August, 1944, they heard the disagreeable news that the regiment was to be disbanded.

Man-power consideration at this time demanded reduction in Royal Armoured Corps units, and 153rd Regiment, as the junior armoured regiment in 34th Armoured Brigade, was selected for disbandment. In exactly one month's fighting the Regiment had lost 19 officers and 99 other ranks and eighteen tanks in action.

"Essex Squadron" with 107th Regiment Royal Armoured Corps (King's Own).

This disbandment of 153rd Regiment Royal Armoured Corps made up casualties in the other regiments of the 34th Armoured Brigade. One complete squadron, however, brought up to full strength with reinforcements from the remaining squadrons, went as a complete unit to 107th Regiment Royal Armoured Corps (King's Own), where it became "C" (Essex) Squadron of that Regiment.

The order of battle of the Squadron was as follows:
Squadron Commander: Major E. C. Garner (Essex Regiment).
Second-in-Command: Captain M. P. Stubbs (Essex Regiment).
Reconnaissance Officer: Captain G. R. Hamber (Essex Regiment).

Four out of the five troop commanders were also Essex Regiment—Lieutenants F. Grundy, K. J. Spratt, J. S. McMartin, and D. O. Thorogood.

It is interesting to note that subsequently Major E. C. Garner and Lieutenant J. S. McMartin were to be awarded the Military Cross, while Captain M. P. Stubbs, Lieutenants J. S. McMartin, K. J. Spratt, and D. O. Thorogood were to be mentioned in dispatches.

The Commanding Officer of 107th Regiment gave permission for all ranks of the Squadron to retain their Essex Regiment cap badges.

It is regrettably impossible to give in detail the story of all the operations in which "C" or "Essex" Squadron was to play a distinguished part between the break-out in Normandy and V.E.-Day.

First at Le Havre, in support of the 49th Division, of which the 2nd Essex was a unit, where, as Major Garner says, "an enjoyable day's shooting was had by the Squadron," and then on into Holland where, in support of the 158th Infantry Brigade (53rd Division), the Squadron held part of the famous Nijmegen corridor which extended up to Arnhem. This corridor, extending only a mile or so each side of the

Army centre line, had to be kept open in order to supply the troops of the Second Army then pressing forward to relieve the hard-pressed 1st Airborne Division in Arnhem itself.

Next, in October 1944, the 107th Regiment became part of "Clarkeforce," a formation under Brigadier W. S. Clarke, the Commander of the 34th Armoured Brigade. This force, operating under command of the 49th Division, was to be launched through a gap to be made by the Division in a "set-piece" attack in the area of St. Leonard, and then to advance northwards in order to protect the flank of the Canadians then engaged in clearing the Scheldt Estuary.

The History of the 107th Regiment, the Royal Armoured Corps (King's Own), says of this period:

"In ten days of continual fighting, the Regiment had advanced approximately twenty-five miles over flat Dutch territory against the enemy rear-guard screen of self-propelled guns and infantry strongpoints. It had destroyed eight self-propelled guns and taken 230 prisoners: its own losses in officers and men were 9 killed and 32 wounded and 1 man captured; it had nineteen tanks put out of action.... Major E. C. Garner, the commander of 'C' Squadron, was awarded the Military Cross for his conspicuous gallantry throughout all these actions."

Then in December came operations up to the Rhine in support of the 15th (Scottish) Division and the 43rd (Wessex) Division, and in February 1945 the support of the 51st (Highland) Division for the advance into the Reich. This was the last operation. The Regiment, now in Second Army reserve for the crossing of the Rhine, was not called upon, because of the high degree of success of the crossing and the subsequent speedy advance into Germany.

V.E.-Day found the 107th Regiment R.A.C. in Nordwalde, near Münster, where a victory salute of twenty-one guns was fired by the tanks of the Regiment.

Shortly after V.E.-Day Major E. C. Garner, M.C., who had been with the 8th Essex, 153rd Regiment, R.A.C. and "C" Squadron 107th Regiment R.A.C. from its formation to V.E.-Day, was appointed Second-in-Command of the 107th Regiment R.A.C., and "C" Squadron was finally commanded until its end by Major I. H. Butler.

Disbandment came to "C" Squadron in February 1946, and so died the last surviving unit of the 8th Battalion The Essex Regiment, later the 153rd Regiment Royal Armoured Corps.

Major Garner says: "We had come a long way from those early

days at Warley Barracks, where the original cadre was formed, and from Bentley Manor in Worcestershire, where we received our intake. There, under the eye of our first commanding officer, Lieutenant-Colonel C. L. Wilson, M.C., the process of turning raw recruits into highly efficient soldiers commenced, and much of the credit for the fine performance put up by the 153rd Regiment, Royal Armoured Corps, and its child, 'C' (Essex) Squadron, 107th Regiment Royal Armoured Corps (King's Own), must be paid to Lieutenant-Colonel Wilson. He set the standard for our behaviour for the rest of the life of the Regiment."

A beautifully made scale model of a Churchill tank now rests in the Regimental Museum at Warley to perpetuate the service of an Essex battalion in the Royal Armoured Corps.

Section II

THE 9TH BATTALION THE ESSEX REGIMENT (11TH (ESSEX) MEDIUM REGIMENT R.A.)

The original 9th Essex was a special service battalion raised at Shorncliffe in August 1914 as part of the 12th (Eastern) Division. It was fighting in France by 1915, where it had a distinguished career. It was disbanded in 1919.

Orders to form a 9th Battalion of the Essex Regiment were again received in 1940. Lieutenant-Colonel H. L. H. Boustead was given command. He was also given a cadre of 10 officers and 120 other ranks, some indent forms for clothing, equipment, and tentage, and a promise of 800 Army intake within the next ten to fourteen days.

On the 10th July, 1940, the cadre, formed at Warley, moved to Park Attwood, Kidderminster, to prepare for and organise the arrival of the 800. It was not possible to have everything ready in ten days, but at least the cadre could, and did, ensure that there would be accommodation and food, kit and clothing within reason. There was also a detailed training programme, so that not a minute would be lost on the arrival of the recruits.

The intake exceeded all hopes. The men came from East Anglia and East London. They were from the ideal age group—twenty-five to twenty-seven—and they one and all had that will and purpose which so characterised the whole of Britain in that summer of 1940.

Twelve weeks later the 9th Essex, now a battalion in more than name, moved to Yeovil, and from there, on the 19th October, 1940, into the area of Lyme Regis and Burton Bradstock to take over beach defence duties from the 8th Durham Light Infantry.

Battalion Headquarters was established at Morecombe Lake, and the strength of the 9th Essex as it took over responsibility for a sector of the Dorset beach defences was 26 officers and 900 other ranks. Major A. G. de la Mare was Second-in-Command, and Captain C. F. V. Bagot was Adjutant.

It is interesting to note that Captain C. F. V. Bagot, Captain H. F. Gormley, Captain J. C. Bowman, Lieutenants J. B. Douglas and R. M. Bate, and Lieutenant (Quartermaster) W. Johncock, who were on the strength at the time, were still on the strength when, on the 14th July, 1944, the 11th (Essex) Medium Regiment R.A. landed in Normandy.

The 9th Essex was now part of the 210th Infantry Brigade and was brigaded with the 8th Essex and 8th Dorsets.

The task of the Battalion was beach defence, and the preparation, maintenance, and manning of these defences filled the Battalion's workaday life. It was a hard life and one not free from danger, as casualties could be sustained only too easily from the numerous minefields, in which it was only too possible to walk as sentry or on patrol.

Every possible opportunity was taken for sport and recreation—in January 1941 the 9th Essex won the 210th Infantry Brigade cross-country race—but such opportunities were rare. The sole reason for the Battalion's existence was beach defence.

To quote from Operation instruction No. 2, dated 15th January, 1941: "There will be no withdrawal from the beaches. Any landing will be defeated on the beaches. Any local counter-attacks will be delivered on to the beaches."

In February the Battalion was transferred to the 226th Independent Infantry Brigade, but although command had changed, the role remained the same until, in May 1941, the 9th Essex handed over positions on the beaches to the 1st South Lancashire Regiment and moved inland to Wardon Hill Camp for training.

The Battalion was there assisted by officers of the 2nd Lincolns, and this team, together with demonstration parties from the 2nd Royal Ulster Rifles, gave valuable help, so that on the 19th June, when the training period ended and the time came to return to the beaches, the 9th Essex felt competent either in a field force or a beach defence role.

During the time at Wardon Hill Camp they were seen at training by Lieutenant-General E. C. A. Schreiber, now commanding the 5th Corps, the formation responsible for the particular section of the south of England in which the area of the 9th Essex lay.

At the end of October 1941, as the autumn and then the winter set in, the dangers of invasion lessened, and the manning of beach guards and permanent observation points was discontinued.

Towards the end of November, the 9th Essex was relieved by the 8th Royal Welch Fusiliers, and moved to the area of Teignmouth and Dawlish, Battalion headquarters being established at Bishopsteignton. Here the Battalion was to remain until the middle of February 1942, when it moved to Exeter.

A series of changes between March and September took the 9th Essex first to Colyton and then back again to Exeter, and then away out of the West Country to move in relief of the 10th Royal Sussex at Deal.

At Deal the Battalion was visited first by Lieutenant-General Sir Geoffrey Howard, the Colonel of the Regiment, and then by Lieutenant-General J. G. Swayne, the G.O.C.-in-C. of the South-Eastern Army.

But these visits and inspections were in the nature of an infantry swan-song, for on the 21st November, 1942, the 9th Essex came under War Office control in order to be transformed into a medium regiment of artillery with effect from the 1st December.

On the 30th November the 9th Essex moved to Snaith and Thorn in Yorkshire. They were dismayed and unhappy as they handed in their infantry arms and equipment, receiving in exchange strange artillery pieces and their associated stores.

Lieutenant-Colonel Boustead made it quite clear that there was to be no looking back. If the need, at the moment, was for tanks, medium artillery, or other supporting arms, and if the task was for the 9th Essex to become an efficient medium regiment of artillery as quickly as possible, then it would be undertaken in the spirit and traditions of the Essex Regiment.

By April 1942 the 11th (Essex) Medium Regiment R.A. could stand alone. Its teething troubles were over, and the feat had been accomplished of converting a complete infantry battalion in a space of four months into an efficient regiment of medium artillery.

In the summer of 1942 the 11th (Essex) Medium Regiment became part of the 9th Army Group Royal Artillery (9 A.G.R.A.) and artillery training went ahead with rapidity.

Lieutenant-Colonel H. L. H. Boustead retained command until July 1943, when he handed over to Lieutenant-Colonel M. Yates, D.S.O., O.B.E., R.A.

Training, ever mounting in scope and realism, was the lot in 1943 and 1944 for every unit earmarked for the second front. It was the lot of the 11th (Essex) Medium Regiment, for it now formed part of the 21st Army Group.

The Regiment landed at Courseulles-sur-Mer on the 14th July, 1944, and was soon in action, the first targets being engaged on the 17th July. From then on the 11th (Essex) Medium Regiment was to be almost continuously in action. First in the battles of the Normandy bridge-head and the break-out. Then across the River Seine to operate against Boulogne, Calais, and Cap Gris Nez. Next forward into Belgium and Holland, for the capture of Breskens, and operations against Flushing and Walcheren. Then came the drive to the River Maas, the attack towards Venlo and Roer, operations against the Siegfried Line and the crossing of the Rhine, until on the 28th March, 1945, the last round was fired against the enemy.

Fifty-one casualties had been sustained during the campaign and 9 officers and men were to be awarded decorations. Seventeen were mentioned in dispatches.

Little remains to be told. With the cessation of all organised resistance in North-west Europe, the life of the 11th (Essex) Medium Regiment became that of any unit in the Armies of Occupation, and when, in December 1945, disbandment was ordered it came as no particular shock to a regiment already run down in strength by the working of the release scheme.

So passed the 11th (Essex) Medium Regiment R.A., a striking example of the versatility of the officers and men of the Essex Regiment.

The unit had completed its task in a spirit of good humour and comradeship and with a reputation and record of which it can be justly proud.

Section III
THE 10TH BATTALION THE ESSEX REGIMENT (9TH PARACHUTE BATTALION)

The 10th Battalion of the Essex Regiment was formed in September 1914 as part of "Kitchener's Army," and became a unit of the 18th Division. In France the Battalion served with honour and distinction until it was disbanded in June 1919.

The 10th Essex was once more formed in July 1940. Casualties in the early months of the war had been fewer than originally anticipated, and the surplus output from infantry training centres not absorbed by existing battalions had been concentrated in holding units.

One of these reservoirs of man-power was the 50th Holding Battalion at Billericay, Essex, commanded by Lieutenant-Colonel T. E. Hearn, The Essex Regiment, and made up of a company some 300 strong from each of four regiments, the Norfolk, Suffolk, Bedfordshire and Hertfordshire, and the Essex.

Here then was a nucleus of further battalions, and so, in the crisis of Dunkirk, the 50th Holding Battalion was split, the four regimental companies going to form the nucleus of the 9th Norfolk, 8th Suffolk, 6th Bedfs and Herts, and 10th Essex.

Lieutenant-Colonel T. E. Hearn was translated from command of the holding unit to that of the 10th Essex.

Remaining in the holding battalion's accommodation at Billericay, the 10th Essex received and absorbed a draft of approximately 600 Army intake class. Fine material of the twenty-six to twenty-eight-year age group call-up, these men were to be the backbone of the 10th Essex and the 9th Parachute Battalion.

On the 31st October the 10th Essex moved to the East Coast, to Dovercourt, there to join the 223rd Infantry Brigade (Brigadier Sir Alexander Stainer, Bart., D.S.O., M.C.) and share in the defences of the port of Harwich. Harwich was a focal point in the defence of the country, and its garrison naturally received its fair share of interest and attention.

Within a few weeks of their arrival in Dovercourt, the 10th Essex had been seen by the Inspector of Infantry, Major-General H. C. Lloyd, by the G.O.C.-in-C. Eastern Command, Lieutenant-General Sir Guy Williams, and by Lieutenant-General H. R. S. Massy, the Commander of the 12th Corps.

But these inspections were only occasional events. The day-to-day life of the Battalion was one of exceedingly hard work on the defences of Harwich, both seawards and landwards. Although with the onset of winter the immediate risk had been lessened, the spring would bring a renewed threat of invasion by sea and air. A port with adequate docks, quays, and anchorages being an early prerequisite of a successful seaborne invasion, there was always a possibility that the Germans might launch an airborne expedition with the object of seizing the landward defences of the port of Harwich and so turn the seaward defences.

Landward and seaward defences were thus of the highest priority through the winter of 1940–41.

The work was hard and many times interrupted by air raids, in which the 10th Essex had their share of casualties, but all ranks felt that their efforts were more than rewarded when, on the 7th February, 1941, the Prime Minister, the Rt. Honourable Winston S. Churchill, visited the Harwich defences and inspected in detail the defence works which were the responsibility of the 10th Essex. Nothing could have told them more clearly the importance of their task than the visit from the Prime Minister.

By this time the 223rd Infantry Brigade (8th Suffolk; 10th Essex; 6th Northamptons) had been made part of the Essex County Division, a formation formed to command and administer the coast defence, beach defence, and other non-field force units across the county. It was commanded by Major-General J. H. T. Priestman, C.B., C.B.E., D.S.O., M.C., who thus had yet another Essex battalion under his command. In his periods in command of the 13th Infantry Brigade, Catterick, the 54th (East Anglian) Division, and the Essex County Division between 1935 and 1941, Major-General Priestman had had under his command the 1st, 1/4th, 2/4th, 1/5th, 2/5th, 7th, 10th, and 70th Battalions of the Essex Regiment.

In February 1941 the Colonel of the Regiment visited the 10th Essex, as he visited every battalion of the Regiment during the war years.

In May the 10th Essex, relieved of defence duties by the 9th Lancashire Fusiliers, moved inland to Colchester for three weeks' hard training. This was followed by a second spell on the Harwich defences which lasted until July. Then came a spell on aerodrome defence, Hornchurch aerodrome being made the Battalion's responsibility.

The stay at Upminster was marked by a visit from Lieutenant-General N. S. Irwin, now the commander of the 11th Corps. General

Irwin at the time of his visit was escorting His Majesty the King of Greece, who visited the lines of the 10th Essex and saw several demonstrations mounted by the Battalion. His Majesty afterwards lunched in the officers' mess.

At the end of January 1942 the Battalion moved to Harlow and in February to Much Hadham, still on aerodrome defence, and then towards the end of May the whole of the 223rd Infantry Brigade moved to Suffolk to relieve the 213th Infantry Brigade in the Woodbridge area.

At Woodbridge the 10th Essex underwent a further three months of coast defence duties. As there was an important installation in the area, the Battalion had a series of visits from high-ranking officers which included Lieutenant-General B. C. T. Paget, Commander-in-Chief Home Forces, and Lieutenant-General K. A. Anderson, the G.O.C.-in-C. Eastern Command.

On the 23rd August, 1942, the 10th Essex was freed from its coast defence role and moved inland to St. Albans. Here the 223rd Brigade came under the 45th Division, but only temporarily, for on the 6th November the Brigade (less the 10th Essex) was converted into the 3rd Parachute Brigade.

The 10th Battalion was bitterly disappointed to be left out, but it was explained that for the moment, because of territorial recruiting requirements, it was necessary to retain the 10th Essex as infantry of the line. However, things changed rapidly, and within a very short time Major-General F. A. M. Browning, the Commander of the Airborne Division, flew to St. Albans, and in his address to the Battalion said it was to become a parachute unit and asked everybody to volunteer. Within a battalion strength of 644 all ranks, 567 volunteered for parachute training.

The 10th Essex thus became the 9th (Home Counties) Battalion of the Parachute Regiment, and formed the third battalion of the 3rd Parachute Brigade.

The extremely high over-all standard required for a parachutist naturally cut down the numbers who were finally allowed to take the jumping course, but nevertheless, by February 1943 large numbers of men of the Essex Regiment, proudly wearing parachutist's wings, formed the nucleus of the 9th Parachute Battalion.

Lieutenant-Colonel T. E. Hearn was still in command, but not being permitted to jump because of his age, had eventually to relinquish the appointment.

In May 1943 the 3rd Parachute Brigade became part of the newly formed 6th Airborne Division. Stationed at Bulford, it took part in a number of airborne exercises in England, Scotland, and Wales.

The object was always the same—an airborne assault on an enemy strong-point. In those early days the limiting factor in training was aircraft. But in January 1944 an almost unlimited supply of Dakotas became available, and the 3rd Parachute Brigade made the first mass drop at Winterborne Stoke.

In May 1944 the 9th Parachute Battalion moved to West Woodhay, and there, from aerial photographs, constructed a full-scale replica of the German battery of four 150-mm. guns at Salanelles, Normandy, which enfiladed the beaches on which the seaborne landings were to be made. Its destruction was essential. So deeply housed in their emplacements that not even the 4,000-lb. bombs of the R.A.F. could penetrate and destroy them, their elimination on D-Day was to be the task of the 9th Parachute Battalion.

On the night of the 5th/6th June the Battalion emplaned and set a course for Normandy. Many aircraft were knocked off their course by flak on crossing the Normandy coast, and some men of the unit were dropped up to thirty miles wide of the selected dropping zone. Owing to the enormous area over which the Battalion had been scattered in dropping, only 150 assorted all ranks arrived on the rendezvous at 5 a.m. on the 6th June, 1944. There were no sappers, gunners, field ambulance personnel, no mine detectors nor special stores, but in spite of all difficulties, the battery was located and overrun.

About 75 of the 9th Parachute Battalion came out of the Salanelles battery on their feet as the Battalion, so greatly depleted, pressed on to the next objective.

During the night 6th/7th June, the Battalion pushed on inland, south of Brevilles to Bois du Mont by Château St. Comme, where it dug in and held repeated German attacks for the next eight days and nights.

It was to remain almost continuously in action all through the severe fighting that was such a feature of the enlargement of, and breakout from, the Normandy beach-head. After the break-out, the line of advance led to Benzeville, where, after three months' continuous and savage fighting, the 9th Parachute Battalion was relieved and evacuated. Just over three months after taking off from England, approximately 75 all ranks returned to Bulford.

In December 1944 Von Rundstedt launched his counter-offensive in the Ardennes. The 9th Parachute Battalion left Bulford on the 24th December, 1944, and was in southern Belgium on the afternoon of Christmas Day. It fought an infantry war until 8th February, 1945, when it was again relieved and returned to Bulford. During this campaign the Battalion never had a really good battle, but only skirmishes. The chief features of this second trip in North-west Europe had been the acute cold, wet, and general discomfort.

The third expedition to North-west Europe was to be for the crossing of the Rhine and the advance into Germany.

At dawn on the 24th March, 1945, the 9th Parachute Battalion emplaned at Gosfield, Essex, in thirty-five Dakotas and took off for Germany. The plan for the 3rd Parachute Brigade was that the 8th Battalion would drop and seize the "DZ" (dropping zone) which was held by the enemy, the Canadian Parachute Battalion would then drop and clear the way for the 9th Parachute Battalion, which would capture the Schneppenberg, a high wooded feature suspected as an enemy gun area and observation post.

The drop at about 10 a.m., the 24th March, 1945, was most successful, 85 per cent. of the Battalion arriving in the rendezvous within thirty minutes of dropping. The objective was quickly taken with several hundred prisoners.

Two days later the advance across Germany began—on foot. There were skirmishes and attacks throughout the long advance which took the 9th Parachute Battalion through Kloster Lutherheim across the River Issel to Erle, and from there to Lembeck. Then twenty-three miles to Graven, to secure a bridge across the River Ems, and on another seventy miles to capture Minden.

All this time the 6th Airborne Division had managed to keep its nose ahead of competitors, but now the 15th (Scottish) Division went forward to capture Celle. Meanwhile, the 9th Parachute Battalion was involved in a full-sized battalion battle for the town of Ratzlingen. The success of the Battalion in this battle was partly due to the fact that the battalion padre, the Reverend John Gwinnett, M.C., moving with the leading company, located an enemy position in a cemetery and signalled their presence by frantically waving his walking-stick.

At Luneberg the 15th (Scottish) Division established a small bridgehead over the River Elbe. This was enlarged by the 9th Parachute Battalion, which rested for one night in the area of Boizenburg. Before dawn, on the 2nd May, 1945, the unit embussed and motored some sixty miles through Gadebusch to Wismar.

The Battalion arrived in Wismar a few hours before the leading Russian tanks arrived from Rostock. It was the end of the War.

Eventually, the 9th Parachute Battalion, relieved by the 5th Essex, moved back by road to Soltau, emplaned, and returned to Bulford.

So ended the Battalion's third campaign. In all, never once did it fail to take its objective at the first attempt in the attack, nor did it ever give an inch of ground when on the defensive, even against vastly superior enemy forces.

From Bulford the Battalion would have gone to take part in the assault on Japan, but the Japanese surrender came before more than an advance party had sailed for India.

The 9th Battalion Parachute Regiment won two D.S.O.s, four Military Crosses, eleven Military Medals, an M.B.E., a B.E.M., an American Bronze Star, and two Croix de Guerre. Eleven had been mentioned in dispatches. It was a notable record. The Essex Regiment has every reason to be proud of this fine fighting battalion. The Eagle had indeed spread its wings.

Section IV

THE 19TH BATTALION THE ESSEX REGIMENT

In the history of the Regiment during the years 1939-45, one must not forget a battalion formed far from the depot, a battalion which fought no action, and yet which in its short life did much to uphold the good name of the Essex Regiment.

This was the 19th Battalion, which was formed in Egypt on the 1st March, 1943, and disbanded in the same country on the 4th August, 1944.

Raised on a modified establishment which gave the Battalion 25 officers and 461 other ranks, the personnel came from the Home Counties Battalion of No. 1 I.T.D., and were about 60 per cent. men of the Essex Regiment. They were, in the great majority, men who had been evacuated to hospitals from the desert fighting of 1942-43.

Lieutenant-Colonel E. S. Bingham, M.C. (Queen's R.R.), was the Commanding Officer, and he was warned that his battalion, immediately it had been equipped, would move to the Sudan, there to relieve the 1st Welch.

Nine of the original twenty-five officers were of the Essex Regiment —Captains W. R. Burroughs, J. R. A. Cooper, P. G. Payne, B. J.

Cornelius, E. N. Gooderson, H. Lambshead, and Lieutenants A. Smith, R. G. Clark, B. A. Coker.

Plentiful stores and equipment were available, and altogether it was an easier task to form the 19th Essex in 1943 than it had been to form the 8th, 9th, and 10th Battalions in the hard days of 1940.

The rank and file, too, were a comparatively easy task, for all were trained men, the majority with considerable battle experience. One could wish that such conditions had existed nine months before, when the lack of trained reserves in the depots led to the disbandment of the 2/5th Essex after the Battle of Deir-el-Shein.

The 19th Essex left Geneifa for the Sudan on the 17th March, 1943, reaching Shellal in Upper Egypt the following afternoon, after some thirty hours in the train. There they embarked in three river steamers to make their way up the Nile to Wadi Halfa. Another train journey brought them to Khartoum on the 23rd March after a five-day journey.

The 19th Essex was the third battalion of the Regiment to serve in Khartoum in seven years. The 2nd Battalion was there in 1936/7, the 1st Battalion in 1940, and the 19th Battalion in 1943/44.

Quartered in Khartoum Barracks (South), the home of the 2nd Battalion in 1936/37, the Battalion came under command of No. 72 Sub-Area.

A week after arrival, the Battalion was inspected by Major-General B. O. Hutchison, C.B., C.B.E., the General Officer Commanding the Sudan, who said that perhaps at some later date the Battalion would be increased to full war establishment and given an operational role. This half-chance of an operational role, a carrot before the donkey's nose as it may have been, was a stimulus, and all ranks of the 19th Battalion went wholeheartedly at their training. Not only content to increase their own efficiency, they even started special weapon-training classes for the Free French units then in Khartoum—a success, despite the lack of a common tongue through which instruction could be carried out.

A duty that fell to the Battalion was to find the main guard at the Palace, residence of the Governor-General, Sir Herbert Huddleston, a task that remained with the 19th Essex almost throughout its stay in Khartoum.

In May a company detachment was sent to Asmara in Eritrea. It was a popular station, for Asmara is cool and conducive to training, and a change from the great heat of a Sudan hot-weather season.

Despite the heat, the main body in Khartoum was by July undertaking elaborate battalion training exercises. The very first scheme dealt with mine-gapping, river crossing, and a dawn attack.

Welfare and leave were not forgotten. Throughout the time the Battalion served in Khartoum, leave could be taken at Erkowit, in the Red Sea Hills, at Asmara, or at Wadi Medani in the Sudan. Erkowit and Asmara were the more popular, for the Eritrean climate is better than that of the Sudan. The Sudan did, however, provide good weekend leave at the Jebel Aulia Dam, about thirty miles from Khartoum up the White Nile, with good shooting, fishing, and bathing.

In November 1943 the whole Battalion was moved to Eritrea for a spell of intensive training. The camp was set up at Cheren, where Christmas 1943 was passed in traditional style. In January 1944 the Essex took part in the 2nd Sudan Defence Force Brigade exercises directed by Brigadier C. Greenslade and held in the mountainous country between Cheren and Agordat.

On the conclusion of the exercise, the whole Battalion concentrated for a five-day rest period at Asmara before returning (less one company) to Khartoum.

The 19th Essex remained in Khartoum and Asmara until June 1944, when, travelling from Khartoum to Asmara and from Asmara to Massawa where the Battalion embarked for Suez, it arrived at Mena, Cairo, on the 29th June.

Here the Battalion was placed under orders for disbandment, and on the 4th August, 1944, after a life of 531 days, the 19th Essex ceased to be recognised as a unit. Many of its personnel were posted to the 5th Essex, then serving in Palestine.

In its short life the 19th Essex had travelled many thousands of miles, had served in Egypt, the Sudan, and Eritrea, and had at all times upheld the honour of the Essex Regiment and of those Regiments of the Line from whom its personnel had come.

Chapter Ten

HOME DEFENCE BATTALIONS
THE ESSEX REGIMENT, 1939-43

Section I

THE NATIONAL DEFENCE COMPANIES

IN 1934, as Hitler became head of the German State and as Mussolini's Italy daily became more bombastic and bellicose, so the needs of war began to receive increasing attention.

The first preliminary stirrings were felt when Territorial battalions in camp for annual training that year each received a War Office letter stating that the formation of National Defence Companies had been approved, and that the 4th and 5th Battalions were to raise a company each and the 6th Battalion two companies.

The duty of these companies—each 1 officer (a lieutenant) and 50 men—was solely that of guarding certain vulnerable points within their recruiting area, it being agreed that in time of war there would be no other troops available for this purpose. Recruiting was confined to such individuals as had already been trained in one of the services and yet were not liable to compulsory recall in an emergency, and who lived within ten miles of one of the vulnerable points (V.P.s) for which their respective companies were responsible. This last condition followed from the fact that after mobilisation men were expected to live at their homes and to report for eight-hour tours of duty on a company roster. These companies, to be known as the National Defence Company of the battalion responsible for raising them, were under the commanding officer of that battalion, and had no connection with other National Defence Companies raised elsewhere in the county.

After the first announcement of the formation of the new companies had appeared in the Press, further publicity was forbidden. Organisation consisted solely in registering the names of applicants: no parades were to be held nor arms and clothing issued or even held on charge, and so not unnaturally the numbers secured were few. The National

Defence Company of the 4th Essex in 1935, for instance, consisted of 1 officer (Major H. J. Young, T.D.) and 2 men.

In 1936 the ban on publicity was removed, and very little energy was necessary to bring companies up to strength.

Immediately after the Munich crisis of 1938, the whole position was closely considered. It was, perhaps, the realisation that the fall of Czechoslovakia in March 1939 had been engineered and accomplished as much from within as by armed force front without that brought home the need to insure against an unseen as well as a seen enemy.

The fifth column, a term that had its origin in the Spanish Civil War, began to be talked of, as did the possibility that war might bring with it attacks on and sabotage of the national effort.

Because of this threat the safety of points valuable to the national economy—aerodromes, magazines, depots, key factories, power stations, viaducts and bridges, junctions, docks—became of increased importance, and the supply of troops to guard them of higher priority.

In the spring of 1939, Colonel H. F. Kemball, T.D., D.L., was given the task of building up and co-ordinating the National Defence Companies. During the summer the lists of vulnerable points grew larger as defence schemes daily grew more detailed. Each month home commands and areas had greater need of men to carry out the multitude of guard duties and the National Defence Companies grew larger. For example, the National Defence Company of the 4th Essex was raised in establishment from 1 officer and 50 other ranks to 8 officers and 238 other ranks, while the number of V.P.s for which it was to be responsible rose from one to five.

Drills were now held—up to six per man each year—and as the companies grew in size and importance, it was intended that they should be grouped and given a commander with a small headquarters. But events were to move too fast, and when the "Precautionary Period" was put into operation on the 24th August, 1939, no group commander had been appointed for the County of Essex.

Two days later Colonel Kemball was summarily ordered to assume command of the Essex group, No. 8 Group National Defence Companies.

This group consisted of four independent and self-accounting companies based on Ilford (one company under Major H. J. Young, T.D.), Southend (two companies under Major C. E. Edwards, D.S.O., M.C., and Major J. N. Coker, M.C.), and Colchester (one company under Major G. C. Benham, M.C.).

Colonel Kemball took as his Adjutant Captain R. A. Chell, D.S.O., M.C. The group was to be the parent of the 7th (H.D.) Battalion—later to be the 30th (H.D.)—and the 70th (Y.S.) Battalion the Essex Regiment.

Section II

THE 7TH AND 30TH (HOME DEFENCE) BATTALIONS THE ESSEX REGIMENT

As members of the N.D.C. reported on being called out on the 24th August, 1939, they were provided with a red armband marked in black "T.A.," issued with a rifle, and given a bounty of five pounds. There was no accommodation, and there were no rations, so each man was put on subsistence allowance of 3s. a day and told to fend for himself.

They were then sent to the various vulnerable points, adding to their commitments as their strength increased. They remained there, self-administered until, on the 1st November, 1939, No. 8 Group N.D.C. was renamed the 7th (Home Defence) Battalion The Essex Regiment, under command of Lieutenant-Colonel H. F. Kemball, T.D., D.L. Major G. C. Benham, M.C., became Second-in-Command, and Captain R. A. Chell, D.S.O., M.C., became Adjutant. Companies were re-lettered as follows:

"A" and "B" (late "X" and "Y" N.D. Companies) under Captain C. E. Edwards, D.S.O., M.C.

"C" (late "V" N.D. Company) under Captain H. J. Young, T.D.

"D" (late "W" N.D. Company) under Captain S. E. Collier.

Later, "B" Company was separated from "A" with Major J. N. Coker, M.C., in command, and a fifth company formed under Captain C. A. Boorman. Battalion Headquarters was at Ingatestone.

The change in nomenclature achieved little. The Battalion was certainly inadequate to defend the three aerodromes and the many V.P.s for which it had been made responsible, inadequate in numbers as well as in weapons. There was not enough of anything except food, for food was always plentiful that first winter.

There was little ammunition, no bombs, no barbed wire, and the cold winter of 1939/40 was upon the Battalion before any greatcoats arrived. At Hornchurch, where five double-sentry posts were mounted continuously, the only greatcoats available were ten, borrowed from a pile of condemned clothing at Warley. The off-coming sentry handed the greatcoat to his relief, and there was little or no opportunity for drying the coat after rain. The supply of gum-boots for marshy posts and patrols at Purfleet was no better. Gum-boots were unobtainable officially, but friends were allowed to help their county by lending them. This was a great help, though, as Major Young says, "It complicated the work of the officers making up the duty roster, which had to be prepared with special reference to the size of a sentry's feet."

But the 7th Essex "managed" and was always in demand. Indeed, calls upon the Battalion grew greater as depots, installations, and aerodromes increased both in size and number. The hard-working "over 45s" worked even harder as the number of guards and patrols increased, till in the early months of 1940 they were only getting every other night in bed.

On the 10th May the war really started, and then, as Lieutenant-Colonel Chell says, "The stampede was incredible. Ten operational controls. News of how Rotterdam aerodrome was taken. Sign-posts taken down, and a division of the field force moving in."

On top of its now almost unbelievable responsibilities over an area of some 3,000 square miles, the 7th Battalion was now required to act as parent to some lusty young-soldier companies. These young-soldier units came into being during the week-end of 18th/20th May, 1940, for the sole purpose of providing immediately additional static guards for aerodromes. Home defence battalions were the nominal source of aerodrome guards, and so those H.D. battalions got urgent instructions to make arrangements to receive all young-soldier recruits from recruiting offices, clothe, house, feed, train, and everything else them, and get a company on to each aerodrome in the County of Essex just as soon as possible. "The task was immense, and the only additional help forthcoming was a steady supply of middle-aged subalterns called up at reckless speed from the Army Officers Emergency Reserve. Of N.C.O.s none arrived, and we had consistently to bleed our five original companies of their junior leaders."

In July 1940 the unit, as Colonel Kemball says, "received a very welcome addition to our strength in the shape of six platoons from the Infantry Training Centre at Warley. These were all fine young men of category 'A,' who had passed through their basic training. Unfortunately, they were posted without officers and N.C.O.s and again the poor old parent unit had to be bled. These young men were split up into two companies, each of three platoons under Captain

J. M. Kyd and Captain G. D. Knight. Their advent considerably eased the strain upon a unit which had operational responsibilities in excess of its man-power."

But although the task was shouldered and willingly done, the 7th Essex was glad when, on the 19th September, 1940, it came to the end of its parental duties, and, divorced from the unit that had raised them, the five young-soldier companies became the 70th (Young Soldier) Battalion The Essex Regiment.

Lieutenant-Colonel R. A. Chell, D.S.O., M.C., took command of the Young Soldier Battalion.

But if the load on the Home Defence Battalion had been lightened by separation from the young-soldier companies, it was still much greater than it had been in the first winter of war. There was now the continual liaison with numerous Home Guard units across the county, and to the trials of busy days had to be added the tribulations of the almost continuous air bombardment suffered by the county of Essex in the winter months of 1940/41.

Days were one continuous round of visiting detachments found by the 7th Essex from Saffron Walden to Colchester and from Tilbury to Earls Colne, visiting Areas or Sub-Areas, liaising with H.Q. 15th (Scottish) Division and other field-force formations thick across the county, all the time producing the proverbial quart from a pint pot as additional calls for guards and escorts were received, escorts for baled-out aircrews and guards on crashed aircraft. On top there was the administration and interior economy of a strong and widely scattered battalion, and the assimilation of the masses of paper in each orderly room basket.

The burden may be said to have got progressively heavier until, about April 1941, the C.M.P. (V.P.)—"Blue Caps" not "Red"— came into being, and began to take over responsibility for certain static guards.

The 7th Essex, for the first time, had a small decline in responsibilities, and Colonel Kemball even found time for leave, the Adjutant remarking rather pointedly, "An uneventful Easter Sunday. The Commanding Officer is on 48 hours' leave."

But even now that the time of the heaviest duties seemed over, life in the Home Defence Battalion was no sinecure and sometimes very irritating.

As, for example, when "M.T.-less days" were instituted to save petrol. A magnificent idea when units were centralised, but almost impracticable when a battalion was scattered in numerous detachments over 3,000 square miles, and with an M.T. establishment inadequate to maintain them, even working seven days a week.

Then there was the "telephone-less" day. It was good fun when the "M.T.-less" and "Telephone-less" days coincided, for then a battalion headquarters was almost safe from interruption and could catch up on some urgent arrears of correspondence.

"8 August 1941. M.T.-less day. Also telephone-less day. Routine work of B.H.Q."

This quotation sums it all up.

Then there was the instruction that said that respirators would be worn on training and in offices for two consecutive hours one day each week. Telephone conversation was wont to fall off during those hours, and "one was able to realise how much time was wasted when the instruction was not in force."

Then in August 1941 a reorganisation of home defence units was ordered, resulting in the 7th Essex extending its already wide commitments to take over further responsibilities in Hertfordshire and Suffolk.

This was followed, at the beginning of September, by a change in command, Colonel Kemball handing over to Lieutenant-Colonel Chell. The whole Battalion regretted Colonel Kemball's departure, for all realised the great services he had rendered since its formation.

In November 1941 there was a change in designation, and the Battalion became known as the 30th (H.D.) Battalion The Essex Regiment.

Lieutenant-Colonel Chell found great changes in the Battalion he had left a short year ago. Of these, perhaps the most noteworthy was the departure of the majority of the original N.D.C. personnel, the nucleus of the unit. The terms of their engagement were so limiting that they could not be moved a distance of more than ten miles from their homes unless they agreed. They had done valuable service in the early days, and their departure was regretted, but they were, in many cases, unfitted for total war.

The 30th Essex now had six companies and a training wing, the latter being located at Ingatestone, with Battalion Headquarters. One of the companies had been training for some months and was made up almost entirely from category "A" men. The other five were spread over the three counties, were still heavy with low-category men, and for the most part were operationally engaged looking after a multitude of vulnerable points. All aerodromes, however, had been handed to the keeping of the young-soldier battalion.

Early in the winter of 1941/42 it became obvious that the unit was to undergo revolutionary changes: over 600 men were to be found for the R.A.S.C. (to be trained as drivers), about 140 were to go to the C.M.P. (V.P.), and nearly 100 to the Pioneer Corps. Replacements came from No. 1 I.T.C., and were younger and of higher medical category than the men they replaced.

The whole aspect of home defence was altering in the light of changed circumstances. Now, in early 1942, the period of the greatest danger from invasion had passed, and a reassessment of the force required for home defence was being made side by side with appreciations of strengths for possible offensive operations overseas. This resulted in changes in role and composition for many units and disbandment for others.

Among other changes was the realisation that the demands of modern war called for younger leaders, and in February of 1942 an Army Council instruction was published which required special reports to be rendered on all officers over forty-five. Lieutenant-Colonel Chell had to write reports on no fewer than 32 of his officers before the Area Commander wrote one on Lieutenant-Colonel Chell himself.

There was a general upheaval, as these older officers were placed in appointments deemed more suitable to their years. Lieutenant-Colonel Chell was replaced by Lieutenant-Colonel F. A. S. Clarke, D.S.O., in June 1942.

The intention was that the 30th Essex, with younger officers and men and more modern equipment, should become a counter-attack battalion. Thus it was, at long last, relieved of all the many static duties, and concentrated at Upminster to train for the new role.

But it was not given long life in its new guise. On the 24th November, 1942, the 30th (H.D.) Essex came under War Office control for disbandment. Lieutenant-Colonel Clarke was one of the first to leave, his place as commanding officer during the disbandment period being taken by Major R. G. Philipps.

Some time elapsed before all the personnel, so carefully collected during the summer, were finally dispersed, and it was not until the 1st April, 1943, that battalion records showed "Strength Nil."

What disembodied shade made that last entry, one wonders? The ghost, perhaps, of one of those gallant men, who, making most incorrect answers about their age and service and with carefully dyed hair and moustaches, joined the National Defence Companies, only to give things away by proudly parading Chitral and Boer War ribbons on their newly issued battledress.

The 30th Essex had had a chequered career, and its misfortune was to be disbanded just when, after so many months of unrewarding toil, it stood at last concentrated and properly equipped.

Section III

THE 70TH (YOUNG SOLDIER) BATTALION THE ESSEX REGIMENT

The German offensive in the West, so swiftly followed by the withdrawals from Dunkirk and the fall of France, left this country disillusioned but determined. The full extent of the menace to which the British Empire was confronted was at last realised.

There was a great upsurge of patriotism, and despite the fact that every man was liable to be called up with his age group under the National Service Act, there were many who wished to volunteer for immediate service rather than to wait for the call-up. Prominent among these volunteers was the youth of the nation.

Recognising this desire to serve, which became very apparent the moment the German assault in the West was launched, a War Office decision to proceed with the enlistment of young soldiers was promulgated during the week-end of the 18th/20th May, 1940. Youths of $17\frac{1}{2}$ to 19 years of age were from that time eligible to volunteer for service in their county regiment. This decision may be said to have killed two birds with one stone. Firstly, it satisfied the patriotic needs of young men below call-up age, and secondly, it tapped an untouched reservoir of man-power and provided an answer to the question of who was going to undertake the ground defence of aerodromes. For the campaign in the Low Countries and in France was showing all too clearly the need to protect aerodromes, not only against bombing, but against hostile airborne landings.

The home defence battalion of each county regiment was selected to be the parent unit of these young soldiers. Over the week-end of the 18th/20th May, 1940, the 7th (H.D.) Battalion The Essex Regiment received orders to prepare to receive young-soldier recruits direct from recruiting offices, and then to clothe, feed, house, train, and organise them into companies with the object of getting formed companies out to aerodromes as soon as was possible.

The first young soldiers to enlist for the Essex Regiment began to appear very shortly afterwards at the 7th Battalion's depot at Upminster, where Lieutenant-Colonel H. F. Kemball and Major R. A. Chell had organised a young-soldier company under Major H. J. Young. It was quickly up to establishment (150 young soldiers), and was followed by the formation of additional companies until in all five had been formed.

The War Office intention was that after fourteen days' preliminary training with the parent unit the young-soldier companies should be posted to take their place in the ground defence organisation at selected aerodromes. The first four companies moved out to Rochford, North Weald, Stapleford Tawney, and Debden. The fifth and last company remained temporarily at Upminster.

Company commanders who went with companies in this initial deployment were Captain L. J. Dilliway, T.D., Captain J. Lewis, D.C.M., Captain A. E. Bunting, Captain T. J. Curtis, and Major W. J. Baumgartner.

A moment's thought will show that an old-soldier unit is not the best parent for a young-soldier unit, but at the time it was "Hobson's choice," for what other parents or foster-parents, suitable or unsuitable, at the time existed? Infantry Training Centres were more than fully occupied, and the field force was either in the process of evacuating itself from the Continent or taking up the best defensive order it could to repel an expected invasion.

However, despite all the more pressing and complex questions of the day, time was found to agree on the formation of young-soldier battalions, and thus sever the ties between them and their parent units.

On the 4th September, 1940, the 70th (Y.S.) Battalion The Essex Regiment was formed at Berkley House, Ingatestone, and consisted initially of the five young-soldier companies already established, together with one company of army class intake men from the 7th (H.D.) Essex. This latter company was primarily men of 23-26 years of age, and was to form the backbone from which many of the original non-commissioned officers of the 70th (Y.S.) Essex were to come.

Command was given to Lieutenant-Colonel R. A. Chell, D.S.O., M.C., who had served with the 10th Essex during the First World War, and who had served since, and indeed before, the outbreak of war in 1939 with the 7th (H.D.) Essex. Major H. J. Young was

Second-in-Command, and continued as such until April 1942. Captain W. G. Wenley, M.C., was Adjutant.

"A" Company was commanded by Captain A. Balden, "B" Company by Captain J. Lewis, D.C.M., "C" by Major W. J. Baumgartner, and "D" by Captain T. J. Curtis. "D" was the depot company at Upminster. "E" Company, commanded by Captain H. W. Silver, M.C., was to take further recruits as they joined. The Battalion was engaged exclusively on aerodrome defence.

Quite naturally there had to be a period in which the 70th Essex found its administrative feet, and before it could assume complete operational control of its duties on aerodromes. So it was the 15th October, 1940, before the new battalion was finally divorced from the parent 7th Battalion.

Those early days were not easy. Training, administration, and operational duties filled every moment, and the staff was inadequate. The establishment of young-soldier companies was raised from three to six platoons, but no second captain was allowed by war establishment to the companies now 220 strong.

Inexperienced but high-spirited young men had to be disciplined, trained, and administered, whilst at the same time carrying out an important operational role in dispersed and distant areas. All this with an inadequate and somewhat ill-suited cadre of officers and N.C.O.s, for by some strange stroke of the pen these battalions were officered by middle-aged subalterns from the R.A.R.O. and A.O.E.R., whose sole experience had been a period of commissioned service during and immediately after the First World War. N.C.O.s were limited in number and of those available many were unsuitable.

The whole of 1941 was spent on static aerodrome defence duties armed with antiquated and obsolescent weapons. Whether such a role was the right one for high-spirited young volunteers is questionable, for although the operational role was a necessary one and at all times efficiently performed, the peculiarly static nature of the duties irked these young volunteers and raised many disciplinary problems.

Even the counter-attack role in the event of an airfield being occupied by the enemy was reserved for the field force. The young volunteers were confined to their weapon pits. It did not take a student of psychology to anticipate trouble.

Officers and non-commissioned officers were forced to wage a continuous war against boredom. During the early part of the year, while the German air attack continued on a large scale, the problem was not too difficult, for an occasional action against low-flying aircraft was a good safety valve. But as raids grew less frequent, so the problem of the young soldier became more difficult.

Increased numbers of aerodromes meant greater dispersion, with added difficulties for Headquarter and company staffs. Early in 1941 the Battalion was stretched by companies and platoons across Essex and Hertfordshire. A detachment was later sent as far afield as Ipswich, where it was heavily bombed, having 1 killed and 11 wounded.

In August 1941 Lieutenant-Colonel H. J. Laverty, M.C., took over command from Lieutenant-Colonel Chell.

The Battalion remained dispersed until the 10th January, 1942, when all ranks were delighted to be withdrawn for a period of training at Leigh-on-Sea. It was the first time, since its formation sixteen months earlier, that the Battalion had been concentrated, and companies now saw each other for the first time. The young soldier was happy to find himself at last part of a battalion of the Essex Regiment and not merely one of a collection of individuals, inadequately armed, saddled with the guarding of an aerodrome which in some cases was non-operational.

At Leigh-on-Sea the Battalion heard of the impending formation of the R.A.F. Regiment to be charged with the defence of aerodromes, and how young soldier battalions were to be reorganised, re-equipped, and rearmed, and given the important counter-attack role.

This reorganisation gave the 70th Essex the carriers, mortars, and all the weapons and specialist equipments they had been so long denied; and removed the feeling of inferiority which had been a basic reason for discontent.

Great progress was made with training but on the 15th February they had to leave Leigh-on-Sea and return once more to their aerodromes. They knew it would not be for long, and the day when the R.A.F. Regiment would be trained and ready to relieve them was anxiously awaited.

Eventually that day arrived, and on the 2nd June, 1942, the 70th Essex was concentrated once more. The new location was Hill Hall Camp, near Epping, whence the unit would carry out its new operational role of counter-attack battalion to the aerodromes of North Weald and Stapleford Tawney.

Major A. L. Semmence joined as Second-in-Command while the Battalion was in Hill Hall Camp, and was to remain until the final disbandment of the unit.

It was hoped that the revitalised and now well-trained battalion would advance even beyond the aerodrome counter-attack role and be included in the field force. But it was now late in 1942 and the military scene was again rapidly changing.

The risk of invasion or even of a large-scale raid was now small. Indeed, it was now Great Britain which was engaged in plans for invasion. The number of overseas infantry divisions had been decided upon, and the call was for specialist and supporting arms rather than for further infantry battalions.

Early in November 1942, Lieutenant-Colonel Laverty was notified of the intenton to disband young-soldier battalions, and on the 30th November the 70th Essex moved to Leigh-on-Sea for dispersal and eventual disbandment.

Bit by bit the Battalion left Leigh-on-Sea, but it was the 31st March, 1943, before final disbandment was accomplished.

The 70th Essex had completed its task which had not been easy. The employment of young, keen volunteers on extremely static and dispersed duties was dictated by the needs of 1940, but whether other and more suitable employment could not have been found is open to question.

The material was excellent, but the manner of its employment was perhaps unfortunate.

Chapter Eleven

THE REGIMENTAL CENTRE, WARLEY, 1939-50

WARLEY BARRACKS, the home of the Depot The Essex Regiment since 1873, held, in the summer of 1939, both the Depot and the 2nd Battalion of the Regiment, the former commanded by Major L. W. W. Marriott.

The Munich crisis of 1938 had focused attention on the many deficiencies in the mobilisation arrangements of the armed forces. A year's grace was given and made full use of, and by August 1939 the scheme for the conversion of the Depot into the Essex Regiment Infantry Training Centre was ready. The solution of the problem had been made somewhat easier by various measures of national defence put into effect during 1939, principally the Militia training scheme, for this had meant the introduction in peace of additional training staff to the Depot and the provision of extra accommodation at Warley.

Thanks to the care and forethought shown throughout 1939 by Lieutenant-Colonel C. C. Spooner, D.S.O., and Lieutenant-Colonel A. H. Blest, the commanding officers of the 2nd Battalion, and by Major L. W. W. Marriott, the twin problems of the mobilisation of the Regiment's regular personnel and the change-over of the Depot to an Infantry Training Centre were satisfactorily dealt with.

Morale was high, and very few reservists failed to report by the appointed time. Many, in fact, threatened the smooth running of the mobilisation arrangements by arriving far earlier than they had been expected. There was adequate barrack-room accommodation, and no difficulty was experienced in finding and dispatching all the drafts that were required.

Perhaps the accommodation and messing of the large numbers of officers who rejoined was the most difficult problem, for the little Depot officers' mess was much too small and the new battalion mess building not yet completed.

In accordance with its war establishment the staff for the Training

Centre was to be found by the Depot staff as augmented to deal with the militia intakes, together with two increments, one from the regular home battalion and the other from the territorial battalions. Not unnaturally the latter contained a considerable number of individuals not yet trained in instructional duties, since with the limited training facilities in, and the recent doubling of, the Territorial Army, its cadre of experienced non-commissioned officers was inadequate.

Lieutenant-Colonel Marriott, now in command of the Infantry Training Centre, met this situation by starting courses of instruction for those inadequately trained, the regular permanent staff assuming additional duties until such time as sufficient instructors were available to fill all vacancies on the establishment.

As soon as an adequate staff of instructors had been provided, training progressed smoothly, special steps being taken to increase the output of specialists over and above the numbers laid down by the War Office. This policy stood the Infantry Training Centre and battalions in good stead. Later, at the time of Dunkirk and after, the demands for specialists became extremely heavy, but the Training Centre was able to meet all such demands, both as regards officers and other ranks.

Right from the earliest days, great care was taken to screen all intakes for potential officer and non-commissioned officer material, such personnel being passed into pre-O.C.T.U. instruction as soon as they had finished their period of basic training.

Although the training of the many hundreds of men in the Centre was the greatest official responsibility of the Commanding Officer, perhaps the biggest problem for Lieutenant-Colonel Marriott was the safety of this large but concentrated community from enemy air activity. For Warley obviously lay on one of the main routes of enemy aircraft approaching London.

The official statistics of enemy air activity in the area of Brentwood and district are as follows:

Number of H.E. bombs dropped	1,018
Occasions when incendiary bombs were dropped	108
Parachute mines dropped	18
Flying bombs	19
Long-range rockets (V2)	32
Number of alerts	1,262

The first high-explosive bomb dropped at Goldings, Great Warley, on the 23rd July, 1940, and the last—a V2 rocket—fell at Hutton Park on the 27th March, 1945.

But despite air-raid distractions, and, even after the withdrawal from Dunkirk, of an operational role, the Training Centre lived up to its name, and in general personnel sent away with drafts were of a good standard in training and fitness.

One of the very first drafts to be sent away went to the Royal Scots Fusiliers—a disappointment to those drafted that they were not to serve with the Regiment—but they were very well received, and it may please those who went to know that the Commanding Officer of the R.S.F. Battalion wrote: "Ayrshire has sent many farmers to Essex in the past, so it is only right that we should have some Essex soldiers in return—a very fine draft, and I am delighted to have them."

In April 1941 Lieutenant-Colonel L. W. W. Marriott was posted to command of the 2nd Battalion, and his place at Warley was taken by Lieutenant-Colonel T. O'C. Doherty.

Lieutenant-Colonel Marriott had had an arduous and exacting tenure of command. The day before he left, the Centre was seen by the Inspector of Infantry, Major-General D. G. Johnson, V.C., D.S.O., M.C., who, in a letter to Lieutenant-Colonel Marriott, said: "It was a pleasure to see all your officers and N.C.O.s running a well-organised centre which I feel is the result of much painstaking on your part." Lieutenant-Colonel Marriott's staff had included Major S. H. Andrew, Major Sir George Rowley, Bart., Major H. G. Aylmer, Major (Q.M.) H. G. Ricketts, and R.Q.M.S. F. W. Waddell.

The first small contingent of the Auxiliary Territorial Service joined the staff of the Essex Regiment Training Centre almost immediately after mobilisation, and their strength was gradually built up throughout the war, until there was a complete A.T.S. company of some 240, which carried out most efficiently the greater part of the essential administrative duties of the Centre.

An important member of the A.T.S. community was Regimental Sergeant-Major Pouch, daughter of a very old member of the Regiment, Lieutenant-Colonel (Q.M.) H. R. Pouch, M.B.E., at the time serving in the Middle East.

The introduction of the A.T.S. was not without its effect on the Warley way of life, as is shown by the following minute taken from the Officers' Mess Minute book for 1943:

"The A.T.S. officers' overpowering urge to knit in the mess

precincts gained a blitzkrieg victory over a somewhat dazed and unprepared male opposition. Field officers and certain of the more senior captains were, however, excused the arduous duties of wool winding. As an act of grace, it was hoped that A.T.S. officers will undertake the more urgent underwear repairs for the unmarried male members of the mess."

One is told, too, that the first reaction of the P.M.C., on hearing that A.T.S. officers were to use the officers' mess as full dining members, was to go and remove a lurid Hogarth "Rake's Progress" print from the ante-room where it had hung so long, and move it to a more suitable room, inaccessible to A.T.S. officers, in the mess building.

In 1941 a general reorganisation and amalgamation of infantry training centres took place, the I.T.C. The Essex Regiment becoming, on the 14th August, No. 1 Infantry Training Centre, designed to train recruits for the Essex Regiment and the Royal Fusiliers. There was an element of doubt as to whether such an amalgamation would work out, but it was at Warley a great success.

The "Royal Fusilier Chronicle" at the time said: "We were naturally a little apprehensive at first of a strange orderly room, but the Essex Regiment have left us in no doubt of their determination to welcome us and help us in every way."

Lieutenant-Colonel T. O'C. Doherty had little time to do more than see the reorganisation through before, in accordance with the policy laid down that the first Commanding Officer would be from the senior of the grouped regiments, he handed over to Lieutenant-Colonel H. H. Cripps, D.S.O., The Royal Fusiliers, who was to retain command until May 1943.

The balance was kept at all times between Fusilier and Essex officers, a Fusilier commanding officer having an Essex Second-in-Command, and vice versa. The same principle applied, as far as was possible, throughout the permanent staff.

So when, in May 1943, Lieutenant-Colonel T. E. Hearn took command, he found Major C. Portway, M.C., T.D., who had been Second-in-Command to Lieutenant-Colonel Cripps, and who, in his turn, had to give place to Major G. L. Cazalet, D.S.O., M.C. He also found at Warley Captain (Q.M.) E. H. Crane and Regimental Sergeant-Major A. F. Sutton, D.C.M.

Later that year the Regiment lost an outstanding personality, and many an old "Pompadour" a personal friend, in the death in Warley Woods Hospital of Captain Crane, for the past twenty-five years a tower of strength in orderly room and quartermaster stores, as well as on the cricket, football, and hockey grounds. He was succeeded by Lieutenant T. G. Gagen from the 2nd Battalion.

On the 1st April, 1944, an appropriate date, the Essex Regiment was for the first time since 1873 uprooted from Warley Barracks and sent to Squires Gate Camp, Blackpool. Warley Barracks were wanted as a D-Day assembly area.

It took five trains and one horse-box to move the Centre, but it was done. The odd box was for "Bess," the C.O.'s mare, for Lieutenant-Colonel Hearn apparently thought she would benefit from the sea air.

About 2,600, including the A.T.S. company of 240, had to be moved and reaccommodated in Squires Gate Camp, which was a holiday camp, and most unsuitable to house an I.T.C. There were no training grounds, the troops lived in small chalets which looked like bathing huts, and the whole camp was always deep in sand, which blew in incessantly from the sand dunes facing the camp.

On arrival no one knew a parade ground existed until tons and tons of sand had been moved, and everyone, officers included, for four nights a week were on sand-moving fatigue, a new one for the Regimental Sergeant-Major. Some previous unit with a passion for tidiness had apparently pulled up all the spear grass on the nearby dunes, not realising its importance. Thus, when the wind blew, as it often does at Blackpool, the sand dunes moved into camp. There was sand everywhere, even under the eaves of the chalets, and as the weight increased, so roofs collapsed, engulfing the beds below in sand and broken roof.

The Essex, and perhaps the Royal Fusiliers, too, thought Southend-on-Sea a better place, and all were pleased to be back in Warley by mid-July.

Resettling in at Warley was not assisted by the "Doodle-bug" epidemic which started in July, and a later visitation of V2s was a nuisance, three falling in the barrack area. One destroyed the old stables, one fell near the married-quarter block, then occupied by the A.T.S., and one dropped near the Chapel. But luckily there was little damage, except to the stables and gymnasium, and relatively few casualties.

Towards the end of January 1945, Lieutenant-Colonel Hearn was asked to train a number of young Dutchmen, the nucleus of the armed forces of liberated Holland. They had mostly been in the resistance movement, were well educated, and easy to train.

Their arrival was an event of importance to Warley, and their tremendous keenness an inspiration to everyone. One of the most remarkable features was their deep religious background and their desire to attend services at the Regimental Chapel.

Warley was visited, between January 1945 and September 1946, by the G.O.C. of the Dutch forces in England, Major-General van Voorts Evekink, by the Dutch Minister for War, M. Meyren, and by H.R.H. Prince Bernhardt. The latter had lunch in the officers' mess, a great occasion.

In all, about 3,500 Dutchmen were trained at Warley, and in recognition of their services to the Dutch nation, Lieutenant-Colonel T. E. Hearn and Regimental Sergeant-Major A. F. Sutton, D.C.M., were both awarded the Order of Oranje-Nassau, the presentation being made by M. Meyren.

In addition, the Dutch authorities presented a silver cup and a silver cigar box. The cup was given for the purpose of an annual football match between the training establishment of the Royal Fusiliers and the Essex Regiment, the silver box going to the losing side. At the end of 1950 the cup rests with the Essex Regiment.

The text of the final letter of appreciation from the commander of the Dutch troops in England read as follows:

"Now that training of Netherlands troops at Brentwood is coming to an end, I consider it my duty and privilege to express my heartfelt gratitude and deep admiration to the Commanding Officer and all ranks of No. 1 I.T.C. for the important share they have had in the training of personnel for the new Netherlands Army.

"It is to my very deep regret that I am not able personally to be present today; accordingly, I have prepared the message, in order that I may express the deep appreciation which is mine, of the high standards ever demonstrated by the entire staff of No. 1 I.T.C. while carrying out the task of training Netherlands personnel.

"I wish to congratulate you on the, in my opinion, excellent results of the training of about three and a half thousand Dutch, between January 1945 and now. They came to the United Kingdom in order to be instilled with the theoretical and practical military knowledge and training which have led the British Army to victory and to the liberation of my country. It is my honest opinion that they have had the best possible training a soldier can get.

"The Dutch officers and men who have been attached to No. 1 I.T.C. desire to offer a tangible proof as a token of their gratitude, and with a view to the sporting qualities of the British people, they thought they could not do better than present a silver challenge cup as prize for the winner of a yearly football match to be played by the Royal Fusiliers and the Essex Regiment.

"I hope that this cup will be an annual reminder of the high appreciation which the Dutch trainees feel for their British instructors and friends."

Among all the war-time activities it had been found possible, as a variation of training, to hold tattoos at Warley in 1943 and 1944. After V.E.-Day in 1945 it became possible further to extend these activities.

An ambitious project was staged in June and was a complete success, some 15,000 people seeing the tattoo, with a net profit of £1,250. This was divided equally between the regimental charities of the Royal Fusiliers and the Essex Regiment. It is difficult to name all those who were responsible for this notable event, but Captain G. Shadbolt (R.F.) and Regimental Sergeant-Major A. F. Sutton, D.C.M. (Essex), were outstanding in their efforts towards its success.

Then again in June 1946, another and perhaps even better tattoo, despite the difficulties of the release scheme. This time 23,000 saw the show, and the charities of the Royal Fusiliers and the Essex Regiment each benefited by £1,000, a notable achievement, and a fitting reward for the enormous amount of hard work by organisers and performers.

In mid-December 1946, Lieutenant-Colonel T. E. Hearn handed over the command he had held for three and a half years to Lieutenant-Colonel S. C. W. W. Rea, O.B.E.

Among those on the permanent staff of the training centre during the period of command of Lieutenant-Colonel Hearn were: Captain R. Wilson (R.F.), Captain H. Bestley, Captain D. H. Ford, Major G. L. Cazalet, D.S.O., M.C. (R.F.), Major S. H. Andrew, Major H. G. Aylmer, Major W. S. Smith, Captain G. Shadbolt (R.F.), Captain (Q.M.) T. G. Gagen, the Reverend G. M. Lister, R.S.M. A. F. Sutton, D.C.M., and O.R. Quartermaster-Sergeant B. Kirby.

The departure of Lieutenant-Colonel Hearn marked the turning-point at Warley. Until then, the emphasis had all been on expansion and training for war; and even though it was a year after V.J.-Day, the training requirements of the armies of occupation and the training of the Dutch personnel had kept No. 1 I.T.C. working at full pressure.

Now came the divorce of the two Regiments which had worked

together so harmoniously for so long. Infantry training centres were replaced by primary training centres, that of the Royal Fusiliers being set up at Hounslow and that of the Essex Regiment at Warley.

The association of the two Regiments at Warley had been a most happy one, not only for individuals, but for the two Regiments, and although the break was inevitable, it was none the less regretted.

The departure of the Royal Fusiliers and the Netherlands personnel left Warley seemingly very empty after the crowded years that had gone before.

Before passing to the Primary Training Centre, it is necessary to remark briefly on two items that deserve their place in Regimental history, the presentation made in 1943 to the U.S.S. *Essex*, and the Regimental Museum.

In a letter in October 1942, the Colonel of the Regiment wrote to all battalions of the Regiment serving at home to say that he was in favour of a suggestion to present the U.S. aircraft-carrier *Essex* with an Essex Regiment Eagle Crest.

The idea was eagerly taken up, and shortly Lieutenant-General Sir Geoffrey W. Howard was able to write to the United States Naval Mission in the United Kingdom and suggest this presentation from the Regiment of the County of Essex to the aircraft-carrier *Essex*, named from the county of Essex, Massachusetts.

"Essex" is a traditional name for a warship of the United States Navy, and a ship of that name has figured in the U.S. Navy List for over a hundred years.

The idea of the presentation was gratefully accepted, and in January 1943 the "Eagle" was handed over at the United States Naval Headquarters in London, the Captain of U.S.S. *Essex* subsequently signalling "Please convey to the Colonel of the Essex Regiment and his officers and men my thanks and appreciation for their thoughtful gift. We shall bear it with honour throughout what we hope and expect will be a long and successful career." It was. Altogether, the U.S.S. *Essex* steamed 244,000 miles during the war, and her aircraft accounted for 740 Japanese planes in the air and 791 on the ground—a magnificent achievement of which the "Eagle" may well be proud.

The Regimental Museum was established before the war at Chelmsford by the interest and energy of Colonel H. R. Bowen, D.S.O., D.L. It was moved and settled at Warley in the winter of 1946/47. This move, together with the continuing interest of Colonel Bowen, gave the Museum a new lease of life, and in the three years between 1947 and 1950 it gained greatly in size and regimental interest, and had begun its object of maintaining and building up still further the important regimental *esprit de corps*. The Museum, in fact, had become a regimental institution, comparing more than favourably with others of its kind.

No. 44 Primary Training Centre rose like the phœnix from the ashes of No. 1 I.T.C. on the 21st November, 1946. It was commanded by Lieutenant-Colonel S. C. W. W. Rea, O.B.E.

This new centre was responsible for the primary training of army intakes from the County of Essex, and it was visited very early in its career by the G.O.C.-in-C. of the Eastern Command, and by the commander of the East Anglian area.

These visits proved the forerunners of a yet more important visit, for on the 18th March, 1947, Warley was visited by the C.I.G.S. Field-Marshal Viscount Montgomery of Alamein. It was only a brief visit, but the Field-Marshal found time to inspect the training, and walked through the Depot gardens to see the Chapel. He then took tea in the officers' mess, accompanied by Lieutenant-General Sir Evelyn Barker, K.B.E., C.B., D.S.O., M.C., the G.O.C.-in-C. Eastern Command.

A more intimate visit was when, on the 1st May, 1947, Lieutenant-General Sir Geoffrey Howard paid a visit to Warley at the wish of the serving and retired officers of the Regiment, so that they could express the appreciation and gratitude which were felt for the great services rendered to the Regiment by General Howard during his twelve years as Colonel. It is pleasing to record that on this occasion a message of gratitude was sent to Lady Howard, who had never spared herself in the Regiment's interests, particularly in the war years. There will be many who served in North Africa, in Italy, Iraq, Burma, Palestine, Holland, or Germany who remember with gratitude the parcels of comforts which arrived so regularly owing to Lady Howard's activities, and which were so great a boon to all ranks.

At the same time that the P.T.C. was set up in 1946, the Depot of the Regiment was reconstituted on a post-war basis.

It had a strength of 3 officers and 14 men, and was planned, not for training, but to hold and administer up to 100 all ranks, thus being capable of dealing with all regular personnel coming from overseas on leave, for discharge, and so on.

It was commanded in the first instance by Major S. H. Andrew.

The P.T.C. did not have a long life. By mid-1948 it had been disbanded, but not before some 5,000 men of Essex had passed through its ranks on their way to the various units and arms of the service. They had all spent the initial six weeks of their army life at Warley, and it is not too much to hope that the whole of their service was influenced by this contact with the traditions and manners of the Essex Regiment.

As the months passed, numbers at Warley grew fewer until the small post-war depot staff alone remained in those echoing barracks that had known such crowded years.

But Warley, empty as it now was in 1949 and 1950, remained, as ever since 1873, the home of the Regiment.

Chapter Twelve
THE ESSEX REGIMENT CHAPEL

THERE is an old story that when the Roman Legions were stationed in Britain, the men of the Legions were gathered together from time to time for their religious services in tents of goatskins—"a caprarum pellibus" or more shortly "capella," in which some think the word "chapel" has its origin. Ever since those days effort has been made to ensure the fighting men of our land having appropriate opportunity and place for corporate worship. In Essex such endeavour has found pleasing and fitting shape in the Chapel of the County Regiment.

Warley Barracks became in 1842 the depot of the Honourable East India Company. At first the riding school had been used for church services, as is shown by a recommendation of the Commandant at Warley Barracks dated the 13th March, 1843, "that the riding house should be allowed to stand, as it would prove very useful as a place of worship." When the barracks were extended in 1855, the plans included the erection of the present Chapel, built in 1857 to the design of Sir Matthew Digby White. The Chapel, to seat 600, was built at a cost of £2,147, the largest sum that the Commissioner for Affairs of India was prepared to sanction.

After the disasters of the Mutiny in 1857 the entire administration of India passed into the hands of the Crown, the East India Company regiments becoming part of the British Army, and in 1861 control of Warley Barracks passed to the War Office.

The Cardwell reforms of 1870 followed, and in 1873 the depot companies of the 44th (East Essex) Regiment and the 56th (West Essex) Regiment, the "Pompadours," were brought together at Warley. They were accompanied by the depot companies of the East Essex and West Essex Militia. Thus was established at Warley a regimental centre for the regular and militia regiments of the county of Essex.

The early grouping of regiments raised in the county led logically to the major reorganisation of 1881, when the system of county regiments was inaugurated, the 44th and 56th Regiments becoming the 1st and 2nd Battalions The Essex Regiment, while the Essex Rifles and West Essex Militia became the 3rd and 4th Battalions of that Regiment.

Warley Chapel has therefore regimental connections as far back as 1873, but the earliest memorial to the Regiment is a brass plate on the north wall, giving the names of those of the 56th Foot, the "Pompadours," who fell in the Nile Campaign of 1884/85.

The second earliest memorials are those in connection with the South African War of 1899-1902, in which the 1st, 2nd, and 3rd Battalions, together with personnel from the 4th Militia Battalion and Volunteer Battalions, all served, as did Mounted Infantry Companies formed from personnel of the Regiment. The memorials include a plate to "The Essex Regiment, South Africa, 1899-1902," as well as brasses in memory of individuals who died during the campaign. Of these, the plate erected to the memory of Lieutenant F. N. Parsons, V.C., is perhaps the most notable. Lieutenant Parsons was awarded the Victoria Cross posthumously for great gallantry at the Battle of Paardeberg.

The First World War

The very great losses sustained by the Regiment in the First World War are reflected by the numerous memorials to the fallen now in the Chapel.

The initial memorial was unveiled on the 21st May, 1921, by Lord Lambourne, C.V.O., the Lord-Lieutenant of Essex, and was dedicated by the Bishop of Chelmsford. It was to the fallen of the 1st and 2nd Battalions, and was placed in the middle of the South Wall.

It consists of a fine alabaster mural tablet emblazoned with the crests of the two Battalions, a shelf supporting a cedar box containing the Roll of Honour Books, and a central plaque of white marble inscribed: "To the glory of God, and in memory of 185 Officers, 3,244 Warrant Officers, Non-commissioned Officers and Men of the 1st and 2nd Battalions, The Essex Regiment, who fell in the Great War of 1914-1918."

This bare statement is silent witness to the glorious and gallant part played by the two Regular Battalions in the First World War.

The Dedication of the Chapel to the Regiment

On the 25th February, 1925, official sanction was given to the proposal that the Chapel should be recognised as the Essex Regiment Chapel.

This proposal had been put forward by Major-General F. Ventris, C.B., Colonel of the Essex Regiment, in response to a strong feeling that the dedication of the Warley Garrison Chapel to the Regiment would have the much-to-be-desired effect of forming a closer link between all units of the Regiment, and also strengthen the connection between the Regiment and the County.

The Essex Regiment thus achieved the distinction of being the only line regiment with a chapel of its own. It owes much to Sir Bertram Cubitt, K.C.B., D.L., for his help at the War Office in obtaining sanction, and a memorial to him was placed in the Chapel in 1948.

The ceremony of dedicating the Chapel took place on the 1st March, 1925, and was performed by the Chaplain-General, Bishop Taylor Smith. The ceremony was made all the more impressive by the laying up of the King's Colours of the 10th and 11th Service Battalions and the 1st and 2nd Garrison Battalions of the Regiment.

Dedication within the Chapel

It is not possible to name all those whose early interest and energy led to the present beauty of the Chapel, but certainly the Reverend A. J. Wilcox, C.B.E., C.F., Colonel and Mrs. A. P. Churchill, Lieutenant-Colonel R. N. Thompson, Lieutenant-Colonel A. E. Maitland, D.S.O., M.C., and Lieutenant-Colonel A. E. M. Sinclair-Thomson, D.S.O., were outstanding in their efforts.

Within the scope of this history it is not possible to do more than catalogue briefly and in chronological order the more important of the many presentations that have been made. It is hoped that those who read will come and see this inspiring memorial.

Lectern Bible, Altar Service Book, and Book of Common Prayer	July 1925	Presented by Colonel T. Stock, C.M.G.
The Colours of the 5th Battalion Local Militia (The Essex Fencibles, 1808–16)	26th January, 1926	Transferred from the Shire Hall, Chelmsford
The 4th Battalion Memorial Window	28th March, 1926	Presented by the 4th Battalion The Essex Regiment (T.A.)
The 4th Battalion Memorial Pew (This Pew was inscribed in		

1948 with the sign of the 4th Indian Division, the 4th Essex having served with distinction with that formation in North Africa, Italy, and Greece between 1942 and 1945)

The 4th Battalion Oak Pillar Desk and Roll of Honour

The King's Colour and Regimental Colour of the 3rd (S.R.) Battalion The Essex Regiment	31st October, 1926	Transferred from Harwich Parish Church
The King's Colour of the 15th Service Battalion The Essex Regiment		Transferred from St. Mary's Parish Church, Ilford, where it had been deposited on the disbandment of the Battalion after service in France and Belgium, 1916–18
The Trones Wood Cross	March 1927	Raised in Trones Wood after its capture in August 1918 by the 53rd Infantry Brigade, of which the 10th Battalion The Essex Regiment was part. It stood for eight years, and was then entrusted into the keeping of the Regiment
The King's Colour of the 9th Service Battalion The Essex Regiment	May 1927	Presented to the Battalion in France by the Prince of Wales, it was transferred to the Chapel in 1927
The Gundamak Colour	17th July, 1927	The Colour of the 44th Foot at the Battle of Gundamak in the first Afghan War, 1841. One of the most prized possessions of the Regiment, it was transferred from Alverstoke Parish Church, where it had been for many years

The Crimean Colour of the 56th Foot	17th July, 1927	This colour was carried by the 56th Foot from 1826 to 1864, and saw service in Ireland, the West Indies, Canada, England, Gibraltar, Bermuda, the Crimea, and India
The 6th Battalion Memorial Window	31st July, 1927	Presented by the 6th Battalion The Essex Regiment (T.A.)
Six Choir Stalls	26th February, 1928	Presented by the Borough of Southend
The West Doors	March 1928	Presented by the Borough of Ilford
The 9th Battalion Memorial Window The 9th Battalion Oak Pillar Desk and Roll of Honour	8th April, 1928	Presented by the Old Comrades of the 9th Service Battalion The Essex Regiment, 1914-20
The South Door	17th June, 1928	Presented by the Old Comrades of the 11th Service Battalion The Essex Regiment, 1914-19
The Pulpit	15th July, 1928	Presented by the Borough of Chelmsford
The 7th Battalion Memorial Window The 7th Battalion Oak Pillar Desk and Roll of Honour	1st September, 1928	Presented by the 7th Battalion The Essex Regiment (T.A.)
The Queen's Colour and Regimental Colour of the 44th Foot	26th May, 1929	Presented to the 44th Foot in 1843, they were deposited in St. Peter's Church, Colchester, until transferred to the Chapel
The Queen's Colour and Regimental Colour of the West Essex Militia	26th May, 1929	Previously in the keeping of Colonel A. W. Ruggles-Brise, who now returned them to the Regiment
The 1st and 2nd Battalion Memorial Windows	26th May, 1929	Presented by the 1st and 2nd Battalions The Essex Regiment.

The 11th Battalion Pillar Desk and Roll of Honour	10th June, 1929	Presented by the Old Comrades of the 11th Service Battalion The Essex Regiment, 1914–19
The 5th Battalion Memorial Window The 5th Battalion Pillar Desk and Roll of Honour	23rd June, 1929	Presented by the 5th Battalion The Essex Regiment (T.A.)
The 6th Battalion Pillar Desk and Roll of Honour	29th September, 1929	Presented by the 6th Battalion The Essex Regiment (T.A.)
The King's Colour of the Loyal and United West and East Ham Volunteers	29th September, 1929	Presented to the Volunteers about 1802, the Colour was laid up in Armagh Cathedral until returned to the Essex Regiment
The King's Colour and Regimental Colour of the 4th (Militia) Battalion The Essex Regiment	1929	Transferred from St. Mary's Cathedral Church, Chelmsford, where they had rested since the disbandment of the Battalion in 1908
The Oak Lectern	20th July, 1930	Presented by the Borough of Maldon
The West Window	7th December, 1930	Presented by the Borough of Colchester
The 10th Battalion Memorial Window	7th December, 1930	Presented by the Old Comrades of the 10th Service Battalion The Essex Regiment, 1914–19
The front to the West Gallery	31st May, 1931	Presented by the Freemasons of the County of Essex
The King's Colour and Regimental Colour (Waterloo Colours) of the 2nd Battalion the 44th Foot	10th June, 1931	The Battalion was raised in 1803 and disbanded in 1816 after having greatly distinguished itself in the Peninsula, at Quatre Bras, and at the Battle of Waterloo
Oak Panelling in the Chancel	25th September, 1931	Presented by the Essex Scottish Regiment of Canada

The Parclose Screen	26th June, 1932	Presented by the Royal and Ancient Order of Buffaloes in Essex
The Militia Memorial Window	25th June, 1933	Presented in memory of those of the two County Regiments of Militia, the Essex Rifles and the West Essex, who gave their lives in the Great War 1914-18
The King's Colour of the 13th Service Battalion	30th May, 1935	This Colour had been previously laid up in the West Ham Parish Church
Oak Pillar Desk and Roll of Honour of the 1st and 2nd Battalions (from 11th November, 1918)	30th June, 1935	Presented by the 1st and 2nd Battalions The Essex Regiment.

There are in addition many memorial panels, pews, and mural tablets, but, unfortunately, it is not possible to enumerate them here.

The Prayer for the Regiment

"O Lord, our Heavenly Father, send Thy Blessing upon the Essex Regiment. Strengthen us to whom its honour is entrusted, that we may prove worthy of its best traditions. Keep us true to King and Country, and, above all, true to Thee. As the Star in the East pointed men to their Saviour, so may His Light in us point men to Thee. May He fill us with a passion for Freedom, Justice, and Right, and with that Love greater than which no man hath. We ask it for His sake, Jesus Christ, our Lord. *Amen.*"

This beautiful prayer is known and loved throughout the Essex Regiment, but its source and authorship seem obscure.

The Reverend Matthew Tobias in his book, *Collects for the British Army*, says of the prayer that it was already in use in the Regiment in 1930 when he compiled his book of collects.

The first recorded instance of its use is at the Dedication Service of the 4th Battalion War Memorial, but the general opinion and recollection seems to be that the prayer was introduced to the Regiment by Bishop Taylor Smith, Chaplain-General to the Forces, about the time of the Dedication of the Chapel.

It is the prayer now regularly used at the Chapel Services.

In his book Mr. Tobias gives also another very lovely collect where reference is made to the main points of the Regimental history and emblems.

"O Lord, our stony rock and our defence,[1] hear us, we pray Thee, Thy servants of the Essex Regiment, and ever bear us as on Eagles' wings,[2] in the faith and truth of Him Who is now our shield and buckler,[3] Jesus Christ our Lord."

Long custom, however, has endeared the former prayer to the heart and sentiment of the members of the Regiment, and it is the one used on all official occasions.

The Chapel in the Second World War

The Chapel, in the heart of the Regiment at Warley, was, during the Second World War, in grave danger of destruction or damage by enemy action.

Despite the severe bombing—1,018 high-explosive bombs fell on Brentwood and district, with numerous incendiary bombs, flying bombs, and rocket bombs—it was decided not to remove the Colours to a temporary place of security, but to leave them in the Chapel. For the Regimental Chapel was rightly judged to be a source of encouragement and inspiration to all ranks under training at Warley.

This courageous decision by Lieutenant-General Sir Geoffrey Howard and Lieutenant-Colonel L. W. W. Marriott, the Commanding Officer of the I.T.C. in 1940, had the reward it deserved, for with the exception of two plain-glass windows shattered by the blast from long-range rocket bombs falling within the barracks area, the Chapel suffered no damage.

Throughout the war, in addition to the official services, the Chapel was much used by individuals for times of quiet and personal meditation, devotional reading, and talks with the Padre, the Reverend G. M. Lister, M.C., M.A., C.F. Confirmation classes were held in the Chapel, and during the war period many candidates were confirmed there by the Bishop of the Diocese.

In addition, some found in the Chapel organ a great source of joy,

---

[1] 56th Foot badge, Castle and Key of Gibraltar, with "Montis Insignia Calpe." (Psalm xviii. (P.B. version) : "The Lord is my stony rock and my defence.")

[2] 44th Foot badge, Eagle of the 62nd French Regiment. (Exodus xix[4]: "Ye have seen how I bare ye on eagles' wings and brought you unto myself.")

[3] A shield, the Arms of the County of Essex, worn as a badge. (Psalm xci. (P.B. version): "His faithfulness and truth shall be thy shield and buckler.")

particularly those in the Training Centre who were organists in their home towns and villages.

The men of the Royal Netherlands Army, under training at Warley, and their padres made much use of the Chapel, and also of the Church hut which belongs to the Chapel.

In this Church hut Mrs. Lister and her splendid band of helpers ran a Social Club for the men and women stationed at Warley. This work was of inestimable value before the N.A.A.F.I. and welfare services were fully developed, and indeed served a very useful purpose throughout the war years.

During 1944, when the Infantry Training Centre was transferred to Blackpool, the only Regimental link left at Warley was the small Depot party and the Regimental Chaplain. The Chapel, as ever, played its important part in the life of the garrison, now not a training centre, but a community, completely wired in and cut off from the outside world, awaiting D-Day. Many services were held in the Chapel, and very large numbers attended the special Services of Intercession before their departure.

The Regiment owes a very great debt of gratitude to the Reverend G. M. Lister for his care of and interest in the Chapel through those difficult war years, and indeed through all the twelve years since he assumed the Chaplaincy in 1938.

The Post-war Years, 1945–50
The Salamanca Eagle

The first and most important addition to the Chapel after the end of the war was when, on the 29th September, 1947, the Eagle Standard of the 62*ieme* Regiment, captured from the French at the Battle of Salamanca on the 22nd July, 1812, by Lieutenant W. Pearce of the 2/44th Foot and restored to the keeping of the Essex Regiment by command of His Majesty King George VI, was laid up in the Chapel.

On capture the Eagle had been laid up in the Chapel Royal, Whitehall, now the Museum of the Royal United Service Institution. There it remained until 1829, when it was removed, first to the old Armoury in Birdcage Walk, then to Wellington Barracks, and finally, in 1855, to the Royal Hospital, Chelsea. It remained there until its restoration, by the command of His Majesty King George VI, to the Essex Regiment at a ceremonial parade at the Royal Hospital on the 28th September, 1947.

Additional Memorials

The difficulties of the post-war years retarded plans for further memorials and improvements to the Chapel, but nevertheless the following and many individual memorials have been dedicated:

The Essex Home Guard Memorial Window	7th November, 1948	Presented by all ranks of the Essex Home Guard
Brentwood School Memorial Pew and Book Rest	8th May, 1949	Presented by Brentwood School in memory of the Old Boys of Brentwood School who fought and died with the Essex Regiment 1914-18 and 1939-45
Felsted School Memorial Pew	2nd July, 1950	Presented by the Old Felstedian Society in memory of all Old Felstedians who served with the Regiment
The Memorial Bells	2nd July, 1950	This chime of 13 bells, housed in a temporary structure, forms part of the memorial to all ranks of the Essex Regiment who laid down their lives in the Second World War. These bells were subscribed for by the people of Essex and by past and present members of the Regiment
The Font	2nd July, 1950	Presented by the Officers, Warrant Officers, and Sergeants the Royal Fusiliers, to commemorate the many friendships formed during their tour of duty at Warley, 1941-46
Lych-gate	2nd July, 1950	Presented by Colonel Stuart S. Mallinson and Mrs. Mallinson in memory of their son, Major M. S. Mallinson, M.C., and the

men of his company ("C" Company 1/4th Essex) who fell with him on the 21st April, 1944

Thus we find at the end of 1950 the following Colours and major memorials in the Chapel:

- 22 Regimental Colours.
- 9 Unit memorial windows.
- 9 Rolls of Honour.
- 27 Memorial pews.
- 40 Memorial panels.
- 8 County Memorials such as the bells and pulpit.
- 10 Mural tablets.
- 8 Private memorials, together with presentations such as Communion Plate, Altar Frontals, the oak panelling in the Chancel, and the South Door.

This list of memorials and presentations is surely proof that the first part of the original purpose leading to the dedication of the Chapel to the Regiment—that it would assist in forming a closer link between all units of the Regiment—has been fully realised.

Civic Sunday Service

In conclusion, one perhaps cannot do better than to mention the Civic Sunday Service instituted in 1946 and since held annually.

This service, intended to foster still further the good relations between the County and the Regiment, is attended by the Lord-Lieutenant of the county, together with the High Sheriff, the Mayors of all the Boroughs, the Chairman and Members of the Essex County Council, and the Chairmen of all the Urban District and Rural District Councils of the county.

By this service does the Chapel link county and Regiment, and so achieve the second part of the original purpose in seeking the dedication of the Chapel to the Regiment.

Chapter Thirteen

THE ALLIED REGIMENTS FROM THE DOMINION OF CANADA AND THE COMMONWEALTH OF AUSTRALIA

IN 1926, as part of a scheme for the closer linking up of the armed forces of Great Britain and the Dominions, the Esssex Regiment was associated with the Essex Fusiliers, Canadian Militia. This Battalion became constituted in 1927 as the Essex Scottish (Highlanders). A further change made the title the Essex Scottish Regiment of Canada, and it was under this title that the Regiment came to England in July 1940 as part of the 2nd Canadian Division.

In 1927 an alliance was made between the Essex Regiment and the 44th Battalion of Australian Infantry.

The early history of these two Regiments and the notable part they played in the First World War has been told by Mr. John Burrows in his histories of the Essex Regiment.

It remains, therefore, to tell in brief the story of those Regiments in the Second.

Section I

THE 1st BATTALION THE ESSEX SCOTTISH REGIMENT OF CANADA

The Essex Scottish Regiment has a long background of history in the militia of Essex County, Ontario. Its beginnings date back to 1763, and the Essex Militia has participated in the War of 1812, the Rebellion of 1837-38, the Boer War, and the First World War. In 1927 the Regiment became constituted as the Essex Scottish (Highlanders), and adopted its present Highland dress.

On the 3rd September, 1939, the Battalion mobilised for war under Lieutenant-Colonel A. S. Pearson, and trained in Windsor and at Camp Borden, Ontario. As part of the Second Canadian Division, the Battalion proceeded to England in July 1940, where it became at once committed to the defence of the southern coastal areas. When duties permitted, training exercises were conducted to complete the battle training which had been started in Canada.

[1] For this chapter see maps facing pages 218 and 428.

In May 1942 intensive assault training was commenced on the Isle of Wight to prepare the Battalion for inclusion with the force that struck at Dieppe, France. Although the raid was planned for the first week in July, unfavourable weather and tide conditions caused a postponement.

On the 19th August the Essex Scottish, under Lieutenant-Colonel F. K. Jasperson, landed at Dieppe on a most unfavourable stretch of the beach, charged with the task of clearing the main part of the town. Enemy resistance was extremely fierce, and so heavy was their fire that three stubborn attempts to cross the sea wall failed. Everywhere along the coast extremely heavy casualties were suffered by the raiding force. When the eventual withdrawal was ordered, so few landing craft remained undamaged that only 2 officers and 49 other ranks (27 of whom were wounded) returned to England out of the assaulting battalion.

The lessons learned and the experience gained in the planning of the Normandy landings in 1944 were at this grim cost to the Battalion. Bravery during the fighting was unexcelled; the names of Majors J. A. Willis (K/A), Lieutenant J. C. Palms (K/A), and Private James Maier shine with honour.

Rebuilding the unit was a difficult task for those who remained. Training started at once under Lieutenant-Colonel J. H. Mothersill. The names "Spartan," "Dig," "Outburst," "Harlequin," "Frosty," "Push," and "Step" suggest the nature of the training schemes undertaken to train the Battalion, with other units of the Division, in the role of breaking out from a bridge-head. From May 1943 onwards, the Battalion was under the command of Lieutenant-Colonel B. J. S. MacDonald.

In early 1944 the training tempo heightened, and visits from His Majesty King George VI and high-ranking Army officers placed a final emphasis on preparation for battle. Exercise "Kate" at Scunthorpe, Lincolnshire, involving storm-boat practice, was the final stage in training, and back at Denton Camp, in Kent, the Battalion heard the news of three Canadian infantry divisions landing in Normandy on the 6th June. The balance of the month was spent in waiting and in briefings for conduct in battle. On the 30th June, 1944, the Essex Scottish prepared to move to France.

The crossing was uneventful, and on the 5th July the Battalion disembarked at La Valette, France. After a few days, a front-line defensive position was occupied at Eterville, under continuous enemy shelling and air attack. In the days that followed, the Essex Scottish shared in the stern task of the Canadian Army to hold the German Army in the Caen perimeter while the Americans swept around through Brittany in their drive towards Paris.

On the 20th July the Battalion, having been assigned a reserve role with 6th Canadian Infantry Brigade, became involved in the battle of Ifs. The following day, the Battalion area was overrun by enemy tanks and infantry and casualties were very heavy. This fighting at Caen proved to be desperate and costly for all the units. The enemy's stubborn defences and strong reserves survived the shock of the battle but the purpose of keeping his best formations engaged in this sector had been accomplished.

Towards the end of the month, the Battalion, under the command of Lieutenant-Colonel T. S. Jones, sent "D" Company in to attack some high ground near Verrières. The success of this attack resulted in the award of the M.C. to Major T. E. Steele, and did a great deal to restore morale.

On the 7th August, the Essex Scottish participated in the great armoured break-out from the Caen bridge-head. Although Lieutenant-Colonel T. S. Jones was wounded, Major J. W. Burgess took charge of the column and led the way on to the objective, which was completely cleared with great success. This break-out proved to be the climax of the Caen battle, and a few days later, under Lieutenant-Colonel P. W. Bennett, the Battalion set out on the pursuit to Falaise, which was reached after a series of brilliantly conceived moves.

After very little rest the Battalion set out on the drive to the River Seine, pursuing a badly beaten enemy. Near Elbeuf, on the Seine, an enemy stand caused heavy casualties as attacks were sent in to dislodge them from high ground.

The month of September saw the Regiment's return to Dieppe. Its liberation squared accounts for the losses of 1942 and provided an opportunity for a fitting memorial service to those of the Essex Scottish who fell at Dieppe. A few days later, having been directed on Ostend, the unit succeeded in securing the capitulation of the coastal fort at Westende with 316 prisoners. This incident is an important page in the Regiment's history, as the citizens of Westende renamed the street that leads to the fort after the Essex Scottish.

The next move was to a defensive position in the dock area of Antwerp, where during an enemy counter-attack Lieutenant-Colonel Bennett was wounded. Lieutenant-Colonel J. E. C. Pangman joined the unit, and shortly afterwards plans were laid for the Second Division to assist in the clearing of the port of Antwerp.

On the 2nd October, the operation to free the Scheldt Estuary began. The Château and Fort of Merxem fell to the Battalion, and a northward march in the nature of a pursuit carried the attack as far as the defences which guarded the South Beveland Peninsula. Just inside the Holland border "C" Company, under Captain S. B. MacDonald, assisted the South Saskatchewan Regiment, and themselves captured about 150 prisoners.

The Essex Scottish led the attack that resulted in the defeat of the enemy in South Beveland. An armoured drive on the 24th October did not meet with success, but the infantry on foot crossed flooded dyke lands and fought bitterly to secure an intermediate objective. Further fighting in appalling conditions ferreted the enemy from dykes and causeways, and by the end of the month the port of Antwerp was wrested from the enemy's grip.

After a week's rest in Bonheiden, near Antwerp, the Battalion moved to the defence of the Nijmegen salient, where most of the winter was passed in patrolling for information. Christmas was celebrated with a regimental dance at the Winter Garden in Nijmegen, and the performance of Padre Joe Cardy's concert party at the Town Hall in Hook.

For a few days the Battalion formed part of an army mobile reserve south of s'Hertogenbosch, but soon returned to its defensive role in the line.

In February 1945, 21st Army Group began the battle of the Rhine, and the Essex Scottish attacked on the 19th near Louisendorf, Germany, in an armoured drive to cut the Goch-Calcar Road. "B" and "C" Companies got very badly cut up going in, and the remaining troops suffered heavily during enemy armoured counter-attacks that night. Enemy opposition all round was much heavier than expected, but the unit, though suffering extreme losses in men and equipment, held on in reduced strength, enabling the Brigade to secure a complete victory. How Battalion Headquarters, "A" and "D" Companies got cut off and yet managed to beat off numerous attacks reads like an unbelievable story.

The Regiment once again reorganised and re-equipped without rest, and on the 1st March attacked the Hochwald. Here was another relentless enemy stand, and "C" Company, fighting into the edge of the forest that day, made this engagement famous in the history of the

Canadian Army. The inspiration for the attack was that of Major F. A. Tilston, whose conduct and example, though he had been wounded three times, won for him the Empire's highest award—the Victoria Cross.

The order was "Attack again." On the 8th March, the ancient Roman town of Xanten fell after bitter fighting. The Essex Scottish fought into the north-west suburbs and took about 250 prisoners after killing a great number of fanatical paratroops. This attack ended the operation for the Battalion in the clearing of the west bank of the River Rhine. Casualties had been very heavy, and throughout the standard of personal gallantry, as evidenced by the decorations won by individuals, had been the highest.

A period of rest followed in mild weather on the edge of the Reichwald Forest overlooking the River Rhine. Each day training, sports, and recreation restored team spirit and morale. Upon the large-scale crossing of the Rhine, the Essex Scottish moved to the east bank by a bridge at Rees, and commenced a series of moves by which northern Holland was to be cleared. The battle for the Twenthe Canal, a long armoured drive to Nijverdal, the crossing of the Overijsselsch Canal passed by in quick succession.

A major effort, led by "B" Company under Major A. J. Hodges, resulted in the capture of the town of Assen. The pursuit was relentless, and by the 14th April the unit was in the outskirts of Groningen, the largest city in north Holland. Fighting across defended canal lines and subjected to intense small-arms and flack-gun fire, "A" Company rushed a bridge leading into the central part of the city and secured it intact. This tactical success resulted in the subsequent early capitulation of the commander and garrison of the city, and in the award of the D.S.O. to Major D. W. McIntyre.

The next major offensive, after a few days' rest near Groningen, was directed at the city of Oldenburg, Germany. The Essex Scottish formed part of a force protecting the left flank of the British advance on to Bremen. In northern Germany a series of skirmishes with an enemy which sought to impose delays preceded the fall of Oldenburg and on V.E.-Day the Battalion was out of contact with a beaten, retreating foe.

After the cessation of hostilities, the Battalion, under the command of Lieutenant-Colonel K. W. MacIntyre, D.S.O., did a tour of two months' policing duty in Germany between Oldenburg and Wilhelmshaven. During this time the process of reorganisation, demobilisation, and providing volunteers for the Pacific Force, were the paramount objects of concern. Study, rehabilitation, and recreational programmes kept the days full for the majority of the Battalion.

The alliance of the unit entered into in 1926 with the Essex Regiment of the British Army was further strengthened by exchange visits with the 2nd Battalion The Essex Regiment which was in Unna, Germany, doing occupational duty. During one of such visits the Essex Scottish pipe band played for the British Regiment's guard mounting in their town square. The Essex Scottish Regiment was the only unit in the Second Division to engage in such good-will exchange visits.

Early in July operational duties ceased, and the move to friendly Holland was the first stage in the return to Canada. Late in September the Essex Scottish moved to England for final leaves before embarkation for home.

Before embarkation, the Essex Scottish held their farewell parade at Blackdown, near Aldershot. Here, on Thursday, the 18th November, 1945, the Battalion, 500 strong, with drums and pipes and the band of the Essex Regiment on parade, formed up for inspection by Lieutenant-General Sir Geoffrey W. Howard, K.C.B., C.M.G., D.S.O., D.L., the Colonel of the Essex Regiment.

In his address, the Colonel of the Regiment referred to the magnificent record of the Battalion in all the battles in which it had fought. He said how proud the Essex Regiment was to have such a fine Regiment allied to it.

And so the Essex Scottish, their task accomplished with honour and great distinction, returned to Canada, bearing with them the good wishes and friendship of the Essex Regiment.

APPENDIX

SOME STATISTICS—1st BATTALION THE ESSEX SCOTTISH REGIMENT, 1939-45

Casualties
   Killed: 36 officers and 483 other ranks.

Honours
   1 Victoria Cross (Major F. A. Tilson)
   5 D.S.O.s
   5 O.B.E.s
   10 M.B.E.s
   12 M.C.s
   1 B.E.M.
   3 D.C.M.s
   1 Bar to M.M.
   1 Second Bar to M.M.
   15 M.M.
   49 Mentions in dispatches
   13 Foreign decorations

Section II

THE 11/44TH INFANTRY BATTALION (CITY OF PERTH REGIMENT) OF AUSTRALIA

As with the 2/4th Battalion The Essex Regiment, so was the 44th Battalion (West Australian Rifles) denied an active role during the Second World War, and given the unspectacular but nevertheless necessary role of garrison duty and draft finding.

When the Australian Imperial Force (A.I.F.) was formed soon after the outbreak of war in 1939, a large number of officers and other ranks from the 44th Battalion were used to help form the hard core of three expeditionary-force battalions raised in West Australia.

At least some of the 44th Battalion were soon in action in the Middle East in the perilous days of 1941 and 1942, and it was a strange accident of war that brought together officers of the Essex Regiment, the Essex Scottish Regiment (Canada), and the 44th Battalion (West Australian Rifles) as prisoners of war in Oflag 79, Brunswick, Germany.

In February 1945 these officers, still prisoners, prepared a signed message of greeting to the Colonel of the Essex Regiment, the Colonel of the Essex Scottish Regiment, and the Commanding Officer 44th Battalion Australian Military Forces (West Australian Rifles), and among the signatories were Captain R. A. E. Conway, 44th Battalion Australian Infantry, captured at Tobruk on the 3rd August, 1941, and Lieutenant W. T. G. Cloutman, captured at El Alamein on the 27th July, 1942.

Drafting and garrison duties for the 44th Battalion continued for five years. Then, in 1944, it was disbanded, and its members were used as reinforcements for the various A.I.F. battalions.

Under a post-war reorganisation of the Australian Military Forces the 44th Battalion (West Australian Rifles) was reconstituted and designated the 11/44th Infantry Battalion (City of Perth Regiment).

Chapter Fourteen

THE ESSEX HOME GUARD
By Major P. R. Finch, T.D., R.A. (T.A.)

IN most memories the official birth-date of the Home Guard is fixed as the 14th May, 1940, the day on which Mr. Anthony Eden made his famous broadcast announcing the formation of the Local Defence Volunteers and calling for recruits for the new force. But in several parts of Britain—among them our own county of Essex—calls for voluntary defence service had already been sounded, and partly answered.

As early as December 1939, Colonel Stuart S. Mallinson, C.B.E., D.S.O., M.C., D.L., J.P., the future Commander of "J" Sector Home Guard, had written to the Lord-Lieutenant urging the creation of such a force; and his letter, forwarded to the Under-Secretary of State for War, had produced the reply: ". . . I rather think that soon after Christmas there may be a move made. . . ." In the following March the Lord Bishop of Chelmsford, Dr. Henry Wilson, had written upon the same theme in the *Chelmsford Diocesan Chronicle*: "I would like to see a town-guard enrolled, consisting of men from forty to sixty years of age . . . to give unpaid service in guarding buildings . . . and also as a protection against what is by no means an impossibility, the landing by parachute of bodies of German soldiers. . . ."

In the same month a national newspaper reported on "The County of Essex Volunteer Corps"—"this vanguard of Britain's part-time army,"—which was indeed, in spirit even if not in fact, the beginning of the Essex Home Guard. The Corps was formed of men over military age who were prevented for various reasons from joining any of the recognised National Defence Services. Having no uniforms, they paraded in their own clothes and wearing armlets; having no weapons, they used drill-purposes rifles borrowed from local units of the Officers' Training Corps. The Essex Volunteer Army Force, as the Corps was later called, soon enlisted the support of the Lord-Lieutenant, who became its Patron, and the help of the Territorial Association, which gave the Force the use of the South Street Drill Hall, Romford. But before the matter of official recognition could be resolved, the greater national scheme was made public, and the Volunteer Army Force was accordingly absorbed into the L.D.V. Its existence, however, enabled the Lord-Lieutenant, within twenty-four hours of Mr. Eden's broadcast, to report that Essex already had an organised body of men 400 strong.

In the early morning hours of the 15th May, a dispatch-rider from Eastern Region Civil Defence Headquarters at Cambridge brought a letter from the Regional Commissioner, Sir Will Spens, to the Lord-Lieutenant, Colonel Sir Francis H. D. C. Whitmore, K.C.B., C.M.G., D.S.O., asking him, firstly, to put forward (after consultation with leading Territorial Association and British Legion officers) the name of a suitable L.D.V. Commander for Essex; and, secondly, to attend a conference on the L.D.V. at Cambridge later that day.

Within a matter of hours the Essex Commander had been selected. He was Colonel Sir Edward A. Ruggles-Brise, Bt., M.C., T.D., D.L., M.P., an officer whose military and public service had already won him considerable distinction. Together, he and the Lord-Lieutenant went to Cambridge, where they were told that the L.D.V. was " 'a Rural scheme' applying mostly to villages and not to large towns or to places where troops were quartered." The areas commanded by the County Commandants were to conform in each case to the area controlled by the Chief Constable of the County. Similarly, an L.D.V. Company Commander's area was to be that of a Superintendent of Police, and a Platoon Commander's that of a Sergeant or Inspector of Police. Sections were based upon the parishes, and were to vary in strength from upwards of 6 men. The duty of the section was to remain in its parish unless ordered elsewhere by Regular troops, and to attack enemy troops within the parish. Each man was to be given a steel helmet, arms, uniform, and thirty rounds of ammunition.

The conference over, the Lord-Lieutenant and Colonel Ruggles-Brise returned to begin the work of organisation. A list of possible officers had already been prepared at Chelmsford, and to this further names were added, together with the police divisions of the county. Letters were then sent off to all those named, asking each to act as Local Defence Officer for a number of specified villages and to begin enrolling recruits at once. And as the Local Defence officers went to it, Colonel Ruggles-Brise turned to gathering about him the nucleus of a county Headquarters' staff. Brigadier-General C. G. Charlton, C.B., C.M.G., D.S.O., Brigadier-General J. T. Wigan, C.B., C.M.G., D.S.O., T.D., D.L., Colonel R. C. O. Parker, O.B.E., T.D., D.L., Lieutenant-Colonel K. E. Jameson, D.S.O., D.L., Lieutenant-Colonel A. Sinclair-Thomson, D.S.O., D.L., Major G. V. L. Prowse, D.L.,

Captain (later Lieutenant-Colonel) G. Wells Jennings, and Captain (later Major) G. V. N. Ridley were among the first to be given Headquarters' appointments. Meanwhile, the Essex L.D.V., with its companion organisations in Hertford and Suffolk, had been placed under the command of General Sir Charles Deedes, K.C.B., C.B., C.M.G., D.S.O.

No matter that authority had ruled the L.D.V. to be a "rural scheme," in town and village alike there was enthusiasm for the new force. Volunteers had started giving in their names at local police-stations even before Mr. Eden had finished speaking on that evening of the 14th May, 1940. And what variety of experience there was in the material! In the Braintree area, for example, the call brought forth old gunners, infantrymen, and cavalrymen; men who had seen service in the Royal Navy and the Royal Flying Corps; men who had served with the Engineers, the Service Corps, or the Medical Corps. This was the pattern all over the land. Few worried because arms and ammunition were as yet little more than promises; the will to win through was just as strong with cudgels and borrowed shotguns.

Some volunteers turned to more subtle weapons. One, a former battery sergeant-major of the Royal Horse Artillery and a publican, put a very heavy chain and padlock on one of the handles of his beer-machine. "This is one way of carrying out your orders, sir," he explained to his officer. "You said that we were to use every possible method to destroy these adjective Germans, so this is a special thirty-six-gallon cask for them if they should come. The ——s are sure to be hot and thirsty when they get here. I shall have to leave my little old pub, and they'll have a free hand. That cask contains stuff that looks like beer, smells like beer, and very possibly tastes like beer, but is actually the best arsenical weed-killer I could buy. If two hundred of the ——s drink it, that will be two hundred less we shall have to destroy."

In those early days there was so little for detachments in the way of arms and equipment that when the Zone Headquarters' accounting system was begun, all that was needed was a small, ten-columned notebook which Colonel R. C. O. Parker himself purchased at a Chelmsford stationer's. When weapons and stores did arrive, "it was merely a matter of throwing stuff into lorries and getting it out." "It" was received eagerly enough, cleaned and distributed, and explo red and practised with, sometimes in the strangest of training places. Picture the Debden Green volunteers at drill and musketry in a disused slaughterhouse; those of Debden in a windmill; those of Hadstock in a chapel decorated with pious texts and exhortations. No one then foresaw that the small trickle of rifles would become, over the years, a flood of arms of all kinds in abundance, or that Colonel Parker's small notebook would eventually be supplemented by a desk-top-size ledger listing over 500 different types of equipment. In the beginning it was a matter of rifles, denim uniforms, and—for the lucky few—L.D.V. armbands and five rounds of small-arms ammunition. Add to this some forage caps, and you have the dress and equipment of the first L.D.V. patrol ever to operate. Numbering 10 volunteers, it was sent out from Wickford by Colonel H. W. Burton, O.B.E., M.P., the Local Defence Officer, and its uneventful, but exhausting, exploit was recorded by Press photographers and news-reel cameramen.

On the 12th July, 1940, Zone Headquarters published its first Part II Order, which divided the Essex Zone L.D.V. into the following battalions:

No. 1 Battalion Essex L.D.V.

Commanding Officer: Colonel H. W. Burton, O.B.E., M.P.

Companies at Canvey Island, Southend-on-Sea, Rochford, Rayleigh, and Wickford.

No. 2 Battalion Essex L.D.V.

Commanding Officer: Colonel Sir F. Carne Rasch, Bt., D.L., A.D.C.

Companies at Maldon and Danbury.

No. 3 Battalion Essex L.D.V.

Commanding Officer: Brigadier-General J. T. Wigan, C.B., C.M.G., D.S.O., T.D., D.L.

Companies at Pitsea, Stanford-le-Hope, Tilbury, Grays, and Purfleet.

No. 4 Battalion Essex L.D.V.

Commanding Officer: Sir Charles Bressey, C.B., C.B.E.

Companies at Romford.

No. 5 Battalion Essex L.D.V.

Commanding Officer: Brigadier-General C. H. de Rougemont, C.B., C.M.G., D.S.O., M.V.O., D.L.

Companies at Laindon, Billericay, Brentwood, Ingatestone, and Stapleford Abbotts.

No. 6 Battalion Essex L.D.V.
Commanding Officer: Lieutenant-Colonel K. E. Jameson, D.S.O., D.L.
Companies at Chelmsford.

No. 7 Battalion Essex L.D.V.
Commanding Officer: Lieutenant-Colonel A. M. Turner, D.S.O., D.L.
Companies at Boreham, Witham, Kelvedon, and Copford.

No. 8 Battalion Essex L.D.V.
Commanding Officer: Major-General C. Kirkpatrick, C.B., C.B.E.
Companies at Colchester, Boxted, Halstead, and Yeldham.

No. 9 Battalion Essex L.D.V.
Commanding Officer: Major Wyndham Birch, D.S.O., M.B.E.
Companies at Brightlingsea, Thorpe-le-Soken, Clacton, Walton, and Mistley.

No. 10 Battalion Essex L.D.V.
Commanding Officer: Lieutenant-Colonel C. M. Davies, D.S.O.
Companies at Ongar, Epping, Harlow.

No. 11 Battalion Essex L.D.V.
Commanding Officer: Major G. G. Gold, T.D., D.L.
Companies at Waltham, Braintree, and Easter.

No. 12 Battalion Essex L.D.V.
Commanding Officer: Brigadier-General C. G. Charlton, C.B., C.M.G., D.S.O.
Companies at Dunmow, Saffron Walden, Stanstead, and Newport.

In addition, there were two independent companies: one formed from employees of the Essex Rivers Catchment Board, and the other from employees of the County of London Electric Supply Company. The whole was divided into Western and Eastern Groups. The Bishop of Chelmsford was appointed Honorary Chaplain to the County Zone and the Lord-Lieutenant became its Honorary Commander.

Notice that the County Zone did not include metropolitan Essex, which fell within the London Area and was divided into "J" and "K" Zones, the former embracing Waltham Abbey, Buckhurst Hill, Loughton, Chigwell, Chingford, and other places in that vicinity: and the latter, Barking, Dagenham, Becontree, Goodmayes, and Chadwell Heath. On the 10th July both zones were adopted by the Essex Territorial Association: adopted is the word, because until then they had been orphans in the world of administration. However, this was a temporary and unsatisfactory solution; for while administered by Essex, the zones remained under London District for operations, and had perforce to serve two masters. So it was to London District that both zones shortly after went. When, on the 3rd August, all Home Guard battalions (as the L.D.V. units had then become) were affiliated to their County Regiments and given permission to put up the badges of those regiments, the county association was preserved in "J" Zone, where Colonel Mallinson insisted that his Essex units were affiliated to the Essex Regiment. In "K" Zone no effort was made to link the units with the county, and the Essex battalions went with the rest in affiliation to the Royal Fusiliers.

Before this happened, there fell to "J" Zone the signal honour of receiving a visit from H.M. the King. This notable event took place on the 20th July, when His Majesty, accompanied by a large number of distinguished officers and personages, inspected units of the Zone, and took the salute from more than 2,000 denim-clad Defence Volunteers.

Space permits only the briefest reference to the growth of the Essex Home Guard battalions. Grow they did, particularly after the introduction of compulsory service in 1942; and even before this time, new general service and specialist units were thrown off by the original battalions. In the Essex County Zone, commanded by Colonel Ruggles-Brise, the Post Office Home Guard units were formed into the 13th Essex Battalion by August 1940; two months later the 14th was formed from the Grays and Purfleet companies of the 3rd; in the following June the Halstead and Yeldham Companies of the 8th went to form the 15th Essex Battalion; in September 1942, the Southend company of the 1st Battalion became the 16th Essex Battalion; about the same time, the 17th was formed from the southern companies of the 9th, and the 18th from the Copford and Kelvedon companies of the 7th; in November, the Grays companies of the 14th Battalion were reorganised into the 19th; and in June 1943, the 20th and last general-service battalion of the Essex Home Guard was formed from the Hornchurch, Upminster, Emerson Park, and Rainham Road Companies of the 4th Battalion. And in "J" Zone there were eventually six Essex Battalions, the 51st, 52nd, 53rd, 54th, and

56th, the last being formed, in March 1942, from a Company of the 54th Battalion. To these twenty-six Battalions must be added the specialist Home Guard units formed within the county—Coastal Defence Artillery, Heavy and Light Anti-aircraft Artillery, the Rocket Batteries, and the Home Guard M.T. Column—and also those Battalions that were Essex by location but Fusilier (and so London) by affiliation.

Each of these Home Guard units has a story within its own right, but it must suffice to mention only some of the features by which they will be best remembered and which made each just that much different from its neighbours. In the 2nd Battalion, for example, there was the "Crouch patrol," a Home Guard force manning nine commandeered craft and operating on the lower reaches of the River Crouch. And for a time there was a similar patrol of the 9th Battalion on Hamford Water, with headquarters at the Walton Yacht Club. From the 6th Battalion came the Home Guard Camouflage and Deception School. The 10th was justly proud of its Musketry School and range, and the 16th had its armoured train, the *Terror*. The 4th Battalion had its own Officer Cadet Training Unit, and "J" Sector, a School of Arms dating from L.D.V. days and probably the first of its kind in the country.

As the Home Guard expanded, so more and better weapons came along—rifles and ammunition in plenty, grenades of many types, sub-machine carbines, Browning automatics, Northover projectors, and Smith guns. Training, which in the beginning had been elementary in the extreme, naturally became more and more ambitious. There were demonstrations, courses of instruction at Warley, Dunmow, Colchester and other centres, Home Guard schools and camps, field-firing ranges, battle inoculation, and assault courses. From 1941 onwards, as many as 600 Home Guards would be under canvas in the "J" Zone camp at Chigwell Row over a summer week-end. And about the same time the most notable of the Essex Zone camps began its career at Weald Park, staffed in the main with instructors from the Warley Depot. Weald Park is particularly associated with two officers—Major P. L. M. Battye, M.C., of the Welsh Guards, its first Chief Instructor and Commandant, and Major Cyril Edwards, D.S.O., M.C., T.D., J.P., of the Essex Regiment, who was Major Battye's successor. Weald Park was the first large camp in the Essex Zone where Home Guards practised with live ammunition, and in its heyday it accommodated a 1,000 men and more at a time. Two other popular and older training centres were Tollesbury and Bradwell, where in November 1940 Brigadier H. G. Seth-Smith, D.S.O., had built field-firing ranges.

In the beginning the Home Guard had a fourfold role—to observe enemy landings; swiftly to pass information of those landings; to deny movement to the enemy; and to safeguard important points against surprise attack. Road-blocks had risen everywhere; in the County Zone alone there were nearly 400 for which the Home Guard was responsible. Then came pill-boxes, and then a whole series of fashions in defence—village defence schemes, "defended localities," "nodal points" and "keeps," and battle and garrison platoons. At times it seemed that as fast as one defence scheme was devised, another took its place; and some Home Guards were tempted to believe that the life of a defence scheme was precisely that of the tenure of appointment of the Regular Army commander in the neighbourhood. Particularly varied at one time was official ruling on whether the Home Guard should have a static or a mobile role. Lieutenant-Colonel J. O. Parker tells of Brigadier J. A. A. Griffin, D.S.O., Commander of East Essex Sub-District, who "cheered us all by reading out a poem:

"HOME GUARD TRAINING

"*The Brigadier we had last spring*
Said, 'Static roles are not the thing;
As mobile as the midnight flea,
Is what the Home Guard ought to be.

"*Accordingly our schemes were set—*
To make the Home Guard thirstier yet;
And all agreed that Brigadier
Must have some interest in beer.

"*He went; another came instead,*
Who deemed mobility quite dead,
And thought the Home Guard, on the whole,
Far safer in a static role.

"*We did not mind. Our Home Guard 'hut'*
Is sited well for 'staying put.'
We'll see that in our battle keep
There's no impediment to sleep.

*"Besides, some fresh and fertile brain
Is bound to change it all again,
And perch us, possibly, up trees—
Like monkeys and the Japanese.*

*"No doubt some high strategic plan
Beyond the ken of common man
Dictates these changes in our job
From 'mob' to 'stat' and 'stat' to 'mob.'*

*"Still, it would help us all to know
More positively where to go,
In case, when Boches do appear,
We cannot find a Brigadier."*

Change of role was the hall-mark of steady progression from a rough-hewn *franc-tireur* force to a powerful, if fantastic, citizen army. Not only were there changes of this kind; there were also changes in administration and command. The County Zone, which was led almost until his death, in May 1942, by Colonel Ruggles-Brise and subsequently commanded by Brigadier-General Charlton, was decentralised in July 1942. The battalions of the Zone were then formed into four administrative groups, while remaining under the appropriate Regular commanders for operations. Then, in the summer of 1943, Home Guard Sectors with a definite operational function took the place of Groups as the stage was set for Operation "Overlord."

For the Essex Home Guard, the operation was "Overlord Defence," involving the protection, in conjunction with Regular troops, of the embarkation ports; defence of the Sea Raid zone; patrols and picquets for the marshalling areas; coast-watching; guarding vulnerable points; and giving assistance, as the Home Guard already had done in no small measure, to the Civil Defence Services. In Essex, the main area of activity was Marshalling Area "S," of which the focal point was Tilbury, and hereabouts more than ninety-seven posts were manned by the Home Guard. There was no mustering of the Home Guard to carry out this vital commitment; but many did more than their full share of night duty—and their civilian work as well. Some found themselves guarding road junctions or railway bridges, or standing-by at certain headquarters and localities; others did duty at outlandish places on the coast whose very names suggested desolation. Some posts were manned by night, and others the day round; some were manned throughout by Essex men, and others were handed over for short periods to men from inland or neighbouring counties—from Suffolk, Northampton, Hertford, Buckingham, Bedford, and Huntingdon. From Marshalling Area "S" along the entire Essex coast, Home Guards were on the watch. In the Marshalling Area itself, the 3rd Battalion alone had "to find 840 men weekly to guard posts at Vange, Stanford, Orsett, Mucking Ford, East Tilbury, and Tilbury." Nearby, the 16th Battalion was furnishing 7 officers and 113 other ranks every night for picquet duty or coast-watching at Landwick Cottages, Belfairs, Fisherman's Head, Asplins Head, Havengore Bridge, Wakering Stairs, and Shoeburyness Point. The 1st, 2nd, and 10th Battalions shared posts on the Dengie Peninsula, taking fresh problems of administration and supply in their stride; and still farther north the 8th, 9th, 17th, and 18th Battalions stood guard along the coast and round the port of Harwich, the defence of which they shared with the Royal Netherlands Brigade. Nor were the womenfolk idle: Home Guard Auxiliaries gladly undertook canteen and messing duties more arduous than ever before, and manned headquarters' switchboards.

In most parts of the county "Overlord" duties began on the 29th April, 1944, although in a few instances communications were fully manned by Home Guards and Auxiliaries before this date. As success was granted to the Normandy landings, so the burden on the Home Guard was eased, and on the 3rd September the few remaining guards and picquets were stood down. The Home Guard had been ready for such attempts as the enemy might have made to wreck the smooth machinery that was to convey the armies of liberation to imprisoned Europe. That no attacks were made was, perhaps, the greatest tribute of all to the quality and character of the citizen army.

With victory assured, there was little left for the Home Guard. On the 11th September, 1944, compulsion was ended; on the 1st November, *Fallow*, the code word for "stand down," was received; and on the 19th of the same month, some 900 Home Guards, representing all the Essex units, attended a Service of Commemoration at Chelmsford Cathedral. Throughout the county, battalions now arranged their own Stand Down ceremonies, many of these being held on Sunday, the 3rd December, when representatives of wellnigh every Home Guard unit in the country paraded in London before H.M. the King.

Stand Down—and then, in December 1945, Disbandment. But for the Essex Home Guard that did not mean oblivion. A rightful memorial of their courage and devotion may be seen in the Chapel of the Essex Regiment at Warley, where a stained-glass window commemorates "the services of 115,000 men and women of Essex who served in the Home Guard 1940-45 in defence of Great Britain and for the preservation of liberty and freedom."

That the memorial should take this form was the suggestion of Colonel Stuart S. Mallinson, and widespread approval of his idea was reflected in the instant response by Home Guards of "J" Sector and the former Essex Zone when subscriptions were sought, and in the attendance of nearly 500 Home Guards at the Service of Dedication on the 7th November, 1948.

The lights forming the window show "St. Roger and St. Ethelburga, both connected with Essex. St. Ethelburga, the first Abbess appointed to the Abbey of Barking, was chosen as a tribute to the great services of the womenfolk of the county.... St. Roger (Roger Niger de Bileye (Beeleigh)) was Archdeacon of Colchester and later Bishop of London. He is represented as a bishop, and holds a model of old St. Paul's Cathedral, the choir of which he rebuilt. In the pillars of ornament are (left) the arms of the See of London and (right) the arms of Beeleigh." Below are named the twenty Battalions of the County of Essex Home Guard and the six Essex Battalions of "J" Sector, London District Home Guard. Across the window runs a paraphrase of the seventh verse of the thirty-eighth chapter of the Book of the Prophet Ezekiel: "Be thou prepared and be thou a guard unto them."

★   ★   ★   ★   ★   ★

These were the Battalions of the Essex Home Guard, their headquarters and their Commanding Officers:

Crouch Sector: Colonel R. C. O. Parker, O.B.E., T.D., D.L.

1st Battalion Essex Home Guard
Headquarters: Wickford.
Commanding Officers: Colonel H. W. Burton, O.B.E., M.P.
　　　　　　　　　　Lieutenant-Colonel S. Mapleson.
　　　　　　　　　　Lieutenant-Colonel H. Langdon Dowsett.

2nd Battalion Essex Home Guard
Headquarters: Maldon.
Commanding Officers: Colonel Sir F. Carne Rasch, Bt., D.L., A.D.C.
　　　　　　　　　　Lieutenant-Colonel B. H. Bright, M.C.

16th Battalion Essex Home Guard
Headquarters: Southend-on-Sea.
Commanding Officer: Lieutenant-Colonel J. Dalton White, T.D.
Estuary Sector: Colonel E. A. W. Lake, C.B.E.

3rd Battalion Essex Home Guard
Headquarters: Stanford-le-Hope.
Commanding Officers: Lieutenant-Colonel R. Neave.
Lieutenant-Colonel F. Hughes, M.C.

14th Battalion Essex Home Guard
Headquarters: Fondu Works, West Thurrock.
Commanding Officers: Lieutenant-Colonel A. V. Hussey, O.B.E.
Lieutenant-Colonel H. Ashton, M.C., D.L.

19th Battalion Essex Home Guard
Headquarters: Grays.
Commanding Officer: Lieutenant-Colonel W. R. McLaughlin, O.B.E.
Colchester Sector: Brigadier H. G. Seth Smith, D.S.O.

8th Battalion Essex Home Guard
Headquarters: Colchester.
Commanding Officers: Major-General C. Kirkpatrick, C.B., C.B.E.
Lieutenant-Colonel A. J. R. Waller, D.L., J.P.

9th Battalion Essex Home Guard
Headquarters: Weeley, then Mistley.
Commanding Officers: Lieutenant-Colonel Wyndham Birch, D.S.O., M.B.E., D.L.
Lieutenant-Colonel J. W. Boardman.
Lieutenant-Colonel G. Blewitt, D.S.O., M.C.

17th Battalion Essex Home Guard
Headquarters: Colchester.
Commanding Officer: Lieutenant-Colonel J. O. Parker, T.D., D.L.

18th Battalion Essex Home Guard
Headquarters: Blackheath.
Commanding Officer: Lieutenant-Colonel C. G. Mangles, M.C.
Dunmow Sector: Colonel J. Cooper Bland, M.C.

7th Battalion Essex Home Guard
Headquarters: Witham.
Commanding Officers: Lieutenant-Colonel A. M. Turner, D.S.O., D.L.
Lieutenant-Colonel R. W. Macdonald, C.I.E., D.S.O.

11th Battalion Essex Home Guard
Headquarters: Shalford, then Braintree.
Commanding Officers: Lieutenant-Colonel G. C. Gold, T.D., D.L.
Lieutenant-Colonel J. Cooper Bland, M.C.
Lieutenant-Colonel K. S. Richardson.

12th Battalion Essex Home Guard
Headquarters: Stansted.
Commanding Officers: Brigadier-General C. G. Charlton, C.B., C.M.G., D.S.O.
Brigadier W. H. Anderson, C.B.E.
Lieutenant-Colonel T. Slingsby, M.C.

15th Battalion Essex Home Guard
Headquarters: Halstead.
Commanding Officers: Lieutenant-Colonel F. Colvin Watson, O.B.E., M.C., D.L.
Lieutenant-Colonel D. B. Rose.
Ongar Sector: Colonel C. M. Davies, D.S.O.

5th Battalion Essex Home Guard
Headquarters: Brentwood.
Commanding Officers: Brigadier C. H. de Rougemont, C.B., C.M.G., D.S.O., M.V.O., D.L.
Colonel H. R. Bowen, D.S.O., D.L.
Lieutenant-Colonel C. S. Duffus, O.B.E., M.C.

6th Battalion Essex Home Guard
Headquarters: Chelmsford.
Commanding Officers: Lieutenant-Colonel E. A. W. Lake, C.B.E.
Lieutenant-Colonel W. C. Neild, M.C.

10th Battalion Essex Home Guard
Headquarters: Harlow.
Commanding Officers: Lieutenant-Colonel C. M. Davies, D.S.O.
Lieutenant-Colonel C. H. Gould.
Romford Sector: Colonel P. C. Henderson, O.B.E., J.P.
4th Battalion Essex Home Guard
Headquarters: Romford.
Commanding Officers: Sir Charles Bressey, C.B., C.B.E.
Lieutenant-Colonel P. C. Henderson, O.B.E., J.P.
Lieutenant-Colonel H. B. Pett, M.C.
Lieutenant-Colonel M. R. W. E. Mount.
Lieutenant-Colonel F. Graham.
20th Battalion Essex Home Guard
Headquarters: Hornchurch.
Commanding Officer: Lieutenant-Colonel A. W. Durrant, D.S.O.

13th Essex (35th G.P.O.) Battalion Home Guard. Specialist Unit
Headquarters: Colchester.
Commanding Officers: Lieutenant-Colonel A. W. Gaze, M.C.
Lieutenant-Colonel R. N. Hamilton.
Lieutenant-Colonel T. Bagley.
"*J*" *Sector Home Guard:* Colonel Stuart S. Mallinson, C.B.E., D.S.O., M.C., D.L., J.P.
51st Battalion Essex Home Guard
Headquarters: Chingford.
Commanding Officer: Lieutenant-Colonel S. Pickis, M.M.
52nd Battalion Essex Home Guard
Headquarters: Chigwell.
Commanding Officers: Captain Hedges, M.C.
Lieutenant-Colonel C. Gresham Chappell, J.P.
53rd Battalion Essex Home Guard
Headquarters: Wood Green.
Commanding Officers: Lieutenant-Colonel S. Shaverin, M.B.E.
Lieutenant-Colonel I. V. Coote, D.L., J.P.
Lieutenant-Colonel H. A. Linfoot, D.S.O., M.C.

54th Battalion Essex Home Guard
Headquarters: South Woodford.
Commanding Officer: Lieutenant-Colonel V. D. Walker, D.S.O., M.M.

55th Battalion Essex Home Guard
Headquarters: Walthamstow.
Commanding Officer: Lieutenant-Colonel C. S. Harrison.

56th Battalion Essex Home Guard
Headquarters: Waltham Abbey.
Commanding Officers: Lieutenant-Colonel H. F. Kidd, M.B.E.
Lieutenant-Colonel Mansfield Dyson.

Chapter Fifteen

THE ESSEX REGIMENT, 1945-50

EARLIER chapters have attempted to bring the long history of the Essex Regiment forward another short span of years. They have tried to tell the story of the Regiment up to the eve of the Second World War and to chronicle with impartiality the fortunes of units, present and past, during that war.

They have sought to show happenings in the years immediately following the cessation of hostilities until, their tasks honourably accomplished, the Battalions came home, the First from India, the Second from Italy, the Fourth from Greece, and the Fifth from Germany to await whatever fate should have in store.

It remains to continue the story of the Battalions that are still in being, for many have gone, and the Regiment is now tragically reduced.

The Essex Regiment, which in the First World War maintained thirty-one battalions and a peak of twelve in the Second, at the close of 1950 had been reduced to two active battalions.

Yet the supreme importance of first-class infantry has not been disproved, and in the present era of disturbed international relations the reduction of infantry and the denigration of the regimental spirit is a matter for profound regret and disquiet.

But before dealing with the units of the Regiment that still remain, it is perhaps suitable here to include some account of happenings since the war which affect the Regiment as a whole, the amalgamation of the Regular battalions, changes in the colonelcy of the Regiment, the Freedom of the county towns and boroughs, and the return to the Regiment of the Salamanca Eagle.

Section I

THE REGIMENT, 1945-50

On the 14th December, 1946, Lieutenant-General Sir Geoffrey W. Howard, K.C.B., C.M.G., D.S.O., D.L., retired from the appointment of Colonel of the Essex Regiment, a position he had held for twelve years.

All ranks took this retirement as a personal loss, for his wholehearted interest in his Regiment, his vigorous personality, and long military experience had been of the greatest value in keeping to the fore the best interest of the Regiment.

The Regiment had been doubly fortunate that Lieutenant-General Howard's colonelcy had covered the war years. Perhaps only one who has been concerned in the editing of the regimental history, and who has had access to the many personal letters that passed between the Colonel of the Regiment and commanding officers can know to the full the intimate relationship built up by General Howard and the trust placed in him by all commanding officers, whether old Essex officers or newcomers from other regiments temporarily in command of an Essex battalion.

No trouble was so great when shared with the Colonel of the Regiment. Thus throughout the war years we see commanding officers turning to him for advice and help, whether it was the 5th Battalion on the eve of battle in Italy wishing to safeguard battalion funds, or the 1st Battalion from the jungles of Assam and Burma praying for a draft of officers trained by and belonging to the Regiment.

The place vacated by Lieutenant-General Sir Geoffrey Howard was taken by Brigadier G. H. Wilmer, D.S.O., M.C., and the Regiment was fortunate to have his great experience to help solve the many perplexities that arose in the years of reorganisation and reconstruction that followed the end of the war.

But the Regiment was not to have Brigadier Wilmer as its Colonel for long, as he vacated the appointment at his own request early in 1950. His place was taken by Brigadier C. M. Paton, C.V.O., C.B.E.

The Restoration of the Salamanca Eagle

The Eagle of the 62nd French Regiment, captured at Salamanca in 1812 by Lieutenant Pearce of the 2/44th Regiment, had been first laid up at the Chapel Royal, Whitehall, now the Museum of the Royal United Service Institution. There it remained until 1829, when removed first to the old Armoury in Birdcage Walk, then to the newbuilt Wellington Barracks, and finally, in 1835, to the Royal Hospital, where William IV directed it should "remain as a memorial of the Valour and Discipline of His Majesty's Land Forces."

It so remained until Sunday the 28th September, 1947, when the Eagle, together with trophies claimed by other regiments, was handed over at a ceremonial parade in the grounds of the Royal Hospital, held by Command of the King, to mark the symbolic importance of the transfer of the trophies to the Regiments into whose keeping they were now entrusted.

At the parade the Eagle was handed by Pensioner J. Sitton to the Governor of the Royal Hospital, General Sir Clive Liddell, and accepted from him by Lieutenant-General Sir Geoffrey Howard, representing the Essex Regiment.

Lieutenant-General Sir Geoffrey Howard gave the Eagle to the Essex Regimental Party, commanded by Major J. M. Woodhouse, which then marched off to the tune of the Regimental March played by the band of the Scots Guards.

The next day, Monday the 29th September, 1947, the Salamanca Eagle was laid-up in the Regimental Chapel, Warley, at a most inspiring special service. Before the service the parade under command of Lieutenant-Colonel S. C. W. W. Rea, O.B.E., was inspected by Colonel Sir Francis Whitmore, Lord-Lieutenant of Essex, who was accompanied by Lieutenant-General Sir Geoffrey Howard and by Brigadier G. H. Wilmer, the Colonel of the Regiment. The whole ceremony, whether at the Royal Hospital, Chelsea, or at Warley, was most impressive and worthy of the occasion.

It was fitting that Lieutenant-General Sir Geoffrey Howard received the Eagle on behalf of the Regiment, for it was entirely owing to his personal efforts that this coveted trophy was at last returned to the Regiment for safe keeping.

Section II

THE SIX FREEDOMS

On Saturday, the 25th May, 1946, the Colours of the Regular and Territorial Battalions, the 1st, 2nd, 4th, and 5th Battalions The Essex Regiment, were on parade together for the first time in the history of the Regiment. With them were the Colours of the 6th and 7th Battalions, with escorts, both these old battalions, now units of the Royal Artillery, having retained the right to carry Colours on prescribed occasions. In addition, the Salamanca Eagle was paraded with a suitable escort. This event was, of course, before the official return of the Eagle to the Regiment, and the Standard was on loan for the parade from the Royal Hospital, Chelsea.

Special arrangements had had to be made, for the Colours of the 1st Battalion had to be flown back from Egypt, where they had been deposited on the outbreak of war, while those of the 2nd and 5th Battalions had to be escorted home from Germany, both Battalions at the time forming part of the British Army of the Rhine. The 4th Battalion was serving in Greece, and their Colours, too, had to be specially conveyed home.

The Freedom of the County Borough of Southend-on-Sea

The ceremonial occasion that caused this historic gathering of the Colours was the equally historic occasion when Southend became the first Borough in the county to confer upon the Essex Regiment, "proud of the unsurpassed record and glorious tradition created by your most distinguished Regiment . . . the privilege, honour, and distinction of marching through our said Borough on all ceremonial occasions with bayonets fixed, drums beating, and colours flying."

Starting with a Drumhead Service in Chalkwell Park, conducted by the Archdeacon of Southend and the Reverend G. M. Lister, M.C., M.A., C.F., Chaplain to the Essex Regiment Chapel, and attended by the Mayor (Alderman S. F. Johnson, J.P.) and Corporation and a large gathering of civil and military dignitaries, the representative detachment of the Regiment, commanded by Lieutenant-Colonel T. E. Hearn, then marched through the town to Clifftown Parade. There was read the text of the scroll giving the Council's resolution to confer the "Honour of the Freedom" upon the Regiment, the scroll afterwards being presented to Lieutenant-General Sir Geoffrey W. Howard.

On the conclusion of the ceremony, the Regiment then marched with Colours flying, drums beating, and bayonets fixed through the centre of the town, afterwards being most hospitably entertained by the Borough. A keepsake of a new two-shilling piece was given by the Mayor to every officer and man on the parade, in addition to admirable entertainment.

The memorable occasion was made even more distinguished for the Regiment by the presence of General Sir Ian Hamilton who, at ninety-three years of age, had made the journey especially to attend. Sir Ian Hamilton commanded the Mediterranean Expeditionary Force employed in 1915 to force the Dardanelles, and of which the 1st Essex, in the immortal 29th Division, formed part.

The Freedom of Chelmsford

"That the Borough of Chelmsford, being the County Town of Essex, in recognition of the distinguished services of the Essex Regiment on the field of battle, and also as a token of appreciation and remembrance of all the Essex men and women who have served and are still serving in all Arms of His Majesty's Forces, do hereby confer upon the Essex Regiment the Freedom of Entry into the Borough and the privilege of marching through the streets of Chelmsford with bayonets fixed, drums beating, and colours flying on all lawful occasions without let or hindrance."

It was to receive this honour that a detachment of the Regiment, under command of Lieutenant-Colonel T. E. Hearn, paraded in the stadium of the Chelmsford City Football Club on Monday, the 27th May, 1946.

The scroll, surmounted by the different arms of the county of Essex and the Borough, with the badge of the Regiment and the list of battle honours, was presented with appropriate ceremony by the Mayor to the Colonel of the Regiment, after which the detachment, headed by band and drums, marched through the town and up the High Street to salute the Mayor of Chelmsford outside the Shire Hall.

At the saluting base with the Mayor stood Lieutenant-General Sir Geoffrey W. Howard, Colonel of the Regiment; Lieutenant-General Sir Oliver Leese, the G.O.C.-in-C. Eastern Command, and Major-General Anderson, Deputy Commander of Operations, United States Air Forces in Europe, who earlier in the day had been made a Freeman of the Borough of Chelmsford in commemoration of his period as Commanding General of the Eighth Bomber Command in Essex during the Second World War.

At the conclusion of the parade the Regiment was entertained in traditional style by the Borough of Chelmsford.

The Freedom of Colchester

"To Lieutenant-General Sir Geoffrey W. Howard, K.C.B., C.M.G., D.S.O., D.L., Colonel, the Officers, Non-commissioned Officers, and Men of the Essex Regiment.

"We, the Mayor, Aldermen, and Burgesses of the Borough of Colchester in the County of Essex, acting by the Council, appreciating the famous record and glorious traditions of your most distinguished Regiment over many years of loyal and devoted service to our beloved

King and Country, and being desirous of fastening the mutual attachment which is now and has for long been enjoyed between our Borough and the Essex Regiment, in which Regiment so many of our men of Colchester have been proud to serve or are continuing to serve, and being desirous also of recognising the gallantry and achievement of the Regiment since its formation and especially in the war of 1939–1945 DO HEREBY CONFER upon the *Essex Regiment* the privilege, honour, and distinction of marching through the streets of Colchester on all ceremonial occasions with bayonets fixed, colours flying, drums beating, and bands playing. IN WITNESS whereof, we have caused our Corporate Common Seal to be hereunto affixed this 30th day of May 1946."

That very day a detachment some 400 strong and representative of all Battalions of the Regiment, and under the command of Lieutenant-Colonel T. E. Hearn, paraded outside the Town Hall, Colchester. Here it was inspected by the Mayor, who was accompanied by the Colonel of the Regiment and the Honorary Colonels of the Territorial Battalions.

In his speech the Mayor asked the Regiment's acceptance of the highest honour the town could bestow upon the Regiment, a token of their gratitude and high regard, and referred to the long and inspiring record of battle honours and to the great traditions and great gallantry of the Regiment.

The detachment, exercising its newly granted privilege, then marched with bayonets fixed and Colours flying through the town, headed by the band and the silver drums of the 2nd Battalion, being afterwards admirably entertained by the Borough.

The Freedom of the County Borough of East Ham

Then, on the 20th August, 1946, another Freedom was granted to the Regiment, that of the Borough of East Ham. Once more Lieutenant-Colonel T. E. Hearn led a representative detachment, this time to Plashet Park, East Ham.

There, with impressive ceremony, was read: "That the Council of the County Borough of East Ham, in recognition of the gallant and distinguished services of the Officers and Men of the Essex Regiment in the Service of their Country, and in particular throughout the Second World War, and in special appreciation and remembrance of all Essex men and women who served in all Arms of His Majesty's Forces, do confer in perpetuity upon the Essex Regiment the privilege, honour, and distinction of marching through the streets of East Ham on all ceremonial occasions with bayonets fixed, colours flying, drums beating, and bands playing."

The scroll was presented to Lieutenant-General Sir Geoffrey Howard, who accepted it on behalf of the Regiment for which as Colonel he had done so much. It was almost the last ceremony in a most distinguished colonelcy.

The detachment then gave a General Salute to the Borough of East Ham, and marched away through the Borough in traditional style, Colours flying, bayonets fixed, drums beating, and bands playing. The ceremony terminated with the entertainment of the Regiment by the County Borough.

The Freedom of Ilford

The fifth Freedom was that of the Borough of Ilford, which was granted to the Regiment on the 14th June, 1947. It was accepted on behalf of the Regiment by Brigadier G. H. Wilmer, the Colonel of the Regiment.

As was very appropriate, the Freedom made special mention of the 4th Battalion of the Regiment: "Borough of Ilford to Brigadier G. H. Wilmer, D.S.O., M.C., Colonel, the Officers, N.C.O.s, and Men of the Essex Regiment.

"We, proud of the unsurpassed record and glorious traditions of your most distinguished Regiment through loyal and devoted service since its formation in 1741, and especially in the last war, desire to recognise the affection with which the Essex Regiment is held by the people of Essex.

"We also desire to acknowledge and cement the close bond existing between our Borough and the Essex Regiment, and in particular the 4th Battalion, in which so many of our inhabitants have with pride and distinction served, and are continuing to serve.

"We therefore confer upon the Essex Regiment the honour and privilege of marching through our Borough on all ceremonial occasions with drums beating, bands playing, colours flying, and bayonets fixed."

The detachment of 200 Essex officers and men from the East Anglian Brigade Infantry Training Centre and No. 44 (Essex) Primary Training Centre was commanded by Lieutenant-Colonel A. Noble, D.S.O., T.D., D.L., the Commanding Officer of the 4th Battalion.

After a Drumhead Service at the Ilford Football Club Ground, attended by some 3,000 people, and conducted by the Vicar of Ilford, the Mayor's Chaplain, and the Reverend G. M. Lister, M.C., M.A., C.F., the detachment marched past the Mayor at the Town Hall, thus exercising the newly granted privilege of marching through the Borough "drums beating, bands playing, colours flying, and with bayonets fixed." Subsequently the detachment was most hospitably entertained by the Borough.

The Freedom of Romford

The sixth and last Freedom to be granted to the Regiment, the Freedom of the Borough of Romford, was conferred on the 20th September, 1947. It was the first Freedom to be granted by the Borough.

The Mayor, in presenting the scroll to Brigadier G. H. Wilmer, D.S.O., M.C., Colonel of the Regiment, said: "The Essex Regiment has a record which cannot be surpassed by any regiment in the British Army. It is a matter of pride to us that many hundreds of Romford men have been members of the Regiment and have helped to create those traditions, and write into the pages of history those battle honours which we recall today. It is our Regiment: we have a personal attachment to it. . . ."

Receiving the scroll, Brigadier Wilmer thanked the Mayor, his Councillors, and the people of Romford for the great honour they had conferred on the Essex Regiment.

After saluting the inhabitants of Romford by a General Salute, the detachment of the Regiment, commanded by Lieutenant-Colonel H. J. Laverty, D.S.O., M.C., then marched through the centre of the town with band and drums playing the Regimental march, Colours flying, and bayonets fixed, being subsequently entertained most hospitably by the Borough.

* * *

So was brought to a conclusion a series of honours to the Essex Regiment, possibly unequalled by any regiment of infantry of the Line, honours that add lustre to the already rich traditions of the Essex Regiment. As a memento of these occasions, the Regiment presented each of the six Boroughs with an inscribed silver salver, and a set of Mr. J. W. Burrows' *History of the Essex Regiment*.

(*Agenzia Fotografica Nazionale, Venezia*)
THE DRUMS OF THE 2ND BATTALION THE ESSEX REGIMENT BEAT RETREAT IN THE PIAZZA SAN MARCO, VENICE. 20TH MARCH, 1947.

THE RETURN OF THE SALAMANCA EAGLE TO THE REGIMENT.
Lieutenant-General Sir Geoffrey W. Howard receives the Eagle from General Sir Clive Liddell, Governor of the Royal Hospital, Chelsea. 28th September, 1947. (Major J. M. Woodhouse in command of the Regimental Party.)

The Colours of the 4th Battalion The Essex Regiment being received from the Colour Party of the Regimental Depot on the reconstitution of the Territorial Army. Gordon Fields, Ilford. 17th May, 1947.

The King's and Regimental Colours of the 1st, 2nd, 4th, 5th, 6th, and 7th Battalions of the Regiment, the Salamanca Eagle, and the Silver Drums of the 2nd Battalion. 25th May, 1946.

Top Row: 5th Battalion, 6th Battalion, 7th Battalion. Bottom Row: 2nd Battalion, 1st Battalion, 4th Battalion.

Section III
THE AMALGAMATION OF THE 1ST AND 2ND BATTALIONS

On the 3rd November, 1948, amalgamation of the 1st and 2nd Battalions (44th and 56th) took place, and thus, after a period of over 200 years, the two Battalions ceased to have a separate existence.

The ceremony took place at Colchester, representative detachments of the two Battalions being formed up in line with their Colours. The parade was first inspected by the Lord-Lieutenant of Essex, Colonel Sir Francis H. D. C. Whitmore, K.C.B., C.M.G., D.S.O., T.D., J.P., attended by the Colonel of the Regiment, Brigadier G. H. Wilmer, D.S.O., M.C.

Both Battalions then marched past in line to their old Regimental marches. Then, re-formed into line, the two Battalions were addressed, first by the Colonel of the Regiment, and then by the Lord-Lieutenant. Both stressed the fact that on this parade both 44th and "Pompadours" were ceasing their careers as separate Battalions, and that the ceremony was symbolic of the merging of the two into one, and that from the ceremony would arise a new battalion, the 1st Battalion The Essex Regiment (44th and 56th Foot), a unit that would zealously maintain the traditions of both the original 44th Foot and the "Pompadours."

After the addresses the Colours of both Battalions were marched off, the two Battalions then closing to form the new 1st Battalion The Essex Regiment (44th and 56th Foot). The Colours were then marched on once more, and the new Battalion, under command of Lieutenant-Colonel C. A. Southey, marched off in column of route to the strains of the Regimental march.

Section IV
THE 1ST BATTALION THE ESSEX REGIMENT (44TH AND 56TH) 1948-50

Earlier chapters have taken the story of the 1st Battalion through from 1929 to 1939 and on through the days of war and the years that followed until, on the 3rd November, 1948, the 1st Battalion was merged with the 2nd Battalion, and an amalgamated unit, the 1st Battalion The Essex Regiment (44th and 56th), was created.

It remains, therefore, to tell the story of this Battalion from November 1948 to the end of 1950.

This history has shown how in 1946 No. 1 Infantry Training Centre at Warley was changed to No. 44 Primary Training Centre. With the change came a need for a centre to deal with the second stage of training—arms basic training. The first step towards the grouping of East Anglian regiments was taken when, in November 1946, the East Anglian Infantry Training Centre was established at Colchester and given an establishment that allowed for one company from each regiment in East Anglia.

From this stage it was comparatively easy to leaven the whole with individuals from the Regiment selected to be the first, on the subsequent reorganisation of infantry, to carry out the role of Group training battalion. The selected unit was the 1st Essex, and on the 15th May, 1948, the Battalion took up its new role, the arms basic training unit for all regiments in the East Anglian Brigade.

Lieutenant-Colonel C. A. Southey was the Commanding Officer, and the Battalion in its new role remained at Colchester.

There is little to record of those two years at Colchester, two years of repetitive training that seemed to know no finality. All the teething troubles of a grouped infantry system, coupled with a shortage of regular personnel, and what at times appeared a superfluity of National Service men.

The training battalion was the hub of the new system, and as such the 1st Essex received its full share of attention.

In January 1949 the Battalion was visited by Field-Marshal Sir William J. Slim, the Chief of the Imperial General Staff. He was followered later in the year by General Sir Evelyn Barker, the G.O.C.-in-C. Eastern Command, and by his chief of staff, Major-General E. B. Bastyan. Early in 1950 Lieutenant-General Sir Gerald W. R. Templer, the new G.O.C.-in-C. of the Command, came to see the Battalion.

In October 1950 Lieutenant-Colonel T. L. G. Charles, D.S.O., took over command. Very soon afterwards it was learnt that because of a planned increase in the number of field formations in the British Army, there was an added need for active units. All infantry battalions engaged in brigade training duties were to be relieved on a reformation of the war-time training centre system.

The end of 1950 saw the 1st Battalion, very much under strength, engaged in the reorganisation necessary to turn it once more into a line battalion and to take its place in the British Army order of battle.

Section V

THE 4TH BATTALION THE ESSEX REGIMENT (T.A.), 1948-50

The Territorial Army was re-established on the 1st January, 1947. On the 1st May, 1947, the 4th Battalion The Essex Regiment was re-formed as infantry, the only Territorial battalion of the Essex Regiment to be revived in its old role. The 4th Essex was brigaded with the 4th Royal Norfolk and the 4th Suffolk in the 161st (Independent) Infantry Brigade Group T.A.

The 161st Infantry Brigade had, up to 1941, except for a short period when the 1st Hertfordshire Regiment was included, been an all Essex infantry brigade. Then, as this history has shown, the 1/5th and 2/5th Essex left, their places being taken by the 3/7th Rajputs and 4/7th Rajputs. Finally, in 1942, the departure of the 1/4th Essex to join the 5th Indian Infantry Brigade left the 161st Brigade an all Indian formation which subsequently served in the Western Desert and the Far East. Now once more an East Anglian infantry brigade, the 161st Brigade, contained the 4th Essex, sole surviving unit of Essex Territorial infantry.

Lieutenant-Colonel A. Noble, D.S.O., T.D., D.L., took command of the Battalion. He was quickly joined by a nucleus of pre-war and war-time officers and warrant officers, which included Major G. A. Eden, Major H. J. Young, M.C., Major J. Watt, D.S.O., M.C., Major T. W. Grist, M.C., Major R. A. Plackett, and Captain G. E. Smith, M.C. Major H. R. Pouch, M.B.E., was appointed Quartermaster. Regimental Sergeant-Major C. J. Rose, D.C.M., rejoined as a company sergeant-major, and Regimental Quartermaster-Sergeant N. T. Croucher rejoined in his old appointment. The Honorary Colonel was the Right Honourable W. L. S. Churchill, O.M., C.H., T.D., LL.D., M.P.

On the 17th May, 1947, the Colours of the Battalion, since 1939 in safe keeping at the Regimental Depot at Warley, were handed back in a ceremony at Gordon Fields, Ilford, attended by the Lord-Lieutenant of Essex, Colonel Sir Francis H. D. C. Whitmore, K.C.B., C.M.G., D.S.O., T.D., J.P., the Colonel of the Regiment, and very many friends of the Battalion. With this ceremonial return of the Colours the Battalion may be said to have lived again.

Recruiting was slow. A firm foundation was laid by the re-enlistment of many who had served with the Battalion during the war, but after a year, at the time of the first post-war camp in July 1948, the strength was still only about 120. Even so, the 4th Essex had a strength much in advance of the majority of infantry battalions in the Territorial Army. This first camp was held at Languard Fort, Felixstowe, and was attended by a high proportion of those then on the strength, 17 officers and 77 other ranks.

Before the 1949 camp, Major Eden relinquished the appointment of Second-in-Command, his place being taken by Major H. J. Young, M.C. Another change about this time was the appointment of Major D. J. Palmer, M.B.E., M.C., as Quartermaster, and in the spring of 1950 R.S.M. J. Jones left the Battalion. He had had the possibly unique experience of being Regimental Sergeant-Major to the 1st and 2nd Battalions as well as the 4th Battalion.

The 1949 camp, the first full fifteen-day camp, was held at Roman Way Camp, Colchester. In 1950 camp was held at Bodney, Stamford, where opportunity was given to work with armour once more and carry out live firing with all weapons except the 6-pounder anti-tank guns, which went to a firing area at Lulworth.

In July 1950 the first drafts of national service men began to join the Battalion on completion of their eighteen months' training in the regular army. The strength rose to about 350 towards the end of the year, but there it was to remain, save for voluntary enlistment, until the spring of 1951, because of the decision to extend the period of regular national service to two years.

It is at this point, at the end of 1950, with the great innovation of the introduction of national service men into the Territorial Army yet uncompleted, that we must leave the 4th Battalion of the Regiment.

EPILOGUE

So the long annals of the Essex Regiment dating back to 1741 have been brought forward another short step. It can only be hoped that the story of service, valour, and cheerfulness this history has tried to tell will be read with pride and affection by the many Essex men and women who cherish their county Regiment.

"Dutiful to its masters, merciful to its enemies, it clung steadfastly to its old simple ideas—obedience, service, sacrifice."
(*History of the British Army*, Sir John Fortescue.)

APPENDICES

APPENDIX I

ROLL OF HONOUR (1939–45)

(*This List has been compiled from official War Office sources*)

> Where is the number of our English dead?
> Edward the Duke of York, the Earl of Suffolk,
> Sir Richard Ketley, Davy Gam, esquire;
> None else of name; and of all other men
> But five and twenty. O God, thy arm was here;
> And not to us, but to thy arm alone,
> Ascribe we all!
>
> HENRY V.

Surname and Christian Name	Army Number	Rank
Abbay, John R.	69159	Lieutenant
Abramovitz, Joseph	6021252	Private
Adams, Henry T.	6032064	Private
Adams, William	6008570	W.O. Class II
Adlington, Leslie R.	200904	Captain
Ager, William H.	6016748	L/Corporal
Aldridge, David E.	5784056	Private
Allen, Francis T.	6025804	Private
Allen, Frederick	6010930	Private
Allen, John A.	14664004	Private
Allen, Maurice A.	14406524	Private
Allen, Thomas H.	6021779	Private
Ambrose, William L.	151297	Lieutenant
Amies, Thomas D.	6024588	Private
Anderson, Henry	1074807	Private
Andrews, Alfred E.	6007678	Private
Andrews, Alfred E. G.	5574163	Private
Andrews, Douglas H.	6029096	Private
Andrews, John R.	3252907	Private
Anslow, James A.	6099063	Corporal
Anthony, Leslie J.	6022916	L/Corporal
Appleyard, Gilbert O.	6016989	Private

ROLL OF HONOUR (1939–45)

Surname and Christian Name	Army Number	Rank
Argent, Charles	6024936	Private
Arkell, George	108856	Private
Arnold, Charles J.	6029097	Private
Arstall, Herbert	3455758	Private
Arundell, Frank	14392026	Private
Ashworth, Alexander J.	14410101	Private
Atkinson, Walter	1739243	Private
Attwood, George V.	6019990	Private
Attwood, Richard D.	6017486	Private
Austin, Frank R.	6021257	Private
Averill, Leonard A.	5734515	Private
Avitabile, Natale	6019500	Private
Ayres, Norman E.	105110	Major
Bagley, Edward J.	6021282	Private
Baines, Alfred J.	107013	2/Lieutenant
Baird, Malcolm	13097036	Private
Baker, Charles G.	6031386	Private
Baldwin, John	14622080	Private
Bally, St. J. C.	256115	Lieutenant
Bambridge, Edwin J.	5951488	Private
Bambridge, Harry J.	6013118	Private
Bance, William J.	6025232	Private
Banks, Alfred W.	6024552	Corporal
Banks, Ernest	5731840	Private
Bannatyne, Patrick G. D.	6477553	Private
Barber, Herbert J.	5780733	L/Corporal
Barker, Eric	14641709	Private
Barnes, Frederick H. V.	5952592	Private
Barnes, John W.	6027103	Private
Barnes, Walter J.	6010471	L/Corporal
Barnett, Albert T.	14552763	Corporal
Barnett, Arthur S.	5954295	Private
Barrett, Arthur G.	6016639	Private
Barrett, Edward F.	6021794	Corporal
Bartels, Leonard F.	6015619	Private
Barton, George W.	6011311	Private
Basham, Cyril G.	6016460	Private
Bass, William M.	6010752	Corporal
Bastable, Cyril	6030130	Private
Baston, Newman L.	5387160	Private
Bates, Eric C.	6018480	Private

Surname and Christian Name	Army Number	Rank
Bates, James A.	6027111	Private
Bearman, George A.	6011601	Private
Beckett, Alfred	6010773	Private
Beecroft, Hector	6398667	Private
Beeston, John W.	4923419	Private
Bell, Alfred R.	6023603	Private
Belshaw, Hugh	14488750	Corporal
Benford, E. A.	6013003	Private
Benjamin, Michael	6021279	L/Corporal
Bennett, Frederick	3866166	Private
Bentley, Gerald D. J.	14739946	Private
Bentley, Ivan	6011684	Private
Bettell, Higgins F. H.	6019175	Private
Betts, Henry B.	5932623	Private
Bidgood, James S.	6027069	Private
Birch, Charles A.	6021192	Private
Birden, Ivor	4080212	Private
Bishop, Edward G.	14405645	Private
Bishop, William W. C.	2066996	Private
Bissley, Frank B. L.	153305	Lieutenant
Bixby, Raymond F. G.	6016069	Private
Black, William	3251981	Sergeant
Blacknell, Edward G.	6011613	Private
Blackwell, Donald E.	5115895	Sergeant
Blain, John M.	3252996	Corporal
Blake, Ronald W.	14653743	Private
Blakeman, Richard H.	6009542	Private
Bland, Edgar C.	6011095	Private
Blessley, Dennis M.	184583	Captain
Block, Frank P.	6018541	Private
Bloomfield, Victor A.	6016892	Private
Bolitho, Herbert T. H.	5442789	Private
Bond, Alfred J.	6012877	Private
Bond, Frederick A.	6024591	Corporal
Bonnell, Henry	6351180	Private
Bonnett, Albert F.	14659782	Private
Bosley, William R.	4076733	Private
Bottomley, Samuel	14612722	Private
Boughey, William H.	5110298	Private
Bounds, William C.	6012731	Private
Bourne, John E.	5381564	Sergeant
Boyd, John W.	3252828	Private

ROLL OF HONOUR (1939-45)

Surname and Christian Name	Army Number	Rank
Brackenbury, Donald	13022570	Private
Bradley, Anthony	6029679	Private
Branch, Herbert W.	6024958	L/Sergeant
Brett, Leslie V.	6022184	Private
Brewer, Harry T., M.M.	6007953	Corporal
Brewin, James H.	4981097	Corporal
Brighouse, William	3864454	Private
Brindle, Arthur	6008229	Private
Bristow, William A.	6013961	Corporal
Britton, Elijah	6023615	Private
Broad, Cyril A.	6022965	Private
Brooks, Phillip H.	183486	Lieutenant
Brooks, Raymond	4617527	Private
Brotherton, William G. H.	6014342	Private
Brown, Charles W.	14576980	Private
Brown, George	3252915	Private
Brown, George E.	4698398	Private
Brown, Harry P.	6012973	Private
Brown, James	3252831	Private
Brown, John J.	6019513	Private
Brown, Nelson E.	14655899	Private
Brown, Robert J.	6013539	Private
Browne, James	6010864	L/Corporal
Browne, Reginald C.	124242	Lieutenant
Bruce, Wilfred W. P.	6019514	L/Corporal
Bruckman, Robert J.	6027131	Private
Bryan, Hubert	6005224	Sergeant
Bryant, Eric W.	6027461	Private
Bucknill, Edward T.	6017628	Corporal
Buckoke, Dennis L.	6023622	Private
Bugg, Arthur John	6018514	Private
Bungard, James, M.M.	315398	Lieutenant
Burge, Charles H.	5616729	Private
Burgess, Norman	3390697	Private
Burke, John E.	253488	Major
Burland, George	6009839	Sergeant
Burnett, Frederick S.	6006867	Private
Burton, Bertie W.	6007484	L/Sergeant
Burton, Charles E.	6011859	Private
Burton, James A.	6013540	Corporal
Burton, William J.	6016785	Private
Burtwell, Malcolm G.	6019368	Private

Surname and Christian Name	Army Number	Rank
Butler, Percy E.	186201	Captain
Butler, William H.	6028924	Corporal
Byam, George V.	6013784	Private
Byrne, Patrick	6026158	Private
Cable, John	6024606	Private
Calvert, Derrick G.	96685	Captain
Camfield, Maurice I. G.	14671212	Private
Campbell, Leslie T.	6010503	Private
Canner, Ernest J. J.	6024004	Private
Canning, Robert	6030887	Private
Cannon, Thornton G. L.	300401	Lieutenant
Capel-Dunn, Dudley C., O.B.E.	64026	Colonel
Caplin, George	1787721	Private
Carey, Sidney E. C.	11255328	Corporal
Carlyon-Hughes, Basil J., T.D.	2939	Captain
Carpenter, Albert J.	14581170	Private
Carrigan, Robert T.	6021326	Private
Carrington, Joseph	6025838	Corporal
Carroll, Bernard C.	269804	Lieutenant
Carson, James C.	5385205	Private
Carter, Charles W.	751178	Private
Carter, Dolphus	29763	Private
Carter, Samuel J.	5771025	Private
Carter, William J.	6032170	Private
Cassidy, Patrick L. A.	6014524	Private
Cassie, Joseph G.	3252998	Private
Catchpole, Phillip G.	6020538	Private
Cavson, Arthur E.	5193753	Private
Chadney, Geoffrey V.	89779	Lieutenant
Chambers, Clarence	3715835	Private
Chambers, Thomas	3445779	Private
Chance, Kenneth	14509845	Private
Chandler-Honner, Harold	149011	Captain
Channell, Alex F.	300354	Lieutenant
Channing, John R.	5836206	Private
Chaplin, Edward B.	6030361	Private
Chapman, Frederick	6023345	Private
Chapman, George A.	6007418	Private
Chappell, Ernest J.	14640735	Private
Chappell, William J. C.	5570615	Private
Chapple, Albert G.	14606386	Private

ROLL OF HONOUR (1939-45)

Surname and Christian Name	Army Number	Rank
Charlesworth, Edwin I.	287840	Lieutenant
Charlton, George G.	6019761	Private
Charlton, Thomas	3252917	Private
Chatters, Ronald A.	6016380	Private
Chell, Peter J.	130865	Captain
Chenery, Gordon	6013687	Private
Cherry, Arthur	3714738	Private
Cheshire, Cyril H.	6019926	Private
Chesney, Leslie T.	14384366	Private
Chippett, Reginald C.	6022433	Private
Church, John P.	6016765	L/Corporal
Church, William R.	6021363	Sergeant
Civica, Bruce	6011096	Private
Clarabut, Harry H.	6011440	Private
Clark, Arthur S.	5948416	Private
Clark, George	6013174	Private
Clark, George E. A. E.	6010974	Private
Clark, John	6030269	Private
Clark, Joseph	6027295	Private
Clark, Kenneth J.	6025844	Private
Clark, Stanley W.	6011703	L/Corporal
Clarke, Alfred B. W.	182503	Lieutenant
Clarke, Eric W.	6024619	L/Corporal
Clarke, Frederick S.	6011244	Private
Clarke, George W.	6022023	Private
Clarke, Stanley	3531842	L/Sergeant
Clarke, Wilfred E.	1571116	Private
Clayton, Leonard W. C.	235338	2/Lieutenant
Cloake, Frederick S.	6014481	Private
Coe, Walter, M.M.	6025259	Corporal
Coghlan, Patrick M. F.	70525	Lieutenant
Colbourn, Leslie W.	6025505	Private
Cole, Wilfred A.	6027738	Private
Colebourne, Arthur L.	5776549	Private
Collett, Ronald E.	6026915	Private
Collins, Thomas L. A.	5837393	Private
Colvill, Harold	6031819	L/Corporal
Colyer, Douglas W. C.	14576948	Private
Combstock, J.	5628925	Private
Commons, Frederick	6024021	Private
Compton, Arthur	14499218	Private
Connelly, James	3252875	Private

Surname and Christian Name	Army Number	Rank
Constable, Robert	6005622	Private
Cook, John E. G.	5832958	Private
Cook, Stanley	4745463	Private
Cook, William H. J., D.C.M.	6007186	Colour-Sergeant
Cooke, Arthur	6018166	L/Corporal
Cooke, Arthur R.	237678	Lieutenant
Cooke, Reginald C. A.	6020593	Private
Cookson, Walker	5569750	Corporal
Cooper, Arthur D.	6019486	Private
Coot, Arthur A.	6027888	Private
Corder, Fred	1607306	Private
Corkland, Cecil	6027469	Private
Cornelius, Brian J.	174404	Lieutenant
Cornell, Arthur E.	6011196	L/Sergeant
Cotton, Joseph C.	6855291	Private
Cousins, William J.	6012847	Private
Covernton, Charles T.	262377	Lieutenant
Cox, Edward J.	6020163	Private
Cox, Walter E.	14659787	Private
Cox, William G.	6022978	Private
Craig, George	6010375	Sergeant
Crane, Edward H.	73869	Captain
Cranham, John W.	14727760	Private
Creesey, Leslie C.	6021330	Sergeant
Crockford, Ernest A.	6020079	Private
Croft, Henry	6024687	Corporal
Crofts, Bert A.	6020360	L/Corporal
Crook, Frederick W.	6021321	Private
Crozier, Leslie G.	6011659	Private
Crump, Edgar	14585206	Private
Cuff, Reginald J.	6028954	Private
Cullen, Michael J.	130060	Captain
Cullen, Patrick	5957579	Private
Culling, William	6010289	L/Sergeant
Currie, Ronald	6019913	Private
Curtis, Thomas B.	14407242	Private
Cuttill, Victor	6012323	L/Sergeant
Cutting, George C.	6029258	Corporal
Cutts, Harold	4694367	Corporal
Dalby, Hendry	1799810	Private
Dallow, Walter C.	6025516	Private

ROLL OF HONOUR (1939-45)

Surname and Christian Name	Army Number	Rank
Daniels, Alfred J.	6011466	Private
Dann, Joseph C.	6012149	Private
Dann, M.	6013695	Corporal
Darrant, Victor H.	6013553	Private
Davies, Douglas H.	6016629	Private
Davies, John E. C.	14239179	Private
Davies, John L.	6022030	Private
Davies, Renie	3915323	Private
Davis, Harry B.	6020576	Private
Davis, James A.	6012523	Corporal
Davis, William H.	6020070	Private
Davison, Peter D.	331870	Lieutenant
Dawson, Thomas H.	14406414	Private
Day, Stanley John	6010527	W.O. Class II
De Cort, George W.	6009591	Private
Deacon, Leslie C.	6014788	Private
Dean, John T.	14638176	Private
Dear, Norman H.	105584	Lieutenant
Death, Paul W.	6020179	Private
Demmon, Jack P.	6018502	Private
Denny, Stanley A.	6022217	Private
Denny, Wilfred G.	6012099	Private
Denton, Frederick	3252925	Corporal
Denton, John S.	4622308	Private
Denyer, William A. J.	6018478	Private
Dines, Frank	6011863	Private
Divall, Francis J.	6016729	Private
Dix, Ronald L.	6022221	Corporal
Dixon, Albert J.	14618039	Private
Dodd, George D.	6007839	L/Corporal
Dodge, Alan	14415670	L/Corporal
Donohue, Frank	1824175	Private
Dover, Frank	6019545	Private
Dowsett, Clifford H.	6021368	L/Corporal
Doyle, James D.	3910693	L/Corporal
Drain, William H.	6011718	Private
Drury, Charles H.	6019959	Private
Drury, Harry G.	6019983	Private
Duddy, William	3252782	Private
Dunbar, William R.	3251886	Private
Dunkin, Donald	6028187	Private
Dunlop, Benjamin	3859515	Private

Surname and Christian Name	Army Number	Rank
Dunn, Arthur P.	14675256	Private
Dymond, John H.	5624084	Private
Eassom, Horace	6022928	Private
Eatough, Harold B.	3389040	Private
Edge, Walter	14659844	Private
Edgeley, Norman	6031943	Private
Edgell, Edwin G.	6014457	Private
Edrupt, Keith D.	143520	Captain
Edwards, David V.	1609705	Private
Edwards, Frank	6012733	L/Corporal
Edwards, Frederick S.	6020509	L/Corporal
Egalton, Henry A.	13019018	Private
Elder, James	3254265	Private
Ellen, Victor S.	6027768	Private
Elliott, Frederick V.	6025076	Private
Elliott, Frederick W.	6028401	Private
Ellis, Leonard H.	6022077	Private
Ellson, James R.	112868	Captain
Emmerson, K. S.	14549642	Private
Emmett, Norman E. H.	1137830	Private
Endersby, Harold F.	6025871	Private
Enscoe, Sidney A.	14203632	L/Corporal
Evans, Rhys L.	6012735	Private
Evans, William	3912191	Private
Evans, William G.	6030169	Sergeant
Evans, William T. G.	14567181	Private
Everett, Samuel F.	6021389	Private
Everitt, Frederick E.	6024970	Private
Everitt, Jack L.	6024971	Private
Everson, Harry H. S.	6013766	Private
Fairhurst, Edward E.	6018528	Private
Farnam, Peter	162578	Major
Farraway, Arthur L.	6020077	Private
Farraway, Robert A.	6019549	Corporal
Faulkner, George N.	6010772	Corporal
Feak, Frank C.	6014702	Private
Fidgett, Percy H.	6016373	Sergeant
Fileman, John M.	6024980	Private
Finley, Robert	6025877	Private
Fisher, David H. W.	6012937	Corporal

ROLL OF HONOUR (1939–45)

Surname and Christian Name	Army Number	Rank
Fisher, Raymond	6016369	Private
Fisher, William F.	6026891	Private
Fishman, Monty E.	14296004	Private
Flack, George	6010834	Private
Flack, Victor	6021416	Private
Flanagan, John W.	4105610	Corporal
Fletcher, Leslie C.	6013318	Private
Flint, James H. J.	6021400	Private
Flint, Ronald B.	5990091	Sergeant
Flynn, John P.	7020936	Private
Ford, Bernard S.	6014813	Private
Forman, Alec	6026425	Private
Forrester, James A.	6011750	Private
Foster, Herbert L.	6016480	Private
Fountain, Edward	6010669	L/Corporal
Fountain, Edward	6011223	Private
Fowler, Henry F.	6019554	L/Corporal
Foyle, Kenneth	14649258	Private
Fradin, Henri J.	255790	Lieutenant
Francis, James M.	6020049	Private
Francis, Leonard E.	6016265	Private
Fraser, Donald J.	6025152	Private
Fraser, William J.	5948921	Private
French, Basil B.	160537	Captain
Frier, Norman J.	191459	Captain
Frost, Albert J. E.	6012696	L/Sergeant
Frost, James G.	6029916	Private
Fry, H. L.	77661	2/Lieutenant
Fry, Ronald A.	14413056	Private
Furness, Frederick	4449221	L/Corporal
Futer, John H.	6013717	Private
Gage, John	3251945	Private
Gallacher, Patrick	3252801	Private
Galpin, William H.	6012566	Private
Gamson, Archibald G.	3252802	Private
Gapes, Alfred W.	6013273	Sergeant
Garbutt, James	6023160	Sergeant
Gardiner, Robert H.	6013178	L/Corporal
Gardiner, Robert T.	5055544	L/Corporal
Garland, Lindsay E. A.	6012353	Sergeant
Garrad, Lionel C.	6021986	Private

Surname and Christian Name	Army Number	Rank
Garratt, William	14650332	Private
Gartin, Samuel	6021429	Private
Gascoyne, David A.	6023162	Corporal
Gatward, Douglas	182322	Lieutenant
Gee, Robert	4754190	Private
Genders, Henry J. K.	50950	Captain
Genge, Dick E.	14659438	Private
Gibbs, David M. H.	149014	Captain
Gibbs, Ernest G.	5822542	Private
Giddings, Joseph H.	6099643	Private
Gillett, Thomas F.	6021843	Private
Gilliland, Henry J.	3445607	Private
Gilson, F.	130335	Captain
Gingell, Basil G., M.C.	182323	2/Lieutenant
Ginn, Charles J.	14426313	Private
Godsafe, Albert J.	6012011	Private
Golding, Joseph R.	6012067	Private
Golding, William C.	6022238	Private
Goldstone, Donald	6016973	Private
Golledge, Reginald G.	6023676	Private
Goodridge, Edward G., M.M.	6028900	Private
Goodspeed, Leslie A. G.	873144	Private
Goodwin, Charles L.	6014881	L/Corporal
Goodwin, Eric	6016185	Private
Gore, Albert E.	6024690	Private
Gorell, Frank	14545842	Private
Gould, David D.	6012686	Private
Gould, Horace	6009756	Private
Gourley, Samuel	3252808	Private
Goward, Frank G.	14631619	Private
Gowers, Maurice	6009238	Private
Graham, Douglas C.	6016846	L/Corporal
Grant, George	3252810	Private
Gray, Alfred V.	6025891	Private
Gray, Frederick A. W.	6011249	Private
Gray, Gordon H.	6013689	Private
Gray, Stanley A.	6014532	Private
Gray, Walter T.	5731278	Private
Greaves, Albert E.	3252934	Private
Greaves, Joseph	4616935	Sergeant
Green, Kenneth F.	268556	Lieutenant
Green, Louis W.	3253017	Private

ROLL OF HONOUR (1939-45)

Surname and Christian Name	Army Number	Rank
Green, Richard J. J.	6014236	Private
Gretton, Joseph H.	6013213	L/Corporal
Gridley, Alfred C.	6004568	Private
Gridley, George A.	6018321	Private
Griffiths, Alfred G.	6026922	Private
Grigg, Denis W.	292691	Lieutenant
Grove, George F.	6023166	Private
Guest, Robert	3973418	Private
Guest, William	6026923	Private
Gunn, Alfred	6030165	Sergeant
Guy, Sidney T.	6019019	Corporal
Hall, Reginald A.	6013152	Private
Hallett, William F.	6021462	Private
Hamilton, Richard D.	6021453	Corporal
Hammerton, Albert E.	6028212	Corporal
Hanlon, John	3254283	Private
Hanson, R. W. D.	14219229	Private
Hardie, William B.	3251964	Private
Harding, Keri	249243	Major
Harrington, John W.	6023167	Private
Harris, Richard T.	269935	Lieutenant
Harris, George F.	6013251	Corporal
Harris, Gerald P. S.	6012265	Corporal
Harris, Sidney W.	6019755	W.O. Class II
Harrison, Albert M.	6011779	Private
Harrison, George	6027938	Private
Harrison, Norman F.	255789	Captain
Hasler, Clement K.	6013109	Private
Hathorn, Douglas McF.	72458	Captain
Hatten, Charles	6011848	L/Corporal
Haviland, Cyril A.	6019973	Private
Hawkes, Thomas F.	6011862	Private
Hayes, James P.	14609334	Private
Haynes, Charles G.	6029076	Private
Haynes, Edward R.	6014131	L/Corporal
Haynes, Harold G.	6008030	Corporal
Heard, Henry J.	6013081	Private
Hearn, Charles R.	6008693	Private
Hedger, John F.	6016649	Private
Hedges, Henry	6030339	Private
Held, Stephen G.	6027114	Private

Surname and Christian Name	Army Number	Rank
Hempstead, Stanley	6014969	Sergeant
Hennessy, George	5385782	Private
Hewitt, Richard	14642701	Private
Hickingbotham, Victor O.	14385477	Private
Hicks, Herbert J.	6021243	Private
Hicks, Leslie	14229311	Private
Hilden, Mark	6011170	Private
Hill, Robert A.	6022038	Corporal
Hills, John J.	6012107	Sergeant
Hilton, Harold	3716745	Private
Hockley, Alfred G.	6021216	Private
Hodges, Ernest A.	6013712	Private
Hoggins, Fred S.	6021215	Private
Holdaway, Charles A. J.	5728891	Private
Hollands, Alfred	6010388	Corporal
Hollis, John	14207832	Corporal
Holton, Sydney	6009344	Private
Hood, Henry J.	14415798	Private
Hopkins, Frederick	6010938	Private
Hopkins, James	6022039	Private
Hopkins, Rhydwyn	3910713	Private
Hopkins, Thomas A.	6019580	Private
Horobin, Hector R.	189420	Lieutenant
Horrex, George D. A.	6028234	Private
Horsfield, Frederick M.	3648	L/Corporal
Horsley, Ronald	6019583	Private
Houston, James I.	53748	Major
Howard, George F.	6009723	L/Corporal
Howard, John	307944	Lieutenant
Howard, Stanley V.	6027780	Private
Howarth, Jack	3455018	Private
Howitt, John L. D.	111949	Lieutenant
Hoy, William S.	6016602	L/Corporal
Hudson, George, M.M.	6021493	L/Corporal
Huggett, Harry F.	5184808	Private
Huggins, Arthur R.	6019587	Private
Hughes, Clifford	6028990	Private
Hughes, Frank W.	4041867	Private
Hughes, Walter J. F.	6027269	Corporal
Hull, George N.	6008951	Corporal
Hulme, John R.	6027957	Private
Humphrey, Frederick G.	5833296	Private

Surname and Christian Name	Army Number	Rank
Humphries, Arthur J.	6007290	Private
Hunt, Leonard R.	6026802	Private
Hunt, William P. C.	6012102	Private
Hurley, Robert J.	14393513	Private
Hylands, Howard T.	6030162	Sergeant
Imeson, Harry	6027958	Private
Ince, Walter	6010905	Private
Iron, L.	6024211	Private
Irvin, Leslie	4395556	Private
Isaac, Alfred L.	6032024	Private
Ives, Francis	6010666	Private
Ivory, Frederick C.	6021498	L/Corporal
Jackman, George J. H.	6021509	Private
Jackson, George, D.C.M.	6021512	Private
Jackson, Graham M.	90231	2/Lieutenant
Jackson, Walter F.	6027653	L/Corporal
Jacobs, David	14584442	Private
James, Robert B., D.S.O.	53746	Lieutenant-Colonel
James, William S.	866172	Private
Jarvis, Samuel S.	156612	Lieutenant
Jay, Alan Ernest	14429459	Private
Jay, Carl J.	6012071	L/Corporal
Jennings, Benjamin W.	6009764	Corporal
Jennings, Cyril H.	6016191	Sergeant
Jennings, Frederick H.	6006318	Corporal
Jesse, Arthur W.	6016852	Private
Johnson, Edward	14394050	Private
Johnson, Peter	3252683	Private
Johnson, William E.	6021217	Private
Jones, David L.	5382119	Private
Jones, Dennis	14509597	Private
Jones, Frank	6012495	L/Corporal
Jones, Griffith C.	6025917	Private
Jones, Harry A.	6022681	Private
Jones, Leslie C.	6021988	L/Corporal
Jones, Thomas D.	14618091	Private
Joslin, Christopher J.	14631516	Private
Kain, Edward G.	6011426	Private
Kane, Henry	3252866	Private

Surname and Christian Name	Army Number	Rank
Kaser, Robert	6014311	Private
Kaye, Laurence C., M.C.	92981	Captain
Keating, Frederick J.	6009803	Corporal
Keeble, Olley	6021989	Private
Keeble, Robert A.	6024667	L/Corporal
Keeley-Callan, Robert E.	6019950	Private
Keen, Leslie A.	14436040	L/Corporal
Kelly, Thomas J.	6009317	Private
Kemp, Ernest C.	6013334	Private
Kemp, Frank	14612755	Private
Kemp, Maurice H.	6031640	Private
Kerlogue, Leslie W.	6014642	Private
Kermode, William V.	6021528	Corporal
Kerry, Douglas W.	6022043	L/Corporal
Ketley, Richard C.	6024556	Private
Ketteley, Francis J., M.C.	185232	Major
Keynes, Gerald L.	6028251	Private
Kidman, Sailor M.	14724256	Private
Kilburn, Arthur	7389867	Private
Kimmence, William A.	6031981	Private
King, Alfred C.	6021534	Private
King, James W.	5572711	Private
Kingsbury, Leslie	6028961	Private
Kinsalla, Patrick	6025921	Private
Kirby, Leonard W.	6009303	Corporal
Kirkpatrick, Samuel	3254298	Private
Kitchen, Albert J.	6021524	Corporal
Knight, Charles H.	6010192	C.Q.M.S.
Knight, Samuel	6027106	Private
Knivett, Stanley J.	6024671	L/Corporal
Lacey, George	14516562	Private
Lacey, Raymond G.	4982820	Private
Lampard, William G.	300213	2/Lieutenant
Lancaster, James	3252945	Private
Lane, Geoffrey G.	5729514	Private
Lane, William J.	6006127	W.O. Class II
Langridge, Robert G.	6024697	L/Sergeant
Langrish, Lawrence W. J.	6010581	L/Corporal
Langston, Gordon E.	6013216	Private
Langstone, Henry A.	6021542	Private
Lanzer, Reginald	6031700	Private

ROLL OF HONOUR (1939-45)

Surname and Christian Name	Army Number	Rank
Laplain, James F., M.M.	6019600	Sergeant
Lardner-Burke, Dermot W.	152611 (v)	Lieutenant
Larter, Harold K.	6023279	Private
Larter, Vernon	14434512	Private
Lavender, Harry G.	6023398	L/Corporal
Lawrence, Archie	6005395	Sergeant
Lawrence, Cecil H., M.C.	126184	Lieutenant
Lawrence, Thomas A.	6026467	Private
Lawrie, Walter G.	6019602	Private
Layzell, Stanley W.	14713168	Private
Leckie, Archibald	6021559	Private
Leet, Edward	6009952	L/Corporal
Leftly, Henry A. E.	772858	Corporal
Lenn, Stanley F.	6107160	Private
Lennox, Andrew A.	6085619	Private
Levy, Benjamin	6019604	Private
Lewis, Donald P.	14421875	Private
Lewis, John T.	6013076	Private
Lewis, Philip	4080271	Private
Lindsay, John J.	6008308	Private
Lines, Charles E.	6012392	Private
Llewellyn, Richard E.	6021543	Corporal
Lochmiller, Harry J.	6009845	W.O. Class II
Lofthouse, James W., M.M.	3252946	L/Corporal
Love, Thomas R.	6010249	Private
Love, William H. J.	5876474	C.Q.M.S.
Lowe, Henry H.	6019607	Sergeant
Lowe, John N.	176280	Captain
Lowe, Robert A.	172310	Captain
Lucking, J. T.	6007254	Private
Luetchford, Sidney	6089972	Private
Lumbers, Frederick A.	5957607	Private
Lund, Thomas	3860732	Private
Luxton, James	14626136	Private
Lynn, Robert A.	4981235	Corporal
Mabbett, W. E.	6029052	Private
Macklin, Henry C.	6009915	Sergeant
Maiden, William	14540173	Private
Mallinson, Michael S., M.C.	153306	Major
Mallinson, Telford	14590802	Private
Maltby, Charles H.	3253040	Private

THE ESSEX REGIMENT

Surname and Christian Name	Army Number	Rank
Mancini, John G.	6023189	Private
Mann, John	148596	Captain
Mann, Keith W. M., M.C.	17788	Captain
Manning, Arthur H.	226199	Lieutenant
Mapes, Percival F. C.	6008980	Private
Marjoram, Aubrey, M.M.	6029281	L/Sergeant
Marjoram, William A.	314920	Lieutenant
Marlow, John A.	219189	Lieutenant
Marsh, Dennis G.	14549716	Private
Marsh, Edward H.	6013480	Private
Marsh, Roy L.	6012839	L/Corporal
Marshall, Gilbert G.	6025330	Private
Marshall, Harry	6021602	Private
Marson, James	9901	Sergeant
Martin, Albert E.	6021887	Private
Martin, Arthur	6027993	Private
Martin, Cecil E.	6025547	Private
Martin, Harold	3865952	Private
Martin, James A.	6003809	Sergeant
Martin, Joseph	6026324	Private
Mason, Edgar C.	3253041	Private
Masters, Frederick P.	6016712	Private
Matthews, William F.	6030003	Private
McCarthy, Jeremiah	6025023	Private
McCarthy, Thomas J.	6007942	L/Corporal
McCormack, William	6007889	Private
McDermott, John	4623646	Private
McFarlane, Hugh	3253196	Corporal
McGlinchey, James	7076310	Private
McGowan, Patrick	14437699	Private
McGuire, John	3253073	Private
McKnight, Alexander	3245334	Private
McLeish, Robert	13097884	Private
McNamee, John	6013145	Private
McVey, Charles I. V.	5126517	Private
Meacock, Ernest F.	6016685	Private
Mears, Ralph C.	6025643	Private
Menote, Frederick T.	14712975	Private
Mercer, Leonard C.	6021894	Corporal
Messias, Sidney W.	14511507	Private
Metson, Thomas J.	6022044	Private
Miles, Nathaniel R.	6027116	Private

ROLL OF HONOUR (1939-45)

Surname and Christian Name	Army Number	Rank
Mill, Findlay	2755868	Corporal
Miller, Reginald H.	6022261	Private
Miller, Ronald E.	304135	Lieutenant
Milligan, Samuel	2604693	W.O. Class I
Mills, Herbert J.	6023018	Private
Mills, Robert M.	6018328	Private
Milton, Benjamin C.	6008052	Private
Monk, Charles F.	6025093	Private
Monk, William A.	6025941	Private
Monti, Alfred J.	3254308	Private
Moore, Albert	14405894	Private
Moore, Kenneth	14003034	Private
Moran, Thomas G.	14424344	Private
Mordecai, James R.	6013715	Private
Morgan, Horace C.	6023308	Private
Morley, Arthur H.	6011661	Private
Morrell, Leonard V. W.	6027375	Private
Morrill, Edward G.	14726590	Private
Morrison, David D.	3253099	Private
Mortimer, John	6012800	L/Corporal
Morton, Walter B.	5393352	Private
Mott, Alec J.	6016232	Private
Mulvaney, Lucieu A. J.	6014793	L/Sergeant
Mummery, George H.	6024817	Private
Murphy, John W.	867301	Private
Murray, Thomas	6026835	Private
Murray, Thomas	30871	Private
Musgrave, William G.	6023746	Private
Musselwhite, Frederick	6019869	Private
Myers, Frederick C.	5946924	L/Sergeant
Nabarro, Benjamin	14412854	Private
Nellis, James F.	6021900	Private
Nelson, Eric P.	189421	Captain
Nesmyth, Henry S.	6016386	L/Corporal
Nevill, Cyril	4922214	Private
Neville, Stanley V.	6012753	Private
Newell, Foch	6013840	Private
Newman, Charles H.	6031784	Private
Newman, Henry W.	6011916	Private
Newton, Stanley C.	6031228	Private
Nicholson, George C.	6021622	Private

THE ESSEX REGIMENT

Surname and Christian Name	Army Number	Rank
Nicol, William	6027379	Private
North, Ronald	14200601	Private
Northeast, William R.	6022049	Sergeant
Nosworthy, Thomas R.	14653866	Private
Nutley, Leonard H.	6024096	Private
O'Flanagan, Bernard O.	285253	Lieutenant
Ogden, Henry	14229215	Private
Old, Enoch J.	6029750	Private
Old, Thomas	6012699	Private
Ottley, Henry W.	6013859	Corporal
Overton, Ronald E.	6011737	L/Corporal
Overton, William H.	14579864	Private
Owen, Cecil G.	6028013	L/Corporal
Owen, George H.	6019778	Private
Owen, William B.	6010087	Private
Oxborrow, Raymond G.	186208	Lieutenant
Packer, Frederick J.	6012347	Private
Paling, George S.	6018746	Private
Pallett, James E.	6020596	Private
Palmer, Cecil F.	6024729	Private
Palmer, Frederick F.	6027535	Private
Palmer, John A.	6028295	Private
Parker, Albert W.	6029338	Private
Parker, Cyril A.	6018637	Sergeant
Parker, Edwin	6013094	Corporal
Parkinson, Stanley	4622194	Private
Parrott, Harold T.	6018540	Private
Parry, David H.	5057877	Private
Parry, John L.	14690261	Private
Parry, Peter F. M.	117954	Lieutenant
Parsley, Stanley L. M.	14618128	Private
Parton, Leonard	11005756	Corporal
Passfield, Alfred	6024179	Private
Pattle, T.	176027	Lieutenant
Paulin, John W.	6013578	Private
Paxton, George A. M., M.C.	8189	Lieutenant-Colonel
Payne, William A. G.	6011593	L/Corporal
Peacock, Stanley G.	6019799	Private
Pearce, Albert G.	6002969	W.O. Class II

ROLL OF HONOUR (1939-45)

Surname and Christian Name	Army Number	Rank
Pearl, Richard C. T.	6010379	Private
Pearman, Charles W.	6010320	Private
Peirce, Stephen M.	6009248	Sergeant
Pentney, Reginald	6010832	Sergeant
Perkins, Norman	3911474	Private
Petre, Gerald M. M. L.	711216	Major
Petticrow, Roland W.	6016317	Private
Phillips, Reginald A.	6019856	Private
Phillips, William J. A.	14639543	Private
Pickering, Matthew	3456737	Private
Pimblett, Henry	14657975	Private
Pincus, Monty	6027117	Private
Pinnell, Ronald G. W.	6013922	Sergeant
Pitt, Alfred J.	6026928	Private
Pitt, Leslie	6930	Sergeant
Pitteway, Thomas G.	6014462	Corporal
Playle, Mark C.	6013366	Private
Plumb, Clifford	6030753	Private
Plummer, John W. P.	6019253	Private
Pollard, Herbert C.	4983692	Private
Pollard, Ronald J. H.	6027028	Private
Polson, Henry W.	6006474	Private
Popper, Harry	6027174	Private
Porter, Ernest C.	6008793	Private
Poulter, Frederick A. C.	6009869	Private
Powell, Albert	5127059	Private
Powell, Leslie G. W.	5193608	Private
Power, Henry	3251847	Private
Preston, David J.	6025651	Private
Price, Clifford	6022280	Private
Price, George E.	6012003	Private
Price, Horace	4077657	Private
Price, Kenneth G.	4034611	Private
Price, Kenneth P.	5393607	Corporal
Procter, Bertie J.	6025954	Private
Procter, Herbert	6012156	Private
Proctor, James T. H.	3461409	L/Corporal
Pugh, George E. H.	6028313	Private
Pullen, Joseph H.	6285939	Sergeant
Purcell, George J.	20817	Major
Purdy, John W.	4622202	Private
Purkis, Robert C.	258690	Lieutenant

E.R.—38

Surname and Christian Name	Army Number	Rank
Purrington, Henry M.	5623583	Private
Pymer, William F.	6019871	L/Sergeant
Randall, Arthur E.	5618850	Private
Randall, Basil J.	5384875	L/Corporal
Randall, Edward S. C.	6014741	L/Corporal
Randall, Reginald P.	6014776	L/Sergeant
Randle, Norman	4923532	Private
Rathe, Thomas L.	14615696	Private
Rawlingson, James S.	6011467	Private
Raymond, Herbert	6013823	Private
Read, Albert J.	6141966	L/Corporal
Read, John H.	6028444	Private
Reader, Thomas E.	6016980	Private
Reed, Geoffrey F.	14579870	Private
Reeder, Thomas J.	6026724	Corporal
Reeve, James	6022056	Private
Reeve, Reginald W.	6022285	Private
Regan, Harry	14207054	Private
Reid, William F.	6026343	Private
Reynolds, Robert W.	14391974	Private
Richards, Roland	5890313	Private
Richardson, Percy A.	6013524	Private
Richardson, W. H.	6017681	Private
Ridgewell, Leonard C.	6024854	Private
Riley, Henry	5193316	Private
Riley, Joseph	3252719	Private
Ring, Frederick G.	6026839	Private
Ripley, Nelson	6008002	Sergeant
Rivers, Edgar A.	300382	Lieutenant
Roberts, Alfred	6008182	Private
Roberts, Edgar	4190323	W.O. Class II
Roberts, Fred	6025698	Corporal
Roberts, George	6026040	Private
Robinson, Charles C.	14301087	Private
Robinson, Colin H.	74668	Major
Robinson, Ronald C.	220627	Captain
Rogers, Charles P.	5188893	Private
Rogers, Ernest A.	6016961	Private
Rogers, George	6006205	Sergeant
Rogers, George H.	6016870	Private
Rogers, James A. J.	6011590	Private

ROLL OF HONOUR (1939-45)

Surname and Christian Name	Army Number	Rank
Rogerson, John	3457316	Corporal
Roote, Clifford J.	6012080	Private
Rose, Harry J.	6013422	Private
Rose, Jack	4625973	Private
Rose, Travers L.	258050	Captain
Rose, Valentine H.	6014664	Corporal
Rosenbloom, Frederick	6021676	Private
Rosier, Edwin D.	14558788	Private
Ross, Alfred A.	14550376	Private
Rosser, David W.	3810543	Private
Rostron, Edward	3450569	L/Corporal
Rothery, Henry	3599466	Private
Rothwell, Gordon H.	3909938	Private
Rowe, Geoffrey W.	5729106	L/Corporal
Rowe, John E.	6007775	Sergeant
Ruglys, Harold C.	6025174	Corporal
Russell, T. J.	6028320	Private
Saberi, Thomas	6026732	Private
Sadler, Frank	4623777	Private
Samuel, Frederick C.	6012134	Sergeant
Sanders, Stanley W. G.	6014357	Private
Sargent, George	6026521	Private
Sargent, Miles	6013470	Private
Sargent, William H.	6030870	W.O. Class II
Saunders, Harry W.	6028043	Private
Saunders, Robert R.	5671979	L/Corporal
Savill, Percy J. B.	121354	Captain
Savory, James J. F.	6011582	Corporal
Saych, Reginald	6009269	L/Corporal
Scott, Albert W. G.	6023444	Private
Scott, John	6011988	Private
Scott, Walter F. C.	6019925	Private
Scowen, Walter	6011787	Private
Seagram, Arthur W.	6013711	L/Corporal
Sear, James J.	6031922	Private
Seddon, Walter	3451842	L/Corporal
Sellars, Norman D.	260147	Captain
Semmens, Albert L.	14330799	Private
Senft, James	5577428	Private
Senior, William A.	6010414	Private

Surname and Christian Name	Army Number	Rank
Sewell, Leslie W.	14208558	Private
Sharp, Ernest E.	6026846	Private
Sharp, George W.	6024734	Private
Shaw, Alfred	14710339	L/Corporal
Shaw, William T.	6016934	Private
Sheenan, James J.	3253058	Sergeant
Shelley, Terence G.	6026138	Private
Shepherd, John W.	7942560	Private
Sherfield, Dennis G.	4923361	Private
Sheridan, John	6013649	Private
Shields, Norman	3865858	L/Corporal
Shoesmith, John	6016357	Private
Shorter, Harry	6019786	Corporal
Shrimpton, Harry W.	6022059	Private
Shuster, Stephen	6027109	Private
Silverstein, Leon J.	6028493	Private
Simmons, Albert V.	6013163	Private
Simmons, Frederick P. A.	14618156	Private
Simpson, Edgar	421142	Private
Simpson, James	3657831	L/Corporal
Simpson, Kenneth F.	14499964	Private
Sims, C. W.	852839	Corporal
Single, Geoffrey R. C.	109539	Lieutenant
Singleton, Herbert	13103237	Private
Singleton, William A.	6027686	Private
Skeggs, Robert	14401788	Private
Skerrett, John	3456355	L/Corporal
Slobom, Herbert L.	6013727	Corporal
Smith, Bertie W.	14655617	Private
Smith, Cecil A.	14288525	Private
Smith, Cyril E.	247046	Lieutenant
Smith, Denis W.	182327	Major
Smith, Edward	6024118	Private
Smith, Edward S. G.	5730330	Private
Smith, Frank E. L.	6014812	L/Corporal
Smith, Frank G.	6014218	Private
Smith, Frederick	6014578	Private
Smith, Henry G.	6025111	Private
Smith, John	14229222	Private
Smith, Leonard	6010336	Private
Smith, Philip H.	130561	Lieutenant
Smith, Ronald G.	14207073	Private

ROLL OF HONOUR (1939-45)

Surname and Christian Name	Army Number	Rank
Smith, Roy A.	6013415	Private
Smith, Samuel C.	6019902	Private
Smith, Thomas G.	6025659	Private
Smith, Thomas W.	4922059	Private
Smith, William C.	6012152	L/Corporal
Smith, William H.	3444679	Sergeant
Smithson, John L.	14659779	Private
Sneddon, R. McN.	1141149	Private
Snow, Frank A.	6923545	Private
Snow, James W.	14213880	Private
Snow, Patrick A.	6016202	Private
Snowden, Derek	14408635	Private
Snoxell, Horace F. W.	6011070	Sergeant
Sorby, Wilfred	14351999	Private
Sparkes, John E.	6027229	Private
Speight, John H.	6005319	Private
Spinks, Alfred H.	6029291	Private
Spooner, Walter T.	6023456	Private
Spragg, Leslie A.	6027692	Private
Spraggons, George W. C.	6022306	Private
Springham, George D.	6021925	Private
Stanfield, Charles W.	4918925	Corporal
Staples, William F.	6024123	Private
Steedman, Alexander S.	189327	Lieutenant
Stebbings, Alfred G.	14242086	L/Corporal
Stephenson, John	6024894	Private
Stephenson, Thomas F.	14405171	Private
Stevens, Albert T.	6027012	Private
Stevens, Kenneth	14437905	Private
Stevens, Stanley W.	6010369	Private
Stewart, Daniel L.	100683	Lieutenant
Stewart, James A.	6019789	Private
Stiles, Donald F.	6016313	Private
Stiles, Reginald W.	14655620	Private
Stockburn, Harry	3252960	Corporal
Stokes, Sidney L.	314187	2/Lieutenant
Strachan, Robert M.	3254224	Private
Strangleman, Cecil E.	14744326	Private
Stratton, Henry T.	6026815	Private
Street, Percy C. W.	6016151	L/Sergeant
Stroud, Roland H.	6289969	Private
Strutt, Arnold G.	6016275	Private

Surname and Christian Name	Army Number	Rank
Stuart, John	3252272	Private
Summers, Douglas J.	6011667	L/Sergeant
Sutherland, J.	2877612	Private
Suttie, Edwin C. N.	3251790	Private
Sweeting, Charles M.	6012290	Private
Sweetman, Cyril L.	6005804	Private
Tattersall, Major R.	6019343	Private
Taylor, John B.	3191538	Private
Taylor, William C.	6012325	Private
Taylor, Rodney C.	6024128	Private
Teague, Stanley	14330803	Private
Tempest, Harry	4923784	L/Corporal
Templeman, Leonard G. E.	6026905	Private
Tewkesbury, George	6023048	Private
Thom, William	14613272	Private
Thomas, Charles W.	5389619	Private
Thomas, George E.	6012473	L/Corporal
Thomas, Harry P.	4074475	Private
Thompson, Kenneth H.	6011512	Private
Thornton, Frank J.	288937	Lieutenant
Thornton, George A.	6009497	Private
Thornton, Hanson	4624028	Private
Thredder, Robert L. C.	10081004	Private
Thresher, Allan	14631146	Private
Thulbourn, Derrick S.	14328571	Private
Thurlow, Alexander C.	6012085	Private
Thwaites, Nembhard J.	303860	Lieutenant
Tidman, Arnold C.	6011938	Private
Tillott, William L.	14586601	Private
Tongue, Leslie W.	14550399	Private
Toswell, Reginald G.	5875829	Sergeant
Tough, Ernest J.	14529015	Private
Townson, Edward	14303114	Private
Tucker, Alfred W.	6008687	W.O. Class II
Tull, James W.	6026265	Private
Turner, Charles W. G.	6028503	Private
Turner, Sidney H.	6025388	Private
Tuvey, Henry J.	6013193	Corporal
Tweedie-Smith, John P.	33369	Captain
Twiddy, Jack	6022140	Private

Surname and Christian Name	Army Number	Rank
Ulph, Ronald A.	203093	Lieutenant
Uncles, Ernest	6024495	Private
Upton, Norman R., D.S.O., O.B.E.	5059	Lieutenant-Colonel
Usher, Sidney E.	6025417	Private
Van Bergen, Arthur C.	5124843	Private
Vine, Raymond A. B.	5504883	Private
Wadman, Herbert G.	6028113	Private
Wagstaffe, Bertram H.	6011118	L/Corporal
Wakeling, Horace	6014396	Private
Walford, James	6022095	L/Corporal
Walker, Charles F.	6021776	Private
Walker, Edward T.	6025396	Private
Walker, George	6008011	L/Corporal
Walker, Harold G.	6022143	Corporal
Walker, John R.	4983805	Private
Wallace, William J.	6021758	Private
Wallis, Ronald	6031382	Private
Walsh, Daniel	14573615	Private
Walters, Richard	6005291	W.O. Class II
Walton, Thomas	3661928	Private
Warburton, Thomas	3252971	Private
Ward, Frederick T.	6021956	Private
Warner, Charles	6012600	Private
Warren, Edward R.	5958154	Private
Washbourn, Arthur C. S.	6021778	Private
Washington, George	6019999	Private
Waters, William J.	6015522	Corporal
Watkins, Norman J.	6022096	Private
Watson, Alfred J.	6021759	Private
Watson, Edward T.	14655454	Private
Watson, James A.	6017604	Private
Watts, George	6021959	Private
Watts, John W.	4922354	Corporal
Waylett, Douglas H.	6011858	Private
Weakford, Edward	6023057	L/Sergeant
Weatherley, P. E. J. H., M.C.	112978	Captain
Weavers, Clifford S.	6016483	Private
Webb, Arthur J.	6021773	Private
Webb, G. F.	14284305	Private
Webb, Herbert E.	14591777	Private

Surname and Christian Name	Army Number	Rank
Webb, Keith	4079043	L/Corporal
Webb, Leonard A.	3651907	Private
Webster, Ernest	3450257	Private
Webster, James W.	6012106	Sergeant
Weller, James R.	6016987	Private
West, Alfred W.	6022097	L/Sergeant
Westcott, Eric J.	6021770	Private
Westwood, Stanley C.	6027197	Private
Whalley, William A.	6016648	Private
Whelan, Graham F.	14558800	Private
Whiskin, Frederick P.	6020059	Private
Whitaker, Walter	4537529	Private
White, Charles J. H.	6025180	Private
White, Ernest A.	6022152	Private
Whiteley, Albert	1578128	Private
Whitley, Derek T.	271896	Lieutenant
Whymer, Claude	6020527	Private
Whyte, Gerald A.	182382	Lieutenant
Wilder, Wallis	6013644	Private
Wilkinson, Alfred	14403884	Private
Wilkins, Douglas P.	5953323	Sergeant
Wilkins, William H.	6012666	Private
Willey, Reginald C.	14330805	L/Corporal
Williams, David R.	4079426	Private
Williams, Edwin J. C.	91764	Lieutenant
Williams, Harry E.	14614821	Private
Williams, Peter	6025707	Private
Williams, Thomas	4922092	Private
Williams, William	6013528	Private
Williamson, Adam R.	3251802	Private
Williamson, Frederick G.	6013736	L/Corporal
Williamson, George S.	2610	L/Corporal
Willingham, Frank A. C.	14655913	Private
Wilson, Alexander G.	6013353	Private
Wilson, Edward	14659809	Private
Wilson, Edward	6013157	Private
Wilson, Henry F.	6016306	Private
Wilson, Robert A.	6021771	Private
Winstone, Ernest H.	6011429	Private
Wiseman, Samuel	6025991	L/Corporal
Withers, Alfred J.	6026566	Private
Wood, Douglas B.	6027278	Private

Surname and Christian Name	Army Number	Rank
Wood, Douglas G.	4079196	L/Corporal
Wood, Henry B.	6012032	Private
Wood, Samuel	3911670	Private
Wood, Walter A.	6012118	Private
Woodison, Stanley	6020494	Private
Woodley, Reginald E.	6013197	Private
Woods, Joseph William	6028114	Private
Woodward, Vincent	14658046	Private
Woodwards, Robert J.	6013461	Private
Wootton, Morrison J.	72751	Captain
Worthington, Ronald A.	14612497	Private
Wren, Ernest E.	6019299	Private
Wright, Frederick G.	4923019	Private
Wright, Thomas C.	6022010	Private
Wyatt, Arthur E.	6016299	Private
Wymer, Sydney G.	5836340	Private
Young, Frank R.	6012092	L/Corporal
Young, Walter G.	6025189	L/Corporal

APPENDIX II

HONOURS AND AWARDS WON BY OFFICERS AND OTHER RANKS OF THE REGIMENT DURING THE SECOND WORLD WAR, 1939–45

(This list has been compiled from official War Office sources)

> But he'll remember with advantages
> What feats he did that day; then shall our names,
> Familiar in his mouth as household words,—
> Harry the King, Bedford and Exeter,
> Warwick and Talbot, Salisbury and Gloucester,—
> Be in their flowing cups freshly remember'd.
> HENRY V.

FRANCE AND BELGIUM, 1940

6008398	Andrews, G.	Private	Mention	20.12.40
10020	Blest, A. H.	Lieutenant-Colonel	Mention	26.7.40
95631	Browne, D. W.	2/Lieutenant	Mention	20.12.40
6009700	Clarke, C. T. V.	L/Corporal	M.M.	22.10.40
6018333	Coffee, S. H.	Private	Mention	20.12.40
50249	Cramphorn, J. F.	Captain	Mention	20.12.40
5999085	Green, W.	W.O. Class II	Mention	20.12.40
6002768	Head, L. J.	Sergeant	M.M.	22.10.40
95497	Irwin, A. S.	2/Lieutenant	M.C.	22.10.40
5999253	Lewis, R.	W.O. Class II	Mention	26.7.40
6028870	Lorraine, P. P.	Private	M.M.	12.8.41
36865	Sheffield, G. N. H.	Captain	M.B.E.	11.7.40
48277	Smith, W. S.	Captain	Mention	26.7.40
6190605	Sutton, A. F.	W.O. Class I	D.C.M.	11.7.40
104	Wilmer, G. H.	Brigadier	Mention	26.7.40
14970	Wilson, C. L.	Major	Mention	20.12.40

THE MIDDLE EAST

6029006	Adlam, D. L.	Corporal	Mention	24.6.43
6010746	Applebee, F.	Sergeant	D.C.M.	24.2.42
6016682	Bacon, S. C.	L/Corporal	Mention	6.4.44
6014395	Bardell, A.	L/Corporal	Mention	13.1.44
6013529	Bartlett, E. N.	L/Corporal	M.M.	19.8.43
180247	Beech, D. J.	Lieutenant	M.C.	28.1.43
180247	Beech, D. J.	Lieutenant	Mention	24.6.43
88354	Gregory, H. C.	Captain	M.C.	28.1.43

HONOURS AND AWARDS

837518	Blows, C.	Private	Mention	30.12.41
6007953	Brewer, H. T.	Corporal	M.M.	22.7.43
36468	Brooks, C. A.	Major	Mention	14.2.46
6008270	Burgar, A. J.	Sergeant	M.M.	29.11.40
6012348	Calder F. J.	Private	Mention	30.12.41
6025836	Calvert, M. H.	Private	M.M.	24.2.42
6021210	Carter, G. Z. F. M.	Private	M.M.	18.2.43
6014477	Chapman, E. K.	Sergeant	D.C.M.	24.9.42
70699	Chappell, L. W. A.	Captain	Mention	30.6.42
70699	Chappell, L. W. A.	Captain	M.C.	18.2.43
6018673	Churan, C. A.	Private	M.M.	24.2.42
6005912	Clark, A. G.	C.Q.M.S.	Mention	30.12.41
6012035	Clarkson, R. W.	L/Corporal	M.M.	31.1.41
6006826	Cogan, C. H.	W.O. Class II	Mention	30.12.41
235720	Conder, J. B.	Lieutenant	M.C.	23.9.45
89063	Cooke, T.	Captain	Mention	6.4.44
70186	Cooper, E. B.	Captain	M.C.	14.2.46
90215	Cooper, J. R. A.	Captain	Mention	9.8.45
6008121	Copley, W.	L/Sergeant	Mention	15.12.42
6010732	Cordery, A. F.	Private	M.M.	24.2.42
6005337	Cornell, W. E.	W.O. Class II	D.C.M.	21.10.41
6019762	Cronk, N.	Sergeant	M.M.	25.11.43
74755	Cullen, A. L.	Captain	M.C.	14.2.46
6011109	Daisley, E.	Private	Mention	30.12.41
5998338	Dalley, C. E.	W.O. Class II	Mention	13.1.45
6010527	Day, S. J.	W.O. Class II	Mention	24.6.43
18333	Drury, G. H.	Major	Mention	30.12.41
18333	Drury, G. H.	Major	Mention	13.1.44
46094	Dyer, H. T. J.	L/Corporal	M.M.	14.2.46
143520	Edrupt, K. D.	Captain	Mention	6.4.44
6010866	Eldridge, A. W. G.	Private	M.M.	19.8.41
2940	Finn, J. F., M.C.	Major	Mention	13.1.44
6016369	Fisher, R.	Private	Mention	14.2.46
6020871	Furnival, S. G.	L/Corporal	M.M.	24.2.42
6024989	Gardner, H. G.	Corporal	Mention	6.4.44
39650	Gibson, G. M.	Colonel	Mention	24.6.43
39650	Gibson, G. M.	Colonel	Mention	14.10.43
190300	Gillmore, M. I.	Captain	Mention	30.12.41
182323	Gingell, B. G.	2/Lieutenant	M.C.	24.2.42
6022034	Gladwell, A. G.	L/Corporal	Mention	15.12.42
6021433	Glibbery, J. T.	L/Corporal	M.M.	19.8.43
6028900	Goodridge, E. G.	Private	M.M.	19.8.43
6009580	Grantshaw, G.	Private	M.M.	24.2.42
6012892	Green, G. C.	Sergeant	Mention	13.1.44

THE ESSEX REGIMENT

141761	Grimley, B. F. H.	2/Lieutenant	D.S.O.	21.10.41
130061	Grist, T. W.	Captain	M.C.	25.11.43
217422	Hailes, C.	Lieutenant	M.C.	19.8.43
6009204	Hayes, C. W.	Corporal	D.C.M.	24.2.42
6014978	Hazell, W. B.	Private	M.M.	19.8.43
6016667	Hazle, E. B.	Private	D.C.M.	24.9.42
6019216	Heasman, J. T.	Corporal	Mention	6.4.44
56702	Higson, J. F.	Major	M.C.	24.2.42
6020904	Hill, W. A.	Corporal	B.E.M.	4.1.45
5880542	Horne, T.	Sergeant	M.M.	28.1.43
6009723	Howard, G. F.	L/Corporal	Mention	1.4.41
6021493	Hudson, G.	L/Corporal	M.M.	22.7.43
6021513	Jackson, G.	Private	D.C.M.	22.7.43
6010334	James, F. G.	L/Corporal	Mention	1.4.41
53746	James, R. B.	Major	D.S.O.	19.8.41
53746	James, R. B.	Major	Mention	19.8.41
53746	James, R. B.	Lieutenant-Colonel	Bar to D.S.O.	1.6.43
53746	James, R. B.	Lieutenant-Colonel	Mention	24.6.43
2731889	Jones, T. S.	W.O. Class II	M.M.	25.11.43
185232	Ketteley, F. J.	Captain	M.C.	22.7.43
185232	Ketteley, F. J.	Captain	Mention	13.1.44
237737	Lambshead, H. T.	Lieutenant	M.C.	9.8.45
6019600	Laplain, J. F.	Sergeant	M.M.	17.6.43
126184	Lawrence, C. H.	2/Lieutenant	M.C.	21.10.41
20962	Littlehales, R. W.	Major	Mention	30.6.42
66669	Lovelace, A.	Lieutenant	M.B.E.	30.12.41
177788	Mann, K. W. M.	2/Lieutenant	M.C.	24.2.42
6011819	Marchint, G. H.	L/Sergeant	M.M.	24.2.42
6029281	Marjoram, A.	L/Sergeant	M.M.	19.8.43
250694	Mason, S. G.	Lieutenant	Mention	6.4.44
6014592	Matthews, C. B.	Private	M.M.	24.9.42
6009855	Mead, T. L.	L/Corporal	M.M.	24.2.42
6007527	Miles, T. A.	W.O. Class II	Mention	24.6.43
73369	Muirhead, T. D'A.	Lieutenant	M.C.	19.8.41
143513	Nelson, C.	Captain	Mention	15.12.42
6013244	Nethercoat, T. C.	Private	Mention	6.4.44
6701	Nichols, J. S., M.C.	Lieutenant-Colonel	D.S.O.	21.10.41
6701	Nichols, J. S., D.S.O., M.C.	Lieutenant-Colonel	Mention	21.10.41
6701	Nichols, J. S., D.S.C., M.C.	Lieutenant-Colonel	Bar to D.S.O.	24.2.42
39065	Noble, A.	Lieutenant-Colonel	Mention	30.6.42
39065	Noble, A.	Lieutenant-Colonel	Mention	24.6.43
39065	Noble, A.	Lieutenant-Colonel	D.S.O.	19.8.43

86229	Parker, C. P. N.	Major	Mention	6.4.44
9333	Paton, C. M.	Lieutenant-Colonel	Mention	9.9.42
9333	Paton, C. M.	Lieutenant-Colonel	Mention	24.6.43
6010301	Peacock, C. H. E.	Private	Mention	30.12.41
72881	Plackett, R. A.	Major	Mention	6.4.44
73724	Pouch, H. R.	Lieutenant-Colonel	M.B.E.	6.1.44
6022284	Raby, W. R.	Corporal	Mention	6.4.44
74668	Robinson, C. H.	Major	Mention	30.12.41
6019924	Rodbard, C. A.	Private	Mention	15.12.42
6010523	Rose, C. J.	W.O. Class I	Mention	24.6.43
6010523	Rose, C. J.	W.O. Class I	D.C.M.	25.11.43
23890	Salew, N. R.	Lieutenant-Colonel	Mention	6.4.44
6013711	Seagram, A. W.	L/Corporal	Mention	6.4.44
5734005	Skuse, F. C.	Private	Mention	9.8.45
51291	Smith, D. J. M.	Major	D.S.O.	28.1.43
6012886	Smith, G. T. H.	Corporal	M.M.	24.2.42
6016230	Smith, R.	L/Sergeant	M.M.	14.2.46
131085	Sowerby, W. F.	2/Lieutenant	Mention	30.12.41
140610	Spicer, A. G.	2/Lieutenant	Mention	30.12.41
65836	Stevenson-Hamilton, I. J. D.	Captain	D.S.O.	24.2.42
65836	Stevenson-Hamilton, I. J. D.	Captain	Mention	24.2.42
6014427	Stringer, J.	Private	M.M.	19.8.43
6016803	Taylor, H. T.	L/Corporal	Mention	24.6.43
6016803	Taylor, H. T.	L/Corporal	M.M.	19.8.43
6018320	Tedder, J. S. A.	L/Corporal	M.M.	22.7.43
6021944	Thompson, H.	Corporal	M.M.	19.8.43
6011121	Thornhill, A. T.	L/Corporal	Mention	30.12.41
6016880	Tokeley, R. C.	Sergeant	Mention	9.8.45
5875829	Toswell, R. G.	Sergeant	Mention	14.2.46
10365	Trollope, H. C. N.	Brigadier	Mention	13.1.44
56703	Waite, W. N. C.	Captain	Mention	30.12.41
138043	Watt, J.	Captain	M.C.	17.6.43
138043	Watt, J.	Captain	D.S.O.	19.8.43
6013605	Wheeler, R. G.	C.Q.M.S.	M.M.	14.10.43
6021949	White, A. H.	Private	Mention	6.4.44
6021185	White, E. H.	Private	M.M.	24.2.42
6010512	Wiley, L. A.	Private	Mention	13.1.44
6025409	Wiseman, C. W.	Private	Mention	14.2.46
73727	Young, H. J.	Captain	M.C.	19.8.43
73727	Young, H. J.	Captain	Mention	13.1.44
112978	Weatherley, P. E. J. H.	Captain	M.C.	22.7.43

INDIA AND PERSIA AND IRAQ COMMAND

6014518	Francis, E. C.	C.Q.M.S.	Mention	23.12.43
23475	French, J. L.	Brigadier	C.B.E.	1943
6002173	Ketley, L. G.	Sergeant	Mention	5.8.43
105112	May, V. A. L.	Captain	Mention	5.8.43
6016443	Rivers, G. A.	W.O. Class I	Mention	5.8.43
27403	Upton, P. V.	Major	M.B.E.	5.8.43

SICILY

6028982	Carpenter, C. C. F.	L/Corporal	Mention	23.3.44
53746	James, R. B., D.S.O.	Lieutenant-Colonel	Second Bar to D.S.O.	21.10.43
26342	Rea, S. C. W. W.	Lieutenant-Colonel	Mention	23.3.44
10365	Trollope, H. C. N.	Colonel	C.B.E.	1943

ITALY

6014624	Armsby, A. F.	Corporal	M.M.	4.5.44
6027818	Barber, W. W.	Private	Mention	29.11.45
47360	Barrett, F.	Major	Mention	29.11.45
113508	Beckett, D. A.	Major	D.S.O.	27.4.44
180247	Beech, D. J., M.C.	Captain	Bar to M.C.	22.8.44
5384774	Bishop, R.	L/Corporal	M.M.	23.3.44
6024951	Bishop, R.	Corporal	M.M.	24.8.44
5783290	Boakes, F. A.	L/Corporal	Mention	29.11.45
284013	Brangham, W. T.	Captain	Mention	29.11.45
6018146	Bridgman, J. W.	Sergeant	Mention	29.11.45
6013961	Bristow, W.	Corporal	Mention	19.7.45
6016833	Brown, J. F.	L/Corporal	Mention	11.1.45
315398	Bungard, J.	Lieutenant	M.M.	1943
6024602	Butterfield, E.	L/Corporal	Mention	23.5.46
138041	Buzza, W. W.	Captain	Mention	29.11.45
6022069	Cardy, A. L.	Private	Mention	29.11.45
6016966	Chambers, R. E.	Sergeant	B.E.M.	9.1.46
6013543	Chattaway, R.	L/Sergeant	Mention	19.7.45
6021327	Clatworthy, V.	L/Sergeant	Mention	19.7.45
6007186	Cook, W. H. J.	W.O. Class II	D.C.M.	24.8.44
87564	Counsell, D. C.	Major	M.B.E.	28.6.45
87564	Counsell, D. C.	Major	Mention	29.11.45
6014857	Cox, R. H.	W.O. Class II	Mention	11.1.45

6019756	Craven, R.	L/Corporal	Mention	23.5.46
285626	Cresswell, W. R.	Lieutenant	Mention	19.7.45
6014454	Cross, J. R.	Sergeant	M.M.	24.8.44
6012365	Croucher, N. T. H.	W.O. Class I	Mention	11.1.45
6012365	Croucher, N. T. H.	W.O. Class I	Mention	29.11.45
6022028	Dale, E. J. P.	L/Sergeant	M.M.	23.3.44
63925	Davey, N. G.	Major	M.C.	8.3.45
3532485	Davies, E.	Private	M.M.	21.9.44
45299	Drury, H. J.	Major	M.C.	29.6.44
214611	Edwards, A. M.	Major	Mention	23.5.46
6014658	Ellis, E. W.	Corporal	M.M.	24.8.44
6019994	Ellwood, W. C.	L/Sergeant	D.C.M.	13.1.44
6028931	Elsmore, G. N.	Private	M.M.	23.3.44
6019754	Erith, W. C.	Private	Mention	11.1.45
6022079	Fenn, E. T.	L/Corporal	Mention	11.1.45
6021417	Fincher, H. B.	Corporal	M.M.	6.4.44
6013676	Fisher, C. L. R.	Corporal	Mention	19.1.45
6013676	Fisher, C. L. R.	Corporal	M.M.	13.12.45
68034	Foster, I. P.	Captain	Mention	29.11.45
88345	Gregory, H. C., M.C.	Major	Bar to M.C.	24.8.44
187126	Griffen, W. F.	Captain	M.C.	28.12.43
130061	Grist, T. W.	Major	Mention	11.1.45
3254285	Hastie, J.	Private	M.M.	6.4.44
6019569	Hatcliff, S. A.	L/Corporal	Mention	29.11.45
6016667	Hazle, E. B., D.C.M.	Corporal	Bar to D.C.M.	3.8.44
5778332	Hill, F.	Corporal	Mention	29.11.45
53875	Hinde, P. C.	Lieutenant-Colonel	D.S.O.	23.8.45
53875	Hinde, P. C.	Lieutenant-Colonel	Mention	29.11.45
6021862	Jeal, F.	L/Corporal	Mention	19.7.45
92981	Kaye, L. C.	Major	M.C.	23.3.44
132270	Kenrick, C. J.	Major	M.C.	26.4.45
6002173	Ketley, L. G.	Sergeant	M.M.	23.3.44
258293	Lane, E. H.	Lieutenant	Mention	19.7.45
6014492	Law, E. F.	Corporal	Mention	23.5.46
145888	Lee, A. R.	Captain	Mention	23.5.46
52778	Lee, J. W. G.	Major	D.S.O.	6.4.44
6024704	Leppard, P. J.	Corporal	Mention	24.8.44
6011946	Lewis, P. G.	Private	M.M.	24.8.44
109050	Liddell, D. O.	Major	M.C.	6.4.44
5888672	Lloyd, J.	L/Corporal	Mention	29.11.45
3252946	Lofthouse, J. W.	L/Corporal	M.M.	6.4.44
6012435	Lungley, A.	Sergeant	Mention	19.7.45
5193930	Mahoney, J.	Private	Mention	11.1.45
153306	Mallinson, M. S.	Major	M.C.	20.7.44

6025936	May, R. C.	W.O. Class II	Mention	29.11.45
90300	Maytham, P. L. N.	Captain	Mention	29.11.45
251446	McClair, A. R.	Captain	Mention	9.11.44
6021581	McQueen, J.	Corporal	Mention	11.1.45
6008074	Mummery, A. H.	Sergeant	Mention	11.1.45
5780938	Nunn, E. J.	L/Corporal	Mention	23.5.46
6018296	O'Donoghue, J. E.	Corporal	M.M.	24.8.44
77280	Ostler, A. L.	Captain	M.B.E.	21.12.44
255608	Owen, F. J.	Captain	Mention	29.11.45
255608	Owen, F. J.	Captain	M.C.	13.12.45
9333	Paton, C. M.	Brigadier	C.V.O.	20.7.44
9333	Paton, C. M.	Brigadier	Mention	11.1.45
6014633	Penson, H. W.	C.Q.M.S.	M.M.	23.3.44
6014212	Piper, L. T.	L/Corporal	Mention	11.1.45
6022284	Raby, W. R.	Sergeant	Mention	11.1.45
26342	Rea, S. C. W. W.	Lieutenant-Colonel	O.B.E.	13.12.45
87542	Reeves, N.	Captain	Mention	11.1.45
6016955	Richardson, R.	Private	Mention	19.7.45
6010523	Rose, C. J., D.C.M.	W.O. Class I	Bar to D.C.M.	24.8.44
6018400	Roy, F. J.	Sergeant	Mention	11.1.45
6018400	Roy, F. J.	Sergeant	Mention	29.11.45
6016424	Shortland, I.	C.Q.M.S.	Mention	19.7.45
6014466	Smith, D. D.	Sergeant	M.M.	23.3.44
6014668	Smith, H. C.	Sergeant	Mention	11.1.45
6016130	Smith, K.	Private	M.M.	24.8.44
6007420	Stanford, J. L.	Sergeant	Mention	29.11.45
6009450	Stebbing, M. A.	Private	Mention	19.7.45
6013533	Stephenson, G.	Private	Mention	19.7.45
193814	Stringer, L. E.	Major	Mention	23.5.46
247778	Stuart, G. W. W.	Captain	M.C.	10.5.45
6012679	Swann, W. J.	Sergeant	D.C.M.	6.4.44
3249134	Syme, G. D.	Sergeant	M.M.	6.4.44
264954	Taylor, A. H.	Lieutenant	M.C.	21.9.44
6013733	Thomson, J. W.	W.O. Class II	Mention	23.5.46
197244	Thulbourn, I. D.	Captain	Mention	29.11.45
71272	Trimble, C. O. P.	Major	Mention	23.5.46
6016590	Ward, E. S.	C.Q.M.S.	Mention	29.11.45
6016590	Ward, E. S.	C.Q.M.S.	B.E.M.	13.12.45
226600	Warne, J. P.	Captain	Mention	29.11.45
6014661	Watts, J. A.	Private	Mention	11.1.45
4616884	Whitaker, A. A.	Corporal	Mention	11.1.45
6012203	Whitby, S. M.	Sergeant	B.E.M.	13.12.45
6021670	White, E. J.	L/Corporal	Mention	24.8.44
75464	Whiteley, N.	Major	Mention	11.1.45

117140	Whyte, C. E. A.	Captain	Mention	19.7.45
6016706	Wilkinson, T.	Sergeant	Mention	11.1.45
6031800	Wisbey, W.	L/Corporal	Mention	23.5.46
6027444	Wood, S. J. H.	Private	Mention	27.11.45
6013461	Woodwards, R.	Private	Mention	19.7.45

G.O.C. C.-IN-C. CENTRAL MEDITERRANEAN FORCE

6026397	Chinnick, H. H.	Corporal	M.M.	10.5.45
111734	Croft, N. A. C.	Major	D.S.O.	15.3.45
6012239	Eve, G. M.	L/Sergeant	M.M.	10.5.45
6012900	Hutton, G. F.	W.O. Class II	Mention	22.2.45
6012900	Hutton, G. F.	W.O. Class II	D.C.M.	15.3.45

BURMA AND INDIA COMMAND

172308	Baker, H.S.	Lieutenant	Mention	19.7.45
180248	Black, G. W.	Captain	Mention	19.7.45
6009536	Bright, J. B.	Sergeant	Mention	19.7.45
6024252	Brommick, A.	Private	Mention	19.7.45
6016416	Brown, R. F.	W.O. Class II	Mention	19.7.45
189417	Brownless, R. S.	Captain	Mention	19.4.46
6018573	Churan, C. A.	Sergeant	Mention	19.7.45
63304	Church, P. J. B.	Captain	Mention	27.9.45
149012	Clark, P. H. C.	Captain	Mention	10.1.46
5998323	Cooper, W. F.	L/Corporal	Mention	19.7.45
6026968	Cottle, S. R.	Private	M.M.	5.10.44
132172	Dawkins, A. F.	Major	Mention	5.4.45
132172	Dawkins, A. F.	Major	Mention	27.9.45
201475	Deed, F. J.	Captain	Mention	27.9.45
143519	Drake, S. E.	Captain	Mention	27.9.45
251525	Earley, D. F.	Captain	Mention	19.4.45
14612364	Ellis, L. W.	Private	Mention	19.7.45
90845	Fairhead, J. D.	Major	Mention	5.4.45
90845	Fairhead, J. D.	Major	Mention	19.7.45
86515	Franklin, P. H. A. L.	Major	Mention	19.7.45
200906	Garon, F. J.	Captain	Mention	9.5.46
6018303	Goodhew, A. L.	Private	Mention	19.7.45
6008429	Grimwood, R. le V.	Private	Mention	5.4.45
6025014	Heath, H.	L/Corporal	Mention	19.7.45
6003818	Jackson, S. W. E.	C.Q.M.S.	M.M.	8.2.45
151595	Johnston, J. H.	Captain	Mention	27.9.45
182324	Jones, H. M.	Captain	Mention	5.4.45
182324	Jones, H. M.	Captain	Mention	10.1.46
31652	Jones, H. F. H.	Major	M.B.E.	16.12.43
6009281	Klintworth, C. J.	Sergeant	Mention	19.7.45

6003074	Larcher, W.	W.O. Class I	Mention	16.12.43
12139	Laverty H. J., M.C.	Lieutenant-Colonel	D.S.O.	22.6.44
12139	Laverty, H. J., M.C.	Lieutenant-Colonel	Mention	19.7.45
198325	Levy, G. L.	Captain	Mention	10.1.46
66669	Lovelace, A., M.B.E.	Major	Mention	5.4.45
66669	Lovelace, A., M.B.E.	Major	M.C.	28.6.45
186205	Lowe, E. R.	Captain	Mention	9.5.46
176280	Lowe, J. N.	Lieutenant	Mention	27.9.45
6031414	Mariner, C. D.	Private	Mention	5.4.45
164773	McArthur, I. C.	Captain	Mention	10.1.46
200838	McCrossan, G. J. M.	Captain	Mention	19.7.45
6028826	Mower, A.	Private	Mention	5.4.45
87166	Nicholson, J. A.	Major	Mention	5.4.45
6009130	Peacock, H. J.	C.Q.M.S.	Mention	5.4.45
6027027	Phillips, J.	Sergeant	M.M.	17.1.46
6027791	Reeve, J. A.	Sergeant	M.M.	22.3.45
13021495	Rigby, P.	Private	Mention	19.7.45
6011310	Robinson, H. A.	W.O. Class II	Mention	19.7.45
6009770	Root, G.	Sergeant	Mention	19.7.45
258050	Rose, T. L.	Captain	Mention	10.1.46
6023225	Sammon, T.	L/Corporal	Mention	19.7.45
6009669	Slaughter, C. B.	W.O. Class II	Mention	10.1.46
247046	Smith, C. E.	Lieutenant	Mention	10.1.46
6012886	Smith, G. T. H., M.M.	Sergeant	Bar to M.M.	8.2.45
117137	Telford, E. C.	Major	Mention	10.1.46
5059	Upton, N. R., O.B.E.	Lieutenant-Colonel	D.S.O.	28.10.42
199757	Waddell, F. W.	Major (Q.M.)	M.B.E.	19.7.45
34939	Walker, G. H.	Lieutenant-Colonel	Mention	5.4.45
34939	Walker, G. H.	Lieutenant-Colonel	Mention	19.7.45
117139	Walker, L. G.	Major	Mention	19.7.45
6016205	Watkins, L. H.	Sergeant	Mention	19.7.45
138044	Watts, P. E.	Captain	M.C.	5.11.42
138044	Watts, P. E.	Captain	Mention	5.4.45
543943	Way, R.	Corporal	M.M.	28.6.45
232202	White, G. J.	Captain	Mention	19.7.45
6007391	Wildey, G.	W.O. Class I	Mention	19.7.45
6010007	Willis, J.	Sergeant	Mention	19.7.45
219190	Withey, G.	Major	Mention	10.1.46
6021077	Wybourn, M. W.	L/Corporal	Mention	19.7.45

NORTH-WEST EUROPE

50932	Bagot, C. F. V.	Major	Mention	10.5.45
324279	Barnes, C. L. A.	Lieutenant	M.C.	12.7.45

77102	Barrass, P. R.	Major	Mention	22.3.45
155091	Barrett-Lennard, D.	Lieutenant	Mention	4.4.46
6025238	Benson, K. A. G.	Corporal	Mention	8.11.45
26904	Boustead, H. L. H.	Lieutenant-Colonel	Order of Oranje Nassau	
95631	Browne, D. W.	Major	M.C.	19.10.44
6343307	Bucknell, F. S.	Corporal	M.M.	3.5.45
58152	Butler, M. A. H., M.C.	Lieutenant-Colonel	D.S.O.	12.4.45
5783267	Burt, B.	Private	Mention	22.3.45
44851	Charles, T. L. G.	Lieutenant-Colonel	Mention	22.3.45
44851	Charles, T. L. G.	Lieutenant-Colonel	D.S.O.	21.6.45
165804	Clarke, A. M. S.	Captain	Mention	8.11.45
39270	Clover, S. K.	Major	Mention	8.11.45
39270	Clover, S. K.	Major	M.C.	24.1.46
6025259	Coe, W.	Corporal	M.M.	19.10.44
230132	Cooper, H. A. S.	Lieutenant	M.C.	12.4.45
296029	Cooper, J.	Lieutenant	M.C.	19.10.44
6085856	Danby, G.	Corporal	Mention	9.8.45
6013793	Dean, H.	Private	Mention	4.4.46
129619	Dyer, I. C.	Major	Croix-de-Guerre 1944	
314168	Dyne, N.	Lieutenant	Mention	8.11.45
56468	Eden, G. A.	Lieutenant-Colonel	Mention	2.8.45
56468	Eden, G. A.	Lieutenant-Colonel	Bronze Cross (U.S.A.)	
45027	Elliott, G. G.	Lieutenant-Colonel	D.S.O.	23.1.46
6297840	Farmer, J. C. A.	Corporal	Mention	8.11.45
269415	Filby, R. G.	Captain	Mention	22.3.45
269415	Filby, R. G.	Captain	M.C.	12.4.45
269415	Filby, R. G.	Captain	Croix-de-Guerre	3.4.45
74019	Foote, C. J. A.	Major	Mention	8.11.45
74019	Foote, C. J. A.	Major	M.B.E.	24.1.46
105585	Garner, D. W. B.	Major	Mention	9.8.45
137394	Garner, E. C.	Major	M.C.	26.10.44
6019561	Giles, J. R.	Private	M.M.	19.10.44
4451961	Glendinning, E.	Sergeant	Mention	8.11.45
66419	Greene, J. S.	Captain	M.C.	21.6.45
4039193	Head, L.	Sergeant	Mention	4.4.46
6023170	Hill, I. E.	Corporal	M.M.	24.1.46
6139928	Holdaway, J.	W.O. Class II	Mention	4.4.46
14591153	Holland, F.	Private	M.M.	1.3.45
117134	Holme, M. W.	Major	M.C.	1.3.45
117134	Holme, M. W.	Major	Mention	22.3.45
6024348	Hutton, W.	Sergeant	Mention	4.4.46
14499454	Jordan, J. H.	Private	M.M.	21.12.44
228411	Keeling, C. D. E.	Captain	Mention	10.5.45
27218	Kelly, A. H.	Major	Mention	4.4.46

149494	Kirkman, M.	Major	M.C.	21.12.44
149494	Kirkman, M.	Major	Mention	4.4.46
170473	Kirkwood, J. F.	Captain	M.C.	21.4.46
14655880	Laver, M.	Private	Mention	4.4.46
6020117	Lawson, R. G.	Corporal	Mention	4.4.46
228210	Leavey, M. H.	Lieutenant	M.C.	19.10.44
6013686	Leggett, G. S.	Corporal	Mention	4.4.46
174453	Lipscombe, J.	Captain	M.C.	22.1.46
53459	Lewsey, T. L. W.	Major	Mention	8.11.45
6011899	Lloyd, E. J.	Corporal	Mention	4.4.46
162659	McMichael, W. F., M.C.	Major	Bar to M.C.	20.1.45
6004943	Mayes, F.	Sergeant	M.M.	24.1.46
14409372	McDougall, G.	Private	Mention	4.4.46
2353299	McLaughlin, D.	Private	Mention	4.4.46
232545	McMartin, J. S.	Lieutenant	M.C.	24.5.45
232545	McMartin, J. S.	Lieutenant	Mention	9.8.45
65826	McMillen, C. J. S.	Captain	Bronzen Kruis	1944
4030860	Morgan, A. W.	W.O. Class II	M.M.	1.3.45
6008074	Mummery, A. H.	W.O. Class II	D.C.M.	24.1.46
242311	Murphy, M. M.	Lieutenant	Mention	8.11.45
334125	Newcomb, W. M. C.	2/Lieutenant	M.C.	12.7.45
6018485	Newton, C. J.	Sergeant	Mention	4.4.46
—	Orr, J. N.	Lieutenant	M.C.	1944–5
86229	Parker, C. P. N.	Major	M.B.E.	29.3.45
69160	Parry, A. J. M.	Major	Mention	10.5.45
69160	Parry, A. J. M.	Major	M.C.	24.1.46
5615111	Piper, W. M.	Private	Mention	4.4.46
14574505	Pullen, E.	Corporal	Mention	8.11.45
307164	Quickenden, R. W. J.	Lieutenant	M.C.	12.4.45
6022000	Ringrose, R. W.	Sergeant	Mention	4.4.46
6030756	Saffrey, A.	Private	Mention	4.4.46
77097	Salmon, C.	Captain	Mention	4.4.46
314214	Sellors, R. B.	Lieutenant	M.C.	1.3.45
—	Selvage, D. J.	Captain	M.C.	1944–5
4586565	Shaw, B. J.	Private	D.C.M.	1.3.45
6016424	Shortland, I.	C.Q.M.S.	Mention	8.46
6011168	Sizzey, H. C.	Corporal	Mention	22.3.45
5947042	Skeels, J. W.	Sergeant	Mention	22.3.45
14207071	Skittrall, W. J.	Sergeant	D.C.M.	12.4.45
14207071	Skittrall, W. J.	Sergeant	Mention	10.5.45
14207071	Skittrall, W. J.	Sergeant	Croix-de-Guerre	27.4.45
5998308	Smith, R.	W.O. Class II	M.B.E.	24.1.46

HONOURS AND AWARDS

6022005	Spearman, G. H.	L/Sergeant	Mention	4.4.46
271319	Spencer, J. L.	Captain	Mention	8.11.45
243204	Spratt, K. J.	Lieutenant	Mention	10.5.45
6009450	Stebbing, M. A.	Private	Mention	4.46
14406007	Stephenson, A. P.	Private	Mention	4.4.46
514104	Stewart, W. A.	Major	Mention	2.8.45
6007498	Stothert, E. J.	Sergeant	Mention	9.8.45
78984	Stubbs, M. P.	Captain	Mention	4.4.46
5771582	Sturman, C. G.	Sergeant	M.M.	19.10.44
176913	Taylor, A. D.	Captain	Mention	4.4.46
6025714	Thompson, G. J.	C.Q.M.S.	Mention	4.4.46
304704	Thorogood, D. O.	Captain	Mention	4.4.46
164769	Townrow, J.	Captain	M.B.E.	11.10.45
14643368	Tyrell, V. F. C.	L/Corporal	Mention	10.5.45
299737	Vince, A. A.	Lieutenant	Mention	9.8.45
299737	Vince, A. A.	Lieutenant	M.C.	24.1.46
6010022	Walters, W. I.	Corporal	Mention	22.3.45
780818	Ward, S.	C.Q.M.S.	Mention	22.3.45
4923814	Whitehall, H.	Corporal	M.M.	19.10.44
117140	Whyte, C. E. A.	Captain	Mention	8.46
164774	Wilkins, P. J.	Major	M.C.	1.3.45
4105525	Williams, W. E.	Corporal	M.M.	21.12.44
301627	Woodbridge, L. O.	Captain	M.B.E.	24.1.46
6007569	Worwood, W. A.	L/Corporal	M.M.	19.10.44

SPECIAL OPERATIONS

6021252	Abramovitz, J.	Private	Mention	1.11.45
6012241	Bailey, E. D.	Private	Mention	26.7.45
149013	Coe, F. G.	Lieutenant	Mention	27.4.44
6014285	Dale, E. C.	Private	Mention	14.9.44
573051	Dennis, W. H.	Private	Mention	1.11.45
6016265	Francis, L. E.	Private	Mention	19.4.45
6096797	Hartley, L. H.	Private	Mention	9.11.44
6013031	Hewett, H. E.	Sergeant	Mention	23.1.47
6019825	Hicks, J. A.	Private	Mention	26.7.45
79651	Hopwood, H. G. L.	Lieutenant	Mention	5.7.45
79651	Hopwood, H. G. L.	Lieutenant	Croix-de-Guerre	
15338	May, K. F.	Lieutenant-Colonel	O.B.E.	29.6.44
201147	Milton, J. W.	Lieutenant	Mention	27.4.44
73369	Muirhead, T. D'A., M.C.	Lieutenant	Mention	1.3.45
86959	Murray, M. H.	Lieutenant	Mention	27.4.44
33927	Newman, A. C.	Lieutenant-Colonel	V.C.	19.6.45

33927	Newman, A. C.	Lieutenant-Colonel	Mention	20.12.45
94409	Roderick, J. M.	Lieutenant	M.C.	5.7.45
6016266	Rowland, J. P.	Private	Mention	9.11.44
6014270	South, J. W.	Corporal	Mention	3.8.44
17774	Starkey, N. L.	Lieutenant	M.B.E.	26.7.45
6014360	Thompson, R.	Private	Mention	5.7.45

OTHER AWARDS (BIRTHDAY HONOURS, NEW YEAR HONOURS, AND SPECIAL AWARDS)

Capel-Dunn, D. C.	Colonel	O.B.E.
Chell, R. A., D.S.O., M.C.	Lieutenant-Colonel	O.B.E.
Hearn, T. E.	Lieutenant-Colonel	Order of Oranje Nassau
Irwin, N. M. S., D.S.O., M.C.	Major-General	C.B.
Martin, T. A.	Lieutenant-Colonel	M.B.E.
Read, R. V., C.V.O., D.S.O., M.C.	Colonel	C.B.E.
Salew, N. R.	Lieutenant-Colonel	O.B.E.
Sutton, A. F., D.C.M.	W.O. Class I	Order of Oranje Nassau

APPENDIX III

AWARD OF THE VICTORIA CROSS TO LIEUTENANT-COLONEL A. C. NEWMAN

MAJOR A. C. NEWMAN was embodied in September 1939 with the 1/4th Battalion The Essex Regiment, and served with that Battalion until February 1940, when he was given command of No. 3 Independent Company raised within the 54th (East Anglian) Division.

He served with the Company in Norway from March to June 1940.

On the formation of No. 1 Special Service Battalion in November 1940, Major Newman became Second-in-Command. When the Commandos were formed in March 1941, Lieutenant-Colonel Newman was appointed to command No. 2 Commando, which he led in the raid on St. Nazaire in March 1942.

For his services in the operations, Lieutenant-Colonel Newman was awarded the Victoria Cross. The official citation reads:

"H.M. the King has recently approved the award of the Victoria Cross to Lieutenant-Colonel Augustus Charles Newman, The Essex Regiment (attached Commandos) (Salford, Bucks).

"On the night of the 27th/28th March, 1942, Lieutenant-Colonel Newman was in command of the military force detailed to land on enemy-occupied territory and destroy the dock installations of the German-controlled naval base at St. Nazaire.

"This important base was known to be heavily defended, and bomber support had to be abandoned owing to bad weather. The operation was therefore bound to be exceedingly hazardous, but Lieutenant-Colonel Newman, although empowered to call off the assault at any stage, was determined to carry to a successful conclusion the important task which had been assigned to him.

"Coolly and calmly he stood on the bridge of the leading craft, as the small force steamed up the estuary of the River Loire, although the ships had been caught in the enemy searchlights, and a murderous cross-fire opened from both flanks, causing heavy casualties.

"Although Lieutenant-Colonel Newman need not have landed himself, he was one of the first ashore, and, during the next five hours of bitter fighting, he personally entered several houses and shot up the occupants and supervised the operations in the town, utterly regardless of his own safety, and he never wavered in his resolution to carry through the operation upon which so much depended.

"An enemy gun position on the roof of a U-boat pen had been causing heavy casualties to the landing craft, and Lieutenant-Colonel Newman directed the fire of a mortar against this position to such effect that the gun was silenced. Still fully exposed, he then brought machine-gun fire to bear on an armed trawler in the harbour, compelling it to withdraw, and thus preventing many casualties in the main demolition area.

"Under the brilliant leadership of this officer the troops fought magnificently and held vastly superior enemy forces at bay, until the demolition parties had successfully completed their work of destruction.

"By this time, however, most of the landing craft had been sunk or set on fire and evacuation by sea was no longer possible. Although the main objective had been achieved, Lieutenant-Colonel Newman nevertheless was now determined to try to fight his way out into open country and so give all survivors a chance to escape.

"The only way out of the harbour area lay across a narrow iron bridge covered by enemy machine guns, and, although severely shaken by a German hand-grenade which had burst at his feet, Lieutenant-Colonel Newman personally led the charge which stormed the position, and under his inspiring leadership the small force fought its way through the streets to a point near the open country, when, all ammunition being expended, he and his men were finally overpowered by the enemy.

"The outstanding gallantry and devotion to duty of this fearless officer, his brilliant leadership and initiative, were largely responsible for the success of this perilous operation, which resulted in heavy damage to the important naval base at St. Nazaire."

LIEUTENANT-COLONEL A. C. NEWMAN, V.C.

(*Top left*) LIEUTENANT-COLONEL R. B. JAMES, D.S.O.
Lieutenant-Colonel James was awarded the D.S.O. with two bars before being killed in Normandy, July 1944.

(*Top right*) REGIMENTAL SERGEANT-MAJOR C. J. ROSE, D.C.M. (AND BAR).
1/4th Battalion The Essex Regiment.

(*Below*) L/CORPORAL E. B. HAZLE, D.C.M. (AND BAR).
1/4th Battalion The Essex Regiment.

[617]

APPENDIX IV

COMMANDING OFFICERS, 1929-50

Section I

COLONELS OF THE ESSEX REGIMENT, 1929-50

Major-General J. C. Harding-Newman,
  C.B., C.M.G.   1929-35   (5.1.29-2.2.35)
Lieutenant-General Sir Geoffrey W. Howard,
  K.C.B., C.M.G., D.S.O., D.L.   1935-46   (3.2.35-13.12.46)
Brigadier G. H. Wilmer, D.S.O., M.C.   1946-50   (14.12.46-15.3.50)
Brigadier C. M. Paton, C.V.O., C.B.E.   1950-   (16.3.50-   )

Section II (a)

LIEUTENANT-COLONELS COMMANDING 1ST BATTALION THE ESSEX REGIMENT

G. H. Wilmer, D.S.O., M.C.	1931-35	(26.9.31-21.2.35)
A. E. Maitland, D.S.O., M.C.	1935-36	(22.2.35-22.7.36)
R. V. Read, D.S.O., M.C.	1936-38	(23.7.36-1.9.38)
G. A. M. Paxton, M.C.	1938-41	(2.9.38-1.9.41)
C. M. Paton, C.V.O.	1941-44	(2.9.41-1.9.44)
L. W. W. Marriott	1944-47	(2.9.44-1.9.47)
C. A. Southey	1947-48	(2.9.47-3.11.48)

Section II (b)

LIEUTENANT-COLONELS COMMANDING 2ND BATTALION THE ESSEX REGIMENT

H. R. Bowen, D.S.O.	1928-32	(2.3.28-1.3.32)
H. Gordon	1932-36	(2.3.32-1.3.36)
C. C. Spooner, D.S.O.	1936-39	(2.3.36-31.7.39)
A. H. Blest	1939-42	(1.8.39-31.7.42)
F. A. S. Clarke, D.S.O.	1942-45	(1.8.42-31.7.45)
R. L. Telfer	1945-48	(1.8.45-16.2.48)
C. S. Mills	1948	(17.2.48-3.11.48)

Section II (c)

LIEUTENANT-COLONELS COMMANDING 1ST BATTALION THE ESSEX REGIMENT (44TH AND 56TH FOOT)

C. A. Southey	1948–50	(3.11.48–1.3.50)
T. L. G. Charles, D.S.O.	1950–	(2.3.50–)

Note 1.—Since the amalgamation of the two Regular Battalions on 3.11.48 two Lieutenant-Colonels are included in the regular establishment. Lieutenant-Colonel C. S. Mills filled this appointment.

Note 2.—During the war period from 1940 and up to the amalgamation of the 1st and 2nd Battalions on 3.11.48, owing to service exigencies, Lieutenant-Colonels C. M. Paton, C.V.O., F. A. S. Clarke, D.S.O., L. W. W. Marriott, and R. L. Telfer did not take over their allotted commands. The chain of command for this period was as follows:

   1st Battalion—Majors W. P. Williams and K. F. May, Lieutenant-Colonels J. S. Nichols, D.S.O., M.C. (The Border Regiment), E. W. Towsey, O.B.E. (The West Yorkshire Regiment), G. H. Walker, C. S. Mills, and C. A. Southey.

   2nd Battalion—Lieutenant-Colonel A. H. Blest, Major C. L. Wilson, M.C., Lieutenant-Colonels A. H. Blest, L. W. W. Marriott, J. F. Higson, M.C., G. G. Elliott, D.S.O. (The Queen's Own Royal West Kent Regiment), N. W. Finlinson, D.S.O. (The South Staffordshire Regiment), Major C. L. Sayers (Duke of Cornwall's Light Infantry), Lieutenant-Colonels M. A. H. Butler, D.S.O., M.C. (The Prince of Wales's Volunteers), E. S. Scott, M.B.E. (The Buffs), V. C. Magill-Cuerdon, G. H. Walker, T. L. G. Charles, D.S.O., Major C. J. S. McMillen, Lieutenant-Colonels C. A. Southey, C. S. Mills, and Major G. G. Stevens.

Section III

4TH BATTALION THE ESSEX REGIMENT (TERRITORIAL)

HONORARY COLONELS, 4TH BATTALION THE ESSEX REGIMENT

Brigadier-General J. T. Wigan, C.B., C.M.G., D.S.O., T.D., D.L.	1922–45	(22.1.22–20.1.45)
The Right Honourable W. L. S. Churchill, O.M., C.H., T.D., LL.D., M.P	1945–	(21.1.45–)

LIEUTENANT-COLONELS COMMANDING 4TH BATTALION THE ESSEX REGIMENT

J. L. French, T.D. (Brevet-Colonel)	1928–36	(26.2.28–25.6.36)
G. M. Gibson, T.D.	1936–39	(26.6.36–31.5.39)

In the spring of 1939, an increase of a second battalion was ordered. The 4th Battalion was designated the 1/4th Battalion and the 2/4th Battalion raised separately.

LIEUTENANT-COLONELS COMMANDING 1/4TH BATTALION THE ESSEX REGIMENT

G. M. Gibson, T.D.   1939–41   (1.6.39–21.11.41)

From 21.11.41 to May 1946, when the 1/4th Battalion was placed in suspended animation, the chain of command was as follows:
Lieutenant-Colonels A. Noble, D.S.O., T.D. (1941–44), L. W. A. Chappell, M.C., Major H. C. Gregory, M.C., Lieutenant-Colonels V. C. Magill-Cuerdon, A. Lovelace, M.B.E., M.C., R. E. O. Bell (Sherwood Foresters), and L. W. W. Marriott.

On the reconstitution of the Territorial Army on the 1st May, 1947, the 4th Battalion The Essex Regiment reappeared in the Territorial Army order of battle.

LIEUTENANT-COLONELS COMMANDING 4TH BATTALION THE ESSEX REGIMENT

A. Noble, D.S.O., T.D., D.L.   1947–   (1.5.47–   )

LIEUTENANT-COLONELS COMMANDING 2/4TH BATTALION THE ESSEX REGIMENT
(TERRITORIAL)

Lord Edward Hay   1939–40   (1.6.39–3.8.40)

Note.—From 3.8.40 to December 1945, when the 2/4th Battalion was placed in suspended animation, the chain of command was as follows:
Lieutenant-Colonels J. W. Hurrell, M.C. (The Bedfordshire and Hertfordshire Regiment), C. S. Mills, J. L. L. Lotinga, M.C. (Royal Fusiliers), C. L. Archdale (Manchester Regiment).

Section IV

5TH BATTALION THE ESSEX REGIMENT (TERRITORIAL)

HONORARY COLONELS, 5TH BATTALION THE ESSEX REGIMENT (TERRITORIAL)

General the Viscount Byng, G.C.B., G.C.M.G.,
  M.V.O., D.C.L., LL.D.   1919–35 (3.2.19–2.8.35)
Colonel Sir F. Carne Rasch, Bart., A.D.C., T.D., D.L. 1935–50 (3.8.35–26.9.50)

LIEUTENANT-COLONELS COMMANDING 5TH BATTALION THE ESSEX REGIMENT
(TERRITORIAL)

C. Portway, M.C., T.D. (Brevet-Colonel) 1928–36   (13.1.28–11.1.36)
W. L. Ridley   1936–38   (12.1.36–27.9.38)
H. C. N. Trollope, D.S.O., M.C.   1938–39   (28.9.38–31.5.39)

In the spring of 1939, an increase of a second battalion was ordered. The Battalion recruiting zone was divided geographically, the 1/5th Essex becoming the West Battalion, the 2/5th Essex the East Battalion.

LIEUTENANT-COLONELS COMMANDING 1/5TH BATTALION THE ESSEX REGIMENT
H. C. N. Trollope, D.S.O., M.C.   1939–41   (1.6.39–30.11.41)

Note 1.—Owing to the 2/5th Battalion being placed in suspended animation and disbanded in November 1942, the 1/5th Battalion was redesignated 5th Battalion The Essex Regiment.

Note 2.—From 30.11.41 to 24.4.46, the chain of command of the 1/5th and 5th Battalion was as follows:
   Majors P. V. Upton, J. R. Nott, Lieutenant-Colonels B. G. Allen (The Sherwood Foresters), W. L. R. Benyon (The Royal Welch Fusiliers), E. E. Owen, W. L. R. Benyon, W. A. Heal, O.B.E. (The Suffolk Regiment), Major B. H. Craig (The Buffs).

LIEUTENANT-COLONELS COMMANDING 2/5TH BATTALION THE ESSEX REGIMENT
C. Portway, M.C., T.D., D.L. (Brevet-Colonel) 1939–40 (1.6.39–15.4.40)

Note.—From April 1940 to the disbandment of the 2/5th Battalion in November 1942, the chain of command was as follows:
Major C. A. Brooks, Lieutenant-Colonel C. M. Paton, Major C. A. Brooks, Lieutenant-Colonel K. F. May.

On the 1st May, 1947, the Territorial Army was reconstituted, the 5th Essex being allotted an anti-aircraft role and designated 646 H.A.A. Regiment R.A., T.A.

Section V

6TH BATTALION THE ESSEX REGIMENT (TERRITORIAL)

HONORARY COLONELS, 6TH BATTALION THE ESSEX REGIMENT
The Lord O'Hagan   1926–36   (31.7.26–11.12.36)
Hon. Colonel E. J. Upton   1936–42   (12.12.36–3.2.42)

LIEUTENANT-COLONELS COMMANDING 6TH BATTALION THE ESSEX REGIMENT
C. A. Bailey, O.B.E., T.D.   1929–33   (30.9.29–29.9.33)
P. L. Grimwood, M.C., T.D.   1933–37   (30.9.33–29.9.37)
R. W. Wren, T.D.   1937–38   (30.9.37–1.11.38)

On the 1st March, 1938, the 6th Battalion was converted to a searchlight role and split into two units, becoming the 1/6th Battalion The Essex Regiment (64th Searchlight Regiment) and 2/6th Battalion The Essex Regiment (65th Searchlight Regiment).

Lieutenant-Colonels R. W. Wren, T.D., and P. L. Grimwood, M.C., T.D., commanded the respective units. Lieutenant-Colonel R. W. Wren, T.D., later became Honorary Colonel of the two units.

In 1940 these two Battalions became units of the Royal Artillery.

Section VI

7TH BATTALION THE ESSEX REGIMENT (TERRITORIAL)

HONORARY COLONELS 7TH BATTALION THE ESSEX REGIMENT

Brevet-Colonel H. F. Kemball, T.D.   1924–50   (3.5.24–2.5.50)

LIEUTENANT-COLONELS COMMANDING 7TH BATTALION THE ESSEX REGIMENT

F. R. Waller, T.D.   1930–34   (17.2.30–16.2.34)
C. D. Martin, O.B.E., T.D.   1934–39   (17.2.34–16.2.39)

On the 15th December, 1935, the 7th Battalion The Essex Regiment (Territorial) was converted into a heavy anti-aircraft unit, designated 59th (The Essex Regiment) H.A.A. Brigade R.A., T.A.

APPENDIX V

THE ESSEX REGIMENT

REGIMENTAL DATES, SERVICE, AND BATTLE HONOURS SINCE FORMATION

Section I

1ST BATTALION THE ESSEX REGIMENT (44TH REGIMENT OF FOOT)

1741. Raised by Colonel James Long as the 55th Regiment of Foot, the personnel coming mainly from Northern Ireland and the Scottish Border.
1748. Renumbered the 44th Regiment of Foot.
1782. Designated the 44th or East Essex Regiment. (First County connection.)
1881. Designated 1st Battalion The Essex Regiment.
1948. On the 3rd November, 1948, the 1st Battalion The Essex Regiment was disbanded. After disbandment, personnel of the 1st Battalion were amalgamated with personnel of the disbanded 2nd Battalion to form a new battalion of the Regiment designated "1st Battalion The Essex Regiment (44th and 56th Foot)."

1745. Five companies of the Regiment served at the Battle of Preston Pans.
1755–60. North America, with Braddock's Expedition, and occupation of Canada.
1775–79. War of the American Revolution; occupation of New York, Battles of Brandywine, Germanstown, and Monmouth Courthouse.
1794. War with France: capture of Martinique and Guadaloupe; service in Flanders 1795. Capture of St. Lucia.
1801. Egypt: Battle of the Pyramids and the Siege of Alexandria. (The first Battle Honour, "*The Sphinx superscribed 'Egypt'* " to be borne on the Regimental Colour. A Sphinx now forms part of the Regiment's cap badge.)
1809. Capture of the Ionian Islands.
1813. Peninsular War—occupation of Tarragona.
1814. North America. Battle Honour "*Bladensburg,*" and occupation of Washington. Repulse before New Orleans.
1824. Burmese War. Battle Honour "*Ava.*"
1842. Afghan War. Last stand at Gandamak.

1854-55. Crimean War. Battle Honours *"Alma," "Inkerman,"* and *"Sevastopol"* (Sergeant W. McWheeney awarded the Regiment's first Victoria Cross).
1860. Chinese War. Battle Honour *"Taku Forts"* (Lieutenant R. M. Rogers and Private John McDougall awarded Victoria Cross).
1899-1902. South African War. Battle Honours *"Relief of Kimberley," "Paardeberg," "South Africa"* (Lieutenant F. N. Parsons awarded the Victoria Cross).
1914-19. The First World War. Gallipoli, France, and Belgium. The Regiment as a whole was awarded sixty-two Battle Honours, of which ten are borne on the King's Colour of each Battalion of the Regiment. Of these ten, the 1st Battalion shares with other Battalions the following: *"Gallipoli," "Somme," "Arras," "Ypres 1917," "Cambrai."*
1919-22. Service in Ireland against Sinn Fein.
1934-35. Plebiscite duty in the Saar Region of Germany.
1936-38. Active Service in Palestine.
1939-45. Battle Honours have yet to be awarded. The Battalion saw service in the Sudan, Iraq, Syria, the Western Desert (Tobruk and Ed Duda) and in Assam and Burma.

2ND BATTALION OF THE 44TH (2/44TH REGIMENT OF FOOT)

1803. A second Battalion of the 44th or East Essex Regiment was raised.
1816. The 2/44th Regiment was disbanded.

In the short period of its existence, the Battalion, known as the "Little Fighting Fours," served with great distinction, gaining four Battle Honours for the Regiment: 1810-13 Peninsular War, Battle Honours *"Badajoz," "Salamanca," "Peninsula."* At Salamanca the Eagle Standard of the 62nd French Regiment was captured by Lieutenant W. Pearce (an Eagle badge is now used by the Regiment). 1815 Battle Honour, *"Waterloo."*

Section II

2ND BATTALION THE ESSEX REGIMENT (THE "POMPADOURS," 56TH REGIMENT OF FOOT)

1755. Raised by Lord Charles Manners as the 58th Regiment of Foot. The men were recruited from the north of England, principally from Newcastle and Gateshead.
1757. Renumbered 56th Regiment of Foot.
1782. Designated 56th or West Essex Regiment (First County Connection).
1881. Designated 2nd Battalion The Essex Regiment.

1948. On the 3rd November the 2nd Battalion The Essex Regiment was disbanded. After disbandment, personnel of the 2nd Battalion were amalgamated with personnel of the disbanded 1st Battalion, to form a new battalion of the Regiment designated "1st Battalion The Essex Regiment (44th and 56th Foot)."

1762. Expedition to Havannah. The Regiment's first Battle Honour "*Moro*" was gained at this, the Battalion's first battle engagement. The Regiment was the only one to be awarded this Honour. The Battle Honour "*Havannah*" was also awarded.
1779–83. The Great Siege of Gibraltar. For this Service the Castle and Key, superscribed "*Gibraltar* 1779–83," and with the motto "*Montis Insignia Calpe*" underneath, was authorised to be borne on the Regimental Colour. (A Castle and Key forms part of the Regiment's cap badge.)
1793. War with France—occupation of Martinique, and seizure of St. Lucia and Guadaloupe.
1799. Expedition to Holland.
1809–10. East Indies. Seizure of Rodriguez. Raid on St. Paul's, Bourbon, and capture of Mauritius.
1842. Canada, Maine–New Brunswick dispute.
1853. Bermuda.
1855. Crimean War. Battle Honour "*Sevastopol*."
1856. Close of Indian Mutiny.
1885. Nile Expedition. Battle Honour "*Nile*."
1901. South African War. Battle Honour "*South Africa*."
1914–19. First World War. France and Belgium. Of the ten Battle Honours borne on the King's Colour of all Battalions of the Regiment, the 2nd Battalion represented the Regiment at "*Le Cateau*," "*The Marne*," and "*Ypres* 1915," and share with other Battalions of the Regiment the following Battle Honours: "*Ypres* 1917," "*Somme*," "*Arras*."
1919–23. Malta and Constantinople.
1930–31. Disturbances in Peshawar City and operations on the Kajauri Plain.
1935–36. Special Service, Sidi Barrani, in Western Desert of Egypt.
1939–45. Battle Honours have yet to be awarded. The Battalion took part in the campaign in France and Belgium 1940, and the subsequent withdrawal from Dunkirk. Landing in Normandy on D-Day 1944, it fought throughout the campaign in North-west Europe.

2ND BATTALION (2/56TH REGIMENT OF FOOT)

1804. A second Battalion of the 56th or West Essex Regiment was raised at Farnham, Surrey, and disbanded in 1817 at Chatham. The Battalion served in India between 1807 and 1817.

3RD BATTALION (3/56TH REGIMENT OF FOOT)

1813 (November). Raised at Horsham, Surrey, and disbanded in October 1814. Served in Holland at the Battle of Merxem and Siege of Antwerp. Here, perhaps, it would not be out of place to put on record an unusual Regimental custom—the playing of Irish airs on St. Patrick's Day. Although no date can be fixed when first commenced, the custom has been traced back to 1881, when it was well remembered by the late Chelsea Pensioner J. Sitton. It can therefore be assumed that the custom was in vogue prior to this date.

The reason for the custom is no doubt due to the many Irishmen enlisted in the two Regiments in the early period of their history. In fact, the Regimental Museum possesses an old 56th Regiment Recruiting Poster calling for County Limerick and Kerry lads to join the "Pompadour" Standard.

Between the years 1749-1896, the 44th Foot served no less than thirty-nine years in Ireland, their 2nd Battalion (2/44th Foot) being actually raised there; likewise, between these dates, the 56th Foot served, in broken periods, a total of twenty-eight years in Ireland.

Section III

3RD BATTALION THE ESSEX REGIMENT (ESSEX (RIFLES) MILITIA)

Descended from Essex Trained Bands, which in 1588 were reviewed by Queen Elizabeth during the Spanish Armada alarm. Fought at Siege of Colchester 1648 and Battle of Worcester 1651.
1757. Essex Militia Regiment formed from Trained Bands was reorganised into 1st or East Essex Regiment Militia and the 2nd or West Essex.
1759-62. Embodied for home Service—Seven Years War.
1778-83. Embodied for home Service—American War of Independence.
1792-1816. Embodied for home Service—Napoleonic War.
1854. Embodied as Essex Rifles for home Service—Crimean War.
1881. East Essex (then known as Essex Rifles) became 3rd Battalion The Essex Regiment and West Essex 4th Battalion The Essex Regiment.
1902. 3rd Battalion The Essex Regiment on Service in South Africa. Battle Honour "*South Africa.*" 4th Battalion contributed a Mounted Infantry Section.
1908. Reconstituted as Special Reserve battalion and designated 3rd Battalion The Essex Regiment. 4th Battalion disbanded.
1914-18. Great War. Service in England and Ireland, mainly used in a training and draft-finding role.
1919. Demobilised.

Section IV

4TH, 5TH, 6TH, 7TH BATTALIONS THE ESSEX REGIMENT (TERRITORIAL)

During the Napoleonic War, from 1797 onwards, numerous Volunteer Corps were raised in Essex. In 1808, five battalions of Local Militia were formed, largely taking the place of the Volunteer Corps. These battalions were, however, disbanded in 1816.

1859. Independent companies of Volunteer Riflemen organised.

1860. These were formed into three Administrative Battalions, with Headquarters at Chelmsford, Plaistow, and Ilford.

1867. 2nd Volunteer Battalion reorganised into two Battalions, with Headquarters at Plaistow and Silvertown.

1883. Volunteer Battalions incorporated in the Essex Regiment as 1st Volunteer Battalion The Essex Regiment (Ilford), 2nd Volunteer Battalion (Braintree), 3rd Volunteer Battalion (Plaistow), and 4th Volunteer Battalion (Silvertown).

1900–2. Detachments from the four Volunteer Battalions served with the City Imperial Volunteers in the South African War. A Special Service Company was also formed to reinforce the 1st Battalion The Essex Regiment in South Africa. This company was subsequently relieved by a second company, who in their turn were relieved in 1902 by a Special Service Section. Battle Honour "*South Africa.*"

1908. The four Volunteer Battalions were designated 4th, 5th, 6th, and 7th Battalions (T.F.) The Essex Regiment, with Headquarters at Ilford, Chelmsford, West Ham, and Hackney.

1912. Hackney Companies of the 7th Battalion transferred to 10th London Regiment and 7th Battalion Headquarters moved to Walthamstow.

1914–19. First World War—all battalions mobilised for active service to form the 161st Infantry Brigade. July 1915, embarked for Gallipoli, to be followed by service in Egypt and the Palestine Campaign. The Brigade took part in many engagements against the Turks, gaining ten Battle Honours for the Regiment, the Honour "*Gaza*" being one of the ten borne on the King's Colour. Battalions of the 161st Brigade also share the Battle Honour "*Gallipoli.*" During the war, all Battalions of the Brigade formed 2nd and 3rd Line Battalions. By December 1919 demobilisation was completed.

1920. In February, the 4th, 5th, 6th, and 7th Battalions were re-formed as the 161st Brigade of the Territorial Army.

1936. 7th Battalion was taken from the Brigade, and became 59th (The Essex Regiment) A.A. Brigade R.A.

1938 (November 1st). The 6th Battalion was divided into 1/6th and 2/6th

Battalions, taking on a searchlight role. (Designated in 1940 as 64th and 65th Searchlight Regiments R.A. respectively, the two units became regiments of the Royal Artillery.)

1939. In the spring, the remaining infantry battalions of the Regiment, the 4th and 5th, were duplicated. The 4th Battalion was renumbered 1/4th, the 2/4th being raised separately. In the case of the 5th Battalion, the Battalion was split on a geographical basis, personnel from the West forming the nucleus of the 1/5th, and those from the East the 2/5th. The 2/5th Battalion was subsequently disbanded in November 1942, the 1/5th being designated 5th Battalion the Essex Regiment.

1939–45. During the war the 2/4th Battalion was retained in England. The 1/4th Battalion went overseas in 1940, and served in West Africa, Egypt, Cyprus, and Palestine before joining the Eighth Army in June 1942. The Battalion subsequently served in the Western Desert of Egypt, from El Alamein to Tunis, and in Italy and Greece.

The 2/5th went overseas in 1940, serving in West Africa, Egypt, and Iraq. It was disbanded after the Battle of Deir-el-Shein (1942).

The 1/5th went overseas in 1941 to serve in Egypt, Iraq, and Syria. Designated the 5th Battalion in 1942, it took part in the Italian Campaign of 1943/44 as a unit of the Eighth Army. The Battalion later returned to the Middle East, and finally served in the North-west Europe campaign.

The 1/4th, 2/4th, and 5th Battalions were placed in suspended animation in May 1946, December 1945, and April 1946 respectively.

1947. On the reconstruction of the Territorial Army on the 1st May, the 4th Battalion was re-formed as infantry, the 5th Battalion becoming a unit of the Royal Artillery.

Section V

8TH (CYCLIST) BATTALION THE ESSEX REGIMENT (TERRITORIAL)

1908. Raised as the 8th Essex Cyclist Battalion, with four companies in Suffolk.
1911. Renamed Essex and Suffolk Cyclist Battalion.
1912. Divided into two separate battalions, the Essex Companies becoming the 8th (Cyclist) Battalion The Essex Regiment.
1914. Mobilised and at war stations on the East Coast by the 5th August. The unit volunteered for service overseas, but was retained in the United Kingdom, though personnel served overseas in practically every battalion of the Regiment.
1920. Disembodied, and not re-formed as infantry in the new Territorial Army.

Second and third line units were formed during the First World War.

Section VI
SPECIAL SERVICE BATTALIONS RAISED DURING THE FIRST WORLD WAR

9TH, 10TH, 11TH, AND 13TH BATTALIONS THE ESSEX REGIMENT

The 9th and 10th Battalions were raised at Shorncliffe in August and September 1914 respectively. The 11th Battalion was raised at Shoreham in September 1914, and the 13th Battalion ("The Hammers") at West Ham, December 1914.

All four battalions served in France. The 9th Battalion was the first to arrive, in May 1915, shortly followed by the 10th Battalion in July, the 11th in August, and finally by the 13th Battalion in November 1915.

These battalions saw much fighting, and between them took part in most of the major battles. They claim a worthy share in four of the ten Battle Honours borne on the King's Colour—"*Somme,*" "*Arras,*" "*Cambrai,*" "*Ypres*"— and in addition the 9th and 11th Battalions added to the Colours of the Regiment "*Loos*" and "*Selle.*" Lieutenant F. B. Wearne, of the 11th Battalion, was awarded the Victoria Cross.

12TH, 14TH, 15TH, 16TH, 17TH AND 18TH BATTALIONS THE ESSEX REGIMENT

Of these, the 15th Battalion, constituted from the 2/4th Battalion the Essex Regiment, was sent to France May 1918 as a B1 Unit, but, due to good service, became an A battalion. It took part in the occupation of Lille, the crossing of the Scheldt, and the advance through Flanders. The remaining battalions were formed for draft finding and home service duties.

GARRISON BATTALIONS

During the First World War, 1st and 2nd Garrison Battalions of the Regiment were also formed. They served in Egypt and India.

VOLUNTEER BATTALIONS

Five Volunteer Battalions were recruited, and were liable to serve in case of invasion or when a state of national emergency was declared by Parliament.

Special Service Battalions, Garrison Battalions, and Volunteer Battalions were disbanded at the end of the First World War.

Section VII

NEW BATTALIONS 1939-45

7th Battalion The Essex Regiment.—Raised in 1939 for home service and disbanded in 1943.

8th Battalion The Essex Regiment.—Raised in 1940, and served as infantry (principally on beach defence duties) until at the end of 1941 it was converted to an armoured-corps role, and designated the 153rd Regiment Royal Armoured Corps.

Landed in Normandy, and fought until August 1944, when it was disbanded, one squadron, "C" (Essex) Squadron, being transferred to the 107th Regiment R.A.C. Finally disbanded in 1946.

9th Battalion The Essex Regiment.—Raised in 1940, and served as infantry (principally on beach defence duties) until in November 1942 it became the 11th (Essex) Medium Regiment R.A. The Regiment landed in Normandy in July 1944, and was continually in action until V.E.-Day. It was disbanded in December 1945.

10th Battalion The Essex Regiment.—Raised in 1940, and served as infantry (principally on beach and aerodrome defence duties) until November 1942, when it was converted into the 9th Parachute Battalion, to become in 1943 a unit of the 6th Airborne Division. Dropped on D-Day, 6th June, 1944, the Battalion took a conspicuous part in the campaign in North-west Europe.

19th Battalion The Essex Regiment.—Raised in Egypt in 1943 and disbanded in that country in 1944.

30th Battalion The Essex Regiment.—A redesignation of the 7th Battalion.

70th Battalion The Essex Regiment.—A young-soldier battalion. The unit was raised for home defence purposes in 1940, and was disbanded in 1943. It was engaged in the task of aerodrome defence throughout its existence.

APPENDIX VI

"ED DUDA: OUR ACTION OUTSIDE TOBRUK"[1]

BY LIEUTENANT P. P. S. BROWNLESS, 1st Battalion The Essex Regiment

WE had formed part of the "beleaguered garrison" of Tobruk since the 18th October, 1941, and for about the last fortnight there had been many rumours of the coming desert "push." One morning we saw the first formation of British planes since leaving Egypt. A few days later the 14th Brigade, with the 4th Battalion Royal Tank Regiment, after fierce fighting made a large gap in the enemy lines in the western sector of Tobruk, round the Bardia road. This was done to enable the Eighth Army, which was advancing from the frontier, to link up with the garrison of Tobruk. We were in the reserve line at the time, and were anxiously wondering what we should have to do. We did not wait long. Three days later we were to go into action at dawn. We spent that night by the Bardia cross-roads. Occasionally a few shells would land nearby. The night seemed tense. Groups of soldiers were lying down talking. There were lorries and ambulances scattered on either side of the road. The tanks had already gone up. I was called to Company Headquarters to receive my orders. "Jock" Nelson,[2] my Company Commander, had gone up into the Black Watch positions to have a look at the objective. He did not return till after dark. When I arrived at the hole which was Company Headquarters, he was talking about the Black Watch, and the grave of one of them, who had died heroically, and whose equipment and rifle were laid out on his grave. Browne,[3] our Second-in-Command was, as usual, full of beans and cheerful.

The plan for the next day was roughly that we were to capture and hold Ed Duda, a ridge about nine miles south of the Tobruk perimeter, thus cutting the Trigh-Capuzzo road, which runs over the top of it, and was the enemy's main supply road. The tanks were to go in first, and we were to go in when the tank brigadier sent back that he was ready for us. We were to advance right on to the objective in lorries in extended formation, the carriers first, then "D" Company, "C" Company, "A" Company, and "B" Company. "D" Company had to push straight for the far side of the objective, "C," my own company, were to cut the road on the left, and "B" on the right. "A" Company were in reserve.

I gave out my orders, and then chatted to my men for a while. Most of them were rather quiet, except for two, who seemed to have obtained a large dose of rum from somewhere. Presently Jock came round calling for me and

[1] See map on page 82.   [2] Captain C. Nelson, O.C. "C" Company.
[3] Lieutenant R. C. Browne.

said, "Here, Philip, have some wheesky." This was the first whisky we had seen in Tobruk. I got an hour or two's sleep, and at three o'clock in the morning we moved out to the starting-point, well outside the Tobruk perimeter. Our occupation of Ed Duda was supposed to coincide with the New Zealanders' occupation of Sidi Rezegh, about four miles south-east of it. As there was no sign of the New Zealanders, we had to wait. We waited till lunch-time, and though there was still no news of them, the Brigadier decided not to wait any longer. The tanks went in, and we followed soon afterwards.

We moved off, in our lorries, with the carriers in front and armoured cars on our left flank. After a mile or more we halted behind a slight fold in the ground. They started to shell us, but most of the shells fell short. I told my platoon to fix bayonets and remove respirators. I made them get off the lorries and lie down, as they were shelling a little more. I was keyed up: I think they were too. I do not think I was really frightened. Then on the lorries again and forward we went. This large number of lorries advancing steadily together, and filled with soldiers all ready to leap off and fight, looked most impressive. We were going as fast as we could over the rough desert. I kept telling the driver to get on. Shells were landing amongst the column. A dud shell landed five or six yards from our lorry. Overhead I noticed a formation of bombers. Suddenly, I saw a curtain of sand shoot into the air not 200 yards in front, and heard deafening explosions. The bombers had dropped the whole of their load on the company[1] in front of us. We heard afterwards they had killed 2 officers and 16 men. We were near the ridge now and were going all out. We passed some wire and a few old enemy positions. We stopped at the bottom of the escarpment, and my platoon leapt off the lorries. I put two sections forward, and one following twenty yards behind, all in extended order, and started moving east, along the bottom of the escarpment. The shelling was extremely heavy. Shells were landing all round us. I kept them moving as hard as I could. We kept lying down as the salvos started to land, but the men were marvellous the way they were up as soon as I shouted "Up." We passed the signal officer looking very white. One of my men fell, hit in the crutch. Then we passed two knocked-out carriers. They were lifting Lawrence[2] out of one. I think he was probably dead then. There were many cries for stretcher-bearers. Browne came up with our platoon, and we wheeled round and started to advance over the escarpment. Two Italians came out of a wadi waving white rags. To my bewilderment they were followed by another thirty or so. I left one man to guard them till Company Headquarters turned up. Looking back a few moments later, I saw Jock making them sit down in the middle of the shelling, as if it were a picnic and asking if any talked English. I ran in front of the platoon to hurry them up. As we advanced over the top, shells were bursting everywhere. The road was 150 yards in front, with a continuous storm of shells bursting down its length, and knocking the telegraph poles about like pea-sticks. I kept shouting to the sections to keep well spaced. We reached the

[1] "D" Company.   [2] Lieutenant C. H. Lawrence, M.C.

road, which was our objective. There were some deafening explosions as shells landed right amongst the platoon. I was blown over, and so were some others. I felt myself, and was surprised to find I was all right. I could not see a thing. The dust cleared. It was obvious that if we remained in the area they were shelling on that rocky ridge there would not be many of us left. To my astonishment none of the men immediately round me had been hit. I shouted "Advance!" and moved 100 yards forward of the road, made the platoon get down, and placed my sections, one covering the road and the other two forward. The shelling quietened a bit, and I had time to look round. Twenty-four Section had lost 3 men, one of them L/Corporal Stevens, a man I had become very fond of; he had a shell-splinter through his head. Another man had a shell-splinter through his boot, but said he was all right. Worst of all, "Eddie" Slater, my platoon sergeant, had been wounded very badly in the back. Sergeant Lydiate, then a section commander, took over platoon sergeant.

Suddenly I noticed down below three German tanks moving up towards us. We were on the top of a bare rise, with no cover anywhere, and if they had come on, could have mowed us down, as all our tanks had gone. It seemed hopeless. I sent off a message to Company H.Q. to get some tanks up. "D" Company, some of whom had been shot up by the tanks, then came running back up the escarpment. Not only were they on the run, but they were likely to attract a lot of fire if they did not get down. Browne and I ran forward, stopping groups of men, and making them get down, and getting them sorted out in sections. They had lost all their officers, except Mann,[1] who was stuck the other side of the tanks. We got everything ordered, and then waited anxiously to see what the tanks would do. They had stopped. To our relief one of our own light tanks came up behind us, and I expected some Matildas to follow up behind. The light tank opened up, firing over the top of us, and the Germans replied with one or two shells. For some queer reason, after the exchange of several shots, the Germans cleared off. We waited. There was quite a lot of shelling going on behind us. A small staff car appeared tearing up the road towards us. Two bursts from one of our Bren gunners sent it crashing off the road, with the driver sprawling dead over the wheel. Shortly afterwards a lorry came up from the same direction, with three Germans in the front and several in the back. Quite a few people fired at it. It crashed spectacularly into a heap of gravel. As it crashed one German fell dead on his face with a grenade in his hand, and another leapt from the lorry, as it was still travelling fast, landed flat on his back, got up, and sprinted away up the road. Several men fired. He seemed to have been hit, but still ran on. There was more firing, and he fell twice, only to get up and go on again. One of my men ran after him. He had fallen over again, and when this man reached him, he found that he had at least four bullets through him. With help he was still able to walk. There were two German sergeants on the back of the lorry. We ordered them out. One of our men "cuffed" one of them who showed unwillingness

[1] 2/Lieutenant W. K. M. Mann, M.C.

to comply. I demanded his pistol, and he undid his belt and slung it on the ground. I very nearly hit him again. There was quite a lot of food on the lorry, a quantity of which I collected later. I found a packet of unopened German mail, which I kept for future perusal.

Some German prisoners came up from down in front of us. Four of them were staggering along with one of our casualties on an old door. They reminded me very much, in their helmets and tunics, of the German soldiers of our cartoons. We sent them down to Battalion H.Q. on their own. A closed lorry came out of a wadi and started moving up towards us. Some idiot opened up with an anti-tank rifle at a thousand yards, and though we afterwards found out that he wounded one of its occupants it turned round and got away. Later a "German people's car" appeared, coming up the ridge, with two apparently khaki-clad figures in it. I shouted, "Hold your fire!" At fifty yards I gave the Bren gunner the tip to put a couple of bursts into it. He did, putting his bullets accurately through the bonnet. (I smiled afterwards when I discovered the engine was not in the bonnet, but under the back seat.) They accelerated, but stopped suddenly as both of them were hit through the knees. The ubiquitous Browne drove them back to the R.A.P. Another lorry was shot up on the road that night. The same process had been going on down at "A" Company's end of the position. Our score so far was two lorries, one burnt-out ammunition lorry—this had been going off in explosions, with some spectacular showers of sparks when we passed it earlier: it had been shot by the tanks—two small staff cars, and a "German people's car."

That night, we changed our dispositions, my platoon moving to the rear side of the road. After sending back many messages, we at last managed to get up a few picks and shovels, and got some sort of a hole dug for everybody. Thank heaven we did.

I shall not now try to describe the battle as a whole in detail, for, being in the middle of such an exciting and complex run of events, there are many trivial occurrences which have impressed themselves heavily on my mind, whereas certain of the most essential parts of the battle I hardly remember. I relate them as they stick in my mind.

That first night no rations arrived, and once I had seen the digging started, I went, with my batman and a corporal, on the "scrounge." Earlier I had combined the duty of disarming the two German sergeants with that of "whipping" three tins of jam and a box of German "comforts" off their lorry. We returned to their lorry, and collected enough biscuits to last the platoon for a while, and a ten-pound tin of pickled cucumber. We collected some cans of water off another lorry, and then I had a careful look over the "German people's car." Needless to say, we were not the first to get there. Some others had collected chocolate off it. However, a careful examination revealed a boxful of cigarettes hidden neatly under the canvas hood. There was enough for everybody in the platoon to have a packet.

The next day shelling began soon after dawn, and continued intermittently all day until darkness brought us quiet. It was a sample of what we were to endure for a fortnight. We were in position on the top of a bare escarpment astride a main road, and six or eight miles in front of the nearest unit. We had no artillery near enough to give us effective support, or to engage in counter-battery fire. The enemy guns could pound us at their leisure. Not only were we on his main "tarmac" road, but if we succeeded in holding Ed Duda, were likely to make a corridor for the oncoming Eighth Army, and thus provide it with a secure base from which to deliver its next blow at Benghazi. The Germans who remained between us and the coast east of us already considered themselves cut off. We divided our time during the day between cowering in the bottoms of our very inadequate holes, eating, and digging. A little more than a foot down you hit rock, which had to be smashed with a sledge hammer and pulled out in lumps. We acquired some sandbags, and built up the walls of the pits, camouflaging them as carefully as we could. We made the pits just big enough for two men to sleep in. Later on, using some angle-iron pickets as a framework, we roofed in one-half of each weapon pit with a double layer of sandbags, leaving the other half open. This gave us overhead cover from shell-splinters, but left an opening large enough for two men to fire from conveniently in any one direction. It was not long before other platoons began to follow our example. I think the idea was originally my batman's.

We were shelled with everything, from small-bore high-velocity guns to nine-inch howitzers. Quite a few of the nine-inch shells were "duds." It was a remarkable sight to see such massive projectiles bounce off the ground, and travel for another 200 or 300 yards, making a queer jerky noise as they spun askew through the air, and then rolling over and over as they hit the ground. The next day, during a lull, I went over to see Alec Clarke.[1] He and his platoon sergeant were sitting in a queer sandbagged construction. They were a little bit shaken, but had not been wasting their time. They had quite a stock of "acquired" food in one corner. I was allowed to try a handful of sauerkraut out of a large round tin. I had to see the Company Commander about several things, and so set out for Company Headquarters. Shelling started, and my batman and I went flat as a salvo landed twenty yards in front of us. We ran over to Company Headquarters to find the sergeant-major covered in dust amid some tumbled sandbags, and looking rather numbed. He asked where Mr. Browne was. "He was just standing there," he said, pointing to a crater the other side of the sandbags. Jock Nelson was running over to a body. I ran over too. It was Browne, his limbs twisted horribly, but his face untouched, looking life-like, except for his eyes, which were still. A shell had landed at his feet as he was talking, and blown him thirty yards away. Had the shell landed a few seconds later, I should have been beside him. So died one of the youngest and bravest soldiers I have known. Only a few days before he had repeated several times, "If I get one, I hope it is a gonner."

We were mortared heavily at various times. The Germans used about

[1] 2/Lieutenant A. A. Clarke.

eight mortars at a time, and divided the area into quarters, each of which they concentrated on in turn, and always fired rapidly. How I remember lying flat in the bottom of my weapon pit with my batman, terrified as we listened to the swish of bombs as they came down, and then the deadening crash as they landed all round us. When they landed particularly near, I used to give Sergeant Byrne a shout, to make sure they were all right. I heard someone shouting for stretcher-bearers nearby. Like a fool I jumped out of my hole and ran over, the bombs landing all round me. Why I was not hit I do not know. Two of my men, Clark and Rogers, were lying badly wounded in the foot. They had been lying side by side in a shallow pit, and the cap of a mortar bomb had blown through the parapet, catching them both in the foot, and then gashing one of them in the face. Two stretcher-bearers arrived in time to save me from the unenviable task of trying to remove the torn boots, and get on a field dressing. It was not long before the mortar fire had lifted and they were being carried away, shouting the usual sort of wisecracks as they waved good-bye from their stretchers. "There's two as knows 'ow to to take it," remarked one of the men. It was the last time we were to see those two. Three days later the hospital ship they were on was bombed and sunk outside Tobruk harbour, and they went down with her.

We were counter-attacked in all six times. They all meant a lot of shell, mortar, and small-arms fire, but I was never actually attacked on my own platoon front. One attack, however, will remain vivid in my mind to the end of my days. I usually spent a large part of my day looking through my field-glasses. On the 29th November, about midday, I spotted what I thought were tanks moving in our direction near El Adem. Later I became certain they were tanks manœuvring, and reported it to "Jock," who duly 'phoned Battalion Headquarters. I remember my batman saying to me, as I stood watching through my glasses, "Take it easy, sir, you will wear yourself out worrying." A while afterwards, coming from exactly the opposite direction, I picked out, two or three miles away, a party of about 60 men marching down the road towards us. I could not tell whether they were Germans or not. I guessed they were British prisoners being marched away from Sidi Rezegh. I went over to 13 Platoon area to get a better view. Almost immediately a runner came over shouting, "Stand to! We are being attacked." Shelling had started. As I ran back, I remember seeing an Italian automatic lying in the sand beside the road. Shelling became heavier, and then to my surprise our forward anti-tank guns started firing. I saw what was happening. German tanks were standing 1,000 yards off our position and shelling us. They started closing in. It was late in the afternoon, and the sun was behind them. Three of our tanks came up on the side of our position, later joined by a fourth. They were Matildas. They started withdrawing in pairs, firing as they went. As the heavy tanks got nearer the position, the German light Mk. IIs moved up on our flank, and swept the area with machine-gun fire. The anti-tank guns in front of us were knocked out one after another. Their little two-pound shells were bouncing off the German tanks. Every gun which opened fire was silenced. When they got in close, the tanks were firing their stubby 75-mm. guns at point-blank range at our men's "sangars"[1] in front of us, blowing them to pieces, one at a time. Two men lying in range with an anti-tank rifle made a last effort. They fired several well-aimed shots at the tank in front of them. A few seconds later they were blown to pieces. The position of those two forward companies was hopeless. Infantry were following up behind the tanks, and were already in some of our knocked-out positions. Some posts continued firing. The German tanks, twenty of them, fanned out, and formed a line right across the middle of the battalion position. Our four tanks had cleverly withdrawn behind us to a hulls-down position. You could see plainly German infantry with our prisoners behind those tanks. It was a muddle. I expected the Germans to sweep on over the rest of our positions. There was nothing to stop them. It was starting to get dark, however, and we had kept so still that I think they were under the impression that they had taken the whole position, and any small parties which were left would get away in the dark. Also, had they come on, our four tanks would have engaged them from hulls-down positions as they lumbered at short range over the skyline. As it was, they had halted just short of where our tanks could engage them.

It was dark. I saw some men coming back through our position. Some of them were from "D" Company, and there were some men who had got out from "A" and "B" Companies. We stopped a lot of them and put them in with our sections. Jock Nelson did great work organising these stragglers, many of whom, being without officers, would have strayed from the scene of the battle had it not been for him. I remember going round my sections and telling them if the tanks came in, they were to remain absolutely still until infantry came really close, and then to give them everything they had got. I remember going back to my pit determined, come what may, to sit in that pit and fight it out. My batman and I arranged our clips of cartridges on the sandbags round the top of the trench. I had a rifle as well as a pistol. My batman, to my surprise, produced no less than one hundred and seventy rounds of ammunition from his person. I looked with some comfort at those rows of brass cartridges.

We could hear our tanks coming up behind us, their engines groaning as they manœuvred into formation. Suddenly our guns started shelling very accurately just behind the German tanks. Some guns had been brought up near us specially for the job. It was during this that Captain O'Reilly, who had been taken prisoner earlier, jumped out of the hole his German guard had allowed him to get into, and sprinted through the shell bursts to our own lines. The shell fire stopped, and our tanks started moving through our positions towards the Germans. There were about twelve of them. As soon as their lumbering forms were sighted by the Germans, the area broke into a blaze of fire. White-lighted tracer shells scorched the air. The German light tanks, with their heavy

[1] Breastworks of loose stone.

machine guns, were blazing strings of tracer bullets at the tanks. Our tanks deployed. They too were firing furiously. There was confused firing for some time. The Germans showed no sign of withdrawing. One of their tanks had flames pouring from it. The air was full of tracer bullets. I saw the squadron commander's tank push forward in front of the others, firing hard as he went right amongst the Germans. Our tanks started to withdraw. Several of them came straight down the road. One of them had three terrified German prisoners, hands up and no hats, running along in front of it. The squadron commander's tank crawled out last. It had been hit and its engine timing had gone wrong. As it pulled off to the right it kept stopping and was hit several more times. The German tank was blazing faster. Things seemed worse. I expected the Germans to follow this up.

There was a long lull, during which one could do little but wait. Our own tanks kept moving about behind us, and some more came up to join them. At last, at about eleven o'clock, after an interminable wait, our tanks started moving into attack. One column of them was coming straight at our bunch of weapon pits. I got out of mine to lead them through. This was necessary, as all the weapon pits had built-up sides, as they could not be dug down owing to rock, and a tank going over would have pushed in the walls and crushed the occupants. While I was doing this the Germans spotted our tanks, and let loose a storm of fire at them. Some bullets ricochetted off the tanks, and I hastily withdrew to my hole. There followed a muddled and most furious battle. The air was lit up with tracer bullets and shells. Some bullets cut the parapet of our trench. I watched a lot of it through my periscopic binoculars. Our tanks pushed right into the German tank line. In the darkness the Germans shot at everything just to make sure. All the "shot-up" cars and lorries were, by this time, on fire, and continued burning for the rest of the night. Tanks were moving about in different directions all over the position. One German tank crashed up to our weapon pits, went straight over two of the only three pits in my platoon which could be dug down into the ground, wheeled round just in front of my hole, and trundled off in another direction. Luckily it did not come over ours. The anti-tank gun on my left had just had one of its men shot through the head. I was so tired out with excitement that I found I had dropped off to sleep—how long for, I do not know. The firing was still as furious as ever. Gradually the battle seemed to move away. Our tanks were forcing theirs off the ridge. Farther they went. Suddenly there was a scream as two companies of Australians, collected from nearby—nobody seemed to know why they were there—ran in with the bayonet. Most of the German infantry surrendered. The "Aussie" commanding officer had refused our colonel's offer of a carrier, saying, "No thanks, Colonel, I'll go in with the boys." He was wounded in the leg. The Australians then took over our lost positions, and we, having lost two companies almost complete, formed a composite battalion of two companies of Essex and two of Australian.

We "stood down," and after I had visited the sentries I got some sleep. The next morning we started straightening things up. Several men's packs were riddled with bullets. A tank had gone over the shell-hole in which we had stored our emergency rations, and ground them to powder. The burnt-out lorries were still smoking. I walked over to see the Australians, and gave them a can of water we had taken off one of the lorries, as they were short of it. I passed a knocked-out anti-tank gun, its gun shield riddled with heavy shot from a German tank. We were shelled a lot during the day. I had put the oldest soldier in my platoon to do the cooking. I had installed him in a trench of his own, at one end of which he fixed a fireplace with some iron bars. It was a good deep trench, and he was able, by this arrangement, to carry on his primitive culinary efforts without interruption by shell fire. It was a picture to see him sitting in this trench, seated on a ration box and wearing a cap comforter, and feeding the fire. He took a lot of trouble, but was rather conservative about food. One day I found a small sack of lentils in a German lorry, and gave them to him, suggesting that he should thicken up the "bully" stew with them. I asked him why he had not put any in the next day, and he said they were too hard, and he thought would spoil it. I told him to soak them that night, and gave him a direct order to put some in the next stew. The next day we had a really thick bully stew.

That night I took a patrol out to cover the Trigh-Capuzzo road, a dusty motor track below us. Soon after going through our wire, I saw below in front of us what looked like a man standing. We lay down quietly and watched. It did not move, so I sent my scout to find out what it was. He fixed his bayonet, moved quietly away, and then rushed it with his bayonet, to find it a pile of stones. We moved on past a crashed Junkers 87 into the cover of a wadi, and then carefully down one side of this, till we came to some built-up shelters. We searched these systematically. There were quite a number of Italian carbines and some old greatcoats and tunics. My batman found two packets of cigarettes. I made note of a barrel of wine. We moved quietly out of the wadi and into the plain. We lay up thirty yards from the dusty road near some German tents and some knocked-out vehicles. We lay there till three in the morning. It was bitterly cold, and there was no sign of any movement. On the way back, about half-way up the wadi, I stopped the patrol and signalled them to get down. I thought we were being watched from the high ground on our left. I could see what I was almost certain was a head, which moved slightly amongst the small dry desert shrubs. I watched for some time. It is very easy when you are excited to see things at night, and I was afraid this was what I was doing. But as I watched it moved again, and my batman, who was on my left, crawled up to me and whispered, "There is somebody there," and pointed exactly where I was looking. It was useless to rush up the steep slope at them, especially as we did not know how many there were, so I decided to move the patrol in pairs round the next corner of the wadi, move farther back, get on to the high ground, and then move forward and see what was there from higher ground. I had the only "tommy gun," and was behind a bump in the ground, so decided that I and my batman would remain there till last to cover the others as they moved. I signalled two men at a time and pointed where they were to go. Last of all, we hurried round the corner. We moved some way back along the wadi, and then started to climb out of it. The scout in front of me was challenged by one of our listening posts. I was surprised they were as far out as this. They made so much noise that I felt it unwise to start crawling back along the high ground. I warned the sergeant in charge of the listening post that there was movement not far in front, and then went back into our lines.

The next two nights we were told that there might be some New Zealand patrols in the area. Their recognition signal was the firing of three green Very lights. The Germans, however, frequently made lavish use of Very lights of different colours, and for several nights there was a most colourful display of these in all directions, and our signal was virtually useless. The second night some green lights went up on our left. The next day we received information that two companies of New Zealanders had taken up a position there. That afternoon I was sent out with a patrol to make contact with them. We set out in the approximate direction: on the way we disturbed a hare, the only one I saw in the desert. After about a mile we spotted their position, and somebody walking towards us. He was the New Zealander company commander, a tall dark man. I shook hands with him, gave him the compass bearing to our position and the distance, and after a chat, returned home. I believe I was the first member of the garrison of Tobruk to meet a member of the oncoming Eighth Army.

About midday the next day there was a lot of cheering as an Eighth Army carrier rushed up to our position. There was a New Zealand officer in it, who had run the gauntlet to get back to Tobruk. They were running out of shells at Sidi Rezegh, and he hoped to arrange for some to be sent, but nobody knew how. That night the whole of the New Zealand Divisional Headquarters and 13th Corps Headquarters with all its transport came through, and we directed it behind our position and then into Tobruk. They had had rather a rough time getting through. Sergeant Byrne swaggered over to one lorry which had stopped and had a word with the driver. The driver seemed rather "done in," talking a lot about being shelled all day and going past places with the enemy only 1,000 yards away. Sergeant Byrne looked at him, and pointing down the road with his thumb said, "Well, you'd better 'jiloh,' mate, they're only 300 yards down the road." The conversation stopped; the lorry went on. This line of transport, with a good many stops, took all night to come through. I went back to my hole for the last part of the night and got some sleep, for the platoon had been working, deepening their weapon pits. When I was awakened for "stand-to" at dawn, they were still passing through, and to my horror were coming straight over the middle of our position in full view of the enemy, where, in a very short time, when it was light, they would attract the fire of every gun the Germans could use. I ran half a mile up the road, stopped a lorry, and with some difficulty persuaded the officer in charge of it to drive off the road and down into the low ground out of sight of the enemy. I warned the other lorries after him, and before it became really light all transport was clear of the position.

During the morning a light tank with an artillery officer in it was knocked out in front of the position. The officer was killed, but the other two crawled in later. Captain Gardiner,[1] of the 4th Battalion R.Tks., who was in command of the half-squadron of tanks with us, asked me if I was going out that night if I would bring the body back. It was some way away from the tank. There were four abandoned enemy guns out in front of us, complete with ammunition, and to prevent the enemy moving them at night, we always put a standing patrol out there after dark. I took the patrol out to the guns, and after my batman and I had looked through the dug-outs, put them in position in front of the guns. My batman and I then went over towards the tank, but it was burning rather brightly, so I left it alone. About an hour earlier, just after dark, one of the tanks, seeing a light in it, and thinking there was probably somebody there, had put a shell through it. It had unfortunately burst into flames. So the pair of us went back to the guns, and then moved carefully along the escarpment in the other direction. It was a beautiful moonlit night, and the reflection on the desert was a queer hazy white. We went some way and then stopped. There were some vehicles moving beyond us, and after listening for a while I decided that they were trucks, and seemed to be moving in our direction. As there were only two of us, and we had been up most of last night, and would be on patrol the next night, I decided to return. We went past the guns, and I told the corporal there to be on the look-out, and also mentioned it to "Jock" before going to bed. There the matter was unfortunately dropped. The next morning Gardiner took out his half-squadron of tanks east along the escarpment on a reconnaissance. I watched them go. When they were about 1,000 yards away there was a quick exchange of shots, and then two of the Matildas came trundling back as hard as they could go. When they reached our position Gardiner jumped out of his tank, came running over to me and shouted, "Do you know what in the devil's over there?" I said I did not, and asked him what had happened. He said he had just had five of his seven tanks knocked out. The noise we had heard the night before must have been the Germans bringing up one or perhaps two 88-mm. guns. Ten minutes later one of our ambulances drove straight up to the disabled tanks to remove the wounded, and was allowed to do so unmolested by the enemy. I felt rather guilty. The Germans, already in strength on two sides of us, were pressing in on to the third: not a very comfortable position.

Later, some fighting broke out in the same direction near the New Zealanders' position at Bel Hamed. There was a lot of shooting, but we could only guess what was happening. Late that afternoon "C" Company of the 4th Battalion the Border Regiment were put in to attack and clear this area. They partially

[1] Captain P. Gardiner V.C., M.C., Royal Tank Regiment.

succeeded, but at the cost of seventy-five per cent. of the company killed or wounded.

Another night I wandered over to Company Headquarters rather late. As I stepped inside the dug-out, I was greeted by the sergeant-major "Have you seen my armoury, sir?" "What have you been doing now, Sergeant-Major?" He took me outside, and showed me a German machine carbine and fifteen Mauser rifles laid out in a row, with sixteen sets of German equipment laid out behind them. A German patrol, led by a warrant officer, had come in through the thinly held rear of our position, past Battalion Headquarters, and when challenged by our sentry at Company Headquarters announced, in English, that they were cut off and wished to surrender.

During all this time the shelling and mortaring continued during the hours of daylight, taking its steady toll in casualties. Just before light one morning, two Germans came walking up the road, talking loudly, and walked into "B" Company's listening post. They were taken prisoner. They did not seem in the least bit worried, and explained that we were surrounded and about to be wiped out. The listening post was due to come in: it was beginning to get light. They looked round in the half-light, and saw that there were a lot of Germans nearby. They sprinted back to our positions and gave the warning. When the attack came in, ten minutes later, it was already daylight, and it was driven off without difficulty. Two Germans with flame-throwers were shot down on our wire.

Some fresh tanks came up in the middle of the morning, and three foolishly moved across the exposed side of the position and shelling began immediately. A salvo of nine-inch shells came over, one of which, a lucky shot, hit one of the Matildas over the driver's seat. To my surprise, two men were helped out of the turret not badly hurt. The other two were killed. It burnt for several hours, ammunition going off in a spectacular shower of sparks every so often. I looked at the tank later, and its front was blown wide open, the heavy armour splayed like the petals of a giant flower.

Not long after dark a noise was heard down below the escarpment. A German half-track lorry drove up to our wire. It ran into the wire, and then several Bren guns opened up on it. A German had the audacity to reply with two bursts from his machine carbine. He was shot down. Some "goodies" were collected off this lorry. In the morning a Hurricane circled playfully round our position, and then dived and "strafed" the middle of it. Fortunately, nobody was hit. About this time there was a lot of enemy movement on the nearest ridge up the road two miles in the El Adem direction. Through glasses you could see them digging. There was, annoyingly, no artillery near enough to engage them.

The next night I had most of my platoon working, putting up more barbed wire. About ten o'clock, just before the colour-sergeant was due up with the ration truck, an aeroplane circled low over the position. It dropped a flare, and I shouted to people to keep still. It dropped five flares, one on each corner of the position and one in the middle. It circled round several times, and then a ration truck started to come up the back of the hill. The plane dived and machine-gunned it. We waited, wondering what was going to happen next. The plane circled round again, and then flew off. It had obtained the information it wanted.

The following night we were told that our bombers were to raid El Adem aerodrome. This cheered us immensely. It was from El Adem that the dive-bombers used to come regularly every day before the push started and bomb our positions in Tobruk, when we had no air support of any sort. Many of the guns that had been shelling us without interference for days past were also in the area of the aerodrome, and we wished them all the hate that steel and explosive could produce. We heard some planes in the distance. Then they started dropping flares over El Adem. They seemed to be doing this in a slow and deliberate way, as if they were saying, "Yes, we will drop them just exactly when it happens to amuse us, and meanwhile you can just wait and cower." Then, after a good many flares had been dropped, the air was suddenly alive with quick flashes of the bombs. The thunderous roar went on for some time. It was delightful to hear.

The next morning, when it was light, as we looked out in front of us over the flat two-mile-wide plain down below, strewn with knocked-out transport, stores, and tents, and on to the escarpment the other side, we saw that the enemy were on the move. Along the top of this escarpment, a little over two miles away, an endless stream of enemy troops, lorries, and guns were moving in a westerly direction. Could it be a withdrawal, or were they concentrating for an attack from the west? We watched. Through my glasses I picked out some tanks. Two companies of New Zealanders from Bel Hamed had moved in the previous night and took over from the Australians. A new Second-in-Command had also arrived in the Battalion, and he was over with the New Zealanders. I walked over to meet him and see what he was like. He seemed "snappy," but quite agreeable. Soon we noticed some German infantry well extended moving up to our ridge. There was a company of them or more. They had set some machine guns well back which had started to machine-gun us. This went on in a very thorough manner all the morning. One man in 13 Platoon was hit through the neck. The Germans did not attack, as we expected, but took up positions at the foot of the escarpment, where we could not see them.

We found out afterwards that they had actually built some sangars near the top, just out of sight, but quite near our position. All these were left when I went out later, with two stick-grenades on the parapets. Their object was apparently to prevent us from interfering with the movement of their army. One of their machine guns was particularly active. A tank came up, and from its turret you could spot where the gun was. The tank fired about a belt of ammunition at it. The gunner said he could not hit it, as his gunsight only went up to 1,500 yards. The enemy gun was still firing furiously. One of the Bren gunners climbed on to the tank, set his sights at 1,800, and started shooting. Another man with a captured spandau also climbed on to the tank. He started firing too. There was an exchange of bursts, and the enemy gun never fired again. I collected it the next day. Some enemy transport started moving in the plain, nearer us. One of our anti-tank guns fired a few shells at them. Two Vickers machine guns opened up on them, and with effect. They were spotted by the enemy artillery, and some shells landed a few yards from them. I expected them to take this as a warning, but the crews took no notice of the shells and continued firing their long well-aimed bursts. They were firing at extreme range, though, and not as effective as they might have been. It was a magnificent sight to see Rommel's army, complete, on the move. It was tantalising that though they were in such a vulnerable position, we seemed unable to do anything about it. The Air Force did not attack them, there was no artillery at the moment near enough to engage them, and the tank squadron commander, a real battle-worthy major, was furious with the armoured cars just behind because they would not go out and attack. He said his tanks were so slow they would be knocked out before they got there, but the armoured cars with their speed could do the job all right. He had sent back for some cruiser tanks, and presently three of them sped up to the position, and taking no notice of anybody, ran on to our small minefield. The first one set off three mines, and had both tracks blown into the air. After that they considered themselves *hors de combat* and did nothing. A troop of artillery did move up somewhere near, and just at the right time. There were a lot of lorries moving in the plain now. A group of about seven had gathered in one place and you could see them moving what looked like bodies from one truck to another. The artillery officer ranged on to them. A green Very light was fired from the group of lorries, and immediately, as if in answer, a salvo of shells landed right in the middle of them, then a second and a third. One lorry pulled away, the rest stayed there. I went out there the next day, and there were a number of dead round the lorries. I did not succeed in getting any watches off them: I did, however, get a bottle of Chianti and a small bottle of beer from a half-track lorry there. The back seat was covered in congealed blood. One of the corpses had fallen in a most unnatural posture. His arms were stretched out sideways, and one leg, the lower part of it torn off, was sticking in the air with the two bones protruding out of the stump.

As we watched the far escarpment, we noticed shells landing amongst the transport. Those shells did not come from the Tobruk side: somebody was harassing them from the other side. I then began to think that it was a genuine enemy withdrawal. Guns from Tobruk were brought out to join in the shelling. Soon their shells were whispering as they passed high over our heads, and we watched them land on the columns.

The enemy continued to machine-gun us. A message came up from Battalion Headquarters. We were to do something about it: send out a patrol. This was fantastic, with a whole German company below us covering the lower slopes of the ridge. However, it had to be done, and as I was the only officer left in the company other than "Jock," the Company Commander, I was detailed to take it out. I detailed two sections, and gave out orders. I decided to make quickly for the top of the biggest wadi. This would mean a minimum of open ground to cover. Then I would move with a section extended up either side of the wadi, and move down it by bounds from one bend to the next, one section lying down covering the other. By this means, only enemy in that particular wadi could engage us, and we should be on the higher ground. This would be of particular advantage when using grenades. I anticipated a blood bath. We took out two Bren guns, I had the "tommy gun," and we loaded up with a large number of grenades. I thought these the best things for clearing a stretch of wadi. At eleven o'clock, we were just going over to the gap in the wire on the way out, when heavy mortaring started. We took shelter in "D" Company's weapon pits. The mortaring was heavy, and a bomb landed on the side of our parapet. It partly buried myself and the other men: I was very deaf. After this fire had lifted, I quickly cleaned my "tommy gun" and we set out. We reached the wadi and then moved cautiously down it. There were tense moments as the riflemen moved carefully up to peep round the corner into the next bend. To our surprise and intense relief we arrived near the bottom to find the wadi empty. I moved the sections forward into some banks of soft sand, where they could cover the bottom of the escarpment in both directions. There was no sign of movement. Just then we saw a car coming along the track in front of us, followed by a motor-cycle. I waited till it came within 250 yards of us, and then shouted, "Corporal Hill, three bursts on it." The car started slowing down. "No. Twenty-two section—two hundred—three bursts—— Stop!" I shouted. The car had stopped and two men in khaki battledress I had not seen before got into it. I looked through my glasses. There was no doubt about it, and the two men on the motor-cycle were also in khaki. I sent two men over to the car. There were seven New Zealanders in it! They drove off, and I never discovered where they came from.

The Germans had left, and probably under cover of the mortar fire, half an hour earlier. This was too good to be true. I decided to have a look round some of the tents. We found a food store in one of them, which was fiercely guarded by a terrier, who I suppose had been there for nearly a fortnight waiting for his German master to return. There was nothing very interesting, but we helped ourselves to a few tins of food and some black bread, which we had learnt was rather palatable. There were a lot of empty beer bottles round the tents. We failed to discover any full ones. In one store tent, though, we found some band instruments and drums, and somebody actually found a signed photograph of the band. I thought we really ought to go back and report the valley clear, though the temptation to stay and look through more tents was strong, for I love looting. We returned in correct formation, but carrying three bugles, two drums, three flutes, a ukelele, and our pockets and equipment bulging with food.

That afternoon it was announced that the Colonel[1] would inspect the Battalion by platoons. So the battle was over. That night we heard that the nearest Germans were fifteen miles away. This was the fourteenth day on Ed Duda. We had been shelled almost continuously in the daytime during that period, had been counter-attacked six times, and had lost some 240 men and exactly half our officers. We had been completely overrun by German tanks. On that fateful evening the Divisional Headquarters in Tobruk had given us up for lost, and ordered the closing of the gaps in the wire behind. Afterwards, the General had sent up a message, "By holding Ed Duda you have won the battle." The padre was busy burying some of the dead who had not already been buried. There was a small group of people round him. It was now that it was all over, and we began to look round and see who really was missing, that we felt their loss. I could not help thinking particularly of three officers, all of whom had joined the Battalion together. They were of the best, young—all only just over twenty—all genuinely keen to get to grips with the enemy, and all died bravely when they did. One was blown thirty feet into the air, another cut nearly in half when his carrier was knocked out, and the third riddled with machine-gun bullets from a tank.

The Colonel was due to inspect the platoon in five minutes' time. I formed them up, and had a quick look over them. My heart sank. We really had been busy cleaning the weapons and greasing our boots and trying to make ourselves look tidy. But never before had I seen such a scruffy, dirty-looking lot of bodies in the King's uniform. I must have looked as bad myself, but we could not help it. The Colonel strode up, walked quickly round the ranks, and asked one or two of the men questions. He then turned to me and said "Excellent! Well done; excellent." I saluted, and as he walked off turned round and dismissed a platoon of which I was very proud.

[1] Lieutenant-Colonel J. S. Nichols, D.S.O., M.C.

INDEX

In view of the many names in the text, the index is to some degree selective. For example, names which appear in the appendices but not in the chapter text have been omitted.

Many place-names in the text are villages and hamlets of little but momentary tactical importance. Some of these, particularly locations below battalion headquarters level, will not be found in the index.

A

Abbay, Lieut. J. R., 146–7
Abbotsbury, 9th Essex on beach defence at, 487–8
Abbé d'Monte Cassino, 1/4th Essex attack the, 306–20
Abeele, 152
Abyssinia, 7, 13, 14, 27, 29, 39
Acquaviva, 5th Essex at, 376, 378
Acre, 8; 2/5th Essex at, 459
Adair, Major-General A. H. S., 339
Adams, Capt. C. P., 416
Adaradeb, 1st Essex in action near, 32
Adarama (Sudan), 30
Addario, 5th Essex at, 373
Ainsworth, Lieut. E. G., 372, 388
Air bombing, references to, 35–7, 46–7, 50, 56, 61–2, 73, 80, 116–17, 136–7, 145, 159, 208, 308, 460
Air Force—*see* Royal Air Force
Air supply in Burma, the system of, 97–8
Akarit, 1/4th Essex at battle of Wadi, 289–91
Alamein, 1/4th Essex before battle of El, 266–78; 1/4th Essex at battle of El, 279–84
Alam-Halfa, 1/4th Essex in the battle of, 276–8
Aldeburgh, 2/4th Essex at, 349, 351
Aleppo, 69
Alexander, Capt. F. R., 172, 175, 242
Alexander, General Sir Harold, 276, 306, 322, 336, 448
Alexandria, 9, 14, 70–1, 302, 303, 371, 421
Allen, Lieut.-Col. B. G., in command 5th Essex, 364–7, 369, 372, 375–6, 378, 435
Allfrey, Lieut.-General C. W., 159, 373, 419
Alliquerville, 2nd Essex at, 205
Alost, 136
Alston, Capt. A. E. C., 447, 452, 453, 465, 467, 470
Altun Köpri, 1/5th Essex at, 364–5

Amalgamation of the Regular Battalions, 128, 246, 569
Ambala, 2nd Essex at, 12
Ambrose, Lieut. W. L., 62
Amey, R.S.M., G. W., 441
Amritsar, 2nd Essex at, 12
Amriya (Amryia), reference to, 70–1, 260, 264, 460
Anderlecht (Brussels), 2nd Essex at, 138
Anders, General, congratulates 1/4th Essex, 331
Anderson, Lieut.-General Sir K. A., 489, 499
Anderson, Brig. W. H., 558
Andrea (Andria), 1/4th Essex rejoin 4th Indian Division at, 324
Andreoli, 5th Essex at, 400
Andrew, Major S. H., 519, 523, 525
Andrews, Pte. G., 156
Andrews, Lieut. H., 297
Ankrett, Sgt. W., 160, 197
Anti-Aircraft Command, 21–2; 2nd Essex under, 130; T.A. units with, 474–84
Antria, 1/4th Essex at, 325
Antwerp, 216, 483, 540
Applebee, Sgt. F., 88
Arab Legion, the, 43, 45, 47, 54, 60
Arakan, 1st Essex in the, 91–5
Archdale, Lieut.-Col. C. L., 355
Archi, 389
Arezzo, 324, 331
Arielli, 5th Essex on line of River, 414–17
Armies:
 British: Black Sea, 11; B.E.F. 1940, 135–56; First, 1/4th Essex with, 298–301; Second, 2nd Essex with, 160–97, 222–3; Eighth, 71, 78–89, 260–84, 285–301, 303–5, 321–32, 371, 421, 459–73; Ninth, 368–71; Tenth, 366–7, 458–9; Fourteenth, 60, 90, 120
 Canadian: First Army, 2nd Essex with, 198–221, 223–40
 French: 136
 U.S.: Fifth Army, 305–20, 373, 476

INDEX

Armies—*continued*
  German: 5th Panzer Army, 301; 6th Army, 144; 7th Army, 180, 203
Armsby, Cpl. A. F., 419
Army Council, 1st Essex thanked by, 6; 5th Essex thanked by, 20
Army Rifle Association, 3, 4
Arnhem, 223, 225; 2nd Essex in second battle of, 235-7, 492
Arras Day, commemoration of, 14
Arromanches, the landings at, 162, 490
Ashton, Lieut.-Col. H., 557
Asmara, 503, 504
Aspeleares, 2nd Essex at, 140
Atbara, 1st Essex at, 28-33, 40
Atessa, 5th Essex in, 389, 399-400
Athens, 1/4th Essex in, 332-6
Atkins, Lieut. T. W. G., 252-3, 268
Attwood, Pte. (1st Bn.), 10
Auchinleck, General Sir Claude, 68, 71, 126, 257, 262, 269, 458; extract from despatches of, 471
Australia, armed forces of—*see* Regiments
Auxiliary Territorial Service, the, 519
Aventino, the River, 390-400
Avesnes-en-Val, 211
Avigliano, 1/4th Essex at, 304
Aylmer, Major H. G., 519, 523
Aylsham, 355
Ayres, Major N. E., 161

B

Baalbek (Syria), 1/4th Essex at, 303
Bad Kleinen, 5th Essex at, 432
Baghdad, 42, 44, 47, 54-6; 1st Essex enter, 58; references to, 59, 367, 454-5, 458
Bagley, Lieut.-Col. T., 559
Bagot, Captain C. F. V., 494
Bagush Box (Maaten Bagush), 257, 362, 451
Bailey, Col. C. A., 20, 23
Baines, 2/Lieut. A. J., 145
Baird, Lieut. G. J. D., 422
Balden, Capt. A. D., 440, 514
Baldwin, Lieut. C., 372, 392, 402, 422
Bally, Lieut. St. J. C., 420
Bangalore, 1st Essex at, 95, 97, 122, 125-6
Banks, Lieut. S. G., 252, 279
Baquba, 2/5th Essex at, 458
Barambe (Ranchi), 1st Essex at, 123-4
Barge, Lieut. K. R., 422
Barkakawa, 90
Barker, General Sir Evelyn, 129, 198, 525, 570
Barlaque, 2nd Essex force River Mark near, 220
Barlow, Lieut.-Col. F. S. S. (S.W.B.), 193
Barnsdale, Lieut. R. D., 453

Barrass, Major P. R., 154, 162, 170, 172, 174-5, 192, 197, 199, 206
Barrett, Capt. F., 357
Barrett-Lennard, Capt. H. D., 194, 197
Barry, Lieut. W. J., 215
Barskamp, 5th Essex in action at, 427, 428
Barton Stacey, 2nd Essex at, 159
Bas Breuil, 2nd Essex at, 193-7
Basra, 42, 44, 49
Bastyan, Major-General E., 570
Bate, Lieut. R. M., 494
Bateman, Brig. D. R. E. R., 284-5, 288-9, 297, 307, 312
Bathurst, R.Q.M.S., J., 154
Battalions—*see* Regiments
Battaye, Major P. L. M., 552
Baumgartner, Major W. J., 513-14
Bauvin, 2nd Essex at, 142
Bawli Bazaar (Arakan), 1st Essex occupy, 92-4
Bayeux, 156, 162; 2nd Essex in capture of, 163-7
Beal, 1/5th Essex at, 358
Beard, Major C. F. M., 362, 368, 372, 388, 399, 402, 422
Beaulieu, 2nd Essex await D-Day at, 161
Beazley, Capt. J. E., 307, 311-12
Beckett, 2/Lieut. A., 252
Beckett, Major D. A., 252, 266, 271, 279, 284, 309, 311-17, 321-2, 324, 330-1
Beech, Major D. J., 265, 279, 281, 284, 302, 316
Beisan, 45
Beit Lid (Palestine), 5th Essex stationed at, 421
Bel Hamed, 83
Belgium, campaign of 1940 in, 135-56
Bell, Lieut.-Col. R. E. O., 338
Bellechem Bosche, 2nd Essex at, 140-2
Benares, 2nd Essex at, 12
Bengal, Japanese threat to, 90-1
Benghazi, 71; 1/4th Essex at, 284
Benguema (Sierra Leone), 2/5th Essex at, 446-7
Benham, Major G. C., 506-7
Bennett, Lieut.-Col. P. W., 540
Benyon, Lieut.-Col. W. L. R., in command 5th Essex, 376, 390, 391, 393, 396, 401-3, 409, 412, 414, 415, 419, 422, 424
Berchem-St. Agatha, 2nd Essex at, 138
Beresford-Peirse, General Sir N. M. de C. P., 71, 257, 451
Bergin, Pte. (1st Bn.), 104
Bergues, 2nd Essex withdraw through, 149
Berlin, 2nd Essex in, 242
Bernay, 153
Bernhard, H.R.H. Prince, 238; visits Training Centre at Warley, 522

INDEX 649

Bernières-Bocage, 2nd Essex at, 170, 175
Bestley, Capt. H. R., 523
Biddulph, Lieut.-Col. J., 191-2
Bidwell, Sgt. P., 197
Biferno, the River, 375
Billericay, 497
Bingham, Lieut.-Col. E. S., in command 19th Essex, 502
Birdwood, Field-Marshal Sir William, 12, 351
Bishop, Major D. M., 490
Bishopsteignton, 9th Essex at, 495
Bizerta, 476
Blackpool, the I.T.C. at, 521
Bleckede, 5th Essex at, 434
Blerick, 2nd Essex hold the area of, 223
Blest, Brig. A. H., 17, 21; in command 2nd Essex, 130-40, 156, 157; reference to, 354, 517
Blewitt, Lieut.-Col. G., 557
Blida, 1/4th Essex at El, 292-8
Boardman, Lieut.-Col. J. W., 557
Bodo (Norway), Essex Territorials at, 359
Bois de St. Germain, 2nd Essex at the, 179-85
Bois du Mont, 500
Bokajan (Assam), 100
Bollebeke, 136
Bolton, Lieut. C. N., 252
Bombay, reference to 1st Essex at, 90, 125, 128
Bond, the Rev. B. K., 302, 451
Bone, 59th A.A. Regt. deployed at, 476
Boorman, Capt. C. J. A., 507
Borde Hill, 2nd Essex at, 158
Botley, 159, 353
Boucher, Major-General C. H., 336
Boucher, Capt. J. A., 233
Boulton, Major R. G., 482
Boustead, Lieut.-Col. H. L. H., 14, 17, 131, 149; in command 9th Essex, 493, 495-6
Bowen, Col. H. R., 12, 13, 18, 524, 558
Bowman, Capt. J. C., 494
Bradford, Sgt. (2nd Bn.), 148
Braintree, 440
Brentwood, 14, 15, 518
Brentwood School, 536
Bressey, Sir Charles, 549, 558
Brest, 131, 153
Brewer, Cpl. H. T., 302
Brigades, British:
   Cavalry and Armoured: 4th Cav., 44, 60, 61-2; 5th Cav., 66-7; 2nd Armd., 274; 32nd Armd., 78-89; 34th Armd., 489-91
   Lorried: 18th Lorried Inf. Bde., 330; 139th Lorried Inf. Bde., 242

Brigades—continued
   Airborne: 2nd Indep. Para., 415; 3rd Para., 499-502; 5th Airborne, 201
   Infantry: Canal, 26; 5th, 114; 11th, 16, 138-9; 13th, 4-5, 7, 243, 421-33; 14th, 4, 78, 85; 15th, 4; 16th, 8, 78; 21st, 32; 23rd, 28; 1st Essex with, 69, 89, 90-124; 25th, 2nd Essex with, 134-60, 354; 29th, 124, 263; 56th, 2nd Essex with, 160-242, 244; 69th, 189, 289; 72nd, 1st Essex with, 125-7; 139th, 333; 140th, 354; 146th, 212, 219, 236; 147th, 219, 236; 151st, 175; 153rd, 298; 158th, 491; 161st, 1, 17, 20-2, 248-51, 255-8, 349, 357, 361-2, 440-52; 162nd, 248; 163rd, 349-53; 168th, 197; 201st (Gds.), 298; 210th, 488, 494; 213th, 499; 214th, 158; 223rd, 498-9; 226th, 488, 494; 231st, 163-4, 189, 369
   Indian (Motorized): 3rd, 69; 161st, 274-5
   Indian (Infantry): 5th, 1st Essex, 67-9; 1/4th Essex, 259-301; 7th, 289, 291, 297, 300, 306; 9th, 277-8; 10th, 1st Essex, 33-41; 11th, 257, 451; 17th, 366, 403, 414; 18th, 366; 2/5th Essex with, 453-72; 19th, 1/5th Essex with, 364-419; 21st, 403, 411, 415
   Australian: 20th, 70
   Canadian: 6th, 540; 11th, 417
   New Zealand: Armd., 420; 4th, 83, 268; 5th, 399; 6th, 278, 307-9
   South African: 2nd, 275
Briggs, Major-General H. R., 261
Bright, Lieut.-Col. B. H., 556
Brightlingsea, 440
Bristow-Jones, Lieut. L. J., 103-5, 110, 111, 121
Brooke, Lieut.-General Sir Alan, 132
Brooks, Major C. A., 440-3, 448, 453, 466-8, 472
Brooks, Lieut. P. H., 453, 469
Brooks, Brig. W. T., 26, 28
Broome Park, Canterbury, 489
Browne, Major D. W., 153, 156, 175, 179, 184, 189, 199, 210, 215, 217
Browne, Lieut. R. C., 87, 630, 634
Browning, Major-General F. A. M., 499
Brownless, Capt. P. P. S., 78-94, 117, 630-45
Bruay, 2nd Essex at, 132-3
Brussels, 2nd Essex in defence of, 136-40
Buceels, 2nd Essex at, 175-9, 190
Bucknell, Lieut.-General A. H., 161
Buhot, 2nd Essex on D-Day at, 164-5
Bulford, 500-1
Bullemore, C.Q.M.S., J., 143
Bunch, 2/Lieut. A. W., 252
Bunda Buka, the, 34
Bunting, Capt. A. E., 513
Buqaq (Iraq), 5th Essex at, 364

Burg-el-Arab, 1/4th and 5th Essex at, 302, 369–70
Burgar, Sgt. A. J., 33
Burgess, C.Q.M.S. G., 419
Burgess, Major J. W., 540
Burma, the campaign in, 37, 99–122
Burnham, 248
Burroughs, Capt. W. R., 502
Burrows, Lieut.-Col. (A.I.F.), 85
Burrows, Brig. J. J., 268
Burrows, Mr. J. W., 1, 11–12
Burton, Sgt. B., 204
Burton, Col. H. W., 549, 556
Burton Bradstock, 494
Buru Jird (Persia), 365
Butana Bridge, 39
Butcher, Lieut. R. T., 362
Buthidaung, 92
Butler, Major I. H., 492
Butler, Lieut.-Col. M. A. H., 223, 225–9, 232–4, 236–7
Butler, Captain P. E., 215, 236, 237
Butte Du Gros Orme, 169
Buzza, Capt. W. W., 362, 368, 372, 388, 399, 402, 404

C

Caen, 156, 176, 179; Essex Scottish in break-out from, 540
Cairo, 1st Essex at, 8–10
Calcutta, 13, 90–1
Caldari, 5th Essex at, 403, 417
Calvert, 2/Lieut. D. G., 145, 156
Calvert, Pte. M. H., 88
Campbell, Brig. L. M., 421
Camphin, 2nd Essex at, 146
Campobasso, 324
Canada, forces of—see Brigades/Regiments
Cannon, 2/Lieut. T. G. L., 172
Canty, R.S.M. D., 276
Cape Verde Islands, the 1/4th and 2/5th Essex prepare for offensive action against the, 256, 447–8
Capel-Dunn, Capt. D. C., 357
Cardy, the Rev. J., 541
Cariappa, General, 60, 363
Carolin, Major R. E. G., 7, 20
Carpenter, Brig. J. O., 158
Carter, Lieut. G. E. M., 453
Carvin, 2nd Essex at, 134, 211
Casa Luciense, 420
Casa Salvini, 417
Casoli, 393
Casone, 403
Cassino, 1/4th Essex in attacks on Monte, 306–20
Castel di Sangro, 420
Catterick (Yorks), 1st Essex at, 3–7
Cawnpore, 2nd Essex at, 12

Cazalet, Major G. L., 520, 523
Celenza, 379
Central Mediterranean Force (C.M.F.), 1/4th Essex with, 303–38; 5th Essex with, 371–420, 424–5
Chakyang (Assam), 116
Chandler-Honnor, Capt. H. E., 362, 368, 372, 395, 411
Chapman, Sgt. E. K., 263
Chappell, Lieut.-Col. G. Gresham, 559
Chappell, Lieut.-Col. L. W. A., 252, 264, 269, 271, 273, 279, 291, 297, 304; in command 1/4th Essex, 316, 324, 327–8, 329–30
Charleroi Canal, defence of the, 138–9
Charles, Lieut.-Col. T. L. G., 14, 17, 154, 243–5, 570
Charlton, Brig. C. G., 547, 550, 558
Château Turcq, the, 61, 63
Chathill, 443
Chekrema (Assam), 105, 107
Chell, Capt. P. J., 162, 195, 197
Chell, Lieut.-Col. R. A., 507, 509–11, 513, 515
Chelmsford, presentation of silver bugles at, 15, 16; 1/5th Essex on embodiment at, 357–8; presentation of Freedom of, 565
Cherbourg, 131, 156
Chester-le-Street, 351
Cheswema (Assam), 103–4, 112, 115
Chhartapur, 97
Chindwin, the River, 99, 119
Chinnery, 2/Lieut. G. F., 422
Chittagong, 1st Essex at, 91–2, 94
Churan, Sgt. C. A., 88, 104
Churchill, Col. A. P., 11–12, 529
Churchill, Rt. Hon. W. L. S., on campaign in Syria, 66; on Beauman Div., 153; inspects 10th Essex, 498; Honorary Colonel 4th Essex, 571
Civic Sunday, the annual service at the Chapel, 537
Clacton, 2nd Essex at, 160–1; reference to, 349
Clark, Major-General George, 41–2, 44, 47, 49–50, 53–4, 56, 58, 59, 61–3, 65
Clark, Lieut. L. M. L., 402, 422
Clark, Lieut. R. G., 416, 422, 503
Clarke, Lieut. A. B. W., 402, 411
Clarke, Pte. C. T. V., 146, 156
Clarke, Lieut.-Col. F. A. S., 5, 511
Clarke, L/Sgt. S., 115
Clarke, Brig. W. S., 492
Clay, Capt. J. G., 279
Cloutman, Capt. W. T. G., 545
Clover, Capt. S. K., 453
Clyde, Pte. R., 419
Coe, Lieut. F. G., 453, 472
Coffee, Pte. S. H., 156

INDEX 651

Coghlan, Lieut. P. M. F., 311, 312, 314
Coker, Lieut. B. A., 503
Coker, Major J. N., 506-7
Colchester, 1st Essex 1929, 2; 2nd Essex, 11; references to, 16, 21; 1st Essex 1948, 128, 570; 2nd Essex 1948, 246; 2/5th Essex, 440-2; presentation of Freedom of, 565-6; amalgamation of regular battalions at, 569
Colle Croce, 5th Essex at, 420
Collier, Capt. S. E., 507
Colvin, Brig. Sir Richard, 2, 6
Comber, Major P. D., 115, 121
Congress Revolution, the, 90
Consalvi (Conselve), 321
Constantinople, 2nd Essex at, 11-12
Conway, Capt. R. A. E., 545
Cooper, Capt. E. B., 453, 467, 470, 472
Cooper, Lieut. H. A. S., 234
Cooper, Lieut. J., 177
Cooper, Lieut. J. R. A., 279, 502
Cooper-Bland, Col. J., 557
Coote, Lieut.-Col. I. V., 559
Corbridge, 443
Cordery, Pte. A. F., 88
Cormeilles, 2nd Essex capture, 199
Cornelius, Capt. B. J., 503
Cornell, Cpl. (5th Bn.), 382
Cornell, P.S.M. W. E., 68
Coronation duty, 14, 15, 21
Corps:
  British: 1st, 198-221, 223-40; 2nd, 132-52; 5th, 159, 373-419, 486-8, 494-5; 8th, 179, 186, 190; 9th, 299-301; 10th, 284-5, 321-30, 420-1; 12th, 190, 223-4; 13th, 78, 88, 257, 261-76, 362, 375, 402; 30th, 78, 161-98, 276-98, 461-73
  Dominion: 1st Australian, 65; 1st Canadian, 235; New Zealand Corps, 307-20
  Indian: 15th, 91; 21st, 366; 33rd, 116, 119, 121
  Polish Corps, 331
Cortina, 245
Cosham, 2nd Essex at, 158
Counsell, 2/Lieut. D. C., 252, 279
Courage, Lieut.-Col. A. D. G., 475
Courmeilles, 2nd Essex capture town of, 199
Courmeron, 191-2
Courseulles-sur-Mer, 496
Cowes, 159-60
Cowley, Major W. G., 15
Cox, Brig. C. H. V., 69, 89
Cox, Capt. J. S., 19
Craig, Major B. H., 434
Cramphorn, Lieut.-Col. J. F., 134-5, 138-9, 142, 147, 150, 156, 201, 357, 435

Crane, Capt. E. H., 142, 147, 520
Creedy, Sir Herbert, 16
Creese, Lieut. R. M., 252
Cripps, Lieut.-Col. H. H., 520
Crocker, Capt. M. H., 486
Croucher, R.Q.M.S. N. T. H., 571
Cubitt, Sir Bertram, 529
Cullen, Major A. L., 435, 453, 472
Cumming, Major G. F. H., 476
Cunningham, General Sir Alan, 71
Curtis, Capt. T. J., 514
Cyprus, 10, 26, 27, 89; 1/4th Essex in, 258-9

D

Dagenham, 248, 349
Dakar, reference to attacks on, 254
D'Albiac, Air Vice-Marshal J. H., 43, 48
Dale, Cpl. E. P. J., 385, 387, 419
Dalldorf, 5th Essex at, 430
Daltongunj, 91
Damascus, 8, 59-60, 61, 66, 459
Daniell, Lieut. P. W., 453
Dann, Lieut. R. P., 372, 402, 422
Davey, Lieut. N. G., 357
Davidson, Lieut. J. M., 402, 411, 422
Davies, Lieut.-Col. C. M., 558-9
Davies, Lieut. S. F., 279, 294
Davis, Pte. (1st Bn.), 32
Davis, Lieut. G. M., 422
Day, the Rev. S., 268
Day, C.S.M., S. J., 302
De Gaulle, General, 59, 68
De Jager, Capt. R. W., 422
De La Mare, Major A. G., 494
De Rougemont, Brig.-General C. H., 549, 558
De Winton, Brig. R. M. W., 244
Deal, 360, 495
Dean, Lieut. H. B., 279
Dear, Lieut. N. H., 279
Death Valley (Assam), 117-18
Deedes, Sir Charles, 547
Deir El Abyab, 266
Deir-el-Shein, 266; the battle of, 459-73
Deir-ez-Zor, 67-9, 459
Dendre, River, 140
Dentolo, River, 414
Dentz, General, 65
Deolali, 1st Essex at, 127
Dhanbad, 90
Dieppe, 539-40
Dill, General Sir John, 9
Dilliway, Capt. L. J., 513
Dimapur, 100-1, 112, 119, 122
Dinant, 136
Dipetuli (Dhipatoli), 122-3
Ditton, Major M. A. H., 478

Divisions:
  British Armoured and Cavalry: 1st Armoured, 153, 269-70, 330-1, 464; 1st Cavalry, 41, 44, 45, 64; 6th Armoured, 299; 7th Armoured, 168-74, 242, 257, 298, 299; 79th Armoured, 236
  Polish Armoured: 216
  British Airborne: 1st Airborne, 237; 6th Airborne, 201, 500-2
  British Infantry: 1st, 139, 489; 2nd, 95, 103, 113, 114, 124; 3rd, 132; 4th, 137-8, 335, 424; 5th, 3, 7, 243, 375, 402, 420-34; 6th, 65, 69; 13th, 339; 15th, 429, 492, 501; 29th, 29; 36th, 124-7; 43rd, 186, 360, 434-5, 489-90, 492; 45th, 499; 47th, 158-60, 354; 49th, 175, 198-241, 491; 50th, 156, 160-90, 224, 263, 264, 280, 285, 286, 289, 291, 463, 487; 51st, 205, 224, 281, 289, 492; 53rd, 491; 54th, 20, 248-51, 349-55; 56th, 356; 59th, 190-7; 70th, 69, 78-89, 90-122; 78th, 375, 376, 378, 402
  U.S.: 2nd U.S. Armoured, 186; 104th U.S. Infantry, 217, 220
  Indian Infantry: 4th, 257, 259, 278-339; 5th, 33, 39-40, 258-9, 261-77; 8th, 362, 364-418, 455-73; 10th, 49, 60, 67, 261-2, 326, 328; 14th, 91; 26th, 94
  Dominion and Commonwealth—
  Canadian: 1st, 236, 375, 402, 403, 404; 2nd, 538-44; 3rd, 158, 235; 4th Armoured, 216, 218; 5th Armoured, 236
  Australian: 7th, 60
  New Zealand: 2nd, 263, 266-8, 273, 277, 278, 304, 307-20, 389-400, 402, 420
  South African: 1st, 261, 269, 461
Enemy:
  German: Panzer Lehr, 169; 2nd Panzer, 184-6; 15th Panzer, 439, 465; 16th Panzer, 375; 1st Parachute, 313, 376, 403, 404; 21st Panzer, 266, 280; 90th Light, 268; 164th Infantry, 294; 245th Infantry, 430; 276th Infantry, 185; 305th Infantry, 325; 336th Infantry, 330; 346th Infantry, 240; 352nd Infantry, 168
  Italian: Bologna, 277; Pistoia, 288
  Japanese: 31st Infantry, 104
Djebel Garci, 1/4th Essex at, 291-8
Dobree, Brig. T. S., 371, 378, 380, 386, 390, 397, 398, 402, 405, 410, 412, 418, 431
Doherty, Lieut.-Col. T. O'C., 26, 135-6, 138, 140, 147, 519, 520
Don, 142
Dorchester, 353
Douglas, Lieut. J. B., 495
Douma (Damascus), 66
Dover, 5, 153, 353, 360
Dovercourt, 497
Doyle, Major R. M., 252
Downs, Cpl. B., 168
Drucquer, Capt. J. K., 460, 469
Duffus, Lieut.-Col. C. S., 558
Dunkirk, 2nd Essex in withdrawal from, 135-56
Dunn, Brig. P. D. W., 66
Durban, 256, 361
Durham, 160
Durrant, Lieut.-Col. A. W., 559
Dutch forces, training at Warley of, 522-3, 535
Dyer, L/Cpl. H. T. J., 472
Dyer, L/Cpl. (2nd Bn.), 151
Dyson, Lieut.-Col. M., 560

E

Earls Colne, 440
East Ham, presentation of Freedom by, 566-7
Ebbs, Lieut. H. F., 422
Ed Duda, the battle of, 76-89
Eden, Mr. Anthony, 33, 546-7
Eden, Major G. A., 571
Edhessa (Edessa), 1/4th Essex at, 336-9
Edrupt, Lieut. K. D., 272, 279, 294
Edwards, Lieut. A. M., 279
Edwards, Col. C. E., 484, 506-7, 522
Egypt, the Western Desert of, 13, 68, 70-89, 257, 260-84, 459-73
Eighth Army, the—*see* Armies
Einbeck, 2nd Essex at, 243
El Adem, 73, 74, 78, 83; 1/4th Essex at, 284
El Alamein, 1/4th Essex hold part of front at, 266-78; the battle of, 279-84; 2/5th Essex at, 460-1
El Blida, 1/4th Essex attack at, 292-8
El Daba, references to, 362, 453, 460
El Hamma, 285-9
El Hamman, 463
El Tahag, 361, 451
Elbe, crossing of the River, 426-9, 501
Elbeuf, 540
Eldridge, Pte. A. W. G., 53, 65
Elliott, Major E. I., 360, 361, 372, 376, 387, 390, 399, 402, 404
Elliott, Lieut.-Col. G. G., 161, 162, 164, 170, 173; in command 2nd Essex, 174, 175, 177, 180-1, 183-5, 187-95, 199, 201-6, 208-12, 214-15
Elsmore, Pte. G. N., 387, 419
Elst, 2nd Essex at, 224-6
Emanuel, Lieut. C. A., 422
Enfidaville, 1/4th Essex at, 291-8

Epping, 248
Erbil (Irbil), 2/5th Essex at, 457
Eritrea, 27, 29, 32, 34–41, 503–4
Esschen, 2nd Essex attack at, 218
Essex College, 241; Essex Ridge (Ruweisat), 270–1, 276; Essex Squadron (107 R.A.C.), 491–3; Essex (Verrières) Wood, 168–74
Essex Home Guard, 546–60
Essex Regiment:
Comforts Fund, 133, 414, 525; Prayer, 533; Museum, 430, 524; Chapel, 527–37; Colonelcy of, 3, 128, 246, 561–2; Depot, 517–26; of Canada, 241–2, 538–44
1st Essex: leaves Colchester for Pembroke Dock, 2; moves to Catterick, 3; in the Saar, 5–6; Catterick, 7; moves Palestine, 7; in Egypt, 9; returns Palestine, 9; in Egypt and Cyprus, 10; dispositions on outbreak of war, 11, 26; in Egypt, 26–8; the Sudan, 28–33; operations against Gallabat, 34–9; in Palestine, 40–2; operations in Iraq, 42–58; in Syria, 59–69; at Tobruk and Ed Duda, 70–89; in India 1942–3, 90–1; in Arakan, 91–5; L.R.P. Assam and Burma, 95–122; India and England 1944–48, 122–8; amalgamated with 2nd Battalion, 128, 246, 569
2nd Essex: reference to the, 7; in Malta (1919–21), 11; in Turkey, 12–13; in India, 12–13; in Egypt and the Sudan, 13–14; at Warley, 14–17; reference to, 28; deploys for A.A. defence of London, 130; mobilisation, 130–1; France 1939–40, 131–5; operations in Belgium and France ending at Dunkirk, 135–56; home defence, 157–60; joins 56 Independent Inf. Bde., 161; the landing in Normandy, 162–3; operations in France, 162–212; in Holland, 212–40; in Germany, 240–3; in Italy, 243–6; amalgamated with 1st Battalion, 128, 246, 569
4th Essex: reference to, 14, 17, 19, 20, 21, 22, 23; raises a second line battalion and becomes 1/4th Essex, 23; 4th Battalion re-formed 1946, 571–2
1/4th Essex: formation organisation, 23; reference to, 27; embodiment 1939, 248; home defence, 248–51; in West Africa, 252–6; Egypt, Cyprus, and Palestine, 256–60; the Western Desert to El Alamein, 260–79; at El Alamein, 279–84; in Tunisia, 285–302; in Italy, 303–32; in Greece, 332–9
2/4th Essex: formation, 23; story of, 348–55

Essex Regiment—*continued*
5th Essex: reference to, 17, 20, 21, 22, 23; duplication of, 23; re-formed 1947 as anti-aircraft artillery, 435–6
1/5th (5th) Essex: formation, 24; embodiment, 357; on home defence, 357–61; the Middle East, 361–71; re-designated 5th Bn., 368; with Eighth Army in Italy, 371–420; the Middle East, 421–4; the campaign in N.-W. Europe, 424–35; post-war re-formation, 435–6; reference to, 502
2/5th Essex: formation, 24; embodiment and home service, 440–4; West Africa, 445–50; Middle East, 450–9; Western Desert, 460–73
6th Essex: references to, 17, 19, 21, 22; converted to anti-aircraft role, 22
1/6th Essex in World War II, 478–80
2/6th Essex in World War II, 480–4
7th Essex: references to, 17, 19; converted to anti-aircraft role, 21; reference to, 23; short war history of, 474–8; 7th (H.D.) Essex formed 1939 and converted (1940) into 30th (H.D.) Essex, 507–12
8th Essex: at home as infantry, 486–8; converted into 153 R.A.C., 488–9; in Normandy, 490–1; Essex Squadron 107 R.A.C. formed from, 491–3
9th Essex: at home 1940–42, 493–5; as 11 Medium Regiment R.A. at home and in N.-W. Europe, 495–6
10th Essex: at home, 497–9; as 9th Parachute Bn. at home and in N.-W. Europe, 499–502
19th Essex: 423, 502–4
30th Essex—see 7th Essex
70th Essex: 502–4, 509
Essex, U.S.S.R., presentation to, 524
Esson, 197
Esteuelles, 142
Eterville, 539
Ettershank, 2/Lieut. R. H., 372, 382, 384–5
Euphrates, the River, 49, 54, 60, 68, 69
Eusanio, 5th Essex at, 415–16
Evans, Lieut. J. R., 279
Evans, the Rev. H. B., 278, 279
Eve, Brig. R. A. T., 245
Evershott, 488
Evetts, Brig. (Major-General) J. F., 8, 9, 10
Exham, Brig. K. G., 241–4

F

Fadden, Capt. J. F. B., 252
Fairford, 2/4th Essex at, 351
Falaise, references to, 186, 190, 197, 540
Falluja, 1st Essex in operations at, 49–54, 56
Famagusta, 258

INDEX

Farr, Lieut. D. S., 252
Fasula, Palestine, 1st Essex at, 8
Fatnassa Hills, 1/4th Essex operate in the, 289-98
Faulkner, Major A. C., 482
Felixstowe, 20, 572
Felsted School, 536
Ferrier, Major, 233
Field, Sgt. F., 13
Filby, Capt. R. G., 184, 195, 233, 234
Finlinson, Lieut.-Col. N. W., 215, 217, 219, 222
Finn, Capt. J. F., 442, 445, 453
Fisher, Capt. D. J. V., 252, 272-3, 279, 304
Fisher, Pte. R., 468, 472
Flatman, Pte. L. A., 412
Foggia, 5th Essex occupy, 373-5
Folliott, 2nd Essex at, 170, 174, 175
Fontaine, River La, 210
Foote, 2/Lieut. C. J. A., 252
Ford, Capt. D. H., 523
Forêt de Bretonne, 2nd Essex in, 203-4
Forêt de Grimbosq, 2nd Essex in, 190-7
Forêt de Nieppe, 147
Forge-à-Cambro, 2nd Essex capture, 190-2
Fort Keary, 116-17
Fort St. George, 126-7
Foster, Capt. I. P., 361
Fountain, Pte. E., 62
Fountain, 2/Lieut. R. L., 154
Fowler, Capt. A. G., 252
Foy, 2/Lieut. M. V., 138, 142, 152
Fradin, Capt. H. J., 168, 175
France, 5, 6; campaign of 1940 in, 135-56
Francis, Pte. L. E., 473
Franklin, Major P. H. A. L., 26, 32, 71
Free French Forces, references to, 59, 60, 69
Freedom of County Towns and Boroughs, 563-8
Freetown, 1/4th Essex at, 252-6; 2/5th Essex, 446-9
French, Capt. B. B., 107, 121
French, Lieut.-Col. J. L., 18, 19, 20, 23
French West Africa, 253-4, 449
Freshwater, 160
Freyberg, Major-General B. C., 266, 286, 307, 389, 397, 400
Frinton, 160
Fromelles, 146-7
Fuka, 255-6, 452
Furnival, L/Cpl. S. G., 88

G

Gagen, Capt. T. G., 154, 521, 523
Gahagan, Major D. R., 153, 486, 490
Galal, 460
Gallabat, 33; operations against, 34-42
Gallipoli Day, commemoration of, 29
Galloway, Major-General A., 308
Gambellara, 352
Gambier, Pte. A., 464, 471
Gant, Pte. W., 242
Garner, Major E. C., 490-3
Gauchin Legal, 2nd Essex at, 132
Gaza, 423
Gaza Day, commemoration of, 18, 249, 255
Gaze, Lieut.-Col. A. W., 559
Gedaref, 33-4, 37, 39
Gello, 325-6
Genders, Capt. H. J. K., 26, 32
Ghent, 5th Essex at, 425-6
Ghor Otrub, the, 34, 38
Giaggiola, 330-1
Gibbs, 2/Lieut. (Capt.) D. M. H., 362, 368, 372, 388, 389
Gibson, Col. G. M., 19, 23, 248-50, 252, 255, 257, 258, 446
Gibson, Major J. G., 357
Giffard, General Sir George, 253
Giles, Pte. J. R., 177
Gingell, 2/Lieut. B. G., 81, 87
Gio Jello, 324
Glibbery, L/Cpl. J., 295
Gloucester, H.R.H. the Duke of, references to, 19, 20; visits 1/4th Essex, 259; sees 1/5 Essex, 365; and 8th Essex, 458
Glubb Pasha, 45, 54
Godwin-Austen, Lieut.-Gen. A. R., 88, 362
Gold, Lieut.-Col. G. G., 550, 558
"Golden Square," The, 42
Gondar, 33
Gooderson, Capt. E. N., 503
Goppe Bazaar, 1st Essex at, 92-4
Gordon, Lieut.-Col. H., 13-14
Gordon Fields, Ilford, re-establishment of 4th Essex at, 571
Gormley, Capt. H. F., 494
Goslar, 5th Essex at, 433
Gott, Brig. W. H. E., 257, 260
Gould, Lieut.-Col. C. H., 559
Gowlett, Sgt. (1/4th Essex), 315
Graham, Major-General D. A. H., 160
Graham, Lieut.-Col. F., 559
Grant, Capt. K. M., 110, 113
Grantshaw, Pte. G., 88
Granville, 179-80, 187
Graves, 2/Lieut. T. G., 252
Gravesend, 360
Gray, Lieut.-Col. C. A., 461, 463, 467, 470
Greece, 1/4th Essex in, 332-9
Greece, H.M. King of, sees 10th Essex, 499
Green, Brig. M. A., 253, 447
Green, 2/Lieut. P. J., 138, 140, 143
Green, C.S.M., W., 156

INDEX

Greene, Major J. S., 26, 47, 55, 68, 70–1
Gregory, Capt. C. A., 5
Gregory, Major H. C., 252, 261, 278–9, 284, 288, 295, 300, 313, 316, 325, 330
Gridley, Pte. A., 151
Griffen, Major W. F., 372, 387, 388, 395, 402, 403, 409, 412, 413, 416, 419, 422
Griffin, Brig. J. A. A., 553
Grigg, Lieut. D. W., 204
Grimley, 2/Lieut. B. F. H., 41, 55, 63–4, 68
Grimwood, Lieut.-Col. P. L., 20, 21, 23, 483
Grist, Major T. W., 252, 260, 274, 571
Groningen, 542
Grosse Gronau, 430
Grube Heinitz, 5
Grundy, Lieut. F., 491
Gueron (Bayeux), 167
Gulliver, R.S.M., J. R., 242, 243
Gurdon, Brig. E. T. L., 157
Gurkha Rifles, the—*see* Regiments
Gwinnet, the Rev. J., 501

H

H1, H2, H3, H4, 42, 46, 48, 50, 59–61, 363, 455
Haalderen, 225, 229, 234–5
Habbaniya, Iraqi attack on, 42; operations to relieve and occupy Baghdad, 48–58; 1/5th Essex at, 363; 2/5th Essex at, 454–5
"Habforce," formation and operation in Iraq and Syria of, 44–65
Hadera (Palestine), 70, 261, 459
Haifa, 8, 10, 27, 40–5, 59, 363, 371, 425, 454, 460
Hailes, Lieut. C., 279, 289, 292, 302, 343–7
Haining, Lieut.-Gen. R. H., 10
Haiya, 39
Halbert, Lieut. J. F., 362, 422
Hale, Capt. P., 242
Halfaya, 1/4th Essex at, 261–2
Hallouf (Tunisia), 268–9
Halstead, 440
Hamber, Capt. G. R., 490, 491
Hamburg (Saar), 5
Hamilton, General Sir Ian, 564
Hamilton, Lieut.-Col. R. N., 559
Hammond, Pte. (1st Bn.), 111
Harding, Brig. (Lieut.-General) Sir John, 244, 257, 328
Harding, Lieut. G. F., 372, 391, 402, 407, 422
Harding-Newman, Major-General J. G., 18
Harington, General Sir Charles, 11
Harlow, 499
Harrison, Lieut.-Col. C. S., 560
Harrison, Capt. N. F., 177

Hartigan, Lieut.-Col. (N.Z. Forces), 81
Hartnell, Lieut.-Col. S. (19th N.Z.), 264
Harvey, Major-General C. O., 456
Harvey, Lieut. J. W., 402, 407
Harwich, defence of the port of, 441, 497–8
Hassetche (El Haseke), 69
Hastie, Pte. J., 407, 412, 419
Hathorn, Capt. D. McF., 402, 406, 411
Hawkins, Capt. E. A., 252, 279
Hay, Lieut.-Col. Lord Edward, 23, 348, 351
Hayes, L/Sgt. C. W., 88
Hayes, the Rev. J., 422
Haynes, Capt. R. J., 107, 113, 121
Haynes, Pte. (1st Bn.), 15
Hazle, L/Cpl. E. B., 318, 320
Head, Sgt. L. J., 156
Heal, Lieut.-Col. W. A., 424, 426, 433
Heard, Capt. H. E., 252
Hearn, Lieut.-Col. T. E., references to, 5, 154; in command 10th Essex, 497–9; in command No. 1 I.T.C., 520–3; references to, 564, 565, 566
Hearne, Capt. A. F., 167
Heath, Major-General L. M., 33, 39
Hedges, Capt., 559
Hedley, Lieut.-Col. D. T., 480, 483
Helleburg (Hellebrug), 2nd Essex at, 211–12
Henderson, Col. P. C., 559
Henley-on-Thames, 351–2
s'Hertogenbosch, 541
Hervey, Sgt., 1st Essex, 104
Hessbeck, 426
Heteren, 225
Hexham, 251, 349–50, 359–60
Higson, Lieut.-Col. J. F., 26, 32, 43, 71, 81, 87, 88, 92, 161–74, 244
Hill, Cpl. I. E., 412
Hill, Major R. A., 435
Hill, Capt. R. C. G., 372, 387, 388, 389, 393, 395, 399, 402, 404, 418, 422
Hills, Major A. J., 441, 448, 453–4, 455
Hinde, Capt. P. C., 137
Hipper, the, 445
Hitler, reference to death of Adolf, 429
Hobart, Brig. J. W. L. S., 249, 252, 255, 441, 445, 447, 449
Hochwald, the, 541
Hodges, Major A. J., 542
Holme, Major M. W., 162, 165, 169, 170, 172, 174–5, 179, 183, 189, 194, 197, 208, 215, 220, 232, 233
Holmes, the Rev. R. J., 372, 388
Home Guard, the Essex, 546–60
Homs, 61, 63, 64, 66
Hooton, 2/Lieut. D. J., 422
Hopegood, Major C. J. I. F., 13, 26
Hopwood, Lieut. H. G. L., 358–9, 362
Hornchurch, 498

Horne, Sgt. T., 284
Horobin, Lieut. H. R., 362, 368
Horrocks, Lieut.-General B. J., 284, 299, 301
Horsbrugh-Porter, Lieut.-Col. A. M., 331
Horsington, Lieut. J. S., 304
Houston, Lieut. J. I., 26
Houtkerque, 149
Howard, Lieut.-General Sir Geoffrey W., in command 5th Div., 3; becomes Colonel of Regiment, 3; reference to, 7; visits 1st Essex in Egypt, 10; at presentation of silver bugles, 16; message to 1st Essex 1940, 32, reference to, 105; visits 1st Essex in India, 123; reference to, 215; inspects 1/4th Essex, 249; visits 2/4th Essex, 353; visits 1/5th Essex, 360; visits 9th Essex, 495; and 10th Essex, 498; references to, 524, 525, 534; inspects Essex Scottish Regiment of Canada, 543; retirement of, 561-2; references to, 563, 564, 565, 566, 567
Howard, Lady, 133, 414, 525
Howard, Lieut. W. P., 402, 407, 411
Howell, Major H. F., 135, 138, 142
Howes, Lieut. W. H. W., 372, 402
Huddleston, Sir Herbert, 503
Hudson, Capt. (R.A.), 406
Hudson, L/Cpl. G., 302
Hughes, Lieut.-Col. F., 557
Hunter, Major-General A. J., 6
Hurrell, Lieut.-Col. J. W., 351-2
Hussey, Lieut.-Col. A. V., 557
Hutchison, Major-General B. O., 503
Hutton-Rudby, 2/4th Essex at, 354

I

Ifs, the battle of, 540
Ijssel, the crossing of the River, 236
Ikingi (Alexandria), 5th Essex sails for Italy from, 371
Il Calvario, 390-400
Ilford, 19, 20, 21, 248, 348-9; presents Freedom, 567; re-establishment of 4th Essex at, 571
Imphal, 90, 119, 120
India, 12-13, 30, 90, 91-5, 99, 126; British forces leave, 126-8
Indian Army—*see* Regiments
Infantry battalions—*see* Regiments
Infantry Training Centre, Warley, 517-26
Ingatestone, 507, 513
Inverary, 2nd Essex at, 161
Iraq levies, the, 48, 50
Iraq, the revolt in, 42; 1st Essex in suppression of, 42-58; references to, 89, 362; 1/5th Essex serve in, 363-7; 2/5th Essex in, 455-8

Irbid, 45
Irbil, 2/5th Essex at, 457
Irwin, 2/Lieut. A. S., 146, 147, 156
Irwin, Major-General N. M. S., 254, 498
Isernia, 375, 420
"Island," 2nd Essex on the, 224-37
Italian campaign, 1/4th Essex in the, 303-32; 5th Essex in the, 371-421
Italian East Africa, reference to, 29, 30, 33
Italy, at war with Abyssinia, 7, 13; reinforcement of her garrisons in East Africa, 27; declaration of war by, 30

J

Jackson, Pte. G., 273, 292, 346
Jago, Sgt. (2nd Essex), 223
Jalahalli (Bangalore), 1st Essex at, 126
James, Lieut.-Col. R. B., 26, 51, 53, 54, 55, 64, 65
Jameson, Col. K. E., 547, 550
Japan: entry in war, 89; threat to Bengal, 90-1; 1st Essex in operations with army of, 91-5, 99-102
Jasperson, Lieut.-Col. F. K., 539
Jay, L/Cpl. (1st Essex), 32
Jebel Mazaar (Syria), 5th Essex at, 423
Jennings, 2/Lieut. D. B., 147
Jericho, 41
Jerusalem (Normandy), 173
Jerusalem (Palestine), 5th Essex win 5th Division football at, 423
Jessami (Assam), 116, 117
Jhansi, 123
Jhingergacha (Bengal), 91
Jisr-el-Majame, 45, 454
Johncock, Lieut. W., 494
Johnson, the Rev. A. D., 249
Johnson, Major-General D. G., 519
Johnson, Alderman S. F., 564
Jones, Capt. H. F. H., 135, 138, 139, 141, 142, 144, 147-8
Jones, R.S.M., J. R., 572
Jones, Lieut.-Col. T. S., 540
Jordan, the River, 45, 363, 454
Jouffra, 61
Juaye Mondaye, 2nd Essex attack, 169

K

Kabrit, 303
Kade, 220
Kafr Kanna, 9
Kajouri Plain, 2nd Essex in operations on the, 12-13
Kalyan, 125
Kamjong (Assam), 119
Kantara, El, 363, 371

INDEX 657

Kapellan, 483
Karkur, 259
Kassala, 30, 32-3, 39
Kasteel, 222
Kaye, Major J. P., 362, 368, 372, 381, 383-5
Kaye, Major L. C., 361, 368, 372, 381, 384-6, 387-8, 393, 395
Keeley-Callan, Pte. (5th Bn.), 387
Kelly, Major A. H., 26, 56
Kelvedon, 249, 440
Kemball, Col. H. F., 478, 506-10, 513
Kemball, Lieut.-Col. R. F., 475, 478
Kenrick, Capt. C. J., 283, 294, 311, 316, 329
Kent, H.R.H. Duke of, 15, 19
Keruma (Assam), 102, 104, 112
Kesselring, Marshal, 324
Ketley, Sgt. L. G., 389, 398, 399, 419
Ketteley, Major F. J., 264, 279, 289, 295, 297, 311, 314
Keys, 2nd Essex in Ceremony of the, 15
Khamsa, 262
Khan Nuqta, 1st Essex at, 55
Kharasom Kuki (Assam), 116
Khartoum, 1st Essex at, 28-9, 32; 2nd Essex at, 13-14; 19th Essex at, 503-4
Khashm-el-Girba, 39
Khassa (Gaza), 5th Essex at, 423-4
Khunti (Ranchi), 90-1
Khyber Pass, 2nd Essex in the, 12
Kidd, Lieut.-Col. H. F., 560
Kiddapore, Calcutta, 91, 95
Kidderminster, 486, 493
Kidzemetuma (Assam), 116
Kifisia (Greece), 1/4th Essex at, 336
Kifri, 366
King George V, H.M., 19
King George VI, H.M., reviews 1/4th Essex, 301, 325
King, Pte. C. H., 387, 396
King, Sgt. T., 273
"Kingcol," 1st Essex with, 44-58
Kingston (Jamaica), 225
Kingstone, Brig. J., 45, 50, 54
Kington, 157
Kirkpatrick, Major-General C., 550, 557
Kirkuk, 43, 364-5
Kitchener, 2/Lieut. H. D., 422
Kloster Lutherheim, 501
Knight, Capt. G. D., 509
Knight, Lieut. R. V., 472
Knox, Mr. G. G., 5
Knox, General Sir Harry, 16
Knutsford, 156
Kohima, 99, 101-2, 112-14, 116
Korteheide, 2nd Essex capture, 222
Krumesse, 5th Essex on V.E.-Day at, 431
Kukis, the, 102
Kyd, Capt. J. M., 509

E.R.—42

L

L'Epinette, 147
L'Haute Deule Canal, 2nd Essex hold the, 142-6
La Bagotiere, 191
La Bassée Canal, 2nd Essex hold line of, 142-6
La Bourdonne, 204
La Calonne, the River, 199
La Croix des Landes, 181
La Hutte, 153
La Panne, 152
La Valette, 539
La Venna, 414
Lake, Col. E. A. W., 557, 558
Lake, Capt. P. B., 448, 453, 458
Lambert, R.S.M., R. A., 401
Lambshead, Capt. H. T., 503
Lambton Castle, 350
Lampard, 2/Lieut. W. G., 372, 384, 385, 387
Lance, Major G. C. P., 181
Lanciano, 305, 321, 402-3, 416-19
Landi Kotal, 2nd Essex at, 12
Langheide, 2nd Essex at, 222
Lardner-Burke, Lieut. D. W., 422, 427
Larino, 5th Essex at, 375
Lashbrook, Lieut. H. S., 453
Latakia (Lattaque), 5th Essex at, 368-9
Launay Ridge, 2nd Essex attack on, 185-90
Laverty, Lieut.-Col. H. J., 515-16, 568
Law, Capt. M. I., 362, 368, 372, 396, 402, 419, 422
Lawrence, Lieut. C. H., 64, 68, 80, 87
Le Bourget, 153
Le Bray, 152
Le Breuil-en-Ange, 199
Le Doulieu, 148
Le Hamel, 2nd Essex land on D-Day at, 164-5
Le Havre, 2nd Essex in Operation "Ansonia," 205-11; reference to, 491
Le Mesnil, 192
Le Paradis, 146
Lebanon, the, 59, 368-9, 423
Lebeeke, 140
Lee, 2/Lieut. A. R., 362
Lee, Major J. W. G., 404-5, 412, 419, 422
Leese, General Sir Oliver, 122, 278, 326, 369, 565
Leggett, Cpl. G. S., 412
Leghorn, 59th Regt. (7th Essex) at, 477
Leigh-on-Sea, 515-16
Leiston, 349, 352
Lembeck, 501
Leonhout (Loenhout), 2nd Essex attack at, 216-17

INDEX

Leppard, Cpl. P. J., 387
Les Landes, 180-1
Les Orailles, 179-81
Lesquin, 132
Lewis, Capt. J., 513-14
Lewis, C.S.M., R., 156
Lewsey, Capt. T. W. L., 252
Liddell, Sir Clive, 563
Liddell, Major D. O., 401-2, 405-6, 407, 411, 412, 416
Lille, 132, 136, 142, 144, 146
Lille St. Hubert (Holland), 222
Lillebonne, 211
Linfoot, Lieut.-Col. H. A., 559
Lipscombe, Capt. J., 419, 422
Lister, the Rev. G. M., 414, 523, 534-5, 564-8
Littledale, Lieut. A. M. J., 26
Litton Cheney, 487
Lloyd, Lieut.-General H. C., 159, 497
Lloyd, Lieut.-Col. J. E., 484
Lloyd, Brig. W., 68
Lochner, Brig. R. G., 456, 457, 461
Lockhart, Major-General R. M. M., 126
Loder, 2/Lieut. T. C., 362
Loenhout (Leonhout), 2nd Essex at, 216-17
Loftus, Lieut.-Col. E. A., 18
Lofthouse, L/Cpl. J. W., 406, 412
Lombardy Plain, 1/4th Essex operate in the, 331-2
London, 1st Essex march through, 6; 2nd Essex assist in anti-air defence of, 130
Long-Price, Major D. E., 125, 154
Long Range Penetration role, 1st Essex on, 95-122
Lord-Lieutenant of Essex, references to the, 2, 6, 14, 15, 16, 132, 249, 435, 547, 563, 569, 571
Lorraine, Pte. P. P., 156
Lotinga, Lieut.-Col. J. L. L., 354
Louisendorf, 541
Louvain, 136, 137, 144
Lovelace, Lieut.-Col. A., 47, 96, 101, 106, 107, 108, 111-12, 123, 337, 338
Lowick, 442-3
Lubeck, 429; 5th Essex in the advance to the Baltic and, 431
Luchow, 5th Essex at, 434
Luckock, Major-General R. M., 16
Lumley (Sierra Leone), 254, 446
Luneburg, 434-5, 501
Lydda, 43
Lygett, Pte., 10
Lyme Regis, 9th Essex at, 494
Lymington (Hants), 2nd Essex embark for Operation "Overlord," 162
Lyne, Major-General L. O., 242
Lyster, Major J. N., 362, 368, 372, 379, 380, 382, 387, 388, 391, 393, 395-9, 402, 404, 417, 422

Mc

McComish, Lieut. J. R., 422
McCreery, Lieut.-General Sir Richard, 327-9
McDougall, Pte. G., 419
McIntyre, Major D. W., 542
McIntyre, Lieut.-Col. K. W., 542
McLaughlin, Major (N.Z.E.F.), 86
McLaughlin, Lieut.-Col., 557
McMartin, Lieut. J. S., 491
McMichael, Major W. F., 211, 215, 232-4
McMillen, 2/Lieut. C. J. S., 26

M

Maas, 2nd Essex in operations up to the River, 216-24
Maaten Bagush, 257, 362
Macedonia, 1/4th Essex in Western, 337-8
Macdonald, Lieut.-Col. B. J. S., 539
Macdonald, Lieut.-Col. R. W., 558
Macdonald, Capt. S. B., 541
Madras, 126
Mafraq, 43, 45, 46
Magill-Cuerdon, Lieut.-Col. V. C., 241, 330, 337, 442, 448
Maier, Pte. J., 539
Maitland, Lieut.-Col. A. E., 6, 7, 529
Mallins, Major S. O'C., 26
Mallinson, Major M. S., 317, 318, 321, 536
Mallinson, Colonel S. S., 536, 546, 547, 551, 556, 559
Malta, 7; 2nd Essex stationed in, 11
Mancelli, 5th Essex in, 417
Mangles, Lieut.-Col. C. G., 557
Manipur Road, reference to the, 99
Mann, 2/Lieut. J., 362
Mann, Capt. K. W. M., 82, 87, 115, 121
Manning, Lieut A. H., 372, 384, 385, 387
Manningtree, 440
Mapleson, Lieut.-Col. C., 556
March, Lieut. D. W., 453
Marchint, Sgt. G. H., 88
Marcq, the River, 132
Mareth Line, the forcing of the, 285-9
Margate, 152
Mariani, 100
Marindin, Brig. P. C., 91
Mariner, Pte. C., 104-5
Marines, the Royal, 254, 360
Marjoram, L/Sgt. A., 295
Mark, 2nd Essex force crossing of river, 220-1

INDEX

Marriott, Brig. J. C. O., 32
Marriott, Lieut.-Col. L. W. W., 20; in command 2nd Essex, 157–61; in command 1/4th Essex, 338; in command 639th Garrison Regt., 480; in command Infantry Training Centre, 517–19; reference to, 534
Martin, Lieut.-Col. C. D., 20, 21, 23
Martin, Pte. (1st Bn.), 104–5
Mason, Lieut. S. G., 279
Massy, Lieut.-General H. R. S., 497
Mathews, Brig. F. R. G., 424
Matmata Hills, 1/4th Essex attack in the, 285–8
Matthews, Capt. W. A., 279, 300–1
Maungdaw, 92
May, 2/Lieut. G. C., 384–5
May, Lieut.-Col. K. F., 26, 28, 38, 45–6, 50, 53–4, 56, 58–9, 65; in command 2/5th Essex, 453–5, 460, 461, 462, 465, 469, 471–2
May, 2/Lieut. V. A. L., 362
Mayer, Lieut. E. R., 279
Mayne, Major-General A. G. O. M., 258, 366
Mayu Peninsula, references to the, 91–2
Maxwell, Lieut. D. L., 372, 382, 384, 385
Mead, Cpl. T., 88
Meares, 2/Lieut. G. C., 145
Meavaines, 164–5
Medjez-el-Bab, 1/4th Essex attack at, 298–301
Megas Linin (Greece), 1/4th Essex attack, 335
Meggy, Major E. R., 350–1
Merema, 103
Mersa Matruh, 9, 14, 72; 1/4th Essex break-out from, 260–6
Merville, 146
Merxem, 541
Messe, Marshal, 301
Messervy, Major-General F. W., 257, 451
Messias, L/Cpl. S. W., 412
Mestre, 2nd Essex at, 245–6
Metemma, 1st Essex in operations towards, 34–9
Meteren, 149
Meurchin, 2nd Essex at, 133–6, 142–6
Meyadin (Mayadene), 69
Middle East, the, 7, 13; garrisons sent to war stations, 29; 1st Essex thanked for services in, 33; safety of, imperilled by Iraq rebellion, 44; reference to, 59; 1st Essex leave, 89; 1/4 Essex and 2/5th Essex arrive in, 256; 1/5th Essex in the, 257–371; 2/5th Essex in the, 450–73
Militia Act of 1939, The, 17
Miller, Lieut. R. E., 186
Miller-Jones, Lieut.-Col. T. W., 476
Mills, Lieut.-Col. C. S., 17; in command 1st Essex, 122, 124, 125; takes command 2nd Essex, 128; in command 2/4th Essex, 352–4
Milton, 2/Lieut. J. W., 87
Milward, Brig. C. A., 12
Minden, 483, 501
Minqa Quaim, 1/4th Essex with N.Z. Div. in break-out from, 266–8
Mishiefa, 260
Mishmah Ha Emek, 8
Misurata, 301
Miteiriya Ridge, 1/4th Essex on, 280–1
Moascar, 1st Essex at, 10, 26
Mobbs, R.S.M., A. J., 13
Moerdijk, 2nd Essex at, 221
Mohumi (Assam), 101–5
Mollem, 136
Molln, 429; 5th Essex at, 430
Monastery Hill, Cassino, 1/4th Essex attack, 306–20
Mont St. Amand (Ghent), 5th Essex at, 425–6
Monte Barone, 399
Monte Cassino, 1/4th Essex attack, 306–20
Monte Falcone, 377, 399
Monte Ferano, 379
Monte Mitro, 377–8
Monte Odorisio, 418–19
Montgomery, Field-Marshal Lord, reference to, 132; with 2nd Essex at Bayeux, 179, reference to, 190, 216, 225, 228, 276, 278, 373, 400, 425; sees 5th Essex, 425; visits 8th Essex, 487; references to, 488, 490; visits Warley, 525
Montvilliers, 205
Monunirel, 2nd Essex occupy, 167
Moreton, the Rev. G., 252
Moro River, reference to the, 403
Mosul (Iraq), 1/5th Essex, 364–6; 2/5th Essex, 454–7
Mothersill, Lieut.-Col. J. H., 539
Mott, Pte. J. E., award of George Cross to, 10
Mount, Lieut.-Col. M. R. W., 559
Mount Carmel, 45, 454
Mount Tabor, 9
Mountbatten, Lord Louis, inspects 1st Essex, 100
Mower, Pte. (1st Bn.), 104
Much Hadham, 499
Muirhead, Capt. T. D'A., 26, 51, 53, 55, 58, 65, 87
Mummery, C.S.M., A. H., 412
Munich crisis of 1938, references to the, 16, 17, 22–3, 71
Münster, 492
Münster Lager, 434
Murphy, Lieut. N. M., 175

INDEX

Murray, Lieut. M. H. M., 453, 473
Museum, reference to the regimental, 430, 524
Mutaguchi, General, 99
Mytchett Camp, 18

N

Naaf River, the, 94
Nagas, 1st Essex on operations in territory (Naga Hills) of the, 101-20
Naples, 373-4, 425, 476-7
Nash, Capt. M. T., 361, 362
Nasirabad, 2nd Essex at, 13
Natanya, 5th Essex at, 424
National Defence Companies, the genesis of home defence battalions, 505-7
Navy, references to the Royal, 4, 70-2, 252, 258, 445-6, 447, 489
Nazareth, 9
Neame, General Sir Philip, 40
Neave, Lieut.-Col. R., 557
Neder Rijn, the River, 225, 236-7
Needell, Lieut.-Col. C., 475
Neild, Lieut.-Col. W. C., 538
Nelson, Capt. C., 71, 80, 115
Nerhema (Assam), 114-16
Neunkirchen, 5-6
New Arlesford, 2nd Essex at, 159
New Milton, 159
New Zealand forces—*see* Regiments, etc.
Newbold, Major L. A., 140, 142
Newcastle-on-Tyne, 359
Newcastle-under-Lyme, 157
Newman, Lieut.-Col. A. C., 250, 358; award of Victoria Cross to, 515-16
Ngacham (Burma), 117, 119
Nichols, Lieut.-Col. (Major-General) J. S., 23; takes command 1st Essex, 38; references to, 40-5, 47-9, 53-4, 58-67; awarded D.S.O., 68; at Ed Duda, 78-89; awarded bar to D.S.O., 87; leaves 1st Essex, 89; references to, 285, 467
Nicosia (Cyprus), 10
Nieppe, Forêt de, 147
Nieuport, 152
Nijmegen, 2nd Essex in area of, 224-40; Essex Scottish at, 541
Nijverdal, 542
Nile, the River, 32
Ninove, 140
Nispen, 2nd Essex attack at, 218-19
Niton (I.O.W.), 2nd Essex at, 159
Noble, Capt. (Lieut.-Col.), A., 20, 252, 257; in command 1/4th Essex, 258, 259, 260, 262, 264, 265, 266, 269, 274, 277, 279, 284, 288, 291, 294-9, 302, 304, 307, 309, 312, 313, 316, 403, 465, 567, 571

Nordwalde, Essex Squadron on V.E.-Day at, 492
Normandy landings, 2nd Essex on D-Day in the, 162-8
Norrie, General Sir Willoughby, 260, 438, 461, 472
North Africa, the campaign in, 4, 70-89, 260-302
North Weald, 513
North-west Frontier of India, the, 12-13
Northern Command Tattoo 1936, 7
Northumberland, Essex Territorial battalions in, 251-2, 349-51, 442-4
Norway, references to operations in, 250, 349, 358-9
Nott, Major J. P., 357, 361, 362, 364-5, 367
Nowshera, 2nd Essex at, 12-13
Nro, the River (Assam), 106, 108
Nungphung (Assam), 117

O

O'Connor, General Sir Richard, 126
O'Hagen, Lieut. (Q.M.) B., 26
O'Reilly, 2/Lieut. M. D. O., 26
Oexle, Lieut. D. P., 453
Oker, 5th Essex at, 433
Oldenburg, 542
Ongshim, 116, 119
Oostcappel, 149
Oosterhout, 235
Oostmalle, 212
Orcha, 122-3
Orne, 2nd Essex in crossing of the River, 190-7
Orsogna, 321, 403, 417
Ortona, 403, 404
Osborne, Major-General E. A., 9
Osnabrück, 480
Osterburg, 5th Essex at, 433
Ostler, Capt. A. L., 357, 360, 362, 368, 372, 401-2, 422, 435
Oswald, Major O. R. W., 316
Ouffières, 190-1
"Overlord" Operation, 160-1
Owen, Lieut.-Col. E. E., 367, 372, 376, 383, 385

P

Paget, General Sir Bernard, 158, 361, 488, 499
Paglietta, 389, 400
Pagniez, 2/Lieut. F. L. P., 362, 368
Painter, Capt. R. H. A., 134-5, 153, 486
Palestine, 1st Essex in, 7-9, 14, 40-4, 69; 1/4th Essex in, 259; 5th Essex in 371, 421-4
Palfaliphon (Athens), 339
Pallot, Major M. St. G., 181, 188, 194, 195
Palmer, Major B. J., 125, 486

INDEX

Palmer, Major D. J., 572
Palmoli, 5th Essex occupy, 387-8
Palms, Lieut. J. C., 539
Palmyra, 59, 60-5
Pangman, Lieut. J. E. C., 541
Panningen, 222
Parfouru L'Eclin, 180, 185, 186
Parker, Cpl. E., 314
Parker, Col. R. C. O., 547-8, 556, 557
Parry, Capt. A. J. M., 141
Parry, Lieut. P. F. M., 80, 87, 147
Pashan Camp (India), 124
Patna, 90
Paton, Brig. C. M., 328, 442, 449, 453; becomes Colonel of Regiment, 562
Pattle, Lieut. T. H., 279
Paul, Major J. L., 490
Paul, Major W. K., 458, 464, 467
Pawle, Brig. H., 248, 441
Paxton, Lieut.-Col. G. A. M., 5, 9, 26, 28, 32, 33
Payne, Capt. P. G., 502
Pearce, Lieut. W., references to capture of the "Eagle" by, 535, 562
Pearson, Lieut.-Col. A. S., 538
Pederson, Capt. N., 87-8
Pedouze, 198
Pellow, Capt. R. J. N., 302, 320, 330
Pembroke Dock, 1-3
Penson, C.Q.M.S., H. W., 398, 399, 419
Pepper, Brig. E. C., 160, 162, 173, 179
Pepys, Major A. G. L., 11
Perano, 389
Perfect, Lieut. P. R., 453
Perowne, Brig. L. E. C. M., 97, 120, 121, 126
Perry, R.S.M., L., 486
Persia and Iraq Command (Paiforce), 362-3, 365
Perton, Lieut. T. K., 279
Pescasseroli, 420
Peshawar, 2nd Essex in, 12
Petit-Dann, 2/Lieut. H. J. B., 153
Petre, Major G. M. M. L., 154, 162, 169, 170, 172
Pett, Lieut.-Col. H. B., 558
Petticrow, Pte. R. W., 267
Pezzano, 324
Phalempin, 2nd Essex at, 211
Phakekedzumi (Assam), 116, 117, 119
Phekekrima (Assam), 102, 104, 105-11
Philipps, Major R. G., 511
Piazzano, 389
Pickis, Lieut.-Col. S., 559
Pike, the Rev. V. J., 417
Piper, L/Cpl. L. T., 320
Piræus, 1/4th Essex clear the, 333-6, 339
Pitchford, Lieut. S. M., 114
Pitter, Sgt. (1/4th Bn.), 315
Plackett, Major R. A., 265, 571

Plan "D," reference to the, 135
Platt, Major-General W., 29
Plumer, Field-Marshal Lord, 11
"Pompadours"—see 2nd Battalion Essex Regiment
Pont Audemer, 156; 2nd Essex capture, 201
Pont de la Guillette, 175, 176
Pont L'Eveque, 156
Pont-à-Marcq, 2nd Essex at, 132
Pont Mulot, 185-6
Pont-à-Vendin, 142-5
Poona, 1st Essex 1942, 90; 1st Essex 1945-46, 124-6
Poperinghe, 149
Poppel, 2nd Essex at, 215-16
Port Said, 10, 26, 27, 39; 1st Essex (1938-39), 10, 26; 1/5th Essex at, 362-3
Port Sudan, 14, 28, 39, 40
Port Tewfik, 90, 361, 451
Porte, Lieut. B. A., 372, 402, 411
Porter, Lieut. J. A., 279, 453
Portway, Lieut.-Col. C., 18, 20, 23, 24, 436, 440, 441, 442, 520
Poste Restion, 61
Poste Weygande, 61-3
Potts, Lieut. J. P., 453
Pouch, Lieut.-Col. H. R., 249, 252, 571
Pouch, R.S.M. (A.T.S.), 519
Powell, Lieut. R. J., 423, 428-9
Power, Lieut. M. G., 416
Pratt, C.S.M. (5th Bn.), 395
Price, 2/Lieut. C. B., 173
Priestman, Major-General J. H. T., 249, 252, 441, 498
Primary Training Centre No. 44, 525-6
Proom, R.Q.M.S., S. C., 445
Prowse, Major G. V. L., 13, 547
Prudhoe, 359-60
Pullen, Sgt. J., 204
Purdie, Lieut. R. C., 372, 402, 419, 422
Puxty, Sgt. G., 104

Q

Qaryateine (Syria), 65
Qassassin, 89, 361, 421, 451
Qatana, 371
Quesnay Guesnon, 2nd Essex at, 180
Quinin, Lieut.-General E. P., 458

R

Rahman (Tunisia), 292-4
Ramadi (Iraq), 42, 45-9
Ramsden, Brig. A. H., 134, 141, 148
Ranchi, 90, 91, 122-3
Randwijk, 225
Rangazumi (Assam), 106
Rangoon, 1st Essex sail for, 90
Rasch, Col. Sir Carne, 365, 368, 436, 472, 549, 556

Rashid Ali, 42
Ratzeburg, 430
Ratzlingen, 501
Ravensworth, 7
Rea, Lieut.-Col. S. C. W. W., 523, 525, 563
Read, Lieut.-Col. R. V., in command 1st Essex, 7
Red Army, the, 432-3
Redditch, 8th Essex at Bentley Manor, 486
Reeman, O.R.Q.M.S., G., 147
Rees, Essex Scottish cross the Rhine at, 542
Reeves, 2/Lieut. N., 252
Regiments and Batteries—Royal Artillery:
Royal Horse Artillery: "L" Bty., 2nd R.H.A., 262; 11th R.H.A., 269
Regiments, Field Artillery: 1st Fd. Regt., 316; 11th Fd. Regt., 269, 289; 28th Fd. Regt., 35; 31st Fd. Regt., 302-3; 51/69th Fd. Regt., 122; 60th Fd. Regt., 45, 60, 97; 91st Fd. Regt., 427, 429; 121st Fd. Regt., 263, 264, 458-9, 463, 464, 466; 124th Fd. Regt., 464; 185th Fd. Regt., 206; Essex Yeo. Fd. Regt., 73, 271; Kent Yeo. Fd. Regt., 464
Batteries, Field Artillery: 7/66th Bty., 258; 14/16th Bty., 277; 162nd Bty., 143-4; 237th Bty., 45; 239th Bty., 65; 275th Bty., 458, 464, 468-9
Anti-Tank Artillery: 15th Bty., 379; 52nd Regt., 427; 432nd Bty., 299; 439th Regt., 79; 513th Regt., 289
Searchlight Regiments: 64th S.L. Regt. (1/6th Essex, 639th Garrison Regt., 599th Essex H.A.A.), 22, 24, 478-80; 65th S.L. Regt. (2/6th Essex, 607th Garrison Regt., 600th Essex H.A.A.), 22, 24, 480-4
Light Anti-Aircraft Regiments: 169th L.A.A., 65; 646th L.A.A. (5th Essex), 435-6
Heavy Anti-Aircraft: 12th A.A., 258; 59th H.A.A., 459th H.A.A., 21, 24, 474-8; 599th H.A.A., 480; 600th H.A.A., 484
Cavalry and R.A.C.:
4th Hussars, 139
Royal Scots Greys, 41
Composite Household Cav. Regt., 44, 50, 54
22nd Dragoons, 205
27th Lancers, 331
Sherwood Rangers, 167
Warwickshire Yeo., 44
Royal Wiltshire Yeo., 44, 65
Fife and Forfar Yeo., 218-19
Yorkshire Dragoons, 67
3rd Sharpshooters, 222
107th Regt. R.A.C., "*Essex*" *Squadron with the,* 491-3

Regiments and Batteries—*continued*
Cavalry and R.A.C.—*continued*
145*th R.A.C.,* 299-300
153*rd R.A.C., formed from 8th Essex,* 488-91
Royal Tank Regiment: 4th R. Tks., 84; 6th R. Tks. (B Sqn.), 35; 7th R. Tks., 205, 209; 9th R. Tks., 218-19; 46th R. Tks., 277; 50th R. Tks., 379, 405-11
Foot Guards:
Grenadier Guards: 1st Gren. Gds., 139
Scots Guards: 2nd S.G., 15, 359
Irish Guards: 1st I.G., 359
British Infantry:
Royal Scots: 1st R.S., 146; 8th R.S., 490
Queens: 1st Queens, 123; 2nd Queens, 125; 7th Queens, 134, 142, 148
The Buffs: 464, 470; 1st Buffs, 40, 130, 134, 258
King's Own: 1st King's Own, 65, 327; 2nd King's Own, 42, 44, 48, 50-1, 53; 8th King's Own, 148
Royal Northumberland Fusiliers: 2/7th R.N.F., 137, 138
Royal Fusiliers: At Warley, 520-4; 1st R.F., 362, 441; 2nd R.F., 67; 12th R.F., 354
Royal Lincolns: 2nd Lincolns, 494; 4th Lincolns, 212, 213
Suffolk Regiment: 8th Suffolk, 498
West Yorks: 2nd W. Yorks, 28, 274, 277-8
East Yorks: 2nd E. Yorks, 488
Bedfs. and Herts: 1st Bedfs. Herts, 41; 6th Bedfs. Herts, 497
Royal Leicesters: 2nd Leicesters, 125; 2/5th Leicesters, 146, 333
Green Howards: 6th Green Howards, 185; 7th Green Howards, 180
Lancashire Fusiliers: 1st L.F., 423; 9th L.F., 229
Royal Scots Fusiliers: 2nd R.S.F., 423; 11th R.S.F., 229
Royal Welch Fusiliers: 8th R.W.F., 495; 10th R.W.F., 158; 20th R.W.F., 158; 31st R.W.F., 159
South Wales Borderers: 2nd S.W.B., 161, 165, 167, 175, 180-1, 183, 186-8, 191, 193-4, 201-3, 204-5, 208-9, 214, 217, 218, 226, 227, 232, 234, 236, 244, 359
Cameronians (S.R.):, 421, 427, 429
Gloucestershire Regt.: 2nd Glosters, 161, 167, 169, 176, 180, 185, 186-8, 191, 192, 197, 205, 208-9, 211, 217, 220, 221, 222, 227, 230, 234, 236, 240, 244

INDEX 663

Regiments and Batteries—*continued*
British Infantry—*continued*
Worcestershire Regt.: 13, 243; 1st Worcs. Regt., 29
East Lancashire Regt.: 1st E. Lan. R., 5
Duke of Wellington's Regt.: 2nd D.W.R., 97, 114, 116
Border Regt.: 2nd Border 125; 4th Border, 77, 86, 90, 97, 116
Royal Sussex Regt.: 10th R. Sussex, 495
Royal Hampshire Regt.: 1st R. Hamps., 138, 168; 2nd R. Hamps., 8
South Staffordshires: 1st S. Staffs., 90, 127
Dorsetshire Regt.: 8th Dorset, 487
South Lancashire Regt.: 1st S. Lan. R., 494
Welch Regt.: 1st Welch, 502
The Black Watch: 2nd B.W., 78; 5th B.W., 298; 8th B.W., 159
Oxford and Buckinghamshire L.I.: 2nd Oxf. Bucks, 243; 6th Oxf. Bucks, 159
Sherwood Foresters: 1st Foresters, 27
Northamptonshire Regt.: 6th Northamptons, 498
Royal Berkshires: 1st R. Berks., 147
Royal West Kent Regt.: 5th R.W.K., 403, 411; 6th R.W.K., 316
K.O.Y.L.I.: 1st K.O.Y.L.I., 430
K.S.L.I.: 1st K.S.L.I., 127
Middlesex Regt.: 2/7th Mx., 140
Wiltshire Regiment: 2nd Wilts., 421, 427, 429
York and Lancaster Regt.: Hallams, 234
Durham Light Infantry: 1st D.L.I., 86; 2nd D.L.I., 139; 6th D.L.I., 225; 8th D.L.I., 494; 9th D.L.I., 177, 487; 10th D.L.I., 177; 16th D.L.I., 333
Highland Light Infantry: 1st H.L.I., 130; 2nd H.L.I., 39
Seaforth Highlanders: 6th Seaforth, 427
Cameron Highlanders: 2nd Camerons, 8; 5th Camerons, 228
Royal Ulster Regt.: 2nd R.U.R., 8, 494
Argyll and Sutherland Highlanders: 2nd A. and S.H., 418
Parachute Regt.: 9th Para., 432; 10th Essex become the 9th Para. Bn., 497–502
Indian Army:
Guides Cavalry: 465
2nd Indian Field Regt.: 264
The Nabhar Akal (I.S.F.), 329
1st Punjab Regt.: 1/1st Punjab, 275
2nd Punjab Regt.: 1/2nd Punjab, 275
5th Mahratta L.I.: 1/5th Mahrattas, 400; 2/5th Mahrattas, 257; 5/5th Mahrattas, 405, 418

Regiments and Batteries—*continued*
Indian Army—*continued*
6th Rajputana Rifles: 1/6th Raj. Rif., 308–11; 4/6th Raj. Rif., 259, 261–3, 268, 273, 275, 280, 281, 283, 291, 294–8, 309, 312, 313, 321; 6/6th Raj. Rif., 299
7th Rajput Regt.: 3/7th Rajput, 258, 275, 571; 4/7th Rajput, 258, 571
8th Punjab Regt.: 3/8th Punjab, 376, 379, 389, 391, 397, 399, 404, 410, 415
10th Baluch Regt.: 3/10th Baluch, 259, 261–4, 268, 273, 280–1, 325, 327, 333; 4/10th Baluch, 33, 34, 35, 38
11th Sikh Regt.: 4/11th Sikhs, 456, 459, 460, 463, 468, 470
12th Frontier Force Regt.: 1/12th F.F.R., 415; 3/12th R.F.F.R., 39
13th Frontier Force Regt.: 4/13th F.F.R., 68; 6/13th R.F.F.R., 33, 376, 379–80, 389, 403, 404, 415
15th Punjab Regt.: 3/15th Punjab, 415, 417
16th Punjab Regt.: 4/16th Punjab, 297, 451
18th Royal Garhwal Rifles: 3/18th R. Garhwals, 33, 34, 35, 36
1st Gurkha Rifles: 4/1st G.R., 119
2nd Gurkha Rifles: 1/2nd G.R., 456
3rd Gurkha Rifles: 2/3rd G.R., 456, 459–60, 463, 471
5th Gurkha Rifles: 1/5th R.G.R., 389
9th Gurkha Rifles: 1/9th G.R., 294–7, 299–300, 309, 311, 312, 313, 315, 316, 325, 327, 333
Australian Imperial Force:
2/13th Battalion, 84–5
2/17th Battalion, 70, 78
2/24th Battalion, 70
44th Battalion (West Australia Rifles) and 11/44th Battalion (City of Perth Regiment), 545
Canadian Forces:
2nd Canadian Fd. Regt., R.A., 331
5th Canadian Med. Regt. R.A., 331
Essex Scottish, The, 538–44
Regina Rifles, 158
Westminster Regt. (Canada), 305
Irish Regt. of Canada, 417
6th Canadian Armoured Regt., 232
22nd Canadian Regt., 417
South Africa, U.D.F. of:
Kaffararian Rifles, 362
West Africa Force:
4th N.R., 256
New Zealand Expeditionary Force:
2nd N.Z. Cav. Regt., 305
18th N.Z. Inf. Bn., 452
19th N.Z. Inf. Bn., 81, 83, 86, 264, 266–8, 452

Regiments and Batteries—*continued*
N.Z.E.F.—*continued*
  22nd N.Z. Motor Bn., 305
  23rd N.Z. Inf. Bn., 262
  25th N.Z. Inf. Bn., 308
French Army:
  6th Foreign Legion, 61-5
  12ieme Cuirassiers, 143
  106th Infantry Regt., 6
United States Forces:
  3/41st U.S. Infantry, 186
  1/313th U.S. Inf. Regt., 240
  505th Inf. Regt., 428
Enemy Forces:
  3rd Para. Bn., 395
  3rd Para. Regt., 414
  4th Para. Regt., 414
  277th Inf. Regt., 184
  870th Grenadier Regt., 330
  871st Grenadier Regt., 330
  1/916th Grenadier Regt., 168
Reinforcement Company, 2nd Essex 1940, 153-6
Rekoma, 115
Rence, 331
Renkum, 237
Rheims, 1st Essex at, 6
Rhine crossing, the, 501; clearing left bank of, 541-2
Richardson, Lieut.-Col. K. S., 558
Ricketts, Major H. G., 519
Ridley, Major G. V. N., 548
Ridley, Lieut.-Col. W. L., 22-3
Rimini, 1/4th Essex at, 331-2
Risle, the River, 156, 201-3
Ritchie, Lieut.-General N. M., 153, 260, 490
Rivers, Lieut. E. A., 324
Roberts, Major-General O. L., 49, 60
Roberts-West, Lieut.-Col. C. R., 12
Robinson, Major-General A. E., 160, 354
Robinson, Major C. H., 26, 58, 71, 80, 87
Rochford, 513
Romford, 23, 349; confers Freedom on Regiment, 568
Rommel, General Edwin, 71, 72, 256, 260, 261, 459, 461
Roosendaal, the capture of, 219
Rose, R.S.M., C. J., 273, 302, 314, 571
Rose, Lieut. J. R., 279
Ross, Major G. N., 402, 404, 422
Rosieres (Sudan), 33
Rouen, 132, 153
Row, Major A. W. W., 5
Rowley, Major Sir George, 519
Royal Air Force, references to the, 4, 35, 42, 44, 47, 48-50, 62, 67, 72, 77, 97, 208, 308
Royal Engineers, 55, 79, 405
Royal Fusiliers at Warley, 520-5

Royal Marines, references to the, 254, 360
Royal Navy, references to the, 4, 70, 71-2, 252, 258, 445-6, 447, 453, 489
Royal Netherlands Army trains at Warley, 521-2, 535
Royal Tank Corps—*see* Regiments, R.A.C.
Ruatti, 5th Essex at, 403, 412, 413
Ruggles-Brise, Col. Sir E. A., 547, 551
Rundstedt, Marshal von, 430, 500
Russell, General Sir Dudley, 259, 264, 284, 356, 366, 370, 371, 386, 400, 417
Rutbah Wells, 42, 46, 59, 363, 445
Ruweisat Ridge, 1/4th Essex hold the, 266-78, 462, 465
Ryckesvorsel, 2nd Essex attack at, 212-14
Ryes (Normandy), 2nd Essex on D-Day at, 164-5

S

Saar, 1st Essex in the, 4-7
St. Albans, 10th Essex at, 499
St. Germain, 2nd Essex at the Bois de, 179-85
St. Leonard, 2nd Essex attack at, 216-17; reference to, 492
St. Loup Hors, 2nd Essex at, 168
St. Nazaire, reference to the raid on, 359; award of Victoria Cross to Lieut.-Col. A. C. Newman for gallantry at, 615-16
St. Sulpice, 2nd Essex at, 165
St. Vigor-le-Grand, 2nd Essex at, 167
Saiyapaw (Assam), 116
Salamanca Eagle, the return to the Regiment of the, 535-6, 562-3
Salanelles, 500
Salarolo, 1/4th Essex at, 305
Salerno, 425
Salew, Capt. N. R., 20, 26
Salkhad (Syria), 67
Salome, 142
Salonika, 1/4th Essex embarked at, 339
San Angelo, 5th Essex in the assault on, 390-400
San Felice, 376
San Marco, 389
Sanderson, Lieut. E. E., 453
Sandwich, 5th Essex at, 360
Sangro, 5th Essex in the battle of the River, 387-99
Sarsina, 328
Saugor, 99
Saunders, Major J. N., 416, 422
Savill, 2/Lieut. P. J. B., 64, 87
Savio Valley, 1/4th Essex operate in, 328-9
Saxmundham, 2nd Essex at, 349
Sayers, Major C. L., 208, 215, 222, 223
Schiazzamo, 330
Schneppenberg, the, 501

INDEX 665

Scobie, Major-General R. McK., 88, 332
Scott, Lieut.-Col. E. S., 237-9, 241
Scott, Lieut.-Col. (I. A.), 295-7
Seclin, 142
Seine, withdrawal across the river in 1940, 153; 2nd Essex recross in 1944, 203
Semmence, Major A. L., 515
Senior, Brig. R. H., 229
Seth-Smith, Brig. H. G., 553, 557
Sevenum, 2nd Essex at, 223-4
Sfax, 291
Shadbolt, Capt. G., 523
Shaiba, 42-3
Shaqlawa (Iraq), 1/5th Essex at, 365
Shargarh, 99
Shaverin, Lieut.-Col. S., 559
Sheffield, Capt. G. N. H., 138, 140, 145, 147, 149, 150, 156
Sheldrake, Capt. E. J., 20, 252
Sheldrake, Major J. C., 435
Shenstone, Col. G., 18
Shepheard, Major J. K., 456
Sheppard, C.S.M. (1st Essex), 115
Sherborne, 8th Essex at, 487
Shoeburyness, 349
Shorncliffe, 20, 354
Shortland, C.Q.M.S., I., 433
Sibbald, Pte. (1st Essex), 53
Sidi Barrani, 2nd Essex at, 7, 14; 1/4th Essex at, 257; 2/5th Essex at, 451-2
Sidi Bishr, 14
Sidi Haneish, 258; 1/4th Essex withdraw through, 268; 2/5th Essex at, 451
Sidi Mahmoud (Tobruk), references to, 71, 77, 78, 79
Sidi Mamum, 83
Siena, 324
Sierra Leone, reference to 1/4th Essex in, 252-6; to 2/5th Essex, 446-9
Signal Hill, Gallabat, 34
Silver, Capt. H. W., 514
Silver bugles, presentation to 2nd Essex of, 15-16
Silver Jubilee of H.M. King George V, 21
Simla Hills, the, 12
Simpson, Lieut. H. R., 279
Sinai Desert, the, 460
Sinclair-Thomson, Lieut.-Col. A. E. M., 3, 18, 529, 547
Sinclair-Thomson, Lieut. P. A., 26, 28
Single, Lieut. G. R., 291
Sitton, Pensioner J., 563
Ski championships, C.M.F., 245
Skittrall, Cpl. W. J., 195
Sleeuhagen (Brussels), 136
Slim, Brig. (Field-Marshal) Sir William J., 33, 34, 36, 60, 120, 570
Slingsby, Lieut.-Col. T., 558
Small, R.S.M., C. W., 38, 453, 457
Smith, Lieut. A., 503

Smith, L/Cpl. A. J., 318
Smith, Sgt. D. D., 387, 419
Smith, Major D. J. M., 252, 263, 279, 281, 284
Smith, Capt. G. E., 571
Smith, Sgt. G. H. T., 88, 113, 123
Smith, Pte. K., 314-15
Smith, Lieut. P. A. G., 352
Smith, Lieut. P. H., 279
Smith, Sgt. R., 249
Smith, L/Sgt. R., 468, 472
Smith, Major S. J., 482
Smith, Capt. W. S., 156, 523
"Smithcol," operations with, 263-5
Snaith, 9th Essex convert to artillery at, 495
Snelling, Major-General A., 60
Snowdon, Sgt. C. T., 387
Sofaga, 369
Sollum, 72; 1/4th Essex at, 261-2
Somra Tracts, 1st Essex operate in the, 98, 116, 117
Sottegen, 141
Soueida, 66-7
South, Pte. J. W., 473
South Africa, Air Force of, reference to, 35
South Africa, Union Defence Forces—see Divisions and Regiments
South Beveland, clearance of, 541
Southwold, 354
Southampton, 159, 163, 353
Southend, the Freedom of the County Borough of, 564
Southey, Lieut.-Col. C. A., 128, 245, 569-70
Spearman, Cpl. H., 419
"Special Force," 1st Essex with, 95-122; disbandment of, 122
Spencer, Lieut. J. L., 176, 232
Spicer, Lieut. S. C., 297
Spooner, Lieut.-Col. C. C., 14, 17, 517
Spratt, Lieut. K. J., 491
Stainer, Brig. Sir Alexander, 497
Stamer, Brig. W. D., 258
Stanger, Capt. F., 453
Stapelheide, 217
Stapleford Tawney, 513
Starkey, Lieut. N. L., 372, 395
Stayton, Capt. G. N. R., 422
Stead, Lieut. T. R., 318
Stebbing, Pte. M. A., 433
Steedman, Lieut. A. S., 402, 406, 411
Steele, Major T. E., 540
Stephenson, Pte. A. P., 419
Stevens, Lieut.-Col. G. R., 300
Stevenson, Pte. G., 433
Stevenson-Hamilton, Major I. J. D., 26, 30, 35, 71, 80, 83, 85, 87, 92, 94
Stewart, Lieut.-Col. G. W. F., 476
Stiepelse, 428
Stillwell, General, 99

Stockley, Lieut.-Col. R. C., 201
Stonehouse, Pte. M., 419
Stopford, Lieut.-General M., 119, 121
Stokesby, 2/4th Essex at, 354
Strensall Camp (Yorks), 4
Strong, C.S.M., H. M., 249
Stuart, Capt. G. W. W., 330
Stubbs, Lieut. M. P., 491
Sudan, the, 13; 2nd Essex in, 14; 1st Essex in, 28-40; references to, 71, 89; 19th Essex in the, 503-4
Sudan Defence Force, references to the, 29, 30, 32
Suez, 13, 14, 28; 2/5th Essex at Ranpur Camp, 453-4
Suez Canal, the, reference to, 7; safeguarding the, 27; references to, 30, 70, 453-4
Summers, Lieut. G. R., 294
Sunderland, 2/4th Essex at, 350-1
"Supercharge" Operation, 280-1
Suraj-ud-Dowlah, 127
Sutton, R.S.M., A. F., 141, 154, 156, 158, 520, 522-3
Swan, Sergt. W. J., 384, 392, 406, 407, 411, 412, 419
Swayne, Lieut.-General J. G., 495
Swindon, 488
Syme, Sgt. G. D., 412
Syme Battalion, adventures of, 153-6
Symes, Major-General G. W., 95, 97
Symes, Sir Stuart, 14
Symington, Capt. F. J., 362, 368
Syria, the campaign in, references to, 37, 41; operations in, 59-69; reference to, 89; 1/5th Essex in, 368-9, 371, 423
Syrian Desert, crossing of the, 60

T

T3, 61
Tadmor (Palmyra), 61, 64
Tank Corps, the Royal—see Regiments
Tanner, Major W. E., 95
Tansey, Lieut. J. E. A., 422
Tanti, Pte. (5th Essex), 366, 433
Taranto, 303, 332, 372, 373, 421, 425
Tatanagar, 91
Tattoos, military, 7, 16, 523
Taunbro Ghat, 91
Taung Bazaar, 94
Taylor, Cpl. H. T., 302
Taylor, Sgt. J., 140
Taylor, Sgt. L., 419
Teignmouth, 9th Essex at, 495
Templer, Major-General G. W. R., 159, 488, 570
Tenby, 159
Terlingden, 152
Termoli, 321, 375

Territorial Army, 1, 2, 17-24; reorganised and doubled, 22-3; embodied, 24; reanimated 1947, 571
Tezzo, capture by 1/4th Essex, 328-9
Thaw, Lieut. T., 453
Thizama (Assam), 113-15
Thoma, General, 283
Thomas, the Rev. F., 174
Thompson, the Rev. D. W., 448, 469, 473
Thompson, C.Q.M.S. G., 419
Thompson, Cpl. H., 292; patrol report by, 343-7
Thompson, Lieut. M. B., 422
Thompson, Lieut.-Col. R. N., 529
Thorn, Lieut. P. P. S., 422
Thornton, Lieut. F. J., 372, 395
Thorogood, Lieut. D. O., 491
Thorpe-le-Soken, 440
Throckley, 2/5th Essex at, 444
Thulborn, Lieut. I. W., 279
Thury-Harcourt, 190, 195
Tiberias, 9
Tilly-sur-Seulles, the advance to and capture by 2nd Essex, 168-79
Tilson, Major F. A., award of Victoria Cross to, 542
Tobruk, references to, 37, 69; 1st Essex move into, 70-1; life in, 72-8; breakout from, 78-89; reference to, 262
Tonglang, 117
Toswell, Sgt. R. G., 469, 472
Tournai, 136, 142
Tower of London, 2nd Essex stationed at H.M., 15
Towndrow, Capt. E. A., 422
Townrow, Capt. J., 162, 173, 215, 219, 228
Towsey, Lieut.-Col. E. W., 90, 95
Training Centres I.T.C. The Essex Regiment, 517-19; No. 1 I.T.C., 520-4; No. 44 P.T.C., 524-5
Transjordan, 43, 45, 455
Trelawney, Capt. J. G. S., 372, 384-5
Treleaven, Pte. J. R., 142, 146
Trepal (Falaise), 197
Trieste, 2nd Essex stationed at, 243-4
Trigh Capuzzo, the, 82
Trigh El Abaid, the, 77
Trigno, 5th Essex in the crossing of the River, 375-87
Trimble, Major C. O. P., 361, 368, 372, 380-5
Tripoli, 301
Tripoli (Syria), 43, 369, 371
Trollope, Lieut.-Col. H. C. N., 22, 24, 357, 361, 362
Tufillo, 379
Tuker, Major-General Sir Francis, 247, 278, 283, 297, 298, 303, 305
Tulkarm, 421
Tully, Capt. B. P., 302

INDEX

Tunis, the capture of, 299–301
Tunisia, 1/4th Essex in the campaign in, 285–302
Tuoques, the River, 199
Turkey, 2nd Essex stationed in, 11–12
Turner, Col. A. M., 550, 558
Tusom Khulen (Assam), 116, 117
Twenthe Canal, the, 542
Tye, Major M., 362, 368, 372, 388, 393, 422

U

Uelzen, 5th Essex at, 426
Ukhrul, 116, 119
Ulph, Lieut. R. A., 279, 316
Um Zareba, 34
Unna, 2nd Essex at, 240–1
Upminster, 498, 513
Upton, Lieut.-Col. P. V., 357, 361–3, 364, 367
Upton Cross, 21
Utterson-Kelso, Major-General J. E., 158

V

Valberg, 228–9, 235
Valetta, 11
Vander Kiste, Lieut.-Col. E. C., 154, 483
Vasto, 5th Essex at, 418–19
Vaux-sur-Aure, 165
Velp, 2nd Essex capture, 237
Venice, 2nd Essex in, 245
Venlo, 222–3
Ventris, Major-General F., 529
Verrières Wood, 2nd Essex in battle at, 168–74
Vezzani, 5th Essex at, 414–15
Vichy France, reference to Vichy French forces and to, 66, 67, 449
Victoria Cross, award to Lieut.-Col. A. Newman, 615–16; to Major F. A. Tilson, 542
Vierhouck, 147
Villa Grande, 5th Essex in battle for, 403–14
Villa Marcone, 5th Essex at, 414
Villa Rosa, 5th Essex occupy, 404
Vince, Capt. A. A., 163, 175, 189, 195, 197, 203, 211, 215, 228, 242
Vince, Sgt. G. W., 249
Vincem, 152
Volos, 336
Von Arnim, General, 301

W

Waal, the River, 224–36
Waddell, Capt. F. W., 98, 123, 519

Wadi Akarit, 1/4th Essex in battle of, 289–91
Wadi Halfa, 32
Wadi Portella, 306
Wadi Villa, 306, 317
Wadi Zigau, 285–9
Wageningen, 237–8
Waite, Lieut. W. N. C., 26
Walker, Lieut.-Col. G. H., 85, 86; in command 1st Essex, 95–117; repatriated U.K., 123; in command 2nd Essex, 242–3; references to, 357, 361
Walker, Lieut.-Col. V. D., 560
Waller, Lieut.-Col. A. J. R., 557
Waller, Col. F. R., 20, 23
Waller, Brig. R. B., 269–70
Wannock, 24
Wanstead, 20, 478
Wardrop, General Sir Alexander, 7
Warley Barracks, 1; 2nd Essex 1937, 14–17, 130; role during 1939–45, 517–26
Warships:
H.M.S. *Ashanti*, 351; H.M.S. *Berwick*, 445; H.M.S. *Bonaventure*, 445; H.M.S. *Dunedin*, 445; H.M.S. *Fame*, 351; H.M.S. *Hasty*, 258; H.M.S. *Havoc*, 70; H.M.S. *Kandahar*, 71; H.M.S. *Whitehall*, 152
U.S. Navy: U.S.S. *Eagle*, 524
German: *Hipper*, 445
Wash, Sgt. R., 13
Watou, 149
Watson, Major E. I., 162, 170, 172
Watson, Lieut.-Col. F. Colvin, 558
Watson, 2/Lieut. G. H., 135, 138, 151
Watt, Major J., 252, 264, 268, 279, 289, 292, 294, 302, 571
Watts, Pte. G., 383
Wavell, Field-Marshal Lord, 9; quotation from despatches of, 37–8; references to, 39, 44, 71; congratulates 1st Essex, 122, reference to; 256
Way, Cpl. R., 123
Weakford, Sgt. E., 115
Webb, Capt. C. A., 486, 490
Webster, Lieut. F. H. B., 26
Wells-Jennings, Lieut.-Col. G., 548
Wenley, Capt. W. G., 514
West Ham, 19, 22
West Mersea, 440
WestWoodhay, 500
Westende, 540
Western Desert Force, the, 71
Western Desert of Egypt, the, 13, 68; situation during autumn 1941, 70–1; break-out from and relief of Tobruk, 70–89; 1/4th Essex in, 256; the campaign of June to December 1942, 260–84; references to, 361–2
Wetteren, 5th Essex at, 425

INDEX

Wettering Canal, 2nd Essex force the, 233–4
Weybourne, 479, 481
Weymouth, 8th Essex at, 488
Whistler, Major-General L. G., 126–7
White, L/Cpl. E., 88
White, Pte. E. J., 412
White, Lieut.-Col. J., 557
White, Sir Mathew Digby, 527
Whiteley, Capt. W. J., 422
Whitley, Lieut. D. T., 177
Whitmore, Col. Sir Francis (Lord-Lieutenant of Essex), references to, 2, 14, 15, 16, 249, 435, 547, 563, 569, 571
Whittaker, Pte. A. A., 419
Whitwell (I.O.W.), 159
Whyte, Capt. C. E. A., 362, 368, 372, 379, 381, 396, 400, 402, 433
Whyte, 2/Lieut. G. A., 362, 368, 372, 385, 387
Wickham Bishops, 250
Wiffen, Pte. E., 387
Wigan, Brig.-General J.T., sees 1/4th Essex, 249; visits 2/4th Essex, 353; references to, 547, 549
Wilberforce (Sierra Leone), 253–6
Wilcox, the Rev. A. J., 529
Wildey, R.S.M. G., 113
Wilkins, Major P. J., 162, 175, 199, 215, 217, 220, 239
Wilkinson, Lieut. D. A. C., 8, 451, 453
Wilkinson, Major K., 385–6
Williams, 2/Lieut. A. M., 38
Williams, 2/Lieut. E. J. C., 252
Williams, General Sir Guy, 249, 497
Williams, Major W. P., 26, 32, 33, 38
Willis, Major J. A., 539
Wilmer, Brigadier G. H., in command 1st Essex, 3, 5; appointed Brig. 161st Inf. Bde., 6; meets 1st Essex (1948), 128; meets 2nd Essex (1940), 131; (1948), 246; Colonel of the Regiment, 562; references to, 563, 567, 568, 569
Wilson, Lieut.-Col. C. L., 131, 136; in command 2nd Essex, 140–56; in command 8th Essex, 486–9, 493
Wilson, General Sir Henry Maitland, 44, 67, 68, 302

Wilson, Lieut. K. P. L., 26
Wilson, Capt. R., 523
Wingate, Major-General O. C., 95, 97, 112
Winterborne Stoke, 500
Winton, Brig. R. M. W. de, 244
Wiseman, Pte. C. W., 472
Wismar, 5th Essex at, 432; 9th Para. Bn. at, 501–2
Witham, 1/4th Essex at, 249; 2/5th Essex on embodiment, 440
Wollin, C.S.M., T., 486
Wood, Capt. K. D., 422
Wood, L/Cpl. L., 249
Wood, Major R., 490
Woodbridge, 499
Woodford, 20
Woodhouse, Major J. M., 563
Wooler, 250
Woolner, Major-General C. G., 255, 447
Wootton, Major M. J., 359, 361, 368, 372, 381, 384, 385
Worthing, 2nd Essex on beach defence at, 157
Worwood, L/Cpl. W. A., 177
Wren, Lieut.-Col. R. W., 22, 23, 478
Wright, Capt. C. C., 372, 388, 396
Wright, Capt. H. J. L., 453, 458
Wyndham Birch, Major, 550, 557
Wynn, Sgt. (1/4th Essex), 272

X

Xanten, 542

Y

Yates, Lieut.-Col. M., 496
York, H.R.H. the Duke of, 19
Young, 2/Lieut. (Major) H. J., 252, 266–8, 274, 279, 298, 302, 571, 572
Young, Major H. J., 506–8, 513

Z

Zaccaria (Italy), 332
Zetten, 2nd Essex in battle of, 230–4
Ziest, 2nd Essex at, 239–40
Zigau, the Wadi, 285–9
Zinbindjung (Arakan), 94
Zubza (Assam), 112–13

Lightning Source UK Ltd.
Milton Keynes UK
UKHW021033210420
362024UK00007B/251